The British conquered India within two generations, not only because of their military superiority, but also because they deployed a sophisticated intelligence system. In a penetrating account of the evolution of British intelligence gathering in India between the wars of annexation in 1793–1818 and the aftermath of the Mutiny-Rebellion of 1857, C.A. Bayly shows how networks of Indian running-spies and political secretaries were recruited by the British to secure military, political and social information about their subjects. He also examines the social and intellectual origins of these 'native informants', and considers how the colonial authorities interpreted and often misinterpreted the information they supplied. As Professor Bayly demonstrates, it was their misunderstanding of the subtleties of Indian politics and values which ultimately contributed to the failure of the British to anticipate the rebellions and mutinies of 1857. He argues, however, that even before this India's complex systems of debate and communication were challenging the political and intellectual dominance of the European rulers.

Cambridge Studies in Indian History and Society

Empire and information

Cambridge Studies in Indian History and Society 1

Editorial board

C.A. BAYLY

Vere Harmsworth Professor of Imperial and Naval History,
University of Cambridge, and Fellow of St Catharine's College

RAJNAVAYAN CHANDAVARKAR

Fellow of Trinity College, and Lecturer in History, University of Cambridge

GORDON JOHNSON

President of Wolfson College, and Director, Centre of South Asian Studies,
University of Cambridge

Cambridge Studies in Indian History and Society will publish monographs on the history and anthropology of modern India. In addition to its primary scholarly focus, the series will also include work of an interdisciplinary nature which will contribute to contemporary social and cultural debates about Indian history and society. In this way, the series will further the general development of historical and anthropological knowledge and attract a wider readership than that concerned with India alone.

Empire and information

Intelligence gathering and social communication in India, 1780–1870

C.A. Bayly

University of Cambridge

Published by the Press Syndicate of the University of Cambridge
The Pitt Building, Trumpington Street, Cambridge CB2 1RP
40 West 20th Street, New York, NY 10011–4211, USA
10 Stamford Road, Oakleigh, Melbourne 3166, Australia

First published 1996

Printed in Great Britain at the University Press, Cambridge

A catalogue record for this book is available from the British Library

Library of Congress cataloguing in publication data
Bayly, C.A. (Christopher Alan)
Empire and information: intelligence gathering and social communication
in India, 1780–1870 / C.A. Bayly
    p.   cm. – (Cambridge studies in Indian history and society: 1)
Includes bibliographical references and index.
ISBN 0 521 57085 9 (hardcover)
1. Intelligence service – India – History.
2. Communication – Social aspects – India – History.
3. India – Politics and government – 1765–1947.
I. Title.   II. Series.
JQ229.I6B39   1997
327.124′054′09034–dc20   96–13146   CIP

ISBN 0 521 57085 9 hardback

CE

Contents

Maps

Preface

The germ of an idea for a history book is often sown by a contemporary moment. Coming back to India from east and south-east Asia one time in the later 1980s, I was struck by several paradoxes. In India, a society where literacy still struggled around the 40 or 50 per cent level, there flourished a massive publishing industry working in numerous languages and a vigorous, not to say violent, free press which made its contemporaries in 'educated' and 'technological' south-east and east Asia look tame and controlled. In this poor society, some forms of political and social knowledge were remarkably widely diffused: apparently uneducated people would come up to one in the bazaar to discourse on the demerits of Baroness Thatcher or Mr Gorbachev, while educated people in east and south-east Asia, let alone Britain, seemed to struggle to understand anything of the external world. Another paradox: an Indian government which was as inquisitive and paper-obsessed as its colonial ancestor was constantly putting its foot wrong because it was seemingly so ill-informed about happenings in the states and localities. This set me thinking about a study of the 'information order' of British India, a topic that would occupy the dead ground between what is now a vibrant social history of India and its apparently lifeless intellectual history.

This study is mainly concerned with the Hindi-speaking areas of north India, but it reaches out to other regions when particularly important changes originated there. What was emerging in the nineteenth century was, after all, an all-India information order. Equally, in the first chapter I have glanced backwards into the pre-colonial period with some trepidation, but with a firm conviction that historians of Mughal India and the eighteenth century need to be alerted to these important issues. One final point: this book often deals with the colonial power's Indian informants. In the absence of a modern nationalism, these men should not be regarded as 'informers' or traitors. In fact, it was from the descendants of the informants that many of the future nationalists would be drawn.

Large numbers of librarians, archivists and scholars have helped me in this venture. I can only mention a few individuals. At the India Office Library (Oriental and India Office Collections, British Library), Richard Bingle was unfailingly friendly and helpful. At the Centre of South Asian Studies in Cambridge, Lionel Carter responded cheerfully to endless requests for bibliographical help. The following have all provided assistance and advice, though they bear no responsibility for my use of it: Peter Burke, Stephen Blake, Nigel Chancellor, Simon Digby, Michael Fisher, Sumit Guha, Joanna Innes, Muzaffar Alam, Norbert Peabody, Anil Sethi and Thant Myint-U. Katherine Prior proved a just and eagle-eyed critic of the manuscript; among the other readers of parts of the manuscript who provided valuable comments were the readers for Cambridge University Press, Gordon Johnson, Richard Drayton and Robert Travers. Susan Bayly listened patiently to my ramblings on this subject over several years and heroically read rough early drafts. The book is dedicated to the memory of my father, Roy Ernest Bayly, Master Mariner (1917–94), who first told me stories of the East, but sadly did not live to see the book completed.

Glossary

akhbarat	a newsletter; cf. khabr: news; akhbar: newspaper.
Agarwal	a north Indian merchant caste.
banian	an agent or intermediary; cf. bania: a merchant.
banka	a 'bravo' or 'wide-boy'.
Banjara	pack-bullock owner.
bantiria	a forest watchman (Gorakhpur area).
Bedar	a 'tribal' and hunter community (Mysore area).
bhakti	devotion to god (Hinduism).
Brahmin	the Hindu priestly caste.
dak	post, conveyance of mail or people; cf. dak daroga: head postman; dak dauria: runner.
Dharma	righteousness (Hinduism); loosely 'religion'.
chaukidar	a watchman.
dacoitee	gang robbery.
dubash	an agent (lit. 'man of two languages').
Devanagari	the Sanskrit alphabet, used for modern Hindi.
gorait	a village watchman (Banaras area).
Gosain	a Hindu mendicant of Vaishnavite sect (q.v.).
Gujar	a pastoralist and agriculturalist caste of north India.
hakim	a physician in the Greek-Islamic tradition.
harkara	an intelligence agent (lit. 'do-all').
insha	the science of letter-writing: letter book.
jasus	spy.
Jat	a middle agriculturalist caste of north India.
jyotish	a Hindu astronomer/astrologer.
Kallar	a pastoralist and military caste of south India.
Kayastha	north Indian writer caste.
Khattri	a north Indian commercial and administrative caste.
kanungo	a rural registrar under the Mughals.
kassid	a runner.
kazi	a Muslim judge: under the British a registrar in a city.
kotwal	city magistrate: under the British the police chief.

Kumboh	a (Muslim) writer community (Punjab).
mahajan	merchant title (lit. 'great man').
mahzar	a representation to authority.
majlis	an assembly, usually for Muslims.
maulvi	a Muslim cleric.
'Mewia'	a central Indian runner and tracker community.
mufti	expounder of law in a Muslim city.
muhtasib	superintendent of markets and morals.
Nyaya	a system of Hindu logic and philosophy.
Mug	[Magh] the Bengali name for Arakanese Buddhists.
munshi	a writer; secretary.
mushairah	a poetic competition.
nawab	deputy (to the Mughal emperor); a quasi-royal title in the eighteenth century; hence 'nabob'.
panchang	almanac.
panchayat	a tribunal or council.
pandit	a Hindu teacher, often Brahmin.
patwari	the village accountant.
pir	a title for a charismatic Muslim sufi teacher (q.v).
Purana	cosmologies and divine legends of medieval Hinduism.
qasbah	a small town often of Muslim foundation.
Rajput	the military north Indian royal and warrior caste.
sabha	meeting.
samaj	society, association.
sarkar	government.
sati	widow-burning.
Shaivite	a devotee of the deity Lord Shiva.
shastrartha	a formal Sanskrit debate.
Shia	the largest minority within Islam.
Siddhanta	'correct doctrines': Indian astronomy based on precise observation.
Sufi	an adept of mystical and esoteric knowledge within Islam.
Sunni	the majority sect within Islam.
surathal	a representation to authority.
Usuli	a school of Islamic law stressing rational interpretation.
vaidya	a physician within the Hindu tradition.
Vaishnavite	a devotee of the deity Lord Vishnu.
waqai navis	cf. waqai nigar: newswriter.
zamindar	a landowner.

Abbreviations

Actg	Acting.
BC	Boards Collections, OIOC.
BL	British Library.
CPC	*Calendar of Persian Correspondence.*
Cons.	Consultations.
CUL	Cambridge University Library.
Dty	Deputy.
GG	Governor-General.
HI	Elliot, H.M. and J. Dowson, *The History of Indian told by its own Historians.*
HM	Home Miscellaneous Series, OIOC.
IESHR	*Indian Economic and Social History Review.*
JAS	*Journal of Asian Studies.*
JBRS	*Journal of the Burma Research Society*
LH	Garcin de Tassy, J.H., *Histoire de la Littérature Hindouie et Hindoustanie.*
MAS	*Modern Asian Studies.*
NAI	National Archives of India, New Delhi.
NWP	North-Western Provinces.
OIOC	Oriental and India Office Collections, British Library.
Resdt	Resident.
UPCRO	Uttar Pradesh Central Records Office, Allahabad.

Note on transliteration

English transliterations of south Asian words have been in continuous change since 1750. To preserve original usages would give rise to archaicism and inconsistency, but modern scientific transliteration can obscure well-known names and places. Compromise and a degree of inconsistency is unavoidable. In the case of place-names, I have used the forms common in the later British gazetteers, except where contemporary Indian English usage has substituted acceptable alternatives (e.g.,

Kanpur, Pune, Banaras). In the case of personal names I have used modern transliteration except where famous individuals are still known by contemporary forms (e.g., Muhammad Shah, Ram Mohun Roy), or where the indigenous form is uncertain, in which case I have preserved 'corrupt' contemporary versions. With other words, I have used commonly accepted modern forms (thus 'kazi', but 'qasbah'). I have also preserved the transliterations used by modern translators even where they are variants of the norm.

Introduction

A central purpose of this book is to examine British political intelligence in north India between the 1780s and the 1860s. It describes the networks of Indian running-spies, newswriters and knowledgeable secretaries whom officials of the East India Company recruited and deployed in their efforts to secure military, political and social information. It considers how the colonial authorities interpreted and misinterpreted the material derived from these sources. It draws attention to the gaps, distortions and 'panics' about malign 'native' plots which afflicted the system of imperial surveillance within north India and, for comparison's sake, outside its borders, in Nepal, Burma and beyond the north-western frontier. Finally, the book examines the extent to which intelligence failures and successes contributed to the course of the Rebellion of 1857–9, the collapse of the East India Company's government and the form of the following pacification.

The quality of military and political intelligence available to European colonial powers was evidently a critical determinant of their success in conquest and profitable governance. Equally, this information provided the raw material on which Europeans drew when they tried to understand the politics, economic activities and culture of their indigenous subjects. The book, therefore, addresses some of the most traditional as well as some of the most recent and controversial issues in imperial and south Asian historiography.

The study also concerns communication and the movement of knowledge within Indian society, examining the role of communities of writers in the bazaars and the culture of political debate. It is a study of social communication in the sense used in Karl Deutsch's pioneering work.[1] It considers those specialists who helped to articulate indigenous systems of knowledge and keep information, ideas and gossip flowing: the astrologers, physicians, experts in the philospher's stone,

---

[1] Karl Deutsch, *Nationalism and Social Communication. An enquiry into the foundations of nationality* (Cambridge, Mass., 1960); Paul R. Brass, *Language, Religion and Politics in North India* (Cambridge, 1974).

midwives, marriage-makers, and other knowledgeable people who brought news from one community and region to another. It was the density and flexibility of indigenous routines of social communication which explains why north Indians were able to make such striking use of the printing press, the newspaper and the public meeting once those innovations finally began to spread rapidly amongst them in the 1830s and 1840s. While modern Indian history should certainly not be depicted as a single grand narrative culminating in the emergence of nationalism, the density of social communication demonstrated by this book does, in fact, help to explain why political leaders in a poor country with a relatively low rate of general literacy should have been able to create a widely diffused and popular nationalist movement so early.

These two systems – the colonial state's surveillance agencies and the autonomous networks of social communicators – overlapped and interpenetrated. But the overlap was incomplete. The meeting between British and Indian agencies was riven by suspicion, distortion and violence. For here, at the point of intersection between political intelligence and indigenous knowledge, colonial rule was at its most vulnerable. Here, new communities of knowledgeable Indians which used the colonial state's communications and ideologies independently of it, or against it, began to emerge even in the early nineteenth century. As the expatriate newspaper, *The Friend of India*, remarked in 1836, echoing the administrator, Sir John Malcolm, 'our Indian Empire is one of opinion' and 'the progress of knowledge' would probably 'entail the separation of India from England'.[2] A contemporary British officer, seeing a pile of newly printed vernacular books in the office of Mountstuart Elphinstone, Governor of Bombay, exclaimed in similar terms: 'it is our highroad back to Europe'.[3]

Neither Indian historians nor historians of other European dependencies have paid very much attention to the intelligence or propaganda systems of colonial powers,[4] though intelligence studies have become a major industry for European and American historians who have come to regard political surveillance and social communication as a critical

[2] 'Report of the General Committee for Public instruction', *Friend of India*, 27 Oct. 1836; cf. J. Malcolm, *Political History of India* (London, 1826), I, 82. He defined 'opinion' in terms of 'Gramscian' ideological hegemony as 'that respect and awe with which the comparative superiority of our knowledge, justice and system of rule, have inspired the inhabitants of our own territories ...' I am grateful to Mr Nigel Chancellor for pointing out the original reference.

[3] Cited in K. Ballhatchet, *Social Policy and Social Change in Western India, 1817–1830* (London, 1957), p. 249.

[4] But see Milton Israel, *Communications and Power. Propaganda and the press in the Indian nationalist struggle, 1920–47* (Cambridge, 1994).

feature of the modern state and society.[5] Recent works on India have considered the related area of 'colonial knowledge' or 'discourse', focussing on the learned theories of orientalism, rather than on day-to-day information and its sources.[6] Several scholars, too, have begun to consider the 'native informant' and the impact of the press and print capitalism.[7] Nevertheless, state surveillance and social communication remains a poorly studied area. By contrast, some of the more important works of fiction to emerge from the Indo-British encounter are located precisely on that cusp between British intelligence and indigenous knowledge. Rudyard Kipling's *Kim*,[8] to take the most celebrated example, introduces a cast of characters which find pale reflections in this study. In Kipling's novel the reader meets Kim himself, the Eurasian spy in the Great Game of espionage in central Asia, and Hurree Babu, the learned native informant. Alongside them Kipling memorably pictures the eddies of news and gossip flowing down the Grand Trunk Road from Lahore to Banaras, carried onward by Afghan horse-dealers, Hindu bankers and pilgrims destined for the holy places of Hinduism and Buddhism.

The information order

The book seeks to establish a broad framework for the study of these two elements – state's intelligence and social communication – by using the concept of the 'information order'. This term has been adapted from the work of the economic geographer Manuel Castells who has written of the 'informational city'.[9] Castells treats the new information technology

---

[5] For the early modern period, Ian K. Steele, *The English Atlantic 1675–1740. An exploration of communications and community* (New York, 1986); P. Fritz, 'The Anti-Jacobite intelligence system of the English ministers, 1715–45', *Historical Journal*, 16, 1973, 265–89; H.A. Innis, *Empire and Communications* (Oxford, 1990); for the modern period the journal *Intelligence and National Security*, R.J. Poplewell, *Intelligence and Imperial Defence* (London, 1995).

[6] The most celebrated example is Ronald Inden, *Imagining India* (Oxford, 1990).

[7] e.g. Nicholas Dirks, 'Castes of Mind', *Representations*, 37, winter 1992, 56–77; Eugene F. Irschick, *Dialogue and History. Constructing South India, 1795–1895* (California, 1994); Francis Robinson, 'Technology and religious change. Islam and the impact of print', *Modern Asian Studies*, 27, 1, 1993, 229–51.

[8] cf. Thomas Richards, *The Imperial Archive: knowledge and the fantasy of empire* (London, 1993), pp. 22–30, who notes that in *Kim*, social knowledge has become coextensive with military intelligence; in the Indian system they had always been closely allied.

[9] Manuel Castells, *The Informational City. Information technology, economic restructuring and the urban–regional process* (Oxford, 1989). No 'information' can, of course, be perceived and ordered unless the observer has conceptual paradigms within which to apprehend it. Our use of the word 'information', however, implies observations perceived at a relatively low level of conceptual definition, on the validity of whose claims to truth people from different regions, cultures and linguistic groups might

of the late twentieth century as a type of social formation rather than as a simple adjunct to existing economic forces or a neutral technological process. He shows how in north America after 1960, information technology changed the pattern of urban living, speeded processes of de-industrialisation and income differentiation, and 'de-skilled' large parts of the work force, especially those already disadvantaged such as poorly educated minority groups and women. What is important about his approach is that he sees the generators of knowledge, the institutions of information collection and diffusion and the discourses to which they give rise as autonomous forces for economic and social change. They are not reduced to the status of contingencies of late-industrial capitalism or the modern state. Knowledge itself is a social formation; knowledgeable people form distinct and active social segments with their own interests. For Castells, intellectual property, including education, was as much the foundation of social class and economies as financial or landed property was for earlier generations of social theorists. Rather than being residual categories relegated to the end of the history book in chapters entitled 'intellectual developments' or 'communications', these considerations should be central to studies of social change. Such an approach ought to bring benefits to Indian history, a subject whose proponents have until recently been preoccupied with the sociology of institutions to the detriment of the sociology of knowledge. Equally, Indian intellectual history has been more radically divorced from its social context than in many other areas of historical study. It needs to be restored to that context.

What we have called the information order should not be seen as a 'thing', any more than a state or an economy is a thing; it is a heuristic device, or a field of investigation, which can be used to probe the organisation, values and limitations of past societies. It is not separate from the world of power or economic exploitation, but stands both prior to it and dependent on it. It can be considered to have a degree of autonomy from politics or economic structure. Thus some powers, or powerful groups, with finite economic resources and little brute force – the Republic of Venice in the eighteenth century[10] or the House of Rothschild in the nineteenth, for instance – have had exceptionally well-organised and flexible information systems which allowed them to make

broadly agree. 'Knowledge' implies socially organised and taxonomised information, about which such agreement would be less sure. In north Indian languages 'information' would be rendered by words such as *khabr* and *suchna*; knowledge by *ilm* or *vidya*, though under some circumstances vidya might mean something more akin to 'occult' knowledge, while spiritual knowledge would be represented by *gyana* or *jnan*.

[10] Venice maintained a complex system of internal and external espionage, besides controlling the movement of the commercial secrets of glassmaking, etc.

their limited caches of power and resources work harder. Likewise, societies at similar levels of economic development, when judged by per capita income, had different styles of information order which shaped their capacity to change internally or resist external pressures.

In early modern societies, the information order was decentralised, consisting of many overlapping groups of knowledge-rich communities. It was not mediated as in contemporary industrial societies by a dominant state or commercial communications sector. Schooling and literacy were specialist resources open only to particular elites who used their learning as badges of status. Knowledge was only slowly becoming a public good, a citizen's right, or an adjunct of state power. As yet, it was deeply embodied in the status of the particular informant or knowledge community. Kings and their officials collected and deployed knowledge in unstandardised forms because what should be known was not yet determined by any dominant notion of a critical bureaucracy or public. All the same, the school, the royal writers' chancellery, the public scribe, the spy, the runner, the body of physicians and astrologers, and other specialists tended to make up a loosely-knit constellation of powers in society. In Indian soothsaying as in its European equivalent, all these actors were conjoined under the sign of Mercury, messenger of the Gods, or Budh-Graha, affording us an indigenous licence for the category.[11]

Viewed from the perspective of information, however, pre-modern societies differed greatly from one another in the status and uses of literacy and also in the quality and effectiveness of the systems of information collection and distribution deployed by the state and other agencies. Later Tokugawa Japan, for example, supporting more than 40 per cent male education, mass lithography and a system of commercial horseback messengers,[12] stands in sharp contrast to contemporary societies, such as the Ottoman Middle East[13] and South Asia, which possessed broadly similar levels of per capita wealth. In the latter two societies, lithography was slow to develop and a clerical elite mono-polised literacy which was the preserve of little more than 10 per cent of the male population. The level of state surveillance common in Tokugawa Japan was also rarely aspired to in India, though comprehen-

---

[11] The *Bhuvana-Dipaka* cited in M. Ramakrishna Bhat, *Essentials of Horary Astrology or Prasnapadavi* (Delhi, 1992), p. 40.

[12] K. Moriya, 'Urban networks and information networks', in C. Nakane and S. Oishi (eds.), C. Totman (tr.), *Tokugawa Japan* (Tokyo, 1990), pp. 97–124; as early as 1692, 7,300 book titles had been published in Japan. Kyoto alone had 494 publishing houses in the eighteenth century. *No book* was published in India, by Indians, until *c.* 1800.

[13] See, e.g., Cornell H. Fleischer, *Bureaucrat and Intellectual in the Ottoman Empire: the historian Mustafa Ali. 1541–1600* (Princeton, 1986).

sive records of land measurement and assessment had evolved early in the subcontinent. In contrast again, the early modern states of southeast Asia were more concerned with counting people than with counting revenue, partly because they were constrained by shortages of labour rather than of cash. Burmese and Thai rulers, therefore, organised general population censuses earlier than their counterparts in India and parts of west Asia.

These differences were partly determined by economics. Monetised economies required different forms of knowledge collection and archive-making from those where customary labour dues or shares of produce were taken by the elites. At the same time, differences in ideology and religious practice also moulded contrasting information orders. The reformed Buddhist hierarchies of early modern Thailand and Burma, for example, attempted to impart standard rules of life to the wider population[14] in a way which was impossible for the loose networks of Indian Brahmin priests. Monks and kings consequently encouraged a more widespread system of popular education than existed in most parts of north India.

Colonial knowledge

European colonial states faced obvious problems in engaging with the information order of a conquered society, an essential task if they were to build an intelligence system capable of securing their grip on the territory's resources. The conquerors needed to reach into and manipulate the indigenous systems of communication in new colonies. But because these indigenous systems differed from each other in important respects, colonial regimes in turn came to preside over widely differing information orders. Simple difficulties of language made the Europeans initially dependent on the skills of 'linguists', 'translators' and 'men of two tongues' or, as the Hindustani has it, *dubash*s. These informants were inevitably drawn from the very communities which the western powers sought to dominate. Even if they served their alien masters loyally, they moved in realms of life and thought which they wished to keep hidden from the rulers. The basic fear of the colonial official or settler was, consequently, his lack of indigenous knowledge and ignorance of the 'wiles of the natives'. He feared their secret letters, their drumming and 'bush telegraphy' and the nightly passage of seditious agents masquerading as priests and holy men.

Some contemporary social theorists have gone further and concluded

---

[14]   Nicholas Tarling, *Cambridge History of South East Asia*, I, (Cambridge, 1992), 537–42.

that Europeans never knew anything significant about indigenous societies, and indeed can never know anything about them because of European conceptual biases. What passed, or passes, for European knowledge of the Other is, in fact, a mere web of rhetorical devices designed to give legitimacy to conquest.[15] This position is too extreme. European rule over Asians and Africans could not have been sustained without a degree of understanding of the conquered societies. In India, colonial knowledge was derived to a considerable extent from indigenous knowledge, albeit torn out of context and distorted by fear and prejudice. People from different races and cultures, possessing different degrees of power, could and did achieve a broad agreement over claims to truth about the phenomena they observed. This study, therefore, broadly accepts Stuart Schwartz's view that 'despite the haze of linguistic and cultural assumptions that limit observation ... other cultures existed outside the mind of the observer' and they could be observed and understood 'in an admittedly imperfect approximation of a reality'.[16]

In our view, the problems the British faced in understanding and controlling events in south Asia derived as much from the shape of India's information order and the superficiality of colonial rule as from any particular cultural bias or prejudice resulting from the assimilation of knowledge to power. The British never controlled the bulk of capital, the means of production or the means of persuasion and communication[17] in the subcontinent. Because they were not, in general, concerned to spread their faith or mingle their genes with the Indian population, the British could not count on an inflow of 'affective knowledge', that is knowledge which derived from the creation of moral communities within the colonial society by means of conversion, acculturation or interbreeding. Indian Christians and Armenians were, of course, important informants; Eurasians played a big role, especially in the generation of military knowledge for the British conquerors in the later eighteenth century. But the situation was quite different from that obtaining, for example, in early southern Africa where large mixed-race communities and acculturated or converted Africans ('Hottentots';

[15] This position has sometimes been associated with Edward Said, *Orientalism* (1978), but it is much more typical of his radical disciples, see John M. MacKenzie, *Orientalism. History, theory and the arts* (Manchester, 1995).

[16] Stuart B. Schwartz, 'Introduction' in Schwartz (ed.) *Implicit Understandings. Observing, reporting and reflecting on the encounters between Europeans and other peoples in the early modern era* (New York, 1994), p. 19.

[17] This term is taken from Anthony Giddens, *The Constitution of Society. Outline of a theory of structuration* (Cambridge, 1984), and conveys part of what I mean by information order.

Khoikhoi) provided guides, mediators and informants.[18] Again, the British in India could not rely on that 'patrimonial knowledge' on which independent states and some colonial governments could draw. This was the knowledge of the expatriate or mixed-race landowner or commercial man who acted, albeit in his own interest, as the eyes and ears of the colonial government. In India, as opposed to French Algeria or British southern Africa, white or mixed-raced farmers, or sub-imperialist commercial men, such as the Indians in East Africa, were not widely available to create and transmit information to the rulers.

In India, then, the British were forced to master and manipulate the information systems of their Hindu and Mughal predecessors; this was especially true before 1830. Later, there was indeed change in these systems, though this was limited in its geographical range and impact. Indigenous agencies were modified, given new tasks and set to collecting different types of information from their predecessors. Public instruction created a new type of native informant. The statistical movement, which gathered pace after 1830, had a powerful impact. It raised the status of the expatriate expert, the 'old India hand' in the Indian Medical Service or the Posts and Intelligence Department of the Army and gave the colonial authorities a superficial knowledge of conditions in the major stations and among subordinate Indian servants. Away from the purview of the district offices, however, the British were still ignorant of much that was transpiring, as the events of 1857 brutally revealed. Their chain of surveillance was at its most vulnerable where the body of elite, literate officers stretching down from the district town linked up with the hereditary servants and information collectors of the village. This link snapped in 1857, was partly welded together in the later nineteenth century but was rapidly corroded again during the twentieth century. In short, the surveillance agencies of both pre-colonial and colonial government in India were flexible and at times penetrating, but they also seem labile and thinly spread when compared, for instance, to the density of state institutions at village level in Japan. In parallel with political power through long periods of Indian history, information and knowledge was decentralised. From the heyday of Mughal rule to the present this has confronted the emerging state with serious obstacles in its dealings with regional and village elites.

When we move on to consider the broader impact of British rule on the information order of north India, similar patterns will emerge. On the face of it, the simultaneous introduction of public instruction, the

---

[18] Leonard Thompson and Monica Wilson, *The Oxford History of South Africa*, I (Oxford, 1969), 69–70; Robert Ross, *Adam Kok's Griquas. A study in the development of stratification in South Africa* (Cambridge, 1976).

printing press, public debate in newspapers, the English language, libraries and dense archives transformed Indian society in the nineteenth century more thoroughly than colonial capitalism transformed its economy. This study does not, however, go as far as postulating a revolution in mentalities consequent on the rise of 'print capitalism' as Benedict Anderson does for Indonesia and other colonial territories.[19] It argues that north India's reponse to these modern forms of information diffusion and retrieval was determined to a considerable extent by existing communities of knowledge, styles of reasoned debate and patterns of social communication. Even in realms of scientific knowledge such as the disciplines of astronomy, geography and medicine, where western theories and techniques were to achieve dominance in the long term, the imprint of earlier indigenous sciences and the virtue of indigenous practitioners remained significant for most Indians. The information order of colonial India retained distinctly Indian features, even while it was absorbing and responding to the profound influences set in motion by the European rulers. The first chapter examines this indigenous inheritance.

[19] Benedict Anderson, *Imagined Communities* (revised edn, London, 1994).

1 Prologue: surveillance and communication in early modern India

Without good political and military intelligence the British could never have established their rule in India or consolidated the dominant international position of the United Kingdom. During the years of conquest, British knowledge of the country was drawn largely from Indian sources and supplied by Indian agents. This introductory chapter analyses the indigenous systems of political surveillance which the British sought to capture and manipulate in the years after 1760.

Indian statesmen had long been concerned with good intelligence gathering, regarding surveillance as a vital dimension of the science of kingship. Their aim was not to create a police state which monitored the political attitudes of subjects, so much as to detect moral transgressions among their officers and the oppression of the weak by the powerful. Their systems were flexible and adaptable, but in Indian kingdoms the agencies of the state were generally not as densely clustered in the localities as they were in most European and some other Asian societies. For this reason royal intelligence was heavily dependent on informal networks of knowledgeable people. The chapter goes on, therefore, to consider the context of popular communication and literacy in which the royal agents worked, enabling us to conceive of the evolution of the pre-colonial information order in broad terms. It ends by describing the slow and piecemeal process by which the East India Company began to 'know' the country which it ultimately conquered.

Royal wisdom and intelligence: the tradition

In theory, Indian statesmen of the seventeenth and eighteenth centuries saw kingdoms as treasure-houses of knowledge as well as accumulations of wealth and power. For example, the Maratha 'Royal Edict', a Hindu political text of the early eighteenth century, remarked that forts were 'the essence of the whole kingdom'.[1] These forts were not only strong-

---

[1] S.V. Puntambekar, 'The Ajnapatra or Royal Edict, relating to the principles of Maratha State Policy', *Journal of Indian History*, 8, 1929, p. 219.

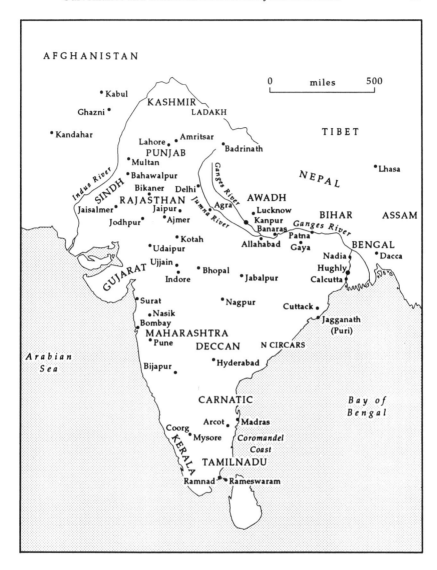

AFGHANISTAN

• Kabul

Ghazni •

KASHMIR

LADAKH

TIBET

0   miles   500

• Kandahar

Lahore • • Amritsar

PUNJAB   • Badrinath

• Multan

• Bahawalpur

• Lhasa

NEPAL

Indus River

SINDH

Bikaner   Delhi •

Jaisalmer • RAJASTHAN

Jaipur •

Jodhpur •   • Ajmer

Agra

AWADH

• Lucknow

• Kanpur

Banaras

Allahabad

Patna

• Gaya

BIHAR   ASSAM

Ganges River

BENGAL

Nadia

Hughly

Calcutta •

• Dacca

Ganges River

Jumna River

• Kotah

• Udaipur

Ujjain •

Indore

• Bhopal   • Jabalpur

GUJARAT

• Surat

• Nasik

Bombay

MAHARASHTRA

• Pune

Bijapur •

• Nagpur

DECCAN   N CIRCARS

• Hyderabad

Cuttack •

Jagganath
(Puri)

Arabian
Sea

CARNATIC

Arcot • • Madras

Coorg

• Mysore   Coromandel
Coast

KERALA

TAMILNADU

Ramnad • • Rameswaram

Bay of
Bengal

1.   The Indian subcontinent c. 1800.

points; they were also stores of knowledge. Each one should be adorned by 'Brahmanas, astrologers, vaidiks [scripture readers], the learned, also surgeons who are versed in mineral medicines', exorcists, wound-dressers and a groups of skilled artisans.[2] In the eyes of these western Indian rulers, collectors of intelligence formed a particularly important class of knowledgeable people. Shivaji, the founder of Maratha power in the late seventeenth century, had set up a large Guide (Jasud) Department to supply such agents. Intelligence agents were attached to forts and counter-intelligence measures were taken to preserve the secrets of their construction.

In this concern for political intelligence the rising kingdoms of the eighteenth century drew on a long tradition. The major ancient texts of political theory consider surveillance in detail.[3] One tenth-century work, which explicitly links political intelligence and the learned sciences, observes that statecraft without spying is like the study of grammar without its most celebrated commentary.[4] Another, 'The Elements of Polity'[5] by Kamandaki (c. 400–600 AD) was copied many times over the following millennium in India, Burma and Java.[6] It advised kings and ambassadors to place spies 'in places of pilgrimage ... hermitages and temples' where they could pretend to study the scriptures.[7] As the priests in a sacrifice are guided by the vedic hymns, Kamandaki urged, so the king should carefully fashion spies 'like vessels for a ritual'.[8] Spies could be of a 'reckless type, mendicant or recluse type, sacrificer or black magician type, or in the guise of persons of noble character'.[9]

The two sides of political intelligence are revealed in these texts. Brahmins, the priestly caste and seekers of hidden knowledge, were to gather the more sophisticated intelligence and communicate it in writing, but the king also needed the services of people with humbler skills. On campaigns, for example, he required runners and trackers, who knew the by-ways, water sources and river fords. The agents should be 'foresters' (tribals),[10] drawn from the domain beyond the arable

[2]   ibid., 228.
[3]   Wendy Doniger with Brian K. Smith (ed., tr.), *The Laws of Manu* (London, 1991), pp. 151, 225–6.
[4]   Pt. Durgaprasada and Pt. Sivadatta (eds.), *The Sisupalavadha of Magha* (Bombay, 1914), 2, 112. This seventh-century AD work stated: 'shabdavidyeva no bhati rajnitir apaspasha': 'statecraft without espionage seems to us like the science of grammar without the Paspasha [the introduction to Patanjali's great commentary on Panini's Grammar]'; I owe this reference and translation to Dr Eivind Kahrs.
[5]   Rajendra Lal Mitra (ed.), *The Nitisara [Elements of Polity] by Kamandaki*, revised with an English translation by Sisir Kumar Mitra (Calcutta, 1982), pp. 266–75.
[6]   U.N. Ghosal, *A History of Indian Political Ideas* (Madras, 1966), p. 395 n.
[7]   *Kamandaki*, xiii, 13, p. 262.   [8] ibid., xiii, 33, p. 269.
[9]   ibid., xiii, 34, p. 269.   [10] ibid., xix, 3, p. 389 *atavika bala*.

which was associated with magic, hunting and asceticism. Even in the nineteenth century, these arts could still bring tribal people close to the springs of power and authority in Indian states.[11]

Surveillance, then, was an important theme in Indian political thought. This was partly a matter of the representation of power: in the absence of local control in detail, the ideal 'universal king' had to be portrayed as an all-seeing icon of royalty. Even in the case of the great Muslim kingdoms of the sixteenth and seventeenth centuries, the detailed descriptions of royal intelligence we encounter may have represented more of an aspiration than a reality. As the allusion to grammar suggests, the texts were also expounding a theory of knowledge: the mind knows the external world through sense impressions, just as the king's wisdom works on the reports of spies to formulate policy.

Practical reason nevertheless played its part. Political surveillance has been vital for all large historical states but it was particularly important to Indian rulers because of certain invariant features of the subcontinent's ecology and society. Despite India's great size, information moved with remarkable speed over long distances. People were always on the move as merchants, pilgrims, soldiers or marriage parties. Although it was not a highly literate society pre-colonial India was a society acutely aware of literacy,[12] where even the poor could gain access to writers and readers at a cost. Knowledge was, however, unevenly distributed within society and kings had to work hard to accumulate information. Families and communities among the priestly and clerical elites attempted to guard knowledge and reserve it for their descendants. Exclusive patterns of marriage reinforced these monopolies of information. Though common languages such as Hindustani had evolved by the eighteenth century, Indians from different regions still found it difficult to communicate with each other and many influential groups recorded information in scripts and dialects which were rendered deliberately arcane.

This posed particular problems for the exercise of state power. While kingship in India may once have been a ritual umbrella opened over a

---

[11] See, e.g., Briggs's report on Bhil–Maratha relations, Bombay Political and Secret Consultations, vol. 60, 22 June 1825, OIOC, cited by Stewart N. Gordon, 'Bhils and the idea of a criminal tribe in nineteenth century India' in Anand A. Yang (ed.), *Crime and Criminality in British India* (Tucson, 1985), pp. 128–39. For the role of forest people in Keralan polities, especially during the revolt of the 'Pychee Rajah', 1799–1805, William Logan, *Malabar*, (reprint, Madras, 1951), I, 542, 546; II, 346–7; A.D. Luiz, *The Tribes of Kerala* (Delhi, 1962), pp. 109–10; for a general narrative, see Home Miscellaneous Series, vol. 607, Oriental and India Office Collections, London [for folio refs. see, C. Hill, *Catalogue of the Home Miscellaneous Series of the India Office Records* (London, 1927)].

[12] See below, pp. 36–44.

diverse range of communities, the nature of the subcontinent's political economy over recent centuries required that kings attempted to retain a tight control over resources and political allegiance. This was because obligations to the state had widely been rendered in cash from at least the thirteeenth century. Rulers needed cash to finance their expenditure on armies and display. To secure it, they required practical information on the doings of peasants, artisans and merchants. The contradiction between a closely-knit, cash-based political economy and a society widely attuned to principles of hierarchy and segmentation placed a heavy significance on information collection.

India's ecology also played its part. Vast distances could be traversed by light horse-carts,[13] camels and bullock trains. The great rivers and the coastline offered opportunities for fast communication, but this was only during the dry season. In north India from June to October, the rains impeded the passage of goods and traffic. Runners operating on the roads had to be doubled from about one every twelve miles to one every six miles[14] simply to maintain a skeleton news service. The business of the state and merchant slowed, but it could not afford to come to a stop. Heavy cavalry wars had to be fought even during the heaviest monsoons because the survival of the state demanded quick action to secure the autumn harvest from enemy marauders. Power in India was not just a matter of assembling tangible resources. Before they could command men and money, rulers had to assemble stores of information and set up networks of communication.

Moral suasion and Indo-Muslim government

The basic Indian agencies of domestic intelligence survived from the early centuries of the Christian era to the end of the nineteenth century. What Muslim rulers, particularly the Mughals, gradually introduced after 1200 AD was a more regular system of official political reporting and a comprehensive grid of regular post stages (*dak chaukis*) under recognised officials.[15] Many words concerning news and communica-

[13] J. Déloche, *Transport and Communications in India prior to Steam Locomotion*, I (Delhi, 1993).

[14] William Palmer, Resident at Pune to Lord Mornington, Governor-General, 6 July 1799, HM 574; cf. relays of 6 miles were customary in difficult terrain, Resdt Mysore to Govt Madras, 20 Nov. 1799, Board's Collections, 76/1659, OIOC.

[15] The fullest description of the Indo-Muslim postal and political reporting system relates to the Deccan; it predated the Mughals, see M.A. Nayeem, *Evolution of Postal Communications and Administration in the Deccan (from 1294 A.D. to the Formation of the Hyderabad State in 1724 A.D.)* (Bombay, 1968); for intelligence, see also Irfan Habib, 'Postal Communications in Mughal India', *Proceedings of the Indian Historical Congress, 46th Session* (Delhi, 1986), pp. 236–52; M.Z. Siddiqi, 'The Intelligence Services under

tion in Hindi and Bengali are, therefore, of Persian-Arabic origin (e.g., *khabr*, news, *akhbar*, newsreport, *dak*, post). In some regions the Brahmin intelligencers of the past were replaced by Muslim gentlemen and Hindus of the upper castes who wrote in Persian. Under the system reorganised by the Emperor Akbar (r. 1556–1605),[16] every provincial and subdivisional headquarters had its 'recorders of events', the *waqai nigar*s who were mainly concerned with revenue matters and *waqai navis*s who dealt with other matters. These officials noted down the happenings of the week and sent their reports to the Emperor by means of runners (*harkaras*). They were despatched under the charge of the head postmaster (*daroga-i-dak*), who was responsible for the safety of royal letters and also for the correspondence of merchants, intelligentsia and ordinary people. Emperors took particular care to prevent the emergence of private or unauthorised daks,[17] though they did not generally attempt to control the movement of individual runners. In the capital an imperial newswriter (*waqai navis*) recorded court events. These included details of the royal routine and diet, the issue of licences, rewards or punishments and 'what marriages and births happen'.[18] When authenticated with the seals of high officials, this diary became an official record.

Along with the head of the runners the head newswriter and his department made sure that the emperor was informed of the intelligence coming in from the regional newswriters. This material was supplemented with reports from a range of secret agents (*swanih nigar*s or *khufia navis*s) who moved around the countryside, listening in at bazaars and checking on the reports of the provincial governors and the official newswriters. The men who headed this system were people of

the Mughals', *Medieval India; A Miscellany* 2, 1972, 53–60; B.D. Verma (ed.), *News-letters of the Mughal court (reign of Ahmad Shah, 1751–2 A.D.)* (Bombay, 1949), pp. i–x; Jagdish Narayan Sarkar, 'Newswriters of Mughal India', in S.P. Sen (ed.), *The Indian Press* (Calcutta, 1967), pp. 110–45; many chronicles mention details of intelligence and post in passing, e.g., M.F. Lokhandwala (ed., tr.), *Mirat-i Ahmadi* of Ali Muhammad Khan (Baroda, 1965), p. 357; Shiva Das Lakhnavi, *Shahnamah Munawwar Kalam*, tr. S.H. Askari (Patna, 1980), pp. 15, 26, 61, 83, 115, 118, 134, 138; Ishwardas Nagar, *Futuhat-i-Alamgiri*, tr. T. Ahmad (Delhi, 1978), passim; for the role of other officers, see, e.g., M.Z. Siddiqi, 'The Muhtasib under Aurangzeb', *Medieval India Quarterly*, 5, 1963, 113–19; Siddiqi, 'The institution of the Qazi under the Mughals, *Medieval India Miscellany*, 1, 1969, 240–60; S.L.H. Moini, 'A critical analysis of the Waqai Sarkar-i Ajmer wa Ranthambore', in Devahuti (ed.), *Bias in Indian Historiography* (Delhi, 1980), pp. 392–4. B.K. Sarkar, *Inland Transport and Communications in Medieval India* (Calcutta, 1925).

[16] Nayeem, *Postal Communications*, pp. 5–6.

[17] e.g., Aurangzeb to an official, J.H. Bilimoria, *Ruka'at-i-Alamgiri, or letters of Aurangzebe* (repr., Delhi, 1972), p. 97.

[18] 'Ain-i Akbari' translated and edited by Francis Gladwin as *Ayeen Akbery or, the Institutes of the Emperor Akber* (London, 1800), I, 214.

importance. Writing to, or about, the emperor was a pious act. Some newswriters were drawn from distinguished literary families and had historians amongst their members;[19] for history writing and newswriting were closely related. Contemporaries stressed the need to select scrupulously honest newswriters. Some surviving periodic newsletters (*akhbarat*s) from the regional newswriters spend many lines describing the author of the letter, the reliability of the information and the method of its transmission. The court newsletters, which detailed the routine of the emperor or provincial governor, were also notable for the precision with which times, places and conversations were recorded.

Various overlapping systems of watch and ward also brought news and information to Indo-Muslim officials. A staff of mace-bearers carried messages around the imperial city or encampment and observed the doings of officials and soldiers. The chief police officer of the town (*kotwal*) had his own staff of constables and nightwatchmen (*chaukidar*s) who patrolled the streets day and night. They observed every house and brought in reports of affrays, murders, marvels and violations of moral law which were recorded in the police diary of the town. These reports were also passed on to the intelligence officials of the court. The civil magistrate (*kazi*), chief cleric (*mufti*) and 'censor' (*muhtasib*) all had a part to play in investigating, recording and alerting authority to commercial, proprietary and moral issues.

In the countryside, watchmen were supported by each village, either on a cash payment or on a share of the grain heap. The office was hereditary and often performed by people of low caste. Village watchmen were sometimes drawn from the same communities as the runners. The watchmen brought news to the headman, village accountant (*patwari*) or chief registrar (*kanungo*) of affrays, assaults, attacks on grain stores and the like. 'Police' constables (*barkandazi*s), sent out from the police station of a village circle kept in contact with these village officials, bringing information to the subdistrict police post (*thana*), sometimes by letter, from whence it could be sent in a newsreport by the newswriter. These constables often wore a gilded badge bearing the title of the emperor, representing the most visible local manifestation of the imperial gaze. Hereditary operators of ferries and 'foresters' who guarded the passes were designated agents and secured on grants of revenue-free land. In addition, the army and other institutions of state alongside magnate households maintained staffs of runners, clerks

---

[19] e.g., the family of Ghulam Ali Azad Bilgrami, famous eighteenth-century Indian writer, A. Schimmel, *Islamic Literatures of India; History of Indian Literature*, VIII, 1 (Wiesbaden, 1973), 45.

(*munshi*s) and newswriters. Even the great Mughal canal systems had their own staffs of watchers to report illegal cuttings by farmers.[20]

These intelligence communities were also enlisted to convey policies of the rulers outward to the population. Officials and runners announced imperial orders and posted signs at the kotwal's platform. The agents of nobles and semi-independent rulers stationed with the ruler or with regional governors listened to the open newsreports as they were read out in court and sent hurriedly written transcripts back to their masters in regional centres.

Social communication and political surveillance

This Indo-Islamic system worked most effectively when it was based on the consensus of the community and rooted in a range of social networks of communication and deference. In addition to the news they garnered through official channels, Indian kings and nobles therefore drew on other sources of information. There was the deep and detailed knowledge of nobles and magnates, such as the Hindu chiefs of Rajasthan, who knew particular regions. This was a *patrimonial knowledge* of the country. Rulers also had access to *affective knowledge*, the knowledge gained through participation in communities of belief and marriage, through religious affiliation and association with holy men, seers, astrologers and physicians.

The populace was expected to play an active part in explaining the state of affairs to the ruler. Documents of 'Representation to the Presence' (*surathal*s or *mahzar*s) were drawn up by notables and officials when issues of fact concerning custom, boundaries, property rights or the doings of officials were in question.[21] Alongside the names of the registrar (*kazi*) and office holders of a subdivision would appear those of its men of status – Sayyids, and Sheikhs, supposed descendants of the Prophet's lineage and *rais*s or 'great men', including Hindus of the commercial castes. These sources of information would act as a check on the direct reports of officials and newswriters.

Indian magnates also had access to the information moving along networks of marriage and kinship. Multiple marriage brought great men

---

[20] Enclosure to G. Blane, Superintendent of the Canal to D. Ochterlony, Resident at Delhi, 9 April 1820, N.K. Sinha and A.K. Dasgupta (eds.), *Selections from Ochterlony Papers in the National Archives of India* (Calcutta, 1964), p. 128; John F. Richards (ed.), *Document Forms for Official Orders of Appointment in the Mughal Empire* (Cambridge, 1986), dct 224b, p. 50.

[21] H.H. Wilson, *Glossary of Judicial and Revenue Terms* (Calcutta, 1864), pp. 320, 494; see, e.g., *U.P. Central Records Office. Calendar of Oriental Records*, III (Allahabad, 1959), pp. 1–13.

a variety of sources of news and gossip. Newsletters were often read out and agents examined during the evening in the emperor's private quarters.[22] Noblewomen sometimes achieved great political independence in India and were in a position to supplement official reports with sources of information drawn from their native territories or kin. Royal ladies carried on independent correspondence under the seals of their husbands, or even under their own seals.[23]

Itinerant specialists were an important source of knowledge for the ruler. Kings and nobles patronised wandering holy-men, astrologers, physicians and even musicians partly because they could bring recent news from their travels. Sufi mystics, especially members of the unorganised Sufi sects, were welcomed by the whole elite. These men made regular pilgrimages throughout India and central Asia. They gave spiritual counsel, practised the healing arts and listened to the concerns of thousands of men and women. Their unworldly status gave them the right and duty to tell men of power the truth without restraint.[24] They carried information between noble houses, and especially between their women's quarters, according to the Venetian, Niccolao Manucci.[25]

Physicians and astrologers performed similar functions. Both these groups of specialists provided valuable secret knowledge. Astrology was a science for predicting the right time for making war, peace or marriage alliances. It was a way of establishing intellectual control in an unstable world. Manucci said of astrologers, 'even the bazaars swarm with these folk and ... they find out all that passes in the houses'.[26] Kings, likewise, called on itinerant doctors to report on the condition of their subjects as well as to reveal new cures and mysteries. The Emperor Shahjahan (r. 1628–57) established a model which was followed up to the time of Ranjit Singh (r. 1799–1839), ruler of the Punjab in the early nineteenth century. One chronicler reported that Muslim and Hindu physicians presented Shahjahan with 'summary reports of the success of their skill in administering remedies'.[27]

Beyond these unofficial agencies lay a petty economy of information.

[22] Francis Gladwin, *The Persian Moonshee* (section 2; extracts from the 'Shahjahan Namah', etc.) (Calcutta, 1801), p. 58.
[23] S.A.I. Tirmizi (ed.), *Edicts from the Mughal Harem* (Delhi, 1971), pp. iii–xii.
[24] e.g., a Mathura seer and Jahangir, 'Tuzuk-i Jahangiri', tr. D. Price as, *Autobiographical Memoirs of the Emperor Jehangueir* (1829, Calcutta, repr. 1972), p. 152; cf. Sheikh Muhammad Ali Hazin in the mid-eighteenth-century, Khairuddin Khan Illahabadi, 'Tuhfa-i-Taza', trans. F.C. Curwen, *The Bulwuntnamah* (Allahabad, 1875), p. 52; Sheikh Ghulam Hussain Tabatabai, 'Siyyar-ul Mutakhkhirin', tr. Nota-Manus, *Seir Mutaqirin* (Calcutta, 1789; repr. Lahore, 1975), II, 524; see below n.34.
[25] W. Irvine (tr.), *Storio do Mogor, or Mughal India, 1653–1703 by Niccolao Manucci* (London, 1907), II, 11–12.
[26] ibid., I, 213.   [27] Gladwin, *Moonshee*, sect. 2, p. 53; Irvine, *Manucci*, II, 217.

*Bazarian*s (or 'bazaar rumour-mongers') were an identifiable group of people who leaked official news to the wider population. They provided grist to the mill of a horde of canny people: midwives, barbers, prostitutes and dancing girls, druggists, bards, itinerant physicians, wandering adepts of the philosopher's stone, amulet sellers, and even sweepers.[28] A good source of day-to-day information were the marriage-brokers, that is women who procured partners for difficult marriages. An eighteenth-century French observer spoke of such a person: 'one of those discreet, shrewd, inquisitive old women, so common in Hindostan where the business of finding a wife or a husband is necessarily contracted by brokerage'.[29]

In principle, the systems of royal intelligence seem dense and intrusive, capable of bringing in a huge volume of information to the rulers. But here some qualifications should be entered. Firstly, the Indo-Islamic system did not apparently compare with the detailed control over information managed by some other contemporary Asian monarchies. In the central domains of the Japanese Tokugawa Shogunate, for instance, households were grouped into fives, and each set to inform on the others. Noticeboards existed in every village on which lithographed copies of all official orders were posted.[30] Secondly, in pre-colonial India, the surveillance and moral suasion exercised by imperial officials did not necessarily give rise to routine bureaucratic procedures. Reports of crimes did not always lead to arrests or punishments by the state, for instance. If they did, rulers did not always inflict standard punishments. Rather, this was a system of watching for infractions of morality or royal right. It was designed to cajole the subject into godly submission, rather than to mount a constant policing of society as some nineteenth century European states attempted to do. Indeed, should a few key people change their allegiance or be eliminated, the system could quickly founder. This helps to explain how Indian states (including the East India Company's dominion) could appear strong and resilient one year and be on the verge of collapse the next.

Even at its height, therefore, the writ of the Mughal Empire could fail to run a few miles from the imperial palace in Delhi. Shiva Das

---

[28] Menials were apparently sometimes used by Indian rulers as informants on 'respect-able' householders, E. Thompson, *Life of Charles, Lord Metcalfe* (London, 1937), pp. 122–3; for professional thief-finders (*Khoji*s), ibid., p. 121.

[29] Ghulam Hussain 'Siyyar,' tr. Nota-Manus, I, translator's Preface, p. 3; cf. *beldars* who knew where to dig wells; finding traces, *ilm-i athar*, necromancy, *ilm-i shoona*, gold extraction, *karahi lena*, etc., E.G. Balfour, *Cyclopaedia of India and Southern Asia* (Madras, 1875).

[30] Chia Nakane, *Kinship and Economic Organisation in Rural Japan* (Princeton, 1975), pp. 69–70, fn.

Lakhnavi (fl. *c.* 1700), who was one of the more independent of the chroniclers, reported on the ambushes of nobles' caravans by rebel Jat countrymen in Hodal, only about sixty miles from Delhi.[31] He noted that two Khans were supposed to be protectors of the roadways, especially the arterial roadway between Lahore and Bengal. The leaders of the caravans were supposed to send prior information about their departure to the Khans who would then escort them from one staging post to the next. On one occasion, merchants who had employed their own guards failed to inform the guardians of the roads of their movements. The rebellious Jats surrounded the caravan with the help of the local villagers and cut the guard to pieces, allowing 'not one of them to escape so as to give information to the Khan'.

Again, while wandering holy-men could be of great use to the state, they could also spread dissidence and bring news to its enemies. Another incident in the last years of Aurangzeb, reported by Shiva Das, conveys a sense of the working of imperial intelligence and of the methods of political dissidents. At the dead of night someone fixed a flag to the railing of the police chief's platform in the central market of Delhi. On it were written the words 'When the king comes out of the Fort, let him beware!' The Kotwal's assistants sent the flag to the Emperor via their master. The newswriters and spies of the city police chief 'entered the details in their reports and submitted the same to his Majesty'.[32] A proclamation was issued to find out who the owner of the flag was. An ascetic of a militant Sikh order was apprehended. He was flogged and died from his punishment, despite the presence of physicians of both the Greek and Indian schools.

Information to knowledge: indigenous constructions of Indian society

We now move from systems of surveillance and consider how the information collected was organised and used by the rulers and social elites. Some writers have argued that the intellectual and administrative techniques of pre-colonial governments were utterly different from those of the early colonial period, but this is an exaggeration. The Indian elites collected, centralised and stored information. They employed concepts of religious community, caste and breeding to distinguish between their subjects. Some of these ideas were taken over and elaborated by the later British rulers. The Indian rulers' search for knowledge, however, was

---

[31] Shiva Das Lakhnavi, *Shahnamah Munawwar Kalam*, tr. S.H. Askari (Patna, 1980), p. 21; cf. Ishwardas Nagar, *Futuhat*, pp. 227–8.

[32] *Shahnamah Munawwar Kalam*, p. 115.

not simply utilitarian or bureaucratic in motivation. Kingship for them was an expression of power, a support of Faith, but also, as the careers of the Emperor Akbar and his more learned descendants remind us, an office directed to knowledge of God and the world. Mughal rule was a discourse amongst the learned and the noble, as well as a system of revenue extraction. The rulers of the seventeenth and eighteenth centuries formulated their information about the country and people in a number of different and overlapping idioms. Among others, we can distinguish a purely empirical idiom, an idiom of spiritual anthropology, one of 'moral ecology' and one of genealogy.

First, then, Indo-Islamic descriptions could be thoroughly *empirical* and analytical about space and time. Precise measurement of time and space was valued; historical time was not 'fuzzy', at least in this tradition.[33] Earlier writers in Sanskrit had perfected the orderly listing of types of people, animals, emotions, forms of speech, and so on.[34] These rational techniques were reinforced by the emphasis on precise testimony characteristic of the Islamic schools. This intellectual discipline of empirical accuracy was to serve some former Mughal administrators well when they later entered British service.

Formal knowledge, the knowledge of geography, resources and statistics, was accumulated by the pre-colonial regimes in much the same way as the future British conquerors were to do. For example, the seventeenth-century courtier, Inayat Khan, included details on the economy and statistics of Tibet, a distant frontier region, in his 'History of Shahjahan'.[35] These he garnered from his father who had led a punitive expedition there. Included are distances, the position of routeways, rivers and sources of fresh water. He also gave details of local products and, in particular, gold-panning farms. All these materials would have been assembled by debriefing harkaras or from eye-witness accounts of the commanders. Later, such materials were recorded more formally. The 'Chahar Gulshan' of about 1760 contains massive details on distances, marches and local resources.[36] Large archives of route maps and 'strip-maps' were accumulated, but Mughal and other indigenous maps rarely 'displayed scalar fidelity in the

---

[33] A brief but clear exposition of this position is found in D. Chakrabarty, 'Modernity and ethnicity in India', *South Asia*, special issue, 17, 1994, 147–9.

[34] e.g., for the eighteenth-century Braj area, G.A. Grierson (ed., tr.) *Bhasha-Bhushana of Jaswant Singh* (Bombay, 1894).

[35] Inayat Khan, *Shahjahan Nama* (ed., tr., W. Begley and Z. Desai) (Delhi, 1990), pp. 218, 233.

[36] e.g. Subhan Rai Khattri, 'Khulasatu-t-Tawarikh' and Rai Chaturman Kayasth, 'Chahar Gulshan', tr. ed. Jadunath Sarkar, *The India of Aurangzib: topography statistics and roads compared with the India of Akbar* (Calcutta, 1901).

geometric sense'.[37] This, along with the general lack of concern for precise political boundaries, probably reflected the absence of a conception of absolute property right such as had developed in contemporary Europe.

While such empirical surveillance of society could be intensive, it was directed to specific rather than general aims. It was often idiosyncratic and rarely correlated in any general matrix of information. In the field of revenue assessment, of course, there existed a sophisticated system based on periodic measurement of fields. The data collected were stored in the records of the village accountant, maintained by the kanungo, and checked by state officials.[38] Sea customs houses minutely registered the movement of ships.[39] By contrast, in levying land transit taxes, the state dealt with great merchants or headmen of communities of traders, and the rulers' commercial information was of a grosser type. Newsletters sometimes mentioned commercial events and the doings of great merchants. Merchants consulted with the market controllers and the kotwal to set fair prices. The state had a commercial memory, but it was a rather limited one.

Census information was apparently less fine-grained than in some other Asian societies such as Japan or Burma, possibly because, in broad terms, it was money rather than people that was in short supply. Household censuses (khanashumaris) were designed for taxation of trades and professions in bazaars and towns.[40] The police sometimes counted the influx of strangers into city quarters.[41] But regular

[37] J. Schwartzberg in J.B. Harley and D. Woodward (eds.), History of Cartography, II, 1 (Chicago, 1992), p. 507; I. Habib, 'Cartography in Mughal India', Medieval India. A Miscellany, 4, 1977, 123–34, esp. 130–4 on the partial shift from route plans to 'medians and parallels'; S. Gole, Indian Maps and Plans from the earliest times to the advent of European Surveys (Delhi, 1989); on deficiencies of Maratha maps, T.J. Shejwalkar, Panipat 1761 (Pune, 1946), pp. 85, 123.

[38] Irfan Habib, The Agrarian System of Mughal India (1556–1707) (Bombay, 1963), passim; full details of local revenue documents in important successor states are to be found in S.P. Gupta, The Agrarian System of Eastern Rajasthan (Delhi, 1987); and in D. Singh, The State Landlords and Peasants. Rajasthan in the 18th century (Delhi, 1990), pp. 5–7, 167–96; 'Khanashumari', H.H. Wilson, A Glossary of Judicial and Revenue Terms (Calcutta, 1855, repr. Delhi, 1968), p. 276; Susan Bayly, Saints, Goddesses and Kings. Muslims and Christians in South Indian Society, 1700—1900 (Cambridge, 1989), pp. 81–2, fn. 16.

[39] Om Prakash, The Dutch East India Company and the Economy of Bengal, 1630–1720 (Princeton, 1985), pp. 27, 221–61; S.N. Sen (ed.) Indian Travels of Thevenot and Careri. Indian Records Series (Delhi, 1949), pp. 2–3.

[40] cf. S.P. Gupta, The Agrarian System of Eastern Rajasthan (Delhi, 1986), pp. 317–33. Khanashumaris were sporadically taken by local administrations until the early nineteenth century, but British officials increasingly rejected them as 'unreliable' bases for population estimates, see Durga Prasad Bhattacharya, Report on the Population Estimates of India, III, 1811–20, Census of India 1961 (Calcutta, 1962), p. 101.

[41] S.N. Sen, Administrative System of the Marathas (Calcutta, 1923), p. 390.

estimates of the whole population were almost unknown. Births and deaths generally remained the purview of genealogical priests. Such computations as did exist omitted low castes, beggars, tribals and nomads, and could only be taken as estimates of population within a large margin of error. When he wanted to find out the size of Delhi's population, the Emperor Jahangir (r. 1605–27) sent the police to count the males gathered in wrestling grounds on the day of a very popular festival. He also counted the number of horses coming into the city for sale and made rough calculation on these rather exiguous bases.[42] Later counts were less hit and miss, but regular censuses were not instituted until the British statistical movement of the mid-nineteenth century.

For plains India, the materials assembled in the 'Institutes of Akbar' (Ain-i Akbari) provided a second stage of knowledge formation and set the pattern for a large number of later topographical works. In the 'Institutes' a heterogeneous set of materials was fused together by the personal concerns with good government of Akbar and his chief minister, Abul Fazl. Revenue and military statistics, fragments of history, regulations for the court and imperial camp and orders for state officials were juxtaposed with remarks on the personal aims and beliefs of the Emperor. Evidently, this was not a gazetteer which processed information as comprehensively as the later colonial or even contemporary Chinese gazetteers. On the other hand, it was by no means a random collection of information. Discussions of astronomical observations, for instance, are placed in front of the section on kingship because regulation of festivals was a prime duty of kings.[43]

One feature of the 'Institutes' and some later Mughal descriptive works was the care taken in depicting Hindu and other non-Muslim religious and social practice.[44] Akbar and his ministers went to great lengths to secure information from often-unwilling Hindu pandits. He staged debates on matters of religion and cosmology and made translations of Sanskrit works.[45] This search for dispassionate knowledge about human faith constituted a kind of *spiritual anthropology*, a blending of the inheritence of Greek observation and enlightened Islamic

[42] 'Tuzuk-i-Jahangiri' tr. Price, pp. 12–13.

[43] S.A.A. Rizvi, *Religious and Intellectual History of the Muslims in Akbar's Reign with special reference to Abu'l Fazl (1556–1605)* (Delhi, 1975), pp. 183–5, 273–4; for contemporary historiography, see K.A. Nizami, *On History and Historians of Medieval India* (Delhi, 1983), pp. 225–44.

[44] Jahangir carried on Akbar's practice of ecumenical debate with the Pandits, but says, anticipating the Christian missionaries, that he 'found it impossible to settle their minds to a steady contemplation of the perfections of the Supreme Being', 'Tuzuk-i-Jahangiri', tr. Price, p. 51.

[45] Rizvi, *Akbar*, pp. 203–22.

sentiment. The Arab travellers Alberuni (in India *c*. 1301) and Ibn Battuta (1304–78) had pioneered this tradition. Muhsin Fani (*c*. 1615–70) was heir to it in his 'Account of all Religions'.[46] This Iranian traveller made a survey of Indian religions by collating personal observation and interviews with the 'high priests' of different communities. In a similar spirit, the 'Institutes' records Hindu cosmological theories and cycles of kingship, descriptions of bathing places and even an account of widow-burning, which was disapproved of by Muslims. There was more to this tradition than rational observation. Abul Fazl, Akbar's minister, was also seeking knowledge of Hindu religion and cosmology because God had given all men some modicum of religious understanding. The Emperor and his Minister believed that a varied and respectful society could be nurtured in India through such mutual knowledge. This tradition remained vital in the eighteenth century and was to influence many Indians who worked in the service of the East India Company.

Under Akbar the interest in the Hindu, Jain and Buddhist tradition had been directed to the great classics of the Sanskrit tradition. The later Mughal intelligentsia became increasingly interested in the details of Indian folklore, arts and music. One important compilation of this sort was Mirza Muhammad ibn Fakhruddin's 'Tuhfat-al Hind' produced for the Emperor Aurangzeb's (r. 1658–1707) son, Prince Jahandar Shah, who cultivated close relations with Hindu notables.[47] In eighteenth-century writings, folktales from Indian and Persian-Arabic sources were brought together in many such compilations.[48] This 're-discovery' of popular culture had something in common with contemporary developments in Europe; it certainly created a body of texts which was consulted by nineteenth-century European devotees of the folkish. But the Mughal investigations also embodied a political strategy. They reflected the growing dependence of Indo-Muslim rulers on the Hindu population. The patronage offered by the later Mughals and many regional rulers to folklore, poetry, dance, music and astrology derived from Hindu sources signalled a programme of political incorporation. Paradoxically, the bringing together of social knowledges by the Indo-Muslim elites

[46] Mushin Fani, 'Dabistan-al Madhahib', D. Shea and A. Troyer (tr., eds.), *The Dabistan* (repr., Lahore 1973), esp. pp. 5, 207, 211 (on *sati*), 284–7 (on 'the Nanac sect', i.e. Sikhs); Schimmel, *Islamic Literature*, pp. 40–1; Fani was probably a Zoroastrian, but his intellectual position was perfectly compatible with that of 'liberal' Muslim thinkers.

[47] H. Ethé, *Catalogue of Persian Manuscripts in the Library of the India Office*, I, (London, 1903), pp. 1, 117–19.

[48] e.g., the work of Mahomed Hasan, a Khattri convert and Faizabad munshi, on the creeds and sects of Hindus and Muslims in India, E.V. Rieu, *Catalogue of the Persian Manuscripts in the British Museum* (London, 1879), I, 64–5.

displayed the limitations and compromises required of imperial authority as much as its solidity and centralising power.[49]

Some learned administrators of the seventeenth and eighteenth centuries wrote in a related idiom which drew inspiration from Greek, Arabic and Persian ethical literature (*akhlaq*).[50] This tradition tended to regard the kingdom as an ideal city, or as a vast human body. These theories of *moral ecology*, as it were, were quite compatible with Hindu learning. They held that the polity, like the body, was subject to diseases, and different regions and races, like different bodily organs, were the seat of different humours which determined moral and physical qualities. These could be kept in balance by a good king, but ineptitude could throw the body politic into disorder. A writer such as Ali Ibrahim Khan (fl. *c.* 1765–93) attributed the decline of the Empire during his own lifetime to the moral and physical indolence of the Muslim cities of the rich and enervating riverain tracts. The peppery, chilli-eating and rebellious Marathas, he thought, represented a choleric irruption from the dry central uplands.[51]

This way of knowing the country was not necessarily exclusive of other modes. The same writer drew on another tradition of understanding human quality, which was *genealogical*. This held that families as well as races could embody innate qualities, whether it was the charisma of the Prophet, still vital among the Sayyids, or the light of Godly rule nurtured even among the most distant descendants of Timur. The Mughals had always been vitally interested in the genealogy of administrative families.[52] Visitors from outside India deposited family pedigrees at court. The interest extended to Hindu royal houses which sometimes acquired fictive genealogies within Islamic history. Thus to Ali Ibrahim Khan and Murtaza Hussain Bilgrami (another eighteenth-

[49] Following Foucault and Said it is often taken as axiomatic that the influence of a knowledge or a discourse both reflects and substantialises the political 'weight' of its authors. Yet we shall suggest that in pre-colonial and colonial times the emergence of systems of knowledge could equally well reflect the weaknesses of power and legitimacy, or situations of intense social competition. Assertive 'knowledges' might grow up on the troubled margins of power. This apparently challenges Foucault's main thesis, but it is consonant with his historical account of the emergence of 'insurgent knowledges' from the margins of post-war French life.

[50] Rizvi, *Akbar*, pp. 365–6; P. Hardy, 'Approaches to pre-modern Indo-Muslim historical writing', in P. Robb (ed.), *Society and Ideology* (Delhi, 1993), pp. 49–71; *Encyclopaedia of Islam*, new edn, I (London, 1960), 325–9.

[51] Ali Ibrahim Khan, 'Tarikh-i-Ibrahim Khan', in H.M. Elliot and J. Dowson, *The History of India told by its Own Historians* [hereafter *HI*], VIII (London, 1877), 263; cf. Ghulam Ali Azad Bilgrami, 'Khazana-i Amira', cit. P. Setu Madhava Rao, *Eighteenth Century Deccan* (Bombay, 1963), p. 227.

[52] Shahjahan enquired into the 'personal and ancestral qualifications' of applicants for land grants and office, 'Ruka'at-i Alamgiri', tr. J.H. Bilimoria, *Ruka'at-i-Alamgiri or letters of Aurangzebe with historical and explanatory notes* (London, 1908), p. 18.

century administrator historian) the house of Shivaji was descended from the last Zoroastrian emperor of Iran whose family had fled to Rajasthan after the rise of Islam.[53] For these writers, even enemies of the Empire needed a royal pedigree. In fact, the elite was more deeply concerned with breeding and gentility ('class' is here anachronistic) than it was with religion and caste. Chroniclers tended implicitly to blame the decline of Empire on royal and noble miscegenation with women of low origins.[54]

This holistic, even humoural understanding of polity, perhaps explains the Indo-Muslim fascination with marvels. Newswriters recorded marvels, but they also appear in memoirs, histories and encyclopaedias. The Emperor Jahangir, for instance, recounted how the Portuguese not only sliced off the leg of a traveller, but then sewed it back on, confirming their status as knowledgeable monsters.[55] Even in the later years of the Empire, newswriters were expected to report on strange events in the animal, vegetable or mineral world – the discovery of pearls the size of limes, for example.[56] The king was the chief natural philosopher as well as ruler and Shadow of God. Marvels, or horrors, might also alert the state to imminent danger. In the later years of the Emperor Aurangzeb, the chief harkara of Delhi, Shankar Rao, reported to the Presence that in the house of the recorder (kanungo) of Narnaul, a nearby town, a supposedly dead woman had given birth to triplets on her funeral pyre. As 'proof of the power of the Lord', one child had survived.[57] While this and similar reports might be regarded as mere filling, as in contemporary tabloid newpapers, something more than inquisitiveness is indicated. Since God alone was capable of overriding the laws of nature, it was vitally important for the king to be alerted to these irruptions in the body politic, so that he could judge whether it betokened divine displeasure. To eighteenth-century Indians, the collection of such information was an entirely rational act, but it was rational, of course, by reference to certain cosmological assumptions.

Rulers needed to have news of moral and religious infractions practised by their subjects, since they were ultimately guardians of Islam and Hindu Dharma (righteousness). Evidently, the close bureaucratic control of heresy and witchcraft which forged the early modern

[53] Ali Ibrahim Khan, 'Tarikhi-i-Ibrahim Khan', *HI*, VIII, 258.
[54] Anon., 'Tarikh-i Ahmad Shah', tr. D. Forsyth, Elliot Add. 30,783, ff. 27b–28, 52b–53, BL; Hardy, 'Indo-Muslim historical writing'.
[55] 'Tuzuk-i-Jahangiri', tr. Price, pp. 124–5; possibly a bowdlerised form of the legend of SS Cosmo and Damian.
[56] Extracts from Delhi *akhbarats*, *Englishman*, 18 Apr. 1834.
[57] Shiva Das Lakhnavi, *Shahnamah Munawwar Kalam*, p. 118.

European state had no equivalent in India.[58] Nor did persecution of rival coreligionists reach the levels of Shia Iran, where the state felt itself under threat from heterodoxy. In India, issues of moral conduct were normally dealt with by arbitration within or between communities. Nevertheless, officials did from time to time enforce outward conformity. Thus brawlers, drunkards, counterfeiters and eunuch-makers were supposed to be expelled from the city by the 'censor' (muhtasib).[59] Certain religious groups whose beliefs or practice had passed beyond the bounds of propriety were also subject to surveillance and harrassment. The Emperor Aurangzeb, apostle of a political puritanism, tried to stop women worshipping at tombs and forbade ecstatic Sufi dancing; he kept a close eye on any religious 'innovations' among his nobles and officers.[60] He also deputed an official to watch over the western ports and suppress the Ismaili sect who were regarded as blasphemous apostates by the orthodox.[61] Again, Aurangzeb tried to extend state surveillance to new areas. Islamic town officials were introduced in parts of the Deccan and Rajasthan where he wished to assert the sovereignty of Islam over Hindu enemies.[62] Hindus who had paid the Emperor's poll tax on them (the *jizya*) were issued with certificates.

This tilt towards orthodoxy and moral surveillance was, however, difficult to maintain. The poll tax was given up and most eighteenth-century Muslim rulers were too circumspect to reintroduce it. Administrators recognised that the law officers' spiritual surveillance could not extend to Hindus. Indian rulers tried from time to time to bring into being a more godly order, but they could not easily construct a persecuting state.[63]

How important, then, was religion to the elite's understanding of society and government? Indo-Muslim traditions of social enquiry and representation were never communal in the sense that they saw India as a field for the conflict of two irreconcilable faiths. This does not mean, however, that officials and writers were unconcerned with differences in

---

[58] R.I. Moore, *The Formation of a Persecuting Society. Power and Deviance in Western Europe, 950–1250* (London, 1987).

[59] A.M and N.D. Ahuja, *Persecution of Muslims by Aurangzeb. Guru Tegh Bahadur's Martyrdom Centenary Publication* (Chandigarh, 1981), pp. 19–20, 31–2, citing J.N. Sarkar, p. 141.

[60] Bilimoria, tr., *Ruka'at-i-Alamgiri*, letter to Muhammad Muazzam about celebration of a pagan Persian festival, p. 5; about drunkenness at a tomb, pp. 69–70.

[61] J.F. Richards (ed.), *Document Forms for Official Orders of Appointment in the Mughal Empire* (Cambridge, 1986), no. 230b, pp. 59–60. 'Some account of the sect of Ismaeliyas ... ', *Calcutta Journal, or Political Commercial and Literary Gazette*, 25 Dec. 1818; draws on Mughal historian Khafi Khan, on Colebrooke and Indian accounts.

[62] Satish Chandra, *Mughal Religious Policies; the Rajputs and the Deccan* (Delhi, 1992), pp. 194–215.

[63] ibid.

religious tradition. Their governing principles were not 'secular' in the sense that religion could be seen as a matter of political indifference. Chroniclers wrote of the persecution of Hindus by Muslims and the retaliation of the latter. A revealing case is the Hindu historian Bahadur Singh's account of the history of Kashmir (c. 1824) which is based on earlier texts in addition to his own sources.[64] He recounts many examples of the rape and murder of Kashmiri Hindus by Muslim soldiers and gangs of insurgents over the centuries. Under Aurangzeb, he says, 'ten seers' (twenty pounds) weight of sacred threads (the symbol of high caste status) were collected from forcibly converted Hindus, many of whom were later to 'reconvert' to Hinduism.[65] Yet the aim of his account was not to raise the general consciousness of Hindus against Muslims so much as to to explain why Kashmiri Brahmins were 'worse than Malechas [sic]', that is dirty foreign barbarians, and why they spread all over the Empire in its decline and 'raised disturbances'.[66] This was not a Hindu chronicler savaging Muslims as such, but an envious clerk attributing the success of his Kashmiri rivals to the degradation of their blood and honour.[67] It was a localised factional discourse rather than a totalising communal one. Likewise, the historian Khairuddin Khan was able to describe at length a conflict between Hindus and Muslims in 1776 in the town of Jaunpur, reserving his choicest invective not for the Hindus, but for 'barbarian' Pathan Muslims.[68] Bringing together religious traditions within the same frame of reference necessarily implied distinguishing between them; it did not, however, imply sustained antagonism between them.

Pre-colonial Indians, then, had an acute sense of religious difference, but this was rarely expressed in broad communal terms. Similarly, they created essentialisations of social types as freely as did later colonial administrators, but these were not yet fixed in a racialist hierarchy. In a sense, the Persian, Turkish and central Asian nobles and intelligentsia who served the Empire could be seen as the first 'orientalists'. For some of them, India east of Delhi, land of the *purbis* ('easterners') was too hot, too full of black men and idolaters. Indo-Muslim travellers were as easily prey to tales of the exotic as early modern Europeans. Bahadur Singh claimed that the females of Kumaon, on the mountainous northern borders of the Empire, were regularly consigned to brothels when their men failed to pay revenue.[69] He had also heard that astrology in the region was so exact that people contracted marriages with an eye to

---

[64] notably the 'Hadikat-al Aklim' of Murtaza Hussain Bilgrami, *HI*, VIII, 180–1.
[65] Bahadur Singh, 'Yadgar-i Bahaduri', tr. Elliot Papers, Add. Mss. 30,786, f. 347b.
[66] ibid., ff. 356b, 357.   [67] ibid.   [68] Khairuddin, *Bulwuntnamah*, pp. 77–84.
[69] Bahadur Singh, f. 296b.

dying on the same day as their spouses.[70] For more rigid Muslims, as for later British missionaries, Brahmins were the particular agents of Satan. Again, bandits were said to abound on India's roads;[71] here was another theme which was taken over and elaborated by the colonial rulers. For one renowned eighteenth-century Sufi of Persian origin, the whole country was a 'dung hill'.[72] For other immigrants it was rich, comfortable and replete with beautiful women and marvels.[73] India was routinely described in terms of races and castes; minute distinctions of skin colour and appearance were noted in police reports or recorded in miniature paintings.

India was thus essentialised and 'othered' (to use the rebarbative modern jargon) in the course of subjection by its Asian conquerors. Nevertheless, no rigid racial hierarchy was constructed by them. Race and caste remained only one signifier among many. These included rank, pedigree, personal appearance and closeness to Sufi masters, or other men of religious power. All people possessed useful virtues and all could achieve merit through bending to God's will.

Finally, it was not the imperial state alone which tried, however fitfully, to sort information and to standardise knowledge in line with political preferences or theories of cosmology and society. Subordinate kings and the later regional rulers did the same thing. In the early eighteenth century, Maharaja Sawai Jai Singh II of Jaipur (r. 1700–43) made a collection of Sanskrit religious works which he had identified through agents posted at the major religious places across the subcontinent. The core of the collection was a library started by his father who had been despatched in Mughal service to many parts of India.[74] Jai Singh's aim was to amass Vaishnavite knowledge and thereby reinaugurate classical godliness. He is known to have tried to reimpose traditional moral rules on ascetic orders and the lower castes.[75] Other Hindu rulers of the late seventeenth and eighteenth centuries had similar goals. This accumulation of Hindu knowledge was different from the purified and nationalistic Hinduism promoted by the western-influenced reformers of the nineteenth century. The focussing of various classical Hindu traditions (*samaj*s) in royal courts and in learned schools such as Nadia,

---

[70] ibid., f. 297.   [71] 'Tuzuk-i-Jahangiri', tr. Price, p. 39.

[72] F.C. Belfour (tr.), *The Life of Sheikh Mohammmed Ali Hazin written by himself* (London, 1830), p. 279, cf. pp. 260–3.

[73] e.g. Mir Sher Ali 'Afsos's 'Araish-i Mehfil', Garcin de Tassy, *Histoire de la Littérature Hindouie et Hindoustanie* [hereafter *LH*] (1875, repr. New York, 1972), I, pp. 125–36.

[74] G.N. Bahura, 'Glimpses of historical information from the manuscripts in the *potikhana* of Jaipur', in J.N. Asopa (ed.), *Cultural Heritage of Jaipur* (Jodhpur, 1982), pp. 104–20.

[75] V.S. Bhatnagar, *Life and Times of Sawai Jai Singh 1688–1743* (Delhi, 1974), p. 337, cf. 264–6, 337–41; A.K. Roy, *History of the Jaipur City* (Delhi, 1978), pp. 27–9.

Banaras or Pune,[76] however, gave rise to an awareness not only of difference but of commonalities in practice and belief. It is difficult to believe that it was colonialism alone which produced a sense of religious self-consciousness among Hindus and Muslims.[77] These earlier, indigenous constructions of society and polity were seized on and manipulated by the British during the colonial era. They also provided a set of images and doctrines which could be projected into the colonial public sphere by Indians, and used to challenge British hegemony.

The 'dynastic security state' of the eighteenth century

The chapter now passes on to the eighteenth century. It argues that while the Mughal information systems were disrupted in some areas, many Indian states intensified surveillance in the course of the struggle to retain economic and human resources. The appearance of foreign enemies, notably the British, made dynastic security their pre-eminent concern.

The sophisticated Indo-Muslim intelligence system had been vulnerable when the populace and magnates challenged the legitimacy of the state. This does not imply that the decline of the Mughals, or of any other pre-colonial state, was primarily caused by the decay of information systems, only that their atrophy was a potent element in that decline once it had begun. Rebels made particular efforts to knock out newswriters and daks. Vested interests in the periphery of Empire combined to deny information to the ruler, or to pollute it. Some symptoms of this decay were already clear by the end of the reign of Aurangzeb. The Emperor complained, with justice, that he had never been told of the imminence of war with the English in 1684–5.[78] John Fryer who visited the Emperor in the 1670s remarked that the great nobles and administrators fighting the Marathas in the Deccan 'live lazily and in pay'. Along with the newswriters and literati, they had an interest in keeping the war spluttering on. He wrote that the generals and newswriters 'consult to deceive the Emperor, on whom he depends

[76] e.g., for Bengal rulers and scholarship at Nadia, S. Vidyabhusana, *History of Indian Logic. Ancient, Mediaeval and Modern Schools* (1920, repr. Delhi, 1971), pp. 392–5, 458–85; Ramcomul Sen on this, *Asiatic Journal*, n.s. xvi, 1835, 43–4; Samita Sinha, *Pandits in a Changing Environment* (Calcutta, 1993), pp. 1–10; Banaras as a place of all-India knowledge, patronised by Shiva, M.H. Sastri, 'Dakshina Pandits in Benares', *Indian Antiquary*, 41, 1912, 7–13.

[77] cf. A. Nandy, *The Intimate Enemy. Loss and recovery of self under colonialism* (Delhi, 1988); G. Pandey, *The Construction of Communalism in Colonial North India* (Delhi, 1990).

[78] I.B. Watson, *Foundation for Empire. English Private Trade in India, 1659–1760* (Delhi, 1980), p. 283.

for a true state of things'.[79] The imperial intelligence services could, of course, hit hard on occasions, as when they captured the Maratha king, Shambaji, in 1689.[80] Yet other Maratha leaders escaped the Mughal net and, by the 1720s, it was the Maratha chiefs and not the Mughals who had the upper hand in the war of information across the uplands of the Deccan. The Mughal attempt at the beginning of the eighteenth century to expel Hindu Khattris from the office of newswriter in the Punjab, because they were thought to be favourable to the Sikhs, was another, self-inflicted wound.[81]

The declining quality of sectors of the Indian intelligence system during the eighteenth century can partly be attributed to economic change. The newswriting literati living in small towns were subject to the same harsh pressures as other elites. Grants of land and pensions lapsed; estates were seized by intruders. The letters of the early eighteenth century from the permanent ambassadors stationed by the Mughal Emperors at the Rajput courts and from Rajput envoys in Delhi are full of complaints about the failure of their salaries to materialise.[82] When rulers farmed out the right to collect taxes to entrepreneurs in order to secure ready cash, this inevitably disrupted the flow of information. Revenue farmers generally maintained agents and even newswriters at the courts of their nominal overlords, but day-to-day matters were dealt with by the magnates, who kept their own books and maintained their own relations with the village accountants and revenue overseers.[83] Thus it was that some of the most powerful men in Indian and British territories in the mid-eighteenth century ran private intelligence services, as well as maintaining armies and private trade. Some of these were farmers of commodities and revenues. Others were great servants of indigenous courts who entered the fray of diplomacy and intelligence in their own interest.[84] One of the most knowledgeable men in the later eighteenth century was the Peshwa's minister, Nana Fadnavis, who ran a famed personal intelligence service. The old Maratha intelligence

---

[79] ibid., p. 282: J. Fryer, *A New Account of the East Indies and Persia* (repr., London, 1909) II, 52, cf. 49; J.F. Richards, *Mughal Administration in Golconda* (Oxford, 1973), p. 233, cf. 76.

[80] Ishwardas Nagar reports many intelligence successes by the Mughal harkaras, *Futuhat*, passim.

[81] Muzaffar Alam, *The Crisis of Empire in Mughal North India* (Delhi, 1986), pp. 197–9.

[82] G.D. Sharma (ed.), *Vakil Reports Maharajgan (1693–1712 A.D.)* (Delhi, 1987) see, e.g., nos. 68, 78, 79, 81, 86.

[83] M. Bajekal notes the decline of state information in Jaipur after revenue farming was introduced, M. Bajekal, 'Agricultural Production in selected Talukas of the Jaipur state, 1700–1770', unpub. PhD thesis, London University, 1990.

[84] e.g. Beniram Pandit, an agent of Warren Hastings and Divakar Pant, T. Shejwalkar, *Nagpur Affairs. A Selection of Marathi Letters from the Menavli Daftar* (Pune, 1954), pp. xxxviii, xxxix.

service, the Jasud department, also survived but now acted as a semi-independent corporation, providing services for different rulers.[85]

Some regions which had once been partially under Mughal surveillance, such as the Jat territories, had become terra incognita to them by the middle of the eighteenth century. In other regions, such as Malwa, flows of political information were abruptly redirected, in this case from Delhi to Maratha Pune. The dislocation of some of the main flows of trade also meant that a private information famine accompanied the collapse of royal intelligence services since credit notes and letters were often carried by the same runners. Until the late 1790s, it remained difficult for commercial people in Banaras to pass credit notes on some larger towns further to the west.

Nevertheless, in the domain of information as in so many other spheres, the eighteenth century retains its paradoxical character. Many sectors of the Mughal comunications system survived, were regenerated, or even expanded. Internal trade continued at a high level in the lower Ganges valley. Pilgrimage and long distance migration was increased by the plethora of aspiring rulers, particularly Rajputs, Marathas and even Sikhs, seeking benediction at the holy places of the Ganges. Powerful people were interested, therefore, in maintaining a basic framework of communications. This came about in two ways. Firstly, the Delhi-centred system of newswriters became a multilateral one.[86] Each significant ruler maintained newswriters at the courts of other big players, and expected to receive their emissaries. This system of 'admitted spies', as a British officer described it,[87] was usually supported by large numbers of hidden agents. Secondly, by appointing the same merchants or officials as head postmasters, the basic system of royal and private mail distribution could be maintained. The result was that regular news continued to come in over vast distances, even in the face of continuous political disturbance. For example, runners could still get messages through from Kandahar in central Asia to Banaras, via Lahore, even during the turbulent years 1780–1820.[88]

Many eighteenth-century rulers were of doubtful legitimacy and were targets of incessant plotting by aspiring kingmakers, mercenary Euro-

[85] Joshi (ed.), *Persian Records*, pp. 21–7; Shejwalkar (ed.), *Nagpur Affairs*, p. li; for Peshwa Baji Rao's intelligence, H.L.O. Garrett and G.L. Chopra, *Events at the Court of Ranjit Singh, 1810–1817* (Lahore, 1935).

[86] M. Fisher, 'The office of Akhbar Nawis. The transition from Mughal to British forms', *MAS*, 27, I, 1993, 45–82.

[87] T.D. Broughton, *Letters from a Mahratta Camp in the year 1809* (repr. London, 1892), p. 25.

[88] Though a 'regular dak' was replaced for long periods by individual harkara runs, see, Abstract of Resdt Lucknow to Govt, 3, 12, 29 Oct. 1798, Wellesley, Add. 13,529, BL.

peans and crowds of envious relatives. The intelligencer and runner, therefore, increased in importance as rulers hired more agents for internal and external surveillance. Nawab Shuja-ud Daulah of Awadh was reputed to be the 'best-informed man in Hindoostan'. The figures are extremely unreliable, but whereas the Mughal Empire was said to have been served by 4,000 imperial harkaras,[89] Awadh alone in the 1770s was said to have had 20,000 harkaras,[90] that is about one spy-runner for every two regular soldiers. Awadh had its own intelligence agents working deep in British Bengal, for example.[91] These figures related only to agents of the state, and numerous others were employed by nobles, landowners and merchants.

As Awadh's political position became more precarious in the 1780s and 1790s, surrounded by the Sikhs and Marathas and subverted by the British, its officials desperately sought increased dynastic security. The Kayastha patriot, Lala Jhau Lal, remodelled the intelligence services to outface his British enemies. Sir John Shore, visiting Lucknow as Governor-General in 1797, wrote, 'The Dauk, an intelligence department was very extensive under Jao Lal.'[92] He went on to allege that it was a 'source of great oppression, as the Hercarrahs were much oftner employed as spies and informers for the purpose of extortion than in their proper duties'. Jhau Lal had amalgamated the offices of revenue manager (diwan) and head of intelligence.[93] He also controlled the Lucknow city police chief and used key men in the army as informers.[94] He had established agents at Delhi and, during the later 1790s, the

---

[89] Danishmand Khan, entry 11 Ramzan 1120 A.H. cit. W. Irvine, *The Army of the Indian Moghuls* (repr. Delhi, 1962), p. 213. I thank Dr Banmali Tandan.

[90] Muhammad Faiz Baksh, 'Tarikh-i Farah Baksh' tr. W. Hoey as *Memoirs of Delhi and Faizabad* (Allahabad, 1889), II, 7; cf. ibid., 18, 69, 319; changes in Jaipur intelligence, Bhatnagar, *Jai Singh*, pp. 307–10, esp. 309; For Tipu Sultan, '*Hukumnamah harkaron*', Asiatic Society of Bengal cat. no. 1681, W. Ivanow, *Concise Descriptive Catalogue of the Persian Mss. in the Collection of the Asiatic Society of Bengal* (Calcutta, 1924), pp. 766–7. I am grateful to Professor S. Bose, Dr S. Digby and Mr N.M. Chancellor, respectively, for locating, translating and commenting on this document.

[91] One Gulab Singh, in charge of the 'Dauk and Hircarrah' Department, was attempting to set up a channel of the Nawab's intelligence between Calcutta and Lucknow, Select Cttee to Capt. G. Harper, 7 Nov. 1770, Orme Mss. OV, 69, f. 110, OIOC.

[92] J. Shore to P. Speke, 5 April 1797, Wellesley, Add. 13,523, BL; cf. Gujarat where the 'chronicler, news-reporter and courier' had infiltrated the revenue offices, M.F. Lokhandwala, tr., ed., Hasan Ali, *Mirat-i-Ahmadi*, (Baroda, 1965), p. 357.

[93] Shore to Speke, 5 April 1797. Jhau Lal, 'an unworthy person', was also allied by marriage with the family of Himmat Bahadur, the powerful Gosain commander, Cherry to Shore, 13 June 1795, HM 577 f. 256; in the biographies in HM 557, Jhao Lal is 'an obscure individual'; see, K. K. Datta, 'Raja Jhaw Lal of the Oudh Court', *Journal of the Bihar and Orissa Research Society*, 23, 4, 1937, 502–15; later, under Nawab Sadat Ali Khan, another Kayastha newswriter 'retained all the powers of conducting the state', Bahadur Singh, f. 378b; cf. ibid., f. 391, Lucknow as an informer's paradise.

[94] Abstract of Resdt Lucknow to Govt, 13 Apr. 1798, Wellesley, 13,529, BL.

roads of the Nawabi were constantly criss-crossed by his horseback despatch riders as he desperately sought for allies among the Marathas and Afghans.[95]

This typical pattern of Indian political change, in which officials merged offices to concentrate power, had been anticipated in Nawabi Bengal. Here, Raja Ram, harkara, 'who was unrivalled in his work'[96] on the troublesome frontier with the Marathas, became governor of Midnapur in 1752–3. He remained 'the Nabob's head spy' and, according to Company sources, a determined enemy of the British.[97]

The intelligence services under powerful head harkaras[98] had also achieved prominence in contemporary Hyderabad. Nizam-ul Mulk (1675–1748), founder of the realm, is reported to have said that his illustrious former commander, the Emperor Aurangzeb, had thrown massive armies at his enemies while he himself had achieved more through good intelligence and the diplomatic arts.[99] On one occasion 'advised by a messenger from God', he spent Rs. 5,000 bribing enemy agents to fail to report his army's crossing of a strategic river.[100] The Nizam also learned much from his close connection with the Sufi orders.[101] These precautions were essential. After 1760 the Nizam's successors found themselves facing not only British and French intrigue, but also the rising power of Mysore which deployed a large and effective secret service.[102] A British officer remembered that in the first two Mysore wars, a letter to Calcutta or between British residents 'was obliged to be written on a piece of paper that might be inserted in a quill', and was not very secure even then.[103] In the last years of Mysore's independence, Tipu Sultan (r. 1782–99) took personal charge of

---

[95] G. Cherry to J. Fullarton, 25 May 1796, Wellesley, Add. 13,522, BL; P. Bradshaw to Mornington, 11 July 1798, Bengal Political Consultations, 10 Sept. 1798, 25, 116/48, OIOC.

[96] Karam Ali, 'Muzaffarnamah', tr. J.N. Sarkar, *The Bengal Nawabs* (Calcutta, 1952), p. 49. Head newswriters (*waqai nigars*) also continued to amalgamate their offices with that of military treasurer (*bakshi*), see case of Shakir-ud Daulah or Mir Kasim, *Imperial Record Department. Calendar of Persian Correspondence* [hereafter CPC], I, 1759–67 (Calcutta, 1911), pp. 258–9.

[97] C.R. Hill (ed.), *Imperial Records Series. Bengal in 1756–7* (London, 1905), I, 100, 120; II, 22, 137, 149.

[98] Mansaram, 'Masir-i Nizami', cited, P. Setu Madhava Rao, *Eighteenth Century Deccan*, pp. 53–5; for intelligence conflicts in Hyderabad see Kennaway letter books, B 6–9, Kennaway Papers, B961/M, Devon Record Office; J.A. Kirkpatrick, 'View of the State of the Deccan', 4 Jun. 1798, Wellesley, Add. 13582, BL.

[99] Mansaram, 'Masir-i Nizami', Rao, *Deccan*, pp. 95–6.

[100] ibid., p. 76.   [101] ibid., pp. 95–6, 114–15.

[102] F. Buchanan, *A Journey from Madras through the countries of Mysore …* (London, 1807), I, 270–1, 276–7, II, 91.

[103] John Kennaway to Lt Col. Harriss, 16 Aug. 1790, B6, Kennaway Papers.

elaborate surveillance operations against potential dissidents inside his kingdom.[104]

Domestic espionage was not neglected in Hyderabad either. The Nizam believed that he had inherited a rigorous moral code from the 'discipline' of the Emperor Aurangzeb,[105] who had stepped up the surveillance of important people on religious and sumptuary matters. The Nizam's own arrangements were fashioned for a still more fearful age. Ibadullah, 'from among the Chopdars [mace bearers]', had the job of reporting on illicit parties among the nobles during the fasting month of Mohurrum.[106] In addition, magnates could mount displays by dancing girls 'only on the occasions of festivals and marriages'.[107] Permission for such dances had to be sought from the Officer of Innovations (the *Darogah-i Bidah*) and were reported by the head harkara to the Presence.[108]

The Peshwa's state similarly kept a close eye on the morals of its wealthier citizens.[109] This followed from the ruler's Brahminical status and the Maratha claim to be a 'Brahman Raj'. As chief preceptor of the people, the Peshwa had the right to adjudicate on serious moral issues such as inter-caste fornication or cow-killing, and to collect fines in punishment. Religious surveillance could thus provide useful extra income. At the shrine of Jagannath in Orissa from which they also drew a large revenue, the Marathas had 'spies over spies' reporting on the collections, according to John Kennaway, British Resident at Hyderabad.[110]

Costly internecine war and, later, the tributary and commercial demands of the British, also forced rulers to raise more from their subjects. To do this they needed to make inventories of resources. The rulers of Bengal in the early eighteenth century had instituted new revenue surveys and rigorous surveillance of criminals. They also introduced audits of grain stores in order to tax the grain trade.[111] Likewise, the first semi-independent ruler of Awadh was advised to base

[104] '*Hukumnamah harkaron*', Asiatic Society of Bengal Library, Calcutta, no. 1,681.
[105] Mansaram, 'Masir-i Nizami', Rao, *Deccan*, pp. 102, 115.
[106] ibid., p. 112.
[107] M.A. Nayeem, *Mughal Administration of Deccan under Nizamul Mulk Asaf Jah (1720–1748 A.D.)* (Bombay, 1985), p. 87; cf. pp. 90–1.
[108] ibid.
[109] Sumit Guha, 'An Indian penal regime. Maharashtra in the eighteenth century', *Past and Present*, 147, 1995, 101–26; public opinion in a village, instigated by caste members, alerted the Patel who involved the *thanadar*, the local representative of government, see the example of a case *c*. 1790, 'Information of Jeewun Bhagwan', Report on the local institutions and fiscal resources of Broach, 31 May 1807, HM 686.
[110] Kennaway's diary, 4–5 June 1799, Kennaway Papers, B10.
[111] C. Stewart, *A History of Bengal from the First Muhammadan Invasion until the virtual conquest of that country by the English, A.D. 1757* (London, 1813), pp. 407, 370–3,

his revenue demand on the 'man's' rather than the 'coward's' rent roll, so assessing the real wealth of the great landholding clans by probing behind the compromises written into the revenue papers.[112] Much later, in the early nineteenth century, John Malcolm reported that Zalim Singh, regent of Kotah in Rajasthan, had 'formed a very extended system of espionage throughout his territories by means of a large and well-educated corps of Brahmin Herkarrahs'.[113] Malcolm compared this to Tipu's intelligence establishment, but the specific concern of the Kotah rulers was to keep track of the opium trade through their territories which was facing heavy British competition and subversion.

Muzaffar Alam and Sanjay Subrahmanyam[114] have argued that it was in the very late seventeenth and early eighteenth centuries that the indigenous state's demands on society and, one must infer, knowledge of its resources, reached its pre-colonial peak. One early eighteenth-century treatise, urging the king to read state documents with care, states that 'Shahjahan was satisfied with oral orders and did not usually sign papers', but 'Aurangzeb made his signature the basis of administration'.[115] Hereafter, the century-long conflict over succession, resources and legitimacy maintained and even enhanced the importance of the intelligence services, written documentation and political reporting. British intervention extended further the gaze of the dynastic security state. With varying degrees of speed and success, the Company was to infiltrate and suborn the agencies of surveillance deployed against it.

Literacy, training and social communication

Knowledgeable and effective government has usually flourished in societies with high rates of literacy and good internal communications. Formal literacy was apparently relatively low in eighteenth- and early nineteenth-century north India. Nevertheless, most north Indians had access to literate people and knew the meaning and power of writing.

drawing on 'Riyaz-as Salatin' tr. F. Gladwin as *A Narrative of the Transactions in Bengal during the Soobahdaries of Azem us Shan . . . (Calcutta, 1788)*.

[112] Muzaffar Alam, *Crisis of Empire*, p. 213, passim.

[113] J. Malcolm, *A Memoir of Central India* (London, 1824), I, 554 n; R.P. Shastri, *Jhala Zalim Singh (1730–1823)* (Jaipur, c. 1971), pp. 340–4.

[114] M. Alam and S. Subrahmanyam, 'L'état Moghol et sa fiscalité (xviie–xviiie siècles)', *Annales*, 49, 1, 1994, 189–218; in the Deccan and the south (pp. 209–10) many of the apparently 'Mughal' administrative and legal forms were introduced in the eighteenth century; in the north, too, the expansion of revenue farming introduced complex new forms of mortgage, lease and hypothecation.

[115] S.H. Askari, 'Mirat-ul-Muluk; a contemporary work containing reflections on later Mughal government', *Indica. Indian Historical Research Institute Silver Jubilee Commemoration Volume* (Bombay, 1953), p. 32.

Changes in doctrine and in economic relations between classes promoted the use of writing, accountancy and the 'technology of the list'[116] within the population at large. Exploiting these trends, the state's agencies of surveillance and communication could penetrate deeply into society, but their competence was limited by the instability of the clerical and commercial elites which were dependent on fickle patterns of trade and revenue extraction under Mughal and post-Mughal regimes.

The level and quality of literacy in India before the early nineteenth century remains guesswork. Indian states were simply not concerned with this question. Anecdotal information suggests that there was considerable variation between regions, classes and castes and even among families of the same status. Though the evidence must be treated with scepticism, established systems of village education in reading, writing and arithmetic for 'clean caste' male children are reported for Bengal, the Punjab and south India.[117] In north India the level of literacy has been lower than in these regions in the past two centuries, and there is no reason to expect this to have been otherwise before colonial rule. The north Indian plains have always been more solidly rural than the coastal regions where petty commerce, specialist artisanship and associated basic literacy were more developed. Even in the north there were significant differences between subregions, resulting from different levels of patronage of basic education by rulers and variable concentrations of merchant and scribal castes. For example, in the Himalayan hill states, the Sikh Punjab and eastern Rajasthan,[118] early nineteenth-century observers recorded relatively high levels of literacy. Here particular dynasties had patronised learning for several generations. In the great cities of the Mughal Empire, the education by private tutors of the well-to-do was matched by training in mosque schools for poorer children; Hindu tradesmen and clerical people also maintained schools for their own offspring.[119] In addition, the towns supported 'vast

[116] cf. Ajay Skaria, 'Power, orality and literacy amongst the Bhils of western India', *Subaltern Studies*, IX (Delhi, forthcoming).

[117] G.W. Leitner, *History of Indigenous Education in the Panjab since Annexation and in 1882* (Calcutta, 1882), p. 21; H. Harkness, 'Remarks on the school system of the Hindus', *JRAS*, 1, 1834, 15–20; but Lal Behari Dey thought that Adam's optimistic account of indigenous education was 'pure myth', *Proceedings of the Bethune Society from November 10 1859 to April 12 1869* (Calcutta, 1870), p. 111.

[118] In Nabha and other states, chiefs who had migrated from the plains kept up 'a degree of hereditary knowledge', J. Gerard, Asst Surgeon, to Capt. C. Kennedy, Asst Dty Supt, Soobhatoo, 20 Nov. 1824, Bengal Political Cons., 7 Jan. 1825, 29, 124/7, OIOC; cf. Major Ludlow's report, For. Pol. Cons. 20 Nov. 1847, 65, NAI, cited, G.C. Verma, 'Educational Development in Jaipur', Asopa (ed.), *Jaipur*, pp. 161–3, which also delineates a flourishing but localised system of schooling.

[119] Narendranath Law, *The Promotion of learning in India during Muhammadan rule by Muhammadans* (London, 1916). The 'patrimonial' nature of these institutions meant

numbers' of public writers.[120] Since there is a broad correlation between urbanisation and literacy, we should assume that, even if there was a drop in overall rates of literacy during the eighteenth century as a result of famine and political disturbance, it was probably not a massive one, because the level of urbanisation did not greatly change over the period.[121] Rising political centres, such as Lucknow, or commercial marts such as Kanpur and Mirzapur, took over from Lucknow, Delhi or Patna as centres of basic education.

The pattern of literacy remained very uneven during the transition to British rule. The ability to read did not imply the ability to write; yet neither did 'illiteracy' preclude sophistication in using others' learning. People of farming background may have attended village schools but this did not necessarily mean that they retained these skills, or ever used them. Even among the elites literacy was patchy. In the early eighteenth century Nizam-ul Mulk expressed astonishment that a key court official was illiterate.[122] Was it more significant that the Nizam thought literacy was the norm among his officials, or that in this case an illiterate could achieve high government office through the patronage of the royal ladies? Maharaja Ranjit Singh of the Punjab was formally illiterate but kept a minute check on the doings of his clerks.[123] In a royal house like that of Hyderabad in the 1810s, two sons were illiterate and three highly educated.[124] Conversely, the assumption that women were invariably illiterate can be challenged. In middle-ranking families women were sometimes taught to read the Koran in Arabic by their fathers, though some high-born women were never taught to read for fear that they might thereby engage in 'intrigue'.[125]

Once we reach the early nineteenth century, the ground becomes a

that they tended to collapse after a generation or two, ibid., pp. 175, 310; cf. Delhi College and Delhi Institution reports, 1829–30, Board's Collections Series, 1255/50501 (2), OIOC. For a general discussion, S. Blake, *Shahjahanabad. The sovereign city in Mughal India, 1639–1739* (Cambridge, 1991), pp. 130–41.

[120] Capt. Williamson, ed. J.B. Gilchrist, *The General East India Guide and Vade Mecum,...being a digest of the works of the late Capt. Williamson* (London, 1825), p. 509: Muslims, Kayasthas and Kashmiri Brahmins became experts in penmanship and calligraphy in 'thousands' in the city of Lucknow, A. H. Sharar, *Lucknow; the Last Phase of an Oriental Culture*, tr. E.S. Harcourt and F. Hussain (London, 1968), pp. 104–5.

[121] Leitner was convinced that the total number of pupils at Punjab schools had fallen by more than 30 per cent since Annexation, *Education*, pp. 1–2. But even his optimistic figures for pre-annexation Punjab, with perhaps 25 per cent of boys at school for some time, do not imply a particularly high rate of overall literacy.

[122] Mansaram, 'Masir-i Nizami', Rao, *Deccan*, p. 119; cf. for an unlettered diwan of Lahore, Harnam Singh 'Sadat-i-Jawid', *HI*, VIII, 346.

[123] Shahamat Ali, *The Sikhs and Afghans in connection with India and Persia immediately before and after the death of Ranjeet Singh* (London, 1849), p. 15.

[124] 'Memorandum on the Nizam's family', Elphinstone Papers, Mss. Eur. F88/3, OIOC.

[125] W. Adam, cited by S. Lateef, *Muslim Women in India* (London, 1990), pp. 46–9; but

little firmer. In the late 1840s in Banaras, before limited British-sponsored public instruction had got off the ground, only one child in 43 was at a recognised school in the urban areas and one in 57 in the countryside.[126] This contrasts sharply with figures of 40 per cent and 10 per cent respectively for Japan a century earlier.[127] Very low literacy rates were also recorded in British jails. In 1838 only 62 of the Agra Division's prison population of 6,009 were reportedly able to read or write and only 14 people were classed as 'educated'.[128] Altogether, a reasonable figure for the early nineteenth century in north India would be that about 20 per cent of males in large towns could at least read and write their names and numbers up to a hundred, 10 per cent in smaller towns, and 5 per cent in the countryside. Even assuming a substantial fall off from 1707, it seems that rates of literacy in Hindi-speaking north India were, formally speaking, somewhat low by European or east Asian standards.

North India was, nevertheless, a 'literacy aware' society, if not a highly literate one. All the commercial classes would know how to count and read simple bills, just as all the Brahmin and writer castes would know the significance of writing and texts. Awareness of the uses of literacy thus spread much further than the number of formal literates suggests. Most clean caste families made use of written engagements for marriage which the barber (the Nai or 'matchmaker') carried between the engaging families.[129] A shadowy popular educator, the Nao Pandey or barber-schoolmaster, carried texts to villages to instruct small boys.[130]

see, Ishwardas Nagar, *Futuhat*, p. 282; Mrs Meer Hassan Ali, *Observations on the Mussulmauns of India* (1832, repr. Oxford, 1917), pp. 4–5.

[126] 'Village schools in the district of Benares', 'Indigenous and other schools in the city, cantonments and civil station', enclosure in Superintendant Schools, Banaras to Collector, Banaras, 31 Mar. 1849, North Western Provinces General Proceedings, Mar. 1850, 107–8, 215/3, OIOC. The earliest 'learned' investigation of schools and literacy in Hindustan was apparently by H.H. Spry thirteen years earlier; the only record of his findings the author has found is in *Friend of India*, 18 Oct. 1838, where he remarks that there was 'no mutual connection between the vernacular and learned schools' but paints a picture of great variation between regions and classes in schooling. Of 1,458 vernacular schools in 'lower Hindustan', 968 were 'without written books of instruction of any kind'.

[127] M.B. Jansen, 'Japan in the early nineteenth century' in Jansen (ed.), *Cambridge History of Japan*, V, *The Nineteenth Century* (Cambridge, 1989), 67.

[128] 'First Report of the Agra School Book Society', *Friend of India*, 28 Feb. 1839 (this was immediately after two severe famines). *Census of British India, taken on 17 February 1881* (London, 1883), I, p. 227, implies that about 9 per cent of males over five were 'instructed' or 'under instruction' in the North-Western Provinces, but that, in addition, another category of people could read but not write, or had the capacity to write their name, etc.

[129] W. Crooke, *An Ethnographic Hand-book for the N.-W. Provinces and Oudh* (Allahabad, 1890), pp. 121–2.

[130] 'Native education in the North-West Provinces', *Benares Magazine*, 8, 1852, 164.

Low-caste people put their signatures to documents of local arbitration.[131] Landholders knew the importance of the village accountant's books and were sometimes required to affix their signatures or marks to revenue documents. Religious initiates printed their garments with letters. Sects fetishised the word of their spiritual guides and engaged in symbolic acts of worship of their writings, even if the majority of members were unable to read the texts themselves. The growing power of text enhanced the power of 'writing people' even if popular mastery of this technique was attenuated.

It was not only the needs of government which was driving the slow and uneven expansion of literacy. The intensity of social communication among Indians had created a talkative, knowing society, highly competitive about the use and diffusion of information, which it was hard for any government to dominate. In India, as elsewhere, a dialogue between the state and elites influenced the development of the information order. The papers of state revenue managers, for example, drew on commercial techniques developed by Hindu and Jain merchants. In turn, the state's officials came to require more standardised presentation of commercial books for any adjudication in which royal justice was involved. In north India this dialogue was associated in popular memory with the name of Todar Mull, Akbar's administrator, who was himself of merchant caste origin. People remembered Todar Mull as a monster of taxation, but also as the figure who standardised the form of commercial ledgers.[132] The state postal system overlapped and formalised the circles of letter-writing among the merchants and intelligentsia. We have little idea of the volume of letters sent by Indians before the 1830s (when it was surprisingly great),[133] but in the commercial city of Mirzapur alone at the turn of the nineteenth century six private entrepreneurs ran express postal services which collected letters for dispatch under state licence to Lucknow, Kanpur, Allahabad and Nagpur.[134] Writing was an art, not merely a convenience. In the seventeenth and eighteenth centuries numerous writing manuals (*inshas*) appeared. These were a medium through which the rulers could publicise their policies and Sufi masters

[131] e.g., a case of a dhobi panchayat recording evidence in a trial *c*. 1810, H.M. Elliot, *Memoirs on the History, Folk-Lore, and Distribution of the Races of the North Western Provinces of India*, ed. J. Beames, I (London, 1859), 281–2; cf. Sykes on 'Land tenures of the Deccan', *JRAS*, 3, 1836, 352–69.

[132] For the Todar Mull legend amongst merchants, C. Smith, Second Judge, Banaras to Register, Nizamat Adawlat, 12 Jan. 1813, Bengal Criminal Judicial Procs., 12 Jul. 1816, 18, 132/43, OIOC.

[133] See below, pp. 216–17.

[134] Actg Magt., Mirzapur to Postmaster General, Fort William, 11 Oct. 1810, Letters of Magistrate Mirzapur, vol. 74, U.P. Central Records Office, Allahabad.

their doctrines as well as a method of instructing young people how properly to address correspondents within and beyond the family.[135] Many institutions possessed stores of information which could be used to maintain prosperity and control, but which could also provide data for the state. Brahmins in villages kept notes of astronomical events and sometimes of births and deaths[136] and received manuscript copies of almanacs from the larger temples.[137] Family priests maintained horoscopes and genealogies over many generations. The priests at the great ritual centres of Hardwar, Allahabad, Banaras and Gaya also kept genealogical records organised by family and caste, noting the periodic journeys of devotees from all over India to make oblations to the ancestors. Temples, religious communities (notably the Jains) and Muslim shrines routinely recorded rules, grants, devotees and donors in the same way. By the eighteenth century these documents were entered in books similar to merchant account books. The merchant accounting system itself became more elaborate over time, spawning cash account books, credit accounts and personal accounts. Large merchant houses would employ clerks to write in Persian and local languages alongside junior partners who had been taught to do the Hindi accounts within the family or in merchant schools.

Political turbulence might destroy caches of information, but it might also provide an incentive for a much closer recording of rights and duties by families who were otherwise illiterate. In Rohilkhand, for instance, an area riven with armed conflict, the 'ten year book' (Dasanni Kitab) was drawn up from earlier documents by local Indian officials, kazis, and holders of privileged land rights in 1210 Fasily (1802) at a general assembly in the town of Bareilly.[138] It recorded the ownership and quality of lands and was an attempt to create a basis for a new consensus about ownership of property. The document was copied privately on a large scale and became the basis for nineteenth-century property mutations and pleadings.[139] Paper records slowly became the preferred form of testimony in adjudications. In Banaras in the 1790s conflicts over rights could still be settled either by investigation of

[135] e.g., Abul Fazl's collection of exhortatory letters of Akbar became a book of instruction for Persian *maktabs*; on *insha*, Rizvi, *Akbar*, ch. 8; some inshas were particularly directed to 'young people', Ethé, *Persian Manuscripts*, I, 1,126–76.

[136] According to a British observer some rural Brahmins also kept daily records of deaths, Asst Surgeon 34 Regt to *Madras Gazette, Calcutta Journal*, 4 Dec. 1818.

[137] See below, pp. 249, 262–3.

[138] Proceedings held by Collector, Bareilly, 7 Aug. 1802, Wellesley, Add. 13,566, ff. 59–63, BL.

[139] Elliot, *Races*, III, 146–8; 'Settlement of Pergunneh Sukrawah, Zillah Farrukhabad', *Selections from the Records of the Government, North Western Provinces* (Agra, 1856), IV, xxii, 252–3, which suggests a regional 'documentary memory' of 100–150 years.

documents or by trial by ordeal.[140] In the late 1820s a dispute over the inheritance of the headship of a monastic foundation in Bharatpur turned on a similar choice. One party wished judgement on 'a paper'. The other asserted his right by pointing to a ceremony in which he had allegedly been invested with the 'Tilak [mark of status], rosary and insignia' of his predecessor.[141]

Slow changes were, therefore, already beginning to break down what appears on the surface to have been a static and hierarchical information order. Popular religion, sectarian movements and the impact of Mughal armies or chancelleries acted as catalysts. In Rajasthan, chronicles and bardic literature, which had previously been transmitted orally, began to be written down in the seventeenth and eighteenth centuries.[142] Muslim models were influential here, but so were internal changes: in a more settled society, ruling houses needed to exhalt their lineages before a wider audience.[143] In Bengal and eastern India large quantities of cheap scriptural texts were being spread among the people at the end of the eighteenth century. For a few rupees one could buy written Bengali versions of parts of the great epics, the Mahabharata and Ramayana.[144] In north India, versions of Tulsi Das's translation of the Ramayana into Hindi, the Ramcharitmanas, grew in numbers after 1700.[145] This mirrored the emergence of Ramlila as a public festival for Hindus. Though Hindu medical scriptures remained the jealous possession of high-caste practitioners, written commentaries on these texts and practical remedies were widely circulated.[146] Dispersed sectarian groups were particularly active in promoting vernacular literature, especially prose literature, as they needed to disseminate standard texts and precepts for people spread across the country.[147] Amongst Muslims, the

[140] 'Translation of sowals or articles of application from Mohammed Naseer Udden, Judge of the Moolky Dewanee Adawlat with the answer to each, delivered by the Resident', Proceedings Resident Banaras, 18 Jan. 1789, U.P. Central Records Office, Allahabad, publ. G. Saletore (ed.), *Banaras Affairs (1788–1810)* (Allahabad, *c.* 1958), I, 101–2.

[141] Political Agent, Bharatpur to Resident, Delhi, 9 April 1831, 'Affairs of Bharatpore', BC, 1369/54486, OIOC.

[142] H. Mahesvari, *A History of Rajasthani Literature* (Delhi, 1980), pp. 68–9, 71–6; N.P. Ziegler, 'Marvari historical chronicles; sources for the social and cultural history of Rajasthan', *IESHR*, 13, 2, 1976, 219–50.

[143] Mahesvari, *Rajasthani Literature*, pp. 75–6.

[144] *Friend of India*, 22 Jan. 1835, says that the whole text of the Mahabharata would cost Rs. 35–48 to copy in Bengali; B.K. Datta, *Libraries and Librarianship of Ancient and Medieval India* (Delhi, 1970), pp. 191–3.

[145] P. Lutgendorf, *The Life of a Text. Performing the Ramcaritmanas of Tulsi Das* (Berkeley, 1991), pp. 9–10, 140–1; there are many more eighteenth-century copies of the work than seventeenth-century ones. The Manas managed to 'synthesise' Hindu tradition.

[146] 'Hindu Remedies for Cholera', *Calcutta Journal*, 2 Feb. 1819.

[147] Paul Dundas, *The Jains* (London, 1992), p. 222; R.S. McGregor, *Hindi Literature from*

translation of the Koran, first into Persian and then into Urdu, pointed to a new emphasis on the vernacular. Urdu became a language of popular religious instruction and of poetry, joining elite and mass.[148]

Anthropologists have criticised the assumption that the spread of writing itself necessarily changed consciousness. Certainly, many Brahmins saw text as an inferior mode of preserving sacred knowledge. Over time, too, texts often became ritual objects which their possessors were incapable of reading.[149] Still, by the eighteenth century, the 'middling sort' of people in north India had greater recourse to fixed texts and to rational rules for the conduct of religion, business and government.

Finally, the expansion of Indo-Muslim military and administrative methods across the subcontinent gave new opportunities to those lowlier communities of knowing people connected with the 'military labour market'.[150] The Mughal and eighteenth-century armies were themselves great forcing-houses of talent and skills. These troopers were often literate because they were drawn from respectable urban elites, unlike their peasant successors in the British armies. Many eighteenth-century authors in Persian and Urdu were soldiers by training,[151] and the army was a career in which boys of humble origin could acquire a broader education as well as writing skills. Because military rewards were often tied to shares in the revenue or graded cash payments, soldiers needed to count and, ideally, to write. Officers in Indian regiments carried boxes of records with them.[152] In one case a middle-ranking soldier enlisted in British service bound crucial letters in his turban as a talisman and a guarantee of protection should his conduct be questioned.[153]

The military labour market broadened out to include such apparently disparate specialists as blacksmiths, gunpowder makers, exponents of the philosopher's stone, wandering letter-writers and regimental accountants, Christian gunners, headmen of pack-bullock caravans and

the beginnings to the early nineteenth Century, History of Indian Literature, VI, 2 (Wiesbaden, 1976); A.W. Entwistle, *Braj. Centre of Krishna Pilgrimage* (Groningen, 1987), pp. 77, 261–7.

[148] M. Sadiq, *A History of Urdu Literature* (London, 1964).

[149] J. Parry, 'The Brahmanical tradition and the technology of the intellect', in J. Overing (ed.), *Reason and Morality* (Oxford, 1985), pp. 200–25.

[150] D.H.A. Kolff, *Naukar, Rajput and Sepoy. The ethnohistory of the military labour market in Hindustan, 1450–1850* (Cambridge, 1990).

[151] *LH*, I, 120–1 (Mir Sher Ali); I, 202 (Amin-ud Daulah), I, 252 (Mir Abdul Jalal), 1, 357 (Mirza Babu Ali Beg).

[152] Mansaram, 'Masir-i Nizami', Rao, *Deccan*, p. 77; but conventions about employment by caste and ethnicity still remained, see, Nayeem, *Mughal Administration*, p. 92; Askari, 'Mirat-ul-Muluk', *Indica*, p. 34.

[153] 'Account of the Banjaras', *Transactions of the Literary Society of Bombay* (London, 1819), 177; cf. Khairuddin, *Bulwuntnamah*, pp. 3–5, 7, where a Brahmin is shamed by having a land deed tied in his turban.

woodworkers. Few of these people were literate in the sense of being able to read and write without aid. They were, however, able to calculate, create templates and memorise operational systems. Men could rise fast from humble social origins in the ranks of eighteenth-century Indian armies.[154] The military camp should be seen as a vast system of schooling and repository of knowledge. The military, like religious sects and the wholesale bazaar, was an institution which broke down older, hierarchical knowledge communities. Pre-colonial India was not on the verge of a modern information revolution comparable to the one which was taking place in 'closed' Japan, but widening circles of sophisticated knowledge and the growing prestige of the written word had created a more self confident set of scribal elites. The most dynamic social formation of the period was not a class defined in a simple economic sense, but the writer's office (*munshi khana*) whose members combined respectable status with access to the charisma of writing. These people, although dependent and humiliated, were to play an important part in the establishment of British rule.

British knowledge and Indian society to c. 1790

This section discusses the sources and quality of British information about north India before the great expansion of the Company's power during the Revolutionary and Napoleonic wars. Until the 1780s, relatively little of its information about the region arose from the direct observation of European officers; most was hearsay. There was no stable body of 'colonial knowledge', but, instead, a congeries of technical commercial information and impressions drawn from diplomatic discourse with Indian states. This was loosely linked to a number of leading ideas about India's political 'constitution' and religious character. India had not yet been firmly relegated to an inferior and exotic status,[155] and Europeans continued to seek answers to questions about human history and knowledge there. Nor had the information available to the East India Company expanded steadily over time. Periods when the Company was quite well informed even about events in Delhi and Agra, far from European commercial enclaves, were followed by long years when almost nothing substantive was known about the political and social evolution of inland India. Once the British had formally become revenue-managers of Bengal for the Mughal Emperor in 1765, however,

---

[154] e.g., *HI*, VI, 287 (Hardas Rai); ibid., VIII, 161 (Muzaffar Hussain), 167 (Kora Mal and Adina Beg Khan).

[155] cf. P.J. Marshall and G. Williams, *The Great Map of Mankind. British Perceptions of the World in the Age of Enlightenment* (London, 1982).

they acquired a great wealth of information about the province and the affairs of northern India from a group of Mughal office-holding families associated with Mahomed Reza Khan, deputy governor in Bengal under Clive and intermittently under Hastings, who provided continuity with the old order. The next chapter shows how this relationship developed over more than two generations, giving the British access to leading indigenous officials in north India, and to the networks of agents, writers and runners they commanded.

Naturally, commercial information about Indian textile production was one area in which the Company developed expertise early. Observation of English textile production and domestic traditions of commercial accounting and reportage provided a foundation for this knowledge. The early consultation books of the presidencies are full of details about the location, production and quality of different styles of cloth. As early as 1639, Henry Bornford[156] wrote a detailed report on the organisation of the cotton trade in India and its overseas markets in central and west Asia. His material was apparently gleaned from discussions with the Company's Indian agents in Agra, Surat and places en route. Though the Company's servants were unable to explain the distribution of factors of production which influenced the structure of textile costs, they did have access to a great deal of raw data about them. Some of this came from the representation or petitions of Indian bleachers, dyers and weavers who had an acute understanding of the economic conditions which bore on their own livelihoods.[157] Other information came from the Company's Indian agents in the various factories who had direct charge of the distribution of cash advances to the producers. Great Indian merchants[158] or headmen of caste groups kept the Company informed about market conditions. Later, Company officers and private merchants began to acquire the services of those permanent commercial agents, banians and dubashs, whose very name ('men of two tongues') points to their wider role as cultural intermediaries and interpreters.[159] Even so, before the 1760s British commercial knowledge was never as full as that of the Dutch who had gained access to Mughal customs records and were consequently able to keep track of all European and Asian shipping in Indian ports. The British did not

[156] K.N. Chaudhuri, *The Trading World of Asia and the English East India Company, 1600–1760* (Cambridge, 1978), p. 243.

[157] ibid., pp. 269–70.

[158] A. Das Gupta, *Indian Merchants and the Decline of Surat, c. 1700–1750* (Wiesbaden, 1979), pp. 80–5, for Nagar Brahmins and Banias whose connections spanned Gujarat and Hindustan.

[159] D. Basu, 'Early banians in Calcutta: the Setts and Bysacks in their own image', *Bengal Past and Present*, 90, 1971, 30–46.

achieve this until after they gained direct control of Indian territory, by which time indigenous shipping had lost much of its importance.[160]

As they moved inland, the British maintained this tradition of detailed cost analysis and observation of forms of production. Company servants complemented direct observation with material drawn from the inland correspondents of the Calcutta dubashs or from private entrepreneurs. These were often Armenians,[161] who often felt compelled to gravitate to the European side. So, R. Barlow's report on the costs of cloth production of Awadh of 1783[162] follows a similar pattern to the earlier material. The information, however, was much sparser when it came to detailing sources of supply. Company servants were generally unaware of the agricultural and political conditions which impinged on cotton cultivation and the procurement of dye, because they knew so little about the social and technical conditions of hinterland trade. By the time the Company and its servants became traders in bulk agricultural produce in the 1790s, the trade in textiles was itself beginning to wane.

Overall, however, British commercial intelligence was effective. It made possible the fine calibration of long-run profits which the Company was able to achieve, while trading in a vast and largely unknown continent clouded by massive political and climatic uncertainties. It also enabled the emergence of a powerful private trade which contributed much to the expansion of British power. One great advantage for the Company was that Indian commercial mentalities, procedures and structures were relatively easily translatable into European economic language. Concepts of profit and loss, double-entry book keeping, rates of exchange and credit notes were common to both sides in the Indo-European trade.[163] Of course, the social and religious values motivating Indian merchants and the controllers of bazaars were often mysterious to Europeans. They could not straightforwardly be read in terms of classical political economy. Fresh from the experience of abolishing 'restraints to trade' at home, Britons were only too quick to write off Indian social expenditures and the political exchange of gifts as bribery and extortion. They often failed to understand that magnates' shares in the produce of markets, or even the location of traders in

[160] Om Prakash, *Dutch Trade*; Das Gupta, *Surat*, p. 280.

[161] ibid., p. 80; R.W. Ferrier, 'The Armenians and the East India Company in the 17th and early 18th century', *English Historical Review*, 2nd ser., 26, 1973, 38–62; P.J. Marshall, *East Indian Fortunes* (Oxford, 1976), pp. 23, 80, 164, 265; M.J. Seth, *Armenians in India from the earliest times to the present day* (Calcutta, 1937), pp. 281–311

[162] R. Barlow's report on trade in Awadh, Foreign Secret Dept Consultations, 6 June 1787, 59, National Archives of India, New Delhi.

[163] See, C.A. Bayly, *Rulers, Townsmen and Bazaars* (Cambridge, 1983), pp. 369–427; K. Chatterjee, 'Collaboration and conflict: bankers and early colonial rule in India, 1715–1813', *IESHR*, 30, 1993, 283–310

markets, was a reflection of social status. Some of them even saw the honorific gifts passed in the Mughal court as 'bribery'.

This does not mean, however, that Europeans were impeded by a 'clash of cultures' from understanding the nature of Indian commercial activity as a whole. Indian trade was not really 'political trade' in Karl Polyani's sense; nor, in practice, did the duties of religion (Dharma) and kingship encompass power and money making (Artha). The critical point here is that Indian merchants were quite capable of separating social and 'protection' costs from the accounting of profit and loss. This was clearly reflected in the very structure of their account books which distinguish between commercial profit and loss and household or establishment expenses, including religious or political ones. Indian merchants might have been predisposed to spend their profits on temples, to the disdain of Europeans, but there was no question about what profit and loss was in Indian commerce. As a result, Indian trade was relatively transparent to Europeans, but conversely, Indians were able to adapt quite speedily to the principles and practice of European traders.

Company servants also accumulated stores of empirical political information which enabled them to deal with the Indian rulers who impinged most directly on their trading interests. From the earliest days continental Europeans, local Christians and Armenians, and Company agents and harkaras brought them gobbets of information on developments in Indian politics. The civil wars after the death of Aurangzeb reduced their understanding of events at the centre of Empire.[164] John Surman's embassy to Delhi on behalf of the Company (1715–17) secured a partial account of events at the Mughal court,[165] but this was soon out of date. The decline of the English factory at Agra[166] following the collapse of the indigo trade and the invasion of Nadir Shah in 1739 reduced news to a trickle. It was in this context that the philosophical and dramatic tropes of Oriental Despotism, sati and decadence flourished. Orientalist fantasy flooded into gaps left by the decline of pragmatic information; it did not always predetermine that information.

The Company was particularly poorly informed about the rise of new regional powers outside the Mughal orbit. The Jats were largely ignored until the 1770s. Then a Jesuit father, Xavier Wendel, who was a strong supporter of the British against the French, established himself in the

---

[164] Das Gupta, *Surat*, pp. 143–7.
[165] C.R. Wilson, *Early Annals of the English in Bengal*, 2, part ii (Calcutta, 1911); D.G. Crawford, *A History of the Indian Medical Service, 1600–1913* (London, 1914), I, 117. The English 'who were very ignorant of the politics and intrigues of the court of Dehly', according to Stewart, used an Armenian intermediary during this mission.
[166] Das Gupta, *Surat*, pp. 143–7.

court of the Bharatpur Jats, and sent regular despatches to the Bengal government.[167] The resulting rush of detail elevated the Jats to a central, and possibly exaggerated, importance. The British fixation with the principality, which persisted until it was finally conquered in 1826, dates from this period.[168] Equally, the north Indian conquests of the Marathas were misinterpreted and views about the Sikhs remained quite inaccurate.[169] Reliable information about events and conditions between Banaras and Bombay remained extremely limited until the 1790s. Even in 1808 the Commander-in-Chief of the Company's Army could state that 'beyond the Jumna all is conjecture'.[170]

The British understanding of Indian society – as opposed to its trades – may have been extraordinarily defective, but this was more the result of a lack of reliable informants than the consequence of orientalist stereotypes. Ideas of Oriental Despotism purveyed by Manucci, Bernier, by Jesuit commentators and by English travellers such as Fitch and Hawkins do not seem greatly to have informed their thinking. These works were not at this time regarded as manuals of political theory for Europeans in India. Rather they were attempts to make room in European mentalities for the great kingdoms of the east. At this period 'orientalism' was largely devoid of significance for the exercising of power within India. Company servants were able to make and maintain relations with Indian powers in a pragmatic way. European assumptions impinged on their actions in another area, however. Most Britons found it difficult to comprehend fully the flexible, interpenetrative systems of rights to shares of produce and political authority which characterised indigenous polity. The British sought for an Indian 'constitution' with well-defined powers and a clear hierarchy of authority. They were confused by the apparent sharing of both authority and power between the Mughal Emperor and the nawabs and nizams. The general British tendency to deny kingly quality to subordinate rulers was denounced by the French scholar Anquetil Duperron,[171] but in fairness one must say that British ideas derived in part from Mughal theory and discourse in which these kings were deemed to be merely landholders, *zamindars*,

---

[167] J. Déloche (ed.), *Les Memoires de Wendel sur les Jat, les Pathan et les Sikh* (Paris, 1979), pp. i–ii; Orme Mss. OV 69, ff. 11, 30, 41, OIOC.

[168] 'The very Palladium of native authority and independence', J.N. Creighton, *Narrative of the Siege and Capture of Bhurtpore in the Province of Agra, Upper Hindoostan* (London, 1830), p. xx.

[169] See, e.g., editor's notes on the misunderstandings in J. Browne, *History of the Origin and Progress of the Sicks* (London, 1787), repr. G. Singh (ed.), *Early European Accounts of the Sikhs* (Calcutta, 1962), pp. 13–43.

[170] Note by Commander-in-Chief, Secret and Separate Dept, 22 Jun. 1808, HM 592.

[171] A.H. Anquetil Duperron, *Recherches Historiques et Geographiques par Anquetil Duperron*, ed. J. Bernouilli (Paris, 1886), p. 145.

even while they were accorded some stately honours. As late as 1800, Wellesley was convinced that Maratha chiefs were in the same position in regard to the Peshwa as the 'territorial aristocracy' of England and Ireland were to Crown in Parliament.[172] As the debate on the settlement of Bengal's revenues between 1770 and 1793 illustrates, most Britons found it difficult to conceive of a society in which there were no absolute proprietary rights in land. The resulting misconceptions did not add up to an attempt to create a stereotyped Orient. Instead, they derived from European and often specifically English, Scottish and Irish experience.

Revenue management and the birth of orientalism

In the early eighteenth century, then, the Company's knowledge of India's interior deteriorated and the European understandings of India, once enriched by the Jesuits and the Dutch, stagnated or were lost. Commercial and political activities between Calcutta and Murshidabad brought a gradual accumulation of information about the textile areas and the environs of both cities. The British conquest of Bengal and assumption of the land-revenue management of Bengal in 1765 resulted in a decisive accession of technical and general information, however. Power over the land meant that Europeans could travel and observe more freely. Under the direction of James Rennell, British mapping now turned from maritime charts to the recording of inland routeways, towns and villages, though it was still concerned with the correction of the knowledge of the Ancients as well as with practical concerns.[173] Power over revenue gave access to a much wider range of information within the Indian polity; it also gave the nascent colonial power a legitimacy in relation to Mughal rule and Mughal sources of information. The disastrous early record of British settlement and taxation of Bengal was no doubt exacerbated by a lack of hard information and a pervasive suspicion among officers that Indians were conspiring to deny them access to it. After 1773, though, a large volume of indigenous revenue records and manuals of procedure were examined. Henceforth, greed rather than ignorance was the root cause of overassessment.[174]

Most importantly, the British could now draw on the political advice and contacts of the branch of Mughal administrative cadre which had been established in Nawabi Bengal since 1704. This had been one of the

---

[172] E. Thompson, *The Making of the Indian Princes* (London, 1943), p. 8.

[173] J. Rennell, *Memoir of a Map of Hindoostan or the Moguls Empire* (London, 1788), pp. iv–xiv, xxvi; R. Phillimore, *Historical Records of the Survey of India*, I, *The Eighteenth Century* (Dehra Dun, 1945), pp. 1–6.

[174] P.J. Marshall, *Bengal the British Bridgehead. Eastern India, 1740–1828* (Cambridge, 1987), pp. 93–137.

most streamlined and effective provincial administrations of the later Empire and it had enhanced its detailed knowledge of revenue and trade in the decades immediately prior to British conquest. From Mahomed Reza Khan,[175] the deputy appointed by Clive to administer the province, the British appropriated the techniques of revenue management and also learned the essentials of diplomacy within the wider Indian polity. Muslim court servants such as this stood at one end of a vast network of 'Persian correspondence' which collated materials from harkaras, news-writers and political secretaries as far as Delhi or beyond.[176] Of course, the Company abused, misconstrued and even damaged sectors of the Mughal information systems. For instance, Warren Hastings abolished the positions of sub-provincial newswriter (akhbar navis) within Bengal, relying instead on his own sources of information.[177] In parts of the provinces of Bengal and Bihar the British co-opted entrepreneurs and 'new men', such as Ramchandra Pandit, administrator and opium agent,[178] in the place of the older official elite. Nevertheless, they made effective use of the network of relatives and connections associated with Mahomed Reza Khan and the families of the governor and kazi of the port town of Hughly. Informants and diplomatists from these Mughal elites, domesticated in Bengal and hence keenly aware of British power, played a crucial role in the subsequent territorial expansion of the Company throughout north India.[179] They also helped to entrench some of the conservative features of the Company's early rule, in particular its reliance on the etiquette, diplomatics and language of the former Mughal Empire.

After the treaty with Awadh in 1765 the British also became more confident in their dealings in Lucknow and Banaras. In both these cities they secured a variety of new informants and agents. These included Muslim court servants such as Tafazzul Hussain Khan and Ali Ibrahim Khan. Information also flowed from up-country connections of Bengal magnates, such as Warren Hastings's agent, Krishna Kanta Nandy, who proved invaluable during the Banaras revolt of 1781,[180] and the north

---

[175] A.M. Khan, *The Transition in Bengal 1756–1775. A study of Saiyid Muhammad Reza Khan* (Cambridge, 1969).

[176] See, e.g., P. Saran, *Persian Documents, being letters, newsletters and kindred documents pertaining to the several states existing in India in the last quarter of the eighteenth century from the oriental collection of the National Archives of India* (London, 1966), pp. 10, 17, 33, 40, 80; cf., e.g., *CPC*, I (1759–67), 25, 33, 273–4, 459; II (1767–9), 664, 763, 776.

[177] Khan, *Transition*, pp. 27–9; Ghulam Hussain, 'Siyyar', tr. Nota-Manus, III, 103–6, 163–4 (abolition of *muhtasib*'s office).

[178] K.P. Mishra, *Banaras in Transition (1738–1790)* (Delhi, 1975), pp. 51, 144–5, 148.

[179] See below, pp. 78–89.

[180] S.C. Nandy, *Life and Times of Cantoo Baboo, the Banian of Warren Hastings* (Calcutta, 1981), pp. 234–69.

Indian merchants who helped finance the Awadh tribute. With the outbreak of European and Indian wars after 1776, Warren Hastings made a vigorous attempt to extend the intelligence gathering capacity of the residencies. In 1782, for instance, James Grant, stationed at Hyderabad, attempted a detailed analysis of the kingdoms of the Deccan. He drew material from the classical works of Abul Fazl's circle, from Indian informants and from the route maps of British officers who had passed through the territory.[181] Similar accounts were put together for parts of the Maratha territories, for the lands adjoining the northern mountains and for Bundelkhand in north central India.[182]

For all this, British comprehension of the subcontinent remained severly circumscribed in 1780. There were several reasons for this. First, hostile powers such as the Peshwa and Mysore, now aware of the Company's threat to their independence, deliberately starved its envoys of information. Residents were cooped up or sent to distant stations to cool their heels. Secondly, while different parties among the British might sometimes be impelled to find new informants and new lines of intelligence during their mutual struggles, conflict could also spread misinformation. This was particularly true during the intense factional battles between Hastings and his enemies on the Bengal Council which further politicised the whole area of information collection. Madras and Bombay nearly ruined the Company between 1776 and 1785 by pursuing their own foreign policy and denying information to Bengal. During 1782–4, again, John Bristow, Resident at Lucknow and an old opponent of Hastings, attempted to undermine his authority in Awadh, spreading news that Hastings has been dismissed and intercepting the letters of neutral British officers.[183] Hastings, however, was sure that Bristow wished to usurp power in Lucknow and established his own flow of information direct from the Nawab and his ministers in an attempt to circumvent the Resident.[184] Hastings found it particularly difficult to maintain reliable channels of information and always felt that European 'adventurers' or his personal enemies were polluting his sources. Even after a firmer line of authority was established within British India, however, special interests constantly manipulated information to suit their projects in Calcutta or London.

[181] J. Grant, 'Political Survey of the Deccan', 1782, Hastings, Add. Mss. 29,209, ff. 383 ff., BL; M. Fisher, *Indirect Rule in India. Residents and the residency system, 1764–1857* (Delhi, 1991), pp. 122–62.
[182] For other collected memoirs of this period, see Hastings, Add. Mss. 29,120.
[183] Haider Beg Khan to Calcutta, 1, 13 May 1783, *CPC*, VI, 264–5, 274; Haider Beg Khan to Tafazzul Hussain, 13 May 1783, ibid., 275–6.
[184] Haider Beg Khan to Hastings, 27 Sept. 1783, ibid., 301; Hastings to Haider Beg Khan, 22 Oct. 1783, ibid., 310.

Finally, the Company's information remained fractured because its officers were puzzled by the organisation and motivating principles of the Indian kingdoms. The structure of decentralised polities made them difficult to comprehend. Observers in Calcutta, for example, had a good idea of what was happening in Lucknow, but were unable to predict the movements or aims of the great revenue farmers of the districts, such as Almas Ali Khan. North, south and west of Banaras even the geographical outlines of the subcontinent were unclear, as was amply illustrated by the fate of Colonel Egerton's expedition from Bombay which was destroyed by the Marathas in 1779. Similarly, Calcutta failed to predict the 'rapid' rise of the Maratha chieftain Mahadji Shinde.[185] Indian political events were, as Hastings's confidant James Grant admitted, 'seen through a distant and obscure horizon, or rather through a mist of ignorance which equally conceals our own strength and that of the powers that oppose us'.[186] For all the empirical detail of his analyses of the Deccan, Grant and his contemporaries had little conception of what drove indigenous politics. The Persians and Afghans, he thought, were barbarians fired with the zeal of Islamic conquest.[187] The pacific Sikh religion, 'did not inspire any ideas of conquest', but nonetheless Sikhs were aggressive because their meat diet did not enfeeble them, as vegetarianism did the Hindus.[188] The Rajputs had been privileged by the 'Institutes of Brahman', but had lately become corrupt.[189] These orientalist stereotypes, it should be noted, were not tools of epistemological conquest, so much as conceptual fig-leaves to conceal desperate ignorance.

The learned orientalism which Hastings promoted during the 1770s and 1780s served another function yet, and was separate from these wilder theories. It was designed as much to confer a degree of respectability on the Bengal government, as it was to 'know' India. It proceeded from 'books', not men, as John Kaye was to assert two generations later,[190] and the investigation of 'Hindoo' and 'Muslim' precedents only resulted in their partial application in the longer term. Hastings and his circle mainly sought to portray themselves as inheritors of the Indian polity as refounded by the Emperor Akbar. They needed to inherit the knowledge, and particularly the political knowledge of the former rulers. Hence Francis Gladwin's translation of Abul Fazl's 'Institutes of Akbar' claimed to depict the 'original constitution' of the

[185] J. Browne, 'Memorandum for Mr. Hastings respecting the state of affairs in Hindostan', 1 Jan. 1785, Hastings, Add. Mss. 29,209, ff. 1–3, BL.
[186] J. Grant, 'A brief state of the British affairs in India at the commencement of 1780', 30 Nov. 1780 cont. to 15 Oct. 1781, Hastings Add. Mss. 29,209, f. 134, BL.
[187] ibid.   [188] ibid., f. 135b.   [189] ibid., f. 136.
[190] See below, pp. 315–16.

Mughal Empire of Akbar.[191] The Asiatic Society of Bengal, founded in 1784 shortly before Hastings's eclipse and departure from India, directed its attention to the improvement of Indian learning for the purposes of governance. A political genealogy and a political theory for Anglo-Indian rule began to be written which portrayed an orientalised British Constitution. Akbar became a kind of Indian Edward I, who had healed the religious and racial divisions between his citizens and made 'Hindostan the most flourishing Empire in the World'.[192] This enlightened Islamic freemasonry, which appealed to the several Deists high in Company service at the time was opposed to the 'Mahomedan tyranny' which characterised the reign of Aurangzeb. By overthrowing Hindu property and abandoning tolerance, this Emperor had destroyed the Indian Constitution in much the same way as James II had overthrown the British Constitution.[193]

This search for true sources of information from those who understood the 'Constitution' was also revealed in the writings and actions of Alexander Dow and Robert Orme, two men who were particularly significant in the creation of a more politically serviceable orientalism. Dow claimed that his own account of the history and structure of the Mughal Empire of 1768 was superior to his predecessors' because he had personally interviewed the Ray Rayan of the Empire,[194] the head Hindu writer of its chancellery, whom he took to be a kind of chief secretary. Dow insisted on the need to consult Mughal office-holders and Brahmins. He denounced Europeans who picked up information from 'inferior tribes, or from the unlearned parts of the Brahmins'. It would be as ridiculous to hope for 'a true state of religion and philosophy' from the lowly as it would be for a Muslim in London to ask coach drivers about Newton or parish beadles about Christian theology.[195] This spirit informed the efforts of William Jones, H.T. Colebrooke, Charles Wilkins and a host of lesser scholars and officials to seek out the 'most learned Brahmins' and construct from them a 'true state' of Hindu Law, religion and literature.[196] The translation of Nyaya

[191] Hastings's minute on the publication of a translation of Abul Fazl, Gladwin, *Ayeen*, I, xiii–xiv.

[192] J.S. Grewal, *Muslim Rule in India. The Assessments of British Historians* (Calcutta, 1970), p. 19; P.J. Marshall, 'The founding fathers of the Asiatic society', *Journal of the Asiatic Society*, 27, 2, 1985, 63–77.

[193] Grewal, *Muslim Rule*, pp. 19–20, 36–7.

[194] Alexander Dow, *The History of Hindostan* (London, 1768), I, appendix, p. 2; O.P. Kejariwal, *The Asiatic Society of Bengal and the Discovery of India's Past, 1784–1838*, (Delhi, 1988); Grewal, *Muslim Rule*, pp. 1–22.

[195] Dow, *Hindostan*, I, xxxvii.

[196] N. Bhattacharya-Panda, 'The creation of the Hindoo Law Code', unpub. seminar

logic and Indian legal doctrine into the categories of European positive law proved much more difficult than this suggested, of course.

After 1785 these diverse and inchoate forms of British knowledge of India were to be rationalised and linked up. The generation of Cornwallis and Wellesley deepened formal oriental knowledge and promoted it as an official discourse in office manuals, gazettes and newspapers. The debate about the Permanent Settlement of the revenues of Bengal and Banaras incidentally founded the Indian statistical movement. A 'native of high birth' was set to write about the land revenue systems in the 'Risala-i Zirat' of 1785.[197] H.T. Colebrooke and A. Lambert's *Remarks on the Present State of the Husbandry and Internal Commerce of Bengal* (1795) later synthesised a mass of revenue and commercial information. The American War and French Revolution forced the Company to take yet closer account of the dealings of Europeans in Indian courts.[198] Most important, as the next chapter will show, the Company set about systematising and collating the material it drew from Indian sources, whether from simple runners and intelligent harkaras, or from newswriters, political secretaries and European travellers.[199] Effective intelligence, especially Indian intelligence, was critical to the Company's success. It was more important than its slender edge of military advantage or its ambiguous capitalist character.

The north Indian information order on the eve of conquest

Indian monarchs had presided over sophisticated and complex networks of surveillance which operated by word of mouth and newsletter. During the late seventeenth and early eighteenth centuries government was becoming more paper-bound; elites were slowly accumulating serviceable knowledge about the land and people. Other European and Asian states could count on much more detailed agencies of information collection and diffusion at local levels; the strength of the Indian system lay in the way it overlapped with a dense network of communication among ordinary people whose news and views were conveyed in part by letter and text, but which was maintained by a range of informal agents: physicians, mystics, astrologers, midwives and barbers. Public arenas of

paper, centre of South Asian Studies, Cambridge, 1993; Samita Sinha, *Pandits in a Changing Environment* (Calcutta, 1994), pp. 221–5.

[197] H. Mukhia, *Perspectives on Medieval History* (Delhi, 1993), pp. 259–94.

[198] 'Notes on Europeans and Asiatics', HM, 556, 557, 558, 577, OIOC.

[199] George Forster's 'remarkably intelligent' letters on the 'country powers of Hindustan' of 1783–4, filed in 1795, HM 685.

discussion and debate had coalesced around bazaar, temple and mosque. Society was certainly becoming more 'literacy aware', even if the absolute percentage of people who could read and write remained moderate by Eurasian standards. Deeper archives were being built up by corporate bodies as well as states, even though they were at the mercy of political fluidity. As many types of knowledge in north India remained specialised, limited to particular communities or professions, the flow of information to the rulers could be abruptly staunched, interrupted by headmen of castes and communities or by powerful people in the villages. Even where centralised knowledge about resources and society was being created, this may have reflected not the emergence of an all powerful state but the need for compromise and concession on the part of the elites.

The British were able, as the next chapter will show, to penetrate and control the upper level of networks of runners and newsletter writers with relative ease. By the mid-nineteenth century their reporting even at village level had improved dramatically, yet they excluded themselves from affective and patrimonial knowledges: the deep knowledge acquired by magnates with roots in the villages and the political sympathy which comes from ties of belief, of marriage and from a sense of inhabiting the same moral realm. In the early days of conquest the gap was not so apparent. Britons married Indian wives and communicated through contacts of mixed race. Some had sympathy with Indian religions; many still gave credence to a view of man and nature which remained humoural. They could call upon Indian texts and Indian informants who were themselves active in the Indo-Muslim attempt to know the resources, religion, folklore and arts of Hindustan. The British, however, were not very interested in affectionately savouring the delights of the land. They sought instead a textual and quantified understanding of the country in order to make it 'progress' and pay. In this scheme value was allocated to religion, caste and tribe according to a hierarchical scheme of 'moral independency' which derived from protestant Christianity and classical political economy. Loving sympathy which had ideally animated even the worst Indian ruler was largely alien to them. Colonial ideas were deeply influenced, especially in the first generations, by Indian knowledge, as we shall see. British understanding, revealingly, was weakest in regard to music and dance, the popular poetry of sacred erotics, dress and food, though such concerns are near the heart of any civilisation.

2 Political intelligence and indigenous informants during the conquest of India, c. 1785–1815

As late as 1785 the British were poorly informed about India outside Bengal and Banaras, Madras and its immediate hinterland, Bombay Island and a few other centres. During wars with the Marathas and Mysore between 1778 and 1783, the Company's effort nearly came to grief when the fast cavalry of its enemies caught its armies badly off balance. Knowledge of the interior of the country, its manufactures, population and agricultural statistics, remained similarly patchy, confined to Bengal and the Madras hinterland. Within a generation all this had changed. In 1808 the Maratha ruler and general of 'predatory cavalry', Jaswant Rao Holkar, remarked on the invaders' 'practice and favourite object' of receiving 'intelligence of all occurrences and transactions in every quarter'.[1] Well-informed residents and Company newswriters reported from all the major Indian courts. The army had created specialist posts and intelligence units. Surveyors and amateur ethnographers had traversed much of central India. The Company's intelligentsia had moved on from the study of classical texts and was now constructing statistical accounts of Indian agriculture, commerce and castes. The results of this surveillance were disseminated in officially-approved journals to a more expert body of civil and military officers.[2]

The expansion of knowledge was not so much a by-product of empire as a condition for it. Recent studies have shown that historians have exaggerated the military superiority of the British in India.[3] Indian armies were rapidly narrowing the gap in technology in the later eighteenth century. Where the British did have a critical advantage,

---

[1] Holkar to Govt, n.d., 'Meer Kurreem Ollah (a person of exceptional character) deputed by Jeswunt Rao Holkar as his vakeel to the Governor-General', BC 236/ 5447, OIOC.

[2] See e.g., W. Dalrymple's *Oriental Repertory*; *Asiatic Annual Register*, and more vigorous advocacy of government policy through *Government Gazette*.

[3] R.G.S. Cooper, 'Cross-cultural conflict analysis. The reality of British victory in the Second Anglo-Maratha War, 1803–5', unpub. PhD thesis, Cambridge University, 1992.

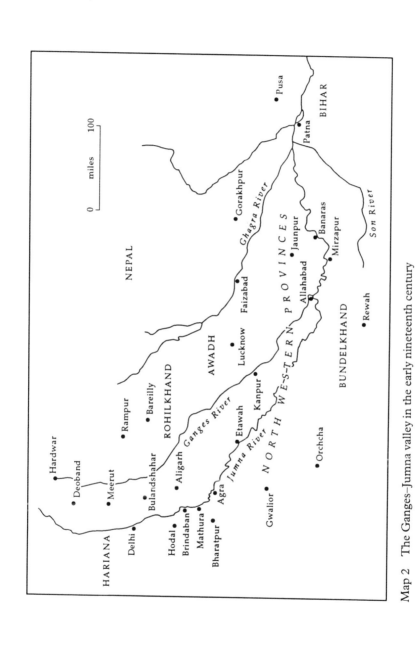

Map 2   The Ganges–Jumna valley in the early nineteenth century

however, was in their political planning and in the cohesion of their ruling group. They were now much more effective at anticipating the alliances and armed resistance of the Indian states. In large measure, this was because they were forewarned by increasingly effective systems of intelligence.

From the time of the Governor-Generalship of Lord Cornwallis (1786–93) onward, the British began to close down bilateral and multilateral channels of information between the Indian powers. Cornwallis's government, for instance, discouraged the client state of Awadh from stationing newswriters at the courts of its Maratha rivals and tried to make the Nawab depend on information from British sources.[4] Later governors-general set out to cut the practical and honorific lines of communication between the Delhi court and the other Indian powers,[5] so terminating the discourse on rights and duties which had informed Mughal rule. Meanwhile, the Company systematically took over Indian lines of communication and established its own. This chapter considers in greater detail the establishments of posts, runners and newswriters which formed a significant but little-studied part of the 'service economy' of eighteenth-century India. It shows how the British penetrated and suborned this system. Finally, it examines the intellectual culture of the native informants whom the British enticed, bribed or bullied into their service.

Posts, carriers, runners and spies

As with the Mughals, post and palankin routes (*dak*) became the arteries of British India. Regular post, with palankins and bearers to convey people and packages, was established between Calcutta, Patna and Banaras by 1775. Extensions to Lucknow and Hyderabad were made in the 1780s.[6] Communication by sea between the Presidencies was improved, especially after French privateers had been expelled from the Bay of Bengal. Elsewhere, until Wellesley's wars, the Company often continued to rely on existing establishments of Mughal origin.

Many of these Indian agencies were no longer run by directly-controlled officials as they had been under the Mughals. Indian powers,

---

[4]   Fisher, 'Akhbar nawis', 62–4; for later discussions of this issue, see 'Oudh newswriter at Rampur', BC 1192/ 3095, OIOC.

[5]   P. Spear, *Twilight of the Mughals. Studies in late Mughal Delhi* (Cambridge, 1951), pp. 6–83.

[6]   P.L. Koffsky, 'Postal Systems of India', *Bengal Past and Present*, 90, 1971, 47–69; M. Fisher, 'The East India Company's "suppression of the native dak"', *IESHR*, 31, 3, 1994, 319–26.

including the Company, farmed out the rights of head postmaster to wealthy men such as merchants or landowners and these maintained their own bodies of runners. The British soon began to be irked by the way in which their communications were intertwined with those of their enemies. For example, the dak on the critical route between north and south India via the Maratha-controlled town of Cuttack had been managed over many years by the family of Mahomed Waris, who were wealthy merchants and shipowners in the town of Thaumnagar.[7] The Marathas and the British both employed Mahomed Waris as postmaster in the province. During the prelude to the Mysore War of 1799, Neil Edmonstone of the Persian Department ordered him to intercept the mails of Bugaji Pandit, Maratha ambassador at Mysore. The intercepted letters included a number sent to the ambassador by the agent at Cuttak of the great Calcutta and Banaras banking firm of Manohar Das under seal of his master.[8] This bank was critical to British financial operations across India, and the incident illustrates how difficult it still was to distinguish between friend and foe, or between the political and commercial spheres in eighteenth-century India. Unfortunately for Mahomed Waris, the banker's agent now complained to the Maratha Governor of his duplicity in manipulating a previously open system of communication in the British interest. The Governor had Mahomed Waris dragged before him and threatened to 'blow him from a gun' unless he, in turn, held up the British mail between Madras and Calcutta. For a time the Postmaster simply directed the British mail onto another route. One despatch, however, fell into the hands of the Marathas. The runner was nearly flogged to death and Mahomed Waris's property was seized by the Marathas.

It was incidents such as this which made the British determined to create their own daks and, wherever possible, to close down the communications of their potential rivals. As political tension rose, British residents put pressure on rulers to allow the Company to open its own daks on their territory. In December 1798, William Palmer, Resident at Pune, informed the chief minister, Nana Fadnavis, that the Governor-General wanted to speed communications between the Company's settlements 'at this critical juncture'.[9] He proposed 'the placing of Hirkarrahs at equal stages on the road between this place

[7] J. Monckton, Pers. Sec. to Govt to Edmonstone, 13 July 1807, 'Donation to Muhammud Wauris in consequence of the losses he sustained in the performance of his duty as dawk moonshy of Cuttack', BC 236/ 5444.

[8] Enclosure, 'Humble petition of Muhammud Wauris', ibid.

[9] Palmer to Govr Genl, 10 Dec. 1798, HM 574; cf. 'Refusal of the Peshwa to admit the establishment of a post through their territory', BC 76/ 1659.

[Pune] and Bombay'. When Peshwa Baji Rao refused to discuss the request for a Company dak, Palmer put it down to 'his own narrow and perverse disposition ... rather than from any maxim or precedent of government'. Rulers, nonetheless, resisted the laying of Company daks because they feared the uses to which the British would put the information so collected. As laying a post was a prerogative of kingship, they also resented the implied dilution of their own authority. Later, when the Peshwa was browbeaten into accepting the British postal system, Palmer complained that he had 'conspicuously refused me the choice of stages and prescribed them himself at great and unequal distances', threatening great delay to British communications.[10]

Indian rulers attempted to evade demands for regular dak, but by 1810 a solid framework of communications was operating. The conquest of Mysore in 1799 allowed the British to strengthen the link between the northern and southern sectors of their power. Thereafter, feeder lines were driven into frontier areas. The government's orders to Charles Metcalfe for his embassy to Kabul in 1809, for example, enjoined him to establish a dak between Delhi and Amritsar if one did not already exist and to take with him the 'requisite complement of officers and runners, securing their protection if found necessary by application to the local authorities'.[11]

In order to create new routes for the regular transmission of information and personnel, the British needed to have access to the great labour force represented by the harkaras. Who were the harkaras of the later eighteenth century and how were they maintained? The sources reveal a hierarchy of agents from the highly educated to the lowly. Some running-spies were officials of royal households or direct dependants of magnates and British officials. Others formed 'intelligence communities' organised under headmen or merchant financiers who were employed by anyone who could afford their services. The word harkara (lit. 'do-all'; 'factotum') had overtones of 'intelligent' activity;[12] the Arabic *kassid* usually meant long-distance runner. *Jasus* implied spy, and did not necessarily indicate a runner, though usage of these terms often overlapped.[13]

Confidential agents achieved high rank and rewards. The Eurasian cavalry commander, Col. James Skinner, recorded that his chief spy had

---

[10] Palmer to Govr Genl, 6 Jul. 1799, HM 774.

[11] Minto to Metcalfe, 20 Jun. 1808, HM 592; cf. W. Kirkpatrick to Ross, 14 Jan. 1787, Kirkpatrick Mss. Eur. F228/1, OIOC; cf. Malcolm to Clive, 4 Aug. 1803, BC 176/3184.

[12] H. Yule and A.C. Burnell, *Hobson-Jobson. A Glossary of colloquial Anglo-Indian and Indian words and phrases* (rev. edn London, 1903), 'hurcarra', p. 430, 'jasoos', p. 453.

[13] Wilson, *Glossary*, 'jasudpatti', p. 234.

been 'brought up' in his own family.[14] Great rulers also maintained bodies of official harkaras with their special dress and staves of office who additionally acted as minor ambassadors and checked on local officials. Thomas Broughton recorded of the harkaras sent with him by a raja in central India that they were 'smart, intelligent fellows ... so generally useful, that, like the ancient heralds, they are looked upon as privileged and allowed to pass unmolested, whereas other travellers would be in the utmost danger'.[15] During the journey, a group of Gujar peasants fired on Broughton's party. The harkaras pacified them and told them that the British had 'passports', but privately called the villagers 'mere *gunwars*, boors', and asserted 'it was always lawful to outwit such fellows by any means'.[16]

Households of nobles, British officers[17] and even merchants had their own bodies of harkaras, but the majority of these were of lower status. Mughal nobles in Delhi had them on their establishments. In Bengal, Warren Hastings's banian, Krishna Kanta Nandy, had several 'pairs', who were paid about the same as doormen and other menial servants (Rs. 3 per month).[18] These were clearly a lower grade than the 'intelligent' harkaras, and may have been drawn from the palankin-bearer (Kahar) caste or from tribals of Orissa. Captain Williamson noted that before the 'pacification' of Bengal, harkaras had been servants who 'travelled beyond the circle of ordinary or daily communication ... What is now commonly called a cossid.'[19] Later, he thought, harkaras in Bengal had become little more than 'running footmen' who were hired simply to confirm the importance of their masters. According to Williamson, the harkara usually carried 'a lacquered walking stick' armed with a square spike ornamented with a fringe of tassels. This stick, carried over the shoulder, was the only distinction between the harkara and the lowly *peon* or footman who sometimes claimed precedence over him.

Among the Indians, the most skilled bodies of harkaras continued to work closely with ministers and newswriters. In post-Mughal governments the man the British called the 'head of the intelligence department' (the *daroga-i harkaron*) coordinated espionage. Influential

[14] D. Holman, *Sikander Sahib. The Life of Colonel James Skinner, 1778–1841* (London, 1961), p. 137.
[15] T.D. Broughton, *Letters from a Mahratta Camp in the year 1809* (repr. London, 1892), p. 12.
[16] ibid., p. 13.
[17] Edmonstone to his brother (WAE), 19 Jan. 1788, Edmonstone Papers, Add. Mss. 7616/1 (grey bound volume), Cambridge University Library.
[18] Nandy, *Cantoo Baboo*, p. 316.
[19] Capt. Williamson, ed. J.B. Gilchrist, *The General East India Guide and Vade Mecum ...* (London, 1825), p. 150.

newswriters would also gather about them runners and agents who were seen as their own particular servants. A British officer in Rajasthan in the 1830s remembered 'the *Ukhbar Nuvees* at Jesulmer, whom I once met coming out of the gate of that city with half a dozen of *hurkarus* before his horse, bearing spears and wands of office, with another attendant carrying a *chata* [umbrella] to screen his delicate person from the sun'.[20] The 'umbrella' was not, of course, employed for cosmetic reasons so much as to indicate the regal status of this king of information.

In addition to the royal officers and the agents supported in noble or private households, there also existed guilds of runners who were employed by the state,[21] landowners, merchants or villages, sometimes on a cash basis, sometimes for a share of produce. The distinction between dependent and hired runners seems clear. In 1796, for example, Sukha Ram Pandit in Hyderabad was said to have 'despatched a *hired cossid*' [my emphasis] along with man of business of his own to a nearby town.[22] Elsewhere, again, the term harkara seems to have become interchangeable with 'post-runner' (*dak dauria*). These were the relays of men living in villages and subsisting on shares of produce who carried royal or, for a price, ordinary mail between one place and another.

During the transition to British rule certain communities, such as the 'Mewias' of Rajasthan,[23] who had been mentioned in Mughal sources, retained their reputation as intelligence workers. In Mysore, the Sultans relied heavily on the nomadic Bedar tribe as an intelligence community.[24] Bedars provided harkaras, post-runners and guides for the military, and a large group of them was settled within a few miles of Tipu's capital at Seringapatam. Their women also became temple dancers and concubines of powerful men, giving their caste an enviable monopoly in the lower echelons of the information order. Bedars were recruited into British service.

As in the case of bullock-drivers, the tight-knit corporate organisations of these communities of harkaras allowed large numbers of them to be mobilised quickly. Rulers and their agents applied for their services to the headmen or officials in charge of runners who usually

---

[20] A.H.E. Boileau, *Personal Narrative of a Tour through the western states of Rajwara in 1835* (Calcutta, 1837), p. 98.

[21] Shejwalkar (ed.), *Nagpur Affairs*, p. lii.

[22] 'Particulars relating to Succaram's messenger', 15 Feb. 1796, 'Correspondence concerning the intrigues of Tippoo Sultan', Kirkpatrick Papers, F228/7.

[23] J. Hoyland (ed., tr.) *The Commentary of Father Monserrate on his journey to the Court of Akbar* (Oxford, 1922), p. 212, cited Nayeem, *Postal Commmunications*, p. 10 n. 81; *Ain*, tr. Blochman, I, p. 252; A.G. Sen, *The Post Office of India* (Calcutta, 1875), p. 63.

[24] 'Hukmnamah Harkaron', Asiatic Society of Bengal Mss.

supplied them in pairs. The pairs worked together and shadowed each other. Sometimes, however, group loyalties could cause problems for an employer. In Lucknow in the 1780s, for example, the Nawab's plans were revealed to his enemies, the Begams (Royal Ladies), because the ruler's post carriers and servants 'went to sleep with their caste-fellows and brothers',[25] who included the runners of the Begams' principal adviser.

At the bottom of the hierarchy of transmitters of information were impressed people of low caste. Enforced running or message-carrying for a superior implied a particularly lowly status. Such operatives, even more than agricultural bondsmen, were regarded as the typical indigenous proletarian. In Banaras people of the untouchable leather and parchment-making caste, the Chamars, had a customary duty to run for men of power. They were called *daurias*, simply 'runners', though success in the lucrative leather business appears to have allowed some of them to buy themselves out of this obligation with a composition fee.[26] In Rajasthan the lowly Mahar caste provided many runners. In Gujarat, Alexander Walker, the British agent, cryptically remarked that the spies were from the same caste as the deeply inauspicious executioners.[27] Where exactly the running or guiding took place was also important. In a swampy region of Rajasthan no caste Hindu would deign to guide travellers along the paths. Here the guides were invariably 'bhungees, or sweepers'.[28] Travelling these paths, particularly at night, exposed higher-caste people to dangerous miasma, ghosts or even pollution arising from the swamps. Really 'dirty' people were required to do really dirty jobs, but equally, such inauspiciousness may have protected the agents from molestation.

Harkaras were apparently trained within their families or were apprenticed to caste-members who taught them skills of running and survival in hostile territory. In the case of superior runners, some descriptions have survived from seventeenth-century Iran of an elaborate system of training through exercise and competition. Safavid runners ran to India and Mughal harkaras to Iran.[29] Their clothing and insignia, as described by the traveller Tavernier, were similar to those of

[25] Faiz Baksh, *Memoirs*, II, 38.
[26] Wajib ul arz of Maulvi Karim ullah, G. Saletore (ed.), *Banaras Affairs (1788–1810)*, I (Allahabad, 1955), 77.
[27] Walker of Bowland Papers, Ms. 13819, National Library of Scotland, Edinburgh. I am grateful to Dr Dilip Menon for this reference; cf., on Mahars, I. Karve and M. Dandekar, *Anthropometric Measurement of Maharashtra* (Pune, 1951), p. 35.
[28] Boileau, *Narrative*, pp. 51–2.
[29] J. Chardin, *Voyages du Chevalier Chardin en Perse et autres lieux de l'Orient* (Paris, 1811), IV, 167–9.

eighteenth-century Indian runners,[30] so it is likely that they were similar functionaries. According to Tavernier, the young Persian runner began walking practice slowly at the age of six or seven. The next year he began to run a league at a time 'at a handsome trot'.[31] The following year he ran two or three leagues. At the age of eighteen, he was given water bottle, bread pan and other accoutrements. As in India, great men attended events accompanied by bodies of runners holding staves; running contests were sometimes arranged between employees of different masters.[32] The best runners could cover enormous distances with few breaks. It was rumoured that some could do 100 miles in twenty four hours, though half that seems to have been the norm on the hazardous routes between Kabul, Delhi, Lucknow, Banaras and Calcutta. Old men in Rajasthan can still remember training of this sort taking place in the 1920s.

A Marathi document of the late eighteenth century records the requirements for different grades of harkara, which included mental as well as physical accomplishments.[33] The superior class of harkara was supposed to be skilled in various forms of classical knowledge, including the Vedas, astronomy or astrology, and vocal music. He should know five languages, 'Dravid [Tamil], Telang [Telugu], Karnataki, Avidhi [sic] and Maharashtra [Marathi]'. He should be able to write in six kinds of script, including joined and simple Dravid and Maharashtra. He should be capable of appearing in different guises, 'having a hardened body', and 'steadfast in bringing news in wartime'. The lower grades were required to command less scriptural knowledge, but even the third grade harkara was supposed to know 'three or four languages' and one script, to be clever and 'capable of appearing in various guises'.[34] The training of these agents ideally involved classical accomplishments in the realm of accumulating and conveying knowledge. It also implicitly recognised the subcontinent as a complex of language communities.

The reputation of the individual agent for honesty and exactitude was critical where a dribble of 'human intelligence' was often all that a commander could count on. The harkara's verbal skills as a reporter and advocate were all important. For reasons of security he only carried

---

[30] Illustration from B. Solvyns, *Costume of Hindustan*, reproduced on cover, *MAS*, 27, i, 1993.

[31] J.B. Tavernier, *The Six Voyages of John Baptist Tavernier* (London, 1678), p. 149; cf. J. Thevenot, *Travels into the Levant* (London, 1686), p. 103.

[32] Tavernier, *Voyages*, pp. 149–50.

[33] 'Qualities of three grades of harkara', in M.M.D.V. Potdar, *Bharata Itihasa Sanshod-haka Mandala Quarterly*, 52, vol. xiii, 4, *shaka* 1855, doct. 21; I am grateful to Dr S. Guha for this reference and translation.

[34] ibid.

written messages as a supplement or key to the verbal messages which he was charged to deliver. He was instructed to convey the messages only to the 'Presence' to which he had been despatched. Above all, a harkara had to get his answer (*jawab*).[35] If a ruler refused to answer a harkara, or had him turned out of the city or the camp on a donkey or with a blackened face, this might mean war, or at least the loss of life or livelihood of the messenger. Harkaras begged for answers, however exiguous.

At important crossing points over rivers or borders, special arrangements were made for all agents who were not passing incognito. Lieutenant Boileau reported, for example, that on the road between Jaipur and Udaipur was the well-supplied village of Nim ka Thana 'which is made over for the maintenance of the *hurkarus* of the Jaipoor state' and its troops.[36] It appears that in this and similar places, part of the revenues of villages was set aside for the maintenance of runners. In Maharashtra there was a territorial tax called 'spy-tax' (*jasudpatti*) for this purpose,[37] but no detailed account of it has come to light.

The survival into the post-Mughal era of this labour-intensive communication system is a puzzle. In the Ottoman Empire, 'running footmen' were used in cities, but the royal mails and other intelligence were carried by fast Caucasian horsemen.[38] Chinese central Asia was served by a 'regular horse dawk'. Even in India we sometimes hear of 'fast camel' and horse dak,[39] and even of the use of pigeons. Why were riders not more generally used? Cost may have been a factor; labour was very cheap in India, and with limited facilities for shoeing horses, it may have been that human runners and palankin bearers could cover a distance not far short of horses for a fraction of the cost. Humans on foot were obviously more skilled at passing treacherous and monsoon-ravaged roads, and harkaras who did not wear livery could probably avoid detection more easily than horsemen. Under the British, horse posts were said to have failed when they had been first introduced.[40] At all events, the system persisted into the 1850s when it was replaced, first by bullock-cart and pony services and then by the railways and telegraph. Even in later times, though, the postal peon trotting across the country-side bore a distant resemblance to the harkara of old.

[35] C. Grey and H.L.O. Garrett (eds.), *European Adventurers of Northern India, 1785–1849* (Lahore, 1929), pp. 66–7.

[36] Boileau, *Narrative*, p. 6.   [37] Wilson, *Glossary*, p. 234.

[38] William Moorcroft minute, 15 Sept. 1814, HM 645; Japanese express messengers in the eighteenth century could ride 70 miles per day, Nakane and Oishi, *Tokugawa Japan*, p. 111.

[39] Thevenot, *Travels*, pp. 75–6.

[40] cf. 'Report on the Affairs of the East India Company', *Parliamentary Papers*, 1831–2, viii, 75.

Whether composed of active intelligent agents or simply running footmen, the combination of the state and private harkara establishments must have added up to a formidable population. Adding writers, it becomes clear that the information service sector in early modern India must have absorbed a considerable amount of manpower. Even in a relatively small town like Jodhpur in the 1820s, for example, 500 members of 'Hurkaru' families or 'messengers of state' were recorded,[41] quite apart from the huge number of private messengers, writers, postal brokers and other agents.

The British come to terms with the harkara

Even though the Company's political intelligence had improved between 1779 and 1785, its military intelligence remained inadequate, especially on the southern flank where it faced the formidable cavalry power of the Mysore state and the Marathas. The Mysore rulers had created a powerful intelligence service and made good use of information from defecting Company troops and the disbanded Afghan Rohilla cavalry who once served the Nawab of Arcot. On the British side, only a few badly paid harkaras were employed by the main columns, according to a scathing report from Col. William Fullarton of the Madras Infantry. While Haidar Ali 'amply rewarded spies and treated English emissaries with utmost severity', the Company was renowned for its 'parsimony', he complained.[42] For example, one of the key intelligence officials never received more than two guineas for dangerous missions. The result was demoralisation and failure. Typically, a Brahmin would 'promise to go into Hyder's camp disguised as a beggar' to discover his movements. Out of sight of British troops, he would 'skulk for a day among the bushes' and would return with fictitious reports or tittle-tattle picked up from 'some wretched inhabitant or Mysorean camp follower, whom he had ventured to converse with while he was gathering fuel or grass for his master'.[43]

This situation changed dramatically towards the end of the Second Mysore War. Hereafter, the British reorganised their military intelligence and cooperation with the civil arm improved greatly. Fullarton himself, a radical critic of the Company, made the breakthrough.[44] In

---

[41] Boileau, *Narrative*, pp. 239; for 'raj hurkarus' in Jaipur, 'Asiatic intelligence', *Asiatic Journal*, 24, 1837, 187 ff.

[42] 'Capt. Fullarton's Hircarrahs', HM 84, f. 913 ff., OIOC.

[43] ibid.

[44] 'Fullarton's hircarrahs'; cf. W.J. Wilson, *History of the Madras Army* (Madras, 1882), II, 86–93.

1782, he wrote *A private account of the state of the Carnatic* (London, 1782), which submitted a long charge sheet against the Company for mismanagement and peculation. His attacks on the failings of his military superiors were as vigorous. Fullarton was among the first Company officers to recognise fully the importance of harkaras in fast cavalry warfare. When Fullarton joined the corps, Col. Lang only employed five 'intelligent hircarahs' and the army suffered from 'a want of a system of intelligence'. Fullarton, however, procured trustworthy middlemen from John Sullivan, Resident at Tanjore, and from the Nawab of Arcot. These agents then employed harkaras on a personal basis. Fullarton had these controllers compete with each other, threatening to kill them if they deceived him. The harkaras were sent out to observe different roads and later examined in the presence of their chief. Fullarton, fully briefed, then interrogated them himself. He would enquire, for instance, where they stopped on the first day, whether they ate at a particular temple refectory or washed in a particular tank, 'occasionally naming villages which did not exist, tanks and choultries [rest houses] which were not to be found'.

Fullarton secured from the Raja of Ramnad in the dry far south of Tamilnadu a body of Kallar tribals 'who were perfectly acquainted with the bye-paths of the country'[45] and stationed them along the roads in pairs. The more 'intelligent' agents were placed at bazaars and temples 'as faquirs, merchants and under various guises'. They 'wrote down everything which occurred' and passed messages to the illiterate tribals who conveyed them to headquarters. In effect, Fullarton had reconstituted under British control the classic Indian intelligence system which allied the writing skills and knowledge of learned Brahmins with the hard bodies and running skills of tribal and low-caste people.

In cases where no news was forthcoming, Fullarton 'assumed that a large body of enemy horse had interposed itself'. Following new rules for 'intelligence, movement and supply', Fullarton marched the army from 'the Coromandel to the Malabar coast through the most difficult and before untried roads', thus scoring one of the first Company successes against Haidar and Tipu.[46] These tactics were later extended to northern and western India where the British faced an equally mobile

---

[45] 'Fullarton's hircarrahs'; for another 'tribal group', the Coorgis, in British intelligence, D. Mahoney to Mornington, 14 Jan. 1800, Bengal Political Cons., 1 May 1800, 3, 117/6, OIOC; for the use of Kallars by Mysore patriots, note by Bentinck, Fort St George Pol. Cons., 27 Jul. 1804, BC 176/ 3184, OIOC.

[46] 'Fullarton's Hircarrahs'; cf. Major Dirom, *A Narrative of the Campaign in India which terminated the war with Tippoo Sultan in 1792* (London, 1794), pp. 154, 201.

enemy in the Marathas. Regular corps of guides began to incorporate harkara reports into books of route maps.[47]

In general, the British widened the purview of the indigenous security state by putting yet more emphasis on surveillance. Ghulam Hussain wrote 'The head harcara or head spy, in several of the best English houses, never fails to become their Major Domo and the hinge on which turn most transactions', despite the fact that he was often of 'the lowest clan'.[48] The harkara's position was, nevertheless, precarious and the more so in the army. George Hadley's Urdu dialogue of 1795 envisages a violent altercation between an officer and a harkara.[49] Thus: 'Call Ram Singh hurkurrah. Go to Ameinaghur, bring exact intelligence where Dummodah is, what he is about and what force he has with him.' Hadley's officer has the cunning to send off another agent to trail the first. The first is found to have neglected his orders and to have fabricated stories about the doings of Damodar, the enemy commander. Brought before the officer, he is told, 'You are a great scoundrel. You did not go to Ameinaghur, and now you come intoxicated before me to tell me lies. If one cannot trust the hurkurrahs we are always in jeopardy, therefore I must hang you.'[50] The errant spy replies: 'Forgive me, sir, it is my fault, I will confess I drank parriah arrack [rice brandy] and fell asleep.' The officer answers: 'You scoundrel, I would certainly hang you, but your father, I hear, is a good, venerable old man. Give him a hundred lashes and turn him out of the service!'[51]

The suspicion which underlay the relationship on and around the battlefield was not fictional. Following intelligence failures at the battle of Assaye in 1803, there were persistent reports that Arthur Wellesley, Col. Stevenson and Shinde had all hanged their head harkaras for dereliction of duty.[52] Wellesley found himself only a mile from the enemy lines when he had been told by the spies that they were ten or twelve miles away. Although properly constituted corps of guides, which were entered in the order of battle, had been established since the days of Fullarton and Wellesley himself had laid down firm rules for 'regulating the Intelligence Department',[53] things could still go wrong. A particular problem in the Maratha lands was that trusted inhabitants

---

[47] e.g. 'Field book of marches of the Army under command of Maj.-General Medows, 1790–1', Mss. Eur. E60–61, OIOC; Wilson, *Madras Army*, I, 336, 367.

[48] Ghulam Hussain, 'Siyyar' tr. Nota-Manus, III, 190.

[49] George Hadley, *A Compendious Grammar of the current corrupt dialect of the jargon of Hindostan* (London, 1796), pp. 197–202.

[50] ibid., p. 201.   [51] ibid., p. 202.

[52] Col. J. Biddulph, *The Nineteenth and their Times* (London, 1899), p. 146; J. Gurwood (ed.) *The Dispatches of Field Marshall the Duke of Wellington, K.G.*, I (London, 1834), 390–3.

[53] ibid., II (London, 1835), memorandum on intelligence, 464–5.

of Bengal, Mysore or the Madras Presidency were as easily recognisable as Europeans, thus the British were 'obliged to employ, as hircarrahs, the natives of the country and to trust their reports'.[54] During the course of conquest and settlement, in fact, the British made use of all the major intelligence communities of the old order for military purposes: Kallars, Coorgis and Bedars in the south, 'Mewias' and Mahars in the west and, in addition, diverse Brahmins and Gosain communities throughout the country.

The other main target of political intelligence was, naturally, the Indian court. In addition to recognised newswriters and public harkaras of the herald type, all the courts of the period were served by large numbers of spies working on behalf of rulers, family rivals and foreigners. These ranged from highly placed advisers who had been 'turned', through to old women and midwives of the women's quarters who provided a 'daily budget of tittle tattle' in return for a few rupees. Agents such as these might be independent operatives who took their intelligence directly back to their masters, or employees of secret intelligence officers (the *khufia navis*s, 'secret writers'), or secret employees of the publicly known newswriters. Elphinstone, stationed as Resident at Pune in 1817, kept a daily diary of intelligence,[55] tracing the activity of spies in the region. He interrogated merchants travelling up from the coast, had spies following the Maratha ruler wherever he went and even placed them with the headmen of villages around the Maratha capital.[56] The Resident was particularly worried about the activities of the 'Bijapur Fuqeer',[57] presumably one of the leading Sufi teachers of that town who had once been correspondents and informants of Tipu and were now thought to be 'tampering' with the loyalty of the Indians in the Resident's guard.

Newswriters: the veracity of political information

An important feature of British intelligence-gathering during the climax of conquest was the intensive use made of the Persian newsletter. In the days of Warren Hastings, these had been collected and sent to Calcutta by Indian administrators such as Mahomed Reza Khan and Ali Ibrahim Khan. The generation of Edmonstone, Cherry and the Kirkpatricks, however, acquired and read in person despatches from Company and

---

[54] *Supplementary Despatches, Correspondence and Memoranda of Arthur Duke of Wellington, edited by his son*, IV (London, 1859), 185.
[55] 'Notebook of intelligence, 22 Sept. to 24 Oct. 1817', Elphinstone Papers, Mss. Eur. F88/3 no. 7, OIOC.
[56] ibid., entry 6 Oct. 1817.   [57] ibid., entry 23 Oct. 1817.

foreign newswriters as well as copies of reports issued directly by Indian courts.[58] Though 'black' or 'native intelligence' was sometimes publicly scorned, access to the detailed information of the 'Persian newspapers' put the Company in a particularly strong position in India. Such a generous flow of indigenous intelligence was not generally available to European conquerors in other parts of Asia or in Africa.

The British, nonetheless, had difficulty in understanding the significance of the newswriter. This was not a system of accredited 'foreign correspondents' or even of resident ambassadors, it was a tolerated espionage system, known and accepted as such, and distinct from the establishments of temporary ambassadors. Broughton, writing from Shinde's camp, mused:

There is a strange custom which prevails at all Indian courts of having a servant ... who is an admitted spy upon the chief, about whose person he is employed; and whose business it is faithfully to repeat all his actions, of whatever nature to his [foreign] employer. Seendhiya [Shinde] has one such in our camp; and we, of course another in his. This latter is a perfect original. He has been in the service of British Residents for more than forty years; and has in the course of so long a period, as may be supposed, picked up a collection of anecdotes of the most extraordinary nature: most of them are entertaining enough, but many not over delicate, and perhaps not always restrained within the strict line of truth.[59]

The newswriters, and in particular the *burains* – old ladies – employed by them as peeping-toms in the women's quarters, kept all India amused for years with a flow of dirty stories until a more severe morality intervened in the 1830s.[60]

In addition to accredited writers at foreign courts, the successor states continued the Mughal practice of having newswriters attached to subdivisional centres, where they could report on the doings of local officials and check on defalcations of revenue. These officials also had the particular duty of passing on the names and rank of important, or sinister visitors moving about the state. F.J. Shore, passing through Awadh in 1828, noted that the 'King's akbarwallas' expected a gift for this office. One said, 'Oh Sir, I am going to announce your coming to the Asylum of the World.' Shore refused on the grounds that he would reach Lucknow before the newsletter,[61] but this was obviously to miss the point of the office. Provincial newswriters such as this were reinforced with another level of back-up intelligence provided by 'secret writers'. In the Rajput states these agents were mobile, moving from

[58] Fisher, 'Akhbar Nawis', 67–70.
[59] Broughton, *Letters*, p. 25.
[60] Westmacott Mss. 'Travels in India', Mss. Eur. C29, f. 289, 24 Dec. 1833, OIOC.
[61] F.J. Shore, 'Private journal', 15 Feb. 1829, Mss. Eur. E307/2 OIOC.

fort-mart to fort-mart and picking up information on the misdemea-
nours of big landholders and local officials.[62] Intelligence from them was
kept separate from ordinary administrative reports (*arzdashts*) and from
the reports of the accredited newswriters. These subordinate writers
were generally suspended once British administration had established
itself.

The right to have newswriters in particular courts meant much more
than simply having access to a flow of information. It implied that rulers
had a legitimate interest in each others' policies and had established a
degree of mutual trust within the all-India system of states. Conversely,
the more newswriters a ruler could establish in another's territory
without reciprocal arrangements, the more sovereignty was effectively
conceded. When he wished to hold out boons to the British, a
competitor for the throne of Awadh is alleged to have assured them that
he would allow them to have 'a [British] newswriter established in every
perguneh [sub-district]'.[63] Acceptance of this level of surveillance
suggested an effective concession of sovereignty to the Company. For a
distinguishing feature of great kings since Akbar had been their access to
continuous flows of local information. Similarly, Abdus Samad Khan of
Hariana, seeking help from the British in 1807, stated that he had earlier
been forced to side with the Marathas against them. He said he feared
that without 'communication' with the British government he would fall
into disgrace like Nawab Bambu Khan 'who in consequence of not
sending information to government' lost possession of his forts to
marauding tribes.[64]

To impede the newswriters of another sovereign, or to expel them,
was tantamount to a declaration of war. Indeed, it suggested permanent
hostility. For even where ambassadors were withdrawn during warfare, it
was customary for newswriters to remain near their posts in order to
alert their masters about the proper time for peace negotiations. In 1787,
Kirkpatrick passed on a complaint from Shinde that the Lucknow court
was obstructing his 'intelligencers' and he asked the British, as the
Nawab's ally, to intervene and prevent further bad feeling.[65] Again, in
1794, when G.F. Cherry was trying to ensure that an anti-British party
did not remain in power in Rampur after a palace coup, the placing and
demeanour of the British newswriter was a critical test of mutual

[62] Personal communication, March 1981, from Dr Madhavi Bajekal.
[63] Resident, Lucknow to Govt, 24 Oct. 1807, 'Intrigues by Members of the Vizier's family against him', BC 248/ 5584.
[64] 'Trans. of *arzi* from Abdoos Summud Khan recd. 23 Jun. 1807', BC 212/ 4735.
[65] W. Kirkpatrick to Harper, 6 Apr. 1787, Kirkpatrick Papers, F228/1; for careful collation of 'Persian news' see entry 19 Jan. 1795 in his private letter book, 3 Dec. 1794–15 Jun. 1795, ibid., F228/3, OIOC.

relations. Johar Mull, the (Khattri) newswriter, was told to withdraw from the Rampur court but to 'maintain a channel of secret communication' with other nobles.[66] The incumbent Nawab, Ghulam Mahomed, wrote of his 'grief and uneasiness' at the writer's departure 'as being an indication of the withdrawment [sic] of the Company's protection'.

In the battles over information which erupted between the major Indian powers, the British tactic was clear. They tried to overawe and suborn the newswriters of Indian rulers situated at Calcutta or other centres of their power, and to short-circuit their harkara and newsletter systems. One trick was to try to undermine the credibility of newswriters by sending back misinformation through other agents such as ambassadors. Again, agents or newswriters of Indian powers who were deemed too clever and effective were rejected as unacceptable. The British also attempted to get behind the agents themselves and attack the ministers in charge of intelligence who had despatched them. Above all, the more able Company officials were avid to receive all the Indian newsreports they could get their hands on. These often gave a better indication of what was happening than the sometimes self-serving reports of their own residents and ambassadors.

Ordinary newsreports were formally documents of almost tedious detail, describing court ritual and gossip and the daily proceedings of the court. Yet there was more to them than met the eye. They conveyed a good deal of social information which was of value to the post-Mughal realm: the rise of new favourites, or the emergence of new factions. Indian rulers were also capable of using the reports to create a climate of opinion or justify a political move to be made. These could be proactive as well as reactive accounts, testimony to a sophisticated set of skills in propaganda. In 1809, for instance, Maharaja Holkar, whom the British regarded as hostile, wished to march to the Deccan with the possible intention of meeting up with the cavalry leader, Amir Khan. Planning to put the British off their guard, Holkar's court released a newsletter which purported to show that the Maharaja was afflicted by supernatural possession:[67] 'The Maharaja became senseless, his jaws locked and it seemed as if death was approaching ... A voice from the Maharaja exclaimed "Do not be alarmed I am your deity".' The ministers asked 'What offence has the Maharaja committed that you vex him so sorely?' The voice replied, 'he has committed numerous offences and now you must conduct him to Jejury and prostrate him at my feet'. An astrologer fixed the following day's march to the temple of 'Khundi Rao at Jejury';

---

[66] Cherry to his Newswriter at Rampur, 19 Sept. 1794, HM 577, f. 81.

[67] 'Translation of an akhbar from Jeswunt Rao Holkar's camp, 7 Nov. 1809', H. Russell, Pune to Gov. Genl 19 Nov. 1809, HM, 596.

this was probably Khandoba, the Maharaja's tutelary deity. Holkar wished to march into the Deccan for political reasons, but by asserting that the god was calling him, he managed to disarm British objections and simultaneously gain credit from his Indian subjects and fellow sovereigns. Likewise, when Ranjit Singh of the Punjab wished to reassure the British about his military movements in 1814, he sent for the newswriter of the Delhi Resident and asked him to alert his master so that their enemies could not sow mischief.[68]

Whereas the open reports of court newswriters were elaborate, intending to give a picture of the multifarious activities of the ruler and his social and diplomatic contacts, military reports compiled by the writers appear to have been more perfunctory. These were digests of harkara information intended to be interpreted by military commanders in the light of information from other sources. Maratha newsletters of 1802–3, which were intercepted by the British, provide some evidence on their form.[69] Much space is given to the size, movement and composition of the force of the potential enemy, in this case the rebel Daundia Waugh. The reports noted the villages where the Waugh's flag had been raised. There is a strong concern with morale: 'the army is willing', 'the foot people [i.e. infantry] are of no account'. In another set of intelligence reports, the troops were said to have been underpaid and underfed and had looted the military bazaar. Above all, the reports detail the possibility of factional realignment and speculate on the chances of detaching one or another war leader or local magnate from an enemy or potential opponent's army. In the case of Daundia Waugh's rebellion, the Maratha authorities wanted most to know how many village leaders and local magnates were prepared to feed and supply the fugitive force.

The newsletter was one of the threads which tied together the 'little kingdoms' and 'segmentary states' making up the all-India polity. At its best, it was a sophisticated system. Despite their complaints, the British continued to use it sporadically right up to 1857. Even thereafter it was never completely ousted by newspapers in the Indian states. Still, it was a fragile system, easily uprooted or subverted. Beyond the Indian plains, as the next chapter will show, it dwindled into oblivion.

Munshis: mastering the mystique of writing

Newswriters were one important group of specialists within a much wider community of writers, many of whom were titled munshi. It was

---

[68] Resident, Delhi, to J. Adam, Sec. to Govt, 8 Oct. 1814, HM 648.
[69] 'Translations of Mahratta intelligence, news from Dharwar', HM 461; intelligence from Holkar's and Bhonsla's camps, 1803, HM 469.

through the good offices of munshis that the officials of the East India Company made tenuous and ambivalent contact with the traditions of statesmanship and knowledge which informed the great kingdoms of the subcontinent. The writer and clerical establishment approximated to an Indo-Muslim bureaucracy which was also acquiring some of the attributes of a middle class. Writers were still divided by caste and religion; they still employed the language of the slave to their masters, and they still depended critically on royal favour. Mastery of the pen, the account books and the politics of the post-Mughal states had, however, given them independent bases of social power. It had also given rise to a tradition of state service above and beyond allegiance to any particular king or dynasty. By controlling diplomatic relations between the small states and the semi-independent provinces of the former Empire and serving the new Company state, writers could enrich themselves and their kin groups, converting grants-in-aid for service into more permanent landholdings. Tension often attended the rise to influence of the writers. In Ranjit Singh's Punjab, the last great successor state to the Mughals, conflict was often acute. In the Sikh army every offence had its fixed price and the commanders of regiments put the finances of their regiments in the hands of 'Persian writers, frequently low intriguing fellows'[70] who plundered the common soldiers. Military revolts here routinely raised a 'cry for the blood of the Munshis'.

In indigenous society, the royal munshi was at the top of a hierarchy which stretched up from the common writer of the bazaar, through the clerks and men of business of Indian commercial firms (munims or sarkars) to the clerks of individual landowners and notables. The commercial communities used their own family members to write the accounts and Bengali or Hindi commercial letters. They needed Persian writers to communicate with the local officials and to check or confirm grants recorded by the registrar (kazi). Complexity of language and multiplicity of scripts therefore increased the number of writers in government and private establishments.

The British encountered munshis first as 'language masters', that is, people who taught them to read and write the Persian script. The relationship was a difficult one. Arrogant British youths were placed under the charge of Persian scholars of learning and, sometimes, of sanctity. Hadley wrote a dialogue for such occasions, and it appears that munshis were treated with derision, as a kind of 'black schoolmaster'.[71]

---

[70] H.M.L. Lawrence, *Adventures of an Officer in the Service of Runjeet Singh* (London, 1845, repr. Karachi, 1975), II, 21. For the rapacity of 'low munshis' in British territory, *Delhi Gazette*, 24 Apr. 1850.

[71] Williamson ed. Gilchrist, *Vade Mecum*, pp. 101–2.

There were constant complaints about their competence. Hadley remarked that few munshis knew English and they were therefore in the predicament of one Mr Hill 'who went to teach English in Holland, but found that he had overlooked the circumstance of his own ignorance in Dutch', consequently master and pupil were unintelligible to each other.[72]

Munshis to Company officials were in an altogether more significant position. Many officials knew some Persian and Hindustani and a smaller number could write sentences. Remarkably few, however, mastered the stylistic intricacies of letter-writing. This was an art in itself, and one with great political significance in the complex polity of eighteenth-century India. In 1790 Neil Edmonstone remarked how dependent the British were on their clerks to read and interpret the letters they received, vowing himself to break this dependency.[73] A generation later, after the ministrations of Fort William College and Haileybury, it was asserted that William Sleeman, tyro of 'Thuggee and Dacoitee' and now Resident, was probably the only British official ever to have addressed the King of Awadh in correct Urdu and Persian.[74]

Expert munshis with long diplomatic experience were an extraordinarily valuable commodity for the eighteenth-century states and for the Company. The best ones could command salaries in excess of Rs. 200 per month.[75] Though these did not compare with the remuneration for British officials in what was a pay scale divided by race, it was good by standards of other Indian employees (ordinary harkaras, for instance, received Rs 2–3 p.m.). The absolute confidentiality of the writers was essential if the diplomatic machine was to continue to function and the British made strenuous efforts to prevent their employees acting as double agents for Indian rulers, something which was common in the practice, if not the theory, of indigenous statecraft.[76] While large numbers of Muslim, Kayastha and Khattri boys entered open educational institutions in the great Indo-Muslim cities to learn basic Persian,

---

[72] Hadley, *A Compendious Grammar*, p. 5.
[73] Edmonstone to his brother, 9 Jan. 1790, Edmonstone Papers.
[74] *Delhi Gazette*, 24 Feb. 1849; cf. Ghulam Hussain, 'Siyyar', tr. Nota-Manus, II, 462.
[75] Abdul Kadir Khan received Rs. 1000 p.m. 'on the highest scale of rewards ever granted to a native', 'Jageer of Moolvy Abdool Kader Khan', BC 1323/52452; the son of Humeed Khan, Head Munshi, was to be specially brought up by the Persian Translator to fit him for service, 'Petition of Sukh Lal', head munshi of Allahabad, Bengal Political Cons. 24 April 1800, 7, 117/6; cf. case of Maulvi Ghulam Makhdum, BC 203/ 4595, OIOC.
[76] Two important informants, Khairuddin Khan and his relative Salahuddin were dimissed for 'intrigues' with the Mughal court and the Marathas, *CPC*, VII, (1785–7), pp. 158, 163; for a later munshi dismissed for 'treason', 'Proceedings relative to the office of native correspondence', BC 1509/59303, OIOC.

accountancy and the Islamic subjects, the type of specialist literary and political education required for high-level political and diplomatic service was very hard to come by. The coded language of political intercourse made reference to Arabic, Persian and even Sanskrit classics. Yet texts were few and far between. Faiz Baksh, the historian of Awadh, remembered the difficulty in acquiring Persian in his home village of Safipur only twenty-four miles from Lucknow where there was no Persian teacher, despite its status as a learned qasbah. He had to come to Lucknow to read the Persian classic, the 'Gulistan', and remembered carrying it under his arm to his teacher.[77] The later generation of the poet Ghalib had equal difficulty in procuring texts and adequate teaching. Naturally, patronage was the key to advancement among writers and political secretaries. In Lucknow, the eunuch statesman Jawahar Ali Khan trained Munshi Faiz Baksh, who himself had another eunuch, Darab Ali Khan, as pupil. Together they read the great classical poets and Sufi saints.[78]

The rituals of writing in the Mughal royal chancelleries had been elaborate. The whole nobility had been brought up to revere the art of insha or letter-writing as a tool of literacy and as a form of regulating proper social relations. The 'letter book' became a key form of instruction in right conduct, and collections from the Mughal period and the eighteenth century were still used as schoolbooks in the mid-nineteenth century. Thus the munshi should be regarded as more than a secretary; he was an expert in diplomatics and social deportment. Proper forms existed to regulate not only political relations but also communication within the Indo-Muslim family.[79]

Mehta Balmukund, munshi to a great Sayyid Delhi noble in the opening years of the eighteenth century, was an influential figure.[80] His collection of letters was used as a teaching tool two generations later. The writer states that the king 'discharges his duties specially with the aid of the epistles of the munshis who are masters of the pen and which by the grace of God are based on a comprehension of the hidden meaning and external appearances'. These writings 'reflect Divine Light', make the Empire 'safe and embellished, teach a lesson to all the rebellious peoples and purify the hearts of sincere followers'.[81] Secular and political knowledge here followed the pattern of divine knowledge, which was divided between the formal lore of the clerics and the hidden

---

[77] Faiz Baksh, *Memoirs*, II, 133.   [78] ibid., II, 193.

[79] 'Insha-i Hari Karan', tr., ed. F. Balfour, *The Forms of Herkern corrected from a variety of manuscripts supplied . . .* (Calcutta, 1781), pp. 123–75.

[80] Mehta Balmukund, 'Balmukundnamah', tr. ed., Satish Chandra, *Letters of a King Maker of the Eighteenth Century*, Delhi, 1972, Introduction, pp. 1–14.

[81] ibid., p. 15.

lore of the Sufi mystics. The regular exchange of loving letters between commanders and nobles, not dry administrative correspondence, was the cement of the polity. For example, the Sayyid states in a letter: 'You have written that the proof of friendship does not consist merely in the exchange of letters'[82] but that appropriately worded ones 'banish every notion of hostility or sedition'. Malicious people may misinterpret communications but, 'Only a lover can understand the secrets of lovers.'[83] Exact wording was crucial in a situation where a large number of oral intermediaries stood between the writer and recipient of a text. Thus a magnate advised another to 'keep open the gates of communication; for it will be productive of an increase in affection'.[84]

Letters in the royal hand were the most honoured writings after the pages of the Koran itself. As another eighteenth-century collection has it, these were 'exquisitely beautiful and expressed in a bold, florid style, the purport concise and to the point, flowing from the amber-scented pen; neither vizier, counsellor, nor secretary having concern therein'.[85] Letters were deemed to preserve the charisma of their writers. The Nizam, like other rulers, gave intense ceremonial importance to the receipt of imperial letters as a sign of submission.[86] The flowery Persian of these epistles was not mere verbosity. Rather they were devices for painting pictures in words and illuminating rank. Letters and miniature paintings were closely paired. According to one letter-book even a son was to be addressed with exquisite politeness: 'My worthy son, the fruit of the tree of my vitals, the plant of the garden of my desire.'[87]

The munshi, accordingly, gave himself an extraordinarily high valuation. Faiz Baksh, for example, contemptuously recorded his dealings with an inexpert writer who, as a mere woman, was working as the secretary of his employer, the Bahu Begam of Awadh. Faiz Baksh asserted that the language of this person, Khair-un Nisa, was 'halting and unsuitable for the rank of her correspondents'.[88] For example, she had addressed a leading official with phrases like 'Whoever says so tells a lie. Beat him with a shoe and turn him out of the city.' Faiz Baksh's letters were written without a first draft in classical style. His attainments purportedly allowed him to insinuate himself into the Begam's service and to 'accumulate information on private matters which it would be improper to mention to others'.[89]

This was the education that the munshis offered their querulous and

[82] ibid., p.26.   [83] ibid., p.73.   [84] Balfour, *Herkern*, p. 13.

[85] 'Shahjahan Namah' tr. ed. F. Gladwin, *The Persian Moonshee* (Calcutta, 1801), p. 51.

[86] Nayeem, *Mughal Administration*, p. 93.

[87] Balfour, *Herkern*, p. 125.

[88] Faiz Baksh, *Memoirs*, II, 185.   [89] ibid., pp. 192–193.

arrogant British charges who revolted against the flowery Persian, preferring the blunt and literal-minded. Far from prizing poetic references, the British translators tended to omit all poetry from the letters and texts they translated.[90] But the 'verses' they pointedly left out may well have conveyed much more than the guarded and complex prose around them. It was in the very twilight of Indo-Persian political culture, as the Rebellion of 1857 gathered, that Ghalib was to sigh over the philistine literalness of the communications he received from the British Commissioner of Delhi.[91] The great days when like-minded men could convey political information and nuance through the language of classical learning were over for ever.

The pedigree and intellectual history of elite informants

Just as the British adapted forms of revenue management from their predecessors, so the rational learning and information skills of India's elites were captured and put to use. During Cornwallis's administration several Indian judges were replaced by Britons because of the Governor-General's rooted suspicion of oriental venality. But until as late as the 1830s the Company's state could not have functioned without highly placed Indian functionaries as munshis and ambassadors. In turn, these 'native servants' helped to perpetuate the archaic, status-conscious character of early British rule. As some members of the Mughal elites were introduced into British service, however, the intellectual and affective principles which had sustained the Indo-Islamic polities were distorted and ruptured. Some Indians responded to this by resisting; others withdrew into a more closely defined religious world, sheltered from the impieties of the Christian invader. Others yet adjusted to the new order and began to forge the mental and moral tools with which to construct Islamic modernism, Islamic purism and the concept of the nation state in India. In the case of some of the ambassadorial, munshi and newswriter families, it is possible to go beyond the bare details of names and paternity to begin to glimpse patterns of career and intellectual lineage. In time a map will be drawn of the social and intellectual terrain which lies between the 'fall of the Mughal Empire' and the emergence of Indian nationalisms.

Most of the Muslims in this emergent clerisy were associated with holy and learned families, protectors of mosques and descendants of saints. A few were the descendants of great Mughal nobles who had

---

[90] Baker Ali to Kazi Mahomed (trans.) 'Intrigues by Members of the Vizier's family against him', BC 248 / 5584.

[91] Ghalib, *Dastanbuy* trans. K.A. Faruqi, (Delhi, 1970), p. 48.

unwillingly taken to the lower status of political secretary.[92] The British were fortunate because the decline of Mughal employment had thrown many of these service families into relative poverty.[93] They were prepared to serve anyone who could guarantee the common peace and the protection of godly society, even if they were undisciplined Kaffirs smelling of impure substances.

The most prominent group of knowledgeable servants of the early British authorities in north India was drawn from the nobility established under the Emperor Muhammad Shah (1719–48). This is not surprising. Without substantial incomes from service these large, high-spending families could not survive. The rulers of the successor states had recalled many of the land grants for service on which they had lived, and the imposition of British rule had squeezed out many sub-tenure holders. The Marathas, Sikhs and other eighteenth-century non-Muslim kingdoms continued to employ Muslims in high positions, but out of prudence they often selected men from relatively humble families, unconnected with the highest nobility.[94] Even the Awadh dynasty had attempted to distance itself from the Mughal inheritance after the defeat at Buxar in 1764.[95] Hyderabad, with its shaky and faction-ridden political system, was perhaps the only successor state where the old noble families found ready service, and even here they were battling against a challenge from the upwardly mobile Hindu writer caste, the Kayasthas.[96] The British were the last resort, and the relatively unprejudiced attitude of eighteenth-century Company servants to matters of religion impressed the Muslim learned, despite the offence given by alcohol and pork.

The most important of these noble servants of the British were families associated with the public offices of Hughly and Murshidabad which had been, respectively, the chief port and capital of Bengal. Descendants of the law officers (kazi, mufti) and governors of Hughly[97]

---

[92] Ghulam Hussain, 'Siyyar', tr. Nota-Manus, III, 192. Ghulam Hussain, himself of noble origin, remarked sarcastically that the British considered 'no office higher' than that of munshi.

[93] e.g., G. Westmacott's regimental munshi, Md. Shufi, from a landed family of Moradabad with five members in the service of Ranjit Singh. He had Rs. 100–150 per annum net of land tax from one village; another produced Rs 300–350 revenue-free. But he had to support five families, and needed Rs 30–40, per mensem, which was not guaranteed in a bad season, Mss. Eur. C29, f. 524, OIOC; cf. below n. 97.

[94] R. Barnett, *North India Between Empires. Awadh, the Mughals and the British* (Berkeley, 1980), pp. 76–7.

[95] Faiz Baksh, *Memoirs*, II, 4.

[96] K. Leonard, *Social History of an Indian Caste. The Kayasths of Hyderabad* (Berkeley, 1978), pp. 27–35.

[97] Mir Sadik, the main Lucknow conspirator in 1807, was son of Lal Mahomed, Kazi of Hughly; his contact in Lucknow was another relation, the former Resident's Munshi,

were found all over north India in the next two generations as writers and ambassadors for the British. These families formed part of a wider group of descendants of people who had come from Persia and north India to serve the Bengal governors since 1700. Several families in this group were Shia Muslims, and the rapid upward mobility of Shias, from within India and from Persia and central Asia, was a phenomenon of the successor states and of the early British service. An important influence on many of them appears to have been the *usuli* tradition of Shia legalism which emphasised the rational sciences and conceded the need to debate matters of custom in the light of reason.[98] Wherever Shia learned families had come to settle, as in Lucknow, Murshidabad and Patna, this tradition was strong. It was an ideal administrator's creed. Shia service families may have felt they had more in common with elite Hindus than they had with poorer Sunni Muslims, their nominal brethren, and this in turn may have enabled them to adapt to British requirements. Bengal, anyway, had been the richest and most relaxed of the imperial provinces and the education imparted by the institutions connected with the mosques and imambaras of Hughly and Murshidabad had been liberal and indulgent to the Hindu majority.[99]

One clear line of intellectual descent had been founded by Mahomed Reza Khan; his administrative lineage was to inform British policy in Bengal and north India for the whole period between 1756 and 1830. Reza Khan was a member of a Persian Shia family of physicians. He became the most important Indian administrator in Bengal under Clive and had an uneasy relationship with Warren Hastings,[100] and was perhaps the last Indian to hold high office in British India until the early twentieth century. Mahomed Reza Khan preserved the ideal of political guardianship enshrined in the 'Akbarnamah' of Abul Fazl,[101] and tried

Mirza Baker, youngest son of 'the late Mirza Cauzim', Mirza Mahomed Kazim, a former Faujdar of Hughly, Clive's chamberlain and informant and a relation of Reza Khan (Khan, *Transition*, pp. 92, 99, 111; Verelst to Mirza Muhammad Kazim Khan, *CPC*, I, 459; same to same, 25 Jan. 1767, ibid., 466). His inheritance when divided was insufficient to support his sons. Therefore having received a 'liberal education', they 'went into the service of the English gentlemen with whom they were acquainted', Bengal Pol. Procs., 15 Sept. 1808 and Secretary's (N.B. Edmonstone's) Report on the examination of M. Sadik and Baker Ali, Bengal Pol. Cons., 4 Jan. 1809, BC 248/ 5584.

[98] J.R.I. Cole, *The Roots of North Indian Shi'ism in Iran and Iraq. Religion and State in Awadh, 1722–1859* (Berkeley, 1988), ch. 1.

[99] The Shia rationalistic Usuli tradition was strong in the institutions associated with the Hughly Imambara. It merged with the liberal tradition of Bengal Sunnis, and was influenced early by European ideas through the Calcutta Madrassah and Muhammad Mohsin's College at Hughly.

[100] Khan, *Transition*, pp. 13–18.

[101] 'Mahomed Reza Khan's description of the former and present state of the country', Wellesley, Add. 12,565, ff. 2–19, BL; Dr Kumkum Chatterjee, 'History as self-representation', *MAS* (forthcoming).

to impress on the British the importance of moderate behaviour and accessible justice. Following the tenets of Abul Fazl again, he stated that 'the tribe of Hindus'[102] could not be subject to the full demands of Islamic law, though he also argued for the ultimate sovereignty of Islam, opposing, for example, British attempts to make Hindu pandits full members of courts of justice.

Ali Ibrahim Khan (d. 1793), who became chief judge of the Banaras Adalat, was originally a protege of Mahomed Reza Khan and had had a chequered career in Bengal and Bihar. A Shia from Bihar, with Murshidabad connections, Ali Ibrahim placed many of his family in local office[103] and initiated their careers as landholders in Bihar and Banaras.[104] Working alongside Jonathan Duncan, Resident at Banaras, he was influential as a go-between for estranged members of the Mughal royal family who had fled to Banaras and Lucknow.[105] Ali Ibrahim Khan established a flexible judicial regime which drew on Abul Fazl's vision of an accommodating Islam, knowledgeable about its Hindu subjects,[106] but stressed again the absolute sovereignty of God's Law. One can speculate that his relationship with the British was an exercise in damage limitation. It would be wrong to regard this man or his peers as collaborators with foreign rule, or as traitors to Islam. Ali Ibrahim was trying to instruct the British in good government because they were servants of the Mughals and 'The Monarch of Islam', the Mughal ruler, remained the pole star of his politics.[107] His surveillance of the royal house was intense and, in addition to the regular north Indian news-

---

[102] Khan, *Transition*, pp. 270–2.

[103] ibid., pp. 225, 294, 345; Ghulam Hussain, 'Siyyar', tr. Nota-Manus, III, 80, IV, 117; Khairuddin, *Bulwuntnamah*, p. 124, Ali Ibrahim 'summoned his own relatives from Murshidabad and gave the appointments as moonsiffs, kotwals and suchlike officers'; S.A.I. Tirmizi (ed.), *Index to Titles, 1798–1855* (Delhi, 1979), p. 10; *CPC*, VII, 298, 411; sends Delhi 'newspapers', ibid., VIII (1788–9), 95, 108, 117.

[104] L.S.S. O'Malley, *Bihar and Orissa District Gazetteers. Patna* (Patna, 1924), pp. 40, 184, 232. Ali Ibrahim had been compromised by his close connection with the family of Alivardi Khan. His Bengal and Bihar career later suffered a setback as the result of a scandalous liaison with a dancing girl. This perhaps explains his desire to establish himself in Banaras.

[105] Saletore (ed.), *Banaras Affairs*, I, 17–31.

[106] e.g., his report to Hastings on trial by ordeal among the Hindus displays considerable knowledge of Hindu Law, 'On the trial by ordeal among the Hindoos', *Asiatick Researches*, I, 1788, 389–404. Jurisprudence seems to have been the Ali Ibrahim Khan family's calling; his maternal grandfather, Maulvi Nasir-ud Din had been trained in the Shia schools of Iran, see Dr Shayesta Khan's forthcoming biography and letters collection to be published from materials in the Khuda Baksh Library, Patna.

[107] 'Tarikh-i Ibrahim Khan', *HI*, VIII, 297; Ali Ibrahim's patriotism and solicitude for the Hindus made him very popular with the local population. When the Prince of Wales tried to secure the Banaras Judgeship for a Briton, even Cornwallis came to the support of a 'black', Bernard Cohn, 'The British in Banaras', in Cohn, *An Anthropologist among the Historians* (Delhi, 1987), p. 432.

letters sent to Calcutta, he kept Cornwallis informed on court politics from his own contacts with the Jats, Marathas visiting Banaras and Muslim officers.[108]

The Khan was himself a skilled Persian and Urdu poet, responsible for an important collective biography of north Indian writers.[109] Through him the British were able to co-opt some of the formidable cadre of Muslim intellectuals who congregated in the cities of Bengal and Bihar. Several members of this connection were later drawn into Wellesley's Fort William College, an imperial academy which was supposed to concentrate the talent of India and educate the young British civil servant. Ali Ibrahim Khan was, finally, a historian and, along with other contemporary administrators in both Bengal and north India, he was an unacknowledged founder of a consciously modern Indian history. Personal involvement in the politics of Warren Hastings's Maratha wars provided him with information for a study which covered the years 1757–80.[110]

Ali Ibrahim was, in his turn, 'patron and master' in the 'principles of rectitude and honour in the service of government'[111] of Maulvi Abdul Kadir Khan, son of Mir Wasil Ali Khan, who had been a servant of Mir Kasim, former Nawab of Bengal. Abdul Kadir, sometime Judge of the Banaras Civil Court, became another pre-eminent early British servant and information collector. The principles of statecraft, like those of religion and science, were passed down the chains of pupil–teacher relationships. Abdul Kadir Khan had strong Hindu connections, spending his later career as an intermediary between the British and Amrit Rao, brother of the Maratha Peshwa, who was an expatriate in Banaras.[112] His preceptor, Ali Ibrahim, introduced him to this sphere of diplomacy and he probably accompanied him on some of his early missions. Abdul Kadir Khan later became the key British negotiator with Nepal, visiting the country several times on British missions and writing reports for them on its trade and topography.[113] This sequence

---

[108] 'Paper of intelligence from Ali Ibrahim Khan', Bengal Secret and Political Cons., 19 Mar. 1788, 3 [P BEN SEC], 9, OIOC. Dr Shayesta Khan reveals that Ali Ibrahim had been Mir Bakshi (paymaster) under Mir Kasim, an office closely associated with the intelligence department.

[109] LH, II, 2–3.

[110] 'Tarikh-i Ibrahim Khan', text and full translation, Add. Mss. BL; cf. H. Ethé, Catalogue of the Persian, Turkish, Hindustani and Pashtu Manuscripts in the Bodleian Library (Oxford, 1930), p. 1,314.

[111] arzi of Munshi Abdul Kadir Khan, c. 1828, 'Jageer of Moolvy Abdool Kadir Khan to be continued on his demise', BC 1323 /52452, f. 432.

[112] W.A. Brooke, Agent to Gov. Genl Banaras to Persian Sec. Govt of India, 30 Oct. 1828, ibid; Tirmizi, Titles, p. 2; the Maulvi also dealt with the Maratha commercial community, Procs. Resdt Banaras, 6 Jul. 1792, vol. 56/1, UPCRO.

[113] CPC, XI (1794–5), 202, 225; cf. Bengal Rev. Cons. 29 Oct. 1792.

of positions is itself revealing. Maratha Brahmin contacts inherited from Ali Ibrahim would have given him an introduction to their caste-fellows among the hill Brahmins who conducted Nepali politics. Abdul Kadir's training in the Muslim sciences and law appears to have fitted him well for the topographical and statistical interests which were prized among Company servants. A report he wrote on the Tarai region below the Himalayas shows how easy it was for him to conceive the world in terms of political economy. He analysed the movements of the borders herdsmen[114] in terms which would not have seemed out of place in Sir John Sinclair's contemporary *Description of Scotland*. Abdul Kadir Khan went on to serve as munshi in the Lucknow Residency.[115] He was rewarded with land in Banaras and, even in retirement, continued to act as an informant and adviser to the British. He played an important role, for example, in helping to compromise the severe conflict which broke out between Hindus and Muslims in the city in 1809 over the status of a Hindu shrine which lay close to a mosque.[116]

A second constellation of families of native informants hailed from the towns of the mid-Ganges valley, Allahabad, Jaunpur, Lucknow, and their associated qasbahs, which were also suffering from the decline of opportunities for service. Typical figures here were Khairuddin Khan Illahabadi, another historian, and his relative Salahuddin,[117] confidential agents to James Browne and James Anderson, British envoys to the Court of the Maratha prince, Shinde. Khairuddin's fundamental loyalty to the Mughal court, over which he had great influence, led the British to suspect him of 'treason', that is partiality to the Mughals, and he left Company service in 1782. After a period with a Mughal prince in Allahabad and Lucknow, he retired to work for the British in Jaunpur where he wrote a number of local histories. Representative of his political views was the 'Ibratnamah' or 'Book of Cautions'[118] which eulogises Nawab Sadat Ali Khan of Awadh, who had been enthroned by the

---

[114] see below pp. 110–11.
[115] 'Conduct of Molavee Abdool Kader in accepting from the late Nabob Vizier a jaghier whilst employed by the Resident at His Excellency's Court', BC 248/5585.
[116] W. Bird, Actg Magt, Banaras to G. Dowdeswell, Sec. to Govt Judl Dept, 28 Jan. 1811, Procs. Agent to Gov. Genl, Banaras, also printed in G. Saletore (ed.), *Banaras Affairs (1811–1858)*, vol. II (Allahabad, 1959), pp. 145–50.
[117] E.V. Rieu, *Catalogue of Persian Manuscripts in the British Museum*, III, p. 946; his brother, Muhammad Salahuddin Khan, was munshi to Capt. James Browne, another one of Hastings's key diplomatists, Singh, *Sikhs*, p. 5; K.D. Bhargava (ed.), *Browne Correspondence* (Delhi, 1960), p. 26, 291; cf. Murtaza Hussain Bilgrami, from the Awadh qasbah of that name, munshi to Hastings's aide Jonathan Scott, who composed a geography and history with a large and detailed Indian component, the 'Hadikat-al Aklim', Rieu, *Catalogue of BL*, III, 992–3.
[118] H. Ethé, *Catalogue of Persian Manuscripts in the Library of the India Office*, I, (London, 1912), no. 483; Fisher, *Indirect Rule*, p. 327.

British, and execrates Ghulam Kadir, the Pathan chief who imprisoned and blinded the Mughal Emperor. For members of this intelligentsia, the Emperor was still the shadow of God on earth and the Empire the plumb-line of universal history. Ghulam Kadir was therefore a figure of primal evil, similar to Dante's Brutus. The travails of the 'moderns' as the Empire disintegrated seems to have been a potent force in the further development of Indo-Muslim historiography. Though this strain of self-awareness came to an abrupt end with the Rebellion of 1857, it is wrong to date the beginning of modern Indian historiography to the simple needs of the modern, that is the colonial state. Self-consciously modern history began with the attempt by the post-Mughal elite to adjust to the rise of Hindus and the British. Equally, this was more than history, it was political philosophy working by example, a discourse intended to turn grasping and rude men, such as the British and Marathas, to God's laws and service of the Empire and to prevent the corruption of public office by venality, irreligion and brutish comportment.

A third group among the informants was drawn directly from the nobility of Delhi or Kashmiri Muslims and Brahmins who had sought service in the capital. After 1803 the city's economy revived rapidly, and one can exaggerate its decline even under the Marathas. Still, the city's elite was certainly in severe distress in the later eighteenth century. Not only were the Marathas and Jats encroaching on landed income which nobles received from the fertile lands around Delhi, but faction at court and a tussle between Sunnis and Shias threatened important revenue-free grants which supported its teaching institutions. By the early nineteenth century British service seemed the only guarantee of a gentleman's competency.[119] Yet that service benefited from the continuing intellectual vigour of the capital. In the very depth of the travails of the eighteenth century, the school of Abdul Aziz and Shah Waliullah[120] had propounded a tradition of rationalistic teaching in Sunni theology, philosophy and law, which was to provide a training not only for Muslim administrators in British service, but also for the leaders of the purist spiritual revival which the British called the Wahhabi movement. Rational sciences such as logic and astronomy had been patronised by the Mughal dynasties in central Asia and north India and these too survived into the eighteenth century. The modernist reformer, Sir Sayyid Ahmad Khan's patron and relative, Khwaja Farid-ud Din

---

[119] Delhi, e.g., Mufti and preceptor families of Delhi seeking British service, BC 1402/ 55500.

[120] See, S.A.A. Rizvi, *Shah Wali-allah and his Times* (Canberra, 1980); Rizvi, *Shah Abdul Aziz. Puritanism, sectarian polemic and jihad* (Canberra, 1982).

Ahmad Khan was a representative of this tradition.[121] A learned astronomer and geographer, he served as Company ambassador to Burma and Persia before becoming superintendent of the Calcutta Madrassah, an advanced teaching institute, maintaining links between the British and the Muslim elite of eastern India. Another similar figure was the Kashmiri, Tafazzul Hussain, who was Asaf-ud Daulah's tutor, and later Awadh's ambassador at Calcutta where he became a confidant of the British. Tafazzul Hussain represented that Shia scientific tradition which we have already encountered in the cities of Bengal and Bihar, but which survived even in the troubled northwest, between Nishapur in Iran, Delhi and Kashmir. Tafazzul Hussain translated Newton and other western scientific works into Persian.[122] A generation later Sir Sayyid Ahmad Khan displayed a similar combination of skills in the Islamic rational sciences, openness to western knowledge and inter-mediary status in relation to the British.

A further significant informant within this group was Munshi Izatullah, officiating Munshi in the Delhi Residency and later compa-nion of the explorer William Moorcroft during his famous journey to Bokhara in central Asia. Izatullah was the grandson of one of the last Mughal governors of the Lahore province, Mir Niamat Khan, who had been powerful in the 1740s and 1750s.[123] Izatullah's high standing among the Punjabi and central Asian Muslim upper classes was of great value to the British, as were his continuing contacts with the powerful Sikh families whom his grandfather had patronised. This influence was so great that Ranjit Singh commonly asked him to sit in his presence and treated his opinions 'with deference and respect which reflect both his ancestry and the value of his opinions on the Punjab'. Izatullah was apparently connected with the Delhi intelligentsia. His precision and concern with exact testimony, a central feature of the Islamic sciences, helped him to adjust to the methods of British information collection. According to Elphinstone, he was 'intelligent, well-informed and

---

[121] According to Sayyid Ahmed's *Sirat-i Faridiya* (Lucknow, 1893), cit. C.W. Troll, *Sayyid Ahmad Khan. A Reinterpretation of Muslim Theology* (Delhi, 1978), pp. 28–9; Farid-ud Din was a pupil of Tafazzul Hussain, Rahman Ali, *Tazkirah-i ulama-i Hind* (Karachi, 1961), pp. 139–40; Nawab Akbar Ali Khan was another Delhi noble who managed the exiled household of Jahandar Shah, the royal prince, in Banaras and acted as intermediary, *CPC*, VIII, 123, 301, 852, 788–9.

[122] S.A.A. Rizvi, *A Socio-intellectual History of the Isna Ashari Shi'is in India (16th to 19th century)* (Canberra, 1986), II, pp. 221–8; Harnam Singh, 'Sadat-i Javid' tr. Elliot Papers, Add. Mss. 30,786, ff. 65b–67; for his role in Maratha diplomacy, 1781–2, David Anderson Papers, Add. Mss. 45,419, ff. 39–45, BL; cf. Edmonstone to his brother, 6 Apr. 1797, Edmonstone Papers, CUL.

[123] Moorcroft to Metcalfe, 2 Dec. 1824, 'Death of Mir Izzut Ollah Khan, and pension to his family', BC 1038 /28641.

unusually methodical'.[124] His extensive travelogues, which were later published in *Asiatic Researches*, represent a halfway point between the Islamic travelogue and British topography.[125] He reports dates, names, distances and physical features with great care, but Izatullah's imaginative world remains that of the Mughal kings and Sufi saints, whose monuments and tombs he always mentions.[126]

One feature of all these intellectuals and servants of state was that they were used to receiving knowledge from abroad. Many of their families had, in fact, come from outside the traditional boundaries of Hindustan. Muslim civilisation, with its Hindu, Jewish and Christian appendages, remained the centre of the world for them. They were accustomed to serving men of different nationalities who, like the contemporary generation of British officials, spoke to them in Persian and knew something of the Persian classics. Theirs was not a narrow or declining tradition, but a universal civilisation. That it was to fall later to the evangelical hubris of the early Victorians and the guns on the Delhi Ridge in 1857, should not lead us to dismiss it retrospectively. Of course, this intellectual culture did have its limitations. Its view of the world outside the Indo-Muslim *ecumene*, or critical public, was circumscribed. It is illuminating that when Bishop Reginald Heber visited Banaras in 1824, Abdul Kadir Khan apparently put it about that the scholarly Anglican was Archbishop of 'Rum', that is Constantinople.[127] Abdul Kadir's was a cosmopolitan vision, but one which still envisioned western Europe as a distant margin of the Ottoman Empire.

The very completeness of the old civilisation generally made it difficult for men to adjust their views of the world appropriately to the speed of change in the early nineteenth century. One exception to this rule was Abu Talib, a munshi who had worked in Lucknow and who later made his way to Europe.[128] Abu Talib's account was later widely diffused in north Indian Muslim centres. It consisted of a dispassionate analysis of the forms of government of Britain, France and the Ottoman Empire,

---

[124] Elphinstone's testimonial, 18 May 1810, ibid.; for Izatullah's diplomacy with Moorcroft, trans. Lahore akhbarats, 19, 20, 21 Sept. 1824, encl. in C. Elliot to Swinton, 8 Sept. 1824, HM 664.

[125] 'Travels beyond the Himalaya' by Mir Izzet Ullah, *Calcutta Oriental Quarterly Magazine*, 1825, repub. *JRAS*, 4, 1837, 283–340.

[126] ibid., 333, on Bokhara.

[127] Bishop R. Heber, *Narrative of a Journey through the Upper Provinces of India*, (London, 1844), I, 169–70.

[128] W. Kirkpatrick had once considered employing Abu Talib in Hyderabad, considering him a man of 'integrity and learning', but not having enough political knowledge outside Awadh, Wm Kirkpatrick to Kennaway, 20 Jul. 1791, Kennaway Papers, F2; for his career, see 'Pension to the son of Mirza Abul Talib', BC 212/ 4732.

which sought to relate them to Mughal examples.[129] Abu Talib was typical of that tradition of rational observation of peoples and faiths which we have called spiritual anthropology.

While the great Muslim servants who filled the office of newswriters and treasurers were the most important Indian informants, other traditions were represented as well. At this time Hindus were less prominent as elite servants and informants of the British in north India. Many great Muslim magnates, however, patronised Hindu families of the writer castes who had taken to Persian, and several of the Company's newswriters are known to have been Khattris or Kayasthas from this background. The Muslim servants also had connections with commercial-caste people (often Khattris again, and Agarwals) who served them as accountants and treasurers and entered British service or aided them informally.[130] In southern and western India, of course, the Indo-Muslim elite families were replaced by Maratha and Telugu Brahmins, though many of these commanded skills similar to those of the northern Muslims. Even in north India, western Indian Brahmin diplomats and traders such as Ramchandra Pandit and Bishambhar Pandit, ambassadors from the Bhonsla court, provided the British with information and contacts as effectively as they managed supplies and revenue farms.[131] Here too must be mentioned the great Hindu and Jain bankers, especially those of Banaras. While men such as Aret Ram Tiwari, Arjunji Nathji, Kashmiri Mull and the Agarwal, Manohar Das,[132] moved the Company's money around India by credit note, the political economic information they provided was if anything more significant. Jonathan Duncan, as Resident at Banaras, held regular interviews with the chief merchants of the city. In addition to telling him the state of exchange on different centres, their agents in far distant towns and personal harkaras were also able to report on significant political and military changes, often before the British got wind of them through their own channels.

Once again, this section has not intended to suggest that the majority of the eighteenth-century Indo-Muslim intelligentsia became 'collaborators' with the British in the modern sense of traitors to a national state.

[129] C. Stewart (tr. ed.), *Travels of Mirza Abu Taleb Khan in Asia, Africa and Europe during the years 1799 to 1803* (1814, repr. Delhi, 1972), pp. 229–79, 167–85; Rizvi, *Shi'is*, II, 230–4; J.R.I. Cole, 'Invisible Occidentalism. Eighteenth century Indo-Persian constructions of the West', *Iranian Studies*, 3–4, 1992, 3–16.

[130] A typical example was (the Khattri) Lala Shimbhunath, former agent of the firm of Bachraj which conveyed the Nawab's 'subsidy' to Calcutta; a 'man of respectability', he was a confidant of Asaf-ud Daulah, but attended the Calcutta Darbar, 'List of vakeels and attendants at the durbar', Wellesley Add. 13,828, f. 292, BL.

[131] Hastings to Beni Ram Pandit, 25 Jan. 1785, *CPR*, VI, 438; Tirmizi, *Titles*, p. 36.

[132] e.g., interviews with principal bankers, Procs. Resdt Banaras, 13 Jan. 1795, vol. 85, UPCRO; Tirmizi, *Titles*, p. 16.

While there are a few examples of Indian information agents in Company service being attacked [133] and of later folklore treating them as 'spies' in a derogatory sense, contemporary opinion was apparently ambivalent about them. Traditional patriotism was not easily enlisted against political servants who had influence with an alien power that might easily need to be courted at some later time. Moreover, these men regarded themselves as physicians of the state. For many, their first loyalty was to the Emperor and they were critical of the arrogance and boorishness of their Christian masters. They argued that their rulers should adhere to established principles in matters of revenue management and justice. Ghulam Hussain Tabatabai's 'History of the Moderns' (c. 1780) complained of the drain of wealth from India, British monopoly of public office and the impoverishment of weavers and the old nobility;[134] he could, indeed, be considered a 'proto-nationalist'. Other writers denounced the British from Warren Hastings[135] downward for violence and peculation. Even a local Muslim judge such as Umer Ullah of Jaunpur fretted about the violence done to local people by the drunken British soldiery.[136] Nevertheless, most of the informants of the British were men of high or noble status and this was of great value to the Company. By contrast, many of the fiercest opponents of the British were people of humbler birth, with less to lose and, possibly, a more developed sense of traditional patriotism. Jhau Lal, the Lucknow head of intelligence who frustrated the British for some years, was an aspiring Kayastha of middling status. The Chitpavan Brahmin diplomatists who opposed the British in central and western India were relatively low on the Brahminic scale. Holkar's literate servants were denounced as men of 'low birth'.[137] The people who surrounded the Begams of Awadh were meritocrats or eunuchs whose loyalty was not compromised by fear for family. While it would be anachronistic to speak of a kind of 'trahison des clercs' among the intelligentsia, it was of great benefit to the British that they could draw so readily on the resources of the talented and formerly privileged. This was a luxury denied to colonial rulers in most other parts of the world, and even to the British themselves in Burma and Nepal, as we shall see in the next chapter.

---

[133]   e.g. 'Assault on the newswriter to the Political Agent in Bundelcund ... by a body of persons belonging to the town of Rypore', BC 618/ 15414, OIOC.

[134]   Ghulam Hussain 'Siyyar', tr. Nota-Manus, III, pp. 32–3, 163–6; cf. Abu Talib, *Travels*, pp. 155–66.

[135]   For an anti-Hastings work, 'Muntakhul-t-Tawarikh', Elliot, 30,786, ff. 106–48, BL.

[136]   *Wajib-ul arz* of Molvi Omerullah, A. Shakespear, *Selections from the Duncan Records* (Banaras, 1873), II, 135.

[137]   e.g., notes on Holkar's agent, Mir Karim Allah, BC 236/ 5447; Prof. Muzaffar Alam drew my attention to this issue.

Penetrating the covered palankin: Madras 1800–1

Between 1790 and 1820 the Company's subcontinent-wide intelligence network began to take shape. A younger generation of experts in Indian politics among military and civil officers coordinated diplomacy and surveillance on the fringes of Empire. George Cherry, once Lord Cornwallis's Persian Translator,[138] became Resident at Lucknow and later Judge in Banaras. He expanded his contacts among pilgrims, merchants and exiles in the holy city. Cherry, in turn, was a confidant of Neil Edmonstone, who later became Wellesley's Persian Secretary and effectively chief intelligence officer in Calcutta. Between 1790 and his death in 1799, Cherry also used his knowledge to advance the careers of the Kirkpatrick brothers whose field of operations was to include Nepal, Hyderabad and Mysore. The young Mountstuart Elphinstone, whose careful intelligence work was to be a major reason for British success in the Maratha wars, was also briefly an associate of Cherry's, and began his career as a writer in Banaras. These men aimed to command the politics of the three remaining great post-Mughal courts in Madras, Hyderabad and Lucknow using the skills of their harkaras and munshis.

Madras, and the Arcot court had proved to be the weak links in British India on several occasions. For this reason, a particular watch was kept on the companions of the dying Nawab Umdat-ul Umara, the short-lived successor of Muhammad Ali who had died in 1795.[139] The fear was that 'discontented partisans' of Ali Hussain, the accepted heir who had been set aside for refusing to hand over the state to the British, would combine with faction leaders within the court and gain control of the Nawab's secret treasure. The aim of Lord Clive, Governor of Madras, was to 'restrain the intercourse of persons with the interior of the palace'[140] by watching and controlling the gateways and in particular by regulating the movement of 'covered palankeens', thought to be the very vehicles of Indian intrigue. What the British were doing, in effect, was to monitor and control the fluid faction-building which customarily took place during the process of succession. New rulers often emerged from among a large number of affines, children and favourites of a former ruler, each contender normally supported by one of the senior royal women. If they failed to control these volatile situations, where

---

[138] Cherry (1761–98) was Lord Cornwallis's Persian Secretary, briefly Resident in Lucknow and then the Governor-General's Agent and Judge in Banaras: C.E. Buckland, *Dictionary of Indian Biography* (London, 1906), pp. 80–1.

[139] N.S. Ramaswami, *Political History of the Carnatic under the Nawabs* (Delhi, 1984), pp. 370–9.

[140] Clive to C. in C., Chepauk Detachment, 6 Jul. 1801, encl. in Clive to Gov. Genl, 15 July 1801, HM 464.

succession was always in doubt, they might be faced with a new and hostile power which could quickly overwhelm their rather exiguous military presence. Company officials tried therefore to impose two new controls on the fluidity of indigenous politics. Firstly, they were determined to make a distinction between an ordinary 'private' household and a royal household in which public and political issues were at stake. While Lord Clive claimed that he did not want to violate usage by interrupting the obsequies of the dead Nawab, he stated that 'the affairs of a great government . . . could not be regulated by the ordinary practice of individual families'. Ultimately, the British were prepared to accept only their nominee, Azim-ud Daulah, as heir, and the consensus of the wider family group and its supporters was set at nought.[141]

As the crisis developed the whole machine of British intelligence was set to limit the 'intercourse' between the inner court and outside powers, who were customarily influential in the choice of successor. This is what lay behind the charge of treason against the Arcot court for communicating with Tipu during the second and third Mysore wars. Wellesley and Clive used this as an excuse to dispense with the embarrassing fiction that Arcot was an independent state. But Arcot's 'man of business', Nejab Khan, was no doubt correct in asserting that diplomatic communication with an enemy during wartime was perfectly consonant with Indian practice. He claimed that he was simply behaving tactfully to Tipu, as Wellesley had enjoined him, and that 'the particular warmth of expressions' used by the Nawab in his letter to Tipu's minister was nothing but an expression of civility.[142] The classical tradition of Indian statesmanship allowed a game of bluff and counter-bluff by letter with enemies and the enemies of enemies. To the British this ran counter to 'the established maxims of the public law of nations'.[143]

Even after the subjugation of southern India, penetrating the covered palankin was to remain a strenuous object for the British intelligence services. A large espionage operation was later established to monitor the contacts of Tipu Sultan's heirs who had been exiled to the British military station of Vellore. Lord Clive submitted to Wellesley detailed reports of every visitor to the princes tabulated under the headings 'names', 'whence' and 'remarks'.[144] The comings and goings of court

---

[141] 'Report by Mr. Webbe and Col. Close on the treaty made with Azim ud Daulah', encl. in Clive to Gov. Genl, 11 Aug. 1801, ibid.

[142] Trans. of paper from Najib Khan to Webbe and Close, 5 Rabi Ahluwal, 1216 AH, ibid; Ramaswami, *Carnatic*, pp. 370–9.

[143] e.g. the Company rejected the argument that it was 'the usage of the native courts to admit vakeels between states at war', Palmer to GG, 2 July 1799, HM 574.

[144] 'Reports of transactions at Vellore for the last month', Clive to GG, 9 Jun. 1801, HM

eunuchs, Sufi counsellors and financial advisers were precisely chronicled.

Gossip, and the politics of the women's quarters: Hyderabad, 1800–3

As André Wink has observed,[145] women had always been central to *fitna* or the process of faction and alliance-building in India. Whereas Muslim powers, and even the Europeans before the late eighteenth century, had used sexual politics as an extension of the arts of diplomacy and intelligence-gathering, the British now began to deny themselves this resource and solace. Most of the well-known empire builders of this period had taken Indian mistresses, often from the Muslim elites. These women improved their language skills and often provided them with extensive, though little-acknowledged Indian contacts which could be tapped for information. Neil Edmonstone, the dominant figure in the Persian and Political Departments for nearly twenty years, had an Indian family which he provided for and maintained quite separately from his European one.[146] Francis Wilford, the head unofficial 'intelligencer' in Banaras following the murder of Cherry in 1799, had an Indian wife and family and maintained a staff of Brahmins and translators. He was later said to have become 'brahminised' over nearly forty years of residence in India.[147] The new official morality sponsored by Wellesley and supported by an official class which was increasingly influenced by evangelical Christianity, began publicly to frown on interracial sexual liaisons. It was, however, the political costs of intervening in the politics of the women's quarters which made the colonial authorities so chary of such alliances: fitna worked both ways and information flowed in two directions.

Such concerns lay behind the celebrated case of James Achilles Kirkpatrick who had an affair with an Indian noblewoman, Khair-un Nissa, while Resident at the Hyderabad Court between 1798 and 1803.[148] James Kirkpatrick, like his brother William, was one of the most influential of the orientalist generation of empire-builders. While

564; Garrison Standing Orders, Vellore, attached to G. Doveton to W. Kirkpatrick, 25 Jul. 1800, Wellesley, Add. 13,587, ff. 42–5, BL.

[145] A. Wink, *Land and Sovereignty in India: agrarian society and politics under the eighteenth century Maratha Svarajya* (Cambridge, 1986).

[146] 'Elmore letters'; note by M.E.B., Edmonstone Papers, CUL.

[147] V.C.P. Hodson, *List of the Officers of the Bengal Army, 1758–1834*, IV (London, 1947), 467–8; *Calcutta Journal*, 27 Jun. 1819; Bholanauth Chunder, *Travels of a Hindoo to various parts of Bengal and Upper India* (Calcutta, 1872), I, 285.

[148] 'Report of an investigation instigated by direction of H.E. the Most Noble Governor General, 7 Nov. 1801', HM 464.

his liaison has been seen as an Anglo-Indian romance, it also provides some insight into the politics of information and alliance in an Indian city. Kirkpatrick's situation came to official light when a Hyderabad noble, Baker Ali, complained that a Muslim of 'great respectability' had asked for his granddaughter's hand in marriage, but that Kirkpatrick, who was having an affair with her, had tried to prevent his suit. Baker Ali complained to Col. Bowen of the Residency Guard and threatened to go to the Mecca Masjid and 'pronounce his dishonour to the whole assembly'.[149] This act would have turned a private affair of the women's quarters, always a most secluded area within Muslim families, into a matter of honour and morality touching the community. The mosque was, after all, the nearest thing to a public political arena in an Islamic society, and this particular mosque, which held a black stone which had supposedly floated to India from the city of Mecca, was virtually regarded as a part of the Kaaba itself.

The situation became explosive when Khair-un Nissa became pregnant. The males of the family agreed to arrange for an abortion, but the Resident 'sent for the principal midwives of the city and deterred them from any attempt of that nature';[150] midwives had always been a major source of information on events in magnates' private quarters. Gossip and faction rose to a crescendo when abusive Persian placards appeared near the Mecca Masjid accusing Baker Ali of prostituting his granddaughter for influence with the British. Placarding the mosque or Sufi shrines was a common means of communicating with the wider community in an Indo-Muslim city.

Bowen and Lt Col. Dalrymple, Commander of the Company's military force at Hyderabad, now took official cognisance of the affair because it threatened relations with the Nizam's court at a critical time a few months before the onset of the Maratha war, when French subversion was still feared in the state. There was, however, some suggestion that Bowen acted out of enmity to Kirkpatrick, who had earlier denied him command of the garrison. Lord Clive, Governor of Madras, was informed, and on his report, the Governor-General instituted an enquiry because the issue had now become one of 'national interest and character'. In particular it was feared that 'an interested combination of the women of the family and even of Bauker [Baker Ali] himself' had sought to compromise the Resident and the security of the Residency.[151]

The role of the women was the other dimension of this story. They appear to have been unusually independent and to have maintained their

---

[149] ibid.   [150] ibid.   [151] ibid.

own written communications with the Resident, and other families within the city. For this was something about which Baker Ali specifically complained.[152] Curiously, the fear that women might carry on 'intrigues', of a political as well as a sexual sort, was advanced as a reason why some Muslim patriarchs neglected to educate female members of their families. Baker Ali's granddaughter must, evidently, have entertained Kirkpatrick privately on at least one occasion. This impression that sexual politics within the noble household cut across the politics of Court and Residency is reinforced by the evidence of Dr Kennedy, the Residency doctor, who like so many of his comperes was an orientalist and intelligence agent. Kennedy received permission from the Nizam's ministers to go into the old city of Hyderabad and meet Sherif-un Nissa Begam, Baker Ali's daughter, mother of the errant lady. This lady appears to have decided that 'since a sin had occurred', her daughter could not be married to anyone other than Kirkpatrick (called here by his Persian title Hismat Jang).[153] The messages emanating from her house were intended to put off the older Muslim suitor and encourage the Resident. Speaking through a fretted screen to Kennedy, Sherif-un Nissa reportedly said 'I wish he [Kirkpatrick] had her ... in the same manner as he might have had her before all the distinctions introduced by Moossa [Moses], Issa [Jesus] and Mahomed were known in the world', a remarkable sentiment for any Muslim woman, let alone an Indian noblewoman in 1800. Kennedy left in a miasma of intrigue. Since he could not see the woman he had spoken to, he gave her a seal to show her father so that he could later prove to Kennedy that she was who she claimed to be. On emerging into the street, the Doctor found that he was being tailed by confidential servants of the Resident and of the elderly Muslim suitor.

In the end, James Kirkpatrick married Khair-un Nissa, but hereafter his career never prospered as before. Wellesley's new moral order for the British in India masked a shift in the nature of diplomacy. The British brought to an end the sexual politics which had allowed Afghans and Mughals successively to take women from the indigenous population of India as a token of their power and as an aid to their influence. The networks of intrigue and information with which aristocratic Mughal and Rajput women had maintained their influence withered in the face of the newly constructed colonial barrier between the court and the home. While such connections might have enriched the knowledge of the British about their Indian subjects, they were evidently too

---

[152] ibid.
[153] 'Substance of a conversation between Sherriffe ul Nissa Begum and Dr. Kennedy', Jan. 1801, ibid.

compromising to permit. In later years missionaries and reformers denounced the helpless dependence of the secluded inhabitants of the women's quarters. These commentators failed to realise that British government had done much to close off the political role of women and the family in its desire to distinguish between public and private information.

Eunuchs and newsletters: Lucknow, 1797–1802

Women were important carriers of information and intrigue in the pre-colonial politics because the exchange of women was a key dimension of the lineage politics of Indian elites. Royal women, and by extension their maids, nurses and midwives, apparently played a much more forward political role than they did in the contemporary Ottoman Empire, where the seraglio was more rigorously secluded. The tribal and Turkish central Asian model of the magnate family had influenced India, whereas the Byzantine model was dominant in Istanbul. Yet Indian rulers did maintain large establishments of eunuchs, and these also were critical carriers of information and influence which began to vanish from the political world at the turn of the nineteenth century. They are too alien – and perhaps too embarrassing – to have received much attention from historians.[154] Indian eunuchs played a similar structural role to the Christian Devshirme levied by the Ottomans in the Balkans, in that they retained connections with their families and acted as communicators between elite Muslims and subjects of different religion. The Awadh eunuch statesman Jawahar Ali Khan, for instance, was said to have maintained close links with Hindus, and Hinduised Muslims, including military communities such as Mewatis, and Chandela Rajputs.[155] Many Indian eunuchs were drawn from rural Rajput and Jat backgrounds and were seized and neutered by roving princely armies. Brought up to be servants and ministers in royal households, they obviously could never father dynasties which would entrench themselves against state power. Their liminal sexual status did confer an important advantage on eunuchs, however: they could move between men's and women's worlds, coordinating information from both. At first the British relied heavily on the knowledge of such men, but they feared eunuch politicians whose independence might pit them against the growing European power. Mahomed Faiz Baksh's 'Tarikh-i Farah Baksh' was partly a lament for the decline of the influence of the old class of

---

[154] E.G. Balfour, *The Cyclopaedia of India and of Eastern and Southern Asia* (Madras, 1858, rev. London, 1885), I, 1060, 'eunuch'.

[155] Faiz Baksh, *Memoirs*, II, 58, cf. 21, 47.

honourable eunuchs, such as Jawahar Ali Khan and Darab Ali Khan, who had served the Begams against the intrusive power of the Company. Not surprisingly Jawahar Ali Khan was denounced as a 'scoundrel' by the British.[156]

One of the last occasions when the old court politics were pitted against the colonial power was during the struggle over the succession of Awadh in 1797–8 when Edmonstone and Sir John Shore, the Governor-General, deposed Vazir Ali in favour of their nominee, Sadat Ali Khan.[157] Here the whole armoury of spies, newswriters, eunuchs and female influence was deployed by both sides. Edmonstone's powerful narrative of the 'revolution at Lucknow' has survived. What the British and their supporters wanted to do was to challenge the legitimacy of Vazir Ali Khan, whom they considered an enemy who surrounded himself with 'panders and low scoundrels' who 'rage for independence from the English'.[158] Vazir Ali also appears to have had the tacit support of the former Nawab's widow, one of the famous Begams of Awadh, who had earlier opposed and been mistreated by Warren Hastings. Edmonstone had picked up 'information on popular sentiments' which, he claimed, branded Vazir Ali a bastard.[159] The heir apparent was supposedly the son of a menial and a servant woman whom the impotent Asaf-ud Daulah had briefly taken into his rooms when she was already pregnant. The chief informant here was a eunuch who was involved in the original deception. It was in matters of legitimacy and succession, and hence in connection with property, that the knowledge of women, eunuchs and doctors[160] was particularly potent. Their influence appears not only in the great courts but among lesser noble families.

Vazir Ali's position was already weak. One of the most powerful men in the state, Almas Ali Khan, eunuch and effective ruler of the western districts of Awadh, had decided to oppose him, though he had not yet decided to support the candidature of the British protege, Sadat Ali Khan. Vazir Ali went down fighting the game of espionage. He

---

[156] 'Narrative of events in Lucknow', encl. in Edmonstone to his father, 21 April 1798, Edmonstone Papers, (red bound volume), Add. Mss. 7616/2, CUL, cf. Shore to Speke, 22 Jan. 1798, Bengal Secret and Political Cons., 30 Jan. 1798, 5, vol. 47, OIOC.

[157] A. Ray, *The Rebel Nawab of Oudh. Revolt of Vizir Ali Khan, 1799* (Calcutta, 1990), pp. 1–107, provides a well-supported but somewhat confusing account.

[158] Edmonstone to his father, 21 April 1798, Edmonstone Papers (no page nos.).

[159] ibid.

[160] Doctors were critical to matters of succession within Muslim families. They could report on births and were also required to report on male impotence which annulled rights of inheritance, see, e.g. 'Marriage in the family of the Nawab of Farrukhabad', BC 1343/53411.

despatched spies to keep him informed of the doings of the Governor-General and of the movements of Sadat Ali Khan who was then at Banaras. Becoming suspicious when invited to the British Residency for the New Year's Day dinner of 1798, he stationed 5,000 of his troops on the one mile between his palace and the Residency along with 'hircarrahs at every fifty yards to carry intelligence'.[161] The critical point was to be forewarned of the approach of his rival Sadat Ali Khan to Lucknow, so Vazir Ali had more agents sent to Banaras to watch for any sign that the British were laying a dak to convey Sadat Ali Khan to the capital. The situation was particularly difficult for the British as Persian newsletters circulating through Banaras 'detailed with perfect exactness the visits made to Sadat Ali by Cherry' explaining the Governor-General's view on the succession. Though every one of the express posts sent or received was specified in the newsletters,[162] the British were lucky the secret dak they had opened to Lucknow was not detected and revealed in the newsletters, while the false ones they had guilefully laid to Jaunpur and elsewhere were noted and published. Thus the British were able to bring Sadat Ali into Lucknow and get him installed as Nawab in place of Vazir Ali. They had outwitted Vazir Ali's party, which included the Begam and her followers who had opposed Warren Hastings nearly twenty years before. They also outmaneouvred Almas Ali Khan who preferred a third solution.

An important aspect of these events was that all the main actors in the case read the newsletters with great care and hoped to outwit their opponents by receiving precise information before them. The purpose of the minutely detailed form of the akhbarats and the great care taken to specify their author and the mode of communication becomes clear. Every single detail of the meetings or letters between one's enemy and his potential supporters needed to be known, so producing a narrative of mind-boggling detail. These court newsletters were, in fact, prophylactics against faction or fitna. Equally, the intensive use of spies was designed to trap enemies before armed conflict broke out and spread public panic. These indeed remained 'dynastic security states' in which information was at a premium. They were testimony to the informational sophistication of Indian society and politics, a sophistication which was India's undoing. Knowledgeable and pliant, the north Indian information order proved too easily subverted by a power which hoarded and controlled information, rather than transacting with it to maintain a system of states.

[161] Edmonstone's narrative.   [162] ibid.

3 Misinformation and failure on the fringes of empire

The British were able to conquer the Indian subcontinent within a period of two generations because they commanded the Indian seas and the Bengal revenues. No less important, however, was the knowledge of the country that enabled the East India Company to use these resources to greatest effect. The subcontinent was straddled by complex and highly sophisticated information systems and the British had learned the art of listening in on these internal communications. By controlling newswriters, coralling groups of spies and runners, and placing agents at religious centres, in bazaars and among bands of military men and wanderers, they had been able to anticipate the coalitions of the Indian powers and to plot their enemies' movements and alliances. It was for this reason, rather than because of any deficiency of patriotism or absence of resistance, that there failed to materialise a general alliance against the British, an alliance of 'all *Puckery wallahs*' or turban-wearers against 'all *Topy wallahs*', or hat-wearers, as Tafazzul Hussain Khan put it.[1]

As they moved beyond the intricate information systems of the Indian plains, the conquerors began to face unforeseen difficulties. In Nepal between 1814 and 1816, in Burma between 1824 and 1826, and on the northwestern frontiers through to the military debacle of 1838–42 and beyond, the British were often confronted by a virtual information famine which slowed their advance and sometimes put the whole edifice of their power in peril. Frontier wars these may have been, but the cumulative financial impact of military and intelligence failures under-mined the Company's government.[2] The long and inconclusive First Burma War forced the Directors to install Bentinck's cost-cutting administration, yet its legacy of debt curtailed the expenditure on

---

[1] Notes on interviews with Sindhia (Shinde), 1781, David Anderson Papers Add. Mss. 45,419, f. 39, BL.

[2] The Burma war alone was supposed to have cost the vast sum of £10 million stirling, *House of Lords Papers*, 1852, n.p., 193, p. 223; another account has £5 million, *Gazetteer of Burma* (Rangoon, 1880), I, 342.

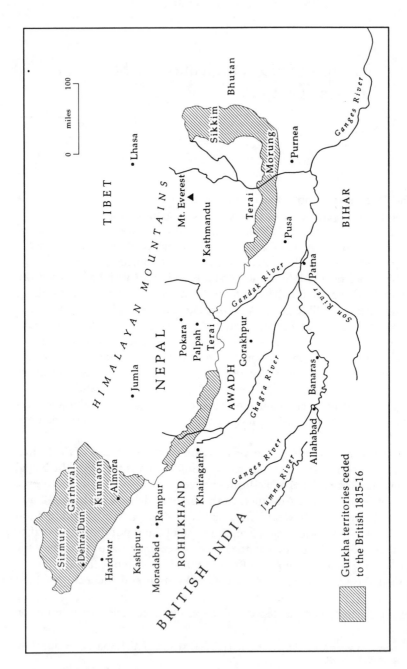

Map 3a Nepal

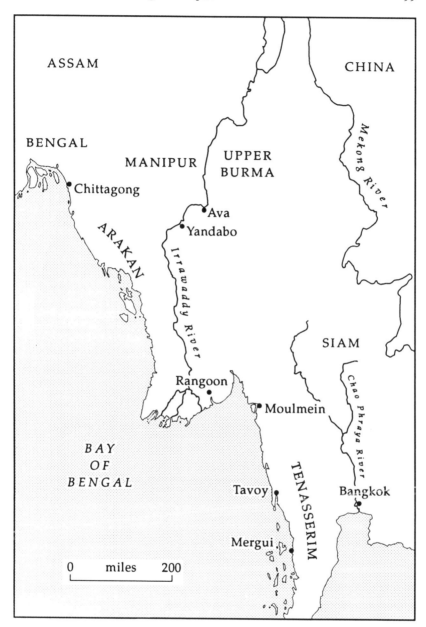

Map 3b   Burma

infrastructure which he hoped would lift the economy out of depression. The study of intelligence-gathering and interpretation during these campaigns serves, therefore, several purposes. It helps explain the ultimate failure of the East India Company; it helps delineate the form and organisation of polities outside the ambit of the Indian system of states. It also throws into higher relief the importance to the British of the information order of plains India.

Gurkha Nepal,[3] an expanding military state committed to neo-traditional Hindu religion, was perched on the northern rim of the Gangetic Valley. It had many links with India. Despite the formidable barrier of the Himalayan foothills, the British could try to penetrate the networks of communication which meandered up into the hills from Patna, Gorakhpur and the cities of Rohilkhand. These were the pilgrimage routes which brought Nepalese Hindus and Buddhists to the holy places of the Ganges, the commercial networks which exchanged plains produce for the wood, herbs, honey and hemp of the uplands, and the connections of 'hill Brahmins' who served the Gurkhas and other local rulers.[4] Company officials might even try to manipulate the hill rulers' keen desire for knowledge of the plains. William Kirkpatrick, who was among the first Company officials to mount a fact-finding mission in Nepal, considered that Indian information, channelled through British sources, might prove a bargaining counter in Kathmandu. Writing to Cherry in Banaras in 1793, he requested a weekly digest of 'Persian intelligence' (i.e. Indian akhbarats) for the Gurkha court, adding that 'they are not indifferent to the political occurrences among their neighbours though they do not appear to be regularly or exactly informed of them'.[5] Precisely because Nepal was not closely tied into the Indian system of reciprocal newswriters, however, the British themselves were only irregularly and inexactly informed of the doings of the Nepalis. The difficult mountain terrain impeded regular dak, but the wary and tightly knit Nepali elite was also able to control the flow of information to its own potential enemies. This was to be true to an even greater extent in Burma, which provided a sharp contrast to the porousness of Indian information systems.

As the British found themselves embroiled in border conflicts with a

---

3   For the war, J. Pemble, *The Invasion of Nepal. John Company at War* (Oxford, 1971); for the Nepal background, D.R. Regmi, *Modern Nepal*, 2 vols. (Calcutta, 1975/6); M.C. Regmi, *A Study in Nepali Economic History, 1768–1846* (Delhi, 1971); Francis Buchanan Hamilton, *An Account of the Kingdom of Nepaul and of the territories annexed to this dominion by the house of Gorkha* (Edinburgh, 1819).

4   Kumar Pradhan, *The Gorkha Conquests. The Process and Consequences of the unification of Nepal with particular reference to eastern Nepal* (Delhi, 1991), pp. 73, 91, 169.

5   W. Kirkpatrick to Cherry, 8 Jan. 1793, Kirkpatrick papers, Mss. F228/ 1.

Nepali state consolidating its power in the foothills and in the recently conquered central Himalayas, they came to realise how limited was their existing data on hill society. In the Calcutta archives a Catholic father's mid-eighteenth-century account of Nepal[6] found its place beside the observations of Captain George Kinloch who had mounted an ill-fated expedition against the Gurkhas in 1767.[7] The ubiquitous Maulvi Abdul Kadir Khan had also gone to Kathmandu on a trade mission from Banaras in 1792.[8] William Kirkpatrick, Francis Buchanan, the naturalist statistician, and sundry military officers who briefly penetrated the country between 1811 and 1813, supplemented this meagre ration of knowledge.[9] What these observers had brought back with them was reasonably detailed information on the routes into the hills and along the Tarai at the foot of the hills. What was lacking was any real knowledge of the key interior logistical lines of the Nepali state in the Kathmandu valley and along nearly a thousand miles of the hills.

The British commanders did have access to some sources which could supplement the patchy and often redundant material gleaned from earlier travellers. First, they began to approach the large numbers of followers of rulers and nobles from Kumaon and other parts of the central hills who had fled their homes during the Gurkha conquest in the 1790s, seeking refuge in British territory.[10] These were mostly descendants of earlier Indian immigrant rajas and their Brahmin court servants and family priests, but some were indigenous Tibeto-Burman Newars of Buddhist cult. These people had taken up residence as a fractious and resentful body of immigrants in the towns of Almora in the west and Gorakhpur in the east. Secondly, the extensive lines of trade between the hills and plains held out hope of informants. Despite warfare and the suspicious 'mercantilist' policy of the Gurkhas, demand for Indian cloth among the Nepali ruling groups had increased. As stability returned to the cities of the Indian plains, demand for timber, hemp and other hill produce also rose. Gosain and eastern Agarwal merchants, who were already well known to the Europeans in Banaras, controlled this trade.[11] Thirdly, the British benefited here, as in other border regions, from the metropolitan character of Indian civilisation. Pilgrimage flourished.

[6] W. Kirkpatrick, *An Account of the Kingdom of Nepaul being the substance of observations made during a mission to that country in the year 1793 by Col. Kirkpatrick* (London, 1811), pp. 380–6, Father Giuseppe's 'Account of Nepaul'; 'A short description of the Kingdom of Napaul', Hastings Add. Mss. 29,210, ff. 1–23, BL.
[7] Ext. from Adjt Genl Fagan to Lt Col. Crawford, 21 Jul. 1814, HM 644; Pradhan, *Gorkha Conquests*, pp. 102–3.
[8] See above, pp. 82–3.   [9] Kirkpatrick, *Account*, p. 270.
[10] 'Emigrants from Nepaul and revolution in that government', BC 204/ 4599.
[11] 'Representation of Geean Gir', encl. J. Duncan to GG in Council, 7 Sept. 1791, Procs. Resdt, Banaras, UPCRO.

Ganges water was conveyed back to Kathmandu by Gosains for its inhabitants' ritual use. The rulers, including the Nepal royal family, maintained large pandit establishments in the holy cities which they visited regularly, reasserting the sacred character of their kingship.[12] Networks of hill Brahmins, in service as family priests, physicians and administrators, spread out into the plains. Among these the most important were the Pants, who traced their origin to Maharashtra,[13] the Tripathis of Kanauj and the Pandes of Kangra. It was the Joshis (from *jyotishi*s, astronomer, astrologer)[14] who were particularly close to the royal families. In the plains joshis were often illiterate palmists and necromancers; in the hills they were literate and powerful. The hill Brahmins were considered to have special privileges and political immunities.[15] Brahmins had played an important role in the diplomacy of the Gurkha conquest and in earlier relations between the hill rajas and the Mughals. The tools of this petty diplomacy were the letter and the harkara. This part of the game and its Brahmin players the British knew very well. After the Company's conquest of Kumaon in 1816, Joshis, Pants and Upadhyayas were to be particularly well represented as writers in British offices.

Large quantities of information had also been built up by the police officials of Awadh and British Gorakhpur whose jurisdictions bordered on Nepal. These officials deployed establishments of musketmen (*barkandazi*s) who formed the local police in frontier communities. Their informants were *bantiria*s, forest watchmen, who since pre-Mughal times had lived on revenue grants in the interior. The Awadh and Gorakhpur officials also kept a close watch on the nomadic herding communities who moved annually from the hill pastures down into the plains, observing military and political changes on their route.[16]

When war broke out in the summer of 1814 the British were forced to create a completely new network of political and military intelligence before they could consider sending their armies up into the hills. One man who seemed capable of putting an effective spy system in place was Thomas Rutherford, Civil Surgeon at the border town of Moradabad. His career during and after the war illustrates the transition from a decentralised and orally-based Indian information system to a more structured, archivally-based British one. Rutherford was typical of his

[12] Kirkpatrick, *Account*, p. 386.
[13] J.C. Nesfield, *The Functions of Modern Brahmins in Upper India* (Calcutta, 1887), p. 31.
[14] ibid., pp. 22–4; H.G. Walton (ed.), *Almora. A Gazetteer. District Gazetteers of the United Provinces of Agra and Oudh*, XXXV (Allahabad, 1911), pp. 93–4.
[15] Father Guiseppe's 'Account of Nepaul', Kirkpatrick, *Account*, pp. 380–6; Pradhan, *Gorkha Conquests*, p. 112.
[16] Wood to Fagan, 15 Jan. 1815; Fagan to Wood, 27 Jan. 1815, HM 651.

period and circle in his command of oriental and medical knowledge and in his unabashed mercenary instincts. His story also provides details of the transaction of information on the margins between the former Mughal and the new Nepali polities.

As war approached, Rutherford wrote to John Adam, Secretary to the Governor-General,[17] that he had 'for the last seven years lived in a state of intimate connection' with the people of Nepal. Commercial contacts and personal observations had given him a close knowledge of the 'manners and customs', routes, bridges and 'several jurisdictions' of the country. He was able to pinpoint the key east–west line of communication in Nepal and suggested ways in which it might be severed. The British armies, heavy in bullock trains and camp-followers, would easily be outmanoeuvred on the hill passes without effective transport. He maintained he could procure Banjara mules, already used in the hemp trade, and surmised that the rumoured wealth of the British would secure numbers of Khasia tribesmen as guides and porters.[18] Hill traders could buy the special deer-skin shoes and warm clothing which the troops would need for the unusual terrain. Supplying food to the army would be a particular problem. Small pockets of grain were sequestered away in the hills. He would need 'secret commissions' to locate them. Here there were no Mughal-style route maps or guide books of harkara reports to locate grain marts as there were in the plains.

Rutherford's knowledge had been assembled while he managed private and Company business in the mountains. He had made the Company's annual 'investment' in hill produce at the town of Kashipur, designed for sale in the plains and abroad. He also managed the Company timber agency at nearby Khairagarh. His own trade in wild hemp, a fibre used in making tough-wearing cloths, associated him with hill landlords who grew the crop for the Indian markets. These, he asserted, were 'a class of people strongly attached to the interests of the British government'.[19] Their income from the trade encouraged the hemp farmers to resist 'Goorkha oppression'. Indian members of the Nepal commercial establishments had been recalled as war broke out, but because they were 'almost naturalised in the country', Rutherford urged that they should also be used to secure 'valuable information' from the cultivators of the interior.

Rutherford's excessive zeal earned him several wiggings from Secretary Adam in Calcutta,[20] but for two years he remained the real innovator in intelligence matters. In November 1814 he began to reorganise the motley crew of employees of the commissariat agency and

---

[17] Rutherford to Adam, 8 Jul. 1814, HM 644.   [18] ibid.   [19] ibid.
[20] Notably, Adam to Rutherford, 20 Oct. 1814, HM 645.

Kashipur Factory whom he was employing as informants.[21] He asked Government to sanction expenditure on a 'pundit for Persian and Newari', an English writer and a larger establishment of runners. As head pandit he had appointed a 'young Brahmin' from the town of Anupshahar, whom he had often sent into Nepal on commercial and diplomatic missions and who was 'well versed in the literature of his tribe, acquainted with the manners, customs, written languages and spoken dialect' of the hills.[22]

Following Rutherford's lead and Calcutta's orders, commanders and magistrates along the whole length of the hills began to improve their own intelligence and commissariat agencies. The appearance of British surveying parties in 1813 and 1814 had been one of the initial causes of war. Once hostilities began, careful surveys were prepared to correct and extend the existing rough route maps. As usual, the advance of the British forces was matched by an advance of formal postal arrangements and the establishment of a dak. In mid-1815, when Lieutenant Roper was officially appointed head of the Intelligence Department under Col. Nicholls, Rutherford's establishment was absorbed into the Company's army.[23] These departments, said the Governor-General, had intercepted letters of the 'highest importance respecting the character and disposition of the court of Cathmandoo and its principle officers in the western portions of the Goorkah [sic]'.[24] As a check on their reliability, the British kept detailed notes on the harkaras whom they employed in Nepal as the war progressed. These do not appear to have been recruited from a particular ethnic or regional group, such as the 'Mewias', Kallars or Bedars of the Peninsula, but were a mixed body, drawn from all the main communities which traversed the hills.[25] There were Kashmiri Muslims, a major trading interest in central Asia, and hill Brahmins (Joshis, Upadhyayas and Tripathis, in particular); there were renouncers, Brahmins of astrologer tradition, and even a few police officers who worked in the British territories or Awadh, but retained family connections in the interior.

While Rutherford stepped forward eagerly, Adam and the military authorities also drew on other men with a knowledge of the hills. They asked Dr Francis Buchanan to revise his old notes taken on journeys in the region several years before,[26] and they alerted David

21 Rutherford to Adam, 21 Aug. 1814, HM 644.
22 Rutherford to Adam, 1 Nov. 1814, HM 646
23 Adam to Gardner, 25 April 1815, HM. 653.   24 ibid.
25 R. Martin, Magt. Gorakhpur, to Adam, 4 Nov. 1814, HM 646; J. Lumsdaine, Dty Commissary Genl to Adam, 24 Jan. 1815, HM 651 (for Kashmiris); R.H. Phillimore, Historical Records of the Survey of India, II, 1800–1815 (Dehra Dun, 1950), pp. 38–47.
26 F. Buchanan to Adam, 19 Aug. 1814, HM 644.

Scott,[27] Magistrate of the border district of Gorakhpur. The military authorities also approached Hyder Hearsey, a Eurasian cavalry officer who had once surveyed part of the Nepal dominions. Hearsey's mastery of Indian languages and friendship with many Afghan irregular cavalrymen made him an ideal intelligence officer, for, as he remarked, 'In mountainous warfare everything depends on information.'[28]

Hearsey concentrated on the western sector of operations. Here Rohilkhand was to be the base for the campaign by General Ochterlony to conquer Kumaon and sever the Nepal kingdom in two. Later, William Fraser, scion of a knowledgeable family renowned in India, took up the role of chief intelligence-gatherer in the region.[29] Against the local Gurkha commander Bam Shah, the 'cleverest and best-informed man among all the Goorkah chiefs', Hearsey pitted the information he gained from Harrakh Deo Joshi, the exiled 'Earl of Warwick' and former political broker of the two hill kingdoms of Kumaon and Garhwal: 'this man is a perfect instrument whose name the Gurkhas dread', and he commanded 6,000 men in Kumaon. He had come to Lucknow as ambassador of the Raja of Kumaon, seeking aid during the Gurkha invasion and had been put in touch with Cherry by the Nawab. Even in exile, the Joshi received a flow of 'perfect' information on events in Kathmandu from agents or, it seems, from his own son who was held hostage there.[30] Rutherford was, for his part, in communication with 'Dho Deo Josee', the family priest of the Raja of Kumaon.[31] While Awadh and the British did not have reciprocal newswriter services with Kathmandu, Ochterlony was able to read accounts of Kathmandu affairs in the Persian newsreports of the small Sikh state of Patiala.[32]

Further to the east, William Moorcroft alerted the extensive connections which he had built up among merchants, indigo planters and horse breeders while Superintendent of the Company's Stud Farm at Pusa in Bihar. David Scott, the Collector, and the military commanders lying to his east in Gorakhpur, began to assemble another set of informants. One important source was the family of the Raja of Palpah (or Butwal) and his pandits and officers. The Raja himself had been in detention in Kathmandu in 1805 and gave a detailed, if outdated, account of the Nepali military establishments.[33] Buchanan later secured information

[27] David Scott to Adam, 12 Aug. 1814, HM 644.
[28] H.Y. Hearsey to Adam, 24 Aug. 1814, HM 644.
[29] M. Archer and T. Falk, *India Revealed. The Art and Adventures of James and William Fraser 1801–35* (London, 1989), pp. 27–35.
[30] Hearsey to Adam, 24 Aug. 1814, HM 644.
[31] Rutherford to Adam, 13 Oct. 1814, HM 644.
[32] D. Ochterlony, Ludhiana, to Adam, 9 Jul. 1814, HM 644.
[33] Moorcroft to Adam, 14 Sept. 1814, HM 645.

from the Raja's uncle. These accounts gave details of Nepal's forces and
of a new east–west road which was intended to tie the straggling Nepali
dominions together. Scott suggested that the Rajput royal exiles and
their dependants living at Gorakhpur should be interrogated about the
hills. The most important resource Scott could locate, however, was the
network of Gosain trading houses based on Patna, Gaya and Banaras
which had branch agencies in the Tarai and the Nepali towns. He wrote
optimistically, for example, of Hari Krishna Das, a former governor of
Morung, who was the 'agent of a banking house at Benares, to which the
Raja of Nypal is indebted'. He was presently in Banaras and could be
tapped for information.[34] These ancient commercial, spiritual and fiscal
links between the hill polities and the Ganges seemed very promising.

In the event, the Gosain and Agarwal commercial houses trading into
the hills proved to be uncertain informants, though their hospices were
the lynch-pins which tied together different polities and ecological
systems. Adam remarked that they might be collecting intelligence for
the British, but might equally reveal an advancing force to the enemy.[35]
The Magistrate of Tirhut in Bihar wrote to William Moorcroft that it
would be extremely dangerous to use them because an important
mahant, Banwari Das, 'has constant intercourse with the interior,
receiving the greater part of his income from the vicinity of Cathmandoo', even though he held a substantial revenue grant in Bihar.[36]
The delicate position of the Mahant and the tight loyalties of the Gosain
mendicants made them 'jealous of persons making enquiries at this
time'. Elsewhere, some commercial interests even abandoned this
degree of ambivalent neutrality. Mahant Hari Sewak at Dehra Dun gave
Gurkha troops 'daily information of our movements and sent supplies of
all sorts into the [Gurkha] fort'.[37] So important were the Gosain
establishments to local society that they had combined with the court
officials to warn the zamindars not to assist the British. The Mahant was
a major proprietor in Dehra Dun and he and others were reported to be
'hostile to the establishment of our power'.[38]

As the Company and Gurkhas squared up to each other along the line
of the Himalayan foothills, the British official mind was invaded by
another chimera. This was the imminent intervention of the Chinese in
the war. Given the critical importance of the Canton trade in opium,
cotton and tea to the British balance of trade in Asia, this is not
surprising. The Qing dynasty had itself been at war with the expansionist

[34] Scott to Adam, 12 Aug. 1814; Adam to Bradshaw, 30 Sept. 1814, HM 644.
[35] Adam to Bradshaw, 30 Sept. 1814, HM 644.
[36] Magistrate of Tirhut to Moorcroft, 6 Sept. 1814, HM 645.
[37] Intelligence from Dehra, Rutherford to Adam, 13 Nov. 1814, HM 646.   [38] ibid.

Gurkha state in 1791–2, and contemporary Chinese documents indicate a keen interest on the part of the Chinese frontier governors in the changing balance of power in the hills.[39] Early on in the conflict, the British registered a rumour that the King of Nepal had sent a letter to the Emperor in Beijing requesting help, and that Chinese troops were being mobilised to intervene.

This happened five years before William Moorcroft and Munshi Izatullah made their celebrated journey of exploration into central Asia.[40] British knowledge of the eastern Himalayan kingdoms and the interior of Chinese central Asia was still negligible. Their desperate search for knowledge of the area during the Nepal war uncovered some ancient commercial and cultural connections between south and central Asia. William Moorcroft announced that he had found a new source of information in a Kashmiri Muslim business house which was established at Patna. Kashmiri families had been an important element in the commercial life of the city for many generations. This house was particularly ancient. It had reportedly been established in about 1620 and maintained agents and depots in Kashmir, Nepal, Lhasa, 'Silink' on the Chinese frontier, and in Dacca. The Patna branch, Moorcroft reported, collected 'otter skins at Dacca and its neighbourhood'. These were transported through Nepal and Lhasa to China, and 'the return of each despatch is made every two years principally in gold'. Otter skins were a prized accoutrement of Chinese imperial dress, and besides, the Kashmiris 'are convenient agents for all kinds of Chinese'. Moorcroft knew the firm's agent well, partly because he had used 'his interests for conveying the practice of vaccination into Kettee China'.[41] So influential was the firm that their agents in Tibet were reportedly given tea from the hands of the Dalai Lama himself when they visited his court. Though Moorcroft doubted this, he accepted that the firm's agents 'wrote generally on all political matters and they were very well informed'.[42]

Moorcroft considered that these Kashmiris were 'deceitful', but since the main agent lived at Patna, the British had great power over him and could exert pressure. Moreover, the Kashmiris had a deep interest in a quick end to the war, even though this might mean British supremacy. Prolonged hostilities would damage their business. Moorcroft sought yet further sources of information. He noted that Mir Izatullah's travels in

[39] See, the Chinese account of the Gurkha war, British Museum, Oriental Antiquities, 1904–4 14.68; Pradhan, *Gorkha Conquests*, pp. 136–7.
[40] See below, pp. 135–8.
[41] Moorcroft's memorandum, 15 Sept. 1814, HM 645.
[42] Moorcroft to Adam, 23 Sept. 1814, HM 645.

the region had revealed a 'good horse dauk in hither China' and that if a spy could be got into Tartary, it would be possible to quickly learn the disposition and attitude of the Chinese. A bizarre pretext had indeed presented itself. Izatullah had reported that the ruler of Kashgar in central Asia had requested 'a hearing trumpet for his wife, who was deaf'.[43] Moorcroft now advised that an ear trumpet be sent up from Calcutta by post so that Izatullah could despatch an 'intelligent man' into the interior with it. This man would be charged to find out whether the public granaries in central Asia were being opened for the use of a mobilised Chinese army. The fate of the ruler of Kashgar's wife's ear trumpet is hidden to history. Suffice it to say that through to the time of Brian Hodgson's period as Resident at the Kathmandu Court in the 1830s and 1840s, Kashmiri firms with trade lines from eastern India into central Asia were used to pick up information on potential Chinese and Tibetan threats to British interests.[44]

Even a year after hostilities began the British had little political and military intelligence from the heart of the Nepal kingdom. Their information was still drawn from exiles and spies who reported on the north–south routeways. They had gleaned a few scraps from one Francis Neville, a contact of Moorcroft. Neville was 'the son of a Frenchman by a native'; his father had served the founder of the Gurkha empire and he himself continued to trade with Nepal.[45] Neville, who spoke fluent Newari, had a good knowledge of the Gurkha military establishments. Most usefully, he revealed to the British the existence of a hidden road which the Nepal government had forbidden to ordinary travellers on pain of death and which was camouflaged with thorn bushes. As often in the course of the nineteenth-century European expansion, scattered representatives of earlier diasporas of Portuguese, Jesuits and pioneering traders of mixed race became valuable informants.

There were two main problems with the information that the British made use of during the first year of the Nepal War. First, the detailed material they managed to assemble on routes and roads did not reveal the difficulties which would face an army moving in such terrain. They underestimated the problems of engaging with a resourceful enemy who could at will withdraw almost indefinitely to further ranges of hill forts. Ochterlony was later to complain that he was drawn into the interior where lines of communication were difficult, the country was full of

[43] ibid.
[44] 'Case of Khwaja Ahmed Ali, a merchant of Patna, imprisoned at Lhasa', BC, 1384/ 55154, OIOC.
[45] Moorcroft to Adam, in Adam to Ochterlony, 3 Oct. 1814, encl. 'Sketch of one line of road to the capital of Nepal communicated by Francis Neville', HM 645.

'pinnacle forts', and 'the expulsion of the Goorkas is not a general wish'.[46]

Secondly, British political appreciation was stymied by their stereotyped construction of the Nepali state as a barbarous tyranny from whose thrall the majority of the hill population were waiting to be liberated. This stereotype derived in part from the early Jesuit accounts of the savagery of the Nepali conquests, their use of the *kukri* knife, supposedly mongoloid appearance, cult of blood sacrifice, and so on. It was reinforced by the reports they received of Nepali 'outrages' on the Indian border, and by the hostility of the refugees in India. While the latter represented much opinion in Kumaon and Garhwal, the British came to realise that refugee information was tainted by 'hope and prejudice'.[47] Thus indigenous reports intensified the orientalist stereotypes. Buchanan, for instance noted that the Newars were 'the most disaffected subjects of the Goorkha, partly from the remembrance of cruelties suffered, partly from religious differences'.[48] Here Buchanan seems to have exaggerated what was a flexible boundary between the Newari hill Buddhism and the Hindu rite of the Gurkhas. The theme of the 'barbarous Gurkha' was kept alive by sundry atrocity stories. British harkaras were tortured with more ferocity than was common in the Indian plains.[49] On the other hand, the rumours that the King of Nepal had sacrificed a Newar boy to propitiate the gods on the outbreak of the war was probably apocryphal. Secure in their prejudices, the British consistently used the rhetoric of liberation from oppression in their manifestos and correspondence in the hills. The Gurkhas took the place of the 'French tyranny' in their minds, as Tipu and the Marathas had done before. This propaganda offensive was hardly a great success. While they were generally able to prize apart elements of a more ephemeral and corporate polity of the Indian plains, the solidarity of the Gurkhas proved relatively impermeable to their wiles, especially in the Kathmandu Valley. Gurkha land policy and their promotion of neo-Hinduism had begun to create cultural homogeneity in the elite and a degree of local patriotism. Consequently, the British found that information on the inwardness of court politics, as opposed to the mere location of routes and forts, was very thin on the ground. Much to their surprise, hill people rarely came to the help of the invaders

---

[46] Ochterlony to Adam, 20 Jan. 1815, HM 647.
[47] Moorcroft to Adam, 14 Sept. 1814, HM 645.
[48] Buchanan to Adam, 19 Aug. 1814, HM 644, f. 309; Kirkpatrick, *Account*, p. 184.
[49] *Memoirs of the Extraordinary Military Career of John Shipp, late a Lieutenant in H.M. 87th Regiment* (London, 1832), II, 99; ibid., 68–70; cf. W. Heathcote to Capt. Faithfull, 29 Jan. 1815, HM 649.

unless they were paid to do so.[50] They put this down to popular fear of the Gurkhas, but it seems likely that, although they disliked Gurkha conquest, white foreign intrusion into a secluded and sacred land, bringing with it significant numbers of Muslims, was resented even more.[51]

The result was a gradual change in British military and political strategy. Outright conquest became more distant as the war ran on. Instead, a policy of restoring the hill kings followed by complete withdrawal seemed increasingly attractive. Military operations would have at least achieved some little gain in the realm of information 'for the chiefs would know that the British were already in possession of whatever knowledge would be necessary to the execution of their ambitions'.[52]

The relative cohesion of the Gurkha polity also enabled it to inaugurate effective counter-intelligence policies. It was not until very late in the war that the British managed to seduce ethnic Gurkha leaders away from their allegiance or recruit Gurkha troops into their army. What little information they received direct from Gurkha sources came either from intercepted letters, or from lowly prisoners and the small number of defectors.[53] Until the beginning of 1816, the Gurkhas were able to limit the penetration of British harkaras. Some were turned back; others were brutally executed. Policies of secrecy generally prevailed in Nepal. A Frenchman who had cast cannon for the Nepali army was killed when he tried to leave the country; ordinary people were excluded from forts and hidden military roads.[54] Gurkha warbands infiltrating the plains made particular efforts to capture and neutralise the police and bantiria establishments, thus hitting directly at the weakest point in the British lines of communication. The Gurkhas also managed to use the commercial and pilgrimage networks down to the plains for their own advantage. In some cases they had the principal agents in their power; elsewhere, as in the case of people with commercial interests in the Kathmandu valley, many wealthy men were inclined to oppose the British anyway. Other individuals who had been slighted or ruined by the British, including the Dewan of the Company's Bareilly Factory who

[50] For a later, sober, assessment of intelligence failures and 'Gurkha fidelity' see 'Sketches of the Later History of British India, vi, the Nepaul War', *Asiatic Journal*, n.s., 1836, 21, 8–9, 120, 121, 129, and p. 172 where 'miserably defective information' is blamed for military failure.
[51] Hearsey to Fagan, 3 Nov. 1814, HM 646.
[52] Buchanan to Adam, 19 Aug. 1814, HM 644.
[53] e.g., depositions in Wood to Fagan, 24 April 1815, HM 654.
[54] 'Sketch of one line of road by Francis Neville', HM 645; Genl Wood to Fagan, 15 Jan. 1815, HM 651.

had been dismissed his post, were reported to be passing information to the hills.[55] The British were particularly concerned when the Gurkhas appeared to be making headway in recruiting restive Rohilla Pathan soldiers to serve against them and were reported to be making secret overtures to the Sikhs.[56]

Company officials also encountered difficulties in their surveillance of the Tharus, a nomadic herding group, who were regarded not only as potential suppliers of the Nepalis, but as a dangerous mobile population which might disrupt the defence of the border villages in Awadh and British territory. The authorities several times considered interdicting travel between the hills and the plains. Abdul Kadir Khan made a detailed investigation of their society and economy by collating the information of Tharu headmen.[57] The creation of a cordon sanitaire along the frontier by relocating the tribal populations as a whole was suggested, but this was ultimately rejected because 'it would deprive the government of revenues, the people of cloths, cottons, muslins, but above all make government unpopular by the interruption of religious rites'.[58]

While the Gurkha regime was regarded as a crude tyranny by colonial officials, it appears to have had a significant degree of archival depth. Conversely, the British were only just assembling the cartographic and social information which was commonplace in the Indian plains. A set of intercepted Gurkha letters warned their leaders against making concessions to the British. The enemy, it said, would not be satisfied with these concessions 'or if he should accept of our terms he would serve us as he did Tippoo from whom he first accepted of an indemnification of 6 crores of Rupees in money and in territory, and [then] wrested from him his whole country'.[59] The writer perceptively went on to argue that concessions of territory would lead the state into a spiral of decline because diminished territory could not support the large army, which was the Gurkhas' only protection. While Nepali historians have written of Nepali nationalism in this early struggle against the British, such a word seems anachronistic. The Gurkha state was seen by its founders as a caste-based raj in which most non-Indic peoples (Newars, Gurungs, etc.) were reduced to the status of lowly serfs.[60] The Gurkha ruling class

[55] Intercepted letter Bam Shah, Almora Subahdar, to Beni Ram, Rutherford to Adam, 1 Oct. 1814, HM 645.
[56] ibid.
[57] Reporting Abdul Kadir Khan's investigations, Wood to Fagan, 21 Jan. 1815, HM 649.
[58] ibid.
[59] Intercepted letter from Ummer Singh and his sons to Raja of Nepal, 2 Mar. 1815, D. Scott, Magt. Rungpore to Adam, 12 Jan. 1815, HM 650.
[60] Pradhan, Gorkha Conquests, pp. 91, 155–95; also Prithvi Narayan, 'Divya Upadesh', tr.

certainly appealed to a state-led Sanskritic Hinduism and a regional patriotism to a greater extent than most contemporary kingdoms of the plains. Yet the most potent force welding together the Brahmin-Kshatriya order was the need to retain the conquered territory already divided amongst the warrior and administrator castes in the form of land grants. Expansion – the rationale of the state – created its own momentum. In its wake a sense of corporate solidarity emerged, but it was as yet the solidarity of a cohesive social elite, rather than that of a nation.

Further indicating the Gurkhas' keen interest in wider imperial affairs, the intercepted letter pointed to the defeat of the British armies at Bharatpur in 1805: 'they have not returned to meddle with Bhurtpore'. The letter also referred to an apocryphal British defeat by Ranjit Singh of the Punjab, but, most revealing of all in view of contemporary Burmese intelligence activities, mentioned the destruction of the East India Company Factories by the Burmese in the mid-eighteenth century.[61] This historical depth in the Gurkha memory and statecraft is further evidenced in other references to affairs many years before. The Nepal rulers were able to recall the early contacts between Warren Hastings and the Nepal government, and the struggles over border villages and trade between the two territories. They claimed that the Gurkhas had helped Warren Hastings during the Banaras rising of 1781 and also gave a self-serving account of the revolt of Vazir Ali and the murder of Cherry in January 1799.[62] The memory of key officers of state was reinforced with documents from the Kathmandu archives. Overall, one gets the impression that the Gurkhas were well served by an efficient record department and by the skill of their Brahmin counsellors.

The Gurkha state was not, of course, a purely pragmatic polity informed by no more than raison d'état. Intercepted letters also revealed a fear that the wrath of the gods had been turned against Nepal by the government's bad treatment of Brahmins who had lost revenue grants and were 'in distress'.[63] Nepali war aims were, nevertheless, clear and militarily feasible. They were to draw the British into the hills, deny them food and information and then cut them to pieces. According to one informant, the Gurkhas said they could not fight the British 'on the plains in the day', but that the British could not fight the Gurkhas in the

in L.F. Stiller, *Prithvinarayan Shah in the Light of his Dibya Upadesh* (Kathmandu, 1968), pp. 35–46.

[61] Intercepted letter from Ummer Singh and his sons to Raja of Nepal, 2 Mar. 1815.

[62] Trans. of a letter from Raja of Nepal to Chandra Shekhar Upadhyaya, 11 Dec. 1814 in Bradshaw to Actg Sec. Govt, 11 Dec. 1814, HM 648.

[63] Intercepted letter from Ummer Singh and his sons to the Raja of Nepal, 2 Mar. 1815, encl. in Scott to Adam, 12 Jan. 1815, HM 650.

hills.[64] Nepalis had tolerable success in these aims. First, they preserved their independence throughout the colonial period. Secondly, and most ironically, their resistance transformed the stereotype of mongoloid barbarity into the imperial myth of the 'plucky little Gurkha' who has lopped heads on behalf of the British Crown for nearly two hundred years.[65] Brian Hodgson later accumulated a vast mass of information about Gurkha politics and society, obsessively watching this dangerous state as Resident in Kathmandu. Nepal was equally sagacious in its careful surveillance of the British and in promoting an information order which opened outward, but not inward.

Hunting the White Elephant: culture and information during the First Burma War, 1824–6

Britain's first confrontation with the Konbaung dynasty of Burma is difficult to explain in terms of economic imperialism. As Douglas Peers[66] suggests, the self-perception of two aggressive but vulnerable empires better explains the origin of the conflict. British India remained touchy about the security of its borders. External foes were always suspected of being on the point of linking up with internal dissidents. During the Burma War the British were constantly on the lookout for unlikely coalitions between the Burmese, Ranjit Singh, the Marathas and Nepal. The mentality of Calcutta and its swollen armed forces had not really adjusted to the end of international war and the establishment of paramountcy. The Calcutta press gingered up the anti-Napoleonic rhetoric of fighting 'tyranny and barbarism' with free-trading hostility to the monopolies and diplomatic conceit of the remaining Asian kingdoms.

On the Burmese side, the stability of the dynasty had been shaken by severe famines in the early years of the century.[67] Burma needed labour. Conquest in Assam and on the Bengal frontier had secured the services of elite Manipuri cavalry, serfs for royal or noble estates and military glory for the King and his commanders. Though the British used

---

[64] 'Deposition of Luman Singh Ale (?), a Gurkhalee of the Nepaul Army now in the Raja's hill corps', Wood to Fagan, 24 April 1815, HM 654.

[65] B.D. Sanwal, *Nepal and the East India Company* (Bombay, 1965); L. Kaplan, *Warrior Gentlemen: 'Gurkhas' in the Western Imagination* (London, 1995).

[66] D. Peers, *Between Mars and Mammon. Colonial armies and the garrison state in India, 1819–35* (London, 1995).

[67] V. Lieberman, *Burmese Administrative Cycles. Anarchy and Conquest c. 1580–1760* (Princeton, 1984), p. 20; H. Burney, 'On the population of the Burman Empire', 1842, reprint, *Journal of the Burma Research Society*, 31, i, 1941, 19–33. Thant Myint-U, 'The crisis of the Burmese state and the foundations of colonial rule in Upper Burma, 1860–1900', unpub. PhD thesis, Cambridge University, 1995.

Burmese military bombast as a domestic justification for hostilities, the war party in Ava really does seem to have believed that Dacca and Murshidabad 'originally belonged to the Arracan Rajah', the Burmese king's liegeman.[68] Bandula (Maung Yit), the commander-in-chief, optimistically prepared silver fetters in which to convey the Governor-General to Ava.[69] But the people were unconvinced that the outcome of the war would be favourable. Burmese knowledge of the British was crude by comparison with the Gurkhas' knowledge of them, as crude, in fact, as British knowledge of the Burmese.

The lack of mutual understanding between the two governments was apparent at all levels throughout the conflict. By aiming a blow at what they took to be the heart of the kingdom and taking Rangoon with an amphibious attack, the British hoped to deal with the Burmese as they had dealt with the Nawab of Awadh or the Sultans of Mysore. Instead, the Burmese forces simply retreated before Sir Archibald Campbell, the British Commander-in-Chief, drawing his armies into danger in the interior. For months the Burmese refused to negotiate and the British learned little about the disposition of Burmese forces or the nature of the regime. The Burmese instituted a scorched-earth and an information famine. As Major J. Snodgrass, moving north from Rangoon, wrote 'Neither rumour nor intelligence of what was passing within his [the enemy's] posts ever reached us. Beyond the invisible line which circumscribed our position, all was mystery or vague conjecture.'[70] That wily old India hand, Sir Thomas Munro, Governor of Madras, saw clearly what was happening. He spoke of 'our ignorance of the country and of the people',[71] compared with 'knowledge of the people' in India. The problem was not Burmese military efficiency, he thought. The Burmese relied on conscript peasant levies rather than professional armies like the Indian rulers, but whereas in India the people were (supposedly) 'relatively indifferent to who ruled them ... in Burma we have no ally and the whole of the people is hostile to us'. Only in Manipur and other recently conquered northwestern parts of the Burmese Empire did the British find subordinate rulers prepared to throw off allegiance to their overlords, a common pattern in India. In Europe or India, Munro continued, the occupation of the capital

---

[68] GG in Council to Select Cttee, Ct of Dirs, 21 Nov. 1823, HM 660; O.B. Pollack, *Empires in Collision. Anglo-Burmese Relations in the mid Nineteenth Century* (Westpoint, Cnct, 1979), pp. 8–37.

[69] Gov. Genl to Dirs, 9 Mar. 1826, HM 660; C.M. Enriquez, 'Bandula – A Burmese Soldier', *JBRS*, 11, 1922, 158–62.

[70] Major. J. Snodgrass, *Narrative of the Burmese War, detailing the operations of Major-General Sir Archibald Campbell's Army* (London, 1827), pp. 15–16.

[71] Munro's Minute, 27 Dec. 1824, HM 665.

'secures the submission of the adjacent country'; not so in Burma where the whole society fell back and reformed itself against the invader, jealously guarding the tiniest morsel of information by terror and a conspiracy of silence. Later reports suggest that the Burmese were deeply suspicious of the Tamil and Telugu Indian trading families amongst them ('Malabar people from the south Deccan') who 'send continual letters' back to India 'favourable to the English',[72] though many Indian immigrants firmly supported the Burmese.

To the more sensitive of the British observers, the Burmese refusal to supply information and aid raised issues of comparison with India. W.E. Fullerton wrote, in a report on coastal Tavoy and Mergui which was finished after the war, the 'mass of intelligence and knowledge possessed generally by the Burmans as a people appears to me greatly less than what belongs to the people of Hindustan or to any other nation of western Asia'.[73] This he put down to the 'utter absence in their society of wealthy or intelligent classes of great proprietors and even of an intelligent hierarchy'. Conversely, the 'great store of equality of which this state of things is productive appears to have been in some respects favourable to the lower classes who are in proportion superior to the rulers, and certainly not inferior to the peasants of India in intelligence and physical strength'. This chimes with some remarks made by Henry Gouger, a British merchant, who spent many years in Rangoon and was imprisoned in Ava during the war. He remarked on the 'liberty and equality of the Burmese servants', 'which would have satisfied the pride of an American help', that is an 'American servant' who refused to accept that status. He thought this was unlike 'the obsequious manners of the natives of British India'.[74] Despite the existence of small numbers of court Brahmins, 'caste is scarcely known or noticed in Ava', wrote Campbell.[75]

Many of the British assertions were clearly prejudiced. Fullerton's view of the low range of general knowledge in Burma is contradicted by Burmese and European sources.[76] Buddhist institutions and the practice of temporary monkhood ensured a much higher level of basic literacy,

---

[72] 'Information from a Burmese writer and from a letter from the Gooroo to the Commander', extract from a private letter from Campbell to Swinton, 20 Jun. 1826, HM 668; but Arakan Brahmins were hostile to the British, evidence of Rev. A. Judson, ibid., 733 ff.

[73] W. Fullerton's report on Tavoy and Mergui, 15 Mar. 1826, f. 1,102, HM 674.

[74] H. Gouger, *A Personal Narrative of two years imprisonment in Burmah* (London, 1860), p. 11; 'The Burmese', *Delhi Gazette*, 1 Jul. 1840.

[75] Campbell to Swinton, 3 Nov. 1825, HM 667.

[76] Manucci recorded of lower Burma, 'It is a kingdom governed by the pen, for not a single person goes from one village into another without paper or writing', cited Lieberman, *Cycles*, p. 104, fn. 129.

simply defined, than existed in north India.[77] The status of township headmen (*myothugyi*s) and the accumulation of mortgaged peasant land in the hands of magnates since the consolidation of the Konbaung dynasty in the 1760s also modifies the picture of a dead-level society outside the court; Burmese society was more finely differentiated by status than the British understood.[78] Again, extensive palm-leaf records of genealogies, landownership and sales existed in pre-colonial Burma. Rigorously administered censuses had been taken at several points in the previous century, notably in 1783, and the state had an abiding interest in the actual numbers of its subjects, which went beyond the revenue statistics so efficiently collected in India.[79] For instance, headmen had to register live and still births and prevent women from procuring abortions.[80] This was because the absence of labour was a critical problem for the authorities, particularly after the famines of the early nineteenth century.[81] The upper levels of administration used written instruments as fully as in India. In Rangoon the British captured route descriptions, lists of supplies and commissariat orders from Burmese files. Even if the lower ranks of the army consisted of an 'impressed peasant levy', its small pinnacle of about 50,000 troops was highly trained and literate. In their dealings with the British, the Burmese were not as 'supercilious' and 'ignorant' as they were depicted. The Burmese population remembered the unavenged destruction of the Company's factories on the Burma coast in 1740 and 1760.[82] The government held written records of dealings with the British back to about 1775 when they had threatened the Company with a war with China and maintained the old 'Mug' King of Arakan in Rangoon as a bargaining counter with Bengal. The problem was that Burmese knowledge had not kept pace with the enormous growth of British power and knowledge in Asia since 1764. They misinterpreted intelligence, putting too much weight on the

---

[77] *Census of British India, 17 February 1881* (London, 1883), I, 227, found 532 of 1,000 males in Lower Burma could read and write, or were at school; Maung Htin Aung, *Epistles Written on the Eve of the Anglo-Burmese War* (The Hague, 1968), pp. v–viii; in theory all male Burmese were taught to read; monks wrote epistles for the majority who could not write.

[78] Lieberman, *Cycles*, pp. 237–8, 252, 254–6.

[79] ibid., p. 45; U Tet Htoot, 'The Nature of the Burmese Chronicles' in D.G.E. Hall (ed.), *Historians of South East Asia* (Oxford, 1962), pp. 50–62.

[80] Burney, 'Population of Burma', *JBRS*, 11, 1921; Daw Mya Sein, *The Administration of Burma* (repr. London, 1973), pp. 45–73; Lieberman, *Cycles*, pp. 173–5, passim.

[81] W.E. Fullerton's report on Tavoy and Mergui, 15 Mar. 1826, HM 674, ff. 603, 1079, 1092; the extreme concern of Burmese authorities with numbers of people was also registered in their desire to stop the emigration of the families of foreign merchants with them, J. Crawfurd's journal, HM 671, f. 77; cf. D. Cox to J. Amherst, Ramree, 2 Jul. 1825, Amherst Papers, 140/24, OIOC.

[82] *Gazetteer of Burma*, I, 295–6, 305.

resistance of Ranjit Singh and other Indian states. Finally, they mistook the failure of some British-trained troops during their conquest of Manipur as a general weakness in the Company's army, an impression confirmed by captured sepoys who were said to be 'amicably disposed' to the Burmese.[83]

Nevertheless, some features of these early analyses by Fullerton, Gouger and others seem to be correct and point us to differences in the information order between two adjacent societies at relatively similar levels of economic development. To a much greater extent than northern India, upper Burma was a homogenous society in which social and political life was channelled through a single powerful royal centre. The networks of Muslim administrators and munshis stretching out to the cosmopolitan centres of the Muslim Middle East, central Asia and even the Malay courts of southeast Asia[84] had no equivalents in Burma.[85] Though a sense of reason of state beyond the will of the incumbent dynasty was probably emerging in Burma, administrators remained personal servants of the monarch, and relatively more dependent on him. The Buddhist Sangha, regularly purged by the incoming monarch, was a state church in the way that the loose networks of Brahmin connections in India were not. New Christian proselytisation was strictly forbidden.[86] Burmese kingship had developed powerful and sophisticated internal espionage systems.[87] Each locality had officers designated 'royal listeners'. The king also appointed his own newswriters and employed a force of mobile spies and informers who moved fast up and down the River Irrawaddy. The distinctions between ordinary peasants and the descendants of state military and labour groups also helped to promote mutual surveillance. All these forms of information-gatherer were closely controlled by the King, princes and royal councillors. Thus bondage and fealty within a royal system had not apparently given way to a concept of dispassionate government service to the extent that it had done in India. The British received little information and no aid from ethnic Burmese during their early encounters with the kingdom. They found it difficult to buy into newswriter, spy or runner services or to secure the compliance of

---

[83] Reported remarks by members of the Burmese court, interview w. Rev. Adoniram Judson, HM 668 f. 733 ff.

[84] British Library Board, *Legacy of the Malay Letter. Warisan Warka Melayu* (London, 1995).

[85] See, e.g., 'Autobiography of a Burmese', *Asiatic Journal*, n.s., 1836, 20, 265–75, esp. 275, on the difficulties of adapting a literate Burmese to British service; for Burmese kingship, Yi Yi, 'The thrones of the Burmese kings', *JBRS*, 43, 1960, 97–123.

[86] E. Judson, *Life of Adoniram Judson* (New York, 1883), p. 143.

[87] Lieberman, *Cycles*, pp. 74, 81, 116, 202.

professional secretaries like the munshis. They were forced to rely on a range of ethnic (Arakanese and Karen) informants for local services. In their dealings with the court, they leant on a heterogeneous collection of Armenians, Kashmiri and Tamil Muslims, European residents and a few old-established Catholic communities. By examining some of these interests in detail, we gain an insight into the degree of, and limitations to, Burma's engagement with the outside world during this period.

When war broke out, Calcutta's knowledge of Burma was very limited. Many of the early deputations and files on Burma available in the Secretariat were dominated by eighteenth-century orientalist concerns for 'Burma books'[88] or by the details of external trade. Successive embassies from that of Capt. M. Symes of 1795 onward had been isolated and humiliated by the court. In 1796–7, Hiram Cox had provided a useful report on commerce, including some details on the trade in raw cotton to China. He had secured information on the position and proprietors of oil wells, anticipating by nearly a century the British interest in oil and the foundation of Burmah Oil.[89] Cox had also interviewed the port-masters (*shahbandars*) of Rangoon and Arakan, respectively a Parsi and an Assamese Muslim, who had provided figures for external trade. The foreign resident merchants of Rangoon sent a petition to the Indian government urging the freeing of trade.[90]

Cox's account of his diplomatic mission was strong on description of the court rituals where he had been slighted and humiliated, but of little real value to an invading army. By contrast, the journals of Francis Buchanan, who had accompanied Symes in 1795–6, had been stronger on statistics and the empirical description of routes, as befitted the first generation of the new self-consciously scientific orientalists.[91] As Marika Vicziany pointed out in relation to the Indian journals, Buchanan's figures were more a rhetorical device that an accurate set of measurements.[92] His dry matter-of-factness concealed a passion for things Buddhist and curiously stereotyped judgements about barbarism and civility. Overall, the most striking feature of these early attempts to gather knowledge was the lack of a serious attempt to come to terms with the Burmese language. The British took their Indian munshis and vakils with them (including Farid-ud Din, Sayyid Ahmad's grand-father), but they had no dedicated Burmese linguist. Only in Assam

[88] e.g., 'Capt. Hill's deputation to Ava', Bengal Pol. extracts, 1 Oct. 1799, BC 72/ 1592.
[89] Capt. H. Cox, *Journal of a Residence in the Burmhan Empire and more particularly at the court of Amarapoorah* (London, 1821), p. 36.
[90] Petition of 19 April 1798, enclosure in Cox to GG, 15 Sept. 1798, BC 72.
[91] Buchanan's Burma Journals, 1795, HM 687.
[92] M. Vicziany, 'Imperialism, botany and statistics in early nineteenth century India. The surveys of Francis Buchanan (1762–1829)', *MAS*, 20, 1986, 625–60.

and among the northern Arakanese was the Persian language and diplomatic etiquette at all serviceable. Even here communication proved difficult.[93]

The brief flurry of interest in Burma, which was typical of the period of Wellesley's schemes for a greater Indian Empire, came to little. British knowledge of the country had hardly increased twenty years later. Linguistic incompetence lasted even longer. As late as August 1825 the Commander-in-Chief of the Burma force was writing to Calcutta complaining of a total failure to establish the rudiments of diplomatic relations and the extreme inaccuracy of all Burmese translations.[94] It was not until the Revd Adoniram Judson, an American minister and Burmese scholar, was released from captivity in Ava on the onset of peace, that the British began to accumulate appropriate language skills.[95]

Quite early in the war, however, the British were lucky enough to secure a new source of cartographical information in the Burmese dominions. A Eurasian from Ava, called Gibson, was accompanying a Burmese mission to Cochin China. This was forced by fire to put into the Malay port of Penang,[96] a British possession since 1786. Capt. Henry Burney, then the leading orientalist official working in south-east Asia, interviewed Gibson whom he found to be 'personally known to the King of Ava and his ministers', and conversant since his birth with 'the language and customs of the Burmese'. He had already made two voyages to Lisbon and had been twice before to Cochin China.[97] Burney quickly found out that Gibson was able to draft a map of Burma, revealing novel detail on the eastern and south-eastern approaches. He was paid Rs. 5,000 for his services. Burney and other officials in south-east Asia supplemented this information with material from expatriate Chinese communities and guild headmen in Penang[98] and Singapore, who knew the situation on the Thai border.

[93] 'Sooja Qazee ... head of that tribe [Mugs] in Arracan' did not know Persian well, T.C. Robertson, Pol. Agent, Chittagong to Swinton, 4 Mar. 1825, HM 665; but earlier the Shahbandar (port master) of Arakan was a 'Cashmerian who speaks the Hindostanee language', T. Hill to Govt, 6 Oct. 1799, 'Capt. Hill's deputation to Ava', BC 72/ 1592.
[94] Campbell to Swinton (private), 6 Aug. 1825, HM 666; Judson noted a case in 1823 when the use of a wrong title in a British letter to the Burmese king was regarded by him as a 'high insult', 'Narrative of Events that occurred in the Court of Ava from 1823 to the end of the war against Burma', Amherst Papers, Mss. F 140/30, OIOC.
[95] Judson, *Life of Adoniram Judson*, pp. 215–87; A. Judson (and others), *A Dictionary of the Burman Language with explanations in English from the manuscripts of A. Judson and other missionaries* (Calcutta, 1826); Anne Hasseltine Judson, *An Account of the American Baptist Mission to the Burman Empire* (London, 1823); Gouger, *Narrative*, pp. 22 ff.
[96] Minute by H. Burney, Penang, encl. Gov. Genl to Dirs, 12 Nov. 1824, HM 660.
[97] Burney to Canning, Pol. Agt Rangoon, 7 Jun. 1824 in Dty Sec. Govt Fort Cornwallis to Swinton, 11 Jun. 1824; cf. Canning to Swinton, 6 Aug. 1824, HM 663.
[98] Enclosure 3 a, intelligence from Prince of Wales Island, HM 666, ff 682–797.

Gibson was another late example of that diaspora of Eurasian and locally resident European military and political entrepreneurs which had spread across south and south-east Asia in the aftermath of the establishment of Portuguese power and the Catholic missions in Goa in the sixteenth century.[99] As cultural brokers and linguists these people were an important source of information for the British throughout India and the eastern Seas. Subrahmanyam has shown how important were the activities of these condottieri, 'renegades' and doctors to the spread of European military and maritime techniques into east Asia.[100] Some French and southern European entrepreneurs had risen to dizzy and dangerous heights in the Burmese, Thai and Malay kingdoms. Gibson himself was a British subject and consequently defected to the British when the war began. His father had been 'a commander in the country service' and he was born in Madras.[101] Trade across the Bay of Bengal between the Coromandel coast and Rangoon had existed for several centuries and had been pioneeered by Tamil Muslim ships' commanders (marakayyar tindals). After the establishment of the Konbaung regime in the 1760s, Eurasians and Europeans had begun to enter the trade in wood, rice, cotton, and calicoes. Cochin China had also become part of this circuit; Gibson had first been there, in fact, on a Dutch brig which sailed from the Danish port of Tranquebar, near Madras. Gibson's geographical knowledge was particularly extensive since he 'had frequently been employed by the King of Ava in compiling maps of different portions of his empire, and of charts and descriptive accounts'.[102] He possessed 'French, Dutch and native maps' of Burma and had a good knowledge of the northeast of Burma and of Tennasserim. He apparently had connections with the tin and birds' nest businesses conducted off its coast. Gibson's account confirms the impression that the Ava monarchy had been attempting in recent years to build up a fuller basis of geographical and demographic knowledge.[103]

Gibson had warned the Burmese King of war with the British and the likely consequences before he went to Cochin China. Although he was

---

[99] Gibson had apparently been educated by Italian missionaries, Canning to Swinton, 6 Aug. 1824, HM 663; for the role of Catholic fathers in Burma, Father Vincentius Sangermano, A Description of the Burmese Empire compiled chiefly from Burmese Documents by Father Sangermano translated from his manuscript by William Tandy D.D. (1833, repr. London, 1966), pp. 277–87.
[100] S. Subrahmanyam, The Portuguese Empire in Asia 1500–1700 (London, 1993).
[101] Sec. Govt Fort Cornwallis, 7 June 1824, HM 663
[102] Minute by Burney in GG to Dirs, 12 Nov. 1824, HM 660.
[103] W.S. Desai, 'A map of Burma (1795) by a Burmese slave', JBRS, 26, 1936, 147–51; cf. contemporary Thailand, T. Winichakul, Siam Mapped. The history of the geo-body of a nation (Honolulu, 1994).

later sent to Rangoon to try to open up a peace communication with Ava, he was of little use to the British hereafter, having been compromised by his earlier defection. This Bay of Bengal trade network, however, threw up other figures who provided the British with insights into Burmese politics once they had taken Rangoon and could impound the ships and warehouses of the overseas trading community. Several of the Muslim ships' captains from the south-eastern Indian coast were interrogated by Campbell's officers to try to ascertain the motives of the court and their likely attitude to peace. This seaborne trade within the Bay of Bengal had been paralleled by a smaller overland trade through Assam to Rangoon and up into the interior. 'Cassayers' or Muslim merchants from Manipur and even a group of 'Mughal' merchants who worked the Ava–Rangoon route were able to fill in Campbell's sketchy picture.[104] Since these men generally knew Hindustani, communication was much easier.

In addition, Campbell was able to interview a number of British and other foreign residents of Rangoon who had managed to avoid being taken back to Ava and incarcerated when the amphibious force stood off the coast. Those who did not escape were debriefed once the war had ended and they had been released under the terms of the peace. This group represents an interesting guide to the foreign commercial and cultural influences to which Burmese society had been exposed on its margins. They included some Tamil Muslims, a Persian trader from Isfahan, a man of Dutch-Thai ancestry, a Burmese-Portuguese, Adoniram Judson and Henry Price, the two American Baptist missionaries, and two British private traders. One of these was Henry Gouger, a free merchant in silk who had been driven out of the Company's territory by the ruthless competition of its commercial agents, against whom he continued to rail.[105] In 1822 he had set up in Rangoon to trade in British cottons which, he deduced from Hiram Cox's narrative, might find a ready market. Gouger had established himself in the city by using, on a smaller scale, those networks which the British government was to use in the war. He first found himself a Burmese translator to negotiate with the local officials. This man was 'A Malabar [i.e., a Tamil] who had adopted a Burmese name',[106] but nevertheless conversed with him in Hindustani. To secure connections in the higher ranks of the Court he then made contact with one M. Lanciego, a French entrepreneur and adviser who had married a favourite sister of the Burmese queen and had secured a noble rank. Lanciego had been driven to the East by the 'changes and chances of the French revolution'[107] and had become a

---

[104] GG to Dirs, 20 Feb. 1828, HM 660. [105] Gouger, *Narrative*, pp. 1–2.
[106] ibid., p. 9.   [107] ibid., p. 7.

'privateer on British commerce'. Though he was 'no lover of the British', he saved Gouger's life and later, reluctantly, provided information on Burmese court etiquette to Campbell.

By far the most useful source of information for the British in the early days of the war, however, came from another and equally ancient commercial network which linked together the countries of west, south and east Asia. This was the diaspora of Armenian traders which had orginally spread out from the Iranian trading town of Julfa, first into Mughal India, and over the later seventeenth and eighteenth centuries into Burma, Thailand and the Malay states.[108] In eighteenth-century Bengal, the Armenian commercial community had provided a vital set of intermediaries and political advisers both for the Company and for private traders. In Burma, after the fall of Rangoon, one Manook Sarkies and his relations became the key linguists during Sir Archibald Campbell's hazardous march into the interior.[109] The Armenians had a vital interest in the orderly continuation of external trade and, being Christians, sometimes gravitated towards the European camp.

Manook Sarkies and his brother Ioze were the major Armenian merchants in Rangoon.[110] They had an extensive trade up to Ava which kept them informed about political developments at the court. A later inventory, produced when Sarkies was in dispute with the Company about compensation, reveals that he traded in indigo, betel-nut and stick-lac.[111] The family also had interests in the birds' nest and beche de mere trades to the south, providing food specialities beloved by all Sinicized populations.[112] Immediately after the fall of Rangoon to the invading force, Sarkies became Burmese interpreter attached to the British headquarters. He demonstrated a great deal of skill in trying to coax the lower echelons of the Burmese court into discussion after the frequent defeats which it suffered. He cajoled intermediaries among old court servants. He pronounced on British strength and their desire for peace in front of big crowds of Burmese and lavished food and drink on the ambassadors. A British officer stated that 'the Manook evidently had a wide latitude in interpretation and used his knowledge of the Burman character'.[113]

As we saw in the case of Nepal, international links of pilgrimage and religious devotion could prove a vital resource in intelligence work and

[108] Lieberman, *Cycles*, pp. 156–9, 257n., 113.
[109] Campbell to GG, 7 Sept. 1825, HM 661.
[110] For references to Armenian networks to Burma, Seth, *Armenians in India*, pp. 571–8, 580–5, 613.
[111] Sarkies Manook to Commrs, Yandaboo, 25 Feb. 1826, HM 668.
[112] W.E. Fullerton's report on Tavoy and Mergui, HM 674, f. 356.
[113] J.S. Tidy to Campbell, 18 Sept. 1825, HM 661.

diplomacy. Though Burma did not possess those close cultural connections which bound the people of the western Himalayan region to the north Indian plains, the links were not negligible. The Burmese had avidly received Indian texts on Buddhism, astrology and medicine for many centuries, and the Konbaung dynasty tried to accumulate further knowledge.[114] The links did not always benefit the British, however. The most important religious institution in the country was the Buddhist Sangha. Regular 'purging' by incoming dynasties and the weight of princely patronage made the monkhood much more amenable to its political masters than the Brahmin priesthood in either India or Nepal. British attempts to employ the 'Raj Gooroo',[115] or chief spiritual preceptor of the Burmese king, as an aid in the process of securing peace proved counter-productive. The Raj Guru and his party had first arrived in Calcutta in February 1823 'with letters from the ministers of the King of Ava intimating that he and others in his train were deputed to Boodh Gaya for religious books',[116] which were to be procured from this ancient Buddhist pilgrimage place in Bihar. The British, however, claimed that they had uncovered evidence that the party was collecting political and military information and trying to make contact with British enemies in the subcontinent. They are supposed to have written to the Sikhs, the Nepalis, and some of the Maratha rulers, soliciting an alliance against the Company.[117] The British believed that an earlier Burmese contact had been made with the Marathas, before their defeat in the war of 1818, through the Burmese Governor of Mergui who had also been allowed to go on pilgrimage to Bodh Gaya and Sarnath, near Banaras. Certainly, there exist Burmese intelligence documents which refer to multilateral links between the Ava court, Tipu Sultan's heirs, the Marathas, Nepal and an unidentified country in the northwest, possibly the Punjab. One of their writers, who had travelled in India, urged a Burmese alliance with Nepal, asserting that the English 'are a people like the banyan tree' which destroys anything growing in its vicinity.[118]

---

[114] In 1807, for instance, a delegation to Banaras from Ava brought back a Brahmin, Govinda, who was later highly placed at court, and Sanskrit books on medicine, etc., U Tin, *Konbaungzet Maha Yazawindawgyi* [Chronicles of the Konbaung dyansty], II, (Rangoon, 1967), pp. 166–7; I am grateful to Dr Thant Myint-U for this reference.

[115] This term is ambiguous. It was sometimes used to designate a senior Burmese court Brahmin. But in this case the 'Rajgooroo' was also serving Buddhist interests.

[116] GG to Dirs, 28 Mar. 1826, HM 660.   [117] ibid.

[118] 'Extract relating to intelligence reporting', Pagan U Tin, *Myanma Min Okchokpon Sadan* ('The Government of the Burmese Kings') (Rangoon, 19), part iii, 70–1. The document, which survived the destruction of the royal archives in 1886, may date from 1813–16 or from the period immediately before 1826. I am grateful to Dr Thant Myint-U for locating and translating it; A.P. Phayre, *History of Burma, including Burma Proper, Pegu, Taungu, Tenasserim and Arakan* (London, 1883, repr. 1967), pp. 224–6.

Similarly, the intercepted letters the Raj Guru's party wrote back to Burma were 'calculated to encourage the ignorant and arrogant court in the prosecution of its ambitions'. These letters reported the Barrackpore Mutiny of the Company's troops and other 'absurd and exaggerated reports ... bearing so striking a resemblance to many of the misrepresentations contained in some of the English journals that they would appear to be derived from one and the same source'.[119] The whole party was therefore brought back to Calcutta from its pilgrimage as prisoners. Yet, so desperate did the British become for any contact or information on the real state of mind of the Burmese war party, that they sent the Raj Guru up-country from Rangoon in the spring of 1825 to intercede with his king. Far from helping the British cause, he seems to have argued for a continuation of the war on the grounds that the Indian sepoys were on the point of mutiny.[120] Brahmins also functioned as royal ritualists and astrologers in this Buddhist polity. It was reported that Manipuri and north Indian Brahmins, who were patronised by the Burmese court, spread propaganda hostile to the invaders 'from hatred to the British rule'.[121]

If the British failed to secure aid or information from ethnic Burmese, they had much greater success as the war continued in attaching non-Burmese to themselves. Divide and rule, seeking out your enemy's enemy, or the 'other's other' brought considerable benefits. It is important to see this policy in formation because, even more than in India, the exploitation of ethnic division provided the underpinning of colonial rule in south-east Asia, and has helped determine the region's politics until the present. The British were encouraged in this policy by the oppressive rule which the Burmese monarchy visited on some of its enemies and ethnic minorities. The army which invaded Burma from Assam and Arakan quickly secured the aid of the 'Mug' people. The word *magh* was applied by Bengalis to the Burmese Buddhists of Arakan 'who had been influenced by the long centuries of contact with Muslim India'.[122] The Arakanese had, in the sixteenth and seventeenth centuries, created a major kingdom between Mughal India and Burma. They had flourished in raiding, slaving and trading across the cultural divide. The Arakanese, therefore, became the major target of the resurgent Burmese empire. Their kingdom was destroyed and they were

[119] GG to Dirs, 28 Mar. 1826, HM 660.
[120] Campbell to Swinton, 4 Feb. 1826, HM 668.
[121] Deposition of A. Judson, J. Crawfurd to Swinton, 12 May 1826, HM 668; Cox, *Journal*, p. 215 on Tamils.
[122] D.G.E. Hall, *A History of South-East Asia* (London, 1981), pp. 411–25; 'History of the Mugs', Hastings Add. Mss. 29,210, ff. 57–68, BL; 'The Aracan Mug Battalion', *JRBS*, 13, 1923, 129–35.

ruthlessly repressed. Some of the most important sacred places in Arakan were the spots where the Burmese had burnt alive the inhabitants of whole villages.[123] As soon as the British troops crossed the border from Chittagong, people began to enlist as guides, casual informers and porters.[124] 'Mug' headmen in Burmese territory wrote to members of an Arakanese refugee colony in British territory apparently offering an alliance to the Company, and obscurely referring to their cosmological legends and holy places.[125] Clearly, here at least was some form of irredentist feeling or spirit of resistance to the Burmese which the British could enlist. Fearing their mass defection, the Burmese defenders of Arakan and Assam sought to revive memories of the earlier terror. The Burmese commanders, for example, collected together three hundred people from various villages. When a 'Mug' asked a Burmese why, he replied: 'Are you mad? Have you not heard what happened? The English have killed our women and children in our own country and therefore the Burmese intend to put every Mug they can get hold of to death. Run away!'[126]

In Burma proper the British also sought allies among the local population. Since the previous century when there had been revolts against rule from upper Burma, the British had believed that the inhabitants of deltaic Burma, the former kingdom of Pegu (or the Talien kingdom), were generally hostile to the Ava government. Equally, the inhabitants of Tavoy and Mergui were expected to be more favourable to the British because they already had trading connections with them.[127] There may indeed have been some inter-regional hostility, but as in the case of twentieth century Vietnam, this was weaker than the fear and hostility with which outsiders were viewed.[128] Moreover, since the British had formed their views in the eighteenth century, the cultural, political and linguistic dominance of upper Burma had been extended. There were no popular rebellions against the Ava monarchy during the war and no court factions supported the invaders, though some magnates soon despaired of winning the war. On the other hand, the British did succeed in finding support among the major submerged ethnic group within Burma, the Karen. The Karen were to be of

[123] G. Drummond to Stevenson, Quarter Master General, Calcutta, 29 Oct. 1824, HM 663.
[124] 'Lists of intelligence', ibid.; T.C. Robertson, Pol. Agent, Chittagong to Swinton, 11 Jan. 1825, HM 665.
[125] Robertson to Swinton, 8 Sept. 1824, HM 664.
[126] 'Deposition of a mug from Cox's Bazaar', encl. J.C. Robertson, Pol. Agt, Chittagong, to Swinton, 21 Aug. 1824, HM 663.
[127] Gov. Genl to Dirs, 30 Jan., 25 Mar. 1825, HM 660.
[128] Peguers were also given the same status as other Burmese citizens, Snodgrass, *Narrative*, pp. 85–6.

particular importance. Not only did they control some of the more important mountain passes, there were also substantial populations of Karens who had been resettled as labour in the plains. Capt. G. Norman of the Political and Intelligence Department wrote that the Karens 'may usefully be employed as emissaries, to watch the movement and report the state and probable view of the enemy ...'[129] Eighteenth- and early nineteenth-century evidence suggests that the old minorities, such as Karens, and Shans, as well as more recently captured colonies of labourers from the northwest, were being absorbed into the mass of Burmese society.[130] A common language, norms of dress and revived Theravada Buddhism were spreading among all sections of the population.[131] This provided the moral underpinning of an apparently arbitrary regime. The suspicions recreated by the coming of the British pointed, however, to the revival and consolidation of these ethnic boundaries when full British occupation ensued after 1886. Difference was enhanced by the rapid success among the Karens of British and American Protestant missionaries. Karen cosmology, which involved legends of sacrificed gods and lost holy books, seems to have provided a fertile ground for syncretism and religious conversion.[132] By contrast in the northern hills which were conquered from the Burman Empire, it was well-organised bodies of Hindu ascetics armed with their sacred books which spread out from the already Hinduised capital cities to the countryside.[133]

This access to information and even logistical support from non-Burmese ethnic groups was never matched by Burmese sources. In part this was a consequence of the markedly cruel punishments meted out to those who broke the information blockade. A Burmese general, who had seized a Tamil Muslim trader attached to the British fleet and conveyed him around the country for interrogation, was publicly disembowelled by his superior because the trader might 'obtain and be able eventually to communicate a correct knowledge to the English'.[134] The inhabitants of Rangoon were bodily moved out of the city on the British attack, under pain of enslavement or death, in order to deny the British support or information. The impermeability of Burmese society was, however,

[129] Encl. in Maj. J. Jackson, Dty QMG, Prome, to Stevenson, QMG, 5 Aug. 1825, HM 666; Snodgrass, *Narrative*, p. 142; Sangermano, *Description*, pp. 44, 110, 290.
[130] Lieberman, *Cycles*, pp. 217–19, 249–50.
[131] ibid., pp. 262–4; cf. Myint-U, 'Burmese State'.
[132] 'The Karens', *Church Missionary Gleaner*, Dec. 1856, 139–40; cf. H.G. Tegenfeldt, *The Kachin Baptist Church of Burma* (S. Pasadena, Cal., 1974), pp. 44–5.
[133] *Friend of India*, 4 Aug. 1836.
[134] Encl. 8, statement of Sheikh Mahomed, *serang*, in Canning to Swinton, 6 Aug. 1824; cf. Campbell to Swinton, Sec. to Govt, 23 Jun., 10 Jul. 1824, HM 663.

founded on more than fear. Burmese did not help the British even though many apparently viewed the war with foreboding, expecting defeat.[135] As Burney wrote, the Burmese exhibited a 'national pride and a peculiarly strong personal interest which every Burman whether willingly or unwillingly must entertain against deserting their chiefs'.[136] Even occupation of part of the country would not snuff this out, he thought. Towards the end of the war Sarkies, the Armenian, was told by a leading Burmese commander that his compatriots were prepared to fight for years against the British, as they had done against the Chinese. They were 'no Bengalees', to submit tamely to their fate.[137] As the king's sister put it, 'The English had no right to the eastern countries, but they could conquer the black strangers with caste [Hindus] because they have puny frames and no courage.' The Burmese should fight on because the defeat of the English would encourage 'the black nations to throw off their yoke'.[138] It is interesting that the British perception of the feeble resistance met by them in eastern India was shared by other Asians, and so early. It may not be fanciful to see remarks such as these as a premonition of that intransigence which would ultimately lead the Burmese to reject the whole British connection.

Right to the end this flawed British intelligence effort had a peculiar quality. There were a number of obsessions. Understandably, officials were concerned for the safety of the European prisoners who had been taken to Ava.[139] This was an issue that bore on the Company's reputation at home and, because several Americans were involved, international diplomacy too. Orientalist myths, however, persisted. There was a stubborn belief that the Burmese had buried vast quantities of treasure in the foundations of the great new pagodas in Ava. Several Europeans, Eurasians and Burmese were interrogated on this point.[140] This greedy, conquistador mentality was no doubt nourished by fears about the growing cost of the war. Finally, there was the legend of the White Elephant. This beast, whose appearance foretold the coming Buddha, was central to Burmese cosmology. The discovery and taming of white elephants, therefore, brought a great access of legitimacy to the monarchy. The British were most anxious to locate white elephants

[135] Aung, *Epistles*, pp. 38–45, where a courtier reports severe public anxiety about British power, contrary to the bravado of Bandula.
[136] 'Memorandum on conversations with Gibson', encl. in Burney to Swinton, 4 Nov. 1824, HM 663; cf. Gouger, *Narrative*, pp. 7 ff.
[137] Campbell to Swinton, 5 Oct. 1825, HM 667.
[138] Reported remarks of King's eldest sister, interview w. Rev. Adoniram Judson, HM 668, f.733 ff
[139] Judson, *Life of Adoniram Judson*, pp. 217–81.
[140] e.g., 'information obtained at Rangoon respecting treasure at Ava', encl. 9, Canning to Swinton, 6 Aug. 1824, HM 663.

themselves and constantly interrogated Burmese prisoners and officials on the matter.[141] Their concern provides a comparison with their equally obsessive interest in the hair of the Buddha supposedly retained by the Kings of Ceylon. Little or nothing was learnt about the white elephants. Like the Burmese kingdom itself, they had apparently vanished into the jungle, untameable.

Evidently, the occupation of Mergui and Tennasserim by the British forces in time brought a great access of information about Burma to the British. In this region they secured documentary evidence from the headmen, especially after a mass revolt of 1826–7 when many of them were dispossessed and killed. The conquerors made partially successful efforts to co-opt the local Buddhist hierarchy into the colonial framework.[142] Yet, excepting the knowledge which came from old-established Jesuit and American Baptist sources, British material on the language, literature, ideology and motivations of the Burmese remained strikingly meagre into the later nineteenth century. The Buddhist Sangha and the headmen establishments were relatively intractable by comparison with the Persian-writing offices of India's decentralised polities. In the Delta after the occupation of 1852 and in Upper Burma after 1886, the British replaced Burmese institutions with a single-mindedness that had not been apparent in India. Burmese resistance and imperial arrogance partly explains this, but the impermeability of the Burmese information order also impeded the imposition of colonial government, the legitimising of capitalism and the spread of European knowledge. This provided a significant contrast to India.

Rumours from the west: between Oxus and Jumna

While the British stabilised their possessions in eastern India as far as the river Jumna, the rise of the Sikh state under Ranjit Singh in the Punjab and the convulsions in the Durrani Empire of Afghanistan continued to cause uneasiness in Calcutta. Zeman Shah's move south in 1798–9 had revived memories of earlier Afghan invasions.[143] The Company also feared French and Russian diplomatic activity in the region. These uncertainties lay behind John Malcolm's embassy to Persia of 1801, Elphinstone's embassy to Kabul of 1808–10, and Charles Metcalfe's associated mission to Lahore and Peshawar of the same years. Metcalfe

---

[141] cf. Sangermano, *Description*, pp. 76–80.
[142] W. Fullerton, Gov. Prince of Wales Island to D. Maingy, Commr Tevoy and Mergui, 29 Aug. 1826, HM 669; D.E. Smith, *Religion and Politics in Burma* (Princeton, 1965), pp. 38–47.
[143] Edmonstone to Elphinstone, 5 Dec. 1808, HM 657.

was told to establish 'regular dawk' between Lahore and Delhi and drawing up a tightly worded treaty of friendship with Ranjit Singh. The purpose was to secure 'the northern route' between Europe and India which 'still remains open to the uninterrupted effects of French intrigue', even though the southern route through the Indian Ocean had now been blocked to the enemy.[144] Security in this region would be a delicate matter. Officials feared that the ruler of the Punjab would resent a British opening to the 'enemy of his own power'.

Spurred on by the desire for exotic knowledge of the lands between the borders of Europe and Asia as much as by diplomatic interests and the desire for trade goods, a bevy of British diplomatists and explorers passed this way over the next three decades. They included William Moorcroft, Alexander Burnes, Claude Wade and Charles Masson. Only with the death of Ranjit Singh in 1839 and Russian movements against the central Asian Khanates was the situation in the northwest deemed to have deteriorated sufficiently for the British to consider direct intervention. The 'forward policy' laid the foundations for the costly British campaign in Afghanistan of 1839–42, and the subsequent conquest of the Punjab and Sindh. These diplomatic moves have been narrated in adequate detail by historians of the foreign policy of British India.[145] This section, however, is concerned with some of the sources of information which the British (and their opponents) were able to use when improvising knowledge of these regions. It is concerned both with the quality of that knowledge and with the light it throws on contemporary social, economic and intellectual processes in the Punjab and the northwest.

One is immediately confronted by a paradox. The northwest was closely linked to Hindustan, and yet it was apparently opaque to the imperial power now poised on its borderlands. Whereas Nepal was a residual Hinduised kingdom isolated by the Mughal dominance of plains India, and Burma was even more remote from the networks of communication which crossed the subcontinent, the northwest was the womb of Indian empires. It had been the broad highroad between central Asia, Iran and the great centres of rule in India. Here a loose Indo-Afghan Empire had emerged in the eighteenth century to replace the Mughals, until it was itself eaten away by the emerging Sikh state.[146] Pathan and Turkish soldiers passed this way to seek fortune. Persian

---

[144] Gov. Genl's minute, 17 Jun. 1808, HM 592.
[145] M. Yapp, *Strategies of British India. Britain, Iran and Afghanistan, 1798–1850* (Oxford, 1980).
[146] J.J. Gommans, *The Rise of the Indo-Afghan Empire, c. 1710–1780* (Leiden, 1994); I. Husain, *The Ruhela Chieftaincies. The rise and fall of Ruhela power in India in the eighteenth century* (Delhi, 1994).

administrators migrated from the town of Nishapur to take employment at the north Indian courts. Khattri houses based on Multan and Pathan dealers moved up and down the trade routes bringing horses, shawls, asafoetida and dried fruits.[147] Itinerant Muslim teachers and doctors moved from their patrons and practices in central Asia through Peshawar to their clients in the plains. Even if there were no regular daks, runners went regularly from Kabul to Banaras in about one month, bringing news of events further to the west or north in Persia and Samarkand.[148] Kabul and Peshawar newsletters were regularly read in Lahore, and were filtered to Delhi.[149] The region was, in fact, a constellation of *vilayat*s or homelands of the Indo-Persian cultural universe, and even during the worst period of political disturbance it was linked by thousands of potential informants.

Yet despite this, the British grasp of events in the northwest and, so far as can be gathered, the indigenous understanding of the conditions of British India, were defective. In the late 1790s, as fear of French ambitions grew, military officers drew on the extensive patrimonial knowledge of George Thomas, the Irish adventurer who had served the Marathas in Hariana. Thomas was well informed about the Hindu Jats and Rajputs of the region, but his comments on the Sikhs were little more than generalities.[150] About the same time, Francis Wilford, the Hessian orientalist of Banaras, commissioned Mughal Beg to make a survey of the southern Punjab and Bahawalpur. These lands he regarded as a fabulous *terra incognita*, which might throw light on the classical geographers. His initiative produced the 'Majmu'a Walforti',[151] 'Wilford's Compendium', a complex and dense document, but one which was more akin to a Mughal route survey than the serried ranks of information which, since the work of Colebrooke and Lambert or Francis Buchanan, were now available on eastern India. As late as 1808, the Commander-in-Chief, planning Metcalfe's mission, wrote that he had found no document 'sufficiently accurate to govern the movements of an army, even on the frontier of our newly acquired territory'. Important fortresses were unmarked. This explained recent reverses. He added that 'beyond the Jumna, all is conjecture'.[152]

---

[147] S.F. Dale, *Indian Merchants and Eurasian Trade 1600–1750* (Cambridge, 1994).

[148] T. Brooke to Edmonstone, personal, 26 May, 1, 4 June, 1808, HM 592.

[149] Ochterlony to Lushington, 12 Dec. 1809, et seq., HM 596; 'Translation of a newspaper from Kaubul', 10 Mar. 1809, Elphinstone to Edmonstone, 16 Mar. 1809, HM 657.

[150] 'Papers of George Thomas arranged by W. Franklin', Wellesley, Add. 13,579, ff. 55–61, BL.

[151] Mughal Beg, 'Majmu'a Walforti', Mss. Eur. F22, OIOC.

[152] Minute by C. in C., copy Secret and Sept. Dept Procs., 22 June 1808, HM 592.

Even the information on which Metcalfe's nearly abortive peace mission to Ranjit Singh's court was based derived from 'an expedition of pleasure' which had taken Capt. Mathews to Lahore in the previous year. Mathews wrote, unconvincingly, of popular disaffection against Ranjit Singh and opined that 'the people's dearest wish is to live under our rule'.[153] He passed on much gossip about Ranjit Singh's poor marital relations and resentment of his humble birth, which seem to have been garnered from bazaar gossip. Mathews's greatest interest was apparently focussed on Lahore's red-light district and the sexual habits of the Sikh soldiery who, he reported, 'bear a great similarity of character to British sailors, spending their money as fast as they get it in the pleasures of women'. By the period of the Nepal War, the British had established a Residency in Lahore and were regularly reading the Lahore newspapers, but information about Sikh politics, let alone the politics of Afghanistan, remained patchy and tendentious throughout the 1820s and 1830s.

Up to the beginning of the nineteenth century the Punjab and the Peshawar region possessed no large states that could concentrate and diffuse information. The rise of the Sikh warbands had cut off and marginalised the Muslim gentry of the small towns which nurtured the administrators and literary men of Hindustan.[154] Lahore was in decline until about 1805, while Amritsar remained a precarious boom town, linked to the cities of Hindustan mainly by the Punjabi shawl merchants settled in Banaras and Patna. The rural Jat society which underlay Sikh, Hindu and Muslim clan groupings was suspicious of towns, and had little truck with the literate Persian culture which had once animated them. Conversely, the Indo-Muslim gentry had little but disdain for Jat country life and religion. It is not surprising that the British received most garbled accounts of the Sikhs and underestimated the resiliance of the Jat clansmen who defeated them at Bharatpur in 1805.

Further to the west, on the Afghan borders, state structures were even weaker.[155] Here the instinct of tribal brotherhoods and the hostility of the rural *mullah*s (religious teachers) kept big government and its scribal apparatus at bay. The British in Delhi had opened some lines of communication with Pathan nobles and merchants in Kabul. They tried, for example, to get the mother of the King of Delhi to transmit

[153] Private letter from Capt. Mathews, Amritsar, to Actg Adjutant Genl, 3 May 1808, HM 592.
[154] Muzaffar Alam, *The Crisis of Empire in Mughal North India* (Delhi, 1986), pp. 200–1.
[155] M. Elphinstone, *An Account of the Kingdom of Caubul* (1815, repr. Karachi, 1972), I, 210–35; for a description of peasant risings led by mullahs, Moorcroft to Swinton, n.d., rec. 28 Sept. 1824, HM 664.

information through a relative in the Afghan royal family in 1808.[156] Elphinstone was also to make use of Bangash Pathan nobles who had fled to India, or made careers there. Archibald Seton, Resident in Delhi, was urged to collect akhbarats from Lahore and the west in the same way as his colleagues did in the Maratha states. But W. Brooke in Banaras was to confess to Edmonstone that intelligence from Kabul was 'precarious and not to be relied upon' and 'numerous rumours are kept afloat which I have not in my power to contradict'.[157] Elphinstone's and Metcalfe's missions were, additionally, met with deep suspicion for the British were seen as 'usurpers of the Mughals, like the Mahrattas'. Even amongst the isolated population of Ladakh, William Moorcroft was later to find that the British were perceived as people who built 'towers' (fortresses?) and then took the land: 'If they build a tower who knows what hurt will come?'[158]

These conditions changed with the consolidation of the power of Ranjit Singh after 1810. Ranjit Singh's state was partly constrained by the interests of the Sikh brotherhood represented in an assembly symbolised by the holy book. Akali chapters still propagated the levelling message of the earlier gurus. European snoopers were struck by the 'haughty, disrespectful' and uncooperative demeanour of the Punjab's 'fakheers'.[159] In other respects, however, the Sikh state began to remodel its central administration as a Mughal state, with its jurists, police chiefs and writers. Here, at last, the British could begin to worm their way into the local channels of communication. They read the regular newsletters which began to be produced by the Lahore court.[160] They also began to filter into the Punjab the descendants of men who had been highly placed in the late Mughal administration of the province fifty years before. Mathews's munshi, for instance, was from a family 'particularly intimate' with Ranjit Singh's father.[161] Most serendipitous of all, the Head Munshi of the Delhi Residency, Mir Izatullah Khan, was, as we have seen, the grandson of a former deputy-governor of

---

[156] Edmonstone to Elphinstone, 19 Oct. 1808, HM 657; cf. 'Employment of Abbas Koolie Khan to transmit intelligence from Cabul', BC 247/5565.

[157] Brooke to Edmonstone, n.d. ? Oct. 1808, (ff. 173–8), HM 657.

[158] A.H. Francke, *Antiquities of Indian Tibet*, II, *Archaeological Survey of India, New Imperial Series*, vol. L (Calcutta, 1926), p. 125.

[159] Mathews to Adjt Genl, 29 May 1808, HM 592; Metcalfe's party was attacked by a party of Akali zealots, Thompson, *Metcalfe*, pp. 98–9.

[160] By 1819 the 'intelligence establishment attached to the Delhi Residency consisted of writers at Multan, Rawalpindi, the King's court, Kabul Kandahar, Herat and Bokhara, C.T. Metcalfe to D. Ochterlony, For. Pol. Dept, 28 Aug. 1819, 72, N.K. Sinha (ed.), *Selections from the Ochterlony Papers (1818–25) in the National Archives of India* (Calcutta, 1964), pp. 89–90; cf. 'Extract of intelligence from newswriter at Lahore', ibid., p. 122.

[161] Mathews to Adjt Genl, 3 May 1808, HM 592.

Lahore. The Mir, persona grata at Lahore, became an expert on Punjab and its dependencies. Other descendants of the Delhi nobility of Emperor Muhammad Shah also proved valuable intermediaries. Mohan Lal, the Kashmiri Brahmin who attended the Delhi College in the 1820s and who accompanied Burnes on his fact-finding mission of 1832, relied on much family knowledge of the region. Other Kashmiri Brahmin families had worked to inform the British and the Sikh administrations of each other's actions. They linked the world of early British Delhi and the Indo-Persian culture.[162]

The very emergence, though, of a more robust and diplomatically acute Sikh state also alerted Ranjit Singh to the importance of controlling intelligence. Within ten years of his conquest of Lahore in 1799, the Maharaja had put in place an excellent system of newswriters and spies which could match anything the British had.[163] The Sikhs patronised the jurist and writer families in many small towns, and brought well-connected Khattri Hindus back into an information system from which many had been excluded at the beginning of the eighteenth century. The Punjab was also relatively easy to police, since the state could position agents on the numerous river crossings to take note of unusual movements and intercept alien harkaras. The result was a sophisticated secret service which Ranjit Singh used most effectively to confront British intrigues and through which he could feed rumours, information and disinformation of his own. His alertness to media of communication is further attested to by the fact that, having at first licensed two lithographic presses in the hope of disseminating the holy book, Guru Granth Sahib, he later had them closed, reportedly on the grounds that printed works might prejudice political control.[164]

The far west and Afghanistan remained 'all conjecture' through to 1842 even though Elphinstone's embassy of 1808–10 had accumulated considerable stocks of information which could be put together with material gleaned from Pathan soldiers in British service. These men were settled in Rohilkhand but retained connections with their homeland. The first Pashtu dictionary in British hands had been assembled by a Pathan nobleman of Bareilly in 1803, prompting Malcolm to

---

[162] H. Sender, *The Kashmiri Brahmins. A study in cultural choice* (Delhi, 1988).

[163] For espionage under Ranjit Singh, Grey and Garrett, *European Adventurers*, pp. 95–9, 290; a Lahore akhbarat noted that Ranjit had ordered that spies for the English should lose their property, noses and ears, C. Elliot to Swinton, 8 Sept. 1824, HM 664; a good impression of the density of information coming in to Ranjit Singh is given in Lala Sohan Lal, *Umdat-ut-Tawarikh. Daftar III*, tr. V.S. Suri (Delhi, 1961), e.g., pp. 58–9, 66, 127.

[164] John C. Lowrie, *Two Years in Upper India* (New York, 1850), p. 184, cit. Emmett Davis, *The Press and Politics in British West Punjab, 1836–47* (Delhi, 1983), p. 16.

recommend a cash prize for him, on the ground that it was well for 'natives of high family' to take a literary turn since this would divert them from 'barbarous habits and martial spirit'.[165]

Elphinstone soon appreciated the 'democratic' and segmented nature of Afghan society and the important role of its tribal mullahs. This tended to confuse and complicate outsiders' attempts to gain a true picture of its politics. Though halted at Peshawar, his staff were able to build up several large memoranda of route maps and reports on lands to the west.[166] Elphinstone interviewed compliant notables and religious leaders[167] and quizzed traders who moved between Peshawar and Kabul. He noted the spread of the Persian wheel throughout the northwest with an eye to propagating it in India. The British also collected information on the population from itinerant Muslim physicians and purveyors of talismans who moved regularly between Peshawar, Kabul, Bokhara and up into Turkestan each spring: 'they traverse great spaces and being everywhere welcomed, they have the best means for observing the manners of the people as well as the nature of the country'.[168] The expedition was able to make its own estimation of distances using a 'perambulator'. More distant routes, however, had to be pieced together from the reports of runners (kassids) at Peshawar. For instance, the route from Raree Bukhur to Hyderabad in Sindh, including a description of soils, towns, villages and local potentates, was devised by cross-checking runners' reports with those of merchants.[169]

While the investigations of Malcolm, Elphinstone and Metcalfe were designed to garner political and economic information, British observation and the interests of their Indian informants were still directed to other more abstract issues: the history of great kings and cities, the location of marvels and hidden human wisdom. As the Portuguese had been driven to the eastern seas partly by the search for Prester John, so Alexander the Great and the lost tribes of Israel haunted the westering movements of British conquistadors as late as the turn of the nineteenth century. Elphinstone, like most who followed him, was fascinated with stories of Kaffiristan. Here ancient, fire-worshipping Aryan colonists were supposed to be standing out against the encircling armies of Islam. It was reported that 'the more Mussalmans a Kaffir kills, he is

[165] Malcolm to Resident, Lucknow, 6 Jul. 1806; A. Seton. Agent, Bareilly to Edmonstone, 10 Jun. 1806, 'allowances to the family of the late Hafiz Rehmat Khan', BC 204/ 4598.
[166] Elphinstone's Ms. Report, HM 658; cf. *Account of the Kingdom of Caubul* (London, 1815).
[167] C. Masson, *Narrative of Various Journeys in Balochistan, Afghanistan and the Punjab* (London, 1842), I, 127, 146, 274.
[168] Elphinstone's Reports, f. 383, HM, 658; cf. Thevenot, *Travels*, p. 81.
[169] Elphinstone's Reports, ff. 209–11.

considered the better man'.[170] Thus the legend of Kaffiristan was lodged in the Anglo-Indian mind long before Rudyard Kipling wrote his story 'The Man Who Would Be King'.

This complex mixture of economic, political and exotic aims also characterised the next great expedition to the northwest, that of the former Superintendent of the Company's Stud, William Moorcroft. Moorcroft, who died on his return from Bokhara in 1825 was one of the great European explorers and antiquarians of central Asia. Using the accounts of Malcolm, Metcalfe and Elphinstone, he added greatly to the stock of British information about the Punjab and the western Himalayas, quite apart from his mapping of Turkestan.[171] A veterinary surgeon trained in the Scottish and Continental schools, his reports were voluminous, empirical and discursive. His description of the varieties, manufacture and trade in Kashmir shawls,[172] for instance, was one of the densest pieces of commercial reporting to pass through the Company's archive in the early nineteenth century.

The networks of contacts and informants used by Moorcroft were an extention to the west of those used by the British during the Nepal War. Pathan horse traders and magnates who controlled grazing grounds furnished him with a stock of information which led through Delhi and Lahore into Chinese Turkestan and the Persian borderlands. Abdul Kadir Khan, the Banaras maulvi, accompanied him on his first journey in Turkestan in 1813. On the 1820–5 expedition he secured the services of Izatullah Khan, whose journal was later published.[173] Alongside 'the Meer' stood Ghulam Haidar Khan, a Pathan soldier, a comrade of Hearsey in the Nepal war and during the Bareilly uprising of 1816. Ghulam Haidar's Mughal-style route description was later expanded by Hearsey using additional verbal testimony, and published in the *Asiatic Journal*.[174] Besides these men of the sword and the pen, Moorcroft depended on the Khattri commercial houses which linked Delhi, Lahore, Peshawar and Kabul with Persia and central Asia. Through the firm of Palmer and Co., he was able to draw from Peshawar on the house of Sant Lal in Delhi to the tune of Rs. 120,000.[175] As he moved up into the Punjab, he was able to tap into wealthy Kashmiri Muslim

[170] ibid., f. 211.
[171] G. Alder, *Beyond Bokhara. The life of William Moorcroft, Asian explorer and pioneer veterinary surgeon, 1767–1825* (London, 1985).
[172] Moorcroft Papers, Mss. Eur D 164, ff. 27–124, OIOC.
[173] 'Izetullah's Journal', 1812, *Calcutta Quarterly Magazine, JRAS*, 4, 1837, 283–340; cf. W. Moorcroft, *Travels in the Himalayan Provinces of Hindustan and the Punjab from 1819–25*, 2 vols. (repr. Karachi, 1979).
[174] 'Mr. Moorcroft's Journey to Balkh and Bokhara. The Journal of Ghulam Hyder Khan, edited with notes by Mr. Hearsey', *Asiatic Journal*, 18, 1835, 107–11.
[175] Moorcroft Papers, Mss. Eur. D 250, f. 28; Dale, *Central Asia*, pp. 56–7.

commercial connections which stretched, as we have seen, to far-distant western China and inland Burma. Besides the politicals in Calcutta, Moorcroft's British connections included agency houses and Company's commercial agents in the down-country cities with an interest in the shawl trade.[176]

Running like a thread, however, through Moorcroft's researches, travels and journals was what must be called the discourse of medicine. It was not simply that Moorcroft and his Indian informants constantly discussed medicine, but that their view of the world was fundamentally formed by it. Moorcroft himself was a physician as well as a veterinary surgeon. He was regularly apprised of new developments in the medical field by his European correspondents. He also corresponded with Company surgeons throughout India and with J. Gibson, Surgeon to the King of Awadh, who was one of his executors. Moorcroft's journals are sometimes interleaved with lurid descriptions of diseases and their remedies. To create goodwill and collect informants he performed minor operations, especially on cataracts, wherever he went. On one day in the Punjab he saw more than 130 patients.[177] The men of this generation had not abandoned the hope that somewhere in the stock of Indian knowledge of flora and fauna, there could be discovered some unknown remedy which would match the fame of cowpox and quinine.

Indians and central Asians, too, were impelled to medicine by practical considerations as well as by the still-powerful tradition of rational science which persisted in the area. Cholera and plague spread north up the trade routes. Moreover, the kingdom of the Punjab was at this time in the control of a man who must be ranked among the greatest hypochondriacs of history. Ranjit Singh inherited the concern for the well-being of his people which caused physicians to crowd the Mughal courts. One-eyed and pock-marked, he seems to have been unusually susceptible to the blandishments of physicians himself. Even in his thirties and forties he complained constantly of his bowels; Moorcroft thought that this was attributable to his consumption of 'fiery new rum of the country', and prescribed the allegedly soothing effects of French brandy.[178] This toning-up was also hoped to extend to his amatory activities, another constant theme in the Anglo-Indian medical encounter of this period.

Since the British were known to possess the secrets of *hikmat* (physic

---

[176] G.R. Kaye (ed.), *India Office Library. Catalogue of Mss in European Languages*, 2, ii (London, 1937), 881–5; cf. e.g., Moorcroft to Palmer, 19 Jan. 1824, Mss. Eur. D250, p. 28, and Moorcroft to J.W. Laing, 26 Apr. 1822, Mss. Eur. D263, f. 61.

[177] Moorcroft Journal, 9 Mar. 1820, Mss. Eur. D237.

[178] Moorcroft Journal, 8 May 1820, Mss. Eur. D 238; cf. Lala Sohan Lal, *Umdat-ut-Tawarikh. Daftar III*, pp. 652–6.

or philosophy) to some degree, they always had an entree into the Sikh court, even when relations were otherwise sour. When Moorcroft arrived at Lahore in 1820, one of his first duties was to 'taste' medicines which Ochterlony in Delhi had sent Ranjit Singh ('elixir of vitriol').[179] As a veterinary surgeon, he was treated in his quarters in the Shalimar Gardens to a daily morning parade of Ranjit Singh's horses. Medical knowledge opened an even more important door. The most powerful man in the Punjab aside from the ruler was Fakir Azizuddin, the King's personal physician and prime minister. Azizuddin, who had been trained in the Muslim sciences and Greek medicine, had first come to the court as a lowly barber-surgeon. He had performed two vital services for Ranjit Singh. He had cured him of a serious disease and had also dissuaded him from confronting the Company in 1809.[180] Moorcroft was able to establish his bona fides and that of the British Government after long medical and political discussions with Azizuddin.

Moorcroft was not simply humouring his Indian connections. The intertwining of pecuniary, orientalist and medical ambitions in his own mind becomes clear in the case of the salts of Jawalamukhi, a place which lay on the shawl trade route near Lahore. The shrine at Jawalamukhi,[181] a goddess shrine in the Kangra Hills, was a sign of wonder, and a lucrative source of donations for its officiating Brahmins. Natural gases were said to explode in flame from a primaeval cave and the local waters were supposed to have a powerful curative property for skin diseases and leprosy. Moorcroft reported that the Emperor Aurangzeb, in his pious fear, had walled in with metal plates the flames, which he considered to be Satan's tongues. After the fires had broken out again with full force elsewhere in the cave, the Emperor made offerings to the Brahmins and hurried away. Moorcroft had other interests. He analysed the Jawalamukhi salts and decided they were of considerable curative value. Sending samples to the Medical Board, he decided that a monopoly of the export of these salts throughout the British Indian territories would bring a handsome profit to himself.[182] European chemists would have to prepare the solution, but in order to 'facilitate its use among Hindoos', each container would have to be stamped after inspection by the chief priest, or possibly by Sikh court officials. To add to its value, he fantasised, the solution could be filtered through a silver model of a sacred Tulsi leaf. To a deist and orientalist of eighteenth-century upbringing this posed fewer difficulties than it might

[179] Moorcroft Journal, 8 May 1820, Mss. Eur. D238.
[180] ibid; Lawrence, *Adventures*, I, 38–40.
[181] *Gazetteer of the Kangra District. Kangra Proper, 1883–4* (Calcutta, 1884), pp. 67–9.
[182] Moorcroft Journal, 29 Mar. 1820, Mss. Eur. D238.

have for an evangelical of the next generation. He approved of Hinduism. Though it was 'obscured by mystic symbols or by circumstantial ceremonies', Moorcroft thought Hindu knowledge was directed to 'the great first cause and least understood Jehovah, Jove or "Lord"'.[183]

Moorcroft's journals reveal a mind poised on the cusp between the classical orientalism of Sir William Jones's generation and the statistical empiricists and empire-builders of the generation of Everest and Burnes. Elsewhere in his travels a similar pattern of interests is revealed. Even in Kashmir and points north, where he wrote reams on shawl weaving, the cultivation of mulberry and the construction of pen-holders, he also kept an eye open for the picturesque and the sublime. He thought he had found the 'seat of Alexander'.[184] The Greek conqueror was a potent figure for Europeans since it represented the first conquest of 'their' civilisation on Indian territory, as much as he represented the universal sultan to Muslims.

After 1830 the British developed a more formidable commercial and diplomatic interest in the northwest. Burnes's and Pottinger's surveys of the Indus anticipated a determined assault on the rulers of Sindh which would, it was hoped, clear another road into central Asia. Russian ventures over the Hindu Kush were regarded with increasing alarm. It is still striking how far the gathering and exchange of information in the region continued to be dictated both among Europeans and the indigenous people by the debates on well-being and the exotic. Medicine and marvels were the symbols which allowed Indian, Afghan and British to overcome mutual suspicion and talk to each other. In Herat in the 1840s doctors were said to hold a very high social position.[185] The chiefs' conversation constantly turned to matters of medicine because they believed that doctors were also dominant in British 'councils'. Most of the Europeans they encountered were surgeons or physicians because the medical services also provided the intellectuals of the Company's government. Indians, Afghans and Persians therefore attributed the wealth of the English to their 'hikmat', physic, that is philosophical knowledge of which medicine was outward manifestation. Tribal councils and ordinary people constantly turned in conversation to the 'healing art'.[186] These 'idiots', moreover, as one traveller put it, 'spend all they possess in the search after the philosopher's stone. They are

---

[183]   Moorcroft Journal, 28 Mar. 1820, Mss. Eur. D238.
[184]   Moorcroft Papers, Mss. Eur. D251, ff. 300–39.
[185]   J.P. Ferrier, *Caravan Journeys and Wanderings in Persia, Afghanistan, Turkistan and Belochistan* (London, 1857), p. 149.
[186]   Masson, *Narrative*, III, 97.

convinced that the English have found it and attribute their riches to that discovery.'[187] Masson also reported that local chiefs engaged him in discussion about medicine and *kimia*, or gold-making, and that they asked particularly about the researches of William Moorcroft who was still remembered.[188] Indian gullibility about the philosopher's stone was perhaps matched by European obsession with the 'white skinned' Kaffirs, which had also attracted Masson's interest.[189] When later embassies brought with them men such as Shahamat Ali and Mohan Lal, Persian-speakers who had been educated in European science at the Delhi College, yet more doors were opened.[190]

Almost everywhere, the medical training of Company servants proved an advantage to them in securing the cooperation of indigenous people. This was important in offsetting the justifiable suspicion with which they were greeted in these vulnerable Asian kingdoms. North and west of the Punjab, however, there was something more than mere curiosity and desire for cure. The most vital intellectual culture in both the Sunni and Shia traditions, which had survived through wars and revolution, was the pursuit of the Islamic rational sciences.[191] Though the syllabus and interests of the major intellectual centres of the north and west became more intransigent and less susceptible to European influences after 1857, in the early nineteenth century they still remained avid for the new learning, especially in astronomy, medicine and chemistry. European travellers with scientific attainments, accompanied by Persian-speaking clerks and soldiers who knew about artillery, were the objects as much of curiosity as of suspicion. By comparison, the intellectual distance between the British and the Burmese, or even the Gurkhas, was much greater.

All the same, the further the British went from Delhi, the weaker became this purchase on indigenous society. In 1839–42 the British expeditionary force to Kabul found itself in an even more exposed position than had its predecessor in Burma in 1825. The intricate politics of the tribal groups on the mountain passes were a closed book. The British had invested too much faith in the power of the Afghan monarchy, which was in reality a mere umbrella over the machinations of tribal faction. Forty thousand troops perished in the disaster, and the British lines of communication crumbled. At this point the older,

---

[187] Ferrier, *Wanderings*, p. 149; Masson, *Narrative*, I, 179–80.
[188] Masson, *Narrative*, III, 97.
[189] ibid., I, 206.
[190] H. Sender, *The Kashmiri Pandits. A study of cultural choice in north India* (Delhi, 1988); see below, pp. 230–4.
[191] J.R.I. Cole, *The Roots of North Indian Shi'ism in Iran and Iraq. Religion and state in Awadh, 1722–1859* (Berkeley, 1988), pp. 1–20; Rizvi, *Shi'is*, II, 224–8.

indigenous networks came into their own again. Despite attempts by the authorities to clamp down on bad news, it was the bankers of the Delhi bazaar who first received reports of the defeat via harkaras from their correspondents in Kabul and Peshawar.[192] One firm even arranged later the ransoming of a group of British women and children isolated in hostile territory.[193] Pathan soldiers with Indian connections and travelling religious teachers were also enlisted to bring information and initiate diplomatic contacts. In 1842, with its horse-dak stopped and its military piquets destroyed, the British Empire turned once again to those humbler Indian experts in communication who had originally given it an entree into the subcontinent.

Knowledge, intelligence and hierarchy

The great states of the Indian plains were built from specialist groups which could bring their skills to the service of the kingdom. These skills ranged from the rituals of divinity to the skinning of animals. Kings were the subtle orchestrators of these diverse skills and knowledges, but arenas of public knowledge existed outside the purview of kings. This was particularly true in the case of the men of the pen, state servants, the munshis and clerks who wrote Persian, understood the management of accounts, and whose knowledge and value survived the rise and fall of kingdoms. The emergence of a definite ethic of service beyond and above the will of any particular king or dynasty was matched by the idea of 'state' which existed beyond the household of the king: 'niche parmeshwar keval sarkar', 'beneath God only the state'. This class of literate specialists, with their dependent scribes, managers and runners, was the dominant feature of the Indian information order. The British tried to co-opt and make full use of it. On the fringes of the subcontinent such networks progressively thinned out and eventually vanished. In Nepal the Persian-writing tradition had made relatively little impact. Instead, a more archaic network of astral and ritualist Brahmins and ascetic traders bound the country to Hindustan. For the British, this proved less useful than they hoped in confronting the tight-knit solidarities of the Gurkha rulers. Here a residual tribal egalitarianism had been fused with an invented Hindu warrior identity to generate a close local patriotism. Little information and few defectors could be prized out of such a society.

This was true to an even greater degree in Burma. Here writers and administrators, like much of the rest of the population, were bonded

---

[192] *Delhi Gazette*, 2 Feb. 1842.
[193] Letter fm Kabul, 25 Dec. 1841, *Delhi Gazette*, 29 Jan. 1842.

serfs of the king. A common language, common norms of behaviour and belief bound together a proto-nation. What we have called affective knowledge was fused with patrimonial knowledge. There was little space yet for administrative skills or universalising cultural norms beyond this ethnicity. For long, no ethnic Burmese were found to write digests and reports on their homelands to help the conquerors, and even if there had been, the British could not yet read them. The colonialists were therefore shut out in a way which had been impossible in India with its international Persian bureaucracy and its rational and descriptive sciences. The British problem in securing indigenous informants and leverage in Burmese intellectual culture persisted into the period of colonial rule. Punjab and the northwest frontier stood somewhere between the two poles of this typology. Here a modified version of the Indo-Muslim state was re-emerging from its eighteenth-century crisis, yet the solidarities of Hindu and Sikh Jat countryfolk and the even closer-knit tribal entities of the north-west frontier remained, for the British, dangerously impermeable beneath the surface networks of Hindu traders and Indo-Muslim court servants.

4   Between human intelligence and colonial knowledge

The next three chapters concern the information order of north India in the early nineteenth century. This chapter considers the strengths and weaknesses of internal surveillance and information collection by the Company's government after 1790. Chapter Five examines the nature of Indian indigenous debate and communications during the transition to colonial dominance. Chapter Six concerns the engagement between British and Indian public debate in the 1830s and 1840s, when statistics, information and education became ideological motifs for an avowedly reforming imperial government.

An impressive range of historical studies have considered the impact of European ideologies on India and the fashioning by the British of categories of difference and backwardness to describe its people, so justifying their dominion.[1] As these studies have grown more sophisticated, historians have come to accept that colonial ideologies were varied, unstable and contradictory; and that they owed as much to debates in European intellectual history as they did to particular Indian circumstances.[2] Equally, British 'constructions' of Indian society were determined by the form and limitations of British military and economic power in the subcontinent and outside. India's alienness could never be too crudely asserted by a government dependent on an army of Indian subordinate servants. It was difficult to sustain an 'apartheid' ideology stressing ineluctable racial difference in a subcontinent where Indians continued to control – albeit under severe constraint – the vast bulk of capital and almost the whole means of agricultural production. Colonial officials, missionaries and businessmen were forced to register the voices of native informants in ideology and heed them in practice even if they despised and misrepresented them.

[1]   Following E. Said, *Orientalism* (London, 1978).
[2]   Most recently, C. Breckenridge and P. Van der Veer, *Orientalism and the Post-Colonial Predicament* (New York, 1993); N. Peabody, 'Tod's *Rajast'han* and the boundaries of imperial rule in nineteenth century India', *MAS*, 30, i, 1996, 185–220; Aijaz Ahmed, *Orientalism and After: ambivalence and cosmopolitan location in the work of Edward Said* (Delhi, 1991).

These chapters attempt to locate so-called orientalist and colonial discourses more precisely in their social and political contexts. Ronald Inden has analysed the leading ideas of Anglo-India through its master texts.[3] But these ideas were abstractions from a body of competing and fractious ideas, principles and rules-of-thumb which were generated by the routine collisions and alliances of colonial politics. British assessments of crime, religion and native lethargy were more often reflections of the weakness and ignorance of the colonisers than a gauge of hegemony. Again, forces were at work in colonial India more general than those unleashed by the East India Company itself. British attempts to describe their Indian subjects in more rigid categories of race, religion and region, for example, were inflected by an international information order which mirrored the creation of a global economy and the rise of the nation state. Orientalism, in Edward Said's sense, was only one among a variety of localised engagements between power and knowledge.

The critical changes in the information order of north India during the early nineteenth century centred around the creation of new, knowledgeable institutions: the army, the political services, the revenue, legal and educational establishments. Almost as important was the emergence of an attenuated sphere of public debate in which European expatriate ideologues and a handful of Indian spokesmen attempted to critique government and society through the press and public meeting. The inverse of this was a relative decline of the importance of those indigenous communities of embodied knowledge which had informed pre-colonial kingdoms. Harkaras, astrologers, indigenous physicians, doctors of Hindu or Muslim law and knowledgeable women were slowly edged away from the political centre.

This information revolution, however, had severe limitations. Away from the hubs of British power and below the level of the district office, the old intelligence communities held their place. It was in the zone of ignorance where the knowledgeable colonial institutions met, but failed to mesh with, the sentiment of the knowing people of the locality, that the stereotypes of Thugs, criminal guilds, religious fanatics and well-poisoners were hatched. In this space arose the information panics which periodically convulsed expatriate British society in India.

In the peripheries, too, British innovations had little purchase on the debates and forms of communication of the older Indian 'public' which centred on mosque, temple and bazaar. As we shall see, British ideological forays into the realm of indigenous science, medicine and religion elicited an immediate and vigorous response from Indian

---

[3] R. Inden, *Imagining India* (Oxford, 1990).

spokesmen, imbued with a sense of traditional patriotism and fortified with a battery of rational procedures for debate.

Orientalism in action. The emergence of the 'political mind'

The shift from embodied to institutional knowledge was very clear in the domain of political intelligence where, by the 1830s, office memory had largely displaced the virtuosity of the munshi and the vakil. This change came about only slowly. Neil Edmonstone, who was to be the most powerful influence on the formation of the Foreign and Political Department of the Government of India, wrote to his brother in 1790 that 'enforced idleness' at the Hyderabad Residency had put time into his hands. He was surprised that no one in the Company's service had 'yet attained a proficiency in the forms of business with the natives, as to be capable of writing (and scarcely of reading) papers without the intervention of a moonshy'.[4] Over the following twenty years, Edmonstone and a few others, such as the Kirkpatrick brothers and Elphinstone, appear to have mastered the art of reading cursive Persian and familiarised themselves with the specialised forms of official letter-writing. Francis Balfour's *Forms of Herkern*, a Persian writing manual, and Francis Gladwin's *The Persian Moonshee* provided a basis for teaching new skills to the next generation of officials. In 1800 munshis began to teach Persian composition to recruits at Fort William College; and Haileybury later employed a Persian 'writing-master'.[5] Language remained a problem, of course. Trying to translate the Company's regulations into Persian, Edmonstone asserted that its rhetorical forms could not accommodate the 'refined terms' and accuracy of English expression.[6] Well into the nineteenth century, officers were still beholden to munshis for complex translation which involved, for instance, verses or literary allusions. The Company's decision to expand the use of English and Hindustani in official business after 1837 was a measure of this continuing frustration.

Alongside the steady, if uneven, acquisition of skills British policy began to develop a routine and a set of guiding assumptions. A 'political mind' began to reveal itself during the wars against Mysore and the Marathas. Wellesley himself propagated a much stronger sense of

---

[4] Edmonstone to his brother (WAE), 9 Jan. 1790, Edmonstone Papers, Add. Mss. 7616/1 (grey loose-leafed vol.), CUL.

[5] C. Danvers, M. Monier Williams et al. (eds.), *Memorials of Old Haileybury College* (Westminster, 1894), pp. 16, 23.

[6] Edmonstone to his father, 18 April 1798, Edmonstone Papers.

imperial mission. His official documents explicitly linked empire-building with the climactic struggle against revolutionary France. More formal organisations for espionage against French personnel and French allies in India were created at the highest level.[7] Edmonstone, followed by John Adam, established the Persian Office as a central intelligence directorate and hived off certain classes of public document, such as diplomatic reports and maps, to confidential sections of the secretariat.[8] For a few years, the Governor-General's private office became a forcing house for political talent and a repository of intelligence which functioned in parallel with the Governor-General's council[9] and independently of the Court of Directors. There was also a perceptible improvement in the quality of intelligence available in Calcutta and London. Regular subject files were created on individuals and topics[10] and the Mughal-style register of titles became another agency through which to check on the dispositions of Indian politics.[11] Rennell's mapping project, now directed from London, began to collate military route plans with diplomatic intelligence.[12]

The government also began to shape information and create propaganda in a more concerted manner. Indian regimes had proclaimed their legitimacy by acts of piety and beneficence, or through routine verbal formulae in charters of appointment. Colonial propaganda was constructive and self-conscious, even if it yet reached relatively few of its subjects. Government printing increased considerably. Wellesley's Persian code of regulations, in which Edmonstone and a number of key munshis had a hand, was intended to be a statement of abstract principle and also an affirmation of the benevolence of British rule which stood beyond 'partiality and favour'.[13] The government determined to lead Indian opinion and issued aggressive proclamations against recalcitrant Indian rulers. In a more positive vein, Wellesley hailed the introduction of vaccination to India between 1803 and 1805 as a particular achievement of British 'benevolence'.[14]

---

[7] British agents spying on the French passed information via Aleppo and Basra to Surat, Bombay and Calcutta, see HM 469.
[8] Edmonstone's memoir of his career in India, Edmonstone Papers, Centre of South Asian Studies, Cambridge.
[9] Wellesley's minute on his private office, 20 Jul. 1801, BC 128/ 2375.
[10] e.g., 'notes on Europeans and Asiatics', HM 556, 557.
[11] The *aiqabnamas*, see, S.A.I. Tirmizi (ed.), *Index to Titles, 1798–1855* (Delhi, 1979), pp. 1–3.
[12] J. Rennell, *Memoir of a Map of Hindoostan or the Moguls Empire* (2nd edn, London, 1785), Introduction.
[13] Edmonstone to his father, 19 April 1798, Edmonstone Papers, 1, CUL.
[14] 'Proclamation in native languages explaining the nature of the "vaccine disease"', Medical Board to GG in Council, 29 Mar. 1803, BC 169/ 2985.

In the Anglo-French wars, 1793–1815, public propaganda and misinformation played a major part. The French published captured documents which were intended to chart British intrigues against the French Empire.[15] The British replied in kind. Official reports from India implicated French officers serving with Mysore, Hyderabad and the Marathas in a worldwide republican conspiracy. The Calcutta government meanwhile became increasingly secretive. More actively involved in the surveillance of its foes, it defined treason more sharply. The government justified censorship of the British press in India on the grounds that critical or radical comments might give comfort to Britain's enemies.[16] Meanwhile, Wellesley and his aides fomented a propaganda campaign in Britain, where a suspicious Parliament and Court of Directors had to be convinced of the need for further costly wars. Semi-official compilations such as *Oriental Repertory* and the *Asiatic Annual Register* were intended to propagate a positive view of the expansion of British dominion. In India, William Kirkpatrick, for example, followed by Mark Wilks accumulated great detail on the supposed 'intrigues' of Tipu with the French and other powers,[17] in order to justify the aggression against Mysore and other enemies. Those in the administration who dissented, such as Joshua Uhthoff, Assistant Resident at Pune, were reprimanded and silenced.[18]

Edmonstone and Adam called into being a demonology of Indian politics which used Indian sources to justify territorial expansion by painting a picture of British strategic weakness. The office mentality so created exercised its sway up to 1857, and even beyond. The key principle was the vulnerability of the British main artery along the Grand Trunk Road and the Ganges Valley. Protection of this route was believed to require vigorous intervention against all adjoining powers. A hostile Punjab, aided and abetted by French or later Russian intrigue, was the worst nightmare. Punjab must therefore eventually fall to British power,[19] but before the happy day of British conquest, the Company would remain vulnerable to a combination between the Punjab and the states on the northern and southern flanks of the Ganges routeway. Residents and their intelligence agencies subjected the Maratha courts

---

[15] Noticed by J.M. Siddiqi, *Aligarh District. A Historical Survey* (Aligarh, 1975), p. 314.

[16] e.g., Wellesley to Dundas, 21 Mar. 1799, E. Ingram (ed.), *Two Views of British India. The Private Correspondence of Mr. Dundas and Lord Wellesley: 1798–1801* (Bath, *c.* 1969), pp. 235–6.

[17] 'Intrigues of Tipoo Sultaun', Kirkpatrick Papers, F228/7.

[18] e.g., J. Uhthoff, writing that Tipu acted 'with common prudence and self-defence', had his despatches censored, W. Kirkpatrick to J. Uhthoff, 8 Mar. 1799, Wellesley, Add. 13,587, BL.

[19] Pte letter from Capt. Mathews to Actg Adjutant General, 3 May 1808, HM 592.

and Maratha princely exiles the towns of Kanpur, Allahabad and Banaras to intense surveillance. While the Hindu–Sikh connection was thought to be guilefully hostile, the Muslim states were wholly and irreconcilably anti-British. Delhi 'that greatest seat of sedition in Hindoostan',[20] had links through the former imperial families in Lucknow and in new Muslim conquest states, such as Tonk, established by the adventurer Amir Khan in central India. The British also anticipated unlikely alliances between Pathan cavalrymen and their old rival, the imperial house of Delhi, and between recalcitrant Hindu Bharatpur and the Rohilla Muslims.

According to the political mind, the mechanisms of these intrigues and alliances were religious connections. Pilgrimages were believed to provide important opportunities for seditious meetings. More insidious were the wandering holy-men who were revered by roving Indian irregular cavalry. The British hoped they could defeat such combinations by deploying orientalist skills, drawing on the wisdom of sound munshis, and by carefully monitoring the opinion of the bazaars in Banaras, Lucknow and Delhi.

Indians entered these intelligence skirmishes with relish. Aware that money and status awaited them if they could uncover a convincing conspiracy, informants fed misinformation into the British intelligence system. A good example of this was the purported attempt of 'Mirza Jungly', brother of the Nawab of Awadh, to turn the British against his brother Sadat Ali Khan in 1807–8.[21] Key players in the plot were the families of Mahomed Baker Ali, chief munshi at the Lucknow Residency, and Munshi Mahomed Sadik. This was a branch of the important Hughly-based connection to which we alluded in a previous chapter. Mahomed Baker 'had the confidence of the British government' and was 'a confidential moonshee, a description of servants of whom Col. Collins [the former Resident at Lucknow] stood in need, on account of his own defective knowledge of the languages of the country, Mirza Bauker being well versed in the English language'.[22]

These two munshis had supposedly been encouraged by Mirza Jungly to write letters which implicated the Nawab in all the worst intrigues the British authorities could imagine. He was accused of maintaining a clandestine correspondence with Amir Khan, the Pathan cavalry leader, Holkar the Maratha enemy of the British and the Raja of Bharatpur,

---

[20] G. Cunningham to Mr Ellis, 24 Sept. 1831, 'Rammohun Roy's representation on behalf of the King', HM 708.

[21] 'Intrigue by Mirza Jungly against his brother the Nabob', ext. from Bengal Pol. Cons., 15 Sept. 1809, BC 248/ 5584.

[22] Secretary's Report on the examination of Mahomed Saudik and Mirza Bauker', Bengal Pol. Cons., 4 Jan. 1808, ibid.

whose forces had humiliatingly defeated them in 1805. One letter claimed that the Nawab was harrassing British merchants; it reported that he wished to secure the return of the city of Allahabad, ceded to the Company in 1802, and was filled with 'aversion and enmity' towards his British masters.[23] The letter, however, appears to have been a forgery designed as part of a plot to blackmail Mirza Jungly. The authorities in Calcutta interviewed the key conspirators and obtained letters in the hands of the Kazi of Hughly which apparently revealed dissension within the family about the plot. The incident gave rise to a debate about the truthfulness of indigenous informants and the reliability of the writing offices. Edmonstone confessed he could not believe that Baker Ali was capable of such deception, but recorded with approbation the remark of Mahomed Sadik that 'as this was Hindoostan no reliance could be placed on the people of the country'.[24]

A similar case involved a 'clandestine and mysterious intrigue', apparently carried on by Raja Ranjit Singh of the Punjab, Maharaja Holkar and Amrit Rao, the Peshwa's brother, through the agency of a Sikh chieftain who had obtained permission to make a pilgrimage to the holy places of the Ganges.[25] The suspect pilgrimage of Mohur Singh was brought to Edmonstone's attention by Thomas Brooke, Agent at Banaras, who was given to superabundant conspiracy theories. Here again it appears that the informant, Shor Singh, had carefully fabricated the whole enterprise to tempt the emerging political service in the hope of financial reward. Brooke, however, took the bait. He made a mental link between the pilgrimage and the rumoured marriage between Ranjit Singh's son and a daughter of the ubiquitous Raja of Bharatpur. He found it particularly suspicious that Mohur Singh had stopped on his journey at a place near Kanpur in the Doab 'where there resides a very holy man, who is, I am informed, the centre of all intrigues. It is from this part of the country our enemies draw their supply of men.'[26] The informant alleged that a harkara from Lahore had arrived in Banaras and was attempting to make contact with the expatriate Maratha prince, Amrit Rao, and that the city was full of ominous rumours against the British. According to an intercepted letter, money was changing hands as Sikh and Maratha business houses transferred funds by credit note. Brooke's imaginings were no doubt intensified by severe heat and a minor earthquake in Banaras.[27]

[23] J. Baillie, Resdt Lucknow, to Edmonstone, 23 Nov. 1807, ibid.
[24] Extracts Bengal Pol. Cons., 4 Jan. 1808, ibid.
[25] GG to Metcalfe, 11 July 1808, HM 592.
[26] T. Brooke to Edmonstone, 4 June 1808: cf. same to same, 1 Jul. 1808, ibid.
[27] ibid.

At this point Edmonstone, the cool Scottish counter-revolutionary, took charge, aided by Brooke's namesake, W.A. Brooke, an older and more experienced officer. Panic was damped down. Thomas Brooke was informed of the danger of surmising 'imaginary but plausible plots'. While the 'disposition to receive such information and the practice of rewarding informants will produce a constant succession of reported plots', a balance must be struck, for 'closing systematically every avenue to secret intelligence would be imprudent in the other extreme'.[28] Instead, further checks were carried out. Bazaar contacts revealed that the money transactions were perfectly ordinary. The story of the runner was reckoned false because he claimed to have made the journey from Kabul with implausible speed. Maulvi Abdul Kadir Khan intervened to pour oil on troubled waters. Most important, the accumulating expertise of the former Persian Office, now Political Department, in Calcutta was enlisted to show that the suspect letter was 'most uncultivated in style' and that the seals were different and the strip of holding paper had been added later.[29]

Periodic information panics of this sort occurred throughout the early nineteenth century. The British became very uneasy during the Nepal,[30] Burma[31] and Afghan wars[32] and at the time of a revolt in the Punjabi city of Multan in 1848.[33] In each case, officials believed that a threatening power beyond British India's borders was in secret communication through religious intermediaries with disaffected powers to the north or south of the Gangetic valley. Seditious forces were uncovered in major cities and officials anticipated discontent in the native army. The irony was, of course, that this merely plausible 'orientalist construct' finally proved to be a premonition. In 1857 a Maratha prince, exiled in a city on the Ganges, combined with disaffected states to the north and south of the valley. Local-level religious leaders proved to be relentless opponents of British rule, and Delhi emerged as a focus of revolt. In this, as in so many other respects, colonial knowledge represented a partially accurate reflection of Indian society and politics distorted by the fear and greed of both colonisers and colonised.

Meanwhile, educational and literary institutions extended the

[28] Edmonstone to Brooke, 30 June 1808, ibid.
[29] 'Memorandum respecting the credibility of a supposed intrigue between Rajah Runjeet Singh and Amrut Row', Procs. Secret and Sept. Dept, 15 Sept. 1808, ibid.
[30] e.g., Rutherford to Adam, 1 Oct. 1814, HM 645..
[31] Resolution of the GG in Council, 5 Nov. 1824, re. the 'spirit of turbulence' in India, HM 663.
[32] e.g., *Delhi Gazette*, 7 Oct. 1841, 5 Feb., 20 Jun. 1842.
[33] *Friend of India*, 16 Dec. 1848; *Mofussilite*, 30 May 1848.

memory and expertise of the state. Fort William College in Calcutta[34] and Haileybury in Britain provided basic training for future civil officers and accumulated larger and more comprehensive holdings of Indian texts than all but the largest Indian libraries. The seizure of Tipu Sultan's library after the fall of Seringapatam gave the British access to a vast new resource of Persian, Arabic and Hindustani texts. The several thousand works it contained were removed to Fort William College. They were then catalogued by Charles Stewart, Assistant Professor of Persian at the College, and deposited in what became the Library of the Board of Examiners, Fort William. Some of the manuscripts, or copies of them, were later taken to Haileybury, probably by Stewart, who became Professor of Oriental Languages there. Others found their way into the Library of the Asiatic Society of Bengal or ultimately to Oxford, Cambridge, and the British Museum Library. This collection of several thousand volumes had been partly built from collections which the Mysore Sultans had seized from their enemies. One large deposit had been captured from the Nawab of Arcot and reflected that state's keen interest in mystical Islamic religion.[35] The Arcot library was a kind of treasury of the lives and sayings of Sufi saints, whose traces gave symbolic cohesion to the state.[36] Other large collections consisted of Arabic and Persian histories and travel accounts and the genealogies of Afghan and Mughal families, which may well have served diplomatic purposes in the pre-colonial kingdoms.

Stewart's catalogue of the library dwelt on Tipu's collection of religious polemic, especially anti-Hindu and anti-Christian polemic.[37] In this, he was contributing to the retrospective justification of the destruction of Tipu's kingdom which was being mounted by Wilks, Kirkpatrick and others. Other 'Mahomedan tyrannies' were also implicated. In all these cases, Indian data and texts were being used to support a colonialist realpolitik. The information and the texts were not in any sense false; they were generated locally and not from a colonial literary matrix. It was the loss of context which occurred as they were appropriated by Calcutta and Haileybury and then returned, abstracted, to the subcontinent, which constituted the 'orientalising'.[38]

[34] Wellesley's minute on College of Fort William, Wellesley, Add. 13,862, ff. 13–31, BL; the 'military academies of France' were a specific model, f. 29.

[35] e.g., Ghulam Abdul Qadir Nazir, *Bahar-i-A'zam Jahi*, tr. S. Muhammad Husayn Nainar, *Sources of the History of the Nawwabs of the Carnatic*, IV, (Madras, 1950).

[36] S. Bayly, *Saints, Goddesses and Kings. Muslims and Christians in South Indian Society, 1700–1900* (Cambridge, 1989).

[37] C. Stewart, *A Descriptive Catalogue of the Oriental Library of the late Tippoo Sultan of Mysore* (Cambridge, 1809), p. 45.

[38] This is, in fact, perfectly compatible with Said's position, *Orientalism*, passim, but later commentators have sometimes implied that any knowledge of the 'native' is impossible.

The growth and imperfections of revenue knowledge

During the first century of British rule, land-revenue emerged as the determining discipline through which the conquerors 'knew' Indian rural society. Evidently, that knowledge was sufficient to the extent that the Company was able to extract from society a massive share, amounting to up to a quarter or more of the value of gross agricultural produce.[39] The receipts from land-revenues dwarfed the profits of British trade with India. From 1806 to 1830 the real rate of revenue per acre may have increased by about a quarter. Yet this policy cannot be said to have been knowledgeable about the inner workings of the rural economy. 'India cannot rise under the present level of taxation', wrote Ellenborough in 1829,[40] and could not therefore afford the produce of British looms. Hundreds of thousands perished in famines in 1833 and 1838. Allowing for hyperbole, a 'melancholy revolution' in landed property did afflict sections of the rural service classes. Agrarian discontent, very widespread throughout north India in the 1830s, was eventually to bring down the Company's regime in 1857, the ultimate proof that its knowledge was defective or partial.

Under the Indian kingdoms revenue management had become an administrative art. The redistribution of grants and rights to revenue remained but one aspect of a much wider science of kingship, whereby the ruler sought to build up networks of political obligation. Under the Company, revenue knowledge was gradually to be separated off, along with agriculture, into a special area of economic information, more divorced from political, judicial and military knowledge.[41] Failures to pay revenue which would once have been written off as grants-in-aid became 'revenue balances'. These increasingly led to the auction sale of underlying proprietary right. In the 1830s and 1840s government abolished grants of revenue and differential rates which had once accrued to holy-men, servants of the state, higher caste landholders and other favoured groups. Accountancy rather than political patronage was henceforward elevated to the top of the hierarchy of administrative skills.

When the Ceded and Conquered Provinces (later NWP) were first settled, this radical separation had yet to take place. Jonathan Duncan's early revenue settlements of the Banaras region (1787–95) had been

<hr />

[39] E.T. Stokes, 'Bentinck to Dalhousie: the rationale of Indian Empire', unpub. paper for 'Study Group on Policy and Practice under Bentinck and Dalhousie', in present author's possession.

[40] Ellenborough to Bentinck, 19 May 1829, C.H. Philips (ed.), *The Correspondence of Lord William Cavendish Bentinck* (Oxford, 1977), I, *1828–31*, 199.

[41] David Ludden, *Agricultural Production and Indian History* (Delhi, 1994), Introduction, pp. i–x.

driven by many principles of the older political economy.[42] Duncan still felt beholden to rely on the former state servants as informants because it was believed that they could interpret the 'ancient constitution' of the respective divisions of the Mughal Empire. Duncan therefore ordered his collectors to accumulate evidence on customary rates of revenue from the 'Canungoes of each pergunneh, and from Cazees, Chowdrees and the most creditable inhabitants of each pergunneh and from the papers of the year 1187 of Raja Cheyt Singh's management'.[43] In general, he sought out creditable and well-born witnesses who could attest to earlier practice. Although he was often rebuffed by the Maharaja, who was understandably jealous of the intruder's power, he found two able informants in Ali Ibrahim Khan and Maulvi Umer Ullah. Both men were members of Mughal administrative families and they were appointed as Judges in Banaras and Ghazipur respectively. Umer Ullah represented the political understanding of his class when he asked the Resident to prohibit the impressment of ordinary people by British troops, whose drunkenness and brawling 'is the occasion of many disputes, disturbances and difficulties'.[44] Drunkenness, 'calumny' and unseemly brawling were blemishes on the face of an irenic polity in the tradition of Akbar.

For his part, Duncan betrayed a deist and classical cast of mind by introducing matters of virtue and benevolence into his revenue arrangements. In Jaunpur he tried to protect the 'descendants of pensioned literati' who still 'retain a considerable degree of learning, and nothing but philosophical pride induces them to live wholly retired in their houses'.[45] He interrupted his revenue arrangements with a morally-inspired campaign against the Rajputs of Bhadohi who were accused of threatening suicide or killing their elderly females in acts of blackmail intended to secure lower rates of taxation for themselves. Duncan denounced their enslavement to 'passions, or ideas of policy' which got the better of their 'reason and religion' and induced them to kill themselves and their old women.[46] He promulgated a special regulation against this practice. It was issued under the kazi's seal and posted in 'Hindee' and Persian on the door of every government building[47] in an unusually vigorous assertion of the state's function as moral regulator.

The days of philosopher kings in either the Scottish or Indo-Islamic

---

[42] K.P. Mishra, *Banaras in Transition 1783–95* (Delhi, 1972), pp. 38–95.

[43] J. Duncan, 'Measures Connected with the Settlement of the Province of Benares', A. Shakespear, *Selections from the Duncan Records, 1787–95*, I (Banaras, 1873), p. 8; cf. 'Report from the Kanungoes', Procs. Resdt Banaras, 7 May, 1794, vol. 55, UPCRO.

[44] *Wajib-ul arz* of Maulvi Omerullah, Procs. Residt, Banaras, 27 Jan. 1788, UPCRO; also Shakespear, *Selections*, II, 131.

[45] ibid., II, 142   [46] ibid, I, 61.   [47] ibid.

tradition were transient, however. Duncan's revenue arrangements and the temporary settlements made between 1802 and 1826 in the Conquered and Ceded Provinces were generally hijacked by powerful nouveaux riches who could combine capital and revenue knowledge. In Banaras the exemplar for this group of men was Mehendi Ali Khan, 'a Persian adventurer'[48] who had already established himself as a major revenue holder for the Company. In 1787 he coerced Duncan into continuing his special terms by threatening suicide himself. Over the next few years his influence grew so great that he became an acknowledged indigenous expert. In 1794 he answered a series of questions from the Resident 'on the state of interior arrangements of the settlement', which became a model for later discussions of revenue in the eastern districts. He explained the sociology and property holding conventions of Rajput landholders in the exact manner of earlier Mughal administrators, but, apparently, he did not dwell on the duties of government to the subject as Reza Khan and his pupils had done. Ramchandra Pandit, another new man who had become the Company's opium contractor, supplied similar dispassionate information on the cultivation of that crop.[49] He was able to give the Resident a full historical account of the Dutch opium trade in the region in the early eighteenth century. His sociology of caste also fed into later colonial descriptions. The Koeris who cultivated the crop were, according to his minute, 'the lowest of the four general tribes of the Hindoos' and were thus known because they grew '*koyrar*, opium, tobacco and vegetables'.[50] He did not, however, mention, or was not asked to mention, the relations of patronage and protection which had once tied together specialist agriculturalists and agrarian magnates.

When Henry Wellesley took over large parts of Awadh from the Nawab in 1802 most of the former collectors of revenue withdrew taking their papers and even in some cases the registrars' papers with them.[51] Over the next decade the British were heavily dependent on nouveaux riches revenue contractors and local writers who could present themselves as experts in the districts. The result was an industry of forgery, enormous peculation and corruption on the part of these interests who falsified revenue papers and title deeds to help themselves to large holdings of land rights, particularly in the Districts of Allahabad and Kanpur.[52] Indian clerks and informants who became landlords and

[48] ibid. I, 27.
[49] For this family of entrepreneurs see K. Chatterjee, 'Collaboration and conflict', *IESHR* 30, 3, 1993, 283–310; Mishra, *Banaras*, pp. 51, 144–5, 148; above, p. 87.
[50] Shakespear, *Selections*, II, 159.
[51] e.g., Collector, Bareilly, to H. Wellesley, 18 Jan. 1802, Wellesley, Add. 13,566, BL.
[52] 'Rent-free tenures', *Friend of India*, 7 Jan. 1836, on forgery in the aftermath of Awadh

promoted their kinsmen as British collectors endeavoured to extract as much as possible from the land. It is not surprising, then, that considerable social and tenurial change was hidden from their eyes. Whole classes of people and descriptions of rights never fully surfaced into view.[53] The undiscovered included household slaves in large Muslim households, and bonded serfs, especially in areas such as south Mirzapur District, where such people were mainly of tribal or very low-caste origin.[54] Women's place in the labour process was hardly understood, and high-caste women were generally invisible until starvation forced them onto the exiguous public relief works during the 1833 and 1837–8 famines.[55] Many classes of sub-tenure holder were similarly ruled out of court by British concern for unitary proprietary rights. Torture by subordinates and racist brutality by British personnel lay well beyond the official ken, or was denied cognisance.[56] While it may be true that in the 1880s the British knew more about their great agricultural populations than any other government in the world, as officials often boasted,[57] this was certainly not true before 1840. These massive gaps in comprehension were slowly remedied by the new official desire for statistics which took hold under Lord William Bentinck and became pressing after 1857. Most important, however, was the growing volume of Indian land litigation which came into British courts after 1830. A new class of Indian pleader came to challenge the monopoly of revenue-knowledge once maintained by the office clerks.

The army as institutionalised knowledge

Even while the British element in the governmental machine in India remained small and widely stretched, the army was becoming a

Cession; but see also, P. Treves to Duncan, Apr. 1789, G.N. Saletore, *Banaras Affairs*, I (Allahabad, *c.* 1959), 105–10, for the history of forgery in north India since Jahangir. This report, apparently drawn up by Ali Ibrahim, provides further evidence of growing 'literacy awareness'.

[53] M. Bhargava, 'Perception and Classification of the rights of the social classes: Gorakhpur and the East India Company in the late eighteenth and early nineteenth century', *IESHR*, 30, 2, 1993, 215–37.

[54] e.g., Banaras Revenue Report, para. 61, Resdt to Govt, 25 Nov. 1790, Duncan Records 16, UPCRO.

[55] S. Sharma, 'The 1837–8 Famine in U.P.: some dimensions of popular action', *IESHR*, 30, 4, 1993, 337–70.

[56] But examples slip through: 'good fun, burning villages!' remarked H.H. Spry of a campaign against the Bhils, *Modern India with illustrations of the resources and capabilities of Hindustan* (London, 1837), II, 119; F. Shore reported British soldiers beating 'blackfellows', Private Journal, 8 Mar. 1829, Mss. Eur. E 307/2, OIOC; Spilsbury's Irish friend generally 'licked', i.e. beat, his servants, G. Spilsbury to E.A. Spilsbury, 9 Aug. 1813, Mss. Eur. D 909/1, OIOC.

[57] W. Crooke, *The North-Western Provinces of India* (1897, repr. Karachi, 1972), p. 303.

powerful, centralised body. It was not only a weapon of terror, but also a large accumulation of institutional knowledge. The European part of this army was no longer a 'passive instrument' but claimed 'the privileges of a citizen' and increasingly presented its views in the public arena.[58] A subaltern noticed that European soldiers became strikingly more literate in the years 1800–30.[59] Meanwhile, large communities of Indian specialists – armourers, salt-petre refiners, horse-keepers, provisioners, carpenters, builders – were employed by it. Literacy among ordinary Indian troops was low, but still much higher than in the population at large and the government attempted to ensure that Indian non-commissioned officers were literate.[60]

The Indian army did not have an organised commissariat until the early years of the nineteenth century,[61] but it rapidly became a most important store of information available to the colonial state, rivalling the civilian service. A shadowy figure called the superintendent of resources appears in the campaigns of the Bengal Army up-country during 1802–5.[62] This officer was apparently responsible for assessing and locating the quantity of grains, fodder, fuel, boats and other items needed by different units. His tasks required close links with horse- and cattle-dealers, grain merchants, ferry- and boatmen. Lists of appropriate merchants who could be trusted in the commissariat business were maintained in consultation with district officers.[63] The army developed close relationships with the controllers of ferries and the tribal watchmen (*paik*s and *ghatwal*s) who had customarily brought information to the Mughals on the movements of their enemies.

This system was centralised and bureaucratic by comparison with that of earlier Indian armies. Previously, individual nobles and war-band leaders had been responsible for equipping their own troops and had often secured supplies from their home landholdings. Most horses in the army were in the possession of members of war-bands, though rulers maintained select stables. Large-scale supplies for moving armies were acquired by foraging and looting, through client groups of Banjaras and other specialists or by farming-out contracts. The new military organisation encouraged the emergence of large-scale, officially approved

---

[58] 'Address to the Officers of the Indian Army', *East Indian United Service Journal*, 5, 1, 1833–4, i.

[59] Shipp, *Memoirs*, III, 79.

[60] Minute on the education of Indian soldiers, 20 Nov. 1828, Bentinck Papers, Mss. Eur. E424/4, OIOC.

[61] Wilson, *Madras Army*, III, 339, 353; IV, 495.

[62] See, e.g., R. Barlow to H. Newman, Superintendent of Resources, 25 Feb. 1818, Banaras Rev. Misc. 24, ff. 76–8, UPCRO.

[63] Bayly, *Rulers*, pp. 217–18.

contractors such as Lala Dharma Das of Agra,[64] or the famous commissariat contractor of the 1840s, Lala Tori Mull. Such magnates monopolised sources of military supply because they were able to control the supply of information to the army. A significant proportion of the later colonial business and clerical elite emerged as military contractors.

In 1822 it was enacted that the Officers of the Commissariat should 'enlarge their enquiries into the resources and capabilities of their respective districts, so as to afford the fullest information on all points connected with military supply'.[65] Their future advancement would 'depend on the zeal and intelligence they may exhibit in developing the resources of the Districts in which they are employed'. Thus regimental commissariat archives were built up during the same period that the records of the magistrate and collector expanded to meet the demand for information generated by the Parliamentary scrutiny of the Company's Charter in 1813.[66] In theory at least, these officers were intended to be experts. No officer was eligible to be appointed until he had passed 'the examination in Native Languages as an Interpreter'.[67] Later, following peculation during the Sikh wars, these skills were made mandatory and officers had to be certified in their 'facility in reading gomashtahs' [agents'] accounts, as presented in Persian or Hindee and in writing purwannahs in the above languages'.[68] Ever increasing concern about corruption and cabals in the Bengal Army had inclined the authorities to try to get a firmer grip on their Indian subordinates in the same way as the civil administration had tried to control the munshi.

Through force of circumstance, the medical knowledge of the army also expanded rapidly. Army medical officers, like their civilian counterparts, were the brains of the colonial establishment. About six per cent of soldiers were expected to need medical attention at any one time.[69] And after the cholera epidemic of 1816–25,[70] to which the army was particularly vulnerable and of which it was the major carrier, the authorities had become even more vigilant. Indian physicians had been

[64] ibid., pp. 214, 314.
[65] Governor-General's Order, 14 Nov. 1822, Commissariat Officer's Manual, 1860 (a compilation of regulations since 1800), p. 327, Military Department Records, [L/Mil] 17/5/1841, OIOC.
[66] This resulted in the census activity connected with the 1813 revision of Charter, preserved in HM 557.
[67] Governor-General's order, 20 Apr. 1835, Commissariat Manual, p. 303, Military Dept Records. [L/Mil] 17/5/1841.
[68] GGO 16 Sept. 1851, ibid. p. 306.
[69] 'Military minutes' 1836, Auckland Add. Mss. 37,714, f. 60 BL.
[70] R. Steuart and B. Philipps, *Report of the Epidemic of Cholera which has raged through Hindostan and the Peninsula of India since August 1817* (Bombay, 1817).

attached to indigenous armies, but their services had been voluntary and were paid for by the individual soldier or his commander.[71] The scale of the new military medical establishment was of a different order. Army medical officers were among the most prolific rapporteurs on disease and theorists of its origins. The large quantities of drugs required by the troops made them avid students of pharmacopoeias and they were among the best connected with Indian physicians who were employed as 'native dispensers'.[72] Lower-ranking Indian specialists – setters of bones, barbers and bleeders, occulists – were taken on as native medical orderlies. Such people provided the nexus through which aspects of Indian medicine were assimilated by the Army and techniques of Anglo-Indian medicine were diffused back into the general population. The cantonment bazaar became a critical focus for the emergence of new, syncretic knowledge communities. By the 1830s, the Army was attempting to produce its own drugs and to set up a laboratory where Indian workmen were employed.[73]

The scale of information and remedies accumulated considerably. By 1840 the army had a well-developed system for the purchase, storage and use of 'Bazaar Medicines and Hospital Necessaries'. Regulations laid down the quantities of medicinal drugs required by Indian and European regiments. A European regiment, for instance, was supposed to hold 1,000 leeches for one month, while a native regiment could make do with a mere 200.[74] The majority of these 'medicines' were in fact commodities such as lime juice, asafoetida, ginger, arrowroot and camphor which would ordinarily have been used in Indian cooking as well as medicine. The extensive use of Indian remedies saved expensive imports of medical supplies from Europe and helped to preserve the older Indian understanding of medicine as a method of improving 'biomoral substance', associated with cooking.[75] Army commissaries drew on the large and complex trade in drugs and natural medicines which connected the subcontinent with the whole of Asia. Groups of men of the gardener castes and tribal people were employed by individual detachments. This, again, had the effect of spreading the money economy into more remote parts of the country.

The army was also at the forefront of the investigation – indeed, the

---

[71] W. Irvine, *The Army of the Indian Moghuls. Its organisation and administration* (Delhi, 1962), p. 25.
[72] Crawford, *Medical Service*, II, 101–23.
[73] 'Asiatic medicines can be substituted for those of South America and Europe', 29 July 1836, Auckland Add. Mss. 37,714, ff. 24b–49b, BL.
[74] Commissariat Manual, [L/Mil]17/5/1841, pp. 282–3.
[75] F. Zimmermann, *The Jungle and the Aroma of Meats. An ecological theme in Hindu medicine* (Berkeley, 1987).

invention – of Indian vernacular languages. Medical officers, like their civilian equivalents, were required to be proficient in Persian and the vernacular. The Bombay Army's experiment in providing European interpreters for every regiment as a check on the activities of regimental munshis and Indian non-commissioned officers was followed in the Bengal Army. Prizes were given to subalterns for learning Persian and the vernaculars.[76] In particular, the Army spread and formalised Hindi written in the Devanagari script. One of the first books every printed in the 'Hindui' language and the Devanagari script was The Soldier's Manual for the Use of Infantry of 1824 and 1828.[77] The soldiers from Awadh used this form of the language and it was soon agreed that medical officers should be proficient in Hindi, not necessarily in Persian or Hindustani written in the Persian script.[78] Another branch of the service which had to work in the Devanagari vernacular were the officers attached to the Trigonometrical and revenue surveys. These departments needed to record the names of villages in Devanagari. The Trigonometrical Survey's form of Hindi transliteration was soon adopted as one of the first formal systems. Benefiting also from missionary efforts, it had become the standard form by the 1840s, ousting John Gilchrist's earlier and cumbersome form of transliteration of Hindustani from the Persian script.[79] Hindi had other redoubts of influence in the Indian states, the commercial communities and the world of the pandit.[80] The colonial military authorities were, nevertheless, a powerful set of allies for it.

The Company's Stud Farm at Pusa in western Bihar also illustrates the growth of institutional as opposed to embodied knowledge within the army. The Mughals had made elaborate arrangements for guaranteeing the provision to the army of good quality horses.[81] They patronised horse fairs and encouraged zamindars to breed horses by means of a system which guaranteed a purchase price at half of an independent valuation (the nisfi system).[82] Imperial officers monitored breeding and an imperial standard brand was provided. Many surviving texts in Persian, Sanskrit or Hindi concern the diseases and care of horses and

---

[76] e.g., Delhi Gazette, 8 Sept. 1849.
[77] J. Harriot, Soldier's Manual for the use of Infantry in Nagri and English Character, I (Calcutta, 1824), II (Serampore, 1828); cf. 'Superintendent, Government Press, Calcutta, ordered to print certain military treatises', BC 229/ 5158.
[78] Military Correspondence Regarding Language Training (c. 1812), Milit. Dept Records [L/Mil]5/ 390 (128), ff. 85–6, OIOC.
[79] e.g., Boileau, Narrative, p. vi.   [80] see below, pp. 295–300.
[81] Gladwin, Ayeen, I, 205–12; Irvine, Moghuls, pp. 49–52; J. Gommans, 'The Horse Trade in Eighteenth Century South Asia', Journal of the Economic and Social History of the Orient, 37, 3, 1994, 228–250.
[82] ibid.

elephants. Elephant mahouts and horse-breeders became politically influential because of their special knowledges.[83] Indian regimes are often seen as agrarian states, but in an important sense they also remained military-pastoralist states. Horsemen from beyond the frontiers of the arable were essential allies for them, gaining honour and wealth in return for protection of royal routeways.

The Pusa Stud inherited some features of this system. Much initiative was left with zamindars, and the Stud's informants included Pathan horse dealers from Rampur and the patrons of the Hajipur horse fair in Bihar[84] whose ancestors had traded animals and exerted influence across many generations. Under Major William Frazer's superintendence (1805–13) the system broke down; the zamindars wrested control from the Stud and the quality of the horses gradually declined.[85] This resembled the typical life-cycle of a Mughal institution in which knowledge and control tended to decay after a generation or two, with zamindars or other magnates building up patrimonial holdings within its shell. But in the longer view, the Pusa Stud was witness to a considerable expansion of information and control. Under William Moorcroft, the Stud became a point of interchange for veterinary knowledge from all over Europe, southern Africa and Asia. The central Asian journeys of Moorcroft and his assistant, Mir Izatullah, were ostensibly scientific expeditions in search of information about sources of cavalry horses, though in truth they became espionage exercises accumulating political data and exotica. Several of Izatullah's family and connections were trained in geographical and animal observation. The vast scale of the Pusa Stud farm, which totalled about 5,000 acres, made of it a potent source of agricultural innovation – and disruption – in the neighbourhood.[86] New varieties of oats for fodder were domesticated in India; new types of canal irrigation were introduced well before the great north Indian canals were planned. Moorcroft and his Indian aides also treated the families of the horse-breeders as well as the animals themselves. Rigid forms of capitalist accountancy were introduced under pressure from the Military Board in Calcutta.[87]

The Company also reached out uneasily to men on horseback through its connections with Skinner, Gardner and Hearsey, leaders of irregular cavalry who preserved the traditions of Mughal cavalry.[88] This had a political purpose because it absorbed pockets of cavalrymen who might

[83] e.g., Saadat Yar Rangin, *Faras Nama e Rangin, or the Book of the Horse by Rangin*, tr. D.C. Phillot (London, 1911).
[84] Alder, *Beyond Bokhara*, p. 114.   [85] ibid., pp. 95–6.
[86] ibid., pp. 99–107.   [87] ibid., pp. 94–107, 192–209.
[88] S. Alavi, *The Sepoys and the Company* (Delhi, 1995), pp. 232–63.

otherwise become disaffected plunderers.[89] Nevertheless, the scale of the operation was smaller than it had been under the Indian regimes. Thousands of men and horses were laid off without employment. 'Arabomania' – the craze for Arab horses among Company officers[90] – led the British to neglect Indian breeds and breeders. Men on horseback beyond the fringes of the arable were regarded as potential banditti. If some of the technical knowledge of the horse-rich communities was learned by colonial veterinary surgeons, their political influence was set at nought in the Company's counsels. This was the context for the exaggerated fears about 'pindaris' (predatory horse) and the alienation between horse-soldiers and the Indian government which caused it much grief from the Tipu's days to the Rebellion of 1857.

Two other important knowledge-gathering institutions connected with the army were the Board of Invalids and the Survey. The Invalid institutions comprised one of the first attempts by the British to order and regulate information about the lives and social background of ordinary Indians. Regimental rolls of recruits were systematically maintained after about 1790. The army also wished to reward and sustain its veterans, establishing invalid *thana*s, or veterans' colonies, which helped maintain the flow of recruits and plant out colonies of useful subjects in dangerous tracts.[91] Because pensions were paid out to soldiers and dependents miles from the nearest station, the military authorities built up personal 'character books' on sepoys and a wide-spread network of surveillance in invalid thanas and recruiting villages. Harkaras were sent to discover whether military pensioners were still alive or whether relatives and others were impersonating them.[92] Former soldiers, planted out in colonies, provided information for the use of recruitment agencies and, in some cases, police intelligence. While the 'loyalty' of old soldiers could never be taken for granted, Indian non-commissioned officers and police remained a critical source of information and political advice for the British through until 1947. It was in the army that many of the first systematic surveys of the health, food and physique of Indians were carried out after 1830. Here was elaborated the first, tentative classification of castes, tribes and racial types. Even if these classifications had little direct relationship to the real

[89] 'Extract Secret Letter from Bengal 21 Aug. 1815', [L/Mil] 5/378, f. 219, ff., OIOC; cf. Adjt Genl to Govt, n.d. May 1815, ibid., ff. 251–5, on Skinner's information and contacts.

[90] Balfour, *Cyclopaedia*, 'horse'; Gommans, *Indo-Afghan Empire*, pp. 96–9.

[91] W. Sleeman, *Rambles and Recollections of an Indian Official*, ed. V.A. Smith (London, 1915, repr. Karachi, 1973), pp. 640–4.

[92] S. Alavi, 'The Company Army and rural society: the invalid thanah, 1780–1830', *MAS*, 27, 1, 1993, 164–8, passim.

policies of recruitment and control, they were an important forcing ground for the colonial anthropology which was to emerge in the later nineteenth century. During the Nepal War for instance, an officer commented that the Pathans were best in attack, Mewatis in retreat, Jats as sharpshooters, and the standard Bengal infantry for slow unspectacular advances.[93]

Though the Great Trigonometrical Survey of India was partly a civilian operation, proceeding in splendid isolation from the more mundane process of building up village maps and revenue surveys, it did act as a conduit for colonial knowledge. This military knowledge was now canvassed regularly in public through *The East Indian United Service Journal*.[94] Surveying techniques were taught at Addiscombe and in Fort William College and the Madras Military Institution.[95] The construction of survey towers and the complex political relations which attended every leg of its progress required a huge effort of human surveillance quite apart from the geodesic and astronomical calculations which were its stock in trade. The expertise of Survey officers in assimilating information about local societies was utilised on many political missions unconnected with the survey itself. Assistant surveyors of Eurasian and Anglo-Indian background were trained in trigonometry and record keeping, while Indian craftsmen at Calcutta, Delhi and Hyderabad were taught how to make and repair the surveying instruments.[96] The Survey of India was probably not of immediate practical value to the British revenue or political authorities. Rennell's maps, which represented a simple accumulation of route plans, continued to be used by military and political officers.[97] The perception of India as a measurable and representable space, however, had a profound longer term effect on Indian society itself. As early as the 1850s, maps were being used by plaintiffs in court cases against British Magistrates and collectors.

'Ground-level imperialism' and local knowledge

In the North-Western Provinces the pacification was still proceeding in the second and third decades of the nineteenth century. Compared with

[93] 'Memorandum of questions with Lieut. Young's replies, respecting irregular corps', Feb. 1815, HM 652.
[94] *East Indian United Service Journal*, 1, 1833–4, i–iii.
[95] M. Edney, 'The patronage of science and creation of imperial space: the British mapping of India, 1799–1843', *Cartographica*, 30, i, 1993, 61–7; M. Edney, 'British military education, map-making and military "map-mindedness" in the late enlightenment', *The Cartographic Journal*, 31, 1, 1994, 14–20.
[96] Phillimore, *Survey*, IV (Dehra Dun, 1958), 24, 62.   [97] ibid., 115.

Bengal, indigenous government had itself become fragmented and decentralised, especially on the Maratha and central Indian marches.[98] Detailed information only became available during the anti-Pindari and anti-bandit campaigns of the 1810s, and through the first organised revenue settlements a decade later. Political information remained military in character. Fast-moving cavalry columns sent out spies while local magnates sent letters to the military and civil authorities tracing the movements of these marauding bands. One commander recognised the danger that 'embarrassment of the public service' would result from the 'transmission by local British authority of every crude and exaggerated native report of the movement of the Pindaries'.[99] Colonial administration remained peculiarly vulnerable to rumours and rumour-mongering not only among its subjects, but also among its own officials.

As the British imposed greater political stability, information-collecting agencies became more effective. Equally, though, the biases, misconceptions and gaps in surveillance of the Company's system became more obvious. In the localities the old communities of knowledge retained much influence. In district offices the writer communities (the *amlah*, or the munshi khana) survived and sometimes prospered. The lack of deep linguistic knowledge among officials and the complex overlapping of written instruments in hybrid language put the chief government clerks into a more powerful position.[100] The munshi khana took root, as it were, using paper to befuddle its colonial masters and also to maintain a whip hand over peasants and merchants. It was this sponge-like capacity of the writer establishments to resist change which caused officials to direct periodic purges against 'the corruption of the amlah' and Anglo-Indian newspapers to demand that Indian head clerks and police chiefs should be replaced by European non-commissioned officers or Indian Christians.[101] It also generated a mountain of paper. An Assam hill raja sensibly asked David Scott, the administrator who was trying to introduce this paraphernalia into Assam, why he wrote down all judicial transactions, including plaints, defence and evidence, when this merely played into the hands of the clerks. Scott replied with false naivete: 'Swurgo Deo, you are of celestial origin, and can recollect everything.

[98] 'Notes on the Police of the N.W. Provinces', *Benares Magazine*, 6, 1851, 851–4.
[99] Extract Pol. Letter from Bengal, 7 Jul. 1817, 'Supposed invasion of the Pindaris', BC 603/ 14491.
[100] See, e.g., on problems of multiple translation, Commr Delhi to C.T. Metcalfe, 16 Oct. 1818, Sinha (ed.) *Ochterlony Papers*, pp. 91–5; the classic work is R. Frykenberg, *Guntur District, 1788–1848. A History of Local Influence and Central Authority in South India* (Oxford, 1965).
[101] *Panchkouree Khan, or Memoirs of an Orderly*, about Indian corruption, appeared in *Benares Recorder* after a spate of letters about peculation on the part of local officials, e.g. ibid., 4, 8 Dec. 1846.

We are earth-bound, and when we go to dinner forget what we have heard in the course of the day.'[102]

Beyond the collectorate or police post the existing patterns of watch and ward and intelligence communities survived, though the British tried, with limited success, to rationalise them. Up to 1840, police organisation remained fragmented. Bodies of para-military musketmen communicated with the exiguous police establishment at subdistrict headquarters, usually by letter and runner. These badge-wearing police agents themselves relied on the reports of semi-official intelligence agents, pilgrims, wandering holy-men or merchants as of old. During the Nepali attack of 1814, for instance, police officers in the far frontier derived much of their information from bodies of pilgrims ('Jatterees', *yatris*) who were moving to the ritual bathing places on the river Gandak.[103] In frontier areas of the North-Western Provinces or Awadh, forest-watchmen or bantirias drawn from Rajput hunting castes had continued to patrol the extremities,[104] supported on small land-grants. They often could not be prevailed upon, however, to provide 'the slightest assistance or information' to their masters.[105]

In plains north India, the local police agent or irregular musketmen relied for reports on a variety of village and township watch-and-ward agencies. In big cities the thanadar of the respective quarters controlled a variety of night-watchmen and informants established on roads and markets.[106] The night-watchmen represented the lowest level of the former imperial power, their night-time cry being 'In the name of the Emperor and the Company.'[107] Night-watchmen also often doubled as town-criers and messengers, announcing official proclamations, orders and prohibitions by beat of drum. The authorities tried to regularise and provide public revenue for a watch-and-ward system which had been funded hitherto by the subscription of the neighbourhood. This caused the house tax riots in Banaras in 1810 and the Rohilkhand towns in

---

[102] N.K. Barooah, *David Scott in North-East India 1802–31. A Study in British Paternalism* (Delhi, 1970), p. 134.

[103] Daroga of Pali, Gorakhpur, 28 Dec. 1814; Daroga of Nitchloul, 30 Dec. 1814, HM 649.

[104] Trans. of a report from the Thanadar of Keykowlee, 21 Dec. 1815; cf. report from Thanadar of Jalla, 24 Jan. 1815, ff. HM 649.

[105] Commander in Chief, Terai, to Ahmuty, 26 Nov. 1805, 'Adjustment of territorial disputes between the Company and the Nepal government', BC 204/ 4600.

[106] e.g., 'Translation of a report on the manner in which the night watch of the police is conducted in Benares in 1781', Duncan to Shore, 18 Mar. 1795, Proceedings Resident Banaras, UPCRO, also printed in Saletore (ed.), *Banaras Affairs*, I, 125–38.

[107] R. Cavendish, Resdt Gwalior to Govt, 10 Jun. 1833, 'revolution at Gwalior', BC 1402/ 55492 (2), OIOC.

1816–17.[108] The townspeople feared that both taxation and policing would give rise to unseemly surveillance. Undoubtedly a degree of routine and regularity was introduced into urban policing by the British. The system, though, remained a pre-colonial one, and estimates of local officials suggested that the vast majority of cases were locally unreported and went unrecorded by the police. A set of reports from the Kotwal of the city of Lucknow survives from the years 1797–8.[109] These record mundane occurrences of theft and violence: an affray between two tradesmen in love with the same boy, a theft by a slave-girl from her mistress, the theft of a raja's Ganges water pitcher, and so on. Thieves were kept at the police-post until punished; debtors were only imprisoned at the behest of substantial complainants. Reports from the 1830s in British-controlled towns suggest that papers were now kept in standard and statistical form.[110] In addition, terms of imprisonment were longer and punishments were more regularised. In other respects routine police surveillance does not seem greatly to have increased or to have become much more effective.

In the countryside the watch-and-ward system remained part of the specialist service agencies supported on percentages of the revenue or grain heap. Going by a variety of names – chaukidars, goraits[111] – these rural watchmen were usually of humble birth or outcaste status and combined menial jobs and message-carrying around the village with official surveillance duties. They answered to the village officers, elders or local zamindar, and were responsible for calling the villagers to the public office and the village accountant whenever required. The British tried, without a great deal of success, to subordinate them to police power and enlist them into campaigns against female infanticide, widow-burning and illicit liquor distilling.[112] The communities of locally-based runners often overlapped with the watch-and-ward agents, reflecting the indigenous idea that informational services formed an inter-locking package. Thus, for instance, in the Banaras region the gorait was a watch-and-ward agent for the community and an informer to the police. He also delivered incoming letters which were passed on from the headquarters post office through the police. It was not until the 1860s that the authorities tried to replace goraits with regular

---

[108] W.W. Bird, Act. Magt., Banaras to Govt, 28 Jan. 1811, and attached 'Petition from the Hindoos and Mussulman of all classes from Saurung Paunee', Saletore (ed.) *Banaras Affairs*, II, 144–55; Bayly, *Rulers*, pp. 323–9.

[109] '*Akhbarat-i Kotwali-yi Lakhnau*', 4 Muhurram 1212 to 17 Dhu al hijjah, 1212, Bodleian Library, Add. Pers. Mss. 2356; Ethé, *Catalogue of the Bodleian*, p. 2,356.

[110] See below, fn. 130.   [111] Wilson, *Glossary*, p. 183.

[112] 'Panchkouree Khan' asserted that this officer was 'called *go-right* because he always *goes-wrong*', *Benares Recorder*, 26 Oct. 1847.

postmen.[113] These community watchmen derived information from unofficial sources, particularly the midwives and barbers who arranged marriage alliances, announced births, marriages and deaths to chief inhabitants, and generally kept up with village gossip.

Knowledge gaps and information panics

The information system of the Company's government in the North-Western Provinces before 1850 was thus a dual one. At the upper levels, in the revenue, machinery, army and political service, a considerable concentration of information and power had been achieved. At the lower levels, however, the older system of decentralised intelligence communities continued. Where they had not decayed altogether they continued to produce imbalanced, uncoordinated and incomplete information. The knowledgeable communities were weakly integrated with the new institutions. The link between state-level and community information systems, always weak, could easily be severed. This happened during the 1857 Rebellion. Much later this form of disjunction reappeared, as British authority began its final disintegration in the region after 1918.[114]

British ignorance in the peripheries can partly be attributed to their failure to avail themselves of much of the contextual richness of the pre-colonial rulers' systems of information. With the exception of Eurasian cavalry officers like Hearsey and Skinner, they were less able to tap into the patterns of ordinary Indian family life, as had all earlier rulers. They also neglected other sources of affective knowledge. For example, they gradually withdrew from involvement with Indian religious institutions, classically a potent source of advice on the body politic for Indian rulers. It is true that Elphinstone and Walker both listened in on information collected by Hindu and Jain abbots and by heads of local Sufi shrines. Archibald Seton at Delhi in 1807 also 'assisted at the meeting of Peerjadas and dervishes',[115] the Sufi notables, and solicited advice on an impending religious dispute between Jains and Muslims. In the process, he visited the school of Shah Abdul Aziz, the leading purist teacher of the city.[116] Missionaries with roots in local convert communities did, of course, provide considerable linguistic expertise and, in the Rebellion of 1857, invaluable political information. Still, as Christians, the British

[113] Board of Rev. to Govt, 30 Nov. 1865, NWP General Procs., 25 Aug. 1866, 179, 438/ 28, OIOC.
[114] On the weakness of the link between *barkandazi* and village watchman, 'Report of the Police Committee', *Friend of India*, 17 Jan. 1839.
[115] A. Seton to Edmonstone, 30 Jun. 1807, 'Disturbances at Delhi', BC 217/ 4758.
[116] ibid.

were slowly retreating from that almost tactile feeling for popular mood which came from participation in Indian worship. The earlier Mughal officials had actually participated in the meetings (*majlis*s) among the faithful which accompanied the Islamic fasting month. They had gone with the Emperor in procession to Lal Kot, thus observing the state of the villages in the environs of the capital. They had processed in the Mohurrum festival, sponsoring *tazia*s (floats) themselves, even when Hindus. But according to a Maratha spy, even Metcalfe, who sometimes processed in Mughal royal pilgrimages, had refused to participate in Holi celebrations on the grounds that 'it was not our festival'.[117] H.H. Spry stated that only European doctors understood the 'prejudice, feelings and domestic manners' of the people. Other officers refused to enter Indian houses 'partly in consequence of the official stiffness of an English functionary', and partly 'for fear of incurring the taint of corruption'.[118] The decline of this affective knowledge of Indian society accompanied the demotion of the officers of advice and counsel (the kazi, mufti and muhtasib). These now became mere subordinate functionaries or, in villages, quasi-castes, having forfeited independent official competence. Progressively the kazi had ceased to be a judge and counsellor of rulers; he became merely a member of a Muslim 'caste' who married people.[119]

The change is marked in the decline of the use of documents which conveyed community knowledge to the rulers. These were the mahzars and surathals, 'general applications or representations'[120] by respectable people cognisant of local circumstances. Documents such as these were still used in the early phases of British rule,[121] but appear much sparser by the 1840s. This may reflect the demise of the sense of state-fostered moral economy as the old Muslim and Rajput gentry declined, and religious authority was distanced from colonial rule.[122] Petitions coming directly to the magistrate's office continued to represent popular grievances. It would be wrong to romanticise pre-colonial government which was often corrupt and oppressive. But under Company rule, police snoopers and the commercial proteges of the government grew in power. In Metcalfe's Delhi system, cohorts of male and female sweepers

---

[117] Thompson, *Metcalfe*, p. 149.
[118] Spry, *Modern India*, II, 247; cf. Heber's remarks on the exclusion of Indians from British society, *Narrative*, II, 11.
[119] Wilson, *Glossary*, p. 272; cf. G. Ansari, *Muslim Caste in Uttar Pradesh. A Study in Cultural Contact* (Lucknow, 1960), p. 61.
[120] Wilson, *Glossary*, pp. 320–1, 494.
[121] e.g. surathal, 12 Oct. 1803, 'attested by the signatures of the Mohrer of the Canongoes and others', 'Rebellions in the Districts of Etawah, Cawnpore, etc.', BC 169/ 2954.
[122] Report of Magt., Allahabad, 1 Sept. 1814, HM 776.

paraded daily at the police office to report doings in peoples' houses; under Mughal government information from such sources was solicited rarely and discreetly.[123]

The decline of affective knowledge went hand in hand with the decline of patrimonial knowledge – the understanding of local circumstances which came from having a direct ownership of property in a region. British indigo planters and merchants were constantly interrogated by officials. John Gilchrist and his partner, Charters, of Jaunpur became vital informants for government[124] and, in the case of Gilchrist, went on to make a major contribution to oriental studies. Landowners with strong European connections, such as Begam Samru, or James Skinner, could still function as intermediaries of great importance.[125] Skinner's compilations 'The History of Castes' and the 'History of Notables' of the Hariana region ('Taskirat-al akvam' and 'Taskirat-al umara')[126] were vital keys to local society, reproducing the material of Persian histories in a form which could be used by revenue officers. Yet sources such as this were unusual. Compared to other colonial societies, where official information was powerfully supported by the expertise of colonists and planters, the administration was often working in a vacuum.

The British were by no means wholly ignorant of the society they were ruling. Conversely, the formal structures of information gathering did not necessarily give them a coherent insight into its workings. Their knowledge was patchy, incomplete and liable to atrophy. They were better at picking up warnings about insurrections than understanding the inner workings of Indian institutions. Colonial knowledge, far from being a monolith derived from the needs of power, existed on different levels which were imperfectly linked.[127] There was the level of formal, learned and abstract knowledge which has become associated with the term orientalism. There was also a level of practical, *ad hoc*, 'satisficing' administration which was not embodied in texts or procedures and

---

[123] Thompson, *Metcalfe*, p. 122; 'Delhi Report', HM 576, OIOC.

[124] e.g., Gilchrist and Charters, Ghazipur, to Duncan, Procs. Resdt, Banaras, 22 Jan. 1793, vol. 61, UPCRO.

[125] See, e.g., James Skinner's detailed report on the likely reaction of different Rajput clans to the abolition of sati, Skinner to Benson, 3 Dec. 1828, Bentinck Papers, Mss. Eur. E424/4, OIOC; his Indian connections used in pursuit of murderers of William Fraser, *Englishman*, 28 July, 1835, *Friend of India*, 23 July 1835; also S. Alavi, 'The Makings of Company Power: James Skinner in the Ceded and Conquered Provinces, 1802–40', *IESHR*, 30, 4, 1993, 437–66.

[126] 'Taskirat-al Akvam' and 'Taskirat-al Umara', Add. 27,255, BL; Rieu, *Catalogue of BL*, I, 65–7; Skinner drew on Sanskrit and Persian sources in compiling these works.

[127] cf. D. Ludden, 'Orientalist Empiricism. Transformations of Colonial Knowledge', in Breckenridge and van der Veer, *Orientalism and the Postcolonial Predicament*, pp. 250–78.

worked on particular local circumstances. This level of coping with India has received less attention than the much-vaunted ideological constructions of its society associated with William Jones, James Mill or Henry Maine. Most of the great compilations of oriental knowledge were themselves inconsistent. Theory rarely absorbed and organised practice. Francis Buchanan's work on India and Burma, for instance, mixed volumes of entirely undigested and sometimes fanciful fact on rivers, forts, roads and markets with occasional forays into environmental race theory and denunciations of the Brahmins.[128] Of course, even the collections of revenue statistics were ideological constructs in some senses. They represented officials' notion of what an economy or a market was. These concepts differed from the indigenous *samaj* or *mandi*. Again, satisficing administration was ideological in the sense that it wished to save money and husband resources. It worked on a deeply recessed British theory of capitalist accountancy in contrast to the notion of protecting but also 'eating up' the subject as befitted an Indian king. Still, this unorganised operation of power made few pretensions to draw general conclusions about Indian society or to compare or contrast it with other societies. It is an error to believe that textualised, learned orientalism ever acted widely or deeply on society, unless its intentions ran with the grain of indigenous ideas or particular bureaucratic requirements or panics. Few officials or soldiers knew or cared about orientalist ideas even in a vulgarised form. The British, for instance, did not invent caste or construct religious identities *ex nihilo*. What they did was to provide conditions, practical and ideological, which allowed people to reproduce these forms of social power and division. British regulation and economic conditions then projected these taxonomies into wider arenas. Change resulted from an unequal dialogue between Britons and Indians.[129]

In the late eighteenth century the British continued, in general, to think about India as a series of polities, possessed of 'ancient constitutions'. By 1830 colonial debates had indeed come to emphasise 'caste' as a distinctive feature of India and much mundane reporting in the localities used caste categories. Pre-colonial political debate and practice was, however, shot through with concerns with caste. These were different from colonial preoccupations, but contributed to them. A feature of indigenous kingship was its duty to preserve the 'order of the castes'. A king's jurisdiction extended to arbitrating on cases of biomoral

---

[128] Vicziany, 'Botany and Imperialism', *MAS*, 20, 1986, 625–60; F. Buchanan, 'Burma Journals', HM, 687, OIOC.
[129] E. Irschick, *Dialogue and History. Constructing South India, 1795–1895*, (Berkeley, 1994), pp. 9–13.

transgression, as, for instance, when marriages between inappropriate partners could not be adjusted locally. The Peshwa's records are full of cases of this sort, requiring details of caste, sub-caste and degrees of consanguinity as detailed as anything which appeared in later British courts.[130] Secondly, political legitimacy required of eighteenth century rulers the protection of Brahmins, the revival of Kshatriya rituals, the amassing of vedic knowledge. The Peshwa's rule or the rule of the Maharajas of Banaras or Nepal were 'Brahmin states', not in the sense that this title recognised them as the dominant caste, but because they were protectors of *Brahman* and its embodied representatives, the Brahmins, who took the state's pious gifts.

Again, the Indo-Muslim states used caste designations in routine administration. Where taxes were levied on 'houses' of residents of a particular centre according to occupations, occupational/caste designations were recorded.[131] The reports of local officers and the representations of communities used caste as a form of identification. Thus an Indian watch-and-ward officer in Gorakhpur in the early nineteenth century could describe a village by saying that it was the habitation of the 'huntsman caste', the Kurwars; other houses were represented as those of Chamars (leather-workers) or Telis (oil-pressers) or Kurmis (peasants).[132] Nomadic people were always referred to with general 'caste' designations: thus 'Dusadhs, Tharus and Goalas'. On the other hand, the superior groups in the village were not identified by caste names; they were simply 'zamindars'.[133] Caste here was used as just one designator of social type, not the only or overridingly important one. Used also were honorific title (Sayyid, Sheikh, Rajkumar, darbari, etc.), lineage, historical association, or propinquity to Muslims saint or Hindu temple. The records of the Kotwal of Lucknow in 1797–8 make similar unsystematic use of caste names, referring at times to Nais (barbers), Khattris and Telis,[134] but elsewhere identifying people by profession, or by their position in the retinue of a particular notable. Caste designation was thus part of a grid which could locate people quite precisely and pass on information to a superior in remarkably few words. Caste

---

[130] S. Guha, 'An Indian penal regime; Maharashtra in the eighteenth century', *Past and Present*, 147, 1995, 101–26.

[131] D.P. Bhattacharya, *Report on the Population Estimates of India, 1820–30* (Delhi, 4 vols., 1962–5); D. Ludden, 'Agrarian commercialisation in eighteenth century south India', in S. Subrahmanyam (ed.), *Merchants, Markets and the State in Early Modern India* (Delhi, 1990), pp. 238–40, for the use of the south Indian *dehazada*, another Mughal-derived census form by the British.

[132] Thanadar's *arzis*, Jan. 1815, encl. in R. Martin, Gorakhpur to Adam, 14 Jan. 1815, HM 651.

[133] ibid.

[134] '*Akhbarat-i Kotwali-yi Lakhnau*', Add. Pers. Mss. 2356, Bodleian Library, Oxford.

designations tended to be used where caste impinged obviously on status, at the extremes of purity or pollution. Its use was inconsistent and it often overlapped with occupation (as in 'my caste is *mahajan*', where mahajan is no more than an honorific for merchants).[135] The word often used for 'caste' in north India was *qaum*, which also meant tribe, community or even nation. Caste designations were used in a similar way to that of numbers and quantities. Sometimes numbers were represented as precise fractions of rupees. Sometimes they were purely nominal, intending to convey 'a lot' (a *lakh*) or 'a little'. Sometimes, again, the numbers were traditional stereotypes, such as 'eighty-four houses of Brahmins'.[136] At all events, the measures used were not standardised and often difficult to correlate with each other. They did not attempt the systematised, generalised statistical view of modern information systems.

Until the 1850s and even beyond much British usage was equally ambiguous and unformed. Under the headings 'caste' were often included purely occupational or honorific designations. For example, the censuses thrown together by Boileau in Rajasthan in the 1820s were derived from and similar to the household enumerations (*khanashumaris*) of the Rajput kings, and used an equally wide range of sectarian, religious, caste and occupational categories.[137] The British revenue business was also constructed in gross caste categories, but this was usually a reflection of the differential revenue rates, tenancy forms or rates of payment in kind assigned to different 'castes' in the countryside. There were ways in which 'caste' had become more important to the British as a way of organising their knowledge of India. In cases brought before criminal courts, and, to a lesser extent civil courts, the castes of suitors, defendants and witnesses were now routinely entered in the records.[138] In the same way, the records of service of Indian subordinate officials routinely recorded caste and sub-caste. Such distinctions, however, only became fully embodied in social processes when they were validated and employed by indigenous agents.

Often the creation of oriental stereotypes was a reaction to fractious

[135] This was the answer given by a number of merchant caste people when asked about *jati* by British customs officials, see Conquered and Ceded Provinces Revenue (Customs) Procs., OIOC.

[136] Vicziany, 'Botany and Empire', 625–60; Guha, 'An Indian Penal Regime', 101–26.

[137] Boileau, *Narrative*, pp. 223–62.

[138] See, e.g., 'Local criminal intelligence', *Benares Recorder*, 11, 15, 18 Dec. 1846. The form of judicial enumeration, including 'sex', 'age', 'religion and caste', is also demonstrated in, e.g., 'Extract from the abstract statement of prisoners punished without reference to the Nizamut Adawlut by the Sessions Judge of Zillah Farrukhabad ... during the month of July 1834' encl. in Register, Nizamut Adawlut to Govt, 16 Jan. 1835, Agra Judicial (Criminal) Procs., Jan. 1835, 151, 231/12, OIOC.

events in India, or to conflicts between official and public objectives which had to be resolved by creating ideological categories. Thus when information panics and ideological frenzies overtook administration, as in the case of Thuggee, widow-burning, human sacrifice or witch-killing, it was evidence of the limitations of colonial power and knowledge, not the effectiveness of its projection on society. As with panics over witches, heretics, Jesuits and freemasons in Europe it reflected the weakness of the new quasi-bureaucratic state in its own hinterland rather than premeditated attempts to master society.

The margins of policing were, therefore, the nursery of practical orientalising where the social Other was discovered. The British regarded something as innocent as wrestling matches as dangerous because they were beyond their ken. In large cities such as Delhi, criminal bosses were said by 'experienced officers' to manage the police officers of the neighbourhoods through their emissaries and henchmen, the wrestlers (*pahalwans*).[139] People gathered at wrestling grounds (*akharas*) which were favourite leisure spots for the lower classes of the town. Gambling houses under the protection of the wrestlers paid off the local police, who had a 'fear of incurring the odium of the mohulla [neighbourhood]'. 'Like the thugs' these criminal gangs all had their own 'customs, meetings and modes of address'.[140] Above all, they had their own dak by which they communicated to cause robberies and affrays.[141] The gangs put spies into the cities who worked as 'artisans, tailors, or pigeon sellers', concealing their true occupation as criminals and seditionists.

In the absence of real intelligence or a fuller understanding of the society they were dealing with, officials took appearances and argot to be symbolic of character and intentions. A senior official in Patna wrote his reminiscences of twenty years' police work in an article on 'Bankas and Swindlers' which was published in the *Delhi Gazette*.[142] *Banka*s or swindlers came in three sorts, he said. There was the 'civil banka' or 'fop', the 'fighting banka' or free cavalrymen of declining status in the native armies, and the common or garden swindler. Of the second sort he remarked, 'Should the banka be a Hindu, if a spearman, he sports an anklet of gold or silver on one of his legs, if a Mahomedan, a small band of bright-coloured silk or cloth above the knee of his horse's near forleg.' In Lucknow the banka often distinguished himself by sporting 'Tartarian cow-tails, four of which ornamented the four corners of his saddle ...' These knight-errant bankas had sometimes offered single combat to British officers who had been forbidden to accept the challenge by Lord

---

[139] *Delhi Gazette*, 5 July 1837.   [140] ibid.   [141] ibid.
[142] 'Bankas and swindlers', ibid., 18 Sept. 1839.

Lake. The third group of 'villains' were particularly prominent in the city of Patna. One such was distinguished by his frizzed hair, his velvet coat of 'European not Chinese manufacture', his expensive shawl and pale green silk trousers. These swindlers, too, had a military character, and often disguised themselves and preyed on merchants. Yet one who has 'obtained some acquaintance with the exterior of native society' can pick them out by their 'tawdry and extravagant dress'. Unfortunately, the writer went on, in Patna 'where the Mahomedans are perhaps more lawless, insolent and licentious than those of any other city under British control' it was necessary to recruit 'third grade' bankas into the police.[143] The problem was compounded by two other features of the inhabitants of Patna. First, they were obsessive bird-fanciers; even labourers took caged birds with them to work. Swindlers made good use of this custom. They hid the jewelled slippers and other items which they stole from rich men in the cages and made off with their loot. Secondly, Patna's women were often involved with bankas. Despite their seclusion they could 'see and hear a lot of what is going on in a great city'. The villains would hang around *pan* (betel-nut) and sweet-meat shops and make contact with women who would pass on information to them about the merchants and their wealth.

These discussions of Indian criminality are revealing. The very retelling of them gave the authors a fraudulent aura of ethnological command, though this often proceeded from relative ignorance. Secondly, the style of presentation of this information was consciously literary: the picturesque and the picaresque were emphasised. The exotic variety of India was there to be enjoyed. It was a genre which was given full expression in Meadows Taylor's *Confessions of a Thug*.[144] Locally, it was superbly represented in the Patna school of miniature painting on micah or paper which vigorously depicted the tribes and castes, pirs and tazias, Gosains and Brahmins for the delectation of passing European travellers.[145] At the same time, there was anxiety. Patna was a cauldron of dissidence and criminality. The Europeans were panicked by the rumour of an uprising here in 1842.[146] Soon afterwards concern about the doings of Islamic extremists (the so-called Wahhabis) was to take root. This vibrant society of pigeon-fanciers and frizzy-haired

[143] ibid.

[144] Meadows Taylor, *Confessions of a Thug* (London, 1839); R. Singha, 'Providential Circumstances: the Thuggee campaign of the 1830s and legal innovation', *MAS*, 27, i, 1993, 83–146.

[145] M. and W.G. Archer, *Indian Painting for the British, 1770–1880* (Oxford, 1955), pp. 27–40.

[146] *Delhi Gazette*, 5 Feb., 20 Jun. 1842.

fops was also thought to be unknowable and dangerous. It had its own secret codes and languages, its own covert dak, its own places of congregation. Very often these panics about covert knowledge and secret communication were preludes to a demand that debased natives in government service should be replaced by 'upright' Eurasians, or even by European lower ranks, who could be relied on to pass proper information to the authorities in the interests of a freemasonry of Christian virtue.

The ordinary signs of character and personality in Indian life were annexed to the prose of criminality. The sweet-meat and pan shop, typical places where information was passed, became dens of vice. The 'Tartarian' cow-tails, a well-known sign of Mughal rank, became the mark of the banka. The courteous speech and 'extravagant style of compliment' of this post-Mughal centre of culture was a sign of untrustworthiness. As in later ethnographic compilations, abusive ditties which linked the 'Thugs of Kukulgaon', the 'Burglars of Bhagalpur' and the 'Perjurors of Patna'[147] were taken as native descriptions of social essence. In fact, they were the result of inter-regional one-upmanship expressed in terms of doggerel abuse. Still, there was no orientalism without fire. Recent research has shown that the decline of the city's eighteenth-century Muslim elite was precipitous.[148] Its resentment of the British and the mercantile nouveaux riches was savage, and was expressed in a variety of Urdu literary forms. The Wahhabi peril may have been a typical 'Green Panic' but Muslims in Bihar and eastern Hindustan were, in fact, embarking upon a programme of purification and self-strengthening which was coordinated by itinerant preachers and private letter-writing. Orientalism was a distorting mirror rather than a purely fictional construct.

This was evident in the case of the Thugs, the most celebrated case of orientalist myth-making. Thug 'language', carefully collected by W.H. Sleeman and his lieutenants and by Meadows Taylor, turns out to be working-class Hindustani slang.[149] The tight-knit religious organisation based on sanguinary Kali worship, was in reality a loose amalgam of militant Hindu devotionalism, goddess cult and Muslim tomb-worship. The fabled centralised direction of Thug bands was probably a myth; mobile robber bands simply moved where the pickings were best. In these cases the 'construction of the Thug' was clearly a reflection of current European ethnographic preconceptions – and their ambiguities. Indians were defined by religion; human communities by speech.

---

[147] *Delhi Gazette*, 18 Sept. 1839, cf. ibid., 13 Mar. 1839.
[148] Kumkum Chatterjee, 'Collaboration and conflict', *IESHR*, 30, 3, 1993, 283–310.
[149] Singha, 'Providential circumstances', pp. 117–19.

Community was an amalgam of environmental and racial features and opinion could wildly swing from one to the other. Thus H.H. Spry, Sleeman's cousin and admirer, presented in the 1830s with a Thug skull, cited the Curator of the Edinburgh Museum's observation that it reminded him of the skull of a slave-trading captain he once saw.[150]

On the other hand, the fact that racial ideologies were introduced into the colonial understanding of criminality by contemporary theory does not mean that no social phenomena were observed, or that the discourse was simply an adjunct to power. The Thug scare itself arose in the context of the western Ganges valley in the first twenty years of the nineteenth century; it was later rediscovered by Sleeman in central India, when the Government wished to intervene in the affairs of tributary princes without paying for full administration. In its first incarnation 'thuggee' arose from an information panic: the feeling of the fledgling colonial administration that it knew nothing of local society and that the locals were combining to deny it information. In Etawah, Thomas Perry, the magistrate and early theorist of the Thugs, observed in 1808 'the greater part of the inhabitants are extremely averse and in fact openly hostile to the forms and principles of our government'[151] and the 'total failure which has attended the ordinary excercise of authority'. Etawah was a frontier region, over which Mughals, Marathas and Awadh forces had fought. It was also a major routeway, close to the important shrines of Brindaban-Mathura. Unstable agriculture subsisted with rich commercial and religious interests. The system of village watchmen had deteriorated badly.[152]

Early in his magistracy Perry was faced with the looting of Rs 60,000, the total holding of the temple of Govindji at Brindaban, and became convinced that the richer inhabitants of his district were prey to organised criminal bands.[153] The first 'tribe' to be isolated were the Budheks. A female Budhek deposed that gangs went as far as Gaya and Patna to the east and the Maratha states to the south; they were protected by headmen. Given the lack of detailed intelligence from local sources, the Magistrate relied heavily on depositions from persons who had been beaten, or at least browbeaten, into giving evidence. In March 1810, one 'Ghulam Hussain, inhabitant of Khira Pergunneh, Shiko-habad', reported that a police officer had asked whether he was a 'thug' and had agreed that he was.[154] The word meant little more than 'cheat'

[150] Spry, *Modern India*, I, 169.
[151] T. Perry to G. Dowdeswell, Sec. Judl Dept, 9 Dec. 1808, Perry Papers, Add. Mss. 5375, Cambridge University Library.
[152] Perry to Dowdeswell, 20 Jan. 1809, ibid.
[153] Perry to Dowdeswell, 26 Nov. 1808, ibid.
[154] 'Examination of Ghulam Hussain', Perry to Dowdeswell, 19 Mar. 1810, ibid.

and was not clearly identifiable with the term 'Phansighar' or strangler which appears in some earlier and indigenous accounts.[155] In his letters of this period Perry alternated between small and capital 't' for the word and sometimes put it in quotation marks. During his first examinations, Ghulam Hussain only reluctantly speculated on 'thugs' or their organisation. He refused to discuss the murders of travellers saying 'I do not know. I have no reliance on the English, whether you intend to kill me or reward me. Therefore I shall not speak.'[156] Later, under pressure from Perry, the Government offered this 'novice thug' a pardon and on 11 April 1810, he made a second deposition under the title 'Translation of the Acknowledgement of Gholam Hossyn Thug'.[157] The concept now became more defined. Ghulam Hussain himself now greatly inflated both the range and the number of Thug bands and their murders. His second statement was followed over the following months and years by growing numbers of 'Thug' depositions which Perry used to put pressure on the government in a campaign to increase his police powers and budget. By 1815 'Thuggee' had been accepted as a specialised and organised crime and the Thugs had been endowed with a caste-like corporate status. Later, under Sleeman, the picture was further elaborated using approvers and reports from his Thuggee and Dacoity Department which generated its own brand of specialised knowledge. Indigenous verification of the Thug theory was sought from a munshi who associated the phenomenon with the collapse of indigenous regimes and the disbanding of their armies.[158] By now, the ideology was fully worked out: Thugs strangled their victims with a knotted silk scarf containing a coin and buried them with a particular style of entrenching tool. They were supposed to worship Kali and had their own special 'language'. None of these features, however, was as important to Perry. His 'Thugs' had usually buried their victims or indiscriminately thrown them down wells.

The creation of knowledge about the 'thugs' was influenced both by bureaucratic politics and by some emerging views about what Indian society was really like. It does not follow, however, that the Thug-finders were uncovering no social processes whatever. Murders and robberies took place in significantly larger numbers along particular routeways.

---

[155] Thevenot, *Travels*, p. 58; 'Tuzuk-i-Jahangiri' tr. Price, p. 57.
[156] 'Examination of Ghulam Hussain', Perry to Dowdeswell, 19 Mar. 1810, Perry Papers.
[157] Encl. in Perry to Dowdeswell, 11 April 1810, ibid; for the reception of the idea of Thug conspiracy by government and the courts, see, Bengal Criminal Judicial Procs., 18 Jan. 1811, 43–8, 130/27, OIOC.
[158] W. Sleeman, *Ramaseeana, or a Vocabulary of the Peculiar Language used by the Thugs* (Calcutta, 1836); cf. M. van Woerkens, *Le Voyageur Etranglé. L'Inde des Thugs, le colonialisme et l'imaginaire* (Paris, 1995).

Certain social groups were more heavily involved in organised robbery than others. Some historians have implicated peasant rebels protected by rural magnates in 'thuggee'.[159] A persuasive argument has been that Thugs were a loose collection of 'men on the road', disbanded Pindaris, irregular cavalrymen and their servants, or grooms without masters or patronage.[160] Certainly, one indigenous elite informant believed this to be the case, though his account was later elaborated by William Sleeman. Necessity forced the unemployed soldiery to robbery and murder in order to survive.

One significant feature of the depositions is the evidence of widespread physical and social mobility which they reveal. The 'Thugs' and their relatives drift in and out of service of the British and Indian regimes as watchmen, inferior police, and bodyguards. Kulloah was 'formerly a Durzee [tailor] afterward he became a Musulman and a "thug"'.[161] Other actors, both 'thug' and victim, were petty cloth and grain merchants and wandering iron-smiths. All travelled large distances, ranging between Patna and Rajasthan, Lucknow and central India, in search of service and income. Many had been temporarily in service with the Afghan cavalry commander, Amir Khan. This was, in fact, the inferior service and provisioning sector of the 'military labour market', described by Kolff,[162] in which both the Company and the Indian rulers were players. This, again, was a social formation with very flexible boundaries. One prisoner, on being asked the origin of 'Thugs', deposed that: 'Ever since the caste of Ufghans, Mewatties and Sheikhs have existed these class of people used formerly to resort to the habitations of those of the Munhar caste, who seeing the immense property that was acquired by them, followed their example.'[163] Evidence such as this recalls many other instances of rapid social change in north India following the settlement of mobile warrior people amongst specialised agrarian service castes. In the loose Hindu–Muslim, urban–rural, mixed-caste societies of entrepreneurs which came into being, parasitism and violence – 'Thuggee' to the British – speedily came into existence.

Surveillance and espionage might well be directed in a haphazard way against marginal elements, but when it came to the invasion of domestic space, the authorities were more circumspect. One of the main arguments for the total banning of sati was the corruption of the system of reporting which had been installed to ascertain when women were

[159] S. Gordon, 'Scarf and Sword. Thugs, marauders and state-formation in eighteenth century Malwa', *IESHR*, 6, 4, 1969, 403–29.

[160] R. Singha, 'Providential circumstances', 97–102.

[161] Trans. of deposition of Nidha, Perry to Dowdeswell, 24 April 1810, Perry Papers.

[162] cf. Kolff, *Naukar, Rajput and Sepoy*.

[163] Trans. of deposition of Nidha, Perry to Dowdeswell, 24 Apr. 1810, Perry Papers.

being burnt 'against their will'. Still, sati was always intended as a step to be taken in front of the community. In the case of female infanticide, secrecy was inherent in the act, and the possibilities of blackmail and corruption by the reporting authorities even greater. In Hindustan, the panic about female infanticide began early. Jonathan Duncan campaigned against it in the 1790s and the issue resurfaced several times through to the 1850s. Gujarat, where the status-conscious Rajputs of Cutch practised it on a significant scale, was the other place where it became a fractious issue, passing out of the realms of administration into those of ideology.[164] Missionary propaganda may have been the trigger for action, but female infanticide was highlighted at times when local authorities were seeking to control the independent high-caste rural communities who practised it. In both Hindustan[165] and Cutch,[166] there is evidence that Indian government servants from outside the district (Muslims and Marathas respectively) helped nudge the issue onto the British agenda either because they abominated infanticide or because they were locked in dispute with local magnates.

To the British, though, 'domestic surveillance' was objectionable and dangerous. It was objectionable because they were seeking to reconstitute the 'fallen' Rajput communities as rural leaders. Insulting them by calling on the testimony of wet-nurses, barber women and village-watchmen – all of whom were low-caste – could only compromise that aim. It was dangerous because the invasion of Hindu and Muslim domestic space in the interests of house taxation or disease control had caused outrage and resistance. 'A system of domiciliary espionage might be prepared to watch over individual cases of birth, and to warn the parents against the destruction of the gift of God.'[167] But this had never been introduced by any 'East Indian government' and 'would degrade the practice of it, and be revolting to those subjected to it'. Because Indian governments, as opposed to those of southeast Asia, had been uninterested in the tight control of personal labour, which was generally in plentiful supply, indigenous systems of domestic surveillance were weakly developed. On the other hand, the killing of children was an affront to the Company's policy of monopolising the power of life and death within its territories. What emerged therefore was an irregular

[164] K.B. Pakrasi, *Female Infanticide in India* (Calcutta, 1970).
[165] *The Missionary Register for MDCCCXXIV containing the principal transactions of the various institutions for the propagation of the Gospel* ... (London, 1824), p. 195.
[166] Pakrasi, *Infanticide*, pp. 22, 25, 27, 32, 37, 42.
[167] A. Burnes, 'Female infanticide in Cutch', *JRAS*, 1, 1834, 193; cf. 'Female infanticide among the Rajpoot tribes in Zillah Agra', *Selections from the Records of the Government, North Western Provinces*, XVI, (Agra, 1852), p. 171, on use of the 'gorait' to report on births.

system.[168] In some areas magistrates insisted that watchmen made regular returns of suspicious infant deaths. In others, these cases only came to court when domestic disputes intervened or attempts at blackmail by the local watch-and-ward establishment broke down.

British attempts to investigate and control the domestic sphere were stillborn. The early and quite limited liaisons between Indian women and British men came to an end. Unlike earlier foreign conquerors, the British denied themselves access to the knowledge, information and gossip circulating in the women's quarters. Thus half the Indian population remained virtually unknown to them. Well into the late nineteenth century, census returns on women and on children under five were wildly inaccurate.[169] Knowledge about Indian women, their life-styles and domestic circumstances was extremely sketchy. The few British doctors and missionary women who entered the women's quarters were appalled by what they took to be the light chatter and erotic banter they found there.[170] The quality of the story-telling and wit among the women, the role of bhakti devotionalism and *pir* cults, was virtually unknown until S.W. Fallon, the philologist, began to record a special 'women's language' in the 1870s.[171] Women as such, rather than women as symbols of tradition, hardly became visible until educational women's missions and a concern for prostitutes arose in those same years. Even then, the British remained remarkably ignorant about a critical area of social life, one where decisions were made and politics was sometimes incubated. This was in marked contrast to colonial Africa where more was known about African domestic life and women, who could sometimes be used as agents for Christianisation and westernisation.

Conclusion

Many pre-colonial Indian states maintained sophisticated archives with long institutional memories. Before the British came there existed cadres of state servants who possessed administrative skills and sought goals which transcended loyalty to the monarch of the day. British rule greatly expanded the density of institutions which collected and processed information to create yet longer social memories. Apart from the myriad overlapping civilian boards and commissions, British government

---

[168] 'Female infanticide in the Doab', *Ledlie's Miscellany and Journal for the North West*, 1, Jul.–Dec. 1852, 105–10.

[169] W.W. Hunter, *Annals of Rural Bengal*, I (Calcutta, 1868) p. 26.

[170] P. Chapman, *Hindoo Female Education* (London, 1839), p. 28.

[171] See below, pp. 358–9.

spawned knowledgeable bureaucracies in the army, police and medical service. Private citizens created oriental institutes, centrally organised business archives and cantonment libraries. The embodied knowledge of Indian specialists slowly gave way to this abstracted institutional knowledge, though mainly at the centres of government and commerce. Similar developments accompanied the emergence of the modern state and capitalist institutions throughout the world. In colonial societies, European rule gave this process a great impetus. The rise of the colonial discourse of religion, caste, race and criminality in India was a consequence of this more fundamental shift in the sociology of knowledge on the margins of government. It cannot be reduced to a simple instrumental relationship with colonial power. Oriental knowledge was one among a large number of specialisms which stood apart from society and surveyed, measured and categorised it. These other specialisms had originated in the contemplation of Ourselves as much as the Indian Other. Often, they were honed by application to nearer Others, the Scottish highlands, Ireland, the English working classes or southern Europe.

These institutionalised forms of knowing, however, were still influenced by people present – and presenting themselves – in Indian society. The colonial information order was erected on the foundations of its Indian precursors. For instance, indigenous police descriptions and sociological understandings of the classes of beings were incorporated into the British canon by means of the testimony of native informants. Of course, this information was reclassified and built into hierarchies which reflected the world view of the Britons of the early nineteenth century. Nevertheless, Indian sociologies, forms of religious thought and beliefs about criminality were active, not passive elements within these constructs, and Indians almost immediately began to critique them from the inside. This is not surprising because, beyond the purview of British institutions, the earlier indigenous networks of knowledgeable people – the runners, village 'intelligence communities', Sufi masters, tribal networks – survived traumatised, but recognisably the same. It was the juxtaposition of the two systems, one of embodied decentralised knowledge, the other of institutions and statistics, which explains a central paradox of colonial rule. So much processed and accessible information about India fell into the hands of the British: 'Our government is a peculiar one', Kipling was to write, 'it gushes on the information front.' But so much of Indian experience, philosophy and sensibility remained outside the purview of the rulers. This paradox was to be brutally revealed in 1857 when a government which now particularly prided itself on knowledge was revealed as unready and ignorant.

5   The Indian ecumene: an indigenous public sphere

So far this study has centred on the relationship between British intelligence establishments and indigenous informants, clerks and runners. By contrast, the following chapter is mainly concerned with communication and debate within the Indian population. India was a literacy-aware society if not yet a society of mass literacy. The elites and populace both used written media in complex and creative ways to reinforce oral culture and debate.[1] Here we try to describe the institutions, tone and scope of the controversies about politics, religion and aesthetics which existed across north India in the eighteenth and early nineteenth centuries. Colonial ideologues and leaders of Indian opinion sought to draw on this tradition of communication and argument when 'public instruction' and 'useful knowledge' became slogans after 1830.

These Indian debates were much more than religious polemic; they were both popular and political. The issues in contention related to religion, but in its public manifestation. They also concerned the interpretations of history and the obligations of indigenous and colonial rulers. Many of the diplomats and munshis we have encountered in Company service played a part in them. Rather than being collaborators with colonial rule, they regarded themselves as mediators between the people and the government, cajoling both towards correct conduct. These discourses on rights and duties informed a sphere of patriotic, public activity, which long predated the consciously nationalist public of the years after 1860, and was to determine its character to a considerable extent.

The Indian nationalism of the later nineteenth century needs a longer perspective. We need to soften the sharp break between tradition and nationalist modernity, and between East and West, which still impoverishes the historical literature. Excellent studies have shown that Indians passionately debated religion before the mid-nineteenth century.[2] Other

---

[1]   cf. R. Finnegan, *Literacy and Orality. Studies in the technology of communication* (Oxford, 1968).
[2]   Kenneth W. Jones, ed., *Religious Controversy in British India. Dialogues in South Asian Languages* (Albany, New York, 1992).

histories reveal how Indians represented shifts in political power through festivals and cultural performances,[3] but historians, following anthropologists, have often over-emphasised the importance of broad ideological principles such as segmentation and hierarchy; this has blighted intellectual historiography. Public opinion – the weight of reasoned debate – was not the preserve of modern or western polities. Ironically, as European observers occasionally admitted, the support of British military detachments tended to make Indian magnates less, not more amenable to the opinion of their subjects. The Indian versions of degenerate Roman emperors – the 'Caligulas and Commoduses'[4] whom Sir Henry Elliot scornfully denounced – were products of British tutelage rather than avatars of the Indian past. Many publicists of the later nineteenth century were drawing on techniques of communication, debate and persuasion which owed as much to Indian norms as they did to Comte or Mazzini. Even after 1885 western public debates had not altogether subsumed indigenous discourse about rights, duties and good kingship as some studies have argued.[5] Recent polemics against the 'derivative' character of modern Indian political ideology have not even begun to characterise indigenous political theory and practice. This chapter considers political theory, individuality, rationality and social communication in the Indian context. These, of course, are all essential elements in the concept of critical politics which developed in the West and they all find a place in Jurgen Habermas's influential discussion of the 'public sphere'.[6] All had analogues within the north Indian *ecumene*.

3 See the contributions in S. Freitag, ed., 'Aspects of the public in colonial South Asia', *South Asia*, 14, i, June 1991.
4 *Friend of India*, 26 Apr. 1849, extracts from *Biographical Index to the Historians of Mahomedan India*.
5 cf. D. Haynes, *Rhetoric and Ritual in colonial India. The shaping of public culture in Surat city, 1852–1928* (Berkeley, 1991).
6 cf. J. Habermas, *The Structural Transformation of the Public Sphere*, tr. T. Burger (Cambridge, Mass., 1992); cf. A.L. Kroeber, 'The ancient Oikoumene as a historical culture aggregate', *The Nature of Culture* (Chicago, 1952), pp. 379–95. For Byzantium, the term ecumene denotes an aesthetic, religious and political community. It expanded the ideal of *oikos* (household) into *koine* (commonalty) (cf. ibid., pp. 4–5). While retaining some sense of patrimonial power derived from the emperor and patriarch, it came to mean 'our common home'. Power here was 'representationally public' (ibid., p. 13), but this does not exhaust the meaning of public, because there was also public, political debate between clerics, philosophers and administrators. This was 'critical' and 'reasoned' in Habermas's sense (ibid., p. 24), though within broad cosmological assumptions (this is also true of the 'modern' West). In some ways the Indo-Islamic world had a clearer sense of 'public'. The ulama and other learned acted as public 'jurisconsults' and 'censors' giving a sense of public beyond the medieval Christian priesthood which was more 'corporate' and introverted in character. In India, however, no single word encapsulated this notion of ecumene; instead it is a composite of communities and groupings of male adults and their dependents: *shura* or *umma*, the body of 'believers'; *dar*, 'homeland' (as in dar-ul Islam), *badshahi* (the common home

I use the word ecumene to describe the form of cultural and political debate which was typical of north India before the emergence of the newspaper and public association, yet persisted in conjunction with the press and new forms of publicity into the age of nationalism. For classical writers, ecumene conveyed the sense of the inhabited or civilised world. In Christian times it came to mean a universal, godly civilisation embodied in a community of affection and constantly renovated through a discourse of worship, rights and obligations. Thus, according to the Oxford English Dictionary, 'the head of the Christian family or *oikoumene* was the Emperor in Constantinople'. Similar critical ecumenes existed in most complex civilisations of the era before print as an ideal of the 'godly city' and as a set of actual political processes. Their relationships to the later imagined communities of print and nationhood need to be examined with greater care.[7]

The ecumene of Hindustani-writing literati, Indo-Islamic notables and officers of state (which included many Hindus) fought its battles with a well-tested arsenal of handwritten media. The guardians of the ecumene represented the views of bazaar people and artisans when urban communities came under pressure. Their connections spread across religious, sectarian and caste boundaries, though they never dissolved them. A common background in the Indo-Persian and, to a lesser extent, Hindu classics enlightened them. The theme of high-minded friendship animated the poets, scholars and officials who conversed along these networks and set the tone for them. Though suffused with pride of country, the ecumene remained cosmopolitan, receiving information and ideas from central and west Asia as well as from within a dimly defined 'Hindustan'.[8] In this sense, it was closer in spirit to the groupings of philosophers, urban notables and officials in the world of late antiquity – the Christian-Greek ecumene – than it was to Habermas's modern public. His public sphere is more sharply separated from the world of intimate social relations; people's judgement is represented through marketed print in an almost mechanical way. The Indian ecumene, however, does bear comparison to the modern European public in the sense that its leaders were able to mount a critical surveillance of government and society. How was this possible in

of the emperor's subjects), or *sarkar* which implies 'public authority' (ibid., pp. 18–20), but comes to mean 'commonweal', implying an entity independent of the incumbent dynasty.

7   B. Anderson, *Imagined Communities. An Inquiry into the Origin of Nations* (Cambridge, Mass., 1993).

8   F. Robinson, 'Scholarship and Mysticism in early 18th century Awadh', in A.L. Dallapiccola and S.Z. Lallemant, *Islam and Indian Regions* (Stuttgart, 1994), pp. 377–98.

a world supposedly encompassed by religious principles and despotic kingship?

Ideologies and social critique

In political theory, the western public emerged from ideological debates which had contested and confirmed authority since the beginnings of Christendom. The dual inheritance of Roman Law and feudal liberties blunted the authority of both King and Pope. The Reformation encouraged personal interpretation of scripture in accordance with conscience. Superficially, 'Islam' and 'Hinduism' appear to weave seamless webs of authority, leaving no ideological space for the emergence of any species of critical public. Islamic Law was both canon and secular law, pre-empting the kind of contestation which developed inside Christendom. The Hindu order, at least as it is interpreted by Louis Dumont, subsumed the political order.[9] The individual will was subjected to the collectivity through the institution of caste and the pragmatics of purity and pollution.

Yet even in theory, still more in practice, authority within these Indian conceptual systems was actually quite friable and ambiguous. In Muslim thought the authority of the sultan was most uncertain and in the Twelver Shia tradition even verged on the illegitimate.[10] The sultan's power was limited by Islamic Law and the interpretation of the learned, but also by the collective authority of the tribe and the general assembly of believers. Sayyids and Sheikhs, who in India were supposedly immigrants from the Prophet's Arabia, claimed special status whether they were learned in scripture or not.[11] Sufi mysticism, which emphasised esoteric religious knowledge, also acted to limit the authority of rulers and clerics. Many Sufis distanced themselves from political power. Their tomb-shrines, headquarters of spiritual provinces, became alternative sources of social power.[12] They took on the title of *shah* or king, and secular kings tried to absorb their charisma.

Though little is made of this in studies of the western public, the notion of individual property right (as an electoral qualification, for instance) lies close to the idea of the public. In India, hereditable proprietary right (*watan, zamindari, milkiyat*) was not subject to

---

[9] L. Dumont, *Homo Hierarchicus. The caste system and its implications* (London, 1970).
[10] S.A. Arjomand, *The Shadow of God and the Hidden Imam* (Chicago, 1984).
[11] e.g., Shaikhs and Sayyids said the *fateha* (Muslim confession of faith) to the dying, Masson, *Narrative*, I, 240.; G. Ansari, *Muslim Caste in Uttar Pradesh* (Lucknow, 1960), pp. 38–9.
[12] R.M. Eaton, *Sufis of Bijapur 1300–1700: Social roles in Medieval India* (Princeton, 1978).

appropriation by the state as Enlightenment thinkers averred. This error was a consequence of the European obsession with Oriental Despotism, which confused the rights of office-holders with the rights of patrimony.[13] Religious donations also functioned as a realm of liberties outside the state's purview in a manner not unlike 'mortmain' in Christendom. It is within the religious corporation that some latter-day Weberians see the beginnings of both transcendent bureaucracy and civil society in Europe.[14] India does not seem to be an exception here. Most important, the notion of government (sarkar) came to hold a virtue beyond the will of the king of the moment, so becoming an equivalent to European 'public authority'.[15] This Indo-Muslim conception of government embodied sophisticated concepts of just and unjust rule, zulum ('oppression'), which could be introduced into popular debate on the merits of rulers through poetic satire, handbills, speeches and by ironic visual displays during popular festivals.

Even the authority of Islamic Law (Shariat) was ambiguous enough to leave room for personal judgement. The 'doors of interpretation' (idjtihad) of the Koran and Sayings of the Prophet were thrust ajar on many occasions in Islamic history. As more rationalistic and legalistic schools of jurisconsults emerged, the independent judgement of the massed doctors of law came to take precedence over both traditional interpretations and charismatic authority. For instance, in the Shia Usuli school of law which became influential in north India after 1780, the independently exercised opinion of the clerics gained increasing authority. In Awadh, the social links of the doctors of law with indigenous administrators meant that their judgements effectively became the opinion of the local political elite.[16] Individual scholars also claimed the right to independent interpretation. To take an example reminiscent of Galileo's struggle with the Church, when Tafazzul Hussain translated Newton into Persian, he was denounced as impious because religious authority still supported Aristotle's earth-centred theory of the universe. Tafazzul Hussain and his supporters, however,

---

[13] B.R. Grover, 'Land rights in Mughal India', *The Indian Economic and Social History Review*, I, 1, 1963, 1–23.

[14] Randall Collins, *Weberian Sociological Theory* (Cambridge, 1986).

[15] Habermas, *Public*, pp. 18–21.

[16] Juan R.I. Cole, *The Roots of North Indian Shi'ism in Iran and Iraq. Religion and state in Awadh 1722–1859* (Berkeley, 1988), esp. ch. 8; Usuli Shias, as opposed to the Akhbari school, emphasised the appeal to consensus, analogical reasoning and the ranking of oral reports on the basis of sound testimony. They sometimes opposed the Nawab and magnates and had deep roots in the qasbah gentry and bazaars of Awadh. They represented a social formation acting as a critical tribunal in matters of public doctrine.

drew on the Koranic verse 'Go even unto China to find knowledge', to argue their case for the heliocentric universe.[17]

The monolithic appearance of Islamic Law was also limited by the concept of custom (dastur). This could be extended to the customary law of Muslim tribes, the kanun or royal law, or even the customs of the infidel subjects.[18] In India, the local law officers adjudicated cases according to Islamic precepts, but Hindus were not bound to submit to their jurisdiction. As Ernest Gellner has shown, the interaction of tribal custom and mystical, embodied Islam (Sufism) created both a theoretical and a historical dialectic which underlay political change in Muslim societies.[19]

The theory of the Hindu Dharmic order was fragile to a similar degree. The purity of the Brahmin and hence his authority was compromised by his position in society. He could withdraw and preserve his purity, like the Sannyasi or renouncer,[20] or he could participate in society and its rituals and risk pollution. Both in theory and in practice, therefore, the Brahmin became a tricky, dangerous commodity, a thorn in the flesh of both king and layman. The non-Brahminism of the late nineteenth century public possessed a deep historical lineage in the popular critique of Brahmin pretensions in earlier centuries.[21] The authority of the king was also compromised. Killing made him unclean; yet he could only uphold Righteousness with the sword. Many verses written in interpretation of the classic political theories are implicit warnings to the king not to transgress the very limited bounds of his authority.[22] The king's authority, as Heesterman argues, was a conundrum; it was also friable.

These structural ambiguities of the key figures in the Indian hierarchy were compounded by two more general concepts which compromised the coherence of authority in general. First, there was the notion of Apadharma, or those conditions under which the ideal, righteous Dharmic order ceases to function. To a greater or lesser extent this idea was used to explain the world as it really existed in the present Age of Iron.[23] Apadharma could be introduced to legitimate violations of caste

[17] Rizvi, Shi'is, II, 228; Troll, Sayyid Ahmad, pp. 144–57.
[18] 'Kanun', Encyclopaedia of Islam. New edn, IV, 556–62.
[19] Ernest Gellner, Muslim Society, (Cambridge, 1981).
[20] J.C. Heesterman, The Inner Conflict of Tradition. Essays on Indian ritual, kingship and society (Chicago, 1985).
[21] E.F. Irschick, Tamil Revivalism in the 1930s (Madras, 1986), pp. 13–20; R. O'Hanlon, Caste, Conflict and Ideology (Cambridge, 1985), pp. 16–35.
[22] Prof. Heesterman remarked that slokas in commentaries on shastric texts on kingship often limited the role of kings even more closely than the rules of the Arthashastra; personal communication, 1992.
[23] P.V. Kane, History of Dharmasastra, II, i (Pune, 1974), 118ff.

rules, the suspension of religious ceremonies, the abandonment of hereditary occupation or the commission of unrighteous deeds by kings and Brahmins. Secondly, influential teachers preached personal devotion to God (*bhakti*) and proclaimed the irrelevance of all worldly hierarchies.[24] Though they were not 'revolutionary' in a modern sense, bhakti movements encouraged people to question social and political authority, and in many cases they prescribed rational rules for social life.[25] Since all power in India was ideologically compromised, the learned and respectable 'middling sort' took it upon themselves to maintain a constant critical vigilance over the doings of state and society.

Norms and contexts of debate

Though authority and sanctity weighed heavily in these Indian debates they might still reflect 'the critical judgement of a public making use of its reason'.[26] Some Europeans saw India as a 'dream society'. Others, however, noticed the existence of rational sciences and modes of debate within Indian traditions.[27] For Hindus, the legends of the Puranas were confronted with the mathematical precision of the Siddhantic star charts. The almanacs of civil and religious events (*panchangs*) which were produced by astronomer-brahmins formed a widespread vehicle for precise, popular knowledge. The existence of the Nyaya system of logic and the formal debate with its emphasis on proof and true testimony refutes the prejudice that magic and trial by ordeal permeated all 'Hindu' systems of adjudication.[28] Several scholars have also noted the steady rise of the rational sciences of jurisprudence, medicine and mathematics among the international Indo-Muslim intelligentsia during the seventeenth and eighteenth centuries.[29] Finally, what Peter Burke

[24] Jayant K. Lele, *Tradition and Modernisation in Bhakti Movements* (Leiden, 1981).

[25] A sect such as the Sadhs outlawed the use of astrology and the concept of auspicious and inauspicious times. Their 'creed' was set out in a number of *hukm* or *adhikar* (rules or orders), see, *LH*, I, 342ff.; W. Allison, *The Sadhs* (Calcutta, 1934).

[26] Habermas, *Public*, p. 24.

[27] B. Matilal, *Nyaya-Vaisesika, A History of Indian Literature*, ed. J. Gonda, (Wiesbaden), 1977, vol. VI, 2; cf. L. Wilkinson, 'The use of the Siddhantas in native education', *Journal of the Asiatic Society of Bengal*, 3, 1834, 504–19. *Panchangs* included astronomical and astrological observations, all the major calendars (Christian, Muslim, Hindu, revenue); later, details of charges and postal services, moral tales, advertisements and political propaganda, see below, pp. 249, 262–3.

[28] The *shastrartha* form continued to be used in Brahminical debates at the major centres in the eighteenth and early nineteenth centuries. Indian commentators stressed the experiential, empirical and rational face of Indian knowledge, see Babu R. Mukherjyea, 'Hindu Philosophy', *Bethune Society*, pp. 227–58.

[29] Francis Robinson, 'Ottomans–Safavids–Mughals: shared knowledge and connective systems', unpubl. Ms.

has called 'literal-mindedness' even seems to permeate the world of theology in the eighteenth and nineteenth centuries when matter-of-fact, but authoritative Persian and Urdu began to oust the prolix and flowery writing of earlier periods in works such as Muhammad Ismail's key text for the 'Wahhabi' reformers, the 'Refuge of the Faith' (*Taqwiyat al-Iman*).[30]

What was the context for these debates on politics and society? Assemblies and places of debate (*sabhas, kathas, panchayats* and *samajs*) represented more than the blind sense of collectivities denominated as tribes, castes or religious sects.[31] Heesterman has argued that the term *sabha* (association) itself originally indicated a meeting in which different qualities of people and opinions were tested, rather than the scene of a pronunciamento by caste elders.[32] A similar point has been made forcefully by Mattison Mines in his recent critique of Dumont.[33] Mines argues that the politics of south India from early times should be understood in terms of the interplay of the 'public reputations' of 'big men' among peasants and commercial people, in competition with each other and sometimes in conflict with the authorities. Even the fabled temple-building of the south represents, in Mines's analysis, not the agency of castes and corporations, but the individual aspirations of patrons expressed through institutions. Thus the words for association – *samaj* and *sabha* – which become part of the western-style debate of the later nineteenth century were not simply communities. Such words could be used to designate collectivities which spilled over the boundaries of social and religious groupings and represented temporary collections of individuals engaged in debate or judgement. The official presentations to authority, characteristic of Mughal and post-Mughal government, were formally organised according to classes of people. Thus the 'Karoris [office-holders], Sheikhs, Sayyids and Mahajans [Hindu magnates]' of a certain subdivision would present evidence to the authority on matters of local conflict or of oppression committed by officials.[34] This was a formula which guaranteed a kind of political representation to influential local people, not to mobilised castes or religious communities.

In the cities of north India, the office-holders, jurists, Sufi elders and

---

[30] C. Troll, 'A note on an early topographical work of Sayyid Ahmad Khan: Asar-al Sanadid', *Journal of the Royal Asiatic Society*, 1972, 143.

[31] R. Inden, *Imagining India* (Oxford, 1991), passim.

[32] S. Vidyabhusana, *A History of Indian Logic* (Delhi, 1971), pp. 22, 27, 263–4, 378–9; for later variations on *sabha*, see Ram Raz on 'Trial by Jury', *JRAS*, 3, 1836, 252–7.

[33] Mattison Mines, 'Individuality and achievement in south Asian social history', *MAS*, 26, i, 1992, 129–56.

[34] See, above, p. 17.

community counsellors were the key people who represented the 'opinion of the locality' to the authorities. They also acted as a critical audience for the rulers' policies. For instance, the judge (kazi) of Banaras led Muslim protests against unlawful changes in city government in the mid-eighteenth century.[35] In 1816 it was the mufti of Bareilly, also a Sufi teacher, who led the popular movement of both Hindus and Muslims against the British authorities when they attempted to introduce house taxation into northern Indian cities.[36] Historically the learned, the local office-holders and the 'honourable' (ashraf) had acted as a check on the ephemeral ruling elites of the Muslim world. The learned and office-holders were drawn from the same families as the urban property-holders and merchants. Their functions were not limited to matters of religion until the colonial powers restricted them to this role. They were doctors, healers of the mind, poets and writers, astronomers and advisers of citizens.

These officers were Islamic in form but non-Muslim people referred to them for adjudication and leadership, and they continued to flourish even in regions where Mughal rule had given way to Hindu or Sikh dynasties in the eighteenth century. Without doubt the question of the representation of Hindus within the ecumene is a complex one. But the model of two opposed 'religious communities' is certainly wrong. Though the religious establishments of the two major religions continued to keep their distance from one another, well-tried procedures of arbitration, joint representation and mutual consultation between Hindus and Muslims had evolved over a long period. Imbalances and asymmetries there were, but the same can be said of the participation of Catholics, Protestants and Jews in the emerging western European public sphere.

The learned and respectable elites kept up a constant conversation on matters of religious wisdom through ritual and official darbars, mosque schools, the Sufi orders and private homes. In early nineteenth-century Delhi bodies of scholars and gentlemen met in the houses of local officers such as the kazi and the sadr-ul-sudr to debate matters as apparently trivial as the licitness of eating mangoes (a fruit not mentioned in the scriptures).[37] There was also a long tradition of free-thinking and debate about the status of non-Islamic religion and culture.[38] Congregational meetings among the Muslim community

---

[35] 'Gyanbaffee Mosque' file, bundle 50, file 97, Judl. 1866, Comr Banaras, Post Mutiny Records, UPCRO.

[36] Address of Md. Ewaz, 27 Rabi-us sanee 1231 Hijree, Bengal Criminal Judicial Procs., 25 October 1816, 29 enc. 3, 132/48, OIOC.

[37] Troll, Sayyid Ahmad, p. 41 (the sadr-ul-sudr was a judge with particular cognisance of matters of religious endowment).

[38] Rizvi, Wali-Allah, pp. 317–42.

during the nights of the month of Ramadan provided a forum for wider discussions on matters concerning the community, and the consensus of these meetings might be conveyed to the rulers.[39] Alongside this, the educated maintained a debate on literature, language and aesthetics through poetry-reading circles or *mushairah*s. The chapter now turns to three forms of public debate centring on public religion, history and literary propriety.

Public doctrine and the ecumene

The guardians of the ecumene among the Muslim gentlefolk were concerned to detect violations in religious law and custom. To an extent, Hindu leaders associated with elite Muslim circles sought to protect and explain the role of their coreligionists within the polity. This was not the blind clash of religious communities, rather a series of transactions about the public face of religious observation. The debate over the rights and privileges of Shias and Hindus among Sunni Muslims was often literate and measured.[40] Even orthodox Sunni participants, for example, allowed that it was legitimate for Shias and 'polytheists' to participate in debates about public doctrine, though they might detest their beliefs. Sunni divines sent their works to Shias. The very practice of 'calling down God's curses' on opponents at the end of such debates can be seen as a way of formalising doctrinal hatred without foreclosing the possibility of dialogue.[41]

The disintegration of the Mughal Empire after 1700 set the scene for the sharpening of debates between Sunnis, Shias and Hindus. These had political, social and ethnic, as well as doctrinal implications. Political change which propelled to power families with Shia connections necessarily raised questions about the limits of royal authority in matters of religion. Conflict within the ruling cliques of Delhi and Hyderabad during the eighteenth century was often expressed in terms of doctrinal difference, while sarcastic comment attributed the political failings of notables to their religious and racial backgrounds.[42] Moreover, these controversies spilled over into political and social matters – luxury, debt and the decline of manufacture as well as 'religion'.[43] Polemic intensified after 1750. The Durrani occupation of Delhi (1759–62) led to a decline of Shia influence and an exodus of scholars, but the refugees later returned to the city with Emperor Shah Alam to wreak vengeance

---

[39] Extract Bengal Pol. Letter 19 Jun. 1807, 'Disturbances at Delhi', BC 217/ 4758.
[40] Rizvi, *Shi'is* II, 19–24, 35–7; A. Powell, *Muslims and Missionaries in pre-Mutiny India* (Richmond, 1993), pp. 43–75; Ethé, *Catalogue*, p. 1,335.
[41] Rizvi, *Shi'is*, II, 88–9.   [42] ibid.   [43] Rizvi, *Wali-allah*, pp. 298–9, 304.

on their opponents. Najaf Khan, protector of Delhi in the 1770s is said to have disfavoured Sunnis.[44] In the same way, the establishment of Shia dynasties in Awadh, and crypto-Shia notables in both Bengal and Arcot, encouraged a vigorous polemical debate between the two confessions. Delhi Sunnis led by Shah Abdul Aziz, and the Lucknow Shia establishment of Maulana Dildar Ali both initiated campaigns of teaching and tract-writing to refute their foes and instil discipline in their supporters. In Delhi and Lucknow the controversy merged into another, that of the Islamic purists against more conservative believers of their own sect, which again provoked a flurry of pamphleteering, debates and religious meetings.[45] These debates (*munazarah*) were governed by certain standards of conduct which implicitly acknowledged the existence of a critical public sphere.[46] Thus Dildar Ali, champion of Shi'ism, religiously sent copies of his works to the Delhi Sunni jurists (although the latter only responded with denunciations).[47] Social and political changes concurrently encouraged Muslim literati to take a greater interest in the newly powerful Hindu rulers and merchants. For example, the historian and administrator, Khairuddin Khan Illahabadi, followed the tradition of Akbar and debated with the Banaras pandits on matters of history and cosmology, showing deep knowledge of their scriptures.[48] In the same way, while the Delhi jurists associated themselves with the Durrani rulers' diatribes against Hindus,[49] the more catholic Mirza Jan-i Janan supported Hindus' right to hold public office and held that their divine heroes, such as Lord Ram, were precursors of the Prophets.

Insistent doctrinal debate and campaigns of purification amongst urban citizens therefore preceded and accompanied the Christian missionary and the 'reform' campaigns of the early nineteenth century.[50] Controversy about public doctrine was in the air. Missionaries found 'the Mahomedan mind in a state of considerable enquiry'.[51] They

[44] Bengal. Pol. Letter, 19 Jun. 1807, 'Disturbances at Delhi', BC 217/4758, OIOC.
[45] R. Russell and K. Islam (tr. ed.), *Ghalib 1797–1869* (London, 1969), I, *Life and Letters*, pp. 32–4.
[46] 'munazarah', *Encyclopaedia of Islam. New edn*, VII (Leiden, 1990), 565–8; Sharar, *Lucknow*, p. 95.
[47] Rizvi, *Shi'is*, II, 137.
[48] Khairuddin Khan Illahabadi, 'Tuhfa-i-Tazah', trans. F. Curwen, *Bulwuntnamah* (Allahabad, 1875), pp. 87–92.
[49] Rizvi, *Wali-allah* p. 303.
[50] This began with the series of Urdu, Hindi and Persian pamphlets denouncing Indian religion released by Serampore missionaries in 1804–6, e.g. 'An address from the missionaries of Serampore to all persons professing the Mohumadan religion', HM 690.
[51] *Church Missionary Record*, I, 2, 1830, 45 (Jaunpur); F. Nizami, 'Madrasahs, scholars and saints: Muslim responses to the British presence in Delhi and the Upper Doab,

targetted towns such as Lucknow or Jaunpur where 'party feeling' between Sunnis and Shias, or between Wahhabis and broad-church Muslims, had already taken root. Muslims, moreover, were already strengthening their popular base before Christian missionaries and the supposedly secular colonial government confronted them. By 1845, Urdu translations of the Koran were in use among the reformist Muslims.[52]

The appearance of print added a powerful new weapon to the arsenal of debate within the ecumene. When Christian missionaries began to pour printed propaganda into north India, its guardians responded vigorously, initiating formal logical contests and written refutations.[53] Missionaries were often surprised by the vehemence with which not only the religious teachers, but also local officers, *thanadars* (superintendents) and kotwals,[54] engaged them in debate. These were not cowed victims of colonial power. These were trustees of a public doctrine which seemed under threat. Rev. C.B. Leupolt, for example, noted of a tour in the vicinity of Lucknow in 1837: 'The Molwee came according to appointment, with an immense retinue of Mussulmans, learned as well as unlearned, and sat outside the tent. He brought a man with pen, ink and paper to note down what was said.'[55] Vigorous responses in pamphlet and placard form often followed Christian attacks on the Prophet. Such works often contained covert critiques of the Company as a secular ruler and were not limited to doctrinal arguments over the veracity of the Koran and Bible. In the 1830s the Muslim police chief of Buxar, for example, revealed to a passing missionary that he had often put a stop to widow burnings within his jurisdiction and denounced the Company for cowardice in failing to confront the issue.[56]

In the Hindu world, too, the activities of Brahmins and ruling-caste men had long transcended their ascribed functions as priests and warriors. Brahmins filled a similar role to Sheikhs and Sayyids as local justiciars, counsellors, literary arbiters, astronomers and doctors. The late eighteenth and early nineteenth centuries saw continuing formal

1803–1857', unpub. D.Phil. diss., Oxford University, 1983; W. Fusfeld, *The Shaping of Sufi Leadership in Delhi. The Naqshbandiyya Mujaddidiyya, 1750–1920* (Ann Arbor, 1981), pp. 1–52; 116–98.

[52] For the history of Urdu translations of the Koran, *LH*, I, 76–87; cf. *Friend of India*, 28 Jan. 1841.

[53] Powell, *Missionaries*, pp. 43–75; *Church Missionary Record [CMR]*, I, 3, 1830, 59, 62; I, 6, 1830, 120–2, 133, 137; I, 10, 1830, 217–19.

[54] e.g., the Sadr Amin and 'The chief native judge' near Lucknow refutes Christianity, *CMR*, 6, 7, 1836, 137–8; ditto, the office manager of the Collector of Ghazipur, ibid., 9, 1, 1838, 15.

[55] *CMR*, 7, 6, 1836, 139.

[56] *The Missionary Register for MDCCCXXIV* . . . (London, 1824), April 1824, p. 195.

debates between different schools of the Hindu learned about scripture and philosophy.[57] But, faced with direct attacks on their spiritual clienteles by Christians, priestly Brahmins had now to defend, to rationalise, to preach and to grasp the new tools of publicity. Some missionaries resorted to physical violence and coercion, such as 'shaking' the fakirs out of their spiritual trance.[58] More often, they found themselves drawn into complex and inconclusive debates which raged around the nature of godhead, the age of the universe and the qualities of good kingship, so touching directly on the political realm and claims to truth of western science. In missionary memoirs we glimpse two Hindu philosophical traditions which engaged the spiritual invader with particular force. First, Advaita Vedantists vigorously asserted the oneness of creation, directly challenging the Christian assumption of the separation of God and his creatures. Secondly, the devotional bhakti tradition afforded ample resources for arguing back against the white man in an idiom which seemed superficially similar. When a missionary advanced on a Hindu priest affirming 'God is love', the priest put his hands on the missionary and responded – to the Christian's irritation – 'I love you.'[59] Hindu devotional love (prem) was here used against Christian love, to diminish the moral, physical and political distance between sahib and 'native'. A generation before the modernist Arya Samaj stepped in to defend ancient religion with print, north Indian Hindu scholars were employing their skills of logical debate to refute, rebuff or incorporate the missionaries. This was no simple Hindu 'reaction' to western 'impact'; instead, the headstrong westerners plunged into a torrent of controversy which had for centuries pitted Vaishnavite scholars against Buddhists and Jains, Siddhantists against the Puranas and devotional gurus against the orthodox. All these formally doctrinal issues, however, bore on the question of good kingship and social propriety.

Speech and critical aesthetic comment

An important precondition for the development of this widespread debate on religion and politics was the flexibility and accessibility of the Hindustani or Urdu language itself (Urdu is used here to mean the more

---

[57] See, e.g., the description of a western Indian debate between Advaita Vedantists and their opponents, J. Howison, *European Colonies in Various Parts of the World* (London, 1834), II, 52–4.

[58] C.B. Leupolt, *Recollections of an Indian Missionary* (London, 1856), p. 56.

[59] e.g., *CMR*, 1, 6, 1830, 128; cf. ibid., 131, 133; ibid., 1, 10, 1830, 243; Leupolt, *Recollections*, p. 82; the missionaries displayed particular interest in Sadhs and Kabirpanthis, ibid., 2, 8, 1831, pp. 178–80; *Miss. Reg.*, April 1824, p. 314.

refined and Persianised form of the common north Indian language, Hindustani). Urdu came to impart to the discussions of the ecumene a popular character which was difficult when Arabic and Persian totally dominated them. The turn towards Urdu in the courts and camps of north India in the eighteenth and nineteeenth centuries represented a deliberate populist strategy on the part of the elite. The emergence of Urdu was attested to by the work of indigenous grammarians as much as by the excellence of its poets. In the late eighteenth century Sirajuddin Ali Arzu, for instance, had critically edited earlier Persian works on Urdu. He argued that this was a true language and proposed a typology which ran from pure Sanskrit, through popular and regional variations of Hindustani to Urdu, which incorporated many loan words from Persian and Arabic.[60] His emphasis on the unity of languages reflected the view of the Sanskrit grammarians and also affirmed the linguistic unity of the north Indian ecumene. What emerged was a kind of register of language types which were appropriate to different conditions of man and society, and even to different times of the day and season.[61] There was a particular variant for the use of women, for court camp and army, for local officials and village registrar. Particular professions, sub-castes and even bands of criminals had their own argot. Sometimes the specific blend of language forms could be used to exclude and monopolise. This, for instance, was a claim commonly made about court and bazaar writers. But the abiding impression is of lingustic plurality running through the whole society and an easier adaptation to circumstances in both spoken and written speech.

Urdu/Hindustani itself had now taken on the character of the public tongue of the ecumene. It was a popular language spread by Sufi saints and Hindu devotees and a language of the court and a discerning literati. The best Urdu could be heard, it was said, at three places: in the court and army bazaar at Delhi, at the flower-sellers' market on the river Jumna, and at the tomb of the saint Shah Madar in Etah district, a resort of horse-sellers, harkaras, palankin-bearers and other common people.[62]

---

[60] S. Kidwai, *Gilchrist and the 'Language of Hindostan'* (Delhi, 1972), pp. 88–9.

[61] J. Majeed, 'The Jargon of Indostan – an exploration of jargon in Urdu and East India Company English' in P. Burke and R. Porter (eds.) *Languages and Jargons* (Cambridge, Mass., forthcoming); D. Lelyveld, 'The fate of Hindustani: colonial knowledge and the project of a national language', in Breckenridge and van der Veer, *Orientalism and the Postcolonial Predicament*, pp. 189–215.

[62] E.B. Eastwick, tr., *The Bagh o Bahar* (Hertford, 1852), pp. 7–8, Munshi's preface; cf. W. Crooke, *Ethnographic Handbook of the North-western Provinces and Oudh* (Allahabad, 1887), p. 84, on 'Madari' palankin-bearers. But see also, A. Rai, *A House Divided. The Origins and Development of Hindi-Urdu* (Delhi, 1984), pp. 246–54, which notes the pre-colonial attempts to 'purify' Urdu of Sanskritic words; Surendra Gopal, *Patna in the Nineteenth Century. A socio-cultural profile* (Calcutta, 1982), pp. 60–79.

Outside centres of high Urdu court culture some Muslims continued to use the Devanagari character. The devotional poetry of the fifteenth- and sixteenth-century Sufi teachers was as likely to be found in the Devanagari as in the Persian script. In the eighteenth century a Sufi teacher of Bihar, writing to the governor of Malwa on the duties of rulers, remarked that 'a king's familiarity with Hindi verses is also very necessary'.[63] According to the writer, the king should consult with 'saintly ascetics', not with 'worldly ulama [doctors of law]' and should espouse 'universal toleration'. Thus regional versions of Hindustani appear to have carried overtones of community and harmony.

The learned reached down to incorporate these more localised language cultures in order to broaden cultural community. Several sources remark on the difficulty of teaching in Arabic or even Persian. Mullahs had to resort to exaggerated mimes of the action when they read out passages from the Arabic or Persian scriptures. One British observer noticed that at Muslim assemblies in which the Fateha or declaration of faith and Arabic prayers were offered, 'the mullah gave the history of the saints', presumably the Shia martyrs, in Urdu 'to enable those present the better to understand it'.[64]

Poetic assemblies held in the court, in the houses of notables and in the shops of bazaar people, spread common standards of aesthetic judgement and common forms of language across the country. Urdu writing was not confined to a self-conscious realm of literature. Instead, it was a discourse among men of weight on matters of aesthetics, health, religion and politics. Aristocratic writers were honoured in this world, but their rank did not exempt their ideas, their forms of letter-writing or their calligraphy, from critical scrutiny.[65] The poet Mir is alleged to have ridiculed the Emperor Shah Alam for his poetry. The Emperor had claimed that he was such a good poet that he could dash off several poems while he was doing his ablutions in the morning; 'Yes, and they smell like it', said Mir.[66] Aesthetic issues could become more directly political. The debate between the advocates of Persian and those of Urdu had ethnic, class, and religious undertones.[67] Though they enjoyed the patronage of the royal family, by the 1840s the proponents

[63] Askari, 'Mirat-ul-Muluk', Indica, p. 31.
[64] Westmacott, 'Travels', Ms. Eur C29 f. 183; Friend of India, 28 Feb. 1839.
[65] A vivid picture of the world of the mushairah is given in Akhtar Qamber, The Last Mushairah of Delhi (Delhi, 1979).
[66] R. Russell and K. Islam, Three Mughal Poets. Mir, Sauda, Mir Hasan (London, 1969) p. 6; cf. pp. 55–8; S.A.I. Tirmizi, Persian Letters of Ghalib (Delhi, 1969), p. xxiii.
[67] Daud Rahbar (tr., ed.), Urdu Letters of Mirza Asadu'llah Khan Ghalib (Albany, New York, 1987), p. xxvii; Tirmizi, Persian Letters of Ghalib, p. xxviii–xxx.

of Urdu were often less consciously aristocratic than the champions of Persian and were more influenced by Indian forms.[68]

One literary form which reflected and perpetuated the memory of the ecumene was the *tazkirah*, or collective literary biography. Literature here went beyond poetry to topics as diverse as medicine and topography. Through such works literary lineages and styles of endeavour could be traced over many generations. Having one's name entered in a major tazkirah guaranteed some degree of literary immortality, and individuality. These collective biographies demonstrate the diverse origins of the people who were known to the Indian critical public. The models were Persian or central Asian forerunners, such as the biographies of the literary men and wits of Kashan, many of whom migrated to India in the thirteenth and fourteenth centuries.[69] Among the noted poets were sons of washermen, water-carriers, tailors, an 'occulist and chess-player', a 'talented man who have himself up to profligacy', 'a great drunkard', and so on. Just as Islam was supposed to pay no attention to class in matters of faith, so in matters of style and literary excellence, men from humble backgrounds could achieve great fame.

In the 1840s Alois Sprenger carried out a detailed analysis of a number of literary biographies, including one of the Persian poets of Calcutta and Banaras, which paints a complex picture of social communication and the geography of the ecumene.[70] The literary men were often drawn from the old officers of the towns and qasbahs, such as the kazi and the King of Awadh's newswriter at Banaras.[71] As we have seen, the connection between political information systems and literary endeavour was very close. Others were dispersed remnants of the Delhi royal house, the Shahzadas of Banaras. Imperial family members who had been exiled or who had fled to Lucknow and Patna became the hubs of patterns of cultural patronage. Many of the people honoured worked in British government offices. They included residency munshis, clerks to the Calcutta Court of Appeal, clerks of the customs department at Banaras, and others in more lowly official positions who still cultivated

[68] cf. R. Russell and K. Islam, *Ghalib, 1797–1969*, I, *Life and Letters* (London, 1969), pp. 79–81.
[69] A. Sprenger, *A Catalogue of the Arabic, Persian and Hindustani Manuscripts of the Libraries of the King of Oudh* (Calcutta, 1854), pp. 23ff.
[70] ibid., pp. 195–306; we have used the term ecumene to describe a *style* of communication but tazkirahs could be used to demonstrate the *geography* of social communication in the sense used by Deutsch. The relative decline of literary and social comment in the western cities, Lahore, Delhi, etc. would be matched in the late eighteenth century by the rise of Lucknow, Banaras, Patna, Hyderabad and their associated qasbahs. Calcutta would become significant for Persian and Urdu scholarship.
[71] ibid., pp. 165–75.

Persian and Hindustani letters. The previously mentioned informant of
the British, Ali Ibrahim Khan, was a prominent member of this group,
and had written a collective biography of Persian poets.[72]

People of poor background were not as evident here as in the Kashan
list. Sprenger, however, listed many humbler authors in a comprehensive
listing of tazkirahs, accounting for more than 1,800 literary people.
Here, for instance, there were druggists,[73] a serving woman,[74] a Hazrat
(one who had memorised the Koran) who kept an apothecary's shop in
the Nakhas cattle market of Banaras,[75] a common writer,[76] a tailor
skilled in *marsiyas* (lamentations on the Shia martyrs),[77] a Hyderabad
'dancing woman'[78] and many others. Hindus accounted for a small but
significant percentage of the list. Most of these were from the Kashmiri
Brahmin, Khattri or Kayastha communities and were traditionally
associated with Persian and Urdu through Mughal service. There were,
however, occasional entries for men of the Hindu commercial castes.
One Eurasian even appeared: John Thomas, a 'soldier-like man',[79] son
of George Thomas, who had founded a small state in Hariana at the end
of the eighteenth century.

So it was not only men of power who participated in the literary
activities of the ecumene. The egalitarian traditions of the Islamic lands
and the community sensibilities of Indian cities encouraged ordinary
artisans and people of the bazaars to aspire to eminence as poets or
commentators. The form of the language was inclusive; it mirrored and
even helped to stimulate the rapid social mobility which was characteristic of post-Mughal north India. Even women wrote and circulated
poems.[80] In Lucknow, noblewomen, courtesans, musicians, dancers
and other cultural performers from poor backgrounds achieved power in
court and urban politics. This gravely offended evangelical Christian
commentators and some later Indian purists, who saw corruption and
decadence in what was actually striking social mobility.

History, libraries and social memory

Alongside questions of public doctrine and literary aesthetics, 'history'
and topography played an important role in maintaining the identity of
the ecumene. History in the Indo-Muslim tradition was, as Peter Hardy
has written, a protean form which merged into poetry, moral and political

---

[72] See above, pp. 81–2.   [73] ibid., p. 207.   [74] ibid., p. 217.
[75] ibid., p. 234.   [76] ibid., p. 282.   [77] ibid., p. 289.
[78] ibid., p. 217.   [79] ibid., p. 299.
[80] *LH*, I, 69–72; cf. Garcin de Tassy, 'Les femmes poetes de l'Inde', *Revue de l'Orient*,
May 1854; Sprenger, *Catalogue of Libraries of Oudh*, p. 11.

instruction, and theology.[81] Amir Khusrau's poetic and panegyric history of the fourteenth century began a tradition which still had its imitators in the eighteenth century when court historians rendered the deeds of the founders of the successor states into ornate Persian. More influential yet in our period was the historical work of Abul Fazl. The 'Ain' and the 'Akbarnamah' were read and discussed extensively by the literati of the successor states and the munshis of the British offices. Besides legitimating the divinely gifted status of the house of Timur, Abul Fazl's history was the philosophy of religious insight teaching by example. Valuing the divine revelation in all mature creeds, his picture of universal harmony, must have seemed particularly apposite to Muslim jurisconsults practising in an age when the 'tribe of Hindus' had achieved much influence in the state. Akbar's debates with his Hindu, Jain, Christian and Parsi subjects were viewed as a template of good government in the eighteenth century. They represented the strain of historical and moral philosophy which inspired Mirza Jan-i Janan to reaffirm the theology of Ibn-i Arabi, and the doctrine of the immanence of God, against the more exclusive doctrines of the Delhi theologians, Shah Waliullah and Shah Abdul Aziz. It inspired that archetypical denizen of the ecumene, Ghalib, to describe ecstatically the sight of the festival of lights, Diwali, at Banaras, 'the Mecca of India'.[82] Despite his earlier adherence to a purist creed, Sayyid Ahmad's description of Delhi diplays similar affection for the Hindu and Jain temples which had arisen in the city.[83]

This sense of the luminosity of place, and of the pleasures and ease of the erstwhile great and culturally diverse empire of Hindustan, was a compelling motif for much of the poetic-cum-historical work of the eighteenth and early nineteenth centuries. Hindus and Muslims, peasant and poet, were united in a wistful remembrance of what was and what might have been. This mode of elegiac historiography reached its fullest expression in the works of 'social poets' such as Sauda and Nazir who elaborated the form called ashob sheher,[84] 'bewailing the fallen greatness of the city', that is the civilisation of Mughal India. It also expressed itself in what is conventionally called 'history' (though the word tarikh does not quite mean history). A good example was the 'Araish-i-Mehfil' of Mir Sher Ali of Narnaul.[85] This writer had a family history typical of

[81] P. Hardy, *Historians of Medieval India. Studies in Indo-Muslim Historical Writing* (London, 1960), pp. 122–31.

[82] Tirmizi, *Persian Letters of Ghalib*, p. xxiii.

[83] Sayyid Ahmad Khan, 'Asar-us Sanadid', trans. as 'Description des Monuments de Delhi en 1852', *Journal Asiatique*, Jan. 1861, 80, 87, 91, passim.

[84] Fritz Lehman, 'Urdu Literature and Mughal Decline', *Mahfil*, 6, 2, 1970, pp. 125–31; Russell and Islam, *Three Mughal Poets*, pp. 1–68.

[85] *LH*, I, 120–1.

the military nobility of the eighteenth century. His father had been commander of the Nawab's Arsenal in Bengal. He himself moved between Delhi, Lucknow and Hyderabad, writing in Urdu under the patronage of Jawan Bakht, son of the Emperor Shah Alam. Late in his life he was introduced by Wellesley to Hasan Reza Khan and settled in Fort William College where he translated the Persian classic, 'Gulistan', under the superintendence of John Gilchrist. Drawing on the work of predecessors, notably Sujan Rai, Sher Ali wrote the history of the kings of Delhi from the Hindu period, described the customs of India's inhabitants, and the topography of each province. Though he recognised distress and decline, the overall tone seems to have been panegyric: 'All the inhabitants of Hindustan are capable, learned and clever and know merit'; the 'majority of grains have a delicious taste ... rice is produced in a paradise on earth'.[86] There are descriptions of the excellence of palankins and other conveyances. He praises the beauty of Hindu women. He dilates on the feelings appropriate to the cycle of the Hindu months in a clear reference to the theory of *rasas* or essences which underlies Hindu aesthetics. But this was no more; after the Emperor Farrukhsiyar, corruption spread, Muhammad Shah became addicted to pleasure and 'the Empire became a sort of market'.[87] Poetry and panegyric in this tone persisted well into the nineteenth century. In 1849, for instance, Maharaja Apurva Krishna Bahadur wrote a historical epic 'The Conquerors of Hindustan' which praised the later Mughals.[88] The Empire had survived the wreck of its sister states, the Safavids and central Asian kingdoms, and even now, this work claimed, the Empire cast a glow like the setting sun. The writer apparently belonged to a family of the Sobha Bazaar, Calcutta, which had acquired its title by giving offerings to an indigent prince who was travelling around India with two mangy elephants.[89] The Anglo-Indian press ridiculed these poetic effusions, but they represent a continuing sense of cultural and political community and of criticism of the ruling powers, which remained strong until it was brutally terminated by the sack of Delhi in November 1857.

Libraries, or rather 'book houses' provided the resources from which this social memory in the fields of history, literature and theology was drawn. Indian libraries were no doubt highly unstable by European standards. Often they were built up out of patterns of princely gift-

---

[86] ibid., 127.
[87] ibid., 136.
[88] 'The Conquerors of Hindustan in Persian and English', *Delhi Gazette* cited *Friend of India*, 16 Dec. 1847; ibid., 3 May 1849.
[89] *Friend of India*, 3 May 1849.

exchange[90] or plunder,[91] as annexes to royal treasuries. Royal and noble libraries were looted by their guardians as well as by external enemies.[92] Many Indian libraries were also exclusive. Temple libraries among Hindus and Jains were generally available only to priests; sacred knowledge was dangerous and had to be stored in safe places.[93] This literary memory, however, was neither negligible nor sealed off from the debates of the ecumene. The largest libraries comprised tens of thousands of volumes,[94] while many thousands of families had smaller collections amounting to a handful of manuscripts. There is some evidence, too, that a more specialist understanding of the library was developing among the elites even before the colonial period; in Jaipur, for example, Raja Jai Singh separated off a study collection from his treasury and this was used by the king and his officials in adjudications on religious and social issues.[95] Though never public, these collections could sometimes serve as a resource for the wider learned community. On occasion the Lucknow Royal Library was asked to produce a text when a controversy between the Muslim learned and Christian missionaries took place.[96] Scholars from outside princely families were allowed to see and copy texts. Sayyid Ahmad Khan, for example, was one person who was allowed to work in the Delhi Royal Library.[97]

Communications and political debate

Historians agree that in the West the public sphere was a domain of communication given form by printed media and the market.[98] Evidently, this key component was lacking from the north Indian scene before the introduction of lithography in the 1830s and 1840s, but the

[90] I.A. Arshi, *Catalogue of the Arabic Manuscripts in Raza Library, Rampur*, 6 vols. (Rampur, 1963–77).
[91] Datta, *Libraries*, p. 84.
[92] Also note the lack of catalogues, A. Sprenger to H. Elliot, 25 Jun. 1847, Elliot Papers, Add. 30,789, BL.
[93] D.C. Dasgupta, *The Jaina System of Education* (Calcutta, 1944), pp. 36–40; John E. Cort, 'The Jain knowledge warehouses: traditional libraries in India', *Journal of the American Oriental Society*, 115, 1, 1995, 77–88.
[94] Sprenger to Elliot, 25 Jun. 1847, Elliot Papers, Add. 30,789; cf. Sprenger, *Report of the Researches into the Muhammadan Libraries of Lucknow. Selections from the Records of the Government of India*, no. 28 (Calcutta, 1896) which records 6,000 volumes in the Topkhana Library and about 1,000 in the Farah Baksh; the private library of Sheikh Mahomed Hazin's family had 5,000 volumes, Belfour, *Hazin*, p. 10; Datta, *Libraries*, pp. 69, 73, 85.
[95] G.N. Bahura, 'Glimpses of historical information from manuscripts in the Pothikhana of Jaipur', in J.N. Asopa (ed.), *Cultural Heritage of Jaipur* (Jodhpur, 1982), pp. 104–5; cf. Arshi, *Rampur*, I, preface p. 1.
[96] *Miss. Reg.*, Aug. 1826, p. 395.
[97] Troll, *Sayyid Ahmad*, p. 104.   [98] Habermas, *Public*, pp. 57ff.

reasons for this remain obscure. Politics may have played a part; several Indian rulers at the turn of the nineteenth century continued to discourage the use of the printing press because it threatened their authority.[99] Rather than being testimony to passivity and the absence of political debate, however, our evidence suggests exactly the opposite conclusion: that royal authority was already too fragile to support this further dissemination of ridicule and *lèse majesté*. This in turn points to a wider reason for the late start of printing. Indians had created a highly effective information order in which strategically placed written media reinforced a powerful culture of oral communication; printing in this sense was not needed until society itself began to change more radically under colonial rule. In the ecumene written media and oral communication complemented each other. Francis Robinson[100] has made a strong case for the dominance of oral exposition and importance of the physical presence of the reputed teacher within the pre-print culture of Islamic north India. Oral exposition, presence and memory were no doubt critical in philosophical debate, and among Hindus and Jains no less than among Muslims. They were also important in poetic and aesthetic discussion. Ghalib, for instance, is said rarely to have purchased a manuscript or book, as he committed to memory anything that he needed.[101] Written media were, nevertheless, an essential part of north Indian critical debate, and could create eddies and flurries of opinion distant from the immediate presence of their authors. Ghalib's proficiency as a letter-writer was as striking as his memory.

While the dismal picture conveyed by Europeans and by Indian reformers was of a society where the communication of knowledge was stunted by hierarchy, there is much evidence to the contrary. We have already noted the speed with which information from the northwest or from Persia was conveyed to Banaras. The combination of harkara information, newsletters and public recitations in bazaars or near the platform of the kotwal's station spread news very quickly across country. During the Nepal and Burma wars, during the Afghan and Sikh campaigns of 1838–52, and during the Multan revolt of 1848 anti-British information and rumour was determindly spread by these

---

[99] e.g. the case in 1849 where the King of Awadh destroyed the Lucknow presses because they had displeased him, A. Sprenger, *A Catalogue of the Arabic, Persian and Hindustani Manuscripts in the Libraries of the King of Oudh*, (Calcutta, 1854), p. vi, or an equivalent case in Punjab, Emmet Davis, *The Press and Politics in British West Punjab, 1836–47* (Delhi, 1983), p. 184.

[100] F. Robinson, 'Technology and religious change. Islam and the impact of print', *MAS*, 27, i, 1993, 229–51.

[101] Russell and Islam, *Ghalib*, I, 38.

means.[102] At the height of the Burma War, Malcolm warned that 'there was a dangerous species of secret war against our authority carried on by numerous tho' unseen hands – the spirit of which is kept up by letters, by exaggerated reports, by pretended prophecies, etc.'[103] Though, as late as 1836, Auckland discounted the influence of the indigenous press itself, he believed that news was still widely disseminated by newswriters and agents of powerful people in whose newsletters 'anything may be inserted . . . without scruple'.

The north Indian case indicates that critical debate within a broad political class could be spread through personal and institutional letter-writing, through placarding and public congregation. In Rajasthan and adjoining areas the bardic tradition and the written stories to which it gave rise also proved capable of carrying subversive political messages. James Tod noted the prevalence of 'licence' and satire, the dissemina-tion of 'truths unpalatable' and 'the absence of all mystery and reserve with regard to public affairs'[104] in the Rajput principalities. All this gives a picture of a lively social and political debate whose existence was reluctantly acknowledged when colonial officials made disparaging references to 'bazaar rumour'.

A similar point was made by Garcin de Tassy on the basis of a lifetime's study of Hindustani literature. It was common to argue that politics and rational discourse had no part in a society dominated by fable. On the contrary, he argued, the western distinctions between politics, literature and history did not really apply. Many so-called 'fables' were strongly political in tone and 'Nous voyons, en effet, que la politique occupe le premier rang dans les fables orientales, et en forme le portion la plus importante . . .'[105] Here he mentions the famous 'Tota Kahani' or 'Tale of a Parrot'. Fables such as this, or the Panchatantra in its various forms, were highly pointed in their characterisation of human types and could be modified in oral presentations to refer to particular political situations. For instance one such story is a fable about diplomacy. A herd of deer hired a jackal to make a compact with a lion, but the jackal betrayed the deer to be eaten because he was the usual

---

[102] Englishman, 12 Jan. 1835; material on Burma, etc.; Banaras 1852, Reade, Contribu-tions, fn., pp. 67–8.
[103] Marginal note to Auckland's minute on the press, 8 Aug. 1836, Auckland Papers, Add. Mss. 37,709, f. 91b, BL
[104] J. Tod, Annals and Antiquities of Rajast'han, or the central and western Rajpoot states of India (London, 1829–32, repr., 1950), Introduction, p. 16; cf. V.N. Rao, D. Shulman and S. Subrahmanyam, Symbols of Substance. Court and State in Nayaka Period Tamilnadu (Delhi, 1992), pp. 1–22 and passim.
[105] LH, I, 10.

recipient of the lion's pickings.[106] This story must have seemed particularly timely in the savage politics of eighteenth century India.

In contemporary west Asia, political debate was carried on in smoking dens and coffee shops.[107] The same was true in India, though here druggists' stalls, selling betel nut, tobacco or medicaments,[108] and sweetshops[109] served as more important forums of gossip and news. In west Asia, again, more resolute protests were made by seizing control of that pre-eminently public place, the mosque, at a time just before the muezzin's call to prayer and making statements critical of the authorities from the minaret. The regularity of this procedure suggests that it was sanctioned by the community, and even reluctantly tolerated by rulers. In India, too, political demonstrations were made at or near mosques. The shrines of saints, or of deceased rulers popularly revered as just men, were also the venue of demonstrations – an indication of the relative importance for the subcontinent of tomb worship and Sufism in both elite and popular life. In Lucknow at the beginning of the nineteenth century, for example, 'oppressions' by the police chief of the city brought together thousands in the garden of the tomb of the late ruler, Shuja-ud Daulah. The crowd called out *andhera! andhera!* 'darkness!, darkness!', that is 'tyranny!'[110] In other incidents, people affixed handbills to points on or near the Friday mosque or royal temple. We have already noticed the use of placards during the celebrated affair of the British Resident, James Achilles Kirkpatrick and the Hyderabad lady.[111] Placards similarly denounced unpopular local Shia officials in Hyderabad,[112] announced changes of regime in Kathmandu,[113] and the onset of the Rebellion of 1857 in Lucknow.[114] Pinning up critical poems in a mordant style, as well as passing them by word of mouth through the bazaar, appears to have been a political form as common as the pasquinade of Baroque Rome. Pasquino was the name given to a 'talking' classical statue near to the church of San Andrea della Valle. It has long been the practice to affix to it lampoons against the Pope or the authorities. Whereas in Rome, pasquinades were afforded legitimacy by

---

[106] C. Bendall, 'The Tantrakhyana. A collection of Indian tales', *JRAS*, 2, 4, 1890, 484; cf. *The Panchatantra*.

[107] Note by Prof. Halil Inalcik in author's possession.

[108] An observation of Prof. Ravinder Kumar.

[109] 'Bankas and swindlers', *Delhi Gazette*, 18 Dec. 1839.

[110] Faiz Baksh, *Memoirs*, II, 285–7.

[111] Above, p. 92.

[112] *Mofussilite*, 11 Feb. 1848 on 'Sunni–Shia disturbances at Hyderabad'.

[113] 'placards have been posted at Cathmandoo threatening destruction to several prominent chiefs and the Resident', the information was sent immediately to Banaras, 'the centre of information about Nepaul', *Delhi Gazette*, 20 Jan. 1841.

[114] Below pp. 323–4.

the statuesque memorabilia of classical republicanism and ciceronian polemic, in India the tombs of just rulers or those Muslim saints, who had been appropriately unimpressed by the powers that be, served a similar purpose.

Political debates over a wider geographical area were carried on by the Indo-Muslim literati through recognised newsletters and also by private correspondence, still often delivered by covert indigenous postal systems. The literature associated with popular Sufi teachers sometimes contained critical comment on rulers, or on various ethnic groups.[115] Hindu sages crafted similar comments on contemporary politics. The poet Kavindracarya wrote verses in honour of the Emperor Shahjahan who had facilitated pilgrimage to Banaras.[116] They were recorded and used on later occasions when pilgrimage rights came under pressure. Shah Waliullah wrote letters to contemporary rulers urging a more strenuously Islamic policy.[117] Such epistles were, of course, destined for the readers of the wider critical ecumene; they were not 'private' letters.[118]

The practice of personal letter-writing also kept the ecumene informed. Figures for the early nineteenth century produced by the nascent British postal authorities suggest that even quite small towns produced a surprisingly large number of letters, perhaps as many as two hundred per annum per head for the literates and people who could afford to have letters written.[119] For men of the pen such as the poet Ghalib, letter-writing was viewed as a necessity of life. This was almost literally the case, because as much paper was spent by Ghalib and his correspondents discussing new remedies and the excellence of various physicians as on the diseases of the body politic.[120] Outside scholarly circles, most towns had substantial communities of bazaar writers acting for ordinary people who could pay them. Village schoolmasters also helped people communicate with their folk 'in distant parts'.[121] Most cities, again, supported large bodies of runners employed by private daks. After 1836, the British tried to suppress these in order to maximise postal revenue, but the impression is that many persisted clandestinely.

[115] Askari, 'Mirat-ul-Muluk', *Indica*, pp. 44ff.
[116] V. Raghavan, 'The Kavindrakalpalatika of Kavindracarya Sarasvati', ibid., pp. 336–7.
[117] Rizvi, *Wali-allah*, pp. 302–3.
[118] cf. David Lelyveld, reported by S. Freitag, 'Introduction' *South Asia*, n.s., 14, 1, 1991, p. 9 and fn. 19.
[119] 'District Dawks', *Friend of India*, 18 Jul. 1850.
[120] e.g., Ghalib to Nawab Alauddin Ahmad Khan, 15 Shaban 1298 (Feb. 1862), Rahbar, *Persian Letters of Ghalib*, pp. 25–6; same to Munshi Hargopal Tafta, n.d. May (?) 1848, p. 57; same to Mirza Shahabuddin Ahmad Khan, 24 Sept. 1861, p. 51; for the social networks in Ghalib's earlier correspondence, Tirmizi, *Ghalib*, pp. xiv, xxiii.
[121] e.g., the case in Westmacott, 'Travels', Mss. Eur. C26, f. 173.

'Native intelligence' continued to move vigorously, transported by runners 'who shift their parcels at every sixteen or twenty miles' and never made unnecessary stops.[122]

As we have seen, the newsletters written from the courts of rulers all across the country were copied by hand in relatively limited numbers. As in the case of later printed newspapers which were read to large groups of people and handed around in the bazaar for several days, the information they purveyed seems to have become public property very quickly. Pages of newspapers were lent by one family to another.[123] Whole copies of newspapers were read out to crowds in the streets in the evening.[124] Professional newswriters moved between the world of the written newsletter and the printed newspaper. Some of these writers also kept lists of subscribers to whose houses they would repair daily in order to read the news from their own manuscript compilations.[125] A combination of these instruments could create a formidable blast of publicity even before the rise of the press. When in the early 1850s, the King of Delhi was maliciously reported to have become a Shia, a whole arsenal of written, lithographed and memorised refutations cannoned back. Ghalib, then poet laureate, was himself asked to write an ode in refutation.[126]

The ecumene was led by respectable men who could draw limits to the actions of government and also seek to impose their standards of belief and practice on the populace. Meanwhile, dense networks of social communication could bring butchers, flower-sellers, bazaar merchants and artisans into political debates and demonstrations. This has been thoroughly demonstrated by the many studies of the taxation riots and religious disputes of the early nineteenth century.[127] These events, however, are evidence of a continuing ecumenical critique; they should not be seen as sudden upsurges of resistance from tyrannised and voiceless subalterns. In 1779 in Lucknow, for instance, there was a celebrated debate between learned physicians who had newly arrived in town,[128] and resident savants who were trying to protect their livelihoods against the newcomers. The invasion of the new men was announced, according to the historian Mahomed Faiz Baksh, by a careful campaign

---

[122] *Mofussilite*, 30 May 1848.
[123] Rahbar, *Ghalib*, pp. 94, 205.
[124] *Friend of India*, 4 April 1850.
[125] Evidence of Chuni Lal, newswriter 'for the public', 'Trial of the King of Delhi', *PP*, 1859, 1st session, xviii, 84.
[126] Rahbar, *Ghalib*, p. xxxiii.
[127] See, K.H. Prior, 'The British administration of Hinduism in north India, 1780–1900', unpub. PhD thesis Cambridge University, 1990.
[128] Cole, *Roots of North Indian Shi'ism*, pp. 55–8.

of slander against existing 'doctors' in the city[129] (slander, of course, itself represents a kind of 'black public'). The conflict came to a head in a public debate. The ostensible subjects of the disputation were rival interpretations of an incident in early Islamic history – a revolt in AD 740 led by Ali Zaid. In fact, the two sides partly represented ethnic divisions, with Persians ranged against Indians. Alongside this there were political divisions, with the supporters of the Nawab and Warren Hastings ranged against partisans of the Begams of Awadh and other groups resisting the Awadh court and the British. The authority of texts and the spoken word were both in contention here.[130] Professional clerics contended with lay literati. Perhaps the most important aspect was the way in which the debate attracted the attention of the whole city with huge throngs of people of all persuasions, numbering more than 1,500, clustering around the house where the contest took place. Finally, order broke down amid Hogarthian scenes of rioting and revelry. As the chronicler wrote, 'It was a marvellous tumult and no-one knew what it was about ... it ended at last, but for some time after it was much talked about and people composed ballads and wrote narratives about it.'[131]

Another example from the first months of British rule at Bareilly in 1804 revealed similar patterns. Fitzroy, a demented magistrate, had struck a Sayyid in a dispute over a garden. The cry went up 'A Seyud has been insulted and struck; our houses are about to be demolished ...' The Governor-General's agent, Archibald Seton, a prolix and learned Scotsman, feared that the 'Green Banner' was about to be raised and the paltry British occupying force in the city would be overwhelmed. To compromise the dispute, 'he went to the Mosque of Moftee Mahomed Ewuz, the most popular and respected Seyud at Barelli, from the purity of his conduct and the sanctity of his manners'.[132] As he entered the mosque, Seton took off his shoes and said to the swordsmen barring his way, 'Do you not see, my friends, that I am prepared to approach a sacred place and meet a holy man.' They respectfully parted and, according to Seton, 'I distinctly heard one of them say to the other "This gentleman is one of us."'[133] The honour of the community was restored by this act of contrition on the part of the Sahib, and, with the aid of two Muslim physicians and the Mufti, the wrong was compromised. The crowds retreated and Fitzroy was bundled out of town under restraint. This story illustrates the ecumene in action, its leading men acting to quell disputes in the same way as the Prophet had compro-

[129] Faiz Baksh, *Memoirs*, II, 44.   [130] ibid.   [131] ibid.
[132] Seton to Wellesley, 22 Jan. 1804, Wellesley, Add. 13,577, BL.
[133] ibid., cf. Seton to Merrick Shawe, 10 Feb. 1804, Wellesley, Add. 13,577, BL.

mised the quarrels of the tribes of Arabia. Here the practice of politics and jurisconsultation was more striking than the 'resistance', for which some historians perennially search. However, resistance was indeed to come when the same Mahomed Ewuz took part in the house tax disturbances of 1816, and fled the city.[134] Faced with open resistance, the British authorities had a tendency to shoot first and consult the ecumene later.

Such standard patterns of political representation and debate embraced Hindus as well as Muslims. Several historians have given us analyses of the political movement at Banaras in 1810 against the new British system of house taxation, emphasising its popular character.[135] From our perspective what is striking is that a vigorous and effective public opinion could express itself in the public arena across the boundaries of caste and religion. Here the ecumene spoke in a Hindu idiom, though Muslims were also active. The protesters presented petitions against the asssessment as discrete communities. One particular market-gardener caste leadership sent a 'letter of righteousness' (dharmapatra) to mobilise its rural supporters, in what was probably an adaptation of the normal method of raising temple funds or seeking adjudication in cases of infringements of caste rules.[136] The action of the Banaras citizens was, however, carefully coordinated between groups. The demonstrators all took a common oath of resistance and congregated in a single spot. Petitions argued the case against taxation in terms of the sanctity of Banaras but also the past and present usage of 'the country of Hindoostan, preferable to the kingdom of the seven climes', acknowledging a sense both of charismatic place and of wider patria.[137] Ultimately, too, they accepted the good offices of the Maharaja of Banaras as an intermediary with the British. Abdul Kadir Khan and another 'faithful old government servant', Akbar Ali Khan, also played the part of intermediaries. Although one historian has denounced them as 'spies' for the British,[138] and they certainly worked to end the

---

[134] Committee at Bareilly to Commrs, NWP, 3 July 1816, 27 and encls., BCJ, 25 Oct. 1816, 3, 132/48, OIOC; Rahman Ali, *Tazkirah-i Ulama-i Hind* (Lucknow, 1914), pp. 24–5.

[135] R. Heitler, 'The Varanasi house-tax hartal of 1810–11', *IESHR*, 9, 3, 1972, 239–57; G. Pandey, *The Construction of Communalism in Colonial North India* (Delhi, 1990) pp. 24–50; S. Freitag, *Collective Action and Community. Public arenas and the emergence of communalism in north India* (Berkeley, 1989), pp. 19–52.

[136] Actg Magt. to Govt, 8 Jan. 1811, Bengal Criminal Judl Procs., 8 Feb. 1811, 1, 130/28, OIOC.

[137] Petition of Mohulla Seedhesree, Bengal Criminal Judl Procs., 5 Jan. 1811, 25, 130/27, OIOC.

[138] Heitler, 'Hartal', p. 251; cf. Actg Magt. to Govt, 28 Jan. 1811, Bengal Crim. Judl, 8 Feb. 1811, 5, 130/28, OIOC.

uprising, these men had high status within both communities. They continued to resemble the munshis and advisers of the eighteenth century rather than the police informers of the nationalist period.

Finally, one should beware of the assumption that, even in cases where religious communities were pitted against each other, rational argument and social communication was totally abandoned. A few months earlier than the house tax affair, Banaras had been convulsed by a riot between Hindus and Muslims over the status of a holy place. In this case the petitioners on the part of the Hindus argued from history and current information. All had been well in Banaras, they said, until the Emperor Aurangzeb had destroyed the harmony between the communities by demolishing a temple; but the Emperor was so powerful that the Hindus had 'necessarily submitted with patience'.[139] Now the Muslim weavers had become 'more bigotted' than Aurangzeb, and the Hindus were forced to respond. Showing an acute awareness of current affairs, they argued that Muslims should concentrate on protecting the holy places of the Middle East against the Arabian Wahhabis who had recently sacked them, killing, it appears, the agent in Iraq of the late Ali Ibrahim Khan.[140]

Elite and mass in cultural performance

In addition to these set-piece demonstrations of discontent, strong political messages could be conveyed through cultural performance which linked elite and populace in enjoyment. Historians have been interested in recent years in the symbolism of festivals such as Ramlila, Holi or, amongst Muslims, Mohurrum and Id.[141] Well before the intervention of nationalist politicians at the end of the nineteenth century, these festivals had become the scene of attempts by magnates to claim new status or bodies of people attempting to assert cohesion or indentity. In this sense, the Ramlila festival, which increased in importance and size in most parts of north Indian in the eighteenth and nineteenth centuries, should itself be seen as a widening arena of public communication.[142] Garcin de Tassy listed many different types of popular literature for recitation at these festivals, including songs,

---

[139] 'Memorial of the Hindoos of the City of Benares', 20 Nov. 1809, 'Disturbances at Benares', BC 365, OIOC; the British were peeved that another important old 'native informant', Bishambhar Pandit, had been involved in fomenting the Hindus.
[140] ibid.
[141] S. Freitag, *Culture and Power in Banaras. Community, performance and environment, 1800–1980* (Berkeley, 1989).
[142] S. Pollock, 'Ramayana and political imagination in India', *Journal of Asian Studies*, 52, 2, 1993, 261–297.

chants, homilies and prayers, all of which could be used to promote cohesion and mutual knowledge.[143] These ranged from laments on the death of the Shia martyrs, through didactic treatises (*risalas*) to what he called, as early as the 1840s, 'national-musical' performances in Indian-owned premises in Calcutta and other cities.[144] This flexible range of media, part-written and part-oral, added up to a wide array of procedures for spreading information, subversion, parody and biting political comment.

A number of different styles stand out. The heroic ballads of warrior heroes conveyed not only tales of ancient valour but observations on right kingship and religious conduct. The 'Prithvi Raja ki Kahani' which told of the last Hindu king of Delhi was a kind of foundation-legend for the high-caste warrior communities. In its full version the story contained not only genealogical and epic material but observations on grammar, diplomacy and other useful arts. Peasants could sometimes be found who had exactly mastered the whole ballad.[145] These legends had a definite reactive and community dimension. The epic of Pabuji, for instance, was circulated throughout Rajasthan by travelling story-tellers with elaborate cloth panels depicting the hero's exploits. In it the Muslim ('Turk') Mirza Khan is anathematised as a cow-killer: 'Oh king of Patan, in your kingdom calves and white cows are slain; at daybreak are slain the frogs and peacocks of the gardens.'[146] Another type of popular story was the social comedy in which stereotyped members of different communities fall into conflict and farce. One typical version was the Punjabi *jhaggra* or *jhannau* in one of which an argument develops between a Khattri woman and a Jat woman.[147] They embody respectively the merits of an acute businesswoman and a sturdy peasant. The Jat woman constantly ridicules the Khattri's assertion of caste superiority. Another version of popular communication was the didactic debate between pupil and master which was found both in the Sufi tradition and in its Hindu form. All these written media and their 'shadow' verbal forms could be used to propagate critical comment and debates on the conduct of both the rulers and society as a whole.

Alongside these, finally, should be placed the performances of wandering cultural specialists: bards, puppeteers, actors and jugglers.

---

[143] *LH*, I, 24–50.   [144] *LH*, I, 41.

[145] *LH*, I, 382–5; *JRAS*, Aug. 1851, 192; this was a source for Tod, *Annals and Antiquities*.

[146] J.D. Smith, *The Epic of Pabuji. A study in transcription and translation* (Cambridge, 1991), pp. 290–1.

[147] D.J. Singh Johal, 'Historical significance of *Jhaggra Jatti te Katrani da*', in F. Singh and A.C. Arora (eds.), *Maharaja Ranjit Singh. Politics, Society, Economics* (Patiala, 1984), pp. 289–91; cf. S. Sagar, 'Social change and the *kissas* of the first half of the nineteenth century', ibid., 292–301.

Bands of these artistes moved rapidly around India often from bases at the major pilgrimage places. They conveyed political and social messages which might originate in either the literate or the non-literate spheres. In Rajasthan and adjoining areas of the Agra Province, for instance, traditional bards (Bhats and Charans), singers of family pride and the heroic exploits of the Rajput rulers, introduced into their repertoire tales of the resistance of the Jats of Bharatpur against Mughal and British. Rather lower down the social scale, courtesans and prostitutes were famous purveyors of music and popular song. Some of their stock in trade were *ghazals* [148] or musical versions of poems which had been written by noted satirists, or even by popular and munificent rulers such as Nawab Asaf-ud Daulah of Awadh.[149] While the British garnered their fair share of sycophantic ditties, they were often the target of attack too. For decades after 1799, any European traveller who wandered into the red light district of Banaras was serenaded from the roof gardens of the courtesans' houses by songs praising the exploits of the deposed Nawab Vazir Ali, who had killed the British judge of Banaras and chief intelligence expert, George Cherry, during the abortive uprising of that year.[150]

Travelling puppet shows and theatrical performances also helped spread subversive political ideas. Thus, in the months before the Vellore mutiny of 1806, it was puppeteers that carried the message that Tipu Sultan's sons were about to regain their power, aided by the French. Several decades later an observer investigated the bodies of actors who took improvised comedies around north India to all the major festivals. Their plays were usually derived from Sanskrit originals but were burlesqued to include contemporary references. The Indians 'are devoted to the type of comedy which the *bazigars* [jugglers] perform at the great occasions, and which often contain political allusions'.[151] One group was attached to a body of irregular Indian cavalry, but was hired from time to time by rich magnates who wanted to entertain their guests. Captain Bevan recorded one such performance which satirised the proceedings in a British criminal court. In the drama the magistrate appeared whistling and striking his riding boots with a cane. The

---

[148] see A. Bansani, 'Ghazal', *Encyclopaedia of Islam*, 2nd. edn, II, 1036.

[149] *LH*, I, 103–4.

[150] Bholanauth Chunder, *The Travels of a Hindoo to various parts of Bengal and Upper India* (London, 1869), pp. i, 283; cf. *LH*, I, 103–4, on Asaf-ud Daulah; for the use of another *ghazal* in a contemporary dispute, Judge Banaras to Register Nizamat Adalat, 12 January 1813, Bengal Criminal Judicial, 12 July 1816, 18, 132/43, OIOC; for use of popular theatre in a political cause, de Tassy, *LH*, I, 24–5.

[151] *LH*, I, 24; cf. 'Dramatic Amusements of the Natives of India', *Asiatic Journal*, n.s., 22, 1837, 25–34.

prisoner was brought in, but the magistrate paid no attention to him as he was flirting with a young Indian woman among the witnesses.[152] During the deposition he continued to make signs and leer at her. Finally, the bearer appeared saying '*tiffin taiyar hai*' ('tea is ready') and the magistrate got up. When the officers of the court asked what to do with the prisoner, he replied 'Dam [sic] his eyes, hang him!' This subversive assault on the white man's justice and lecherousness was, Bevan reported, greatly enjoyed both by the Indian troops and the British army officers present.

The limits of the ecumene

The north Indian critical ecumene as we have described it spilled over the bounds of caste, community and sect; it encompassed a dialogue between elite and popular political culture. It stands as a reminder that Indian minds and Indian social life cannot be reduced to the behaviourist simplicities of hierarchy and segmentation. It takes us beyond the limited and monolithic concept of 'resistance' to the realm of political critique and intellectual history. Yet this is not to say that the ecumene was a seamless web. On the contrary, there were significant breaks and discontinuities in it. For example, while Hindu noblemen, poets and specialists took part in the wider debate and wrote in its languages, Persian and Urdu, the Brahmin establishments stood relatively aloof.[153] Ghalib could say that 'Benares was the Mecca of India', but it is difficult to imagine him participating in the pandits' ritual debates (shastrarthas) in the same way that Khattri Hindus participated in the Persian poetry circles. Even Ghalib had relatively few Hindu literary correspondents. In the case of one of the most prominent, Munshi Hargopal Tafta, it seems that the poet hoped to touch him for money;[154] elsewhere he says he employed 'bunya-language' (shopkeeper talk) with a leading Delhi banker.[155] As a token of the assimilative power of public doctrinal debate, some learned Hindus became Muslims, but the process did not take place in reverse even though poor and unlettered Muslims sometimes venerated Hindu deities.[156] Muslim scholars showed interest in the Hindu classics and literature, but learned Hindus do not seem to have analysed and critiqued the Islamic corpus until Dayananda Saraswati set out to ridicule it. Khairuddin Khan's

[152] ibid., 27.
[153] 'Mahommedan Festivals in India', ibid., 16, 1835, 52.
[154] Rahbar, *Ghalib*, p. 380, n.1.
[155] Ghalib to Nawab Husain Mirza, 29 Oct. 1859, ibid., p. 207.
[156] *LH*, I, 63–4.

debate with the Banaras pandits in the 1770s occurred precisely because he had heard that a rich Bengali 'held no communication whatever with Mussulmans, and avoided even the shadow of a Mahomedan'.[157] Ritual pollution created hairline fractures in cross-community debate. Khairuddin tried to reconcile the genealogy of Adam with the story of the Pandavas of the Hindu epics and some of the Brahmins went along with this. Even so, he asked in irritation, 'what do you know of the Mahomedan religion?'[158] An overlapping debate did not mean equal participation. In fact, when a critical public sphere using the newspaper finally emerged, these inequalities of participation were reinforced by the desire of editors to grasp and hold abstract constituencies of readers' opinions, now more distant from the face-to-face, or pen-to-pen, relations of the ecumene.

Amongst the less privileged, too, social and even economic discourse was still to some extent constricted within what was called the 'opinion of the caste', even if, as in the Peshwa's territories, the authorities intervened to adjudicate and advise.[159] Among the upper castes, extra-caste opinion and debate appears to have influenced these insider debates. So, for instance, social transgressions by an Agarwal banker might have been dealt with by the caste assembly, but it had severe repercussions within the wider multi-caste arena of the market and its rumours, since social and commercial credit were closely bound up. But nobody worried much about what went on amongst the leather workers or liquor distillers. Only bhakti devotion bridged these divides of status, and the sects were becoming increasingly respectable and market-centred in the eighteenth and nineteenth centuries.[160] The ecumene had always worked unevenly beneath the network of the most enlightened intelligentsia. In this, India was not qualitatively different from other societies with emergent public spheres.[161] Nevertheless, the ecumene did display a range of fractures which were widened by the powerful pressures of later colonial politics.

---

[157] Khairuddin, *Bulwuntnamah*, p. 87.

[158] ibid., p. 88. The Bengali eventually shook Khairuddin's hand and said, 'You are a pandit of my religion', but the author clearly took it as the victory of Muhammadan learning!

[159] G.C. Vad (ed.), *Selections from the Satara Rajas' and the Peshwas' Diaries* (Bombay, 1907–11) makes it clear that the rulers' courts acted a role as a kind of 'public tribunal' for intra-caste disputes.

[160] D. Gold, 'What the merchant-guru sold; social and literary types in Hindi devotional verse', *Journal of the American Oriental Society*, 112, 1, 1992, 22–36.

[161] As is made clear by C. Calhoun (ed.), *Habermas and the Public Sphere* (Cambridge, Mass., 1992).

6   Useful knowledge and godly society, *c*. 1830–50

Historians once called the 1830s and 1840s the Age of Reform and discerned in it the beginnings of Indian modernisation. Eric Stokes, in particular, emphasised the influence of utilitarian and evangelical ideas on the Government of India during the rule of Lord William Bentinck and his successors.[1] Later writers, including Stokes himself, abandoned this position and asserted that the conflict of ideologies represented no more than 'one clerk talking to another'. The Age of Reform was rewritten as an age of hiatus, when social change was crippled by economic depression and government penury. This chapter will argue that British reform may well have been contradictory and ineffectual, but the medium of the reformers was no less important than their message. For the deepest changes of this era can be seen in the information order: the rapid diffusion of print media into north Indian society, the further movement of government away from human intelligence to statistical surveys, and the introduction of public instruction as a goal of the state. This chapter will examine these changes and show how the guardians of the Indian ecumene responded to them with speed and flexibility, appropriating some innovations and rejecting others.

Indians and the Anglo-Indian public sphere, *c*. 1780–1830

The British introduced to India not only a knowledgeable bureaucracy but also their own energetic style of public debate. The expatriates never fashioned a creole nationalism. They were too small in numbers, too dependent on Crown and Company and too divided from Eurasian and Indian society by racial exclusiveness to accomplish this.[2] Controversies amongst them raged nevertheless in press and pamphlet and Indian issues became entangled with domestic political divisions. Free mer-

---

[1]   E.T. Stokes, *The English Utilitarians and India* (Oxford, 1959).

[2]   P.J. Marshall, 'The Whites of British India, 1780–1830: a failed colonial society?', in his *Trade and Conquest. Studies in the rise of British dominance in India* (Aldershot, 1993), art. xv.

chants railed against the Company monopoly, especially when its Charter came up for periodic revision. Missionaries attempted to create a godly public sphere in which the paganism of the Company would be argued away and India flooded with improving pamphlets. Fierce controversies over press freedom erupted as Wellesley and John Adam clamped down on newspapers that had substituted sustained political criticism for the grub-street prurience exemplified by James Hicky's *Bengal Gazette* of the 1780s.

Secure in their own sophisticated tradition of communication and debate, Indians were intensely alert to these new styles of political conflict. The intelligentsia of the ecumene denounced or supported Warren Hastings in Persian works which found their way into expatriate debate. In 1787, as impeachment loomed, Hastings's agent, G.N. Thompson, procured petitions in his master's support through the heads of merchant and pandit corporations in Banaras and other cities. Ali Ibrahim Khan, meanwhile, organised a petition from 'the Mussulmans'[3] of the region. Later, the official orientalism of the Wellesley period and aggressive missionary propaganda elicited vigorous reactions from Indian spokesmen. Gilchrist tried to stage debates represented as inimical to Islam at Fort William College and was thwarted by Muslim opposition. In 1804 Raghaviah, an English-educated Tamil, produced a full refutation of the charges levelled against Hinduism by a Company servant, Mr Newham, during a debate in the College and this was later published in England.[4] Raghaviah argued that Newham had exaggerated the 'tyranny of the Brahmin', and went on to urge, with remarkable sophistication, that 'the shastras are copious, and from their equivocal style, our divine legislators gave us an opening to reform any part of them as change of circumstance and vicissitudes of time suggest'. Raghaviah clearly already conceived of Hinduism as an all-India faith, and one which was flexible in itself and accommodating to western knowledge. He anticipated Ram Mohun Roy's modernism by some years, but unlike the Bengali reformer continued to revere the Puranas. Raghaviah went further, denouncing British administrators for their aloofness and craven promotion of Indian underlings, 'without regard to either rank, cast [sic], acquirements, talents or prudence'.[5] Raghaviah's contemporary, Abu Talib Khan, the Lucknow munshi, having written

[3] Thompson to Hastings, 18 Dec. 1787, 'The Nesbitt-Thompson Papers, V', *Bengal Past and Present*, 17, 33–4, 1918, 112; for the role of Tafazzul Hussain, same to same, 12 Feb. 1788, ibid., 18, 35–6, 1919, 181.

[4] P. Raghaviah to W. Kirkpatrick, n.d., including his 'A refutation of Mr. Newham's charges against the Hindoos', which was published in the *Monthly Review*, 1804, Kirkpatrick Papers, Mss. Eur. F228/20, OIOC.

[5] ibid.

his European travelogue, appended to it a defence of Indian treatment of women, a topic of constant controversy during his sojourn in Britain and Ireland.[6] Charles Stewart translated this vigorous polemic and introduced it into the contemporary British debate about the Company's government.

Indian-produced newspapers were not published in any numbers until the 1820s and were not widely circulated west of Banaras until the following decade, but Urdu and Persian printed books found their way up-country earlier, and Indian correspondents entered into debates in English journals. Political information also spread fast, as established networks of bazaar informants picked up hot stories from expatriate journals. During the prelude to the revision of the Company Charter in 1813 and in 1830–4, for example, rumours circulated in the Banaras bazaars that the King of England would intervene against the Company[7] and halt the 'drain of wealth' from India. Indian princes and magnates tried to press their case against the authorities by using European public men and contacts.

The basis for a sophisticated political opposition existed, therefore, as many as sixty years before formal nationalist politics began. As Bishop Heber, who reckoned he had discovered 'Whigs' among the Indian commercial men,[8] perceptively observed, the 'fact is that there is a degree of intercourse maintained between this country and Europe, and a degree of information existing among the people as to what passes there, which considering how few of them speak or read English, implies other means of communication besides those which we supply and respecting which I have been able to obtain as yet very little information'.[9] He commented that the Indian bazaars circulated international news long before official reports arrived on British ships. It was after Bentinck's appointment, however, that the engagement between the Anglo-Indian public and the Indian ecumene began in earnest. Fierce protests against Bentinck's retrenchments from Anglo-Indian Tories[10] and squeals from an army embattled with financial cuts, coincided with greater press freedom and a new public philosophy of information. Indians responded immediately to the change of mood.

---

[6] Abu Taleb, *Travels* (tr. Stewart), pp. 342–51.
[7] For the controversies about the King of Delhi surrounding the Charter revision of 1831–3, HM 708; in 1838 Delhi citizens deluged the editor with Persian letters complaining about new municipal regulations, *Delhi Gazette*, 7 Nov. 1838.
[8] Heber to Wilmot Horton, Dec. 1823, *Narrative*, II, 191.
[9] Heber to Horton, Mar. 1824, *Narrative*, II, 227.
[10] e.g., *Meerut Universal Magazine*, 1, 1835, 1–4.

Useful knowledge and the reformers, 1830–57

European reformers in India looked to Britain for a pattern. The domestic reformist thinking of the 1820s and 1830s laid particular stress on public instruction as a means of spreading civic and religious knowledge. Enlightened people considered themselves duty-bound to supplement state action with privately funded educational campaigns. Their medium was the popular pamphlet fashioned from gobbets of fact and seeded with improving moral sentiments. Directing this movement was the Society for the Diffusion of Useful Knowledge which was founded in 1823.[11] The SDUK was deeply interested in India, both as a moral exemplar for British society and as an arena in which darkness could be dispelled by knowledge of western ingenuity. It published on the exotica of Hinduism;[12] James Mill, 'sole legislator for British India' and scourge of Hinduism, sat on its Committee.[13] In Britain, reformers wrote edifying books and ran evening classes with the explicit aim of diverting workers, especially working-class women, from radical politics and impure fancies. A Calcutta branch of the SDUK was founded in 1839; its aim was similar: to cement faith in the superiority of British rule and also to open the way to godly learning by dispelling the 'erotic fancies' of Hinduism. Proponents of useful knowledge argued that scripture was itself rational fact revealed in that most useful of all books, the Bible. In a similar spirit the Anglo-Indian journal, *Gleanings in Science*, argued in 1829[14] that too much attention had been paid to oriental books and dubious oriental informants. What was needed was precise observation of man and nature in India and its diffusion to European savants and 'enlightened natives'. Well before Indian provincial governments had taken up the cause of public instruction, unofficial schoolbook societies had sprung up in many stations to import, translate and disseminate books for missionary schools and the small number of existing government institutions. The reformers also planned a cheap *fanam* (a fraction of a south Indian rupee) magazine in imitation of Britain's penny magazines.[15] The pressure groups promoting these causes were composed of missionaries, army officers, tradesmen, medical doctors and 'enlightened natives'. Administrators took part as private individuals, though governments sometimes resented non-official intrusion into the domain of Indian education.[16]

[11] See Harold Silver, *The Concept of Popular Education. A study of ideas and social movements in the early nineteenth century* (London, 1965), pp. 210–36.
[12] Especially, *The Hindoos. Library of Entertaining Knowledge*, 'under the direction of the Society for the Diffusion of Useful Knowledge' (London, 1839).
[13] ibid. frontispiece.   [14] *Gleanings in Science*, I, (Calcutta, 1829), preface, i.
[15] 'On the establishing of a fanam magazine', *Friend of India*, 7 Mar. 1839.
[16] *Benares Recorder*, 23 Feb. 1847; *Friend of India*, 28 Feb. 1839; R. Hamilton, sec. to

Official and missionary activities further swelled the huge numbers of books from Britain to India, which amounted in 1839 to 1,469 cwt per annum.[17] This matched exports to the US and British America (including the Caribbean). The books may well have been missionary ephemera; they may have been designed as ships' ballast or simply have sat on library shelves in European stations. But, combined with the products of the now substantial British and Indian printing industries in Calcutta and other centres, the spread of the printed book in a subcontinent where it barely existed a generation before was a striking effect of colonial rule.

Many elite Indians found the movement for useful knowledge congenial. They joined the schoolbook societies and the branches of the SDUK and other similar societies. Indian learned men had customarily built up eclectic libraries. Moreover, the indigenous 'treasury of knowledge', composed of texts from a variety of authors, provided a parallel form to the penny magazine.[18] As early as 1819, for example, an 'ingenious native' proposed that a register of knowledge should be established at the court of Raja Serfojee of Tanjore, where learned men from all over India were wont to gather. It was to include data on inundations, gardening, vaccination, the diseases of coconut trees and a register of births and deaths.[19] The new knowledge spread faster than the printing press. Even a petty raja in the Banaras region had accumulated large collections of western books by the 1830s. He could not read English himself, but showed off his collection to a passing missionary as token of his broad-mindedness.[20] Indian merchants had already set up networks of hawkers to spread exotica and 'Europe goods' into the interior. The 'bookwallah', or retail itinerant bookseller, soon appeared in response to the new demand for information as a commodity.

The concerns of Bentinck and his generation – public instruction, the diffusion of European science, a free press and easy postal communication – all bore the hallmarks of the movement for useful knowledge. The irony was that the 'economical reform' which also lay embedded in Whig ideology discouraged the government expenditure which would have enabled these institutions to flourish. The craze for knowledge had

Textbook Cttee, Meerut to A. Shakespeare, 11 Apr. 1835, NWP Genl Procs., 6 and reply 8, 2 May 1835, 214/24, OIOC.

[17] 'The book trade of various countries', *Journal of the Statistical Society of London*, 3, 1840, 386.

[18] cf., Rieu, *Catalogue of BM*, II, 433–8.

[19] Satyajit Das (ed.), *Selections from the Indian Journals*, I, *Calcutta Journal* (Calcutta, 1963), p. 152 (May 1819).

[20] *Church Missionary Record*, ix, 1838, 48.

been routinely denounced by Tories in India as 'the cant of party';[21] now it was further politicised by the intervention of economic stringency.

Securing a cheap post as a 'means of improvement not as a source of revenue'[22] was a principal aim of social reformers. Rowland Hill, inventor of the postage stamp, and advocate of cheap communication for the masses, also sat on the council of the SDUK.[23] Effective postal communication, now a mundane matter, was then a symbol of the contemporary revolution in information. Bentinck, therefore, attempted to establish a uniform postal system for India.[24] In 1836 private posts were banned by law wherever public dak was available and a fine of Rs. 50 was prescribed for each unauthorised letter. But Indian merchants at Agra and other commercial cities complained that the measure would destroy the great system of 'Hindustani dawk' linking villages with distant cities.[25] The Indian posts, petitioners said, had charged between one and three *pice* regardless of distance or weight of letter; they worked day and night. The letters of impoverished merchants were often carried free as an act of charity, 'and hundreds of poor people are employed in hard labour and run day and night 12 cos or upwards, only at the allowance of Rs. 2 or 3'.[26] All this would disappear if letters were charged by weight and distance, and posts left to a rigid timetable. The issue of postal charges and 'illegal dawks' remained an irritant between government and its subjects for many years. High postal charges appear to have driven 'Hindustani dawk' underground, giving rise to exaggerated fears of secret Indian plots.[27] Later, Anglo-Indian critics were to claim that the 'correspondence of the community at present bears the cost of the entire correspondence of the state', now swelled by increasing numbers of legal documents.[28] While wealthy Indians appear to have used the imperial posts regularly,[29] communication between poorer

[21] *Meerut Universal Magazine*, i, 1835, 227.   [22] *Friend of India*, 19 Jan. 1837.

[23] Alongside him were Lord John Russell, future prime minister, the Hydrographer to the Admiralty, and Henry Hallam, the historian and a source for James Tod's *Rajasth'an, Hindoos*, Frontispiece.

[24] M.H. Fisher, 'Suppression of native dak', *IESHR*, 31, 3, 1994, 311–48; *Friend of India*, 19 Jan. 1837.

[25] ibid., 2 Nov. 1837; 'Petition from undermentioned native Bankers and Merchants' of the NWP, mid-Aug. 1837, NWP Crim. Judl. Procs., 1–5 Sept. 1837, 4, 231/38, OIOC.

[26] 'Petition of the native Merchants, Bankers, etc. of the city of Agra', 23 Sept. 1837, NWP Criminal Judicial Procs., 28 Sept. 1837, 340, 231/39, OIOC.

[27] See Ghalib's comments on the post office, Russell and Islam, *Ghalib*, I, 113–14; cf. *Mofussilite*, 30 May 1848.

[28] *Friend of India*, 2 Dec. 1847.

[29] From figures given in 'District Dawks', *Friend of India*, 18 Jul. 1850. Indian *daks* were gradually supplanted by Company's post after 1836, Fisher, 'Suppression'; see also

subjects may well have fallen victim to high charges, especially during periods of economic distress.[30] This was in sharp contrast to the situation in Britain where access to the post steadily increased popular communication. The information revolution in India may, paradoxically, have been accompanied by a restriction of popular written communication.

When it came to the press, the leaders of the useful knowledge movement faced similar contradictions. Bentinck was more favourable to newspapers than were his predecessors. And he was particularly interested in the expansion of the indigenous Indian press, which he considered too tame and derivative. Andrew Stirling, Bentinck's Persian Secretary, remarked, for example, that the *Jami Jahan Nama* was the best native newspaper in India, but 'never contains any original matter', being composed of Persian translations of articles from English papers and reproductions of newsletters from Indian courts.[31] The Governor-General responded that even this basic diffusion of information from government to the people had a 'salutary operation' and, in time, the Indian press would tend to promote 'useful knowledge'.[32] Bentinck's support notwithstanding, high postal charges and stringent control continued to hold back the press, Indian and Anglo-Indian alike. When opponents of the Government began to rail against sedition in Indian newspapers, the dilemma of colonial government was palpable. It wished to diffuse, but also to control and tax information. 'Our empire in India is an empire of opinion', wrote the *Friend of India*, but, it admitted, there was always a danger that the spread of knowledge would undermine British dominion.[33]

This paradox also helps explain the strident racialism which was now edging out the more favourable orientalist assessment of India from public discourse. If Indians could now share European knowledge through the press and public instruction, then paradoxically, the only justification for their subordination had to be their racial and cultural inferiority. Overt and public racism became more acceptable when Indians began to argue in the same forums and exchange the same ideas as the British. During the Hastings and Wellesley eras, the appropriate public stance for an expatriate had been to stress the wondrous effects of British 'benevolency' in India. Disparaging and racialist stereotypes

NWP General Procs., July 1850, 87–94, 215/5, for native rulers' attempts to break the PO monopoly.

[30] 'Petition of the Native Merchants, Bankers, etc. of the city of Agra', NWP Crim. Judl, 5–30 Sept. 1837, 340, 231/39.
[31] A. Stirling to Bentinck, Calcutta, 1829, Philips (ed.), *Bentinck Correspondence*, I, 139.
[32] Bentinck's minute on the Press, 6 Jan. 1829, ibid., 137.
[33] *Friend of India*, 27 Oct. 1836.

became more common in the 1830s when expatriates began to face real economic and intellectual competition from Indians. But this was a local rhetoric of exclusion. The distant fulminations of James Mill and the domestic missionaries merely consolidated it; they did not create it.

As Stokes demonstrated, another strand in the ambivalent movement to diffuse knowledge in India – and knowledge of India – was provided by moderate Christian evangelicalism. Evangelical influences moulded the thought of many of Bentinck's generation. Covert evangelicalism became particularly prominent, however, in the NWP where James Thomason and his friends gradually rose to influence. For men such as Thomason, denatured systems of Indian thought and communication might yet serve as lowly vehicles for the diffusion of true knowledge. Although Thomason did not become Lieutenant-Governor of the North-Western Provinces until 1843, his evangelical piety and concern for useful knowledge were typical of the leading younger civil servants of the 1830s who had started their careers under Bentinck, Metcalfe and Trevelyan. Thomason, in turn, founded the paternalist tradition of administration which took root in the Punjab during the following generation.[34] Close to the anti-slavery circles of Wilberforce and Zachary Macaulay, he believed that 'we should carry our Christian principles into our daily work as public servants'.[35] The creation of stable property rights and a civil society in India would, he thought, ultimately aid the progress of the Gospel there, but no direct proselytisation should be undertaken. His views mirrored the sentiment of the *Benares Magazine* that 'we want rather books written in a Christian spirit than Christian books'.[36]

Thomason believed that the expansion of knowledge was necessary for the creation of civil society. Noting the large number of lithographic presses which had sprung up in the North-Western Provinces after 1830, he wrote: 'the native mind in this part of the country is undoubtedly making great advances now. A popular and useful Oordoo literature is now forming ... and it is becoming the vehicle for conveying practical and useful knowledge to all classes of the people'[37] and agents of native presses in major cities were circulating books widely through the country. The Government, he believed, had promoted this change by substituting Urdu for Persian as the court language and also by initiating the 'vast circulation' of small elementary books which gave the

[34] R. Temple, *James Thomason* (Oxford, 1893), pp. 98–101.   [35] *ibid.*, p. 72.
[36] cited, *Friend of India*, 4 Jan. 1849.
[37] Thomason to Wilson, 16 Nov. 1847, Mss. Eur. E301/ 10, OIOC; cf. A.K. Ohdedar, *The Growth of the Library in Modern India, 1498–1936* (Calcutta, 1966), p. 122, on the vast internal market for Indian 'bookwallahs'; S. Chaudhuri (ed.), *Calcutta. The Living City*, I, *The Past* (Calcutta, 1990), 128–36.

rudiments of arithmetic and land measurement. He had in mind titles such as the *Patwariyon ki Pustaka* ('village accountants' book') and *Mahajanon ki Pustaka* ('merchants' book').[38]

For the official mind of the NWP Government, public instruction and useful knowledge was closely tied up with agrarian reconstruction. Revenue officers were aware that revenue clerks and middlemen had enriched themselves by manipulating the papers of every settlement since 1802. The authorities had been paralysed in the face of the famines of 1833 and 1838, and feared that they had little control of a countryside which was still armed. Knowledgeable rule and agrarian literacy was to be the panacea for this crisis of Company government and education was the critical ingredient. Thomason rejoiced that, during the settlements of 1836–8, revenue officers surveyed every field and constructed a record of rights which was filed in the collector's office. He believed that there was a direct and powerful inducement for every member of the population to acquire basic literacy and numeracy in order to protect his rights. Books teaching measurement and arithmetic were a significant element in the new vernacular literature.[39]

Government, therefore, began to take a more active role in public instruction during the later 1840s and Thomason pushed through his reforms, instituting a system of village and subdivisional schools throughout the NWP. The new Inspectorate of Public Instruction, under the energetic direction of H.S. Reid, employed Indian subordinates who combined the skills of a traditional munshi with some English education.[40] These men visited village schools and translated classics of English useful knowledge into Hindi and Urdu for their use. Several important vernacular writers served their literary apprenticeship while working on this project.

Following the lead of the new Statistical Society of London, officials also began to collect figures on matters such as literacy and disease from jails, which became institutional experiments for the new policies.[41] Medical, moral and educational concerns merged together in the campaign against infanticide amongst the great agricultural castes. By 1857, village watchmen were supposed to report regularly on births in

[38] e.g., *Mahajanon ki Pustaka* (Agra, 1849) and *Patwariyon ki Pustaka* (Agra, 1849), OIOC; despite his 'modernism' Thomason believed in the use of *inshas* and traditional teacher–pupil dialogues in his educational schemes: 'Hints for promoting national education', NWP Genl. Procs., 28 Mar. 1850, 172, 215/3.

[39] Thomason to Wilson, 16 Nov. 1847, Wilson Papers, 10; cf. Temple, *Thomason*, pp. 138–42.

[40] See below, pp. 229ff.

[41] D. Arnold, *Colonising the Body. State medicine and epidemic disease in nineteenth century India* (Berkeley, 1993), pp. 61–115.

their jurisdiction.[42] Previous censuses had been designed to assist taxation in the manner of the Mughal household computations. Now, the NWP government wanted to secure an accurate count of the actual population. Though it was primitive by comparison with the post-Mutiny censuses, G. Christian's Census of 1851 was a considerable advance on the local enumerations carried out by men such as James Prinsep in the 1830s.[43]

As John Kaye ruefully admitted after the 1857 Rebellion, this statistical knowledge proved of little value in predicting popular sentiment or political events.[44] Even at the time, officials warned that large parts of the countryside were armed and completely out of control,[45] except perhaps for the short time when the settlement officer or a platoon of armed revenue police came by. The statistical movement was also very uneven. Highly competent revenue surveys and gazetteers were created by officials such as Robert Montgomery and R.M. Bird,[46] but the motivating force was factional. Bird and his party were levellers, determined to sweep aside the great magnates, and they wanted to know the detail of every field in order to make their settlements with the village elites. Conservative officers who supported the magnates were more cursory in their investigations. Official knowledge thus remained, even in the 1830s and 1840s, a highly political matter. From the level of the collector up to that of the Presidency, officials and army officers used the new data to press their interests and to fight their corners. While the Indian Government evidently knew much more about local conditions in 1850 than it had done in the time of Warren Hastings, 'men on the spot' could still poison the springs of information.

The changes in the NWP formed, nevertheless, a striking contrast to the sluggishness of Bengal. The press and reforming officials criticised the 'centralisation and secrecy of government' in the Lower Provinces. The obscurantism of the Bengal Government, they said, kept 'valuable information from the public in an age of universal enquiry and unexampled improvement'.[47] In this comparison, the NWP under Thomason scored well. The NWP government had begun to print regular *Selections from Public Correspondence*, partly to head off public and

---

[42] *Benares Recorder*, 26 Oct. 1847.
[43] D. Bhattacharya, *Censuses*; G.J. Christian, *Report on the Census of the North-West Provinces of the Bengal Presidency taken on the 1st June 1853* (Calcutta, 1854), p. 5; cf. 'How the Census is taken in the Mofussil', *Mofussilite*, 18 Apr. 1851.
[44] See below, Ch. 9.
[45] On widespread disturbances in Allahabad district, 'Military Musings', *Mofussilite*, 4 Oct. 1850; same in Bareilly, *Friend of India*, 14 Sept. 1837.
[46] P. Penner, *The Patronage Bureaucracy in North India. The Robert M. Bird and James Thomason school, 1820–1870* (Delhi, 1986).
[47] *Friend of India*, 8 Sept., cf. 16 Dec. 1847, 4 July 1850.

Parliamentary criticism, but partly because the circulation of information was regarded as a good in itself. The *Friend of India* commented that official publication was essential to all those 'engaged in statistical and historical researches' and who need to get beneath 'the mere surface of Indian history'.[48] The massive expansion of revenue information set the NWP aside from Bengal where large zamindars dominated the countryside, and no school of paternalist officialdom emerged comparable to the Thomason circle.

The NWP Government also became more sensitive to the need to make propaganda on its own behalf. It produced tracts in Hindi and Urdu to proclaim the benefits of the new Ganges Canal.[49] During the Sikh War of 1846–7 it embarked on a more direct propaganda effort to counter the popular hostility which was particularly pronounced in the western districts and at holy places, such as Hardwar and Banaras, where Sikh chieftains had previously been lavish donors. Official justifications of the war also appeared in the press.[50] The Hindi book on the rise and eclipse of the Sikhs, *Sikhon ka Udaya aur Asta*,[51] written by Babu Shiva Prasad, Deputy Inspector of Schools, and published in 1851, may have been a cautious support in this campaign. Some of the material in the pamphlet appears to have been taken from Cunningham's recently published *History of the Sikhs*, though it does not reiterate Cunningham's criticisms of British officials. Shiva Prasad's book was one of the first pieces of contemporary history written in the vernacular and in the Devanagari script.

In sum, the new information order was intended to transform the nature of the hybrid Anglo-Indian government which had been inherited from the days of Warren Hastings. R.N. Cust, one of the ablest of Thomason's proteges who was sent into a newly conquered Punjab District in the later 1840s, remarked that Indian rulers had 'expert administrators' and a sense of right and wrong in government, but, 'having no fixed system, and preserving no records, having no printing press at command, the effects are ephemeral and perish with the government that gave them birth'.[52] Cust's own early administrative efforts were designed to improve the recording and transfer of information within government offices. With the assistance of his munshi he

---

[48] ibid., 1 Feb. 1849.
[49] Pt. Bansidhar, *Ganga ki Nahar ka Samkhep* [Sketch of the Ganges Canal] (Agra, 1854), OIOC, VT 1528; cf. *Dak Bijli* (Allahabad, 1856), a promotional work on the wonders of the electric telegraph; cf. *Delhi Gazette*, 26 May 1849, on government propaganda about works of 'public utility'.
[50] 'An intelligent native of this place', *Delhi Gazette*, 11 April 1849.
[51] Babu Shiva Prasad, *Sikhon ka Udaya aur Asta* (Banaras, 1851).
[52] R.N. Cust, *Literary and Oriental Essays*, 2nd ser., 3 (London, 1887), 88.

wrote 'A manual for the guidance of native officials and magistrates in the Cutcheries of the Northwestern Provinces' which was made available in an Urdu edition (*Fihrist Dastur Amal Faujdari*).[53] In it, Cust drew on the methods and terminology of the late Mughal *dastur amal*, but prescribed central 'registers' (he used the English word), which would make it easier to file and trace information.[54] He aimed to ensure that Indian subordinate officials saw their papers as public, not private property, and that the official memory of a district office would survive the departure of the head clerk. Cust wrote this work in simple, matter-of-fact Urdu, with short sentences and English words where necessary. Official manuals and schoolbooks of this sort mirrored the turn of the main reformist Islamic writings of the period towards simpler language. Cust's administrative project remained part of the broader enthusiasm for useful printed knowledge which was the hallmark of the Thomasonian era. He was an indefatigable author, seeing the printing press as a great weapon in aid of Christian proselytisation. Godly information was also useful information, and his early career marked pace with the efforts by missionaries such as C. Pfander and officials such as Herbert Edwardes to batter in what they saw as the crumbling bastions of Islam and Hinduism with printed knowledge.[55]

It was not only government that led the campaign for useful knowledge. The economic pressures of the 1830s and 1840s, and especially the crash of the indigo houses in 1827 and 1847, unnerved the expatriate business community. Correspondents and editors of the up-country magazines cried out for social and economic statistics to help them make sense of their predicament. As an editorial in the *Benares Recorder* put it, after sixty years of British rule, 'we yet know very little of the moral ligatures by which the people are kept together'. What was particularly needed was a good statistical work, especially a scrutiny of the 'mahajun [merchant] system and its working'; like the Jesuits, Indian merchants used secret information for the purpose of 'class aggrandisement'. This, the newspaper argued, was the cause of the monstrously high prices of commodities and the sixty-year stagnation of the country.[56] In local competition, the Europeans had made little headway against indigenous merchants whose inner lines of information and communication were still formidable. Indian merchants, nevertheless, sought reliable trade information themselves and sometimes made common cause with the expatriates against local officials.[57] While, then, the movement for useful

[53] '*Fihrist dastur amal faujdari*', ibid., 89.   [54] ibid.
[55] *Church Missionary Gleaner*, Sept. 1855, pp. 1–15.
[56] *Benares Recorder*, 12 Mar. 1847.
[57] cf. *Benares Recorder*, 4, 11 Dec. 1846, letters re. *Hindee Ukhbar* of Banaras.

knowledge was enlisted in the campaign to establish a colonial moral hegemony in India, its origins and scope stretched far beyond this orientalist discourse, reflecting a much wider change in the international division of labour and knowledge.

Subordinating and recasting Indian knowledge

The controversy between the proponents of English and the classical Indian languages was a symbolic joust between administrative genera-tions. English was already in demand amongst the elites of the coastal areas and Bengali, Hindustani-Hindi and other vernaculars were developing rapidly up-country. Despite the seeming victory of the anglicists, the dominant educational policy of the period was the promotion of western knowledge through vernacular languages and with the aid of indigenous literati. The status of Indian knowledge and Indian informants was much lower than it had been fifty years earlier when Jones and Wilford discoursed with the pandits and munshis. On the other hand, Indian spokesmen immediately began to adapt their own intellectual culture to the new media and ideologies, and penetrated quickly into the heart of the colonial debate.

J.R. Ballantyne, Principal of the Banaras Sanskrit College (1845–62), best represents a new form of constructive orientalism,[58] which historians have often overlooked by concentrating on the anglicists. Believing in the importance of 'national education' in the manner of the Younger Mill, Ballantyne argued that western knowledge, and ultimately Christian enlightenment, could only advance in India through the nuanced use of native languages, particularly Sanskrit, and by co-opting the indigenous intellectual elite, the pandits. Indian educators needed to understand and critique the contents and errors of the Vedas and Puranas, but they also required a method of reasoning and logic which could be adapted to Indian higher education. They would teach the Indian elite by 'moulding what we present to them as nearly as possible in accordance with what is sound in their own systems'.[59] It was here that the Sanskrit science of Nyaya came in. Nyaya was both a phenomenology and a mode of reasoning. It was the second function that appealed to Ballantyne. Although he was a product of the second, and distinctly empirical, wave of Scottish Enlightenment thought, he believed that a proper philosophical grounding was necessary for both

[58] J. Thomason, *Speech Delivered at the Opening of the Benares New College, Jan. 11, 1853* (Banaras, 1853).
[59] Extract from a Report by Ballantyne on Banaras College, 9 Sept. 1847, Wilson Papers, Mss. Eur. 301/10, ff. 204–5.

knowledge and faith. Nyaya, with its concern for rational proof and its progressive reasoning by claim and counter-claim, appeared to fill the need.[60] Accordingly, he tried to revive the traditional scholarly debate (*shastrartha*) as a means of disseminating modern learning.[61]

Like Wilford and Wilkins in an earlier generation, Ballantyne proceeded to collect a large number of texts on Nyaya from the pandit families of Banaras and its environs.[62] This did not occur without resistance from the pandit establishments which, as in earlier forays, resented the appropriation of sacred scripture by Europeans. Still, Ballantyne was able to bring together nearly a dozen texts of the sixteenth to eighteenth centuries from different parts of India which had found their way to Banaras with the migrations of the pandit families. The Sanskrit College Library amassed a large collection of original texts and employed a number of full-time copyists. Some copies found their way back to Wilson in Oxford.[63] Ballantyne's lectures, delivered at the Sanskrit College, expounded Nyaya-Vaisesika, alongside the logic of classical Greece and modern Europe. His students were instructed, for instance, in 'What and how many are the categories of logical statement, according to Nyaya, Aristotle and modern western scientists.'[64] Ballantyne believed that the pandits' teaching system had much to recommend it,[65] but he was pessimistic, believing that there was an absolute ceiling to what his charges could assimilate of western knowledge. This was because individual minds, like a civilisation as a whole, had to go through 'stages' in intellectual evolution. The only way that his students could be introduced to modern analytical philosophy and science was by first taking them personally through these stages. Ballantyne therefore translated into Sanskrit the great classics of western thought – Aquinas, Bacon, Hume – which he believed could straddle the gap between the antique knowledge of the pandits and modern science.[66]

---

[60] J.R. Ballantyne, *Christianity contrasted with Hindu Philosophy* ... (London, 1859), esp. pp. xvi–xviii; cf. his 'Report of the annual examinations of the Benares, 1849', NWP Genl. Procs., April–May 1850, 10, 215/4, OIOC.

[61] e.g., *Chandra Ghumana Vichar (Does the Moon Rotate?) A Question argued in Sanskrit and English by the Pandits of the Banaras College* (Banaras, 1857); cf., descriptions of Ballantyne's attempts to impress the pandits with science in R.N. Cust's diaries, Mar.–Nov. 1852, Add. Mss. 45,394, BL.

[62] J.R. Ballantyne, *Lectures on the Nyaya Philosophy embracing the text of the Tarka Sangraha* (Banaras, 1848), pp. i–ii.

[63] Ballantyne to Wilson, 11 Mar. 1846, Wilson Papers, Mss. Eur. E301/ 10, OIOC.

[64] Anon. (Ballantyne?), 'The Benares Sanskrit College', *Benares Magazine*, 5, 1850–1, 103.

[65] 'The Pandits and their method of teaching', *Benares Magazine* 2, 1849, 353–9; J.R. Ballantyne, *Aphorisms of the Mimansa Philosophy by Jaimini* (Allahabad, 1851), Introduction, p. i.

[66] Anon. (Ballantyne), 'The Benares Sanskrit College', p. 103.

By locating Indian learning and logic on a complex developmental scale, Ballantyne assigned them to a more lowly position than had been common earlier, but he did not erase them. Other officials and educators adopted a similar position. At Sehore in central India, Lancelot Wilkinson tried to expand astronomical knowledge by enlisting the aid of mathematically trained pandits.[67] Alois Sprenger and Felix Boutros were working along similar lines at the Delhi College,[68] believing in the moulding of the indigenous elite to receive the 'higher arts' of mathematics, astronomy and logic. Since oriental learning had ground to a halt at the stage of Aristotle and his Arabic commentators, or at best the Siddhantic pupils of Ptolemy, then it was from that point that native education would have to begin. Men of the stamp of the mathematician Ramchandra,[69] or the historian and astronomer, Sayyid Ahmad Khan,[70] were to aid in the elision of the centuries. While it is true that the constructive orientalists' lessons failed to percolate downward quickly, new communities of knowledge did begin to form among Indians. These were seen among Banaras pandits who participated in Ballantyne's shastric debates, the members of the Delhi Archaeological Society and the mathematical pandits' 'junto' of Sehore. Cliques of this type broadened the range of the critical public and generated innovative responses amongst traditional scholars, as the following two chapters will show.

This more vigorous attempt to subordinate Indian knowledge and modes of communication in the interests of public instruction was also reflected in the making of history and annals, that most political of the sciences. In an earlier section, we have noted the engagement between European and Indian historians. The late-Mughal historian-administrators' discourse of the decline of royal office and the corruption of government, including their assaults on the Company, could be appropriated by the colonial power. It was adapted to disparage Indian government in the light of its own 'constitutional standards'. Between 1790 and 1830, munshis under British patronage wrote numerous works on the topography and history of the new colonial districts.[71]

---

67 See below, pp. 257–60.
68 C.F. Andrews, *Zakaullah of Delhi* (Cambridge, 1929), pp. 40–4; cf. reports on Delhi College and Delhi Institution, 1829–30, HM 1255; Troll, *Sayyid Ahmad*, pp. 146–7; Powell, *Missionaries*, pp. 60–3, 206–225; see the forthcoming work by Gail Minault on the Delhi College.
69 Ramchandra Yesudas, *A Treatise on the problems of Maxima and Minima ... reproduced by order of the East India Company* (1850; London, 1859); Powell, *Missionaries*, pp. 206–25.
70 Troll, *Sayyid Ahmad*, pp. 102–4.
71 J.M. Siddiqi, *Aligarh District. A Historical Survey* (Aligarh, 1981), p. 316; cf. Khairuddin Hussain, 'Tarikh-i Jaunpur', tr. anon., Add. Mss. 3866, CUL; Ghulam Hazrat on

They still drew on the detailed sections of the 'Institutes of Akbar' and later regional histories as models, but the empirical and descriptive elements prevailed over the moral and didactic, reflecting British predilections. These proto-gazetteers, translated from the Persian or Urdu, provided British administrators with basic information on the new territories; they also inscribed the land-controlling rights of particular groups of zamindars whose title was often dubious and recently acquired.[72] By the 1830s, however, the function of Indian histories was less sure. The first generation of British-authored statistical and medical accounts of the districts was beginning to appear, consigning the less precise, but more catholic indigenous versions to the margins. The broad narratives of Indo-Muslim history which set the doings of great dynasties against the history of Islam or of dutiful Hindu kingship seemed less relevant now.[73]

By the 1840s and 1850s larger 'scientific' histories in the style of Cunningham on the Sikhs had also begun to appear, while the moral imperatives of improvement espoused by James Mill were reproduced in the works of the Company's own historians, Edward Thornton[74] and John Kaye.[75] Indian histories began to suffer a relentless assault which reached its apogee in the works of H.M. Elliot, Foreign Secretary to the Government of India. Elliot was an apostle of printed information; with Henry Torrens, he had founded the first newspaper in the NWP in 1831. His *Biographical Index to the Historians of Mahomedan India* appeared in 1849, many years before his more famous posthumous work, *The History of India Told by its Own Historians*. Elliot conceded some value to the factual content of the Persian authors. His broader aim, however, was aggressively ideological and disparaging. Indian history was a 'mere narration of events without speculation on causes and effects'.[76] It failed to penetrate beneath the surface and was consequently unable to remedy the evils of 'despotic government', so that even now 'We behold kings, even of our own creation sunk in sloth and debauchery.' This sentiment perhaps echoed the Foreign Department's desire to annex Awadh. The young radicals and 'bombastic

Gorakhpur, Rieu, *Catalogue of BL*, I, 311, III, 946; cf. ibid., I, 431 (Sangin Beg on Delhi, patronised by Metcalfe), III, 958 (Manik Chand on Agra, patronised by Lushington).
[72] e.g., Shaikh Abdur Rahim, 'Ahsan-ul Kitab wa sifatul Ansab' (*c.* 1840s) on Aligarh, Siddiqi, *Aligarh*, p. 316.
[73] Grewal, *Muslim Rule*, pp. 165–93.
[74] E. Thornton, *Chapters of the Modern History of British India* (London, 1840).
[75] J. Kaye, *The Administration of the East India Company. A History of Indian Progress* (London, 1853); N.N. Singh. *British Historiography on British Rule in India. The life and writings of Sir J.W. Kaye, 1814–76* (Patna, 1986).
[76] Repub. in *Friend of India*, 26 Apr. 1849.

baboos' of new India, Elliot continued, would do well to remember the
appalling tortures inflicted by these ancient kings on rebels, the Hindus
killed by Muslims and the temples razed. A proper history of Mughal
India would make our subjects 'more sensible of the immense
advantages accruing to them under the mildness and equity of our
rule'.[77]

Elliot's specific purpose was to take the wind out of the sails of the
contemporary Indian agitation against the resumption of revenue-free
grants to temples, shrines and learned families by purporting to show
that such rights had always been confiscated at the whim of the ruler.
Indians of all classes constantly complained about the decline of the
great works of the Mughals. Elliot refuted this claim, arguing that the
NWP survey alone 'is sufficient to proclaim our superiority'. Every field
in an area of 52,000 square miles had been mapped and every man's
possession recorded. This eclipsed the 'boasted measurement of Akber
and is as magnificent a monument of civilisation as any country in the
world can produce'.[78]

The British also began to disparage the Persian newsletters which had
once been so important to them. Officials had already ceased to pay for
the prattling of old ladies. One resident, for example, disdained the
collection of 'degrading personal details'[79] purveyed by the 'ukhber
nuwaees, meaning scurrilous rapporteur'. Economic retrenchment and
the new high-minded moralising both counselled the abolition of these
offices.[80] In the 1830s and 1840s the *Englishman* and the *Delhi Gazette*
still published translations of the Delhi newsletters, though elsewhere a
new breed of *mukhbir* or 'native correspondents' began to appear.[81] In
April 1834, to the obvious disdain of the British editors, the newswriters
were writing of the King of Awadh's new palace, the discovery in Bengal
of pearls 'as big as limes', the charismatic status of Timur, the King's
ancestor, the abolition of the pilgrim tax, and the death of Ram Mohun
Roy.[82] The significance of all these matters within the languishing
imperial Mughal discourse can readily be appreciated, but they had
begun to appear trivial to the British. Only reports from the still-
dangerous Sikh kingdom were treated with respect. Newswriters in

---

[77] ibid., but see the later published version in *HI*, I, Introduction, 1–2.
[78] *Friend of India*, 26 Apr. 1849.
[79] Resdt Indore to Sec. Govt, 11 Oct. 1832, 'Residency diaries', BC 1509/59287; cf.
      Resdt Gwalior to Sec. Govt, 30 Oct. 1832, ibid.
[80] Westmacott deplored the sacking of newswriters and their 'old ladies' in Rajasthan,
      'Travels', f. 289, 24 Dec. 1833, Mss. Eur. C29, OIOC.
[81] *Delhi Gazette*, 6 Jan. 1847, on Bahawalpur sawars; ibid., 10 Jan. 1849, on Gujarat
      'newspapers'.
[82] *Englishman*, 18 April, 1834.

Lahore were regarded as useful informants for the northwest and even though Ranjit Singh was failing, his minister, Fakir Azizuddin, who boasted skills in astrology and medicine and knowledge of the Persian classics, was called 'the last of the indigenous diplomatists of Hindostan'.[83] Hereafter, the information flows of the Indian polity declined in importance for the conquerors. Newswriters were gradually laid off, or ignored in many states, and local information was relayed to Calcutta in the more straightforward form of English diaries of political intelligence.[84] The *Benares Recorder* explained the change:

The native style of news-writing is so dry, unentertaining and at the same time so excursive, and particularly in trifles that it requires more than ordinary skill to arrange a native communication into an intelligible shape or form. We are told that a king reigned, built a bridge or musjid [mosque], and died or was murdered. The fine shadowings of thought in describing the operation of many causes which led to his elevation, the policy by which he maintained his power, the opinions of learned contemporaries, in short a philosophical view of cause and effects, are all matters beyond the power of oriental description.[85]

In fact, it was idle to try to find 'moral reflections, abstract reasoning, lofty thoughts or subtle conclusions' in a newsletter. These sheets of intelligence were specifically designed, as we have shown, to report attested fact without opinion. The fine reasoning and the arts of kingship were to be supplied by the verbal information of intelligent harkaras or sage counsellors.

Useful knowledge and the new munshi

The word munshi continued to be used by the indigenous literati into the later nineteenth century, by which time it had become the preserve of consciously conservative men of letters, usually Muslims and Kayasthas. Between 1820 and 1850, however, a new type of munshi began to appear. The older generation of munshi, who had taught the British Persian and done their Indian diplomacy for them, remained firmly rooted in the culture of the ecumene. For them Frankish knowledge was by no means superior to Indo-Islamic knowledge, and it was Abul Fazl rather than Adam Smith who remained their administrative lodestone. The new munshis, however, were tied closely to British patronage and, by the 1850s, most were educated in English.

[83] *Englishman*, 12 Nov. 1843.
[84] But incredible detail still came in from the spies in the Delhi Court; for instance the information that the royal heir was circumcised and hence by family, though not Muslim tradition, unable to succeed to the title, 'Delhi Palace Intelligence', 15–16 Jan. 1849, HM 724a, ff. 42–7, OIOC.
[85] *Benares Recorder*, 3 Sept. 1847.

Many were employees of the Department of Public Instruction. Rather than perusing newsletters and the proclamations of Indian rulers, they translated early Victorian schoolbooks into Urdu and Hindi.[86] Michael Fisher has shown how, between 1820 and 1840, Indians serving the British as semi-independent munshis and clients of individual officers were gradually moulded into a bureaucracy.[87] Here we describe some of the inward changes in literary manners and self-representation which accompanied that administrative change. Rather than diplomatists and natural philosophers, munshis were now expected to be diarists and personal assistants to masterful white men.

One of the earliest of the *évolué* munshis who were brought within the ambit of colonial knowledge was Munshi Mohan Lal of Delhi, a Kashmiri Brahmin from a family with a distinguished history of service to the Mughal royal family, and strong connections to Kashmir, Punjab and the northwest.[88] Mohan Lal's intelligence and adaptability to British modes of thinking brought him to the attention of Charles Trevelyan, who, during the later years of Bentinck's term, reached the apogee of his influence as an apostle of bureaucratic knowledge.[89] Trevelyan was responsible for attracting several learned young Indians to Calcutta.[90] Having been educated in the English Department of Delhi College for three years, Mohan Lal was assigned to a diplomatic and fact-finding mission to central Asia led by Sir Alexander Burnes. Accounts of Mohan Lal's role in this mission served a number of rhetorical purposes in the debate on Indian education and development which filled the pages of the newly invigorated English-language press in north India. The *Bengal Hurkaru*, *Englishman* and other newspapers published regular reports from and about Mohan Lal which were funnelled to them by Dr James Gerard, the medical officer on the expedition. He claimed to have taught Mohan Lal to keep an English diary of his travels in the north-west frontier regions. This ability to speak acceptable English and keep an 'excellent journal' marked him out as a new type of

---

[86] e.g., Munshi Sadha Sukh Lal, see R. Roseberry III, *Imperial Rule in Punjab. The conquest and administration of Multan* (Delhi, 1987), p. 119; for other such munshis, *LH*, I, 89, 155–6, 293–301, 396; III, 9–13, 16; also NWP Government farming out translation to local men, e.g. Munshi Jawahir Lal, Ledlie, Reid and their munshis and Ram Saran Das, note by LG, NWP Genl Procs., 28 Mar. 1850, 173, 215/5.

[87] Fisher, *Indirect Rule*, pp. 339–57.

[88] Sender, *Kashmiri Pandits*, pp. 83–8; H.L. Chopra, *Pandit Mohan Lal Kashmiri*, (Delhi, 1979); Trevelyan's 'memoir', reprinted in Munshi Mohan Lal, *Journal of a Tour through the Panjab, Afghanistan* ... (Calcutta, 1834), pp. ix–x.

[89] Trevelyan was dubbed by north Indian akhbarats the 'knowledge dispensing secretary' whose inquisitiveness was like that of the angels who interrogated the dead at Judgement Day, *Englishman*, 4 Mar. 1835.

[90] e.g. Krishna Rao, son of a former Diwan of Saugor, Spry, *Modern India*, I, 62.

native informant.[91] At the same time Burnes valued his expertise in Persian correspondence, 'the forms of which amount to a science in the East'.[92]

Like the older generation, Mohan Lal had 'accomplished Persian'[93] and delighted the local rulers of a region where the British were beginning to fear Russian influence. His mixture of fortitude and deference was even more to the taste of his superiors. Mohan Lal, unlike most of the 'effeminate' inhabitants of southern Asia, was able to ride for miles with his feet frozen into his stirrups, an appropriate trait now manly exploration on the fringes of empire was beginning to be seen as an indication of racial superiority. He also obliged by declaring to Afghan enquirers 'that there were hundreds of others educated under the patronage of the British Government infinitely superior to himself'.[94] As a consequence, Nawab Jubber Khan, brother of the ruler of Kabul, was considering sending a son to be educated at Delhi College. 'Our young native friend' whose charming, naive English gave promise of better things to come was, it appeared, wonderfully suited to being patronised by the Anglo-Indian public. This was particularly desirable at a time when Raja Ram Mohun Roy had just died in England. Roy's treatment by the Anglo-Indian press had been altogether more circumspect. In semi-ironic tones he was designated 'our illustrious fellow countryman' by the Calcutta British.[95] But the range of his knowledge in Persian, Sanskrit and Christian polemic, and his royal contacts, made him a difficult figure to patronise. It was different with Mohan Lal. The Hindu orthodox in Delhi began to threaten him with excommunication for having passed out of India, Arya Varta, over the River Jhelum to the north. So the Calcutta press could praise Mohan Lal for his compliance while simultaneously mounting a diatribe against the 'native degeneracy' which sustained such superstition.[96]

Mohan Lal was actually less tractable than it appeared. He was soon intruding snide little remarks about the British into his journal and letters. In February 1834 he noted with regret that whereas the British power was now situated only a few miles from Jalalabad, it was 'foreign scholars' who 'wore the crown of knowledge and fame by discovering the treasures of antiquity'.[97] Such niggles broadened out over the next

---

[91] *Englishman*, 17 Apr. 1834; Mohan Lal, *Tour*, p. iv; on the importance of 'drawing and sketching', ibid., p. v; cf. A. Burnes, *Travels into Bokhara, being the account of a journey from India to Cabool, Tartary and Persia* (London, 1834), I, 347.

[92] ibid., I, xii.

[93] *Englishman*, 10 Feb. 1834; Gerard to Sec. Govt of India, 20 Mar. 1834, Bengal Secret Cons., 15 May 1834, 15, OIOC.

[94] *Englishman*, 10 Feb. 1834.   [95] ibid., 11 Feb. 1834.

[96] *Englishman*, 26 April 1834.   [97] *Englishman*, 19 Feb. 1834.

few years into a sustained assault on Company policy in the northwest in concert with British opponents of the Afghan war.[98]

Mohan Lal maintained a wide circle of correspondents in the Punjab. In 1845, during the prelude to the British annexation of the Punjab, the Chairman of the East India Company, James Hogg, judged him to be 'like all natives, intriguing', despite the 'information and services' he had formerly afforded the Government.[99]

Over the years, Mohan Lal's attitude to Brahminical Hinduism also changed. While elite Kashmiri Brahmins, like himself, had tended to assimilate rationalistic ideas from the overwhelmingly Muslim culture of their home state, and Delhi College itself was another arena of such rationalism, Mohan Lal's journeys became a kind of Voltairean tour of the absurdities of pagan religion. While it is uncertain whether he actually converted to Islam, he does appeared to have abandoned Hindu rituals.[100] Ironically, while Mohan Lal's short-lived English education had certainly severed him from the culture of his ancestors, it also provided him with the skills to engage in an assault on 'forward imperialism' within the new public arena. In this respect he was India's first modern anti-imperialist.

Shahamat Ali was another example of the new munshi. He accompanied Claude Wade as secretary during his embassy to Ranjit Singh in 1837–8, and went on to Kabul, a journey which he described in an English journal later published in London. Finally, he became Mir Munshi to Wade when he was resident at Indore, ending his career in the Bhil Agency in central India. Shahamat Ali was a class-fellow of Mohan Lal's in the English Department of the Delhi College and had also been patronised by Metcalfe, Trevelyan and Andrew Stirling (Bentinck's Persian Secretary).[101] He had been briefly 'excommunicated' by the Persian maulvis of the College who refused to eat or drink with him, claiming that he had forfeited his religion by learning English. The caste-like behaviour of the maulvis nauseated, but failed to dissuade him, and eventually Trevelyan was able to pressure them into withdrawing their judgement.[102]

Shahamat Ali's journals, like Mohan Lal's, reveal new attitudes which

[98] *Delhi Gazette*, 17 Dec. 1842, on Mohan Lal's letter to Trevelyan denouncing the Afghan War; Mohan Lal, *Life of Amir Dost Mohammed Khan of Kabul* (London, 1846); some of his critique later appeared in J.W. Kaye, *A History of the War in Afghanistan* (London, 1857–8).
[99] J.W. Hogg to Sir Henry Hardinge, 21 Dec. 1845, Hogg Papers, Mss. Eur. E 342/5, f. 21, OIOC.
[100] Sender, *Kashmiri Pandits*, pp. 86–9.
[101] Shahamat Ali, *The Sikhs*, preface; Fisher, *Indirect Rule*, pp. 346–8.
[102] Shahamat Ali, *The Sikhs*, pp. viii–ix.

would have been strange to travellers of the generation of Izatullah, let alone Azfari, the Mughal noble who had written a travelogue at the end of the previous century.[103] Once again, the writing of an accurate English journal was deemed to be the critical breakthrough into the modern world. At Claude Wade's insistence, Shahamat Ali not only improved himself but 'acquired a habit of writing a journal, and continued the practice in various missions on which that officer was employed'.[104] He recorded routes, quantities and populations. He wrote about the 'despotic' character of Ranjit Singh's government.[105] He bemoaned the meanness of this monarch who, having invested him with a ceremonial garment, then refused to have it delivered to him. He wrote of the glories of the Mughal buildings he had seen. All these would have appeared in classical Islamic travelogues. Yet the tone is different, the landscape is no longer crowded with the relics of great kings, and Sufi shrines are rarely mentioned. The political moves of the British are what define the narrative. Most suggestive is Shahamat Ali's attitude to what he calls superstition, by which he means popular Hinduism and Islam. Such was 'the extent of their superstition', he writes, that the people paid a tithe to holy-men to bless their crops;[106] again, 'many blasphemies' prevailed among the Sayyids and Mullahs of Bahawalpur; these seem to have included excessive polygamy and Sufi devotional singing.[107] This notion of 'superstition' echoes that of his class-fellow, Mohan Lal, and was clearly expected to appeal to a western audience. It also reflected deeper changes in indigenous intellectual culture. One sees in many of these reformist intellectuals of Delhi, including Sayyid Ahmad Khan, the influence of the purist Islam which was then sweeping the Islamic schools of the city. Modernists who came to approve western knowledge and 'Wahhabi' integralists had much in common: disdain for folk religion, spontaneous Sufi devotionalism, syncretic practices and 'innovation' (bidah), or accretions, which is probably what Shahamat Ali has in mind when he uses the word 'superstition'. Reformed thinking of either a modernising or a traditionalist bent fitted well with the ideology and practice of British administration notwithstanding the reformers' revivalist aspirations. A further clue to Shahamat Ali's outlook is provided in his recorded thanks to Captain J.D. Cunningham for lending him a copy of a book on the doctrines of 'Molwee Mohamed Ismael relating to the prevailing abuses and proper reform of the

[103] Ali Bakht Azfari, *Waqi'at-e Azfari. Urdu Translation. Madras Government Oriental Manuscripts Series* (Madras, 1957).
[104] Shahamat Ali, *The Sikhs*, p. xi.   [105] ibid., p. 14.   [106] ibid., p. 124.
[107] Shahamat Ali, *The History of Bahawalpur with notices of the adjacent countries of Sindh, Afghanistan.* (London, 1848), p. xvii.

Mohamedan doctrines in India'.[108] This was probably the *Taqwiyat al-Iman* ('Refuge of Faith'), the key treatise of the Delhi 'Wahhabi' reformers, which he had translated into English.

Compared with Mohan Lal, Shahamat Ali was a loyalist: he believed that the Kabul expedition was correct in principle, but wrong in the execution. This is not to say that he was politically naive; he was acutely aware of the 'rage of party' in England over the Afghan war.[109] His stance, in fact, was more that of an Indian Tory than a disinterested munshi. Elsewhere he remarks in connection with excessive expenditure on 'parties' at marriages: 'I wish the Indians, miserable and wretched as they have become in their pecuniary and political position would learn to be wise.'[110] Shahamat Ali was fully divorced from the intellectual and moral aura of the Mughal Empire.

A third example of the new style of 'native informant' was Babu, later Raja Shiva Prasad,[111] who in his own career linked the age of the last late-Mughal munshis with the public arenas of the Indian National Congress and its enemies. Shiva Prasad was a member of the branch of the great mercantile Jagat Seth family which had taken up residence at Banaras in the mid-eighteenth century. Though Jains, the family's rank in the late Mughal nobility ensured that Shiva Prasad received a classical Persian education as well as a Sanskritic one. He also studied at the Banaras College, before being appointed as a youthful ambassador (*vakil*) of the Raja of Bharatpur. At this time, he later claimed, he was violently 'anti-European', but so appalled was he by his treatment at the Bharatpur darbar, that he resolved 'never again to serve a native'.[112] From 1845 to 1848 he acted as an intelligence officer in various parts of the NWP and the Punjab, ending up as Mir Munshi of the Simla Agency under Herbert Edwardes. Shiva Prasad's transition from a diplomatic munshi to the status of mediator of colonial knowledge was completed in the 1850s when he was appointed Joint Inspector of Schools in the Banaras Circle. Later, he became the first Indian Inspector of Schools, controlling a substantial staff of sub-inspectors, teachers and schoolbook writers. He had already translated a number of works of useful knowledge into Hindi, and implicitly justified British policy in the Punjab.[113] His vision was of a loyalist Hindu polity

---

[108] ibid., pp. i–ii.   [109] Shahamat Ali, *The Sikhs*, p. 549.

[110] Shahamat Ali, *Bahawalpur*, p. xix.

[111] K. Sajun Lal, 'Rajah Shiv Pershad. Early Life and Career', *Indica*, pp. 350–6.

[112] Shiva Prasad to Grierson, G.A. Grierson, *The Modern Vernacular Literature of Hindustan* (Calcutta, 1889), p. 149.

[113] *Sikhon ka Udaya aur Asta*. This work traces the political history of the Sikhs from the collapse of the Mughal empire to the dispersion of the Sikh aristocracy and the passage of the Koh-i Nur diamond to England in the 1840s. It appears to make British

(*dharmarajya*) set within the wider protecting shield of British power.[114] His extremely ambivalent attitude to Muslim rule, and indeed the Muslim presence in India, anticipates an important strand in nationalist attitudes.

Small books and treasuries of knowledge

The first generation of books written by the new munshis for schools and the polite Hindi-reading public combined the Indian form of 'treasury of learning' with that of the British compendia of useful knowledge. Given the extent of colonial patronage, it was gradgrinding British empiricism which usually won out. Basic facts about astronomy, geography and history were crammed into a small compass. An early Hindi printed work, the *Vidyabhasa* of 1839,[115] was typical. In English the title reads 'A treatise on the benefits of knowledge with brief sketches of some of the more important sciences in Hindui.' A disquisition on the wondrous impact of the printed book[116] is followed by sections on the 'science of geography', history (which is a compilation of Greek, Roman and Biblical history),[117] astronomy and chemistry.

Such works were suffused with the western ideology of improvement, but they still left space for Indian reconstructions of their own world. For example, the Hindi book *Patramalika* (1841)[118] illustrates the exchange between British ideas of useful knowledge and Indian learning. Published by the Agra School Book Society, it consists of a series of travel letters written to friends by a pandit of Sehore – the capital of the new astronomy – on a journey to Bombay via Bhopal and Aurangabad. The pandit's travels were recounted in the recognised form of the pilgrimage narrative. He uses the words *achche padarth* meaning 'wondrous things' or 'marvels' to describe his experiences, which previous travellers would have used about temples and holy places. Indeed, he mentions the temples at Bhopal and Nasik,[119] which a traditional *yatri* would have venerated. Few puranic tales are mentioned, however, and views of the gods (*darshan*), seem to be relatively

conquest a 'natural' process following faction and division after the death of Ranjit Singh.

[114] e.g., Shiva Prasad translated and published the laws of Manu in Hindi, *Manava Dharmasara* (Banaras, 1856).

[115] *Vidyabhasa ka phala aur jojo vidya pradhan hai* [a Treatise on the benefits of Knowledge] (Agra, 1839); cf. *Padharthi Vidyasara balakon jan ke liye* [Elements of Natural Philosophy in dialogue form for young people] (Calcutta, 1846), VT 17.

[116] *Vidyabhasa ka Phala*, pp. 8–9.   [117] ibid., pp. 19–22.

[118] *Patramalika. Sehor niwasi Pandit Ratneswaraji ne Sehor se le Bambai tak yatra karne me jojo bare nagar acche acche padarth dekhe unka patra dwara varnan kar uska nam patramalika dhara* (Agra School Book Society, Agra Press, 1841), VT 17.

[119] ibid., 2–3 (Bhopal), 9–12 (Nasik).

unimportant to him. Instead, the pandit had specifically promised to send his friends in Sehore accounts of the schools and *gurus* he encountered.[120] The text includes descriptions of the schools established by 'the old Peshwas'[121] and the various new educational establishments and private indigenous schools of Bombay.[122] He also mentions books he had seen on chemistry and indigenous languages. British officials and engineering works are given space, but this is no paean in praise of western civilisation. It reflects, instead, a pilgrimage in search of Indian learned men whose knowledge had been enhanced, but not created, by their access to western science. Viewed by its publishers as a depiction of useful knowledge, *Patramalika* seems instead to be plotting a map of Indian learning (*vidya*) in which the west has already become marginal.

The debate about women also played an important part in new spheres of useful and uplifting knowledge. Every book published by missionaries and many of their sermons harped on the lack of education and the poor treatment of women.[123] The writers traced the corruption of Hindu society to the inner recesses of the household. Since the sati debate had given an enormous impetus to the Indian press[124] and to public associations and pamphleteering, it is not surprising that the theme constantly resurfaced. What modern, but conservative Hindus needed was a view of the role of women which associated them with the new realm of duty, while distancing them from sacrificial modes of ancient virtue, such as widow-burning, lauded by the Calcutta Dharma Sabha, but deprecated alike by the moderns and the government. Here Shiva Prasad's *Vamamanoranjana* ('Edifying Tales for Women') published in 1849 and 1856 (4 annas; 5,000 copies) was a north Indian example of a hortatory genre which became widespread in Bengal. The collection eulogised a group of good women from Draupadi, heroine of the Mahabharata, through to modern Europeans and Americans. These women represented a variety of virtues from service of mother and father, through service of husband to service of country. Three of the tales had distinct local relevance in Banaras: those about Ahaliya Bhai, the Rani of Indore; the wife of Kalidasa, the ancient sage; and Rani Bhawani, an eighteenth-century Bengali heroine.

Ahaliya Bhai's works of piety were numerous, 'nobody in the whole of India from the Himalayas to Rameshwaram has not heard of Ahaliya Bhai', Shiva Prasad wrote.[125] The citizens of Banaras and its region

[120] ibid., 1–2.   [121] ibid., 9.   [122] ibid., 23 ff.
[123] e.g., Leupolt, *Recollections*, p. 47; P. Chapman, *Hindoo Female Education* (London, 1839).
[124] *Friend of India*, 15 Jan. 1835.
[125] Shiva Prasad, *Vamamanoranjana* [Tales for Women] (Banaras, 1849, 2nd. edn, 1856; printed by Direction of the Lieutenant-Governor), p. 11.

would indeed have known her well as someone who constructed a bathing platform during the great Maratha renovation of Banaras in the eighteenth century. More important, her husband Maharaja Holkar was of lower-caste descent, and she had become joint-protectress of the state as a widow. Rather than becoming sati along with her husband's ten other wives and concubines, the Rani had became a *dharmik stri*,[126] a woman of duty, for the whole of Hindustan (*sara Hindustan*),[127] doing works of righteousness (*punya karma*) which included the feeding of Brahmins, reading the holy books and putting up numerous temples and resthouses. Ahaliya Bhai's righteousness was contrasted with that of the 'Muslim emperor' who was a 'great deviator from prescribed morality'[128] in that he preyed on young and beautiful women. This theme of women and the new Dharma was taken up again in the story of the pious Rani Bhawani of Rajshahi district in Bengal, whose family was in contention with another avaricious and unprincipled Muslim, this time Nawab Alivardi Khan.[129] After the spoliation of the estate the Rani escaped to seek help in Murshidabad from the Jagat Seth. Later, she inherited the now-restored estate and used the proceeds in good works particularly at Banaras. Her house in the holy city became a resort for religious men and she gave rice and grain to the poor.[130] The third story in this collection with local resonances concerned the manner in which the wife of Kalidasa, the poet and sage, had won repeated victories over the pandits in formal debates.[131]

This collection, which was widely used in government and private schools, recast women's public role within a redefined notion of Hindu duty. Women are succourers and nurturers of the family, but they can play a public role as managers and trustees of estates and kingdoms. Exceptional women might be scholars. The Dharma they can best serve is that of pious public works; it is not that of ancient warrior sacrifice. The sociology of the collection is also revealing. Though there are examples of 'good Muslims' in the text, north Indian Muslims of the recent past are portrayed as immoral looters. In the Rani Bhawani story, it is the Jagat Seth, ancestor of Shiva Prasad, a commercial man, who represents the embodiment of princely virtue. These stories were appropriate for publication by a government which promoted limited women's education and kept lists of mercantile Indians who had spent money on charitable works. It appealed equally to Indian commercial people and officials who promoted an all-India vision of Hindu Dharma stressing pious works rather than cult or sacrifice, and who increasingly defined themselves against the notion of Muslim violence.

[126] ibid.   [127] ibid., p. 16.   [128] ibid., p. 13.   [129] ibid., p. 17.
[130] ibid., p. 19.   [131] ibid.

For Indians in the 1840s and 1850s, acting in a public arena came to mean resacralising the land with useful and good works. For instance, the Banaras Missionary, Rev. M. Sherring, noted the activities of a Gujarati Brahmin called Gorji (Gaurji?) who 'has done more to revive Hinduism in this city of late years than any other person'.[132] Having read the *Kashikhanda*, the classical celebration of the sanctity of Banaras, which was now available in lithographed editions for wealthier pilgrims, Gaurji decided to recreate in the real world the ancient sacred geography of the city. He restored or built temples and shrines mentioned in the text, notably the temple of the Goddess Parvatyeswari. Banaras and other cities received many such pious and useful benefactions from lay people during this period[133] for Dharma was now a public Hindu piety operating across the whole of India. The Calcutta Dharma Sabha registered the change by petitioning to manage sacred places in place of traditional specialists.[134] Muslims had, meanwhile, began to redefine Islam by creating their own educational institutions and publishing normative tracts on public behaviour. In 1848–9, for instance, the NWP presses produced a Shia tract on the method of praying,[135] a treatise on the forms of marriage[136] and several other works on Muslim religious rules and decency.

Publishing and the press in perspective

As we have seen, several arguments purport to explain why Indians came so late to the printing press when it was already known to Europeans in their coastal enclaves: for instance, the bazaar writer establishments maintained a monopoly and their product was cheap; there were strong ritual objections to printing religious texts, which alone would have made the press economically viable; the Persian script was difficult even for lithographers; and, finally, indigenous rulers were hostile to the press on political grounds. The Indian case does indeed stand in striking contrast to that of Japan and some parts of China where more intrusive polities, aggressive commercial establishments and centralised political authorities had all been producing information in block-printed form for generations. What is striking about India, however, is that all of these alleged impediments broke down so rapidly between 1820 and 1840. Moreover, it was not only, or even predomi-

---

[132] M. Sherring, *The Sacred City of the Hindus. An Account of Benares in Ancient and Modern Times* (London, 1868), p. 105; *Friend of India*, 5 Apr. 1849.
[133] 'Hindu benevolent trusts in Benares', Reade, *Contributions*, pp. 1–46.
[134] *Chandrika Patrika*, reported in *Friend of India*, 30 May 1839.
[135] Book no 16, *Friend of India*, 5 Apr. 1849.
[136] Maulana Mahomed Bakur Majlisi, 'Turjama Risalah Nikah', ibid., no. 14.

nantly, the consciously modernising sections of the elites which adopted the new medium with such alacrity. The explanation for this rapid change seems to lie in the information order as a whole, rather than in one particular dimension of it. The Indian information order had been complex and flexible, as earlier chapters have stressed. Even before British conquest, entrepreneurs working in the nexus between commerce and government had made use of many different types of written report, legal entitlement and commercial instrument. Information of this sort could circulate yet more easily in printed form. Influential religious reform and sectarian movements had similarly begun to produce large quantities of written prose. They, too, quite suddenly discovered that print was a useful tool with which to discipline and direct their followers.

The luxuriant culture of indigenous political reporting also responded fast to print, once the colonial movement for useful knowledge gave it momentum. Calcutta newspapers registered growing influence up-country before the end of Bentinck's Governor-Generalship. His 'tame' Indian press had shown its teeth in the debates over sati[137] and British intervention in Indian states. Although the *Jami Jahan Nama* was nearer to an akhbarat than a newspaper, despatching only a dozen copies to the major centres of the interior, its official certificate of good conduct did not last long. By 1831, when the British were in conflict with several north Indian courts, the newspaper was being denounced for slander by the Resident at Delhi[138] and the Government ceased to subscribe to it. The Governor-General's enemies had an even blacker view of Indian newspapers. The *Meerut Universal Magazine*,[139] for instance, denounced Bentinck's liberal treatment of their editors, saying that in Bengal and up-country 300,000 people read Indian papers, which disseminated 'abusive calumnies against Europeans of every rank of life'. These were conveyed across country by 'private dawks' at a charge of three *pice* each while the European papers were 'ridiculously controlled' and crippled by postage charges. Certainly, there is evidence that elite Indians quickly became acqainted with the *Jami Jahan Nama* and other papers. Ghalib, for example, denounced it for inaccuracy and contemplated a proposal from a colleague in Calcutta to set up a rival Persian broadsheet.[140] The paper's potential influence was also revealed in 1838. It had stated that 400,000 Afghans were about to invade India and Chandu Lal, the powerful Diwan of Hyderabad, advised the Resident that the *Jam* should

---

[137] *Friend of India*, 15 Jan. 1835.
[138] 'Complaint by Mr. Hawkins of a paragraph in a Persian newspaper about him', BC 53427/1343; cf. *Friend of India*, 20 Dec. 1838.
[139] *Meerut Universal Magazine*, 1, 1835, 115.
[140] Russell and Islam, *Ghalib*, 1, 60.

only be circulated in English for the duration of the war, since the Persian version might undermine the loyalty of Indians.[141] Interestingly, this suggests that the Diwan mistakenly regarded the *Jam* as some kind of akhbarat produced by the Government in Calcutta. Of course, the *Universal Magazine*'s estimate of popular readership was probably far too high, but it does seem that newspapers were borrowed, copied and read out to large gatherings, as earlier newsletters had been.[142] Indians were meanwhile participating in arguments in the Anglo-Indian journals.[143]

In the North-Western Provinces, lithography spread first around government offices and missionary establishments in Banaras, Allahabad and Kanpur. From there Indian printers, mostly Muslims and Christians, took their expertise to the bazaars of the old cities. In Lucknow it was the modernising establishments founded under King Nasir-ud Din Haidar which spread the culture of lithography to the wider community. The Royal Observatory was one such institution. Though a later ruler closed down the Observatory and the associated presses in 1849, the innovation had already taken hold. The printers moved off to Kanpur on the Awadh border and continued to flood the kingdom with the new Urdu literature from there.[144] By the 1840s, the Urdu version of the Koran and tracts of the conservative reformers were beginning to appear in the city. In the 1850s one of the rationalist teachers at the Firangi Mahal seminary had begun to publish a newspaper, *Tilism* which was critical of British policy in the Punjab and later in Awadh.[145] The tone was echoed in the *Dihli Urdu Akhbar*,[146] and the *Kuran-ul Sadin*,[147] both newspapers which consisted of a mixture of bazaar gossip, religious moralising and covert attacks on prominent people, including British officials. In the Punjab, despite the early hostility of the Sikh rulers, by the early 1850s 'little lithographic presses have sprung up all over the country in great numbers for printing Urdu and Persian books'. These 'grew up like mushrooms and often fail like them too'.[148] A printed book

[141] *Friend of India*, 20 Dec. 1838.
[142] The *Satya Pradip* said Indian newspapers were read 'in the evening, sometimes in the open air, to a group of twenty or thirty persons', an adaptation of *sabha* or *majlis* to the new media, *Friend of India*, 4 Apr. 1850; cf. Russell and Islam, *Ghalib*, I, 49–50.
[143] e.g. 'Native of Oude' to *Benares Recorder*, 14 May 1847; 'Anthony' to same, 31 Aug. 1837; 'Hereditary native of Oude' to same, 14 May 1847.
[144] Sprenger, *Catalogue of Libraries of Oudh*, p. vi; Sharar, *Lucknow*, pp. 106–8.
[145] *Tilism*, 1856–7, mimeo. copies, Aligarh University Library.
[146] K.A. Faruqi (ed.), *Dihli Urdu Akhbar* (Delhi, 1972), collected issues; Sharar, *Lucknow*, pp. 104–8.
[147] 'Kuran-ool-Sadeen' on British Government, tr. *Benares Recorder*, 8 Jan. 1847; the Delhi 'Sayyid-ul akhbar' was also a guileful critic, see, e.g., translations of its view on the conquest of the Punjab in *Delhi Gazette*, 14 Feb. 1849.
[148] J. Warren, *A Backward Glance at Fifteen Years of Mission Life* (Philadelphia, 1856), p. 45., cit. Davis, *Press and Politics*, p. 16.

from these presses cost perhaps as little as one-tenth of an equivalent manuscript.[149]

In Banaras, British orientalists, missionaries and the Maharaja[150] had all begun printing between 1820 and 1840. The city, long a centre of gossip and intelligence, quickly became the base for several English-language and vernacular newspapers. *Sudhakar*, the first newspaper in Devanagari and Sanskritised Hindi, appeared briefly in 1847. *Sudhakar* like its sister, the *Benares Akhbar*, adopted a mild anti-British tone. It started a controversy when it bewailed the probable loss of independence by Awadh at a time when the British press was condemning the 'misgovernment' of the kingdom.[151] The *Sudhakar* also took up some of the literary and religious debates which had been characteristic of the Hindu segment of the ecumene. It attacked Ballantyne for misrepresenting the scriptures.[152] It reported that some of the pandits of the city, lamenting public neglect of a Sanskrit work, the Devi Bhagavat, had carefully reconstructed the text, prepared a commentary and were about to publish it at a cost of Rs. 30. Though the work of Ballantyne and his colleagues was probably a spur to them, the pandits were following up on an indigenous literary controversy: one of the leading pandits in the project, a Shakta Brahmin, had a few years previously been involved in a long debate with his peers over the status of the Devi Bhagavat. The *Benares Recorder* remarked that this was 'one of the few' examples of native literary criticism being pursued in a public arena;[153] in fact, though, the Hindi and Urdu newspapers commonly debated equivalent religious and literary issues.

Benedict Anderson has argued that 'print capitalism' heralded a mental and moral revolution in nineteenth-century Indonesia and facilitated the emergence of nationalism by creating new 'imagined communities'.[154] In India, too, it is difficult to imagine the emergence of mature nationalism without the prior spread of the printing press and the newspaper. The range and velocity of the circulation of all types of written materials obviously became much greater with printing. Literati could further standardise written texts and impose new uniformities of

---

[149] ibid.
[150] The Maharaja patronised the Hindi translation of the 'Mahabharata' epic by Gokul Nath in 1828, and cooperated with local Sanskrit scholars, Grierson, *Vernacular Literature*, p. 108, cf. p. 118.
[151] *Sudhakar*, reported in *Benares Recorder*, 15, 19 Oct. 1847.
[152] Vrajratandas, *Bhartendu Harischandra*, (Allahabad, *Samvat* 2019, 1962), p. 190, note, for early Banaras vernacular press, ibid., 189–92.
[153] *Friend of India*, 2 July 1846.
[154] B. Anderson, *Imagined Communities. Reflections of the Origins and Spread of Nationalism* (rev. edn, London, 1991), passim.

interpretation. In time, reading a text could replace the face-to-face charisma of the teacher as the test of correct doctrine.

There were, however, significant continuities in the form and content of communication. As a study of the Krishnaite Radhavallabh texts of the Mathura region has shown, slow processes of standardisation were already taking place before the coming of print.[155] Again, the key categories of manuscript material which had been common before the printing press passed directly into print media. Apart from school-books which disseminated western scientific and moral ideas (though often interspersed with Indian examples and hybrid themes), the most common types of early printed book in north India remained strikingly similar to the types of manuscripts which had circulated before the supposed print 'revolution'.[156] First, there were religious texts: the epics, the Vaishnavite hymns, and the scriptures of sects such as the Radhavallabhs or Sadhs. On the Muslim side, there were Persian and latterly Urdu translations of the Koran, the sayings of the Prophet and various commentaries and lives of Sufi teachers. The second great category comprised almanacs and works on astrology. Medical books, which often combined western remedies with material drawn from indigenous pharmacopoeias, were a third. Antique ballads, stories and novelettes were also popular (though denounced by the British as 'indelicate'). All these types of works had antecedents in the tracts produced and disseminated previously by the armies of bazaar and household scribes. This continuity was a disappointment to those contemporaries who wished to believe that 'print capitalism' would create a revolution in sensibility. R.N. Cust wrote mournfully some decades later: 'How is it that indecent erotics and discordant religious dogma have monopolised a free press?'[157] He also wrote of 'the juxtapositions of astrology with philosophy, the most ancient delusions with the latest discovery ... of Krishna with Mahomet and Paul'. In fact, the very sophistication of pre-print communication, and the canny

[155] R. Snell, *The Eighty-four hymns of Hita Harivamsa. An edition of the Chaurasi Pada* (Delhi, 1991), pp. 334–7.
[156] For the types of early books printed, 'Native Press in the NWP', *Ledlie's Miscellany*, 1, 1852, 201–12; cf. analyses in *Friend of India*, 5 Apr. 1849, 13 June 1850; *Mofussilite*, 20 Aug. 1847; note by Assistant Sec. to Govt on native presses, 13 Mar. 1850, NWP Genl Procs., March 1850, 37, 215/3; compare this with, e.g., *An Alphabetical Index of Persian, Arabic and Urdu Manuscripts in the State Archives of Uttar Pradesh* (Allahabad, c. 1968), cf. J.F. Blumhardt, *Catalogue of the Library of the India Office*, II, 2 (London, 1900). The same categories appear in books printed both in the Devanagari and in the Persian scripts.
[157] R.N. Cust, 'Modern indigenous literature of India', *Linguistic and Oriental Essays*, 2nd ser., 3, (London, 1887), p. 122.

ability of the men of the bazaar to cash in on this type of popular demand explains Cust's apparent paradox.

Print in itself did not create an information revolution. Rather, it speeded up the velocity and range of communication among existing communities of knowledge. It helped transform some actors within the old ecumene into the leaders of a modern public, but it marginalised and subordinated others. Powerful men began to employ tame editors and publishers to attack their rivals. Conservative men of letters quickly took to printing odes and collective poetic biographies. Even the new Urdu and Hindi press drew on the traditions of the newsletter, the ironic ghazal and the tradition of placarding which had characterised the ecumene.

Western knowledge and social conflict

In accounting for Indian opposition to British rule in the generation before 1857, historians have emphasised economic deprivation and the decline of old hierarchies. Indians had, however, always believed the virtuous kingdom to be a repository of learning and godliness as well as a political organisation. When, however hesitantly, indigenous moderni-sers as well as British reformers and officials began to propagate radical ideas using the new media, quite profound social conflicts began to appear. Indian physicians and surgeon-barbers deplored the appearance of British and Calcutta-trained Indian doctors. The learned suspected that Indian Christians – 'the lowest of castes' – were trying to create a monopoly for themselves in the government and missionary printing presses.[158] Many people disliked censuses and other statistical exer-cises[159] because they put power into the hands of low informers and spies. Above all, missionary activity was seen as the precursor of a radical assault on civilisation and learning, not simply a matter of belief. The delicate balance of public doctrines and accepted cults within the ecumene was in danger of being overthrown. Profound intellectual unease, therefore, as much as economic dislocation overtook north India in the 1840s and 1850s. Objections to the new crypto-Christian public instruction[160] converged with opposition to the resumption by govern-ment of charitable and service land-grants.

Outside the main centres of Agra, Delhi and Banaras the success of

[158] Davis, *Press and Politics*, pp. 19–20.
[159] G. Christian, *Report on the Census of the North West Provinces taken on 1 January 1853* (Calcutta, 1854), pp. 218, 330.
[160] *Asiatic Journal*, n.s., 26, 1838, 322–3, noted the mass petitioning campaign by both Hindus and Muslims against the government's new 'English exclusiveness' in the matter of public instruction.

government schooling in the North-Western Provinces fluctuated from season to season. In some places missionaries took over where the government schools failed. Missionary schools were free while the government schools charged up to Rs. 6 per annum which might be one sixth of a father's salary.[161] Missionary schools, however, insisted on teaching the Bible, and this bred resentment.[162] Examples of conversion in Nagpur,[163] Banaras and elsewhere[164] led to affrays and demonstrations. Indians believed that 'you [the British] have already conquered our bodies, and are in a fair way to conquering our minds also'.[165]

The reaction was uneven but sharp. The Calcutta Dharma Sabha was already influential as far up-river as Allahabad.[166] In the later 1840s anti-Christian meetings in Calcutta brought together Gosains, Tantrists, Vedantists, orthodox as well as heterodox. Members reported considerable up-country interest. At one of these a 'Hindoo Society' was founded under the chairmanship of Radhakanta Deb, a great patron of the Dharma Sabha, and a social boycott of those consorting with missionaries was suggested.[167] The towns of the NWP were also canvassed. In 1848 the *Benares Recorder* noted that a kind of 'orthodox society on the model of the *Dhurmusabha* in Calcutta, has been established in Banaras, and is exercising its baneful influence against the interests of the steamer'.[168] There is no reason to believe that Indians, even the most orthodox pandits, were resolutely opposed to all modern technology, such as the Ganges steam-boat. What stirred resentment was the relentless propaganda of the missionaries, associating the visible success of British science – the electric telegraph, the railway, the paper mill[169] – with the coming triumph of Christianity.

For most Indians, the activities of the Department of Public Instruction and its visitors were difficult to disentangle from those of the missionaries. In the aftermath of the famines of 1833 and 1838, Hindu and Muslim orphans were taken to the Agra Christian Orphanage and other missionary schools where they were brought up as Christians. This was particularly shocking to the Muslim religious leadership, who denounced the orphanage in pamphlets and sermons.[170] The level of popular reaction is difficult to gauge, but reports of the Committees of

[161] *Friend of India*, 21 Oct. 1847.   [162] ibid., 23 Sept., 21 Oct. 1847.
[163] *Friend of India*, 15 Feb. 1849.
[164] *Church Missionary Register*, 29, Nov. 1853, 252.
[165] Cited Leupolt, *Recollections*, p. 109.
[166] *Friend of India*, 30 May 1839; in January 1841 Dwarkanath Tagore made a tour of the upper Provinces atoning in Banaras and Gaya for his sins of heterodoxy, encouraging further Dharma Sabha activity, ibid., 28 Jan. 1841.
[167] ibid., 23 Sept. 1847; *Benares Recorder*, 28 Sept. 1847.   [168] ibid., 24 Aug. 1848.
[169] Leupolt, *Recollections*, p. 82.   [170] Powell, *Missionaries*, pp. 159–60.

Public Instruction reported widespread unease and misunderstanding. An article in the *Benares Magazine* (probably by Ballantyne) elaborated on this. Village education, the article noted, was closely tied up with the inculcation of cultural norms and relationships between families of substance and families of knowledge and piety.[171] A general and abstract common education, and one which imparted gobbets of foreign 'general knowledge', through heartless printed books, was both suspect and alien to many. It is not surprising that H.S. Reid, Thomason's active and influential Director of Public Instruction, was known as 'Padre'[172] when he visited village schools. What else could he have been than a priest in disguise?

There was, of course, no homogeneous cultural resistance to public instruction. Rather, sections of the population responded differently. The changes in the information order divided society, marginalising some and promoting others. Thus, according to the author in the *Benares Magazine*, Kayasthas, whose traditional occupation involved making field surveys, were attracted to the pragmatic education of the new schools.[173] Even the Brahmins were gradually shelving the Shastras in favour of 'ready reckoners' and other practical treatises.[174] Those Brahmins who remained teachers were replacing 'divinity, philosophy and law' with poetry, literature and rhetoric. Elsewhere, however, the district school visitor was regarded with contempt and derision, according to this survey. He was 'the man who goes about humbugging people'[175] while the Company 'just puts our money into carts and carries it to Calcutta'. The article recorded a variety of voices. A zamindar thought that the 'glory of religion would pass away' with the coming of village education; another conceded that it might put some kind of a check on the village accountant. A market gardener (Kachchi) said he wanted to emigrate to the canal colonies of the Punjab rather than learn to write. One man reportedly viewed education from a 'communal' perspective: 'As it is now, we have all the hard work and the Toorks [Muslims] . . . have all the fat places. But when we can read and write, the Toorks will be kicked out, and we shall get their places.'[176]

Conclusions

In the generation after 1830 the information order of north India was transformed. Public instruction, along with small books and newspapers, the vogue for statistics and the definition of rights changed the face of

---

[171] *Benares Magazine*, 8, 1852, 'Native education in the North-West Provinces', 158–75.
[172] ibid., 169.   [173] ibid., 163.   [174] ibid.   [175] ibid., 170.
[176] ibid.

government and created new knowledge communities among Indian elites. The older communities of embodied knowledge gave ground before more routinised, abstract information, as the British noted to their cost after the Rebellion. Economic depression highlighted the effects of the new order. Disenchanted expatriate businessmen, for example, attacked Indian merchants and government officials in newspapers and at public meetings; Indian spokesmen argued in response. These changes were, however, most uneven in their effects. While they created arenas in which new publicists ultimately came to the fore, existing authorities, sectarian leaders and magnates were often able to enhance and expand their influence. Yet though there were as many losers as gainers, public instruction, the new media and the diffusion of western knowledge had unsettled society. The dissidents saw the changes not so much a contest between a stagnant orient and dynamic western science, as one between still-vital Indian knowledges and the foreigners' abstract rule-making, which divorced information from godly wisdom.

7   Colonial controversies: astronomers and physicians

The following two chapters examine a series of debates which took place among the British and Indians in the early nineteenth century concerning astronomy, medicine, language and geography. Indian kings had fostered these forms of knowledge because they bore directly on the health and good order of the body politic. For their part, the British believed they could demonstrate intellectual superiority in such disciplines, even while they were uneasily aware that European scientific opinion was itself uncertain and divided. By surveying these debates we can examine British information-gathering beyond the bounds of warfare and statecraft. We also encounter Indians adapting their styles of argument to the new media and using them to conduct polemics about the status of Indian and western learning. The intellectual associations and alliances which emerged from such encounters were harbingers of an Indian nation. Indian protagonists in colonial debates were forming connections across the whole subcontinent and appealing to a national intellectual tradition two generations before indigenous political associations began to emerge.

The shape of the Indian astral sciences

The Indian astral sciences were typical of the knowledges of the ecumene. They were fractious disciplines and also highly political ones because observation of the heavens determined the correct timing for worship, war, politics and agriculture. For their part, the British grappled with these sciences and interrogated their specialists for practical reasons but also because astronomy, since Halley and Newton, had been regarded as a domain of national intellectual triumph. We consider first the Indian inheritance and then the British critical onslaught.

Hindu and Jain astronomy (*jyotishastra*) and their associated mathematics and astrology were designed to foretell auspicious times for rites, alliances and day-to-day transactions.[1] These schools had been influenced over the years by Islamic astronomy (*ilm-i nujum*), which itself drew on Greek traditions of precise observation.[2] Astronomical learning was hierarchically organised. Some classical Sanskrit treatises condemned 'low astrologers' as dabblers in the black arts[3] and Muslims formally disavowed astrology because only God could foretell the future.[4] In practice, though, even purist astronomical schools had established a modus vivendi with astrology, and the most learned men had recourse to seers and necromancers.

These polemical sciences were well adapted to India's tradition of scholarly controversy. Learned men at the great astronomical centres of Nadia (Bengal), Banaras, Gaya, Ujjain and the southern temple towns disagreed about the authority of the puranic legends which placed Mount Meru at the centre of the universe and which invoked cosmological beasts, and concentric circles of salt, curd and buttermilk.[5] Most practising *jyotish*s (astronomers) gave some degree of credence to these legends but also drew on the precise traditions of the medieval Siddhantas ('correct doctrines') whose star tables resembled those of the Ptolemaic or Arab traditions.[6] Some radical Hindu devotional sects, however, denounced all attempts to foretell the future as superstitious[7] and there is evidence of conflict between Brahmins and non-Brahmins over access to astral knowledge.[8] Muslims, meanwhile, argued over the relative authority of Aristotle and the ancient Arab astronomers.[9]

The public sphere of the sciences of the heavens was created by practical need as much as by theoretical debate. In Islam with its lunar calendar and Hinduism with solar and luni-solar calendars, the conduct of worship and sacrifice depended on precise measurement of the days, months and years. Fierce disputes occurred when rival bodies of

---

[1]   David Pingree, *Jyotihsastra: Astral and Mathematical Literature* (Wiesbaden, 1981), *History of Indian Literature*, VI, fasc. 4, pp. 8–56; W. Brennand, *Hindu Astronomy* (London, 1896); R. Sewell and S.B. Dikshit, *The Indian Calendar* (London, 1896); 'The Astronomy of the Hindus', *Calcutta Review*, 2, Oct.–Dec., 1844, 560.

[2]   *Encyclopaedia of Islam*, I (Leiden, 1913), 'Astronomy', pp. 497–501.

[3]   P.V. Kane, *History of Dharmasastra*, V, i (Pune, 1974), pp. 527–8.

[4]   On Aurangzeb's hostility to astrology, Ghulam Hussain, 'Siyyar', tr. Nota-Manus, IV, 139; cf. *Encyclopaedia of Islam*, I, 500–1.

[5]   Pingree, *Jyotihsastra*, pp. 17–22, 41–5. The best brief summary of puranic cosmological literature and bibliography is to be found in L. Rocher, *The Puranas*, *History of Indian Literature*, III, fasc. 2 (Wiesbaden, 1986), pp. 130–1.

[6]   Sewell and Dikshit, *Indian Calendar*, pp. 7–10.

[7]   The twelve *hukm* (precepts) of Birbhan the Sadh *guru* included admonitions against 'superstition', bathing and festivals during the conjunction of the planets, *LH*, I, 342–4.

[8]   K.V. Sarma, *History of the Kerala School of Hindu Astronomy (in perspective)* (Hoshiarpur, 1972), p. 71.

[9]   *Encyclopaedia of Islam*, I, 494–7; 418–501.

observers saw the new moon of the Islamic month of fasting at different times, or when Brahmins announced competing calendars for the most auspicious festivals. These disputes could threaten public order. For example, following a case of violently disputed festival times in Bengal under Mir Kasim (1760–63), the Raja of Nadia had to intervene with a proclamation to settle which of two calendars for a Hindu festival was correct.[10] Similarly, conflicts over times of worship between Sunni and Shia divines opened political divisions in Awadh a few decades later.[11]

Since the luni-solar civil calendar was different from the ritual calendars, disputes could impede the collection of the harvest and the revenues. Rulers, therefore, supported bodies of astronomers to advise them and these were usually distinct from the temple jyotishs. Both categories of astronomer pandit, however, annually received almanacs from the major centres of observation and these were used to adjust local tabulations of political and ritual happenings.[12] Skilled astronomers, who were contemptuous of the slow mental arithmetic of the Europeans, could compute eclipses and other heavenly events with extraordinary speed using cowrie shells.[13] The major Indian regions had different schools of astronomy, but calendrical adjustments had to be made for the whole subcontinent. Astronomy had become, in fact, a form of all-India public knowledge which transcended social status and region.

People who aspired to understand the stars could evidently achieve great political influence. Mrs Meer Hassan Ali, an Englishwomen who married into the Lucknow elite, remarked in 1832 that the astrologer 'can make peace or war, in the family he overrules, at his pleasure'.[14] She reported that the Nawab of Awadh himself had put huge sums of public money into the construction of a dargah for a favourite saint and soothsayer in the hope of regaining his health.[15] Astrologers, like

[10] H. Cavendish, 'On the civil year of the Hindoos and its divisions; with an account of three Hindoo almanacs belonging to Charles Wilkins, esq.', *Philosophical Transactions of the Royal Society of London for the year 1792* (London, 1792), 393.

[11] Cole, *Shi'ism*, p. 141; cf. case mentioned in the Journal of John Riley, Judge of Jaunpur, 1797, f. 12b, Mss. Eur. B 161, OIOC.

[12] Cavendish, 'Civil year', p. 393; Cavendish's article refers to a number of *panchangs* in his possession. There is also a collection of these dating from the 1850s to the 1870s, e.g. *Jantri* (Agra, St. 1907 = 1851) showing the Christian year, Hindu, Fasily and Muslim, in Vernacular Tracts 1528, OIOC; S. Vidyabhusana, *History of Indian Logic*, p. 527.

[13] 'Premier mémoire sur l'Inde, particulièrement sur quelques points de l'astronomie des Gentils Tamoults; sur Pondichery et ses environs par M. Le Gentil', *Histoire de l'Académie Royale des Sciences. Anné 1772. Seconde Partie. Avec les Mémoires de Mathématique et de Physique pour la même Anné* (Paris, 1776), p. 174.

[14] Mrs Meer Hassan Ali, *Observations on the Mussulmauns of India . . . by Mrs Meer Hassan Ali*, ed., W. Crooke, (Oxford, 1917, original 1832), p. 38.

[15] ibid., p. 33; Fakir Azizuddin of the Punjab was also a famous astrologer, *Friend of India*, 12 Oct. 1843.

physicians, midwives and eunuchs, moved between the domestic and the public.

Villagers were as dependent on the astral sciences as kings. In the countryside the foundation of temples properly aligned to the heavenly bodies and even the construction of the humble domestic altar required precision in space and time. The casting of horoscopes and the timing of village festivals depended on the knowledge of the Brahmin jyotish, who was an honoured member of the village elite. Since people thought that heavenly influences affected the life-cycles of all beings, there were auspicious days for sowing and planting and for the mating of cattle.[16] Medicines and aphrodisiacs for human beings were also believed to attain greater power during certain astral phases. The complexities of calculating time for anyone involved in trade, religion or politics were compounded by the superimposition on indigenous systems of time of the Muslim religious calendar, the *fasily* agricultural year and, later, the western calendar. A British observer remarked that the various over-lapping systems of time were so complex that 'a Hindoo has no way of knowing what day of the month it is, but by consulting his almanac'.[17] Almanacs were consequently among the most common form of both written and printed text. They were also among the most complex: early printed almanacs needed additional columns for the Mughal civil year and the Christian one.[18]

Under the Mughals the Indian astral sciences received a new political impetus and a sharper all-India focus. Akbar and Abul Fazl were fascinated by Hindu astronomy and the Hindu and Muslim traditions were cross-fertilised once more, with translations of texts being made from Arabic to Sanskrit and vice versa.[19] Abul Fazl conceived such patronage as part of his plan for a universal monarchy founded on the incorporation of different religious traditions through the exercise of reason (though he, too, was expert at casting horoscopes). In turn, Akbar and Abul Fazl inspired Maharaja Jai Singh of Jaipur, who

[16] 'Note on the Hindu calendar in its relation to agricultural operations', C.E. Luard (ed.) *Indore State Gazetteer*, II, (Calcutta, 1909), 344–8; Ruth S. and Stanley A. Freed, 'Calendars, ceremonies and festivals in a north Indian village. Necessary calendrical information for fieldwork', *Southwestern Journal of Anthropology*, 20, 1960, 67–90.
[17] Cavendish, 'Civil year', p. 392.
[18] In some cases the process went into reverse, A.H.E. Boileau, travelling in Rajasthan in the 1830s, noted that joshis were very widespread in the region, but that very few of them could actually make astronomical calculations even for the purposes of horoscopes; on the contrary, divination by throwing dice, and different forms of necromancy, were pervasive, Boileau, *Narrative*, p. 181. Printing obviously gave as much of a boost to palmistry and necromancy as it did to astronomy/astrology, see, e.g. the tract on palmistry, *Samudrika* (Banaras, 1851), VT, OIOC.
[19] Gladwin, *Ayeen*, I, 260–76, on astronomical eras as they apply to revenue administration, and II, 300–22, on Hindu astronomy.

dominated the final flowering of Indo-Islamic astronomy in the early eighteenth century. Jai Singh's five stone observatories, located at Jaipur, Delhi, Mathura, Ujjain and Banaras, were machines for precise calculation and among the most striking public buildings of the eighteenth century.[20] They implicitly associated his master, the Emperor Muhammad Shah, with the glories of Akbar and, through him, those of his distant relative, the great Samarkand astronomer, Mirza Ulugh Beg, grandson of Timur, founder of the Mughal dynasty. Further, the introduction to Jai Singh's new astronomical tables, the 'Zij Muhammadshahi', specifically reasserted Delhi's status as *dar-al Khilafat*, seat of the Caliphate.[21] Muhammad Shah needed a reform of the calendar because earlier computations were now out of date, but the symbolic aim of refounding the Mughal Empire as a greater Caliphate must have recommended the project all the more. Astronomy was a political science in both the practical and symbolic sense.

Jai Singh's work also subtly asserted the integrity of Hindu universal kingship within the decomposing body of the Mughal Empire. He founded three of his five observatories at important Hindu holy places: Mathura, near the birthplace of Krishna, Banaras, the seat of Shiva and Ujjain, the centre of ancient Indian astronomy. The promotion of astronomical learning represented an aspect of Jai Singh's attempt to centralise vedic and Vaishnavite knowledge.[22]

Though four of Jai Singh's observatories had ceased to function by 1780, the astral sciences did not die out. In Jaipur, royal interest outlasted Jai Singh's death in 1743 and Don Pedro de Silva, a Jesuit missionary, continued to encourage astronomy until his own death about 1794.[23] The Maharaja's grandson, Pratap Singh, made additions to the instruments and collected some new astronomical manuscripts. Jai Singh's Great Sundial (the Samrat Yantra) apparently remained at the centre of religious and intellectual life. Every year on the day of the full moon in June or July (Asadh Purnima) the astronomers assembled

[20] W. Hunter, 'Some Account of the Astronomical Labours of Jayasinha, Raja of Ambhere, or Jaynagar', *Asiatic Researches*, 5, 1798, pp. 177–86. This article contains large sections of the Persian '*Zij Muhammadshahi*'; G.R. Kaye, *The Astronomical Observations of Jai Singh. Archaeological Survey of India. New Imperial Series*, 40, (Calcutta, 1918).

[21] The 'Zij' uses the term '*Dar-al Khilafat Shahjahanabad*', Hunter, 'Astronomical Labours', p. 184. Muhammad Shah's stance reversed that of the purist Aurangzeb in that he stressed his superintending role in religion, reintroduced the practice of royal historiography; Tirmizi, *Titles*, p. x.

[22] V.S. Bhatnagar, *The Life and Times of Sawai Jai Singh, 1688–1743* (Delhi, 1974), pp. 264–8, 337–41; J.N. Asopa (ed.), *Cultural Heritage of Jaipur* (Jodhpur, 1892), pp. 104–5; Jai Singh's text collection is to be seen in the Jaipur City Palace Museum.

[23] Hunter, 'Astronomical labours', pp. 209–10.

there[24] and a flag was hoisted. If it signalled an easterly breeze, this foretold a good harvest; if southerly, the onset of scarcity. Other Maratha and Rajput courts also maintained the astronomical tradition. At Kotah, for instance, the instruments were symbolically built into the wall of the palace-fortress.[25]

In Delhi itself astronomical knowledge retreated to the houses of the Muslim nobility. Jai Singh's observatory, the Jantar Mantar, fell out of use after 1758, but intellectual life survived political revolution and with the substitution of British for Maratha overlordship in 1803, the dormant astronomical tradition revived. Meanwhile, in Lucknow, a city where many of the Muslim intelligentsia had sought refuge, Tafazzul Hussain raised a controversy by translating the western astronomers into Persian.[26] Another eminent contemporary astronomer was Khwaja Farid-ud Din, relation of Sir Sayyid Ahmad Khan, and the man in whose house he was brought up. Farid-ud Din anticipated his grandson as a leading Muslim informant of the British. He had been Vazir at the Mughal court and went on embassies for the Company to Persia and Burma. For a time he was Superintendent of the Calcutta Madrassah, another nursery of the Company's political munshis. Sayyid Ahmad remembered finding the house of one of Farid-ud Din's sons, 'hung with astrolabes, telescopes and astronomical instruments of all sorts'.[27] Sayyid Ahmad's own later switch from Wahhabi-influenced purism to a modernist religious position was heralded by his acceptance, probably in the 1840s, of Copernicus.

British power and Indian science

The British engaged with this still vital astronomical tradition in many different ways. Lewis Pyenson,[28] commenting on Dutch science in Indonesia, rejects the 'instrumentalist' argument that colonial science simply reflected the material needs of colonialism: 'The prosecution of exact sciences in the East Indies did not derive from colonial power; rather power derived from pure knowledge.' While this is an important

---

[24] Oral communications, Jaipur, Delhi, 1992; the ceremony is mentioned in a pamphlet sold near the Jantar Mantar, Daulat Singh, *Astronomical Observatory of Jaipur* (Jaipur, 1981), pp. 18–19.

[25] I owe this information to Dr Norbert Peabody.

[26] S.A.A. Rizvi, *A Socio-intellectual History of the Isna Ashari Shi'is in India (16th to 19th centuries A.D.)*, II, (Canberra 1986), pp. 227–9.

[27] Troll, *Sayyid Ahmad*, p. 147.

[28] Lewis Pyenson, *Empire of Reason. Exact sciences in Indonesia, 1840–1940* (Leiden, 1989), p. 180; cf. Roy MacLeod, 'Passages in imperial science from Empire to Commonwealth', *Journal of World History*, 4, 1993, 117–50; for the general context, Deepak Kumar, *Science and the Raj* (Delhi, 1995).

corrective, the relationship between colonial rule and science in India was more complex than either of these positions suggests. At one level, the new rulers sought political legitimacy by patronising Indian learning. At another, western astronomy was expected to promote Christian knowledge. Competition among British scientific amateurs also played its part. Indians were able to find space for positive evaluations of their own scientific traditions among these conflicting positions.

British astronomy sought, firstly, to appropriate the political legitimacy conferred by Mughal patronage of astral science. T.T. Metcalfe, the British Resident at Delhi, built his own observatory, the Koti Jahan Nama, outside the Kashmiri Gate in 1828.[29] Metcalfe was evidently trying to engage the Indian learned in debates about modern science, particularly astronomy. Later, the Delhi Archaeological Society, which brought together leading Indian and British inhabitants of the city, approached the Jaipur ruler for funds to repair his ancestor's stone observatory. Sayyid Ahmad, by now a junior judge in British service, reserved for Jai Singh's observatory some of his most elaborate descriptions in the 'Asar-as Sanadid' of 1848, a disquisition on the monuments of Delhi as an embodiment of Mughal legitimacy.[30] He exaggerated the indirect contribution of British astronomers to Jai Singh's researches, asserting that Jai Singh brought into astronomy British 'laws' (he uses the English word) and said 'The English participated in the establishment of this Observatory.'[31] The text subtly reinforces the claim of his colonial masters to a predominate share in Mughal sovereignty. Sayyid Ahmad, however, had broader concerns. His emphasis on 'rational proofs' in cosmology embodied the claim that new knowledge acquired by Indians and Europeans since the Ancients could modify established belief. This idea also underlay the modernist Islamic theology which he wished to encourage by 'opening the doors of interpretation',[32] a position abominated by his purist contemporaries. Astronomy, therefore, had implications both for the legitimacy of British rule and for the renovation of the Muslim community.

Lucknow saw similar developments. Here King Nasir-ud Din Hai-

---

[29] As recorded by Sayyid Ahmad Khan in his *Asar-as Sanadid* (1852), and translated by Garcin de Tassy, 'Description des monuments de Delhi en 1852', *Journale Asiatique*, 5th ser., 17, 1860-1, pp. 92-3.

[30] Sayyid Ahmed, 'Description des monuments', tr. de Tassy, *Journale Asiatique*, 1860-1, 5th ser., 16, 537-44.

[31] ibid., p. 540 n., cf. 541; in de Tassy's translation he continues 'en outre, le principal motif qui fit adapter dans cet observatoire grec la base des règles de l'astronomie moderne des Anglais est assez connu'. cf. Troll, *Sayyid Ahmad*, pp. 146-50.

[32] ibid., pp. 144-63.

dar's observatory was for some time managed by a British scientist[33] and liberal Muslim intellectuals were also associated with it. In 1837, for instance, a high-ranking courtier composed and printed an astronomical treatise which included a fierce denunciation of astrologers.[34] The observatory remained a centre of printing, cultural liberalism, and covert British influence, until abruptly closed in 1849 by one of Nasir-ud Din's successors who deeply resented British intereference.[35] In contemporary Banaras, James Prinsep patronised astronomy. A new observatory was planned there in the 1840s[36] and the local British community hoped it would overawe the large jyotish establishment in the city. Meanwhile, a liberal Sikh nobleman, Laihna Singh Majithia, supported the compilation by a Banaras jyotish of an elaborate Sanskrit astrological birth chart (*janampatra*) which diplays the influence of the Hindu, Islamic and western cosmologies.[37] The design appears to draw on contemporary British almanacs, but also included miniature paintings of astrological signs which have a distinctly Banarasi flavour.

More mundane motives were also in evidence among British aficionados of Indian astronomy. The orientalists hoped to advance their own fame and wealth by appropriating the knowledge of the East. Europeans continued to believe that Brahminical lore might reveal facts unknown to western science, and so glorify 'the British name' in Europe. Manuscript collectors were keenly aware that Indian texts could be sold for a considerable profit there. H.T. Colebrooke and H.H. Wilson, William Kirkpatrick and Mark Wilks maintained a long correspondence about Tipu Sultan's calendar and its Tamil Brahmin antecedents.[38] About the same time, Dr Strachey carried out a careful raid on manuscripts around Mysore to the order of the Sanskritist, Charles Wilkins. By 1805 he had collected 1,163 Sanskrit manuscripts and a good number of Hindi and Prakrit ones.[39] Strachey was surprised to have encountered so many Devanagari manuscripts which he attributed to the settlement in Mysore of 'a colony of Northern Brahmans who have recently settled in these parts'.[40] Strachey, however,

---

[33] Phillimore, *Survey*, IV, 115, on James Herbert, astronomer to King Nasir-ud Din Haidar of Awadh, 1831, also Deputy Surveyor General of British India.

[34] *Friend of India*, 2 Feb. 1837.

[35] Sprenger, *Catalogue of the Libraries of Oudh*, p. vi.

[36] *Benares Recorder*, 9, 20 Apr. 1847.

[37] Durga Shankar Patthak, *Sarvasiddhantattvacudamani* (the 'Crest Jewel of the Essence of all Astronomical Systems'), Banaras *c*. 1839, OR. 5259, BL; I am grateful to Dr J. Losty for showing me his unpublished article on this text.

[38] Wilks to Kirkpatrick, 12 Nov. 1809, Mss. Eur. F228/20, OIOC.

[39] Lt Knox to Dr Strachey, 20 June 1805, enclosure in Strachey to C. Wilkins, n.d., Mss. Eur. C 23, OIOC.

[40] ibid.

did not have it all his own way. Indian commercial agents (*dubashs*) at Madras tried to preempt this appropriation by westerners of Indian learning. Strachey complained that one particular Indian merchant, who could speak English, was always a step ahead of him, and this man bought up the manuscripts and presented them 'to poor Brahmans sooner than they should fall into the hands of Europeans'. Not only was jyotishastra an all-India network of techniques, but evidently, some Hindus already regarded Sanskrit learning as a precious resource of a national civilisation.

Next, and contrary to Pyenson's main contention, the British did use western science, and astronomy in particular, to 'reinforce social domination'. As William Hunter stated in one of the first detailed investigations of Jai Singh's astronomy,[41] 'I have always thought that after having convinced the Eastern nations of our superiority in policy and arms, nothing can contribute more to the extension of our national glory than the diffusion amongst them of a taste for *European* science.' Bentinck followed the spirit of this advice, presenting the ruler of Kotah with astronomical instruments, where previous grandees might have presented elephants and shawls.[42]

This is not to say, however, that these debates were simply 'orientalist' or directed solely to the subjugation of India. The British approach to Indian knowledge was deeply influenced by contemporary European controversies. In the eighteenth century, French radicals, especially Voltaire and Bailly,[43] drawing on the orientalist, le Gentil, had sought to undermine the historical status of the Bible by showing that the earliest Indian observations predated the supposed biblical date of creation. Over the next seventy years a whole host of British and European astronomers and orientalists in India and outside – including William Jones, Colebrooke and Bentley[44] – sought systematically to undermine the authority of these Indian observations. They brought forward the date of the Siddhantic calculations to the first millenium AD, so squaring them with the Biblical chronology. By 1820 they had begun to insist that Indian exact astronomy was no more than an imitation of the

[41] Hunter, 'Astronomical labours', p. 210.
[42] Trans. of a *kharita* of Maharao Ram Singh Bahadur of Kotah to Lord William Bentinck; Bentinck to Ram Singh, 3 Jan. 1834, Kotah Archives, Rajasthan (I owe this reference to Dr Norbert Peabody).
[43] Jean Sylvain Bailly, *Traité de l'Astronomie Indienne et Orientale* (Paris, 1787); P.J. Marshall, ed., *The British Discovery of Hinduism in the Eighteenth Century* (Cambridge, 1970), pp. 33 ff. J.F. Nourrison, *Trois Révolutionnaires: Turgot, Necker, Bailly* (Paris, 1885).
[44] The course of the controversy is summed up in G.R. Kaye, *Hindu Astronomy. Memoirs of the Archaeological Survey of India*, 18, (Calcutta, 1924), pp. 1–12, but see, especially, J. Bentley, *An Historical View of the Hindoo Astronomy* (London, 1799).

Greek Ptolemaic tradition, challenging the accuracy and originality of the pandits. An article in the *Calcutta Review* of 1844 expounded and disparaged the mathematical part of jyotishastra. In a classic statement of the link between industrial capitalism and western science, it asserted that the 'mechanical apparatus in one of our great factories' was as superior to the 'rude implements of the Bengal spinners and weavers' as modern algebra was to the 'cumbrous diction' of the medieval astronomer, Brahmagupta.[45]

To this writer the Siddhantas were not rationalistic thought, but 'as dogmatic' as the Puranas. Bhaskara, Brahmagupta and the other medieval astronomers merely replaced the antique sages as figures of blind authority. Indian tradition was valueless, but in introducing western astronomy 'we come with the authority of the very God of Truth'. The problem was that Indian thought, like the Indian polity, was corrupted by tyranny. A writer on Indian mathematics in the *Friend of India* asserted that it was thrown up by a single hero (Bhaskara) 'like a monstrous Indian Empire'.[46]

Over time too, European officials and residents became keener for practical reasons to demonstrate the superiority of their predictions of astral events over those of the Brahmins. The *Benares Recorder* cited a case in 1847 when a Hindu almanac, whose information had been received from a village in Burdwan 'full of humbugging pandit astronomers', had predicted a false time for an eclipse of the sun.[47] It claimed that throughout upper India, government offices were closed, and at pilgrimage places duped Hindus waited immersed in the holy river. Only the observatory attached to the Surveyor General's Office predicted the time correctly, it asserted. Magistrates policing the great bathing festivals over these years delighted in catching out the pandit astronomers in their predictions. The missionaries even tried to turn the ubiquitous almanac, the *panchang*, into a sword of Jesus, printing large numbers of a Christian almanac, *Kristo Panchang*.[48] A variant on the theme was a 'Temperance Almanac', designed for European soldiers as well as Indian elites, which included edifying tales of the fate of drunkards.[49] The official drive for intellectual hegemony coincided with the needs of the embattled expatriate business and commercial classes for a predictable, standard time. In the longer term, Indian merchants, too, succumbed to this imperative.[50]

[45] 'The Algebra of the Hindus', *Calcutta Review*, 2, 1844, 545–6.   [46] ibid., 560.

[47] *Benares Recorder*, 20 April 1847; cf. *Bengal Hurkaru*, 23 Jan. 1823.

[48] *Friend of India*, 21 Dec. 1848; cf. 10 Jan. 1850.

[49] *Benares Recorder*, 2 July 1847.

[50] Dr J. Masselos drew my attention to this important issue, see his 'Bombay time', mss. in author's possession.

Practical orientalism and new knowledge communities

These dismissive assaults on the Indian tradition were only part of the story, however. Other officials and institutions tried throughout the period to promote a cooperative and syncretic approach which was to have much greater influence on Indian mentalities. From the 1790s onwards British observers were taking note of what they thought of as a conflict between the precision of the Siddhantas and the mythology of the Puranas. Some educationists and missionaries urged that the more precise and rational elements within the classical Hindu sciences could be used to undermine the idolatry of the Puranas. In 1834, for example, Lancelot Wilkinson, Assistant Resident in the central Indian state of Bhopal, published a paper entitled 'On the use of the Siddhantas in the work of Native Education'.[51] Here he argued that only by enlisting the better parts of Brahminical knowledge could western ideas be infiltrated into India and native improvement begin. The network of astronomers which spread from cities out to the village jyotish could be used to impart basic European mathematical education. Wilkinson had begun 'experiments' in teaching in a high school at Sehore town which had been founded by the Bhopal court at his urging. Using the Siddhantas and the pandits he enlisted to his cause, Wilkinson claimed success in 'communicating more real knowledge and information than I have done in the previous ten years of my Indian life'.[52] In 1832 the jyotishs had helped calm the fears of villagers on the approach of parties of surveyors from the Great Trigonometrical Survey of India. He reported that the native astronomers had used verses from the Siddhantas to prove to the peasants that astronomical observation was not only harmless, but even pious.[53]

Wilkinson's 'experiment' was at least partly successful. Pandit Omkar Bhatta and other jyotish astronomers at Sehore began to teach Newtonian science using Siddhantic principles. In 1841 Bhatta published a Hindi tract called *Bhugolasara*,[54] which was a comparison of the Siddhantic, Puranic and Copernican systems. The work proceeded in the form of a classical guru–pupil dialogue and in his preface Bhatta sent greetings to other teachers and pupils throughout India.[55] In the dialogue the teacher refutes the Puranic view that the shadow of Mount Meru is responsible for nightfall by enlisting the authority of Bhaskara, a

[51] L. Wilkinson, 'On the use of the Siddhantas in the work of native education', *Journal of the Asiatic Society of Bengal*, 1834, art. vii, 504–19.
[52] ibid., 510–11.   [53] ibid., 511–12.
[54] Omkar Bhatta, *Bhugolasara arthart Jyotish Chandrika, jis me Purana aur Siddhanta ki Kopamikas Sahib ki Jyotish Vidya se Pariksha ki* (Agra 1841).
[55] ibid., p. 23.

leading Siddhantist. Later, the text goes on to introduce Copernican ideas to modify in turn Bhaskara and the Siddhantists. Omkar Bhatta refers to other achievements of western science and technology. The English railways, for instance, are used as a proof of the existence of gravity, since they demonstrate that objects could move fast across the earth's surface without falling into space.[56] Shortly before, the Agra School Book Society had published *Jyotish Vidya ka Varnan*,[57] a brief account of the solar system. Wilkinson's own translation of a major medieval text, the 'Surya Siddhanta', published in Calcutta 1842,[58] was also adopted by the Society. Later, Indian intermediaries, such as Shiva Prasad, inserted modern geography and cosmography into the school textbooks they published for the North-Western Provinces Government.

The Sehore developments became famous, especially among those neo-orientalists, such as Wilkinson, Hodgson, Muir and Ballantyne, who wanted an active policy of public education using indigenous languages and enlisting the indigenous intellectual elite. One protagonist wrote that the Sehore pandits 'have raised active and increasing discussion in all quarters to which their influence extends', including 'Poona, Nagpore, Muthoora, Benares and other places'.[59] Traditional astronomers at these centres responded to the modernisers' challenge with complex and closely reasoned arguments, but there was little agreement amongst them about the status of the Siddhantas and Puranas, let alone the Copernican doctrines.[60] This lively debate illustrates once again the forensic vitality of the ecumene and the capacity of Indian intellectual culture to engage rapidly with new doctrines.

Wilkinson's accounts also indicate some ways in which the new knowledge communities drew on and transformed traditional learning. He gave the example of a Brahmin from Banaras who had been taught the 'chemical vedas' (the Rasayana Shastras) by his physician father. The young man had later learned some principles of modern medicine from a British Assistant Surgeon and had acquired Siddhantic astro-

---

[56] ibid.
[57] *Jyotish Vidya ka Varnan* [A brief account of the solar system], (Agra, 1840, for the School Book Society); see also, Shiva Prasad, *Vidyankar*, (Banaras 1856), pp. 44–6.
[58] L. Wilkinson, *The Goladhia: a treatise on astronomy with a commentary entitled the mitacshara, forming the fourth and last chapter of the Siddhant Shiromuni* (Calcutta, 1842).
[59] 'Cosmopolite' to *Friend of India*, 6 May 1841; cf. ibid., 30 Mar. 1837, Pandits' Sanskrit debate on Copernicus.
[60] e.g. the Ujjain pandits contended 'for the unadulterated Poorans', those at Mathura 'denounced all jyotish, and those at Banaras accepted both the Siddhantas and the Puranas'. Note by J.R. Colvin, Private Sec. to the Governor-General, referred to in Lord Auckland's minute of 24 Nov. 1839, in H. Sharp (ed.), *Selections from Educational Records*. Part I, *1781–1839* (Calcutta, 1920), p. 175.

nomical doctrines from the Sehore teachers. Entering government service, he organised practical demonstrations of the discoveries of modern science at places where he was posted.[61] Another example was given of a Brahmin from Nagpur who had heard of the new learning and travelled to Pune where he studied for a time and observed a variety of 'arts and manufactures'.[62] Returning to Nagpur, this man set up a lithographic press and began printing almanacs corrected with reference to modern algebra and the other mathematics. Such small networks of officials and Indian intelligentsia were to spread and link up between the 1830s and 1870s. They formed the conceptual underpinning for a developing professional class which saw in European science the perfection of an Indian national tradition.

The context of intellectual and social change in places such as Banaras or Pune is relatively well known: what of Sehore? Obviously, the presence there of Wilkinson until his death in 1841 was critical. Becoming a Bombay civil servant in 1824 under the rule of the enlightenment scholar Mountstuart Elphinstone, Wilkinson was an enthusiast. He was prepared to forego leave in order to remain with his Indian charges, and in an exception to the contemporary racial hubris, declared of a pupil, 'He is more fit to be my gooroo (teacher) than my shishya (scholar) in mathematical questions.'[63] On several occasions Wilkinson wrote to the Baptist *Friend of India* and this may indicate evangelical interests on his part. The same is true of his assault on the prohibition against widow remarriage in Bhopal on the grounds that it was 'contrary to God's Law'.[64] Wilkinson also lined up with the 'orientalists' in the language controversy. He advocated Indian education in the vernaculars and Sanskrit and deplored the imposition of English, fearing that his own pupils would never find employment.[65]

Quite apart from the influence of Wilkinson, however, Sehore itself was the kind of cultural crossroads which quickly became a market for new ideas. It was close to Ujjain, a traditional centre of astronomy. The region was home not only to a Maratha Brahmin tradition of learning, but also to a group of Malvi Brahmins from Rajasthan who had acted as intermediaries between the Mughal and Afghan nobles and the Maratha population.[66] Again, Bhopal's aspiring north Indian princely dynasty were generous patrons of learning and maintained close connections with the learned Muslim schools of north India. There were unmistake-

[61] 'Cosmopolite' to *Friend of India*, 6 May 1841; cf. *Benares Recorder*, 2 Jul. 1847.
[62] 'Cosmopolite' to *Friend of India*, 6 May 1841.
[63] Wilkinson's obituary, *Friend of India*, 9 Dec. 1841.   [64] ibid.
[65] *Friend of India*, 6 May 1841.
[66] 'Bhopal', *Imperial Gazetteer of India*, VIII (Oxford, 1908), 128–44; Sehore, ibid., XXXII, 160–2.

able signs of intellectual conflict and social change in the air. Wilkinson's faction of astronomers had links into the court through the diwan (chief minister) of the state. The diwan's son had written a Marathi tract in favour of widow remarriage, as indeed had the Copernican astronomer Shastri Subaji Bapu.[67] This was fertile ground for social as well as intellectual reform. 'Jodhpuri Brahmins' along with some local commercial castes countenanced widow remarriage, though the practice was hotly contested by traditional caste members.[68] This part of central India had thus benefited from its position on several intellectual frontiers. Ujjain and Sehore had given rise precociously to a small critical public without the presence of either a British community or a large Indian commercial city.

Macaulay and the Anglicists may have won the debate about language at a superficial level, but during the 1840s and 1850s the intellectual initiative still lay with men like Wilkinson and their Indian proteges who wished to promote a syncretic public education in Indian languages. James Ballantyne remained a powerful advocate of this approach. In 1857, the very year, as Ballantyne put it, when India was convulsed with blood and horror, he was staging a series of formal debates or shastrarthas in which pandit scholars debated western principles along traditional lines. The set-piece debate of that year was 'Chandra Ghumana Vichar', or 'the question of the turning of the moon'.[69] The argument proceeded with a homely analogy of the way in which a peasant's bullock tethered to an oil press moved round and round in a great circle.

This use of one part of Indian tradition to attack another might be seen as an epistemological equivalent of the political tactic of 'divide and rule'. But it also cautions against the assumption of recent writers that crude disparagement was the dominant mode of British engagement with Indian knowledge. More commonly, influential Europeans held Indians to be trapped at a level of intellectual development similar to that of the Ancient Greeks and Romans. Their knowledge and logical techniques could therefore be put to constructive use. The very act of enlisting some elements of the old intellectual elite in the colonial civilising process, of course, tended to perpetuate them. Rather than sweeping away the old hierarchies, the protagonists of public instruction replaced them with new, syncretic Anglo-Indian ones.

---

[67] Wilkinson to *Friend of India*, 18 Nov. 1841.   [68] ibid.
[69] *Chandra Ghumana Vichar. Does the Moon Rotate? A question argued in Sanskrit and English by the Pandits of the Benares College and James R. Ballantyne. Litt. D. Printed for the use of the College*, (Banaras, Medical Hall Press, 1857).

A revolution in astral knowledge?

These intellectual currents and developments in modes of communication accelerated changes that were already in train. Copernican ideas were gradually taking root amongst the elites in the first half of the nineteenth century. Many modernist Muslims, led by Sayyid Ahmad had embraced the heliocentric view of the universe before 1860. Graduates of the Hindu College, Banaras Sanskrit College and other large institutions were routinely educated in Newtonian science. A number of considerations qualify a picture of western scientific triumph, however. First, the Indian astral sciences were already undergoing a significant transformation before the advent of formal European teaching in astronomy. Quite apart from the syncretic efforts of Jai Singh, and Islamic advances in the astrolabe, there is evidence of an important shift in thinking among learned Hindus towards Ptolemaic, and even heliocentric models. When Bernier visited Banaras in the seventeenth century he was impressed by the dominance among the Brahmins of the puranic cosmological mythology, such as the belief that the universe was created on the back of a giant turtle.[70] By 1824 when Bishop Heber called in on the descendants of these same pandits, he was met with Ptolemy, that is the Siddhantas, and some of his informants even professed a private belief in the Copernican universe.[71] Arguably, the shift from turtles to Ptolemy was more radical than that from Ptolemy to Copernicus.

Secondly, the rise of the Copernican system in India did not hasten the decline of the Puranas, let alone the collapse of the whole edifice of 'false' religion as the Serampore missionaries had hoped. On the contrary, Hindus began to adopt the mental technique, already common among Christians, of hiving off mythology and belief into a separate, transcendant sphere. Raghaviah, the Madras Brahmin who had mounted an early defence of Hinduism, wrote several letters in 1804–5 to William Kirkpatrick about his translations from the Puranas of sections on astronomy and geography. He admitted that this required knowledge of the 'astronomical and geographical principles of enlightened western nations' as well as the Sanskrit, and bemoaned the difficulty of reconciling the 'tedious labour of [European] engineers' with the 'fertile imagination' of the Rishis. Nevertheless, he thought it

---

[70] F. Bernier, *Travels in the Mogul Empire A.D. 1656–1668*, Constable's Oriental Miscellany (repr., London, 1891), pp. 339–40.

[71] Heber, *Narrative*, I, 169; the superintendent of the Vidyalaya (Banaras Sanskrit College) opposed the introduction of the Copernican system but one pandit 'smiled once or twice very slily, and said "*Our people* are taught so and so [i.e. the Siddhantas]"', as if he himself knew better'.

'blasphemous in me as a religious descendant of Divine Brahma if I do not place as much or in comparative degree more belief in the one than in the other'.[72] Another similar case concerns the Bengali family of Pandit Sukh Lal. Sukh Lal's father had been impressed by the Siddhantas and abandoned the 'fantasies' of the Puranas, aiding Sir William Jones in some of his Sanskrit invesigations. The son, in turn, was a skilled astronomer, but refused to forswear the Puranas. To the chagrin of the Serampore missionaries he was carried to the banks of the Ganges on his deathbed.[73]

While Newtonian science was on the formal curriculum of government schools and colleges, there flourished a variety of accommodations between the Puranas, Siddhantas, Islamic astronomy and western science.[74] Puranic beliefs had already been adjusted to the Siddhantic notion of the globe with Mount Meru at its pole. There are several nineteenth century examples of brass globes (bhugolas) inscribed with the Puranic land masses and seas.[75] These were made for teaching purposes and drew on ancient prototypes, but it seems probable that these nineteenth-century versions were made in response to the aggressive teaching of western geography and astronomy in the new government schools and colleges. Astrology also continued to flourish, its practitioners now gaining higher status by using western astronomical calculations to make their predictions more precise. Many of the early Urdu and Hindi newspapers, like their European equivalents, carried astrological predictions. In Agra a large volume of astrological almanacs was printed in the 1850s under the auspices of the Sat Sabha (Society of Truth), a body of astrologers which took to the printing press to spread their skills.[76]

In popular culture the happy mix of puranic cosmology and analytical astronomy became the leading edge of India's print revolution. Almanacs which reported calendrical computations and astral events alongside tales and pictures from Hindu mythology were by far the most

---

[72] Letter no. 1. from P. Raghaviah to W. Kirkpatrick, 1804–5 (undated), Mss. Eur. F 228/20, OIOC.

[73] 'Death of Kalidas Pandit', Friend of India, 28 Feb. 1839.

[74] R. O'Hanlon, Caste, Conflict and Ideology (Cambridge, 1988), pp. 90–1.

[75] See, for instance, the example in the British Museum, Hotung Gallery of Oriental Antiquities, Bhugola, dated Samvat 1915, accession no. OA. 1886.11–27–1; for earlier examples, S. Digby, 'The Bhugola of Ksema Karna: a dated sixteenth century piece of Indian metalware', Art and Archaeology Research Papers, 4, 1973, 10–31.

[76] The Association is mentioned in de Tassy, LH, I, 381 in connection with Chaggan Lal's panchang of which a vast number were printed. There is a copy in VT 1528, OIOC, Panchanga Sambat 1925, Agra, muhar Satsabha, which refers to Pandit Chaggan Lala Jyoti, it has 32 pages and includes predictions of astral events, and a section on palmistry. There are crude line drawings of deities, planets and astrological signs.

common form of printed literature throughout India by mid-century. These soon began carrying commercial advertisments. According to the *Friend of India*, the old written almanacs produced by temple Brahmins were disappearing and 'the publication of these works has fallen into the hands of the bookselling fraternity, a large and growing body'.[77] In the 1840s 4,000 copies per annum of the most important Calcutta almanac were printed at eight annas a copy. Seven in eight of these were disposed of up-country by hawkers who charged a commission of one anna per copy.

Astrological experts also continued to flourish. Joshis, popular astronomer pandits, along with Puraniks (readers of the Puranas), were among the few Brahmin subdivisions prepared to provide their services to low castes and tribal peoples. With the slow improvement of communications, soothsayers and astrologers moved out into the backlands and the camps of the migrant tribals and low castes, bringing the almanac and the horoscope to new audiences. In this way they helped 'bring them within the pale of Hinduism', as one observer put it.[78] The Indian astral sciences were continuing to extend their hegemony over the 'little tradition' of necromancy and divination just as the pioneer peasants conquered the jungle and hill fastnesses.

Finally, as with the ayurvedic medicine considered next, the ancient Indian astral knowledge became a source of pride for an emerging national consciousness. Learned men accepted western doctrines, but at the same time subtly praised the inheritance of Indian knowledge. We see this in the work of Pandit Bapu Deva Sastri, a western Indian who became Mathematics Professor in the Banaras Government College. Sastri, an honorary member of the Asiatic Society of Bengal, revised Wilkinson's *Surya Siddhanta* and published the full text in the Biblioteca Indica series in the 1860s. He subscribed to Newtonian theories, but his text notes were strongly supportive of the medieval sage, Bhaskara, against the charges of inconsistency levelled against him by Wilkinson and his protege, Subaji Bapu.[79]

This politicisation of the memory of Indian astronomy became more pronounced in the second half of the nineteenth century. Western

[77] *Friend of India*, 12 Feb. 1846.

[78] J. Nesfield, *The Functions of Modern Brahmins in Upper India* (Calcutta, 1887), p. 16.

[79] Bapu Deva Sastri, *The Surya-Siddhanta, an ancient system of Hindu astronomy; with Ranganatha's exposition, the Gudhartha Prakasaka*, edited by F. Hall, with the assistance of Bapu Deva Sastrin [sic], *Biblioteca Indica*, 25 (Calcutta 1854–9); cf. *A Translation of the Surya Siddhanta by Pundit Bapu Deva Sastri, and of the Siddhanta Siromani by the late Lancelot Wilkinson, esq. C.S.* (Calcutta 1861), p. 126, note, where Bapu Deva Sastri defends Bhaskara against Wilkinson and his protege, Subaji Bapu; Bapu Deo, or Deva, became an Honorary Member of the Royal Asiatic Society, M.A. Sherring, *Hindu Tribes and Castes as represented in Benares*, (London, 1872), p. 90.

Indian astronomers confidently assigned to 6000 BC the date of the birth of the Ram, which Bentley, the evangelical polemicist, had placed at 961 BC in the early years of the century.[80] Meanwhile, the more sceptical Tilak, leader of the movement for immediate independence, dated the Rigveda, the earliest and the greatest of the vedic books, to not later than 4000 BC 'when the vernal equinox was in Orion'.[81] He hoped this scientific dating would lead to 'a fuller and unprejudiced discussion of the high antiquity of Aryan civilisation of which our sacred books are the oldest record in the world'. So, in the nineteenth century, while the memory of Indian science was newly forged into a national icon, its more lowly practitioners, vitalised by the new media and oblivious to the contempt of white commentators, continued to spread their influence further into the Indian hinterland.

Physic and society

This complex interaction between the British and Indian systems of knowledge can also be seen in the case of medicine. For Indians, medical science was part of a much wider philosophy of influences which also had strong social implications, because the science of ethics was in part an environmental one. As with the relationship between astronomy and astrology, the transformative medical arts were also related to popular practice in subtle ways. Learned practice shared the same moral universe as exorcism and 'white magic'. Some famous seats of exorcism, such as the Balaji temple near Bharatpur and many Muslim shrines, supported exorcists alongside priests who prescribed fasts and ayurvedic remedies for illness. On another conceptual boundary, medicinal chemistry shaded into the search for the philosopher's stone. Thus a sect such as the Sidha ascetics, supposedly spiritual descendants of the ancient Rishis or sages, purified their own substance by ascetic practices to overcome death, greatest disease of all.[82] They were also rumoured to possess the secret of converting base metal into gold, since that, too, involved transforming substance.

Likewise, medical knowledge among Muslims was the disciplined part of a much larger body of lore which included folk belief and esoteric practices. Even elite Muslims believed in black magic and sought ways in which to cast out spirits and transfer evil to enemies and proxies.

---

[80] Kane, *Dharmasastra*, V, i, 484–5.
[81] Bal Ganghadar Tilak, *Orion, or researches into the Antiquity of the Vedas by B.G. Tilak, BA, LLB* (London, 1892), p. iii.
[82] M. and J. Stutley (eds.), *Dictionary of Hinduism. Its myth, folklore and development, 1500 B.C.–A.D. 1500* (London, 1977), p. 276.

Ghalib, for example, once expressed great concern that his brother was possessed of an evil spirit, and detailed his visits to an exorcist.[83] Muslims worshipping at shrines sought to capture the charisma of famous saints in cloth or in waterjars so as to transfer it back to sick people and thereby heal them. For Islam had inherited the Greek asclepian tradition which associated the healer with divinity, and additionally, the tradition of Jewish prophethood in which powers of healing were seen as marks of God. *Hikmat*, like the Sanskritic equivalent, was more than medicine, it was 'natural philosophy', and hakims were doctors of natural law. Here again, their medicinal expertise was believed to have its esoteric side, since medicinal chemistry and knowledge of the properties of quicksilver was an entré into alchemy.[84]

In the Indo-Islamic world as in most other societies kings became patrons of healing, and their own bodies were conceived of as energising, healing agents. Indian rulers were particularly concerned to foster an interchange between Sanskrit and Islamic medical lore, translating the works of Galen into Sanskrit and the medical Vedas into Persian. Despite their hostility to Portuguese political pretensions, the Mughals and their nobles took particular note of the surgical skills which Europeans such as Bernier, Manucci and Surman could bring them. Doctors, like medical remedies, were prized at court; they were passed from one ruler to another as gifts and became politically powerful in their own right. One physician even became governor of Surat.[85] In the early nineteenth-century Punjab, with an ailing king and a society scarified by cholera, doctors wielded even greater influence.[86] Physicians were, in addition, important information gatherers for the state. Those resident in cities held regular councils and could frame broad calculations of mortality rates by ordering the custodians at the city gates (*darwans*) to count corpses passing outside for burial or burning.[87] In villages, Brahmins sometimes kept records of deaths which could provide information for vaidyas.[88] The status achieved by doctors did not, of course, exempt them from the popular belief that they were quarrelsome and incompetent or lechers who used their privileged position to grope female patients.[89]

[83] Tirmizi, *Persian Letters of Ghalib*, pp. xxxv–vi.

[84] *Kimigars*, travelling adepts of the philosopher's stone, also offered mineral cures to the households they visited.

[85] D.M. Bose, S.N. Sen and B.V. Subbarayappa, *A Concise History of Science in India* (Calcutta, 1971), pp. 271–5; Crawford, *Medical Service*, II, 127–8.

[86] 'Fakir Azizuddin of the Punjab', *Friend of India*, 12 Oct. 1803.

[87] Report on plague mortality in Jaipur, Asst Surgeon, 9 Lt Cavalry to Lt-Gov., Agra, 19 May 1837, NWP Genl Procs., 27 May 1837, 16, 214/31, OIOC.

[88] Asst Surgeon 34th Regiment to *Madras Gazette*, cited in *Calcutta Journal*, 4 Dec. 1818.

[89] e.g., Sauda, *Kulliyat*, pp. 150–3 , cited Russell and Islam, *Three Mughal Poets*, p. 50.

As with astronomy, medical practitioners formed a hierarchy, but western observers exaggerated its rigidity and also underestimated the extent to which medical lore had also become a form of wider public knowledge. The most eminent practitioners in both the Sanskritic and the Islamic tradition preserved their own texts and passed them from one generation to the next. Great vaidya families among the Hindus taught small numbers of pupils from their own or related families, and also acted as hereditary physicians to noble and landowning families.[90] Muslim rulers had established medical colleges (tibikhanas) where doctors congregated and which were often associated with the great mosques. There were famous tibikhanas at Hyderabad, Delhi and Lucknow,[91] cities with a reputation for healing expertise. In Banaras the family of Ahsanullah Khan was given Rs. 2,000 revenue-free land as a service grant provided that they distributed free medicines to the poor and gave medical advice to them in perpetuity.[92] Jonathan Duncan continued the grant in 1783, but as with so many service grants, the original purpose of the grant had been overlooked after two generations, and the distribution of medicines came to an end early in the nineteenth century.

Medical knowledge waxed and waned along with the fortunes of the late Mughal service elite. A high percentage of officers of state and military men had some knowledge of medicine, and a good number wrote or transcribed medical or veterinary texts. At least five hundred volumes of Arabic manuscripts on medicine and twice the number of Persian and Urdu treatises existed in the Raza Library of Rampur, one of the eighteenth century's great libraries.[93] Nor was the tradition limited to Muslims; treatment of the diseases of humans, horses and elephants were favourite topics in the emerging Hindi literature of Rajasthan.

It is difficult to get a clear impression of numbers of specialist physicians. Praising a town for the learning of its hakims was an aspect of eulogy from ancient Baghdad through to modern cities like Delhi. At the beginning of the nineteenth century Indian officials in Jodhpur told Boileau that their city's population of nearly 150,000 boasted no fewer than 80 vaidya households with 400 members and 40 hakim housholds with 200 members.[94] In contemporary Jaipur there were 4,500 hakims

[90] T.A. Wise, Commentary on the Hindu System of Medicine (Calcutta, 1845), pp. iv–vi.
[91] Hindu rulers such as Ahaliya Bai also established medical institutions, C.E. Luard (ed.) Indore State Gazetteer (Calcutta, 1909), II, 173–4.
[92] Grant of land to Hakim Abdullah of Banaras, Committee for Hospital Dispensary at Banaras to Lt Gov., 30 Jan. 1837, NWP General Procs., 4 Feb. 1837, 5, 214/30; cf. Reade, Contributions, pp. 4–13; Sharar, Lucknow, 96–8.
[93] Arshi, Rampur
[94] Boileau, Narrative, p. 239.

and 1,250 vaidyas (900 and 230 houses respectively) for a population of about 400,000.[95] Doctors were among the largest learned professional groupings. If we assume two male members of these families 'practised', we have figures of about 1.5 physicians per hundred of the population in Jodhpur and one to every hundred people in Jaipur.

Alongside the dedicated specialists, as in any pre-modern system of medicine, were a host of people with some degree of skill who offered advice or remedies on an informal basis. Medicine merged into other learned subjects, and many ordinary ulama and Sufis had read medical treatises and were prepared to practise within their families or among dependents. Prayer, charismatic touch, exorcism and medicine were all entangled. As in other classical civilisations, certain religious sects held medical ministration to the poor a particularly meritorious act. According to Boileau, the Jutis (or Jettis), a Jain priestly subsect of Rajasthan, practised medicine among the poor 'not for filthy lucre, but simply "pour l'amour de Dieu" '.[96] Again pansaris, who supplied drugs, also seem to have acquired some respectability as independent pharmacists,[97] making up drugs to the instructions of hakims.

Next, there were the humbler medical specialists: barber surgeons who bled people; the potters who were responsible for setting bones; the itinerant eye doctors who removed cataracts;[98] the specialists who dealt with sword wounds; and the various nurses for childbirth, abortion and the diseases of women. Healing was hierarchically graded, and the more demeaning the forms of medicine, the lower the status of the operatives. Medical knowledge embraced a large number of dedicated and part-time people. To these were soon to be added retired Indian sepoys who had been hospital orderlies or pharmacists attached to government dispensaries. Such people began to diffuse some European techniques in their retirement villages.

European doctors and Indian clients

European doctors were in a unique position to act as information gatherers among Europeans and Indians.[99] Able, university-educated

---

[95] ibid., p. 241.
[96] ibid., p. 14; cf. R.H. Irvine, *Some Account of the General and Medical Topology of Ajmeer* (Calcutta, 1841), p. 108.
[97] Sauda, cited Russell and Islam, *Three Mughal Poets*, p. 51.
[98] e.g., P. Breton, 'On the native method of couching', *Transactions of the Medical and Physical Society of Calcutta*, 2, 1826, 344–66; on obstetricians, *Englishman*, 20 Feb. 1834.
[99] M.N. Pearson, 'The Thin End of the Wedge. Medical Relativities as a paradigm of early modern Indian–European relations', *MAS*, 29, 1, 1995, pp. 141–70.

men from relatively humble backgrounds, especially in Scotland and Ireland, were well represented among British military and civilian surgeons, and for them, proficiency in Indian languages was essential.[100] Indians regarded European medicine and surgery with both suspicion and admiration, but European doctors were often able to penetrate into the domestic space of Indian courts. The journal of (Sir) Paul Joddrell, MD, FRS, physician to the Nawab of Arcot in the 1790s, reveals something of the world of learned freelances who existed before the presidency medical services became more formal and disciplined.[101] Joddrell had been sent to Madras following a request by Nawab Muhammad Ali Wallajah to George III. This was a mark of the continuing cultural eclecticism of the Arcot regime which employed Hindu, Muslim and Christian specialists in religion, war and architecture.

Joddrell remained at the heart of the generation of metropolitan medical knowledge even while he worked in India. He regularly received the *Philosophical Transactions of London* and Samuel Simmons's *Medical Facts and Observations*.[102] Madras-bound ships brought him the *Histoire de la Société de Médecine* and equivalent German periodicals. Using Indian information and international connections, Joddrell was able to connect Indian and European discoveries. In September 1792, for example, he read in the London journal *Medical Facts* about a salt found in bamboo.[103] Tracing its Islamic, Sanskrit and Tamil names, he checked his facts with the work of Russell and Patrick. Russell, brother of the Surgeon to the British Factory in Aleppo, had been Joddrell's predecessor in the Nawab's service and had published botanical memoirs of the Coromandel coast. In the following year we find Joddrell entering in his journal an Indian cure for elephantiasis, compounded of arsenic and pepper, which had been recommended by Hakim Athar Ali Khan of Delhi and had found its way into the second volume of *Asiatick Researches*.[104] Joddrell's understanding of India was framed by enlightenment principles. He read the classics, Voltaire, the Scottish philosopher William Robertson's last work *Historical Disquisition concerning the Knowledge which the Ancients had on India* (1791) and confirmed his status as an intellectual radical by perusing Mary Wollstonecraft's *The Rights of Women*.[105]

Joddrell played a minor role in the process of linking together British

---

[100] Crawford, *Medical Service*, I, 488–519.
[101] Journal of Sir Paul Joddrell, Cambridge University Library, typescript, Oriental Faculty Library Cambridge (IB 065); Crawford, *Medical Service*, I, 15.
[102] Journal of Sir Paul Joddrell, entry 24 Jan. 1793.   [103] ibid., 8 Sept. 1792.
[104] ibid., 26 Feb. 1793.   [105] ibid., 11 May 1793.

knowledge of north and south India which accompanied the struggle with Mysore. He was a confidant of John Kennaway, whom he treated for dropsy,[106] and Colin Mackenzie,[107] who was at this time beginning to assemble maps of Mysore. Joddrell quizzed brother surgeons from different stations and acted as a conduit of information in both directions between Britain and India. His relations with Indians were ambivalent. Like his master the Nawab, Joddrell was massively in debt. In ducking and weaving out of the grasp of his creditors, he was several times beholden to the favour of the Nawab and princes. On one occasion, Umdat-ul Umara, the heir to the throne, passed on a report from his spies that Joddrell's servants were on the point of decamping because they had not been paid.[108] Joddrell treated members of the Nawab's family, including women, in their quarters, but he also conducted a private practice amongst Armenians and Indians. Some of Joddrell's patients had sexual problems, but the Arcot nobles also hoped that he might be able to help them with their even more pressing financial needs. On several occasions he was asked to comment on experiments regarding the philosopher's stone. Mimood Sahib said that 'he had been trying for twelve years to convert metals into gold and had at last succeeded'.[109] Joddrell told him that it was 'an imposition', but to no effect. Later, he was consulted by Umdat-ul Umara 'who had been shut up for several days, making gold'.[110]

Joddrell moved easily, if censoriously, in Indian circles. The introduction of vaccination into India after 1800, however, brought sharply into focus the whole question of the status of indigenous knowledge. There were two issues: first, what was the status of the existing 'Brahmin innoculators' and secondly, was there any truth in the assertion that Indians themselves had discovered vaccination with cow-pox. As in the cases of astronomy, language and other vedic sciences, the reaction of Europeans was complicated by their dependence on indigenous networks of information. It was also rendered contentious by the conflict between the British search in India for antique knowledge and their growing contempt for the forms of modern Indian society.

The most sympathetic account of 'Brahmin' innoculation procedures was given by Josiah Holwell in the 1760s. Holwell spoke of the annual appearance in Bengal of Brahmins from Banaras, Allahabad and other holy places of north India, who brought smallpox material smeared on pieces of cotton.[111] They 'examined the spread of the disease' and then

---

[106] ibid., 1 Sept. 1792. [107] ibid., 18 Aug. 1792.
[108] ibid., 8 Oct. 1792. [109] ibid., 30 Jan. 1793.
[110] ibid., 21 Feb. 1793.
[111] Holwell, cited in Williamson, ed. Gilchrist, *Vade Mecum*, pp. 214–17; J. Shoolbred,

moved from door to door in the major towns infecting small children for a fee and abjuring them to pray to Shitala the smallpox goddess. The majority of these children survived, and having the disease in infancy was preferable, of course, to contracting it in later life. This account was reproduced by John Shoolbred, Superintendent General of Vaccine Innoculation in 1803, at the height of the Company's attempt to spread the 'Jennerian discovery' of vaccination. It was reproduced again by John Gilchrist when he prepared his Urdu medical dialogue for the use of doctors in the field. This work (1823) was dedicated to Shoolbred, who in retirement in Britain, had apparently helped Gilchrist with financial support for his linguistic work. True to the spirit of Wellesley's imperial propaganda, Gilchrist's dialogue had the Indian physician, convinced of the superiority of western medicine, praying for the stability of the British Empire (*Vilayat ka Badshah*).[112]

Shoolbred had become ambivalent about the Indian tradition of innoculation. Experience had falsified the notion that Hindus would not mind being injected with the products of a cow,[113] but he continued to hope that the prevalence of innoculation would predispose some higher-caste Indians to vaccinate their children. Existing Brahmin innoculators might also provide informants and operatives to aid the European doctors. On the other hand, Shoolbred believed that Indian practice was dangerous. Brahmin innoculators had spread the disease in Bengal, when it might otherwise only have visited the Lower Provinces once in every ten or fifteen years.[114] Many more children died than would have been the case with vaccination. Shoolbred also doubted that innoculation was widespread or deeply rooted in India. There was little sign of it in Awadh where, according to Holwell, the Brahmin innoculators originated, and seventeenth-century European travellers had got their knowledge of the practice from the Ottoman realms, and not from the subcontinent.

While reluctantly acknowledging the need for native innoculation expertise, the advocates of vaccination reacted with contempt to the idea that vaccination, as opposed to innoculation, was known in ancient India. In 1802 Dr Gillman, Surgeon of the 8th Regiment of Native Infantry, had procured in Bareilly an indigenous medical compendium which included an account of Indian vaccination with

Report on the progress of vaccine innoculation in Bengal from the period of its introduction in November 1802 to the end of 1803 (London, 1804).

112 Gilchrist, *Dialogues*, p. 243.
113 Williamson, ed. Gilchrist, *Vade Mecum*, pp. 214–17.
114 Shoolbred, *Report*, Appendix presented to the Medical Board, 24 Mar. 1804, pp. 67–8.

substance taken from the udder of a diseased cow.[115] Another source reported that a Hindu physician of Bishnapur in Bengal had proposed to protect a child from smallpox by innoculating it with matter from a herd of cattle infected with *gow basant* (cow-pox).[116] These findings led to a vigorous debate in the *Calcutta Gazette*, with medical men 'drawing forth information' on this issue.[117] Shoolbred firmly refuted those Britons, as well as Indians, 'who will have it that the Brahmins know everything'.[118] The Bareilly compendium, he believed, was not a single text but a running compendium of knowledge like those that existed in Europe before the appearance of the encyclopaedia. Inter- polations were easily made. In this case, the text appeared to speak of 'injection' which was unknown in any vedic medical text. Besides, most Indian informants denied that they had heard of vaccination. It was an attempt on the part of the Brahmins, Shoolbred concluded, to buttress their waning authority by appropriating European knowledge. This may well have been true, but if so, the accusation of forgery and bad faith made by European polemicists was inappropriate. To the priesthood all knowledge was implicit in the Vedas, and it was the duty of Brahmins to reveal the hidden meaning of texts by pious interpretation. This theme of the foundational status of Indian medical science was later taken up by the first generation of English-educated Indians, who argued in the same vein that all later knowledge was implicit in the Vedas.

The Pharmacopoeia: a textual window between Europe and Asia

While vaccination and the later public response to cholera proved to be *causes célèbres* in Anglo-Indian medical life, a quieter and longer-term investigation of Indian medicine was also under way. Indian specialists played a critical, though often unacknowledged role in this search for information. Many early European travellers to India, such as Giovanni Careri, had collected botanical samples and made notes on Indian medical practice.[119] As early as 1640, the Dutch in Kerala had attempted to systematise their knowledge of Indian *materia medica* by drawing on written texts and the lore of tribal and low-caste people who

[115] ibid., p. 54   [116] ibid., pp. 59–60.
[117] ibid., p. 52; cf. *Calcutta Journal*, 2 Feb. 1819.
[118] Shoolbred, *Report*, p. 53; cf. Homi K. Bhabha, *The Location of Culture* (London, 1994), pp. 97–100, but note that the tension and ambivalence in the colonial relationship discussed by Bhabha was even more pervasive than he allows. The 'othering' of India was always fatally compromised.
[119] S.N. Sen, *Indian Travels of Thevenot and Careri* (Delhi, 1949), Introduction, pp. i–iv.

were knowledgeable in medicinal plants.[120] As part of the same European scholarly world, the British, too, began to make inventories of plants, herbs and mineral products.

The work of William Roxburgh, first superintendent of the Calcutta Botanical Garden and coadjutator of Sir Joseph Banks gave a considerable impetus to the systematic study of Indian botany.[121] One of the earliest surviving British Indian pharmacopoeias, made in Patna about 1795, with close Indian involvement, appears to be connected with Roxburgh.[122] In the early part of the following century, the rapid expansion of British territory made possible the creation of pharmacopoeias with an all-India reach. There remained the hope that Indian flora might produce novel remedies. The case of gamboge was cited. This powerful purgative had been procured in the Wynad region by Arthur Wellesley's guides during campaigns in 1801–2, though local people were said to have known little of its properties. Later, Whitelaw Ainslie of the Madras medical staff drew together a huge range of materials to publish *Materia Medica of Hindoostan* at Madras in 1813.[123] Ainslie worked at two levels. First, he used the connections of the emerging Medical Service to gather information from doctors and surgeons at other stations. His informants ranged from Tellicherry on the Kerala coast to as far north as Chittor in Rajasthan. He also called on friends in the Asiatic Society, including the Sanskritist, Charles Wilkins, to help in the translation of the many Indian medical texts he had collected.[124] Secondly, Ainslie applied to Indian hakims and vaidyas. An expanded version of his work published in London in 1826 contained substances and remedies drawn from the knowledge of 'other eastern nations', particularly from the Malay world.[125] Another man who consolidated all-India medical knowledge was Dr J.F. Royle, a member of the Bengal Army medical staff, later Professor of Materia Medica and Therapeutics at King's College, London. While in India he had 'made a collection of everything that was procurable in their bazars, tracing them as much as possible to the plants, animals and countries whence they were derived. I had the native works on Materia Medica collated by

[120] R. Grove, 'The transfer of botanical knowledge between Asia and Europe 1498–1800', *Journal of the Japan Netherlands Institute*, 3, 1991, pp. 164–72.
[121] H. Carter, *Sir Joseph Banks (1743–1820). A Guide to biographical and bibliographical sources* (London, 1987), pp. 69–74.
[122] 'Pharmacopoeia', Mss. Eur. E120, OIOC; G.R. Kaye (ed.), *India Office Library. Catalogue of Manuscripts in European Languages*, II, *Minor Collections and Miscellaneous Manuscripts* (London, 1937), pp. 1,100–1.
[123] Whitelaw Ainslie, *Materia Indica, or some account of those articles which are employed by the Hindoos and other eastern nations in their medicines, arts and agriculture* (Madras, 1813, revised edn, London, 1826).
[124] ibid., I, xix.   [125] ibid., I, 49.

competent Hakeems and Moonshees and the several articles arranged under the heads of the animal, vegetable and mineral kingdoms.'[126]

The analyses of materia medica and pharmacopoeias produced by these men illustrate the debates around the status of Indian learning, and of the form of the transformation of Indian into colonial knowledge. Royle and Ainslie still considered 'native knowledge' to be part of Mankind's treasury. Ainslie was concerned to use Indian expertise for the benefit of European medicine. His work was to be 'a kind of combining link between the Materia Medica of Europe and that of Asia', and he carefully distinguished between Indian medicines known in Europe and those 'exclusively used by the Hindoos'. While he considered that modern Indian medicine was 'in a state of empirical darkness', he believed that the ancients had 'made great progress in the arts and sciences',[127] and in practical matters contemporary Indians were quite skilled. They were great observers of the natural qualities of plants and they had achieved 'perfection' in applied arts like weaving and dyeing.[128] He considered that the distinction between theory and practice in Indian medicine had been exaggerated by Europeans. There were, of course, hereditary menial practitioners like bone-setters, leechers and bleeders. But it would be wrong to think that the prohibition on the medical Shastras being read by non-Brahmins meant that medical knowledge was highly restricted. Large numbers of commentaries on the medical Shastras were in circulation in the vernaculars.[129] He took issue with the detractors of Indian physicians, who were 'correct, obliging and communicative'.[130] The Hindu doctors were possessed of 'more learning and less pride than other Brahmins', while the Muslim hakims were 'unassuming, liberal-minded and humane',[131] and often combined their own traditions with the knowledge of the local Hindu doctors. Hindu doctors, for instance, had 'highly praised' the Croton seed (Hind. *nepala*) as a purgative, and their views had been borne out by his Medical Service colleagues. Though they did not know of quinine as such, they did possess effective bark remedies for intermittent fevers.[132]

Royle, too, approved of many aspects of Hindu and Muslim medicine. By the later 1830s when he was lecturing in King's College, London, he had the needs of Europeans going to India uppermost in his mind. Much, he thought, could still be learned from the Indians themselves. He argued that India was a significant source for the knowledge of the Greeks and Arabs in medicine. As in the case of astronomy and

---

[126] J.F. Royle, *An Essay in the Antiquity of Hindoo Medicine* (London, 1837), p. 25.
[127] Ainslie, *Materia*, II, xi.   [128] ibid., II, xxvi–xxvii.   [129] ibid., II, x.
[130] ibid., II, xxxii.   [131] ibid., II, xxxiii.   [132] ibid., I, 125.

grammar, their systems were of high antiquity, and he took the opportunity to refute Bentley and rallied to the support of le Gentil and Playfair, who had admired Indian astronomy.[133]

These medical men approached Indian specialists and Indian texts of every level of sophistication. Ainslie consulted druggists (*pansaris*) of the bazaars, 'an intelligent Ioqui [*jogi*, ascetic] of Benares',[134] 'a learned Parsee vidya of Surat',[135] the native doctors of the Northern Circars,[136] and tribal people from the hill regions of the north and south.[137] Yet the knowledge so acquired was undergoing a subtle transformation of which the Europeans were only partly aware. As we know, Hindu, and to a lesser extent Muslim, pharmacy was one aspect of a much wider grouping of techniques for transforming substance and matter by physical and moral combinations. At one extreme, these included the philosopher's stone, at the other, the art of cookery and the preparation of aphrodisiacs, both of which were gradually excluded from Anglo-Indian physic. Religious practice and bodily regimen were of as much importance as the remedies themselves. The physician's job was to put together a package of religious, dietary, moral and physical remedies which in combination would transform the physical and moral status of the sufferer. The idea was not so much to attack the disease, as in the allopathic tradition, it was more to 'tune up' the patient's body and soul.[138] 'Medicine' had general, religiously sanctioned rules, but in practice it was highly specific to individual, caste and region. This meant that certain diseases were specific to certain climes, and to the people who lived in them, because the vegetable and animal kingdom partook of the natural essences of particular spots. Certain diseases, it was held, were found in parts of the Northern Circars, or in tracts of Gorakhpur. Equally, the phases of the moon and the stars were believed to have a particular influence on the generation of diseases, or rather of the humoural imbalances which registered themselves as 'diseases'. The converse of this was that a wide range of animal, vegetable and mineral substances combined with certain types of religious and bodily practice might help the particular sufferer. Extreme decentralisation of practice, therefore, created a large and intricate pattern of inter-regional and inter-continental exchanges of medical supplies. The collected pharmacopoeia reveal trades which linked Arabia and India, India and Indonesia and even China.[139] Centres such as Patna or Ajmer derived the most common medicines from a broad swathe of territory, relying on

---

[133] Royle, *Antiquity*, pp. 165–70.   [134] Ainslie, *Materia*, I, 103.
[135] ibid.   [136] ibid., I, 108.   [137] ibid., I, 147–9.
[138] D. Frawley, *Ayurvedic Healing. A Comprehensive Guide* (Delhi, 1992), pp. 43–59.
[139] Ainslie, *Materia*; Royle, *Antiquity*; 'Pharmacopoeia', Mss. Eur. E120, OIOC.

the transactions between knowledgeable tribal people, local merchants and the larger wholesale dealers.

The British encoding of these rules and practices exhibited part of this range of virtuosity but excluded much of it. Buchanan, for instance, believed that many districts of north India were bereft of medical knowledge because the people there used only 'spells', abstinence and some vegetable purgatives,[140] despite the fact that Indians would have believed that this was appropriate medicine. Spells were hived off into the category of 'superstition', and prayer and ascetic practices into the domain of religion. The Patna pharmacopoeia includes large numbers of animal remedies, including the meat of fowl, deer, jackasses and combinations of cow-dung and vegetables.[141] Despite the pollution that the animal flesh carried, these were used for the treatment of 'cold' and 'dry' diseases. In time most of them were excluded from western accounts, remedies being separated into those of animal, vegetable and mineral sorts by Royle and his generation. Cookery (the use of substances as simple as tea, cardamum, betel nut) and the philosopher's stone were also radically separated off from medicine.

Cholera, plague and their consequences

In practice, the European collection of Indian knowledge systematised, generalised and abstracted, gradually discarding much of the popular lore and the hierarchy of specialists. This, however, was a long term, piece-meal process. The discourse on inoculation had briefly imposed a wider, imperial agenda on indigenous knowledge. More dramatic by far were the terror, consternation and self-interrogation of both Briton and Indian following the cholera pandemic of 1817 and the outbreak of bubonic plague in central India in the 1830s.[142] These diseases undermined the hegemonic claims of European medicine for many decades and forced Europeans, often surreptitiously, to examine Indian remedies again. The frightful symptoms of these diseases revived fears which had lain dormant since the seventeenth century. Historians have written on both epidemics in recent years. Our concern here is to assess the impact of disease on the engagement between British and Indian knowledge.

As cholera spread along the lines of Lord Hastings's armies it seemed as if the shades of Siraj-ud Daulah and Tipu Sultan had combined to

---

[140] F. Buchanan, ed. M. Martin, *The History, Antiquities, Topography and Statistics of Eastern India* (London, 1838), II, 412.

[141] 'Pharmacopoeia', ff. 170 ff.

[142] D. Arnold, *Colonising the Body. State medicine and epidemic disease in nineteenth century India* (Berkeley, 1993) pp. 116–99.

wreak revenge on the infidel conquerors. The mortality among
European officers and medical doctors was particularly severe. George
Spilsbury, Assistant Surgeon to 2nd Battalion 15th Native Infantry, was
transformed in a few years from a cheerful, lecherous philistine, a true
son of his native Midhurst in Sussex, to a gloomy, exhausted physician
who ultimately translated the *London Pharmacopoeia* into Urdu.[143] It was
the 'worst disease he had ever seen'.[144] Despite the attempts of the
Medical Board to assemble a huge body of information from every
medical man in India, 'I do not think any light will be thrown on its
remote causes.'[145] On the contrary, *quot homines tot sententiae*; the causes
proposed were polluted rice or fish, the foetid atmosphere, the 'want of
electricity'.[146] Dr Tytler said that its origin was a crop of rice cut in 1817
called Puse [in the month *Pus?*], but Spilsbury didn't believe that
because the Bengal troops who always ate *ata dal* (pulses and flour) had
succumbed in their hundreds, while the Madrasis who ate rice had been
relatively immune.[147] While many analyses of the disease and remedies
for it reflected prevailing concepts of western medicine, it also seems
likely that Indian ideas had some influence. Indians tended to attribute
disease to particular atmospheric conditions which transformed human
substance, especially when combined with certain foods. Indian doctors,
too, prescribed violent remedies to heat the body in cases of wasting or
watery diseases. Calomel, brandy, opium and bleeding were resorted to
by doctors on both sides of the racial divide. We can be certain that
many perished from these remedies.

The intellectual shock of cholera was translated back to Europe even
before its deadly reality arrived with the East Indiamen. Latin dissertations from Edinburgh and French and German theses spewed from the
presses.[148] Concern for oriental medical expertise dramatically increased
just at the point when medicine was beginning to be centralised and
professionalised within Europe. Dramatically different positions were
taken between, and within, the two continents. In general, Indian
medical men continued with purging and prescribed fluids, bleeding,
mercury and opium. Some European doctors, against the furious
opposition of their peers, prescribed water and fluids. The doctors in the
field were more likely to be conservative, and the influence of popular

[143] Note by J.A.E.M. on Spilsbury's career, Spilsbury Papers, Mss. Eur. D909/1, OIOC.
[144] G. Spilsbury to E.A. Spilsbury, 7 Jan. 1819, ibid.   [145] ibid.
[146] G. Spilsbury to E.A. Spilsbury, 25 Sept. 1819, ibid.
[147] ibid.; cf. *Calcutta Journal*, 6 Oct. 1818.
[148] e.g., J. Kellie, *Dissertatio Medica Inauguralis, complectus pauca de morba epidemico, qui nomine cholera spasmodica, per Indiam Orientam nuper grassatus est* (Edinburgh, 1820); J. Annesley, *Sketches of the most prevalent diseases of India, comprising a treatise of the epidemic cholera of the East* (London, 1825).

Indian remedies to 'heat' the sickly patient were apparently strong, though rarely acknowledged. Spilsbury's letters refer to hardly any Indians, except the Indian women, presumably his concubines, whom he described in detail to his female relatives. He disapproved of beating Indian servants, but barely mentioned them, except once when he wrote of 'an Haqueem or one skilled in the profession of physic as practised by the natives of Hindoostan'[149] who was also his munshi. It may have been this man who improved his Urdu and sowed the idea for the translation of the *London Pharmacopoeia*.

There were other medical men, however, who developed a much more sustained interest in Indian physicians' remedies for cholera. This shift reflected a growing concern in the 1820s about both the effects of the disease in Europe and the political consequences for the Company. W.G. Maxwell was one of a number of surgeons based in Calcutta and north India who longed that the pages of his tract on cholera's treatment would 'reach the happy Isle [England] before the destroyer gains his strength',[150] but also worried about the fate of those millions of Indians 'beyond the reach of professional assistance'. Maxwell and a small number of supporters believed that no antidote to cholera was in sight, but that the patient should be dosed with copious draughts of water strengthened with vegetable alkalis and acids.[151] This was probably the best that could have been recommended at the time, and ran flatly contrary to the practice of bleeding and the denial of water to dehydrated patients which were common.

Maxwell rested his case on an elaborate physiological argument, a kind of natural religion which stressed water as a gift of God's bounty, and his own experience of the disease when he had given into the craving for water with beneficial effects.[152] Maxwell, however, not only used Indian evidence to support his views, but distinguished between different levels of indigenous practice. He translated and appended to his tract a series of extracts from Mahomed Arzani's 'Tib-i Akbar' of 1593 which recounted the recent outbreaks in Delhi of plague, various agues and what may have been cholera, describing their etiology and suggesting remedies.[153] Maxwell believed that much modern western medical science was of dubious value; medical nativism impelled him

---

[149] Note by J.A.E.M., Spilsbury Papers, 1.
[150] W.G. Maxwell, *A Practical Treatise on Epidemic Cholera, Ague and Dysentery* (Calcutta, 1838), p. vi.
[151] ibid., p. xxvi.   [152] Ibid., Appendix, p. 29.
[153] ibid., Appendix, pp. 27–30; similarly, 'Hindoo remedies for cholera', *Calcutta Journal*, 2 Feb. 1819; Wilson presented a more jaundiced view of native practice in 'On the native practice in Cholera', *Transactions of the Medical and Physical Society of Calcutta*, 2, 1825, 282–93.

towards Sydenham, Culpepper and the English herbalists,[154] while respect for the Muslim tradition brought unani medicine to his attention.

Arzani deserved respect because he had made what Maxwell thought was the right connection between ague, plague and cholera, and because he had noted the alleged tendency of diseases to move towards the west and spread by contagion. He had recommended that the patient be given fluid distilled from 'kid's flesh and spices in copious quantities'. Mahomed Arzani was a rationalistic hakim who believed in observation and the accumulation of evidence. Some modern Indians followed him, but contemporary practice in the bazaars was less enlightened. Most vaidyas and hakims adhered to the biomoral view of disease. They would attempt to heat their patient's essence through the application of powerful poisons of snake venoms and pepper in the form of 'bis barri pills' which were 'bara garram [very hot]'. These were not only expensive, but often fatal.[155]

Maxwell implicitly identified three traditions of 'medical practice'. The first was a textualised rationalistic tradition maintained by a few learned families. The second derived from puranic notions of bodily and moral substance and relied on the ingestion of power pills to enhance the strength of the patient; this was the most common form of medicine among the middle classes. Thirdly, and more shadowy, was the treatment of the poor with spells, abstinence and a little gruel. Maxwell wanted to reveal the textual tradition to the pill doctors. He hoped that 'the present race of hakeems may no longer be discouraged, or amazed or terrified, at the outward glitter and high-sounding fame of European therapeutics'[156] but that there should be laid before them 'the standard works in their own language', which 'would be more succesful than the most accomplished European hakeem who was just commencing practice'.[157]

As with Lancelot Wilkinson and the Siddhantas, Maxwell was one of those neo-orientalists who believed in using the best Indian knowledge and practice to correct its degenerated modern inheritance. Like Wilkinson, Hodgson, and the Serampore Baptists, he was also obsessed with the value of collecting and disseminating Indian information. His frontispiece quoted Bacon on the value of 'facts'.[158] As Wilkinson and Hodgson wished to create 'juntos' of right-minded pandits, so Maxwell wished for 'a commission of enquiry composed of intelligent native

[154] Maxwell, Treatise, p. xi.   [155] ibid., Appendix, p. 27.
[156] ibid., Appendix, p. 28.   [157] ibid., Appendix, pp. 6–27.
[158] ibid., frontispiece.

hakeems' who would investigate and correct native practice with the application of unani and ayurvedic natural medicine.

Professionalisation and hubris

During the 1820s and 1830s the Bengal Medical Service became more cohesive and professional, mirroring developments in metropolitan medical circles.[159] The chorus of contempt for Indian society swelled. Meanwhile, Indian assertions of the strengths of their own medical tradition became more articulate. Some Europeans too, in distant outposts, faced with their own mortality and despairing of western remedies, clung on to the hope that Indian physicians had handed down secret lore still unknown to colonial medicine. Investigations of Indian medical practice and the search for native informants are testimony to a desire to put native physicians in their place, but also to capitalise on whatever strengths 'bazaar medicine' might yet possess. In this Rajasthan proved to be a frontier of medical intelligence, matching in importance the work of translation and systematisation carried out in Calcutta by men such as T.A. Wise and the officials of the new Calcutta Medical College and its associated school.[160] At the Rajasthan courts and in the British district of Ajmer a small British community, isolated from medical expertise and even regular supplies of medicines, lived in a society where royal patronage of doctors had been unbroken throughout the seventeenth and eighteenth centuries. The appearance of plague in Rajasthan in the 1830s and attempts to pen it off from the British North-Western Provinces, heightened this sense of menace.[161]

R.H. Irvine, Assistant Surgeon, was among the first systematically to study and evaluate Indian medical practice in his book, *Some Account of the General and Medical Topography of Ajmeer*.[162] Dismissive of the 'inaccuracy' and literary flair of James Tod, Irvine introduced to Rajasthan the dry topographical style of information collection. Ajmer with its populations of nomads and pastoralists was to be settled, like the Highlands of Scotland, for the benefit of its people. The key to this was the collection of information by an enlightened government. This would

[159] M. Harrison, *Public Health in British India: Anglo-Indian preventive medicine, 1859–1914* (Cambridge, 1994), pp. 1–23.

[160] Wise, *Commentary*, p. xix; Wise derived his information from hereditary families of vaidyas.

[161] cf. R.S. Chandavarkar, 'Plague, panic and epidemic politics in India, 1896–1914' in P. Slack and T. Ranger (eds.), *Epidemics and Ideas. Essays on the historical perceptions of pestilence* (Cambridge, 1992), pp. 203–40.

[162] R.H. Irvine, *Some Account of the medical and general topography of Ajmeer* (Calcutta, 1841).

ensure that the government could avoid famine by knowing the exact stock of grains held in the country. Medical surveillance should be extended so that magistrates could assure themselves that every child had been vaccinated.[163] In Irvine's account, castes were stripped of Tod's colourful legends and histories and reified into hard-edged entities. Irvine's prose was as jagged as the local rock outcrops which he painstakingly recorded. The professionalisation of geology and medicine went hand in hand. His writing was so distant from Tod's heady brew of Sir Walter Scott and the Rajasthan bards, that even the *Friend of India* complained of its stylistic clumsiness.[164]

Irvine's lack of interest in history was, however, counterbalanced by his extreme concern for medicine and pharmacy. He wished to enlist skilled and honest Indian practitioners in his service, noting with distaste that his own Indian innoculators brought in false vaccination returns while privately practising innoculation for fees in the city.[165] He also wished to explode the myths of Indian medicine. He wrote that 'Many Europeans in India are still of the opinion that native hakims and bueds are often superior in knowledge to, are at any rate are [sic] in possession of secrets unknown, to regular practitioners.'[166] They spoke of 'wonderful qualities' in remedies which were no other than the panaceas of 'our sixteenth century pharmacopoeias ... now deservedly neglected'. Some officers even encouraged the men under their command to seek medical aid from the native hakims and vaidyas of the neighbouring town; 'a course which can only throw undeserved discredit on our profession and serve to foster native prejudices against us'.[167] Despite the official opprobium already heaped on Indian medicine, Europeans and Indians, including sepoys who already had access to European doctors, continued to resort to the traditional practitioners. G.E. Westmacott, a surgeon with a Native Infantry regiment in 1830–1, routinely entered in his commmonplace book a sulphur remedy for the treatment of ringworm, 'of high celebrity among natives and strongly recommended by Dr Guthrie of the Bengal Medical Service'.[168] Against this background, Irvine decided to draw up a 'digest of native practice, which the hakims and bueds themselves will allow to be learned in *their* ideas' to show the real state of things.[169] He assembled the physicians of Ajmer and took samples of three thousand remedies from the medicine bags of

[163] ibid., p. 87.   [164] *Friend of India*, 20 Jan. 1842.
[165] Irvine, *Ajmeer*, p. 115.   [166] ibid., p. 153.   [167] ibid., p. 154.
[168] Westmacott, 'Travels', Mss. Eur. C29, f. 501; cf. Indian dexterity in treating Europeans for worms, R.H. Kennedy, 'On Dracunculus', *Transactions of the Medical and Physical Society of Calcutta*, 1, 1825, pp. 167–8; Dr Tytler defends Indian medical practice, *India Journal of Medical Science*, 2, 13, 1835, pp. 8–10.
[169] Irvine, *Ajmeer*, p. 154.

the pansaris of the bazaars whose stalls, far from being mere purveyors of betel nut and tobacco, were at this time chemist shops and stores of practical medical knowledge.[170] From these he selected three hundred of the most instructive remedies which he reproduced with directions for preparations and use and their Hindi and Sanskrit designations.

The purpose of Wise, Irvine and their generation was not always totally to disparage Indian medicine. Nor did they write entirely from ignorance. Irvine, for instance, commented approvingly on the manual dexterity of the hereditary occulists who removed cataracts without the slightest knowledge of anatomy, and of the native barbers and surgeons who amputated limbs.[171] This praise for the practical skill and speed of the Indian practitioners is reminiscent of the comments of le Gentil about Indian astronomers' speedy calculations of the eclipses. As far as medicaments were concerned, the Indians knew many of the efficacious remedies current in the west, reflecting the common Greek inheritance of both western and Indian Muslim medicine. Where Indians could not afford or would not use the quinine, Irvine acknowledged that Indian 'bitter tonics, laxatives and abstinence' might bring about 'a more tardy cure'.[172] Irvine also understood something of the theory of Indian medical practice: 'the hakims and punsaris say efficacy is not in the substance itself but in the combination'.[173] When the British denounced Indian backwardness in theory, they meant their continued adherence to Aristotelian humoural notions which had only recently been abandoned in Europe. The insecurity of European knowledge was a potent element in their rages.

Knowledge battles and social change

The appearance of a professionally disciplined core of British and western-educated Indian doctors did not erase Indian medical knowledge, even among the elites. Wealthy men used both western-trained and Indian physicians, trusting the former for surgery, the latter for internal remedies. Government and army dispensaries also perpetuated the use of Indian remedies for many diseases because of the prohibitive cost of western ones.[174] Eclectic practitioners, pansari shops and printed medical texts which spread into villages promoted a mix of western-style and Indian remedies.[175] After 1850, the indigenous press often recorded

[170] ibid., pp. 123–9.   [171] ibid., p. 122.
[172] ibid., p. 114; cf. Boileau, *Narrative*, p. 70.
[173] Irvine, *Ajmeer*, p. 123.   [174] See above, pp. 156–7.
[175] e.g., the case of the syncretic Persian Hakim, Mahomed Hussain, R. Tytler, 'Native medical education', *Indian Journal of Medical Science*, 2, 13, 1835, pp. 10–12; cf. Babu Devi Dayal who established his own dispensary in a village ten miles from Banaras to

stories of the discovery of adulterated medicines in village shops, indicating the buoyancy of local medical commerce, but also the fears which it roused.[176] Cataract doctors used western instruments;[177] western-type pills and brandy appeared among the bags of herbal remedies.[178] When they could afford what Europeans recommended, and these seemed effective, Indians responded quickly to the new techniques on offer. They also remained conscious of what they thought better in their own learning.[179] The rumours that western medicine polluted or insulted Indian deities did not betoken a general cultural reaction, so much as a rejection of the intrusion by European personnel into Indian domestic space. British medicine in India, before the beginning of the twentieth century, was too poorly funded and too riven with internal contradictions to establish anything like the hegemony over the 'native mind' with which it is sometimes credited. Indians continued to pick and choose remedies, to swap libels on doctors, and to experiment with drugs as they had done before.

Conclusion

Edward Said's followers emphasised orientalism's political agenda in creating 'otherness' more resolutely even than he had done himself. This examination of Anglo-Indian debates about astronomy and medicine has stressed, by contrast, the complexity of the relationship. British observers of India remained uncertain, in the first place, about the theoretical validity and practical success of their own sciences. British herbalism and agnostic relativism challenged the claims of European medicine and astronomy in ways which complicated their practitioners' relations to Indian knowledge. British knowledge in India was, accordingly, contradictory, insecure and driven as much by universalising ideas as by the search for an oriental 'other'. At the same time, the British response was informed by particular local circumstances, not by received ideas derived from metropolitan texts. The growth of professional

wean people from 'talismans', and to provide wholesome Indian and European remedies, Reade, *Contributions*, pp. 20–1; for medical texts, see, e.g., *Rogantakasara* (Calcutta, *c.* 1850), a translation of A.S. Ramsay's *Materia Medica* or Harivilasa, *Rogakarshana* (Agra, 1872).

[176] e.g. *Lawrence Gazette* (Meerut), 18 Sept. 1868, NWP Native Newspaper Reports 1868, p. 455; *Muir Gazette*, 2 Nov. 1868, ibid., p. 516, OIOC.

[177] Breton, 'On the Native method of couching', 357.

[178] e.g., on brandy and opium mixtures distributed by native doctors during cholera epidemic in Banda, *Friend of India*, 5 Sept. 1841.

[179] e.g., Radhakanta Deb to William Cameron, 'Account of the Tikadars', appendix V, *Trans. Med. Soc. Calcutta*, 4, 1830, 41–8; cf. *Indian Journal of Medical Science*, 1, 2, 1834, pp. 34–6.

bodies in India, the competition of Indian practitioners, and the often unacknowledged influence of Indian ideas meant that no coherent body of oriental or colonial knowledge ever emerged. Racism, economic exploitation and orientalism are all valid concepts with which to understand early colonial India, but they were much more tenuously related to each other than recent studies have assumed. By contrast, Indians reacted speedily and pragmatically to the new ideas presented to them. These ideas were as often enlisted to maintain or extend indigenous authorities and statuses as they were to undermine them.

8   Colonial controversies: language and land

As in the fields of astronomy and medicine, the British engagement with the Indian languages and forms of written communication mirrored the changing nature of colonial dominion. It also sheds light on the types of linguist and informant with whom the Europeans dealt, and consequently on new sources of power within Indian society. In the earlier eighteenth century, the British tried to grapple with Mughal diplomatics and to corral its chief expert, the Persian munshi. From about 1760 the massive growth of military activity along the Ganges valley and the swell of peculation and trade in its slip-stream led to an interest in 'Moors' or the 'vulgar tongue of Hindostan' written in the Persian script. The British selected out Hindustani, or Urdu as its more refined form was generally known, as a military and commercial tongue, but also as one which, despite its mongrel origins, could convey a sense of style and aristocracy. After 1840, however, missionaries, populist administrators and officers of the Bengal Army began to register the importance of 'Hindi' written in the Devanagari, or Sanskritic script, though its final triumph was to be long delayed. It was Hindi-writers among the commercial classes, the pandits, and the sepoys of the Bengal Army as much as missionaries and populist officials who promoted the future official 'link' language. Indian agency, as much as colonial policy, remained vital at all stages of this evolution. Their mutual interactions provide the focus for this chapter.

The pre-eminence and decline of Persian

In the 1770s and 1780s Warren Hastings had patronised the study of Persian and the written record of the Mughal Empire as a means of understanding the Indian 'constitution'. By this his generation meant the conventions, ideologies and etiquettes of power which bound together the Mughal elite. The manners of political communication – verbal, ritual and written – were to the men of the eighteenth century the very essence of politics. The huge Fort William Persian correspondence

284

and the expertise of the Persian translators were considered instruments of power as important to British security as the army itself. British experience of Mughal communication and honorifics as much as their knowledge of the 'intercourse of states' in Europe warned that failures of diplomatic etiquette even more than the clash of irreconcilable interest brought war and the disruption of commerce.

The great importance of the Persian munshi in this period has already been discussed. Meanwhile, British Persian scholarship itself was moving on from language teaching and glossary to a concentration on forms of address which reflected these political concerns. Several compilations of Mughal official orders and revenue manuals were produced. The most important of them was probably Francis Balfour's translation of *The forms of Herkern* ('Insha-i Hari Karan').[1] Like so many of those responsible for the forming of oriental knowledge Balfour was a medical doctor.[2] His aim was to ease the difficulty of young civil servants and merchants grappling with the syntactical and orthographical forms of Persian, but also to release them from dependence on the munshi who was 'for the most part unacquainted with the Arabic language, poorly instructed in the principles of grammar, and not sufficiently qualified for the task he undertakes'.[3] Balfour also aimed to produce, with the aid of the eminent orientalist, Charles Wilkins, a more consistent Persian character which 'may receive all the assistance of the [printing] press' and replace the existing script which was 'ill-calculated for becoming a channel of authority or the medium of business over an extensive Empire'.[4]

In the modernisation of Persian, however, an older form was enlisted, the model of letter-writing or *insha* common in Mughal and eighteenth-century courts. The one Balfour used was a specimen of letter-book compiled by 'Herkern [Hari Karan], son of Mutradas, a Kumboh [a 'writer caste'] of Multan', who one day in the reign of the Emperor Shahjahan had sat at 'the seat of Empire, in the city of Mutra' and devoted himself to improving his skills as a munshi.[5] There followed a selection of letters to different classes of people indicating how 'princes write to princes', diplomatics (*firmans, parwanahs*), letters between notables and legal documents including a certificate for the sale of a slave girl.[6] Balfour's translations sought to convey the key features of Indo-Islamic written intercourse within the state and the family.

In the Indian context, Persian or *istimal* (meaning *istimal-i Hindustan,* 'the usage of India')[7] continued to have a dynamic life well into the

---

[1] Balfour, *Herkern*, pp. 1–10.   [2] Crawford, *Medical Service*, II, 153.
[3] Balfour, *Herkern*, p. 3.   [4] ibid., p. 7.   [5] ibid.
[6] ibid., p. 165.   [7] Elliot, *Races*, III, 178.

nineteenth century. Indo-Persian itself was distinct from the western Persian which was developing in the Qajar state. Its flowery prosody, often denounced as decadent, formed an appropriate language for a highly visual and symbolic culture. For an elite increasingly threatened by the assaults of an international English-speaking imperialism and the rise of Hindu dynasties who offered much patronage to Sanskrit, the universal character of Persian as the common language of the ecumene increased its appeal in the aftermath of the decline of the Mughal Empire. This was particularly true for those Iranian and Shia Muslims for whom the decay of Delhi and the rise of Awadh had provided new opportunities. Some of the greatest Indian Persianists, notably Ghalib and Iqbal, were to come late in the history of Indo-Persian and to argue fiercely for the value of Persian and its distinctively Indian character.[8]

Paradoxically, many British also clung to Persian. Indeed, the so-called Urdu that replaced Persian as the court language after 1837 was recognisably Persian as far as its nouns were concerned. The courtly heritage of Persian was also to exercise a constraint on the British cultivation of Hindustani/Urdu. As late as 1840, for instance, a British language snob ridiculed the use of *ki* and *ka* (the Hindustani 'of' as opposed to the Persian '-i') as a 'rising ka-kophany'.[9] The older generation trained in the orientalist tradition as Persian translators in the administrative service saw the assault on Persian as a decline in high standards, amounting almost to a social dereliction. If English gentlemen had to speak to blackfellows, it should be in a patrician language.

The position of Persian was, however, slowly eroded. Administrators found it too complex to transcribe all their documents from vernacular languages through Persian to English. Evangelicals, for their part, saw Persian and Arabic education as supports of Islam and wished to teach in English and the vernaculars.[10] Political suspicion also played an important part. In the mind of some officials, Persian was the language of dissidence and its suppression was therefore desirable on political grounds. For example, R. Cavendish, Resident at Gwalior during a violent change of government in 1833, said that there were two parties in the state and, by extension, across north India: the Imperial party and the British party.[11] While the Company's party was strong now, people said that the King's party would one day be in the ascendant again.

[8]   Russell and Islam, *Ghalib*, I, passim; Sharar, *Lucknow*, pp. 99–100.
[9]   *Delhi Gazette*, 10 Jan. 1840; cf. *Mofussilite*, 24 June 1851.
[10] e.g., *Friend of India*, 15 Jan. 1835.
[11] R. Cavendish, Resdt Gwalior, to Govt of India, 10 June 1833, 'Revolution at Gwalior', BC, 1402/55492 (2).

Cavendish thought that this was not impossible. A 'resolute man' might one day sit on the throne of Delhi. He might be able to 'agitate his rights' through the printed newspapers and Persian newsletters.[12] He might use the reputation of his throne, his seal and the money coined in the name of his ancestor 'for seizing a favourable opportunity for disputing with us the government of the country'.

Cavendish must have known, first, that an eminent Persian scholar, Raja Ram Mohun Roy, had recently been agitating the King's rights in London, using Persian treaties and charters,[13] and secondly, that at this point it was Persian not Bengali or Hindustani newspapers, which were considered the most 'seditious' by the British.[14] Cavendish urged that it was necessary to counteract this malign Royal influence by coining money in the name of the King of England, deciding legal proceedings by jury and not by kazis' pronouncement and by replacing Muslims with Hindus and Eurasians in government service. Most important, the British should abandon Persian as the language of government.[15] What Cavendish was urging, in effect, was a full scale assault on the Indian ecumene, its personnel, its means of communication and its most prized language, Persian. The British adopted all these measures, but they did not avert the final conflict of 1857 which Cavendish had so presciently foreseen.

Hindustani/Urdu, the new imperial language

Suspicion of the political community which still used Persian partly explains the growing importance of Urdu in the British Indian Empire.[16] Urdu, which was usually called Hindustani in its less learned forms, was an Indian, not an international language. It was an elite as well as a popular tongue. Moreover, as the *Friend of India* remarked, anticipating Bernard Cohn,[17] 'Urdu is the language of command ... a poor native when he hears himself addressed in it by a European knows he is to keep his distance. Bengalee is the language of conciliation.'[18]

---

[12] ibid.
[13] 'Proceedings regarding the Royal Family at Delhi – suspension of written communication between the Governor General and the King of Delhi', BC 1368/54481.
[14] See above, pp. 239–40.
[15] Cavendish to Govt, 10 Jun. 1833.
[16] J.R. Ballantyne, *A Grammar of the Hindustani Language* (Edinburgh, 1838), p. viii; W. Yates, *Introduction to the Hindoostanee Language* (Calcutta, 1827), pp. i–iii.
[17] 'The Command of Language and the Language of Command' in R. Guha (ed.), *Subaltern Studies*, IV (Delhi, 1985), 276–329; but this seminal article attributes too great a capacity on the part of the British to 'construct' Indian society independently of the agency of its social formations and knowledge communities.
[18] *Friend of India*, 19 Feb. 1835.

Unlike Persian, Hindustani was a language with which to marshal the lowly servant and sepoy. George Hadley's *A Compendious Grammar of the Current Corrupt Dialect of the Jargon of Hindostan (commonly called Moors)* (constantly reprinted after the early 1770s) was an attempt to come to terms with the popular Hindustani of the British camp and bazaar as it had developed between Calcutta and Delhi since 1765. As Cohn has pointed out, like most other grammars and 'dialogues' it was specifically designed to release Britons from the thrall of corrupt 'language masters' as 'few of the Munshees ... understand English'.[19] Hadley was a soldier with commissary experience. He knew little of, and cared less for, the high Urdu of the north Indian intelligentsia, and saw no merit in a systematic explanation of the language. On the contrary, he endeavoured to explain Hindustani through Indian perversions of English. Thus: 'you lie telling, I certainly punishment will give';[20] 'ship news what?' ('Jahaz ka khubr kya hai?', i.e. 'what is the news from the ships which have arrived from England?').[21]

Like other contemporary examples, Hadley's work is full of mundane words and situations interwoven with a thread of conflict and violence. His dialogues are full of 'a liar you are!', 'false news do not bring!',[22] 'With Persian do not mix it [i.e. Hindustani]!'[23] His dialogue about a spy, in a situation where knowing the language was 'necessary to the preservation of our lives', ends with the drunken agent being flogged and flung out of the camp.[24] There is also an element of shock-horror orientalism which was presumably introduced to sell the work in England and Calcutta as a species of exotic near-fiction. The book was billed as containing notes 'descriptive of various customs and manners in Bengal'. These include an account of 'Muhammadan superstitions', ghosts, and an incident where the servant obsequiously sidles in with the breakfast to ask: 'There is a suckee [sati, widow burning] to-day two miles out of the town. Will master go to see it?'[25] A related compilation of dialogues includes the sentences required to dissuade a sati from immolating herself, but ends with her plunging into the flames.[26]

The enormous purchasing-power of the thirty thousand or more British soldiers and civilians spread along the Grand Trunk Road in the last quarter of the century had created a huge service and information economy among Indians. It was within this community that 'Moors'' and servants' English combined. Difficult to discern in the official records, this fixer's economy resembled a bloated and corrupt version of the traditional *jajmani* patronage system. Intelligence agents, prostitutes,

[19] Hadley, *A Compendious Grammar*, p. v.   [20] ibid., p. 129.   [21] ibid., p. 134.
[22] ibid., p. 129.   [23] ibid., p. 130.
[24] ibid., pp. 197–202.   [25] ibid., pp. 156–61.   [26] ibid., p. 161.

drivers, and innumerable varieties of confidential commercial people subsisted on it. Hindustani was the language of this army of camp-followers. As John Gilchrist's later dialogue has it: 'why does a servant call himself a Sirkar, Baboo, Purvoo, Khuleesa, Mihtur, etc.?' Ans.: 'That he may appear of more consequence in the eyes of his fellow servants.' Reply: 'You are a wag, I see, and know something of men and manners.'[27] A case in point were the Rum Johnnies or Ramzanis, that is low-class Muslims supposedly born in the month of Ramadan, who congregated at Calcutta and up-country stations, offering dubious services of many varieties and 'using broken English with sufficient fluency'.[28] Captain Williamson's *General East India Guide and Vade Mecum* records their existence shortly after describing the charms of 'sable beauties', and insinuates that Ramzani was only a slight change from 'ram juna, a Hindoo dancing-boy'.[29] Even the munshi could become a purveyor of sexual information: he organised the expenditure of the master's house, 'not forgetting those meaner offices ... which levelled all distinction between the man of letters and the common pander'.[30]

A pidgin-Hindustani, like the pidgin-English and pidgin-Chinese of southeast Asia and the China coast, never developed widely in India, however.[31] This reflects the extreme concern with social status among the British in India and, to some extent, their recognition of gentility and class among their Indian subjects. In the south-east Asian pedlar economy of small indigenous merchants and rootless whites, such distinctions did not matter. In India, the expatriate press constantly ridiculed the misuse of Indian languages by the British and poor English among Indians. It is surprising how sensitive Britons who probably knew virtually no Indian literature were to linguistic sloppiness in Persian or Urdu. Incorrect usage would debase them in the eyes of Indian notables. It was better to speak no Indian languages at all. Attempts were soon forthcoming, therefore, from both the British and Indians to establish correct Urdu, *mualla-i Urdu* or 'the language of Hindoostan'. In Delhi, Hyderabad and Lucknow, Indian attempts had been in train since the mid-eighteenth century to formalise the speech. The aim was to preserve much of the Persian vocabulary, thus retaining the sheen of Mughal authority, while reaching out to the common

---

[27] J. Gilchrist, *A Collection of Dialogues English and Hindoostanee* (Calcutta, 1804), p. 147.
[28] Williamson, ed. Gilchrist, *Vade Mecum*, pp. 83, cf. 100.
[29] ibid., p. 84.   [30] ibid., p. 102.
[31] But see, J. Majeed, 'The Jargon of Indostan – an exploration of jargon in Urdu and East India Company English', in P. Burke and R. Porter (eds.), *Languages and Jargons* (Cambridge, Mass., forthcoming). He emphasises the fluidity of 'Urdu' and its tendency to give rise to a written 'jargon'.

speech of the majority.[32] The excellence of the language was measured by the fluency of the great teachers and Sufi masters who taught it, not so much by formal grammatical rules.[33] But like English, Urdu was a cannibal language aspiring to the gentlemanly.

The British 'discovery of Urdu' has always been associated with the name of John Gilchrist. His status as the 'father' of the language has been challenged by S.R. Kidwai who points out that Fort William College, where Gilchrist eventually became Professor, was marginal in the process of refining and codifying Urdu. This took place in the courts of the Mughal successor states and ought to be associated above all with the indigenous poets and grammarians, Mir Taqi Mir and Sirajuddin Ali Arzu.[34] Gilchrist was nevertheless important in recognising the significance of Urdu not only as a critical vehicle for communication, but also as the foundation for a community of information and knowledge throughout the emerging Indian empire.

Gilchrist's work represents a maverick aspect of British information collection about India. Written from the bottom up after intense experience in the field, his *Collection of Dialogues English and Hindoostanee* (1804), sundry glossaries and *General East India Guide* (1825) also capture important dimensions of contemporary social change. Gilchrist had arrived in India in the 1780s but the failure of Calcutta business concerns led to his 'withdrawal' in 1784 to Faizabad in Awadh where he remained for over a decade as an indigo planter.[35] As a private merchant operating in Awadh and adjoining parts of British territories during the consolidation of British power, Gilchrist and his partner Charters fell into dispute with other Europeans, local zamindars and the Company authorities. Several of his aggressive and litigious letters are preserved in the records of the Judge's Court of Banaras.[36] Finding Persian good chiefly for the 'literature of the Moosulmuns ... such as it is', he turned to Hindustani for 'the necessary affairs of ordinary life'.[37] He was unaware of any attempt to set out the linguistic structures or the proper vocabulary of Urdu/Hindustani. All he had to work with was Hadley's and other dialogues which did little more than print specimens of 'the barbarous gabble'[38] which Hadley had picked up from servants or

[32] Amrit Rai, *A House Divided. The origins and development of Hindi-Urdu* (Delhi, 1992), pp. 246–54.
[33] Majeed, 'Jargon of Hindostan', citing Insha Allah Khan, *Darya-e Latafat* (1808, Karachi, 1988) tr. Urdu, by Pt. Braj Mohan; D. Lelyveld, 'Colonial Knowledge and the fate of Hindustani', *Comparative Studies in Society and History*, 35, 4, 1993, 678–9.
[34] S.R. Kidwai, *Gilchrist and the 'Language of Hindoostan'* (Delhi, 1972), pp. 75–7, 88.
[35] J.B. Gilchrist, *Hindoostanee Philology* (London, Edinburgh, 1810) I, vii.
[36] Proceedings of the Resident of Banaras, UP Central Record Office, Allahabad.
[37] Gilchrist, *Dialogues*, p. 15.   [38] Gilchrist, *Philology*, I, preface, i.

sepoys, and which was anyway unintelligible to the villagers. Gilchrist, on the other hand, secluded in 'solitary cogitation' in Faizabad,[39] with occasional visits to Banaras, and 'surrounded by learned Hindustanees',[40] was able to set out the principles of Hindustani philology in the Roman script.

In this work he was associated with the vanguard of the imperial information collectors who were at that time gathered in the region before they fanned out across India: Jonathan Duncan, Archibald Seton and Edward Strachey. While he may not have met the poet Sauda at Faizabad, Gilchrist mentions his works and also draws on the writings of Mir, Dard, and other writers esteemed by the intelligentsia of Awadh in its golden age at the close of Asaf-ud Daulah's reign.[41] Banaras itself remained an important centre of Persian and Urdu writing. As we have seen, Ali Ibrahim Khan, Judge of Banaras, produced literary biographies of Persian and Urdu writers. It is unlikely that Gilchrist, who had a house in Banaras at Shivala and who often had plaints in the Judge's court, did not know him personally. But Gilchrist's close relationship with Indians and their literature did not endear them to him. He complained that only one of the 'dissembling crew' of munshis he employed over fifteen years was honest;[42] he denounced the banias – 'the Indian Israelites' – for their 'shameless rapacity'.[43] His pages are alive with self-pity, racist pejoratives and arcane knowledge.

When Wellesley began to establish his imperial academy, Fort William College, Gilchrist was an obvious choice as Professor of Hindustani. During his period in Calcutta he completed his *Hindoostanee Dialogues*. Its publication was aided by John Shoolbred, Superintendent General of Vaccine Innoculation,[44] for whom Gilchrist included the dialogue between a European and an Indian physician about vaccination (Gilchrist himself had some medical training). Gilchrist did not entirely approve of the 'tide' of dialogue publications, thinking that a systematic grammatical knowledge was to be preferred to learning lines for these typical colonial situations, but he succumbed to the trend. His Indian career finally came to an end when he imprudently organised debates on the propriety of Indians converting to Christianity, and felt that he had been hounded out of office by a combination of Muslims and old India-hands[45] who resented his intrusion into this touchy area. Returning to his native Scotland, Gilchrist was involved in

---

[39] ibid., vii.
[40] ibid., viii.   [41] ibid., xli.   [42] ibid., xxi.
[43] ibid., III, 332.   [44] Gilchrist, *Dialogues*, dedication, p. (i).
[45] Kidwai, *Gilchrist*, pp. 55–6.

a number of somewhat dubious business ventures, but continued to teach and publish on India and Indian languages.

Gilchrist viewed Urdu as the equivalent to English in the British Isles. He compared 'Hindvee', or proto-Hindi, to Saxon and aboriginal Indian dialects to the 'ancient British languages'.[46] Here he wrote as a lowland Scot who had seen Gaelic and Catholic Scotland dissolve in his own lifetime. His view was mirrored by that of his French successor, Garcin de Tassy, who wrote on Hindustani literature for more than sixty years. For Garcin, Urdu was a national language. It stood in the same relationship to Hindi as French did to Bas-Breton or Provençal.[47] Here wrote an unwilling product of the Revolution who had seen the imposition of standard French across the country. Garcin was later to denounce the Hindi language movement as 'une fantasie retrograde'.[48] Gilchrist and Garcin, however, committed an error of categories. Urdu was not a 'national' or even an 'imperial' language. It was the popular language of the ecumene. Its strength was its capacity to soak up and accumulate words from Hindi, Arabic, Persian and even English. Gilchrist's dialogues, for example, show it accommodating new concepts without becoming anglicised. '*Umriku*' (America) appears; so does '*ukhbar ke kagas*' ('newspaper') to distinguish it from the akhbarat.[49] Urdu could also deal with the complexity of the world of paper produced by the meeting of Hindu commercial society and Perso-Arabic systems of land titles. The medical dialogues show words designed for Muslim physic being adapted to new ideas such as vaccination.[50]

Urdu also benefited from being the natural common speech of the Anglo-Indian chancellery, the munshi khana, whose influence expanded rapidly during the early settlements of land-revenue. Brian Houghton Hodgson, orientalist and Resident in Kathmandu, wrote in the 1840s opposing the facile arguments for the introduction of English and the 'young parrots of Bengal' with their Shakespeare and Milton, and supporting the retention of Persianised Urdu.[51] An abrupt switch to English, he thought, would 'give rise to a want of intimate information on the interior economy of this country'. Over generations the rights and duties of people in India had been reduced to 'written instruments of the most complex forms'. He pointed to the 'vast class of subordinate functionaries whose astonishing practical readiness alone ... keeps the Indian administrative machine in motion', without printing or short-

---

[46] Gilchrist, *Philology*, I, xxi–xxx; cf. *Englishman*, 6 Mar. 1835, which urged Indians to learn English as had the Scots, Welsh and Irish doctors who now took science to India.
[47] De Tassy, *Journale Asiatique*, 8, 1826, 231–2.   [48] *LH*, I, 4.
[49] Gilchrist, *Dialogues*, pp. xi, 33.
[50] ibid., p. 221, 'fresh matter' is *tazu pani*; 'lancet' is *nushtur*.
[51] B. Hodgson to *Friend of India*, 16 Mar. 1848.

hand. The culture of the written language was 'the wheel within the wheel of this machine'. In fact, though still strong, the position of Persianised Urdu was less secure than Gilchrist, Garcin de Tassy or Hodgson thought. But before turning to the rise of Hindi, we must consider the precarious survival of another classical language, Sanskrit, which was to influence the fate of Hindi.

Sanskrit and national culture

Even in the early nineteenth century, Sanskrit was still regarded by many elite Britons and Indians as the lingua franca of the Hindu intelligentsia of the subcontinent. It supplied 'refined tastes in competition' and 'strengthened the intellect of youth'; it would seed the vernacular languages and literatures of its progeny: Bengali, Hindi and Gujarati.[52] Like Latin in Europe, it would provide a vehicle for the diffusion of new ideas through native literary societies, and its acolytes might live as far afield as Siam, Kashmir and Travancore.[53] This was perhaps less far-fetched than it may seem. Latin remained a major language of scholarly discussion in Europe as H.H. Wilson's own correspondence with Viennese and Russian correspondents suggests. Likewise, Sanskrit was still used as a written language by pandits and teachers who were moving around India in increasing numbers in the wake of British conquest. Several rulers, including Raja Serfojee of Tanjore, had initiated Sanskrit debates in their courts to which Brahmins from the major centres of learning were invited.[54] In parallel, the first generation of cultural nationalists argued that Government should actively patronise Sanskrit, as even the Muslim rulers, 'though tyrants', had done.[55] Finally, Sanskrit was taught in Haileybury as a paradigm of Indo-European grammar, though this was subject to constant ridicule among the students of the College who, it was claimed, stuffed enough of the 'nausea' into their heads to pass the examination and then instantly forgot it.[56]

British motives in investigating the Sanskrit canon were mixed. Greed for valuable documents was one incentive. Francis Wilford, the 'brahminised' Anglo-Hessian of Banaras, sent many manuscripts of the Sanskrit grammarians to Wilson who regarded them as his 'predeces-

[52] 'Dr. Yates and Sanskrit Philology', ibid., 2 Nov. 1848.
[53] *Calcutta Journal*, 14 May 1820.
[54] cf., e.g., A.C. Burnell, *A Classified Index to the Sanskrit Mss. in the Palace at Tanjore* (London, 1880); R. Mittra, *A Catalogue of Sanskrit Manuscripts in the Library of his Highness the Maharaja of Bikaner* (Calcutta, 1880).
[55] Radhakanta Deb to Wilson, 5 Mar. 1836., Wilson Papers, Mss. Eur. 301/2, OIOC.
[56] *Friend of India*, 9 Jul. 1846, 29 Nov. 1849.

sors'.[57] Later, Edward Fell and James Ballantyne became his purchasing agents for manuscripts. They were both principals of the Banaras Sanskrit College, an institution founded by Duncan in 1792 to make available classical legal expertise to the British courts.[58]

Relationships between British scholars and Indian learned men were tense. The pandits were highly suspicious of the College, and averse to allowing polluted barbarians 'a view of the Shastra', itself a sacred act. Wilford, for his part, railed against the 'blunders, anachronism, contradictions, etc. of the puranics and their followers'[59] who had early on misled him by interpolating a Biblical story into a Sanskrit text.[60] There was also another problem of categories. European scholars wanted to recover the historical genealogy of Sanskrit and the principles of transformative grammar. The pandits, by contrast, wished to record all possible variations of grammar in context: to print out, as it were, a full text of the sacred sounds. To Europeans this seemed mere obscurantism.

The parasitical patronage by the British of some Sanskrit scholarship was significant nonetheless. First of all, British and European preoccupation helped to consolidate the position of the ancient grammarian Panini and the Vyakarna school of grammar as the dominant tradition in the subcontinent. Edward Fell, a former intelligence officer on the Maratha frontier, became Superintendent of the Sanskrit College in 1820. His virtuosity in Sanskrit grammar enabled him to engage in a dialogue with the pandits. He was particularly noted for 'the command he exercised over the system of Panini ... and the facility with which he cited and applied the numerous technical rules of that school'.[61] The phenomenon of wrestling with Panini became more common over the next generation as western-educated Indians lauded Panini as the founder of universal grammar. Panini, the classical sage, became a cultural hero for the Indian nation in the same manner as Bhaskara, the astronomer, and sundry medical authorities. Similarly, the level of support for Sanskrit became a matter of contention between the government and Indian ideologues, who implied that only Indian government could support indigenous 'customs and religions'.[62]

Meanwhile the growing numbers of classically educated scholars

[57] Wilford to Wilson, 3 Apr. 1819, Wilson Papers 1.
[58] Fell to Wilson, 10 Nov. 1821, 7 Mar., 6 Jun. 1822, ibid., 1.
[59] Wilford to Wilson, 3 Apr. 1819, ibid., 1.
[60] Lord Teignmouth, *Memoirs of the Life, Writings and Correspondence of Sir William Jones to which have been added some autobiographical letters addressed by Sir William to Charles Wilkins, Esq.* (London, 1804), Preface, p. xii; a copy with the original letters is in Mss. Eur. C 227, OIOC.
[61] 'Death of Capt. Fell', *Bengal Hurkaru*, 12 Mar. 1824; *Asiatic Journal*, 18, 1824, 265; V. Hodson, *List of Officers of the Bengal Army 1758–1834* (London, 1928), II, 168.
[62] e.g., Radhakanta Deb to Wilson, 5 Mar. 1836, Wilson Papers 2.

turned out by the Banaras Sanskrit College and other institutions began to produce a modernised Hindu tradition for north India, which penetrated schools, colleges and the subordinate services. Ballantyne's enthusiasm was important here. As we have seen, he believed that India would rise through the efforts of its own national intellectual elite, the pandits. The deeper aim was to impart Christian truth. The Serampore missionaries had been sloppy and matter-of-fact in their translations: 'the mere mastery of Grammar and the dictionary does not give one the command of a language. As well it might be expected that the study of a mineralogical cabinet should make a geologist.'[63] What was required was a deep understanding of linguistic and philosophical principles, and that had in principle to be comparative. The encounter between philosophical Christianity and an institutionalised Sanskrit learning in Banaras and other centres consolidated itself after 1840 around the journal *Pandit* and the *Biblioteca Indica* series.[64] It provided a small but highly valued element in the modern Indian sensibility.

The emergence of Hindi

The first official attempt to move away from the Persian script and vocabulary and replace it with the more popular Hindi, using more Sanskrit-derived than Persian-derived words and written in the Devanagari script, was made during the 1830s by Frederick Shore, the idiosyncratic son of Sir John Shore, former Governor-General, in the Saugor and Nerbudda Territories of Central India.[65] His experimental move to Hindi was later reversed by the Board of Revenue and it was not until 1855 that the Devanagari script became acceptable to British courts in central India and 1901 in the North-Western Provinces.[66] It was in areas such as central India, nevertheless, where Mughal influence and Persian literacy had weakened earliest, that indigenous support for the use of Hindi was most likely to complement official initiatives. If Persian had once been extensively used in Saugor and Nerbudda during the Mughal period, it had certainly dwindled in importance by 1750. Marathi had supplanted it as the government language; in Shore's time,

---

[63] Ballantyne, *Christianity Contrasted*, p. 5.; cf. Ballantyne to Wilson, 11 Mar. 1846, Wilson Papers 10.

[64] *The Pandit. A monthly publication of the Benares College – devoted to Sanskrit Literature*, 1 Jul. 1866– , helped to diminish the gulf between the pandits' methods of teaching and comprehension and western academia.

[65] 'Report by the Hon. Frederick Shore on the introduction of Hindosthanee in the Deva Nagaree character in the Saugor and Nerbudda Territories', *Friend of India*, 13 Oct. 1836.

[66] Christopher King, *One Language; Two Scripts; the Hindi movement in nineteenth century north India* (Bombay, 1994).

Marathi, a language close to Hindi, was still used by many pandits and descendants of Maratha administrators.[67] The popular speech was its relative, Hindi, written in the Devanagari script. Ironically, after the British conquest of 1808, the Persian script made something of a comeback and subordinate clerks acquiesced in this because it protected their monopoly of letter-writing. Shore believed, nevertheless, that the Hindus among the clerks could easily be persuaded of the merits of Hindi because it remained their domestic speech and they read the Devanagari script in the course of their worship.[68]

Shore's attempt to put Hindi in the Devanagari script on a par with the Persianised Urdu court language was not repeated for some years. But important as was the debate amongst government officials, the emergence of Hindi in Devanagari as a community of knowledge and communication did not depend solely or even largely on the intervention of civil government. First, missionary and military initiatives were important in promoting and standardising the language. Missionary printing in Sanskrit had made available good Devanagari type and the Bengal Army favoured the eastern Hindi of its high-caste sepoys. Most important, however, Hindi benefited increasingly from the patronage of important groups within Indian society: pandits, the commercial classes and the Hindu rajas.

J.T. Thompson published *A Dictionary in Hindee and English compiled from approved authorities* in 1846.[69] It was sold by all the major Calcutta bookshops and distributed by their agents up-country. This was an important breakthrough: it marked out Hindi as a formal north Indian language, rather than simply as a version of Urdu printed in the Devanagari script. The dictionary incorporated a large number of Sanskrit loan words in place of Persian-derived Urdu ones since the introduction of Persianised Urdu would mar 'the purity of the language'.[70] Thompson's introduction set out the dismal history of Hindi since the 1780s when for a brief time it seemed set fair to become a north Indian equivalent of Bengali and co-equal of the widely used Urdu. As far back as 1785, William Kirkpatrick, then Persian Secretary to the Commander-in-Chief, had urged the authorities in Britain to print a Hindi dictionary.[71] This was in recognition of the number of north Indian Brahmin and Rajput soldiers in the Bengal Army. There were relatively few literate enlisted men, but of these a significant

---

[67] Shore's report, *Friend of India*, 13 Oct. 1836.
[68] *Agra Akhbar*, cited *Friend of India*, 13 Oct. 1836.
[69] J.T. Thompson, *A Dictionary in Hindee and English compiled from approved authorities* (Calcutta, 1846).
[70] ibid., Preface, p. v.   [71] ibid., p. iii.

percentage would have understood the Devanagari rather than Persian script. Kirkpatrick's initiative lapsed because Nagri type was not yet available; the Serampore missionaries only began to make it about ten years later.[72]

After 1800 numbers of Persian, Urdu, Bengali and even Marathi dictionaries appeared. Hindi had to be content with a slender glossary affixed to Captain Price's edition of the *Prem Sagar*,[73] the extracts of Vaishnavite religious and folk-tales used for educating the civil and military services in this second-string argot. Other glossaries were attached to the selections from Hindi literature used in Fort William College. In 1825, Revd M.T. Adam of Banaras compiled a larger glossary,[74] but the problem with this was that the meanings were themselves given in Hindi. Throughout this period of official disdain of the speech, of course, works had continued to be written in Hindi and circulated throughout upper and central India. Many of these were religious, medical or astrological manuscripts. Others were copies of Urdu works in Devanagari, but these paid little attention to specifically Hindi versions of words.

Despite the disdain for Hindi of 'an eminent Sanskritist' who rejected his call for help, Thompson's dictionary of 30,000 entries coincided with a quiet resurgence of the Hindi form of north Indian speech in Devanagari. Again, an important consideration was the character of the Bengal Army. Captain Price had believed the *Prem Sagar* useful for military officers, especially for the linguists attached to regiments. In his own introduction, Thompson made a similar point. A year after publication a Bengal Army Quartermaster wrote praising the work.[75] Thompson, the Quartermaster wrote, was well known for his useful Hindustani glossaries in the Roman script, but this dictionary went much farther. It was a great boon to 'the more adventurous student', in particular 'because all the leading features of the Hindu mythology are clearly explained'. This was, indeed, a striking aspect of Thompson's work which in part reads more like a glossary of custom and religious observance. Thus: *uchchhut tilak*: 'the ceremony of putting rice on the forehead of an image when addressed, or of a *brahmun* when invited to an entertainment'.[76] The names of sages, castes and religious rites are liberally scattered through the work. As Seema Alavi has shown,[77] the

---

[72] Obituary of Charles Wilkins, *Friend of India*, 10 Sept. 1835.
[73] Thompson, *Dictionary*, p. iii; R.S. McGregor, *Hindi Literature from its beginnings to the Nineteenth Century* (Wiesbaden, 1984), pp. 63–7.
[74] Thompson, *Dictionary*, Preface, p. iv.
[75] 'Thompson's Hindee Dictionary', *Mofussilite*, 2 Jul. 1847.
[76] Thompson, *Dictionary*, 'uchchhut tilak'.
[77] Alavi, 'Company Army', *MAS*, 27, 1, 1993, 147–78.

British were concerned to maintain the high-caste status of the Bengal Army. In the 1830s, for example, the authorities had introduced regimental pandits in the hope of reinforcing declining discipline. Officers also believed that military education in Hindi would counterbalance the dominance of Brahmins who were constantly exceeding their notional quota as recruits.[78] The growing repute of Hindi in British circles was therefore partly bound up with anxieties about the state of the Bengal Army, the foundation of colonial rule.

The emergence of Hindi from neglect also illustrates wider intellectual changes. Thompson rejected the vulgar military notion that no learned, that is Sanskrit, words should appear in Hindi dictionaries.[79] Like Ballantyne and Wilkinson, he argued that it was essential for Europeans of all sorts to 'adapt a style that shall show his attainments to be on a par with those of the learned men of the country'. The civilising mission associated with Thomason was now underway. It aimed to create by cross-fertilising different indigenous knowledges 'elegancies of style and delicate shades of meaning' which would hasten the days when 'literature would become an object of more general pursuit in India'.[80]

More critical yet were the changes in Indian social and intellectual life which raised the profile of Hindi. The movement to refashion Hindu Dharma gave it an impetus which European orientalists alone could not have generated. In the eighteenth century the desire of embattled Muslim aristocrats to preserve their status in the face of political decline had encouraged the use of a purified, Persianised Urdu.[81] In the nineteenth century, by contrast, newly assertive Hindu elites tended to favour a Sanskritic Hindi. At the time Thompson published, thousands of printed works in Hindi in the Devanagari script on religious, medical and astronomical topics were coming out of private Indian presses to match the growing volume of official or semi-official publications in the vernacular. Hindi had continued to receive the patronage of Hindu principalities,[82] especially Bharatpur, the Rajasthan kingdoms and Nepal; it also benefited from the growing importance in the colonial towns of Hindu and Jain merchant castes who were less influenced by Persian or Urdu.[83] Hindi was easily instated as the language of Dharmic reformism, just as Urdu was the preferred language of Islamic revival. For while Hindu religious tracts were quite often written in the Persian script, it was more difficult to render Hindu religious and classical words

[78] 'Military Musings', *Mofussilite*, 27 Sept. 1850.
[79] Thompson, *Dictionary*, Preface, p. v.   [80] ibid.
[81] Rai, *House Divided*, pp. 240–8.
[82] McGregor, *Hindi Literature to the Nineteenth Century*, pp. 74–80, 189–208.
[83] For Nepal, *LH*, I, 469; *Friend of India*, 6 Sept. 1838, added that Kayasthas who already knew Hindi for domestic and ritual purposes would eventually fall in behind it.

precisely in it. Moreover, the axis of pilgrimage between Bengal and Banaras was the highroad of Dharmic revival. Here Devanagari in its modified Bengali form with a pronounced Sanskritic flavour was already dominant in the new print media.

The princely states were of great importance in the revival of Hindi. The kingdom of Bharatpur, for instance, along with other eastern Rajasthan principalities, had been patrons of Hindi (locally called Braj Bhasha) in the eighteenth century. Bharatpur, close to the heart of Krishna's land of milk and honey, had sustained a strong Vaishnavite devotional poetic tradition, but even before 1800 a few works had already been written in prose. Some of these were analytical and philosophical texts which may have been influenced by Indo-Persian philosophical traditions.[84] As Mughal influence over Bharatpur's aspiring Jat ruling class receded, Hindi flourished. In 1831, as the British began to consolidate their power in the recently conquered state, G.L. Lushington, Acting Political Agent, found that 'few if any of the Sirdars [chiefs] of this court are acquainted with the Persian language'. He therefore had the munshi draw up his announcements in Hindustani. But even this was unintelligible to the court 'owing to the moonshee's predilection for Persian words and idioms', so he himself read 'the Hindee version which I had caused to be prepared'.[85] For in Bharatpur four out of five of the main departments of government already worked only in Hindi,[86] while the Raja's 'Hindee Pundit' was one of the most powerful influences at court.[87] When the Resident tried to influence the young man's reading, it was through Hindi translations of English and other classics.

British supremacy in Rajasthan also called into question the notion that Persian, or at the least Persianised Urdu, was the natural language of the Indian Empire. In Jaipur and Udaipur, disarmed and conspicuously pious rulers, slipping quickly out of the intellectual orbit of Delhi, initiated a slow switch from Persian to Sanskritic Hindi in the Devanagari character. The old commercial elites had always tended to use Khari Bholi Hindi in their transactions rather than the rural local languages – Bhatti, Mewari and Marwari.[88] Brahmin priests and scholars from the east, seeking patronage in the surviving Hindu states,

---

[84] G. Grierson, *The Bhasha-Bhushana of Jaswant Singh* (Bombay, 1894), pp. 215–16; R.P. Singh, *Rise of Jat Power* (Delhi, 1988), pp. 55–68.
[85] G.L. Lushington, Pol. Agt Bharatpur, to Resdt, Delhi, 11 Jun. 1831, 'Affairs at Bhurtpore', BC 1369/ 54486.
[86] ibid.
[87] Resdt Delhi to Govt India, 10 Dec. 1830, 2 Jun. 1831, ibid.
[88] Boileau, 'Memorandum on the languages and literature of the territories of Buhawalpoor, Jesulmer and Jodhpur', app. to *Narrative*, pp. 263–90.

also introduced their predilection in favour of Hindi. They supplemented a large class of indigenous Brahmins; in the 1830s there were said to be 85,000 Brahmins and 5,500 'sextons' in Jaipur, an astonishing 20 per cent of the city's population.[89] In many parts of Rajasthan and central India, indeed, Persian had never really achieved much prominence. In Jaisalmer there was not a 'single individual who could read even a newspaper written in the Persian character except the British akhbar navis and the people connected with the British government'.[90] Even the rulers of the western Rajput states spoke varieties of 'rustic' Hindi heavily influenced by the prevailing popular speech. In the 1830s this was recognised when the British themselves began to correspond with all the local rulers in Hindi.[91]

The British collection and organisation of data about Indian languages and colonial initiatives in language policy were thus continuously modified by the demands of emerging speech communities within north Indian society. British policy and missionary printing certainly helped create two languages from a single skein of linguistic practices. But powerful forces of social change, partly operating outside the colonial milieu were already prefiguring this linguistic divide.

Indian 'geography': a social science

The previous section attempted to illustrate the social context of British debates about Indian languages. The chapter now moves on to the issue of the land itself, as the concept 'India' was to be an equally important aspect of the emerging national consciousness. The 'sciences of the heavens' had provided an irresistible ideological motif in British debates about India because of the widespread distribution of jyotishs and the implications of Indian astronomy for European religious controversies. What Europeans called 'geography' threw up less highly charged dialogues, but it lay nearer the heart of British colonial information collection.

The Puranas were the source for much Hindu conceptualisation of geography as they were for 'astronomy'.[92] Europeans delighted in disproving the 'wild conceptions of the Poorans' by demonstrating the absurdity of the popular beliefs about the centrality of Mount Meru, or the concentric rings of salt water, butter milk, ghi and so on which were supposed to constitute the face of the earth. True geography as much as

---

[89] ibid., pp. 255–63.   [90] ibid., p. 268.
[91] cf. *Friend of India*, 6 Sept. 1838 ('Choice of character in lieu of Persian in the courts of justice').
[92] Schwartzberg in Harley and Woodward (eds.), *Cartography*, 2, i, 332–87.

astronomy was seen as a way of demolishing heathenism by stealth, and the distribution of globes to schools became a significant aspect of the attempt to spread 'useful knowledge'. The Indian response to these vigorous interventions is reminiscent of that of the astronomers. Raghaviah, for instance, insisted on his right to see spiritual truth in the Vedas and Puranas, even as he tried to adapt the puranic geography to the findings of western science by associating the mythological Jambudwipa with the Indian subcontinent, and the other scriptural 'sea islands' with the continents of European geographers.[93] Indian manuscripts and textbooks of the 1820s and 1830s followed similar strategies, trying to salvage what they could of indigenous lore by associating the known world with the mythical islands. The most subtle manifestation of this response was seen in some of the books issued under government auspices in the late 1840s and 1850s. In Shiva Prasad's Hindi version of Srilala's compendium of useful knowledge, *Vidyankar*, published many times from 1840 to 1880, Copernicus and western geography are adopted but, almost as a compensation it seems, Hindustan is also described by the Sanskritic 'Bharat Khand'. Hindu *tirthas* (pilgrimage places), such as Badrinath, Rameswaram and Dwarka, define its bounds.[94]

As in the case of other Indian knowledges, the pace of westernisation, syncretism and indigenous challenge was influenced by the pre-history of contact between Hindu sciences and the more empirical forms of Indo-Islamic knowledge and skill.[95] Although the Mughals and their successors appear to have used very programmatic forms of route map in constructing their geographical understanding of the empire, larger and more conceptual maps were not unknown. Several world maps were produced from the imperial scriptoria which used Arabic or Turkish originals and depicted the continents with a degree of accuracy which was not far short of that of early Renaissance European maps. Gujarati pilots' maps from the seventeenth century reveal Dutch or Portuguese influences, and present a passable representation of the Indian coastline.[96] Presumably, naval map-making advanced more rapidly than its inland equivalent. The British were to use such maps intensively in the period of conquest, though they disparaged their lack of scale and rarely acknowledged their value.[97]

---

[93] Raghaviah to W. Kirkpatrick, Kirkpatrick Papers 20; this strategy of locating Mt Meru was also adapted by European commentators, *Hindoos*, I, 103.

[94] Shiva Prasad (ed.), Pt. Srilala, *Vidyankar* (lithographed by Harbanslal of Mohalla Pared ki Wali, Banaras, 3rd edn, 1856).

[95] Schwartzberg, *Cartography*, 2, i, 295–331; Gole, *Indian Maps*.

[96] Schwartzberg, *Cartography*, 2, i, 506; cf. the Gujarati Pilot's map displayed in the National Maritime Museum, New Delhi.

[97] Schwartzberg, *Cartography*, 2, i, 123–34.

While relatively accurate physical representations of geographical space were not unknown to Indians, one must question whether the ideology underlying geography was not radically different, at least from that of the nineteenth-century European scientific establishment. The puranic scheme involved the relationship between the material environment and types of human beings. The geograpical units most commonly mentioned were *janapada*s which means something like 'territorial units appropriate to types of people'.[98] In south India this theme in the Sanskrit literature was fully worked out in local Tamil variants: particular ecologies were congruent with such types. There were coastal-type people, black-earth people, dry-land people, and so on.[99] Similar, though less elaborated types appear in both learned and popular lore of north India. For instance, dry and primitive men and women appeared in the dry parts of Rajputana. Boileau translated a well-known ditty thus:

> Carrots for fruit, rank weeds for grass,
> And men exposed behind,
> Women with pendent stomachs too,
> We've reached Dhoondhar, I find.[100]

Another layer in popular 'geographical' sensibility associated places with specialist and prized products. In a society where most people knew the lands beyond their birthplace either through the peculiarities of their merchants or itinerants, or through trade goods, this is not surprising. Geographical and topographical works spent many pages enumerating the climate, fruits, grains and cloths of particular regions. Of particular note were sweets. Sweets became known beyond their lands of production because they were presented and received back as *prasad* (sanctified offerings) in temples and Sufi shrines. They were composed of the qualities of the cattle, rice or pulses of a region reduced to an essence by the application of sugar. The sweets of Bayana near the Bharatpur territory (so close to Krishna's homeland) were celebrated in the 'Ain-i Akbari'.[101] The *barfi* ('snowy') of Mewar 'might have made a Hindu Kitchener turn up the whites of his eyes'.[102] India was divided into an epicurean landscape of mangoes, guavas, bullocks, rice, pickles and medicines, which overlapped the better-known divisions of politics, language or pilgrimage. That sensibility has, of course, survived until today, when many a grandmother packs sweets for her grandchildren to take to distant relatives or friends.

As in the case of Indian medicine, people and substances formed each

[98] S.M. Ali, *The Geography of the Puranas* (New Delhi, 1983), pp. 13–15.
[99] See B. Stein, *Peasant State and Society in Medieval South India* (Delhi, 1980), pp. 55–7.
[100] Boileau, *Narrative*, p. 274.
[101] Gladwin, *Ayeen*, II, 37.   [102] Boileau, *Narrative*, p. 14.

other. One could not say which was prior; the divisions of mankind were responsive to their environment to produce distinct human ecologies. Since spirituality was as much a 'substance' as a 'code', geography in this scheme embraced sociology, religion and natural history. To this extent, our parallel between astronomy and geography is partly a matter of convenience. It would equally be possible to pair geography with religion, or indeed with cooking and medicine. This last point is far from frivolous. People were thought to be transformed by what they ate, drank and breathed. Cooking and medicine, which involved the use of particular substances from known regions, were attempts to capture the essence of certain places. This insight underlies the important work of Francis Zimmermann who showed how people who lived in the 'jungle', that is, in its original meaning, hot, dry and bilious places, differed from those who lived in the easeful, watered places.[103] Medicine and cooking, as transformative arts, could both be used to correct imbalances in nature which arose from too much or too little of a 'good thing'. Islamic sciences which also used notions of humours to explain the different appearance and morality of peoples, fitted easily with this schema. In India it could be used to construct an extremely complex social geography. Ghulam Ali Azad Bilgrami, a late eighteenth century chronicler tried to explain the peculiar features of the Marathas thus:

The reason why this community has a dry and stiff nature is that the food of this community consists of pulses, oils, and chillies; they put hot chillies into everything they eat. That is why their nature has become dry and hot. They always suffer from ailments such as biliousness. They are not accustomed to moderate and useful behaviour. During the last ten or twenty years, ever since these people spread over northern India, the inhabitants of that region have learned to use chillies, a practice which was very rare previously.[104]

The Maratha chief, Balaji, used only the dry grains, bajra and jowar: 'He does not like wheat. He uses pulses and green vegetables. The real profession of these Brahmins is begging ... When beggars become kings, the world is ruined and the substance of religious and learned men is seized from them.' Bilgrami's dietetic theory of the decline of the Mughal Empire was, of course, a strictly logical one, given his premises, which were broadly shared in both traditions of Indian medicine.

This strand of human geography was reflected in the large number of travellers' accounts and indigenous topographical works which linked climates, places, products, the essence of the people and the prevalence of learning and virtue. Mufti Ghulam Hazrat's 'Kifayat-i Zillah Gorakhpur' (Account of the District of Gorakhpur), for instance, which was

[103] Zimmermann, *Aroma of Meats*, passim.
[104] Bilgrami, tr. Madhava Rao, *Deccan*, p. 227.

written under the auspices of British officials, began with the influence of the district's climate.[105] The hills and water of the Terai gave the area its particular human and moral configuration. In one division, water and jungle vegetation 'spoil the atmosphere which in that state gives rise to the phlegmatic and cold diseases'. Moreover, 'The celestial heat and terrestrial cold united together corrupt the humours and affect temperaments, so that everyone according to the strength of his constitution suffers either more or less from cold or hot diseases.'[106] The prevalence of the mountains meant that there were few Muslim men of learning or note in the District.[107]

Geography for such writers meant an understanding of morality and history which was determined by the combination of human essences and natural influences. On the face of it, theories like these did not sit well with the scientific and mensurational ideas which the British brought to the closely defined subject of geography – 'earth measurement'. In practice, though, there was much room for overlap. The British in India were still influenced by more archaic notions of how climate affected human physique and character. Well into the nineteenth century, medical men tried to understand disease in terms of the influence of the moon, foetid air and the predispositions which living in certain types of terrain imparted to human beings.[108] The later discourses of race in gazetteers and ethnographic works – the sturdy mountain man, or the dry farming Jat, the effeminate Bengali fish-eater – selected from and made use of the indigenous beliefs about the connection between moral code and physical substance. The difference was that the Indian classification was more subtle, less absolute. In indigenous thought a balance could and should be achieved between different elements, between Bengali ease and Maratha dryness, for instance.

The European idea of geography could assimilate parts of a number of other Indian traditions of thought and representation besides the complex of climate, cooking and spatial sociology which we have been considering. More precise disciplines of measurement and location were not unknown, despite the clear backwardness of Indian techniques of geometrical land-surveying. Revenue management had required the preparation of myriad rough field maps (naksha zanjir band) by the

---

[105] Mufti Ghulam Hazrat, 'Kifayat-i Zillah Gorakhpur', tr. 'History of Goruckpoor', 1810, Mss. Pers. 1.0.4540, f.1, OIOC; cf. an anonymous indigenous account of the Bhattis, 'a distinct race of men' whose diet marks them out, 'Account of Bhul pargana and fort (Hissar)', Mss. Eur. D165, f.3, OIOC.

[106] Ghulam Hazrat, 'Gorakhpur', f. 2.   [107] ibid., f. 11.

[108] e.g., the Assistant Surgeon, 34 Regt, asserted that cholera attacks were due to 'sol-lunar influence' as he had heard from the Brahmins, Calcutta Journal, 4 Dec. 1818.

agents of the registrar (kanungo).[109] These economically represented village boundaries, soil types and so on. As an observer pointed out, they were constructed more 'like a genealogical tree' than a western map. The same could be said for the Mughal route map which spanned out from a central place, usually a provincial headquarters, noting distances, recording topes, watering places, bridges and fortified points. Rather than maps, these were schematic versions of the sort of travel diaries that Indian officials were wont to make on their journeys. A document such as the 'Majmua Walforti'[110] combined this sort of detailed measurement of distances with the sociological description mentioned earlier.

There was a point at which geography merged into politics, religion and history for these Indian topographers. We might imagine that their geographical world had three layers. At the base there were distance, climate and physical effects; on the second level, the domain of human communities, interacting with the physical environment, drinking in its influences and reflecting its essences. At the highest level, the landscape was composed of testimonies or proofs of the influence of divinity and great men. For the eighteenth-century Muslim this was represented by the doings of Sufi teachers and Muslim kings who had extended the grid of power centred on Mecca and Madina to this far eastern point. The peregrinations of Adam, Alexander, Solomon or the companions of the Prophet, represented the most ancient geographical testimonies of God's greatness. Nearer in time were the doings of the Mughals, the magnificent buildings thrown up by their skilled artisans, and the marks of Mughal honour and honorifics still embodied in the descendants of the great kings. Geographical description here was a kind of itinerant threnody for the relics of the great and the learned. Because Muslims had now fallen into sloth and spiritual lassitude, this was a poignant landscape, redolent of the failure of spiritual conquest, and in the view of some even a *dar-ul harb*, a terrain of war. For the Hindu, the sacred landscape of Bharat, the home of the Gods, represented a comparable geographical hierarchy. Braj, the playground of Krishna, Ajodhya, home-land of Ram, Banaras, Gaya, Ujjain and the other holy places radiated a special essence or taste, of which their people partook. These spiritual homes were part of the greater universal homeland (*mandala*) of India.

Examples of these types of geographical/topographical literature abound. The 'Waqyai-i Azfari',[111] for instance, recounts the journeys of

[109] *Friend of India*, 15 Jul. 1841.
[110] 'Majmua Walforti', 'being a general report made to Lieut. Col. Wilford by Moghal Beg, son of Muhamad Beg Khan on the topography, state of the roads and statistics of the Northwest of India', *c.* 1790, Mss. Eur. F22, OIOC.
[111] Ali Bakht Azfari, *Waqi'at-e Azfari. Urdu Translation. Madras Government Oriental Manuscripts Series* (Madras, 1937).

an exiled Mughal prince throughout north India, and ultimately to the court of Arcot in the south at the end of the eighteenth century. Azfari's understanding of India is mapped out within two overlapping grids, the one the precise statuses of kings, nobles and princes according to Mughal honorifics and marked out through gift exchange and the gloriousness of his reception: the other the charismatic places of Sufi Saints, whose most glorious place is the shrine at Ajmer of Sheikh Muin-al Din Chishti, the spiritual patron of the Mughal regime.[112] While he records these testimonies of greatness and piety with care, dwelling on the glories of Ajmer in considerable detail, his descriptions of British and Hindu activities in India are sometimes cursory in the extreme: Calcutta was merely a 'great city with innumerable people'.[113] This blindness to the non-Muslim and non-imperial was a feature of many of the last generation of true Indo-Muslim savants.

While Mughal Beg's treatise of ten years later, preserved as the 'Majmua Walforti', has some of the same features, this text also displays the precise traditions of the revenue survey and route map. The work was commissioned by Francis Wilford who was concerned to increase British knowledge of the lands beyond the Jumna. As an old-style orientalist, with a hankering for the 'knowledge of the brahmuns' and the lineaments of lost empires, Wilford and his circle no doubt appreciated the detail Mughal Beg accumulated on the buildings, shrines and marvels of Rajasthan, Bahawalpur and the Punjab. Wilford had turned to Sanskrit and Persian 'geographical' texts because he had grown 'really disgusted' with the Brahmins in the realms of philology, religion and literature.[114] He had come into possession of five or six geographical texts, his 'only amusement and only source of delight' as his health failed. This geographical effort was in part directed to reconstructing the geography of ancient India as revealed in the Sanskrit texts and Greek authors. Orientalism, as we have shown, was never purely utilitarian: the release into the scholarly world of information deriving from the Indian empire would 'be worthy of the British nation' and 'acceptable to all Europe' as the President of the Bombay Literary Society had urged.[115] Yet the 'Majmua' was also a military and political account of a country that few officials doubted would one day fall under British influence.

[112] ibid., pp. 10–15.
[113] ibid., p. 31.
[114] Wilford to Wilson, Banaras, 3 Apr. 1819, Wilson Papers, 1, OIOC.
[115] President, Literary Society, Bombay, to President Asiatic Society, Calcutta, 22 Feb. 1806, *Transactions of the Literary Society of Bombay* (London, 1819), appendix B, p. 310.

Surveying and moral dominion

Where Indian accounts sought often to reveal the boundaries of types and conditions of men, British geographical and topographical work was concentrated on drawing boundaries of a political sort for the Indian Empire. From an early period Europeans were concerned with the creation of the boundaries of nation states. Indeed the concept of Europe itself has a hardness not attempted in other great civilisational areas. The limits of the Arab lands, and of 'al-Hind', for instance, were quite malleable and undefined.[116] To some extent these boundaries were purely physical and military. The Bengal Army believed for many years that an appropriate north-western boundary for British India lay on the Jumna River. An invading army from the westward would have enormous difficulty in passing through the drier parts of the Punjab and the Rohtak Division because there were few wells for the armies of bullocks which would have to accompany any serious invasion. Much early geography was, however, designed to seek out the boundaries of ancient kingdoms in a more intellectual exercise in political legitimation. This lay behind the efforts of Rennell and his followers to describe the exact boundaries of the provinces of the Mughal empire; for these had been granted by war or conquest to the British.[117]

It might be thought that the Great Trigonometrical Survey was the pinnacle of a utilitarian imperial scheme which capped a huge effort to locate and extract India's revenues and produce.[118] But as in the case of the politics of boundaries, moral and ideological concerns were pervasive. Matthew Edney's study of the Survey[119] shows the extraordinary bureaucratic chaos and conflict which lay behind the whole map-making enterprise. He argues persuasively that the work of Mackenzie, Lambton and Everest had little benefit even in the medium term for revenue and political officials trying to gain a more precise understanding of their districts. Rather, the Survey drew resources and men from these more utilitarian projects. It was a huge exercise in Newtonian triumphalism. Empire was put to the service of the glories of national science, rather than the opposite.

Fanning out into the Indian countryside, the officers of the Survey and their Indian orderlies were as much evangelists of British superiority as the missionaries themselves. A.H.E. Boileau, First Assistant on the Great Trigonometrical Survey, travelled through western Rajasthan and

[116] A. Wink, *Al-Hind. The Making of the Indo-Islamic World* (Leiden, 1990).
[117] Rennell, *Memoir*, Introduction, pp. xxv–xxx.
[118] Phillimore, *Survey*, IV, passim.
[119] M. Edney, *Mapping an Empire* (Chicago, forthcoming).

Sindh in 1835. His assignment was to help adjust boundary disputes between local chieftains which were becoming embarrassing to Calcutta.[120] Everywhere he took measurements by theodolite and perambulator, and everywhere he sought to impress on the local people, elite and poor, the superiority of white science. One night he laid on a show for the 'intelligent vakeel' of the state of Bikaner. Using British astronomical tables and a chronometer he predicted the emergence of one of the moons of Jupiter from eclipse. The vakil was looking through the lense of the refracting telescope at exactly the time when the moon appeared. Thus 'he was aware of the perfection of that science which enabled a far distant people to predict years beforehand, the exact time of so singular a phenomenon, in the heart of Beekaner'.[121] The poor, of course, could not follow this, but they were sometimes afforded the privilege of a glimpse in the telescope of camels walking with their 'feet upward' and other marvels. Unlike an equivalent English crowd, they were 'quiet' and humble,[122] eminently suitable as subjects for the Empire, in fact.

This quietness was not always in evidence. The surveyors, geographers and other information collectors were often met with hostility. Indians sensed the political, ideological and triumphalist nature of the whole episode of flag-planting, measurement and data collection. During the nights surveying towers were sometimes demolished.[123] Quite what they betokened was probably not known. Boileau himself remarked that their activities must have seemed 'necromancer-like'. By contrast people deplored the demolition by the British of ancient fortresses, popularly seen as familiar landmarks and genies of the landscape. They declared: 'Hindoostan ka nak kut gaia hai' – 'India's nose has been cut off', a particularly humiliating punishment.[124] Another rumour was that the survey was associated with the appearance of pestilence and famine. To secure safe conduct in some areas, the surveyors had to hoist green, Islamic flags on the pinnacles of the Mughal buildings;[125] elsewhere they were required to make offerings to local deities. Even a client of the British such as the Nawab of Arcot had once remarked that a Company survey and census of his territory would

---

[120] Boileau, *Narrative*, p. 1.   [121] ibid., p. 17.
[122] ibid.; cf. Gyan Prakash, 'Science gone native in colonial India', *Representations*, 40, Fall 1992, 153–78. Prakash shows how the indigenisation and popularisation of science undermined its 'hegemonic power'. The elite response to claims of western religious and scientific hegemony, however, was more often to deploy vigorous scientific logic and claim superior scientific status for Indian knowledges. It was to assert higher rationality, not to subvert it.
[123] Phillimore, *Survey*, III, 407–12; IV, 160–3.
[124] Boileau, *Narrative*, p. 151.
[125] Phillimore, *Survey*, IV, 24.

'reduce his honour' in the eyes of other kings.[126] The combination of fear of further taxation and a symbolic struggle over territory combined to impede the spread of colonial information gathering.

Small books and small minds

With the activities of the committees of public instruction and the schoolbook societies, geography also became an important component in the outward diffusion of knowledge by the colonial power and the missionaries. It was expected to aid in the undermining of Hinduism and dispel the idea that India was the centre of civilisation, besides forming new men through the application of 'useful knowledge'. British geography as redefined by eighteenth-century scholars under the influence of Locke and Hume was a heavily empirical subject. The continental European tradition which culminated in Alexander von Humboldt saw geography as a human and natural science, delineating history and culture as well as rivers and cities. Von Humboldt himself denounced the spoliation of the New World by the Iberians and pointed out the great differences in wealth and poverty that he saw there. British geography, by comparison, had largely shorn itself of history and culture. It stressed the dominance of British commerce throughout the globe. Its method was deliberately dry and untheoretical, an antidote to romance and imagination. *The Young Ladies' Geography* of 1757, for instance, was designed to entice its readers from 'obscene and ridiculous novels'.[127]

In general, the new Indian textbooks, both English and Hindustani, were also relentlessly matter-of-fact and empirical. Geography was a science of measurement and description. None of the theoretical concerns of the von Humboldt school or even of the eighteenth-century Scottish philosphers found their way into these works. They were nevertheless, in their own way, shot and shell in the cannonade of the civilising mission. This was recognised by a hostile French reviewer in the *Journale Asiatique* who castigated Indian schoolbooks for inaccuracy in Hindustani and the introduction of English neologisms. It complained that the books carefully avoided the words 'England' and 'English', preferring instead *kampani sarkar* (Company rule),[128] but they would nevertheless 'destroy among the Hindus the threads which attach them to their country, their coreligionists and their castes'.[129]

[126] ibid., I, 3.
[127] M. Bowen, *Empiricism and Geographical Thought from Francis Bacon to Alexander von Humboldt* (Cambridge, 1981), p. 162.
[128] 'Critique Littéraire; livres élémentaires publiés par les Anglais à Calcutta', *Journale Asiatique*, n.s., 1, 1828, 312.
[129] ibid., 307–8.

A typical example was G.A. Nicholls's *Grammar of Geography adapted to the Education of Indian Youth* which went through many editions between 1838 and the 1890s, and spawned many imitations in both English and the vernaculars. It reads much like a compilation of gazetteers, briefly interrupted with unsystematic racialist assertions. 'South Asiatics are in general an effeminate, indolent and luxurious race of men; but evince considerable genius and are remarkable for warm and lively imaginations.'[130] Bengalis were 'weak in body and timid in mind'.[131] North Asians were a 'hardy and wandering race' which periodically overran South Asia and established intolerable despotisms there. Hindustan was derived from the Persian word for 'black';[132] low castes removed filth and were 'deemed the ugliest'.[133] The United Kingdom had achieved 'a considerable degree of influence over many other portions of the globe' and owed this to its manufacturing prowess. Of course, there was no analysis of the progress and consequences of the industrial revolution, which was taken as a natural phenomenon. Another example of this genre, the Revd A.R. Symonds's *Introduction to the Geography and History of India* (Madras, 1845), interspersed a gradgrind text with similar ideological assertions. The Koran, it claimed, was written with the aid of a Jewish Rabbi and two Syrian Christians.[134] The Jats were 'short, black and ill looking'.[135] In so far as this widely used work had a theory of race it was simply 'the will of God'.[136] The chronological table at the end of the book had three divisions: the Church, the History of India and the History of Europe.

The Hindi *Bhugol Darpan Pathshalaon ke liye* (Orphan Press, Agra, 1842) eschewed even this level of comment. It was largely a list of political divisions, cities and rivers. It paid proper attention to *Gret Britan* and asserted that the capital (*rajdhani*) of Hindustan was Calcutta.[137] The 'Description of England' (*Ingland Dwipadipika*)[138] published a year earlier was a compilation of fact, leavened with discreet praise of the British constitution.

The older, humoural components of geography and topography did not simply die out, though. Shahamat Ali, Mohan Lal and men schooled in the new sciences at the Delhi or Banaras colleges, inserted historical legends into their accounts of inner Asia. Even for the British, the myth

---

[130] G.A. Nicholls, *Grammar of Geography adapted to the Education of Indian Youth* (Calcutta, 1838), p. 11.
[131] ibid., p. 25.   [132] ibid., p. 12.   [133] ibid., p. 25.
[134] The Revd A.R. Symonds, *Introduction to the Geography and History of India* (Madras, 1845), p. 32.
[135] ibid., p. 87.   [136] ibid., p. 14.
[137] Pt. Ratna Lala, *Bhugol Darpan Pathshalaon ke liye* (Orphan Press, Agra, 1842).
[138] *Ingland Dwipadipika* [England Described], (Agra, 1841).

of Hindu knowledge continued to have some pull, though this mythical knowledge was now a submerged theme. A typical product of the Library of Entertaining Knowledge, *The Hindoos* (1835), included a long discussion of the puranic continent Jambudwipa which it sought to locate in central Asia, along with Mount Meru.[139] The discovery of ancient caves in the mountains of the region of Bamian, Kabul and Ghazni led the author to assert that this region had probably been the ancient home of the Hindus. Thus the sacred concept of Hindu Jambudwipa had been placed in a specific geographical setting and historicised. Learned Hindu writing elaborated this discursive strategy and used it to protect the veracity of the Rishis and Brahmins by, as it were, secularising their insights. Just as Ram was a historical figure and Bhaskara an antique intellectual giant, so the puranic legends were really misinterpreted testimonies of the great Hindu science of the past. Hindu geographers and astronomers were shown to have identified the 'Arctic home of the Vedas' long before European savants. Indeed, as Tilak was to argue half a century later, the most elevated Brahmins themselves came from those Arctic regions.[140]

Indian geographers, however, refuted the insinuating racism which now permeated even the driest of British textbooks. K.M. Bannerjea, for instance, initiated a long search of north Indian languages, Persian and even 'Chaldean' for the geographical section of an encyclopedia which he had in preparation. His particular target was the 'whimsical' notion, found in Hamilton's *Gazetteer* and then passed on in school geographies, Hindi, Bengali and English, that Hindustan meant 'black-place' in old Persian or, as Bannerjea put it, 'negro-land'.[141] The only derivation of this sort, he said, was to be found in the poet Hafiz, and was unreliable. Hindustan was obviously cognate with the Greek 'India' and referred to the river Indus.

This is not to say, of course, that the notion of Hindu sacred space was expelled from either learned or popular indigenous dialogue. All the Hindu travellers' accounts of the mid-nineteenth century are testimony to the persistence of the notion of *Bharat Darshana*, which implies that since the land was sacred, there could be no geography and no itinerary which was not to some degree an act of worship. India the geographical entity was underpinned by Bharat Varsha and Punyabhumi ('earth which conveys religious merit'). Shiva Prasad's geography in his

[139] *Hindoos*, I, 103.
[140] B.G. Tilak, *The Arctic Home in the Vedas, being also a key text to many Vedic texts and legends* (Pune, 1903).
[141] K.M. Bannerjea to Wilson, 5 Dec. 1847, Wilson Papers 10; cf. *Friend of India*, 26 Aug. 1841.

Vidyankar, which was a typical officially sanctioned North-Western Provinces schoolbook, puts special emphasis on pilgrimage places, Baijnath and Badrinath, Gaya, Banaras, Kanyakumari, etc., in its geographical sections, which otherwise bristle with 'useful knowledge'. The Sehore pandit's *Patramalika* of 1841, mentioned above, is a travelogue of a journey between Sehore and Bombay, which forms, as it were, a pilgrimage to places of knowledge both ancient and modern. Humbler pilgrimage manuals were to form a significant percentage of early Hindi (and Marathi) printed books.[142]

The new syncretic form of a western travelogue which still retains echoes of the charisma of Hindu place is represented by the two-volume work of Bholanauth Chunder, *The Travels of a Hindoo to various parts of Bengal and Upper India*. This was the work of a Brahmo Samajist of Vaishnavite merchant-caste background who kept a diary of his itineraries between 1845 and 1866.[143] His aim was to provide amusement, information and a 'positive history' of the famous places of pilgrimage and legend in eastern and northern India. According to J. Talboys Wheeler, who wrote an introduction to the book, Bholanauth Chunder specifically wished to contradict Hindu 'superstitions' about the holy places.[144] It must have been galling to the new Indian rationalists that, far from eroding idolatry, the railways and better communications had actually increased the pilgrimage trade.

Bholanauth Chunder asserted (here, finally, we find a trace of Hegel): 'We do not want dreamy religious speculations, but practical energy and matter-of-fact knowledge.'[145] At Banaras, for instance, he bewailed the lack of a museum collection.[146] He ridiculed the sannyasis (ascetics)[147] and poured scorn on Brahmins.[148] Following Heber and the studies of James Prinsep, he insists that contemporary Banaras was not shrouded in antiquity, but was a city of no more than two hundred years in age, mainly constructed by the Marathas. He praises British rule as a 'superior civilisation' while still hoping that in his grandchildren's time 'every *dhooty* [wrap], every shirt and every pugree [turban, would be] made from the fabrics of Indian cotton, manufactured by Indian mill-owners'.[149] Yet despite the fact that his aim is iconoclastic demystification, his descriptions of places go far beyond the historical account, or even the picturesque, to become memorials of the sacred. At one point in Banaras, his ironic detachment slips and he remarks 'one

---

[142] e.g., Gurusarana Lala, *Avadhayatra* [a description of sacred places and pilgrimages in Awadh] (Lucknow, 1869).

[143] Bholanauth Chunder, *The Travels of a Hindoo to various parts of Bengal and Upper India* (2 vols., London, 1869).

[144] ibid., I, xix.   [145] ibid., I, 278–9.   [146] ibid., I, 272.

[147] ibid., I, 270.   [148] ibid., I, 41.   [149] ibid., I, 169.

involuntarily performs that *nugur-parikrama* [circumambulation of the city] which is so meritorious in Hindu pilgrimage'.[150] Bholanauth Chunder's Brahmo deism and his acquaintance with western rationalist geographical and travel-writing had pushed him across the conceptual boundary between traditional Vaishnavite pilgrimage and the quasi-modern act of gazing on the glories of India, *Bharat Darshana*. The same can be said of the Arya Samaj, the modernising religious movement. Its founder, Dayananda Saraswati, similarly ridiculed the notion that the Hindu and Sikh holy places conferred automatic merit. With aggressive literal-mindedness the Swami set about refuting all the legends about their origins. Amritsar, far from ever having been a lake of nectar, was so called because the water of the lake had once been 'sweet'. True holy places (*tirthas*), he insisted, were not bridges between heaven and earth but mental disciplines which formed spiritual crossing points to salvation; these included charity, yoga and self-control.[151] Still, the fact that Arya Samaj preachers made a special point of spreading their message against the 'popes of Hinduism' at holy places such as Gaya, Banaras and Mathura, tended in a negative way to reinforce their importance. Orthodox Hindus could always say of them, as they said of the Christian missionaries, that the gods had brought these scoffers willy-nilly to the holy cities.

Conclusions

These studies of the engagement between different types of British and Indian knowledge and their practitioners have revealed some wider patterns. British India was an empire of the sword; it was also an 'empire of opinion', as the *Friend of India* announced. A small expatriate class and an even smaller Indian elite engaged in controversy, producing what are now called colonial discourses. The British sought initially to appropriate and remould, but later to disparage what they thought of as Indian knowledge. Their 'knowledge', though it usually asserted super-iority, was unstable, ambiguous, and often derivative from Indian sources. Meanwhile, Indian elites sought to appropriate parts of this western knowledge, but also rapidly began to celebrate the virtue of what they came to see as national and racial knowledges on the point of dissolution. These controversies influenced debates within the Indian ecumene because many of the issues in contention were central to indigenous conceptions of society and polity. But the rise, efflorescence

[150] ibid. I, 247.
[151] Dayananda Saraswati, *Satyarth Prakash*, tr. *Light of Truth* by G. Bharadwaja (Lahore, 1927), p. 371.

and decline of these debates must be contextualised in broader social and economic processes. The increasingly savage attacks on Indian learning after about 1825 reflected debates in the West and the creation of professions there. They did not simply mask attempts to master India, or to conceive it as Europe's other. Equally, it was the increasing competition which expatriates faced from Indians after 1830, as government servants, merchants, writers of English and even as fledgeling scientists, which intensified the fevered, often racist attacks on the Indian inheritance. Our understanding of 'colonial discourse' must reflect the pervasiveness of Indian agency, of the Indian intellectual challenge, and of Indian cultural vitality. Curiously, the introduction of the 'knowledge is power' theme of Francis Bacon and Michel Foucault into Indian historiography, alongside the behaviourist concept of 'hybridisation', has sometimes served to marginalise Indians and their knowledge as thoroughly as the most hidebound colonial administrative history ever did.

Yet there is another level at which the arguments between Indian elites and the British (or between recent scholars about the texts they produced) conceal more than they reveal. It was the local, decentralised networks of knowledgeable people on the fringes of these pretentious controversies which carried the deepest power of social change. The actors in this sphere were the owners of small lithographic presses; the sellers of herbal pills in western containers; the joshis and puraniks taking printed texts out into the hills; the sepoys returning to their villages with western scalpels, muskets and clocks; the rich villagers who hired local lawyers to procure copies of British revenue maps. This was the critical level of activity. These new techniques and associated knowledges spread along older lines of communication and debate as much as through the post, the cantonments, the new schools and exiguous public libraries.

Anglo-Indian mythology interpreted the dramatic onset of the Rebellion
of 1857 as an acute failure in intelligence-gathering and analysis. Sir
John Kaye, self-appointed historian to the Company, remarked how
rapidly, in a manner 'almost electric',[1] the rebels and the Indian
population disseminated information about British weakness and disas-
ters, in his *History of the Sepoy War*. Kaye's remarks about the inwardness
and speed of Indian communication were strikingly similar to those of
Bishop Heber a generation before, though painted in darker colours. In
common with most officials, he believed that Indian religion was an
important domain of seditious communication. The Dharma Sabha of
Calcutta, the 'great organ of Brahminical reaction', was matched among
Muslims in intrigue by 'venerable *maulavis*' and servants of the declining
Muslim courts of upper India, the 'veritable messengers of evil',[2] who
passed to and fro between the dissident 'baboos' of the Presidency and
up-country nests of treason.

That the British were fighting blind in 1857, and had not been able to
anticipate the storm of mutinies came as a bitter blow to Kaye. In *The
Administration of the East India Company; A History of Indian Progress*,
published in 1853, he had been sanguine about the expansion of colonial
knowledge. During the eighteenth century the 'study of books in India
preceded the study of men'[3] and it was only in 'very recent times that we
have thought it worth while to *know* anything about the natives of India
and to turn our knowledge to profitable account'. Now, the British were
in possession of 'remarkable intelligence' about the Thugs and other
criminal conspiracies. Colonial knowledge had defeated the embodied
knowledge of criminal castes and had unlocked their secret languages.
Even the flow of statistics from the Company's jails had proved

---

[1] *Kaye's and Malleson's History of the Indian Mutiny of 1857–8* (1897–8, repr. London,
     1971), Sir John Kaye, I, 361.
[2] ibid., I, 361, cf. ibid., 363.
[3] J.W. Kaye, *The Administration of the East India Company; A History of Indian Progress*
     (London, 1853), pp. 354–5.

invaluable: 'It was astonishing what a mass of serviceable information was locked up within our prison walls'.[4] In stark contrast, Kaye was forced to conclude after the Rebellion that this was knowledge merely of the 'externals of Indian life', the dry census data of houses, numbers and 'outward appearances'.[5] Bentinck and Thomason's statistical movement had told the British almost nothing about Indian sentiments, politics and beliefs.

So in the aftermath of revolt the old information panics, redolent of 'Thuggee and Dacoitee', returned with a vengeance. The story that the revolt was announced to headmen of villages by the passing of *chapati*s in a kind of chain letter had gained enormous currency.[6] Thereafter, wandering holy-men giving out benedictions were observed at every major point of tension from 1858 until the end of British rule. In the 1880s, the local agents of cow-protection associations were thought to be spreading seditious Congress propaganda.[7] In 1907, the fiftieth anniversary of the Rebellion, the police reported that malevolent holy-men were smearing trees with cow-dung as a prelude to a general massacre of Europeans which would bring to power the so-called extremist leaders of the national movement.[8] The preoccupations of Sleeman's Thuggee and Dacoitee Department retained their fascination in the days of Curzon. It is revealing that surveillance of early Congress agitation was to be placed within the purview of the Thuggee Department's descendant, the Criminal Investigation Department.[9]

Kaye's more chastened opinion had much justification. There had been a subtle change in the quality of information coming in to colonial officials in the 1840s and 1850s. Human intelligence gathered by resourceful harkaras and influential munshis had been replaced by more programmatic material derived from statistical surveys, the courts and reports on the vernacular press. The new generation of officers often regarded the akhbarats with contempt and disdained to pick up the gossip of courts through spies and 'old ladies'. Young and ignorant military officers found it more difficult to communicate with ageing Indian subalterns many of whom had begun their service in the days of Lord Hastings.[10] By the 1850s Anglo-Indian society was more isolated

[4] ibid., p. 400.   [5] Kaye, *Indian Mutiny*, I, 361.   [6] See below, pp. 321–2.
[7] 'Note on agitation against Cow-Killing', 257, vol. 367, Judicial and Public Papers, 1894, OIOC.
[8] U.P. report, Home Political Proceedings, Jul. 1907, 24D, National Archives of India.
[9] C.A. Bayly, *The Local Roots of Indian Politics. Allahabad 1880–1920* (Cambridge, 1975), pp. 127–8.
[10] J.S. Hodgson, *Opinions on the Indian Army* (London, 1857) (orginally published in *Mofussilite*, 1850 as 'Military musings'), pp. 23, 81, passim.

and obsessed with events in England.[11] Eurasians, such as James Skinner and his descendants, with their rich patrimonial knowledge, had less place in it. Of course, there were plenty of voices in army and civilian ranks warning of trouble,[12] and these had grown louder when Indian disaffection had grown strident during the campaigns against the Sikhs. The inability of officials and soldiers to interpret or respond to the messages of unease which came in from so many sources during the 1850s was at least as important as the lack of accurate intelligence of Indian mentalities.

The Rebellion was not brought about simply by military ineptitude and massive failures of intelligence, even though that is what most Britons came to believe. It was the result of two generations of social disruption and official insensitivity, and in some parts of the country rebellion assumed the proportions of a patriotic revolt. This revolt, nonetheless, revealed the strengths and weaknesses of British surveillance of the colonised. Intelligence was vital to the course of events and nowhere more so than in the Punjab and Delhi region. In 1857 a struggle unfolded between the British and the insurgents over the control of modern media of information, which belies the conventional assumption that the rebel leaders were blind traditionalists.

The rapid disarming of the Bengal Army sepoys in Lahore within twenty-four hours of the outbreak of the Mutiny in the Meerut Cantonment was a momentous strategic success for the British. Here speedy and accurate intelligence was their salvation. It may be, of course, that the rebellion was doomed from the beginning. An officerless army of peasant soldiers was set against the forces of the world's greatest contemporary military and technological power. No foreign army was in a position to intervene on the rebels' side, and at the critical moment potential enemies of the British in Persia and Afghanistan were paralysed by internal conflict. If the Punjab had been lost, however, the British would have been unable to move their forces against Delhi, the seat of rebellion, as they did within six weeks of the outbreak. This was a knight's pawn move against the enemy king and it threw the whole revolt off balance thereafter. Without this success the cost to the British government in men and material of suppressing the Rebellion would have been infinitely greater. Empire would have become yet more suspect to opinion in Britain. British prestige would have suffered a

[11] 'Our nearer intercourse with England of itself disconnects further the European mind in progressive ratio from sympathy, and from similar interests with the native mind', *Friend of India*, 23 May 1850.

[12] e.g. *Delhi Gazette*, 2 Feb. 1842; 20 Jun. 1842 (Muslim prayer meetings in Indian cities for British defeat); cf., *Friend of India*, 8 Mar. 1849.

massive blow and domestic finances a crippling setback. As the official Punjab report on the years 1857–8 stated, India would have had to be reconquered 'ab initio' and all British lives outside Bengal 'would have been forfeit'.[13] That this was avoided was largely the result of superior intelligence.

There were twelve simultaneous mutinies among the Hindustani soldiers garrisoning the recently conquered Punjab. The sepoys' plan seems to have been to join with the troops at the large military station of Firozpur. This would have put at their disposal 7,000 barrels of gunpowder and vast stores of weapons. 'Had the disarming not been effected when it was, while the electric telegraph had given us a monopoly of intelligence, it is quite impossible to say what might have happened within 36 hours.'[14] The telegraph had only been opened on 1 February 1855, and in the early days of the revolt electric communications to the west were often sporadic. Nevertheless, information on the Delhi outbreak was passed through from Ambala to Ludhiana, as was the first news of the serious revolt in Jullunder, whose officials had omitted to warn other stations.[15] These critical telegraph messages were supported by more conventional forms of surveillance. Informers working through the Lahore police brought news that the sepoys were organising for mutiny, but wished to see what happened in Delhi before moving.[16] The Firozpur authorities received news of the fall of Delhi to the Meerut mutineers by the tried old system of harkaras. Letters sent through the post by Indian merchants of Delhi to their correspondents in the Punjab were also scrutinised.[17]

This barely adequate intelligence allowed the British to contain the mutinies at most military stations and also to move quickly enough to avert the possibility of civilian uprisings amongst the Province's Hindu and Muslim populations. The Sikhs, recently conquered and resentful of the part played by Hindustani sepoys in their loss of independence, generally remained sullenly inactive throughout the war. But elsewhere the rebels had large pockets of sympathisers. Robert Montgomery, the Chief Commissioner, was aware that this was a war over Indian 'opinion'. One of the first things he did after the disarming of the troops

[13] R. Montgomery, Punjab Administration Report, 1857–8, *Selections from the Public Correspondence of the Administration of the Affairs of the Punjab* (Lahore, 1859), IV, pt 1, 39; copy in Montgomery Papers, Mss. Eur. D1019/3, OIOC.

[14] ibid., p. 2.

[15] G. Ricketts, Ludhiana to H. Lawrence, 11 Jul. 1857, Montgomery Papers, Mss. Eur. D1019/3.

[16] Montgomery, *Punjab Reports*, p. 2.

[17] 'Memorandum of events since we first heard of the Mutiny of Meerut', f. 59, Montgomery Papers, 3.

was to occupy all ferries and passages of rivers.[18] Appreciating the importance of the old pathfinder communities, his lieutenants tried to deprive Gujars of the inflatible skins which they used to cross the rivers. Altogether, the complex river system of the Punjab made it easier to control than the broad, uninterrupted plains of Hindustan. An embargo was placed on all 'suspicious travellers who could not give a proper account of themselves and especially upon fuqeers and other mendicants of a quasi-religious character'.[19] Thousands of Indian light carriages, which used hourly to run the thirty-five miles between Lahore and Amritsar in the days before the railway, were seized by the British authorities.

Next, the 'Native Press was early put under strict censorship'.[20] The authorities imprisoned the editor of the *Moortizaee* of Peshawar for treason and 'the native paper at Mooltan was likewise suppressed'. The editor of the *Chesma-i-Faiz* of Sialkot was ordered to remove his press to Lahore where it was kept under strict surveillance. These newspapers had all earned a reputation for veiled criticism of the government before the outbreak of the revolt, but officials justified the harsh treatment of the press on the grounds that the editors of three of the five Punjab Indian newspapers were 'Hindustanis'. British occupation of the Punjab had seen a rapid growth in the numbers of small lithographic presses,[21] which had been strictly controlled by the Sikh rulers. The British were now reaping the consequences of the information revolution which they had put in train. To a much greater extent than any earlier Anglo-Indian encounter, this was a modern war of propaganda. In form the Rebellion may have seemed like a scattered patchwork of risings, but broader currents of opinion were at work even in areas which did not revolt.

The importance of battle to control the passage of 'sedition' and mould public opinion was demonstrated by new regulations for the control of the Post Office. Since 1836, the government had always controlled the posts closely, suppressing unauthorised 'native dawks'. The main reason for this was financial: the need to maximise revenues from postage duty and stamps. Otherwise, officials had viewed the post, like the press, as benign agencies for spreading useful knowledge. The mood now changed sharply. In each district the magistrate was appointed head postmaster with orders that all Indian letters should be opened and scrutinised by British eyes.[22] The officials 'suppressed

---

[18] *Punjab Reports*, ibid., p. 23.
[19] R. Temple to Sec. Govt India, 25 May 1858, ibid., p. 167; cf. Temple's narrative reprod., supplement of overland, *Friend of India*, 22 Jan. 1859, Montgomery Papers, 3.
[20] *Punjab Reports*, pp. 6–7, ibid.   [21] Davis, *Punjab Press*, pp. 16–17.
[22] Montgomery, *Punjab Reports*, p. 167.

suspicious letters, especially those addressed to sepoys'. The authorities discovered many examples of 'enigmatic' and 'treasonable' messages and were left in no doubt of the widespread popular hostility to their rule.

This leads us to the issue of the communication of dissent and anti-British ideas among the Indian population. The stories of wandering holy-men and chapatis have apparently lent credence to the view that the rebellion was a feudal and obscurantist outbreak. In fact, both traditional and modern networks of information were enlisted by the rebels. It is certainly the case that religious teachers were active in spreading the rebel cause[23] and Muslim religious fighters poured into Delhi from all parts of north and central India, spreading their message in villages along the way.[24] The newly-restored Emperor of India rapidly sent out messengers to the neighbouring territories in order to try to reclaim an authority which had lapsed in 1803. Shortly after the fall of Delhi to the Meerut sepoys, the zamindar of Rewari cut the postal communications along the Grand Trunk Road – at much the same point where earlier Jat rebels had cut the communications of the Great Mughal.[25] There ensued a struggle along the length of Trunk Road to keep the dak running. The ruthless General Neill, commander of the expeditionary force advancing on Kanpur, employed terror tactics with some success. He summarily hanged the headman of a village near a staging-post where dak horses had been killed and punished attacks on the post elsewhere by burning villages. But insurgents continued to attack the telegraphs.[26] On the other side of Delhi, the Punjab officials coerced the rulers of small states such as Jhind and Nabha and others into protecting the British lines of communication.

In British eyes, a most dangerous network of sedition was that maintained by Muslims of the purist Tarikh-i Muhamadiyya ('Wahhabi') tendency. Many officials came to believe that the whole Muslim community was implicated in Rebellion, fuelling the suspicion which culminated in the Patna conspiracy cases a decade later, when Muslims in the capital of Bihar were arraigned for sedition.[27] Herbert Edwardes, the evangelical Christian officer, serving in the western Punjab, denounced the 'rancorous and seditious letters' sent by 'Mahomedan bigots' in Patna and Thanesar, near Deoband, to soldiers

---

[23] See, Farhan Nizami, 'Muslim reactions', ch. 6.

[24] E. Stokes, *The Peasant Armed. The Indian Rebellion of 1857* (Oxford, 1986), pp. 86–90.

[25] ibid., pp. 161–75, see above, p. 20.

[26] 'Allahabad Divisional Report', NWP Police Procs., 26 Apr. 1862, 15–19, 235/51; S.A.A. Rizvi, *Freedom Struggle in Uttar Pradesh*, IV (Lucknow, 1959), p. 713.

[27] P. Robb, 'The impact of British rule on religious community: reflections on the trial of Maulvi Ahmadullah of Patna in 1865', in Robb (ed.), *Society and Ideology*, pp. 142–76.

and civilians serving on the new North-West Frontier.[28] The evidence suggests that some connections within the 'Wahhabi' movement along with some older Sufi networks were used by rebels to try to coordinate different sectors of the resistance, but the official response was out of all proportion to the threat.

The Indian rebels had many other informal agencies of communication to fall back on. Nearly half the public officers in the Punjab were 'Hindustanis' and they tried to maintain a regular communication with their families in the rebel-held territories.[29] Other residents of Hindustan working in the Punjab fell under suspicion. These included domestic servants or labourers on the Bari Doab Canal and, in addition, 'Hindostanee horse-keepers at Ferozepore ... Hindoostanee servants at Murree ... Hindoostanee native doctors at Murree and Umritsur'.[30] Once the British had lost control, the dense patterns of social communication which criss-crossed the Indian plains could rapidly be turned against them by their enemies.

Alongside these older networks, well-tried methods of publicity were also in common use during the Rebellion. In Delhi the ecumene was alerted to danger by the customary placards near the Jama Masjid. When, a few months before the Rebellion, the British had been about to go to war with Persia, 'a small dirty piece of paper with a naked sword and shield' purporting to be a declaration of holy war by the King of Persia was pinned up there.[31] This found its way into written newsletters and the press along with prophecies of the end of British rule.[32]

There was, however, another side to the communication of resistance. In the first place, the role of customary and religious networks among Indians was liable to exaggeration because, after the Rebellion, powerful British voices had an interest in making out that the Rebellion had been a 'caste revolt' or 'Muhammadan conspiracy'.[33] Not everyone agreed. The Acting Lieutenant-Governor of the NWP, E.A. Reade, doubted the whole story of the seditious chapatis.[34] He thought that it arose from misunderstanding of a customary rite whereby families tried to dissipate disease or ill-luck by passing it on to adjacent villages in the form of food or clothing. According to Reade, it was the 'nervous' reaction of

---

[28] Montgomery, *Punjab Reports*, p. 86.   [29] ibid., p. 153.   [30] ibid., p. 8.
[31] Evidence of T. Metcalfe, 'Trial of the King of Delhi', *Parliamentary Papers*, 1859, sess. 1, xviii, 80.
[32] Evidence of Ahsanullah Khan; ibid., p. 72, prophecies of Hasan Askari a healer who frequented the court.
[33] evidence of Deputy Judge Advocate Genl, *Parliamentary Papers*, 1859, 1, xviii, 152–3.
[34] E.A. Reade to J. Kaye, 10 Mar. 1864, Reade Mss. Eur. E124 no. 223, OIOC; cf. narrative of Mainodin, C.T. Metcalfe (ed., tr.), *Two Native Narratives of the Mutiny in Delhi* (London, 1898), pp. 39–41.

J.R. Colvin, Lieutenant-Governor of the North-Western Provinces which drew the attention of district officers to the chapatis and raised the bogey of sedition, thus intensifying an atmosphere of suspicion.

Indian opinion was, in fact, being formed to an equal extent by letters sent through the Post Office, the press and merchant communications – all 'modern' media. The new communities of knowledge created by British rule were at least as heavily involved in rebel propaganda as the older religious and social connections. Even before the Rebellion, for instance, the temperature had been raised by sepoys of the native infantry crowding the Lahore and Firozpur post offices asking for 'news' and 'whether the mail had arrived' and other 'unusual questions'.[35] Most significantly, the remittances which the soldiers had made regularly to their villages in Banaras and eastern Awadh ceased almost completely, and the demand for cash and the price of gold rose sharply in the exchange markets, with merchants also showing signs of panic. At the time, the British authorities were at a loss to explain this stark change in public mood. While it seems unlikely that there was a widespread or tightly organised conspiracy to foment rebellion, the soldiers and bazaar people should be credited with a close understanding of political realities; they had quickly adapted to modern means of communication.

Indians seem to have adapted to censorship, too. The authorities thought that relatively few letters were actually 'treasonable'; the majority both before and after the outbreak of the Rebellion were simply 'cautiously worded', wrapping up political information in everyday phrases. For example, the British read sinister meanings into phrases such as 'white wheat has become very scarce, and country produce very abundant', or 'hats were hardly to be seen, and white turbans plentiful'.[36] According to the authorities, the tone of the letters and of wider public opinion in the Punjab actually deteriorated over the summer, and only with the fall of Delhi to the expeditionary forces on 16 November 1857 was 'disaffection nipped in the bud'. It could be that the British were sometimes reading their own fears into this correspondence, but postal surveillance still produced 'many important and interesting documents' which served to indicate clearly the 'tendency of native opinion'.[37]

That opinion also continued to be formed by the Indian press. In addition to the Punjab newspapers referred to above, the *Sadik-ul Akhbar* and the *Dihli Urdu Akhbar*, two Delhi newspapers, which had been critical of the British before the revolt, continued to publish into

[35] Montgomery, *Punjab Reports*, p. 70.   [36] ibid., p. 190.
[37] ibid., 167; supplement *Friend of India*, 22 Jan. 1859.

the summer of 1857,[38] and carried rebel proclamations. The 'court journal', the *Siraj-ul Akhbar*, now lithographed, though a direct descendant of the old-style newsletter, also carried matters of political interest during the siege and printed rebel proclamations.[39]

Other centres of colonial power distant from Delhi also revealed these contrasting features of the battle over information. Banaras, like Lahore, saw a rapid reassertion of British control. Secure in their links down-river to Calcutta by steamboat, post and telegraph, the authorities were able to act quickly when news of the Meerut mutinies came in. Here the Bhumihar Brahmin royal family, supported for two generations by British power, used its agents to inform the authorities on the course of rural rebellion among its rivals, the declining Rajput clans of the hinterland. The descendants of that most typical of all 'native informants', Maulvi Abdul Kadir Khan, kept a close eye on dissidence among the Muslim weavers and workers of the town. Spies were set on members of the exiled Delhi royal family in Banaras: these far flung branches had long acted as a network of supporters and agents for the Delhi court. But the British also benefited from residual tensions between Hindus and Muslims in the city.[40] Close controls were put on the press and Post Office. When, in September 1857, two Banaras merchants set up an unofficial dak between Lucknow and Banaras, it was revealed to the British by an Indian police officer.[41] The network was broken up and the two merchants were later prosecuted for sedition.

In Lucknow, by contrast, the political and information culture of the old order had survived the British occupation of 1856. As in the classic days of Indo-Islamic urban politics, the outbreak was signalled by the appearance of Persian 'placards' and Hindi and Urdu proclamations urging the citizens to murder Europeans.[42] Alongside anti-British news-papers, the whole panoply of indigenous written communication – akhbarats, *charitas*, *parwanas*, *roznamachas* and the like – were employed to spread the message of revolt and the restoration of the authority of the King of Awadh. Throughout its career the rebel government of Lucknow, supported by its own writers and munshis, kept meticulous records, some of which were later produced in British courts during the prosecution of the rebels. The Awadh leaders, however, used the printing press: the most important proclamation of early August 1857 was lithographed.[43] The court also put into effect vigorous counter-

---

[38] The *Dilhi Urdu Akhbar* and *Akhbar-us Zafar* continued to publish in the rebel interest from Delhi until the late summer of 1857.
[39] 'Trial of King of Delhi', 120–31.
[40] S.A.A. Rizvi and D.P. Bhargava (eds.), *History of the Freedom Movement in U.P.* (Lucknow, 1957–9), IV, 20.
[41] ibid., IV, 45–6.   [42] ibid., II, 5.   [43] ibid., II, 121–2.

intelligence measures, rounding up 'half-castes, Christians, spies and [British] Govt. servants',[44] and restoring the royal harkara system.

These measures were draconian, though not so in comparison with those reportedly taken at Kanpur by the Nana Sahib (the aspirant Peshwa) who executed 'spies', merchants and Bengalis who had communicated with the British and who was said to have ordered that 'every individual who could read and write English, should have their right hands and noses cut off'.[45] It was perhaps the memory of this which caused one enraged army officer to denounce a missionary educationist, shortly after the Rebellion with the words 'What the [Devil] is the good of teaching the niggers, Sir? You taught Nana Sahib, you did, and he learned to read French novels and to cut our throats.'[46] Like the Awadh ruler, Nana Sahib had also moved quickly to send royal proclamations and letters to government servants and magnates in British-held territories commanding their obedience.[47]

Agra, by contrast, was held against the surrounding rebels, as the third, but weakest link in the embattled chain of British redoubts. Here the fear of seditious communication among Muslims became particularly feverish during the summer of 1857. Here, too, the British were put at a severe disadvantage by their own media. News of the Meerut revolt was published in the British and Indian newspapers the day after it occurred.[48] It quickly reached troops in the vicinity of Agra who began to mutiny as soon as the fall of Delhi became general knowledge. The 'baser classes' were soon running riot on the outskirts of the city, though the British were able to maintain a semblance of control through the efforts of 'men of property', notably Tori Mull the military contractor for the Sikh wars.[49] It becomes clear that in the first two months of the Rebellion the British in Agra were totally starved of information. What E.A. Reade called 'mussulmanophobia' swept the station; it was reportedly cultivated by Eurasian clerks who had been prosecuted for debt by the Muslim judge (Principal Sadar Amin) of the city.[50] The Magistrate, R. Drummond, had relied on 'respectable Mahometans for information and advice' and employed them 'almost exclusively' in the police and civil offices.[51] These people were caught between the British

[44] ibid., II, 111.   [45] ibid., IV, 588.
[46] E. Arnold, *Education in India. A Letter from the Ex-principal of an Indian Government College* (London, 1860), p. 8.
[47] Thanadar Mahommed Jaffar to Gen. Keith, 21 Sept. 1857, Bruce Add. 43,996, ff. 121–8, BL.
[48] E.A. Reade to Canning, n.d. Sept. 1857, Reade Papers, 47, Mss. Eur. E123, OIOC.
[49] The major down-river merchant communities were singled out for coercion by the rebels.
[50] Minute by E.A. Reade, Agra, 29 Sept. 1857, Montgomery Papers, Mss. Eur. D1019/3, 135, OIOC.
[51] W. Muir, *Records of the Intelligence Department of the Government of the North-West Provinces of India during the Mutiny of 1857* (Edinburgh, 1902), I, 12.

and popular Muslim resistance. When a few gentry members and numerous ordinary policemen joined the Rebellion, Drummond joined his hate-crazed compatriots and dismissed those few Muslims who had not already absconded, thus destroying his whole information system.[52] Colvin, the Lieutenant-Governor, added to the chaos by replacing Muslims with Hindus in what remained of the provincial administration.

The rebels, advancing from the south, would certainly have taken the Agra fort had they not run out of powder. The Europeans and Eurasians cowered inside its walls, loosing off volleys at shadowy enemies, and were not even aware of the rebels' withdrawal. One of the few positive measures taken at this time was the removal by Reade of the government printing presses from the orphanage at Secundera and his rescue of the 'record of rights', the painfully acquired register of properties which a generation of officials had been assembling.[53] In most stations the mutineers destroyed printing presses along with office records, which they regarded as vital tools of British oppression.

By late August 1857, the Agra authorities began to get the situation under control. A small Intelligence Department was formed under William Muir.[54] This employed a 'large body of well paid and confidential agents' who scouted enemy lines and maintained the links between the forces advancing on Kanpur and the British force besieging Delhi. The first harkara message from Havelock in Kanpur was received on 17 July. But for months the only regular postal correspondence between Britain and Agra was through Rajasthan and Bombay. Muir's job was to prepare daily diaries of intelligence for Colvin and, after Colvin's death from 'apoplexy', for E.A. Reade who became Acting Lieutenant-Governor. He also prepared daily bulletins of mutiny events which were printed and posted round the station to counter the spate of rumours initiated by rebel sympathisers. In addition to spy reports, Muir read the 'Lucknow Urdu paper'.[55] This may have been the *Tilism* ('Magic'), a lithographed newspaper connected with the famous Muslim seminary at Firangi Mahal which continued to publish in the interests of the insurgents during the revolt. His most important source, however, was more traditional. This was the Gwalior newswriter in Delhi whose newsletters were passed on to Agra by the British Resident in Gwalior. Muir recorded that these reports gradually became more truthful.[56] As the Delhi siege proceeded, the akhbarats began to report the British capture of major strongpoints, even though it gloried in the casualties inflicted on the besieging troops. From time to time the British even fed

[52] ibid., I, 13.   [53] Minute by E.A. Reade, 29 Sept. 1857, Montgomery Papers.
[54] Muir, *Records*, I, 16–17; Reade to Canning, 10, 21 Sept. 1857, Mss. Eur. E123; Reade
      to Kaye, 21 April 1874, Mss. Eur. E124, no. 288, Reade Papers, OIOC.
[55] Muir, *Records*, I, 24.   [56] ibid., 97–8.

information into the newsletters themselves in an attempt to undermine rebel morale.[57]

Muir typified the overlap between political surveillance and orientalism. Brother of John Muir of the Sanskrit College of Banaras, he was something of a scholar himself, like many colonial intelligence officials. Before the Rebellion he had kept a weather eye on the doings of the purist Muslims which he interpreted in an insightful, if not sympathetic way. He resisted 'mussulmanophobia' during and after the war. Consequently, it is rather disappointing to find him later writing in such a bland and unreflective way on Islam in his *Mahomet and Islam*, a work which recycled the usual Christian charges of tyranny against the Prophet. It also made the strange assertion that unlike flexible Christianity, Islam was written in stone and had made no attempt to change and develop since the death of the Prophet,[58] a charge that his own official writings and observations of Sufism, syncretism and the emergence of purism rendered absurd. Formal orientalist texts, particularly those of a popular nature, quite often failed to transmit the relatively complex understanding of men actually involved in the governance of India, and cultural historians should beware reading too much into them.

Muir's closest informant during the revolt was not, however, a Muslim but Chaube Ghyanshyam Das,[59] brother of Raja Jai Kishen Das who was later awarded a British honour. Theirs was a landlord family of eastern Hindustan which had served the government as officials for two generations. They were notably pious Hindus and it is possible that their conspicuous loyalty during 1857 was a consequence of the view, shared by the British, that the leaders of the Rebellion aimed to restore Muslim power.

A final dimension of Muir's work highlights the strongly ideological, even irrational, aspects of information collection which the British so often represented as scientific. At the height of the revolt, and at the very time when the sepoys were advancing on Agra, the government tied up much manpower by instituting a detailed investigation into whether European women had been raped before being murdered by the rebels. In 1857, rape was a highly sensitive issue both in India and in Britain, and it bore directly on the honour of the imperial rulers. The report concluded that there was no evidence of rape.[60]

---

[57] ibid., 106–7.
[58] W. Muir, *Mahomet and Islam. A sketch of the Prophet's Life from original sources, and a brief outline of his religion.* (London, 1887: Religious Tracts Society), p. 266.
[59] Reade to Kaye, 21 April 1874, Reade Papers.
[60] Preserved in HM 724a, ff. 633–44, OIOC.

By the late summer of 1857 intelligence in the Agra sector was also being coordinated by Lieutenant Herbert Bruce, a veteran of the force which had pacified Sindh, and who became Inspector of Police in the NWP in May 1857.[61] Bruce's task was to rebuild communications outward from the capital. He was particularly charged with keeping track of General Havelock's small force pressing to relieve the embattled Lucknow Residency, which had rapidly lost touch with its base. Bruce received crucial help from Man Raj, a clerk in the nearby Etawah District Office who sent his own agents to spy on the rebel armies and kept notes on the plunder of villages by insurgents.[62] Man Raj was protected by Abbas Ali, subdivisional officer in the District, who intercepted Nana's letters to local landowners[63] and helped to keep the British lines of communications free.

From late August 1857, Bruce went on the offensive as the death-struggle around Delhi began. In consultation with Havelock, he drew up a petition which sought to convince the Lucknow rebels not to massacre the inhabitants of the Residency, should it fall. They were offered the choice between 'conciliation' or a 'war of extermination'.[64] An agent, Khageswara, was sent to Lucknow to post up the notice on the walls of certain houses. 'The people could not guess from where the papers issued...'[65] Here the British were seeking to turn the indigenous practice of placarding against their enemies. Meanwhile, Bruce was in touch with another sympathiser, Mirza Abbas Beg, who sent information on the position of rebel gun emplacements, and was the first to relay news of the death in the Lucknow Residency of Sir Henry Lawrence to the outside world.[66]

A further figure who emerged as an intelligence expert during the rebellion was Major W.S.R. Hodson.[67] He was appointed Assistant Quartermaster General in charge of the Intelligence Department and helped coordinate the effort against the rebel army in Delhi during the summer of 1857. Hodson also worked with the Agra authorities to keep the dak running between the Punjab and the east.[68] As late as August 1857, it was still being interrupted, its runners being murdered on the road by rebel picquets and reconnaissance patrols. Yet the first

[61] Kaye, *Indian Mutiny*, VI, 76, 78.
[62] Man Raj to Bruce, 9, 11 Sept. 1857, Bruce Add. 43,996, ff. 119–21, BL.
[63] Mahommed Jaffar to Genl Keith, 21 Sept. 1857, ibid., ff. 123–5.
[64] Proclamation, 26 Aug, 1857, Bruce Add. 43,996, f. 104, BL.
[65] 'Statement of Khagesoor', 23 Sept. 1857, ibid., f. 130.
[66] ibid., see the harkara letter in minute handwriting, ibid., f. 172.
[67] G.H. Hodson, *Twelve Years of Soldier's Life in India; being extracts from the letters of Major W.S.R. Hodson, B.A.* (London, 1859).
[68] ibid., pp. 199, ff.

intelligence out of Delhi itself came as early as 2 June, even before the siege had begun. As in the case of Muir's intelligence, the source was akhbarats from the newswriter of a small Indian state, here the Jhind Raj, a Sikh state located about one hundred miles from the capital. These were then copied to the British by G. Barnes, Commissioner of the Cis-Satlaj states.[69] This source continued to be used almost until the fall of Delhi. What is significant about it is that much of the information was apparently collected in the open court of the Emperor.[70] The rebel commanders evidently knew the identity of the Jhind Raja's newswriter and presumably they must have assumed that he would send on secret information, and that this would have a good chance of reaching the British enemy. People suspected as 'news-mongers' were taken and beaten nearly to death by sepoys; fifty Bengalis were said to have been incarcerated for having communicated with the British.[71] But the royal court did not take action against privileged newswriters, even in the death-throes of the Indian polity. The information about rebel positions which flowed out of Delhi gave the British a huge advantage, though the city would certainly have eventually fallen even without these failures of intelligence.

By mid-August Hodson and Montgomery had both set up more direct spy networks in Delhi. Hodson was aided by Maulvi Rajab Ali, the 'one-eyed maulvi'. This man was Henry Lawrence's confidential munshi throughout the early administration of the Punjab.[72] Hostility to the Sikhs appears to have motivated his early connection with the British. The information which came to Rajab Ali and Montgomery, direct from the city and via Jhind, was written in Urdu on small pieces of Indian paper which could be folded up and hidden in a stick or in clothing. Becoming more detailed by the week, they give a dramatic picture of the gradual eclipse of rebel hopes, though it must be said that the writers were aware of what their masters wanted to hear: 'the citizens pray anxiously for the return of British power' was a constant refrain.[73] Divisions within the rebel ranks were detailed alongside attempts to raise morale. The Emperor was said to be using the time-honoured method of speaking to his people by proclamation and corresponded with his erstwhile liegemen in Lucknow. He also wrote and circulated verses, though there were no mushairahs to recall the great days of the

---

[69] G.F. Barnes, Commr Cis-Sutledge Divn to Sec. Chief Commr Punjab, 2 June 1857, 'Reports of spies in Delhi during the siege of Delhi', Montgomery Papers, 3, 174–201, OIOC.

[70] Until the report of 6 Sept. by which time the 'Darbar had dissolved', ibid.

[71] 'Delhi News', 25 July 1857.

[72] Hodson, Hodson, p. 197; 'Delhi News', reports of spies, Montgomery Papers, 3.

[73] e.g., 'Delhi News', 20 Aug. 1857.

ecumene. One poem read ironically: 'I Zuffer ... will seize London for, after all what is the distance from Hindostan?'[74] The arts of astrology were also enlisted to steady the city. One Pandit Hari Chander was reported to be inciting rebels with 'his knowledge of the stars and the occult sciences'. He predicted that 'in this year the sepoys will rule over India'.[75] He urged that Tuesday 21 July should be the day for a mass attack on the British lines: 'The horses' hooves will be steeped in blood and the action will rival the great conflict of the Mahabharut', the famous mythological war. The newswriters further reported that 'native doctors', later joined by the western-trained Wazir Ali from Agra, were dressing the soldiers' wounds,[76] while Muslim holy warriors poured into the city from Tonk to the south and the Indian Pathan homelands to the north. These spies' reports record the last operations of the old information systems of harkara and newswriter. This was also to be the last occasion when the power-holders in Delhi would have recourse to astrology and indigenous medicine until after Independence in 1947.

Consideration of medicine and astrology takes us from issues of communication to issues of knowledge and ideology during the Rebellion. Evidently, this was a complex movement animated by many different arguments and emotions. Three positions, however, dominate the contemporary historical literature. First, Stokes and his followers assert that the Rebellion was essentially a mélange of rural revolts expressing little more than old rivalries deepened by economic stresses.[77] Secondly, historians influenced by the argument that societies are bound together by overarching values have favoured the view that the Rebellion was a legitimist movement responding to the violation of Indian kingship and, in particular, Mughal legitimacy by the British.[78] Thirdly, those who consider that the dominant feature of Indian colonial history was a prolonged resistance to British rule have stressed the rebels' determination to extirpate totally all traces of foreign domination.[79] All these positions have merit, but none of them has paid much attention to intellectual history or to the role of modes of communication, both of which were vital features of the Rebellion.

By examining the information order during the revolt this section has qualified the view that it was simply the 'last stand of the old order'. It has showed that a surprisingly modern battle over the press, posts, print

---

[74] 'Delhi News', 8 Aug. 1857.   [75] 'Newal Spy', 19 Jul. 1857.   [76] ibid.

[77] E.T. Stokes, The Peasant and the Raj (Cambridge, 1978); The Peasant Armed (Oxford, 1986); E.I. Brodkin, 'The struggle for succession. Rebels and loyalists in the Indian Rebellion of 1857', MAS, 6, 3, 1972, 277–90.

[78] F.W. Buckler, 'The political theory of the Indian Mutiny of 1857', Transactions of the Royal Historical Society, 4 series, 5, 1922, 71–100.

[79] R. Mukherjee, Awadh in Revolt, 1857–1858. A study of popular resistance (Delhi, 1984).

and opinion was at the heart of the struggle. Indian leaders showed no abhorrence for the new media when they could control and exploit them. Indians trained in British forms of administration in the army,[80] the administrative services, or even, in a few cases, as doctors, participated on the rebel side. The notion that the rebel leaders were 'feudals' needs to be qualified. Some of them had gone through an English education (even to the extent of reading French novels). Others had shown an interest in western media and ideas.[81] There is no reason why modernising Indian nobles should not have played the same role in the emergence of Indian nationalisms as they did across south-east Asia[82] had not their circumscribed independence been snuffed out by deposition and summary execution.

Though the records of the resisters have been destroyed what little has survived indicates that the Rebellion was also a battle of ideas, 'a mutiny of subordinated knowledges' to use Foucault's evocative phrase.[83] The Urdu pamphlet, 'Advice of the Royal Army' (mid-1857), brings together many of the themes found in proclamations or later expounded by the rebels at their summary trials.[84] It was supposedly written under the supervision of Kishori Lal Lahori and 'was completed in camp during all the confusion of a march and without having the proper printing materials at hand',[85] that is, it was envisaged as printed propaganda. The writer drew on many of the ideological themes of the ecumene. He showed that the Rebellion was foretold by a variety of signs and wonders which revealed that the body politic was diseased. The evidence was found in Sufi dreams, necromancy, analysis of the names of God and astrology.[86] As in most rebel proclamations, unemployment, insults to Indian rulers and to women, and the rise of 'low persons' under British tutelage were presented as causes of the revolt. However, much of the pamphlet concerns the clash of knowledges which we have considered in earlier chapters. European doctors were accused of polluting Indians with filthy treatments,[87] a complaint constantly heard in the bazaars in

[80] Cf. Tapti Roy, 'Visions of the Rebels: a study of 1857 in Bundelkhand', *MAS*, 27, 1, 1993, 205–28.

[81] e.g., *Benares Recorder*, 19 Nov. 1847 on 'hundreds of youths' from new educational institutions who translated mischievous English newspapers for 'Rajahs and Nuwabs'.

[82] The royal families of Yogyakarta and Sulu, for instance, remained important symbols for emerging Indonesian nationalism.

[83] M. Foucault, 'Two lectures' in N. Dirks, G. Eley and S. Ortner (eds.), *Culture/Power/History. A reader in contemporary social theory* (Princeton, 1994), p. 202.

[84] Summary trials, see also Montgomery Report, *Friend of India*, 22 Jan. 1859.

[85] HM 557, ff. 487–665. On the last page of the translation of the document, it is said to have been written 25 Muhurram 1273 Hijri (15 Sept. 1857).

[86] ibid., f. 599.

[87] ibid., f. 497, a doctor in Lucknow gargled and gave the 'filthy liquid' to a sepoy; polluted medicine, using pig fat, wine, etc. For earlier mentions of this theme, e.g.,

earlier years. Another grievance was that learned astrologers had been persecuted or ignored by the British. A story in the pamphlet has an astrologer correctly predicting the colour of a Collector's unborn foal.[88] When he goes on to predict the fall of the British Raj, asking 'Does the Kingdom belong to the natives of India?', he is unceremoniously hanged by the furious official. Again, the writer raged at the innovations stemming from printed tracts and public instruction. He asserts that children in government and mission schools were taught using books that would alienate them from the Prophet: 'in compiling and printing historical works they [the British] invariably selected such passages and stories as were calculated to bring contempt upon the Hindoo and Mahomedan religion'.[89] By contrast, the library in Moradabad which contained [Muslim] lawbooks for the guidance of the Magistrate was burned.[90] English mathematics replaced true religion; girl children were exposed to moral danger in these schools. Boys were expected to reveal the 'errors' of the Prophet. Indians, though, were 'writing back'. At Agra, the Revd C. Pfander had been refuted by Maulvi Rahmatullah[91] and a 'Babu' (Bengali) 'has composed a book in which he has collected one lack and fifty five thousand examples ... of their [British] treachery up to 1848'.[92] While it is startling to be informed that the Calcutta historical school was thriving so early, the broader point is that some of the rebels of 1857 had a world view and an understanding of the consequences for themselves of the information revolution of the early nineteenth century. It is not enough to regard this insurgency of subordinated knowledges as a throwback or the product of an irredeemably conservative society. As we have seen, astrology, medicine and indigenous debates on the rights and duties of government had flourished in the seventeenth and even eighteenth centuries.

Towards a security state? The post-Mutiny pacification

The experience of the Rebellion burned itself into the mind of Anglo-India and policies were evolved to keep a much closer watch on the movements and political opinions of Indians. Official and Anglo-Indian panics about seditious communication and 'native intelligence' were not damped down by the new security afforded by the railway or measures

Benares Recorder, 10 Sept., 14 Dec. 1847; or 'A Word for the Lahore Hakims', *Lahore Chronicle*, 21 Mar. 1857, where a 'respectable' hakim provides material to refute Anglo-Indian calumnies.

[88] 'Advice to Royal Army', f. 625.   [89] ibid., f. 497.   [90] ibid., f. 585.
[91] ibid., f. 505; on Rahmatullah, Powell, *Missionaries*, pp. 263–98.
[92] 'Advice to Royal Army', f. 493.

of control in Indian towns. If anything, the official response became more alarmist. As early as 1860, newly reconquered Lucknow was reported to be in revolt against local taxation.[93] The Anglo-Indian press reported on a campaign of placarding and abuse of Indian subordinate officials. To the consternation of the government, it also pointed to differences between local officers over how to handle the outbreak. Elsewhere, Sir Richard Temple was sniffing treason again as early as 1862. He thought that 'extraordinary exports of grain' from Jabalpur to Bundelkhand in the summer of that year pointed to 'some mischief'.[94] For the small states of Bundelkhand, which had rebelled in the 1840s and again in 1857, were 'a nest of disaffection' even though they were 'in the Lion's grip and surrounded by British troops'.[95] Police informers listened in the bazaars; police superintendents interrogated travelling grain merchants; two rajas were said to be 'enlisting men and harbouring dacoits' and might possibly 'try conclusions with us'.

Well into the 1860s the security services continued to hunt down rebels and their supporters who had gone to ground in sympathetic villages. These operations revealed that whole areas of the countryside remained outside British control. Robert Montgomery, who had been posted as Chief Commissioner of Oudh, attempted to bring Punjab methods of close control and good intelligence back into the still-disturbed territory where the colonial government was working without eyes and ears. The police had disintegrated over large areas of Hindustan and could not be relied on to aid in the discovery of rebels or arms. Montgomery was reduced to crude methods. Large rewards were given to informers or people who revealed the whereabouts of 'proclaimed offenders'.[96] It was suggested that officials should demand one weapon for each male and 'a double number from all Parsees [sic]'.[97] He meant not the merchant community of Bombay, but Pasis, a caste of marginal agriculturalists who were village watchmen but also implicated as 'criminal tribes' in the official mind. Offenders were publicly flogged.

Indian ignorance of the power of the conquerors redoubled the problem of bringing the revolt to a succesful end. For instance, the Raja of Kalakankar, a great landed magnate who had hedged his bets during the revolt, professed continuing loyalty to the Lucknow regime as late as

[93] Dty Supt Oudh Police to Asst Chief Police Lucknow, 14 Jul. 1860, Bruce, Add. 43,996, BL.
[94] R. Temple to G. Campbell, 11 June 1862, Richard Temple Papers, Mss. Eur. F86/50, OIOC.
[95] ibid.
[96] G. Hutchinson, notes on disarmament of Awadh, Montgomery Papers, Mss. Eur. D1019/4, OIOC.
[97] ibid.

September 1858. When secretly visiting a British official in that month, he remarked that he thought that the British would need French help to maintain their grip on India.[98] He surmised that the Indians would have to cede territory to the French, but that they would find the French a useful counterbalance to British power. Here was an Indian leader thinking in broad geopolitical terms, but pathetically ill-informed about military realities. More generally, however, it was the resolute hostility of much of the country which was the main problem faced by the returning British. A rebellious magnate of Azamgarh District, Sungram Singh, managed to hole up in villages across Jaunpur District, where the family had supporters, until 1862 when he was finally captured.[99] Twenty-one villages were punished by having extra police quartered on them, having maintained a three-year silence on Sungram's whereabouts. He was finally shopped by enemies among the local landlords. The Maharaja of Banaras and a rich banker, who both held estates in the District, forced their servants to give information to the police and the fugitive was captured.[100] In another incident, Neamat Ashraf, who had served as the Kotwal of Allahabad under the rebel Maulvi Liaqat Ali, hid for three years in a large village within ten miles of the city. Police informers finally tracked him down and the Head Constable of the subdivision was able to corner him using his contacts among the populace. Both men, it appears, were notable wrestlers and the Head Constable challenged Neamat Ashraf to a match in the compound of the sub-district office. The police officer, 'having got him within the walls, closed the doors and proclaimed him his prisoner'.[101] In an incident more reminiscent still of the Robin Hood legends, the village schoolmaster opened the compound doors and led a crowd of villagers to his rescue. Unfortunately for the romance of the story, Neamat Ashraf was mortally wounded in the affray which followed.

Post-Mutiny panics notwithstanding, the British moved slowly to try to establish a better-informed system of rural police. In the 1860s and 1870s attempts were made to professionalise the police, to unify it as an agency separate from the local Indian officials and to bring town and village watchmen establishments under their control. Numbers of rural police rose slowly throughout the latter part of the century,[102] but many

---

[98] Deputy Commr Partabgarh to Montgomery, 21 Sept. 1858, ibid.
[99] Offg Magt. Jaunpur, to Commr Banaras, 27 May 1862, NWP Police Procs., 30 Aug. 1862, 44, 235/51, OIOC.
[100] ibid.
[101] Inspector General Police to Govt NWP, 29 May 1862, Allahabad Divisional Report, NWP Police Procs., 20 Sept. 1862, 25, 235/51, OIOC.
[102] F. Robinson, 'Consultation and Control. The U.P. Government and its allies, 1860–1906', MAS, 5, 4, 1971, 313–36.

features of the old system remained. The 1860 'Report on Village Police in India' noted that the NWP police were largely ignorant of what was happening in the countryside. They 'know nothing unless they have some tolerably reliable agency in the village'. By comparison, the village watchmen (chaukidars, goraits, etc.) had 'a sort of knowledge and a sort of influence which no police agent could possess'.[103] For the foreseeable future, the government's criminal and political information systems in the countryside would continue to depend on an uneasy cooperation between the thinly-stretched constabulary and village officers who were under the influence of the landowners. The whole system collapsed, for example, when the watchmen staged a strike over pay or police intrusion and threw in their lot with local criminal gangs.[104] Very little information came into the diaries of the village police stations, especially in years like 1862, when bad seasons[105] put great economic pressures on the watch-and-ward agencies, and gang robbery revived. Informed opinion continued to assert that the bulk of minor crimes were compounded locally. Rather than informing the police, for instance, a man who suspected someone of cattle theft would have the animals traced by his private agents and would then hire a professional go-between (dalal) to confront the suspected criminals.[106] A large proportion of the value of the animals would be recovered, but absolutely nothing would have come to the notice of any official agency.

Historians have argued that the Raj of the later nineteenth century was becoming a kind of police state.[107] Certainly, numbers of police were going up. It would be wrong, however, to assume that the police became markedly more efficient. Successes were scored against major dacoit gangs and 'criminal tribes' were surrounded with rules and regulations, but much of the countryside remained out of the ken of officialdom. By the 1920s, the police and political authorities were claiming that the village headman and watchman system was disintegrating,[108] and that the rural society was lost to British control because they could no longer anticipate what would happen there. Despite the weight of revenue

---

[103] Police Committee, to Govt, 10 Dec. 1860, NWP Police Procs., Dec. 1860, 1–8, 235/47, OIOC.

[104] See, e.g., District Superintendant of Police to District Magistrate, Allahabad, 28 Jul. 1889, 209, basta 24b, file no. nil., Records of the Commissioner, Allahabad Division, Allahabad.

[105] IG Police to Govt, 29 May 1862, NWP Police Procs., 20 Sept. 1862, 25, 235/51, OIOC.

[106] Meerut Division Report, IG Police to Govt, 29 May 1862, ibid.

[107] D. Arnold, *Police Power and Colonial Rule. Madras 1859–1947* (Oxford, 1986), pp. 1–6, 230–6.

[108] G. Kudaisya, 'State power and the erosion of colonial authority in Uttar Pradesh, India, 1930–42' unpub. PhD thesis, Cambridge University, 1992.

records, one suspects that the British never really established close, centralised control over the countryside.

Where the authorities did gain a greater purchase on rural society it was less because of more effective government policy than because Indian society itself was slowly becoming more complex, literate and self-aware. Ultimately, it was social change which was to make the British more knowledgeable about their Indian Empire, but also more vulnerable to its internal lines of communication. The postal system evidently did improve at the sub-district level: 'a daily post now reaches every *thana* [village police post]' and 'it is wonderful how correspondence has increased under the new system', stated a senior official in 1866.[109] But he conceded that beyond the thana there was 'great delay and uncertainty', despite hopes for a bi-weekly post to every village. Villagers found it difficult to procure the cheap paper which incurred the lower postal charges.[110] Most letter writers were located in cities and towns. Villagers did not understand how to address letters. Local police and watchmen who delivered the letters from the thanas to the villages, true to their origin as information purveyors rather than mere 'police', levied exorbitant charges on the recipients.[111]

If, even in the deeper countryside, things were stirring, it was because of the slow changes in communication and mentalities brought about by the movement of Indian actors. Vernacular schools run by pandits or maulvis with a minimum of control from the Department of Education, became centres of communication, especially for printed media. Officers noticed that whereas newspapers were rarely seen in villages in the 1840s, by the 1870s, one could be found in most villages. They would be read out to groups of villagers by the schoolmaster or record-keeper, often under the tree at the centre of the village. The patterns of communication typical of the ecumene, which had once been a network for the cities and qasbahs, thus spread into the countryside. Commerce was also wreaking changes. With the development of railways and feeder roads, many more itinerant hawkers reached the bi-weekly village markets and fairs. They distributed cheap lithographic prints of deities and heroes, almanacs and medical recipes. As estates succumbed to rigorous commercial management and the Court of Wards developed, literate estate managers and land agents were to be found in many more villages. Most important, the rapid spread of litigation in the provinces

[109] Offg Sec. Bd of Rev. to Govt, 9 Jun. 1866, NWP General Procs., 30 Jun. 1866, 64, 438/28, OIOC.

[110] 'Abstract of replies recd fm various officers who have been consulted on the subject of revising the present collection of letters', ibid., no. 65.

[111] ibid.

after the Rebellion ensured that a large number of inferior district court pleaders (*mukhtars*) set up in large villages to capture the court cases which arose as the market for land began to develop. Mukhtars made a little money on the side by writing letters or petitions for villagers and providing them with paper.[112] What was happening here was a form of rural class-formation, but, as of old, class power was defined less by material resources than by access to written media, print and urban knowledge. These were communities of knowledgeable people who could act as an intellectual and moral leaven in the rural areas. They replaced the rural jurist (kazi) and registrar (kanungo) families which had comprised the rural literates of the earlier era, but were now increasingly destitute and ignorant of the urban culture to which they had once been linked.

It was the spread of these new knowledge communities which helped colonise the countryside for government and the urban elites. It was they who called in the police to major crimes and began to furnish the state with information about its hinterland through petitions, letters and district newspapers. Conversely, such men provided the rural links for movements which sought to bring the values of the towns to the populace. It was they who brought to the villages the publicists of anti-alcohol and anti-marriage-expenses movements. They linked together the princely and elite backers of the cow-protection societies of the 1880s with the peasant magnates who supported them. By the same token, however, they were also to be the key agents in the slow development of consciousness of wider national issues in the country-side.

Conclusions

Despite the many institutions which the British had established to enumerate and tabulate their Indian subjects and their resources, the Company's government was blown away by a concatenation of revolts which it had failed to predict. Individual leaders and communities which were thought to have benefited from British rule were often among the first to revolt. As with its Mughal forebears, the Company's sophisticated system of local intelligence fell apart quite quickly as key information brokers defected at village and district level. The British survived in part because they had the electric telegraph and could mobilise an international system of communications. Repairing the local networks took longer; and they often found themselves depending on those establish-

[112] Note by Dty Suptdt of Maharaja of Banaras's Family Domains, ibid.

ments of newswriters, scribes and runners which had first revealed the inwardness of the subcontinent to them. If, on the one hand, the British often relied on these older institutions, the rebels and their supporters, on the other hand, were by no means hostile to new modes of communication, if only they could maintain control of them. The press and the colonial post office helped give the Rebellion a shape which made it much more than a congeries of local mutinies and jacqueries. In this sense it looked forward to the nationalist era when control of communications and the capacity to form public knowledge bulked even larger.

10 Epilogue: information, surveillance and the public arena after the Rebellion

The Rebellion was catalyst to many changes which decisively reshaped the information order of colonial north India in the later nineteenth century. It brought about a rapid expansion of the railway network and telegraphic communications. There was a sharp increase in numbers of European military and non-official personnel, followed by Bengali commissariat contractors, wholesale merchants and attorneys, in the cities of the Gangetic plains. This encouraged the English-educated to establish a new range of libraries, educational institutions and public bodies in the cities of the Gangetic plains. The huge internal market of the 'bookwallah' was galvanised by a slow but steady expansion of English and Hindi literacy. All this, in turn, brought more travellers, new commerce and new disruption to the inland market villages. Kaye believed that the 'prodigious triumphs over time and space'[1] represented by the new communications caused the 'Hindu hierarchy to lose half its power';[2] and it is true that the tide of change forced both an abrupt spread of scientific modernism and the rearmament of social conservatism with new methods of publicity and persuasion. Ironically, though, it was the British 'hierarchy' which was in danger of losing 'half its power' to control the direction and political import of the evolving information order. The invigorated Indian press and new-style Indian publicists and social reformers began to outflank the British rulers as innovators in the public arena. They could draw on the skills, connections and forensic techniques of the older ecumene, while at the same time projecting their personalities and ideologies through the printed media and at public meetings. 'Colonial knowledge' of Indian society, always partial and contradictory, now struggled to keep abreast of dynamic developments in elite politics and popular culture.

Superficially, the colonial order emerged strengthened from the ordeal of 1857. The British certainly reinforced their physical control over the towns in the wake of the Rebellion and put in place new

---

[1] Kaye, *Indian Mutiny*, I, 138.   [2] ibid., I, 141.

methods of formal and informal surveillance. Large British forces were quartered in the newly constructed cantonments to protect the European residents. Within twenty years of the pacification urban policing was fairly uniform, although some police establishments betrayed their heterogeneous origins. The relatively modern commercial centre of Mirzapur, for example, had four times the number of constables in the 1860s as did the older pre-British city of Bareilly, where descendants of the eighteenth-century Pathan rulers had continued to run their own police force up to the Rebellion.[3] Nevertheless, in spite of local variations, by the 1860s, most district superintendents of police had effective systems of spies and informers which they used to contain urban robberies, grain riots and outbreaks of sectarian violence during festivals.[4] Magistrates took care to enlist propertied men into the new system of honorary magistracies[5] because wealthy people, especially the trading classes, had generally sided with the British or at least hedged their bets in 1857. Officials had come to believe that pre-Rebellion government had been too official in character; now they regularly consulted 'natural leaders of the people' in local durbars and on expanded municipal boards. The mechanisms of the Court of Wards and the ever more refined systems of rent-rate reporting and revenue settlement also afforded officials increased opportunities for consulting with men of power at estate and village level.

In practice, these mechanisms of consultation were only partly successful in bringing information to collectors and magistrates, and did not always forewarn them of likely breaches of the peace. *Rais*s, or 'men of local influence', were hesitant about compromising their status by too closely associating with officials. For their part, the prejudices of the British against indigenous religious and cultural institutions caused them to exclude well-informed people from the process of consultation. For example, they paid scant attention to priests who controlled bathing festivals or the owners of religious guest houses and this undermined attempts to improve the organisation of pilgrimages and local hygiene.[6] It also allowed new public bodies avowedly working in the Hindu interest to capitalise on discontent and build constituencies. In general, Sufi religious leaders, networks of mosque preachers, temples and monasteries became even more marginal to the British

---

[3] Pres. Municipal Committee Shahjehanpur to Offg Commr Rohilkhand, 10 Jun. 1869, NWP General Procs., 10 Jun. 1870, 226, 438/35, OIOC.

[4] P. McGinn, 'Governance and resistance in north Indian towns, *c.* 1860–1900', unpub. PhD thesis, Cambridge University, 1993.

[5] Robinson, 'Consultation and Control', *MAS*, 5, 4, 1971, 313–36.

[6] K. Prior, 'British administration of Hinduism in north India', 1780–1990', unpub. PhD thesis, Cambridge University, 1990, pp. 195–203.

system than they had been under the Company. This was dangerous, because, regardless of the expansion of the English educated professional class, these institutions remained important focusses of political activity and communication within the ecumene which, though weakened by sharpened distinctions of caste, religion and education, survived on in atrophied form as a network of communication and affective knowledge.

The British surveillance of print

The real struggle was now over the formation of opinion, though few officials could yet see it. One of the skills of the new generation of publicists and the rapidly expanding vernacular press was an ability to link together the older institutions of social communication with the newer associations and urban societies which had sprung up in the NWP among the first generation of English-educated people and the expatriate Bengali population. The British were in two minds about the press. On the one hand, they were still hopeful of using it to gain insights into Indian opinion and spreading western 'enlightenment'. On the other hand, they were now much more suspicious of its potential for sedition. The favour with which Indian newspapers had been viewed in Bentinck's time as disseminators of useful information had evaporated during the Rebellion. Many editors in north India were suspected of sympathy with the rebels and their sour criticism of the authorities throughout the fighting was generally regarded as bordering on sedition.

During the twenty years following the Rebellion, direct attacks on the government in Indian newspapers were rare. Indeed, those implicated in the Muslim purist movement or so-called 'Wahhabi conspiracy' based in Patna used handwritten media to communicate with each other, partly because they feared press censorship.[7] The government, however, remained alert to the danger which the threat was thought to pose to the public peace and public morals. Sectarian battles between modernist and traditionalist Muslims, Sunnis and Shias, and between Ahmadiya and orthodox, were carried out with the greatest violence in the printed media; in these campaigns glancing blows were struck against British rule and western civilisation. The authorities also believed sedition and immorality were linked. They clamped down harshly on 'indelicate' and 'obscene' publications. Remarking on the publication of two 'obscene' books by an Agra press, the Director of Public Instruction stated in

---

[7]   P. Robb, 'The impact of British rule on religious community: reflections on the trial of Maulvi Ahmadullah of Patna in 1865', in Robb (ed.), *Society and Ideology*, pp. 142–76.

1870[8] that such material 'arms the native mind against female education' and 'poisons the mind of youths in the large towns'. He added that for every 'one who reads the cheap trash at nine annas per copy there are hundreds who hear the libidinous suggestions and allusions'. Towards these productions, and others in English or Indian languages which urged sedition, the policy should be 'Parisian', that was one of full censorship. The DPI sometimes complained that Indian editors were not cooperative in informing on their peers who published indelicate or obscene material; this was possibly because British prudery extended to innocuous love stories.[9] Popular erotic literature was as important as religious controversy in keeping the press solvent.

Too heavy censorship would, by contrast, deny useful information to the people and to the government: the DPI remarked that the 'naturalness of the Native Press forms its chief value to the state as an indication of public sentiment, so long as it is carefully watched and judiciously fathomed and reported by the Reporter [on native newspapers]'.[10] This argument was ingeniously used by Indian editors seeking to prove their usefulness and loyalty. One remarked that the press was now like the akhbar naviss of the past, who brought essential news to the ruler, even if it proved unwelcome.[11] The press certainly began to take on some of the functions of the circular letter or *fatwa* in religious disputes after 1850.[12]

In order to limit possible danger from the press without completely hamstringing it, the government introduced a series of severe but flexible controls. Editors were subject to the forfeit of large deposits if they went wrong.[13] Surveillance of vernacular newspapers was increased, with the Reporter on the Native Press making regular weekly extracts from newspaper comment on political, religious and social matters. These extracts were circulated to civil officials and the police. Newspaper surveillance was gradually withdrawn from the Department of Public Instruction, where it had originated, into the realm of political surveillance and counter-intelligence.

Officials were even more ambivalent about the value of entering the public arena directly by sponsoring editors or newspapers. They made

[8] Director Public Instruction to Govt, 18 Feb. 1870, NWP General Procs., 19 Mar. 1870, 63–5, 438/35, OIOC.
[9] ibid.
[10] Director, Public Instruction to Government, 23 Feb. 1875, NWP General Procs., April 1875, 5–8, vol. [P] 54.
[11] *Nur-ul-Absar* (Allahabad), 15 Jun. 1870, NWP Native Newspaper Reports, 1870, p. 245, OIOC.
[12] S. Lavan, *The Ahmadiyah Movement. A History and Perspective* (Delhi, 1974).
[13] N. Barrier, *Banned. Controversial literature and political control in British India, 1907–47* (Delhi, 1976), pp. 1–6; J. Natarajan, *History of Indian Journalism* (Delhi, 1955).

some efforts to use the patronage of the Education Department to reward and punish editors. The loss of a hundred guaranteed sales to the Department could make the difference between success and failure for a struggling broadsheet. On the other hand, sponsored newspapers were not necessarily successful. For example, Munshi Sadha Sukh Lal, a loyalist who managed what officials thought was the 'best-run news-paper', was firmly rejected by the Indian public.[14] The government said this was because his newspaper was 'revolutionary of the old ideas', but it was really because Sadha Sukh Lal had been appointed Chief Government Translator and, playing a part in monitoring the press himself, he was regarded as a turncoat.

A few officials, who saw how politically important the press was becoming, urged a more active role on the government. A.O. Hume, future founder of the Indian National Congress, thought officials should carry out an active propaganda war on behalf of British rule. Govern-ment should be based on 'the will of the majority' and 'the disregard of this principle was the ultimate source of the Mutiny'.[15] Government, however, could also mould that will. In 1863 Hume founded, with the aid of Kunwar Lachman Singh, an important native informant of Bulandshahar and early writer of Hindi prose,[16] The People's Friend which was soon circulating hundreds of miles from its Etawah base. With experience of the Rebellion fresh in his mind, Hume saw the need for a 'loyal, sensible and moral vernacular newspaper' to oppose the 'lying calumnies or shameless misrepresentations' circulated by the disaffected. These had been notable 'from the very outset of the late disturbances (contradicted at most by a government Proclamation, that not one in a hundred saw and no one believed)'.[17] Hume's publication plans fitted in with his general interest in popular education as a means of counteracting anti-colonial sentiment and fostering populist empire loyalism. He urged heavy local investment in schools, paying careful attention to the deliberations of municipal bodies and the founding of useful agricultural fairs.[18] Unsurprisingly, Hume's popular imperialism never took root. His demands that The People's Friend should be seen and approved by Queen Victoria smacked of presumption, and the Lieutenant-Governor tartly observed that he hoped that the newspaper

14   Director Public Instruction to Sec. Govt NWP, 22 Feb. 1864, NWP Genl Procs., 10 Jun. 1865, 162, 216/19, OIOC.
15   A.O. Hume, Chairman Municipal Cttee Etawah to Commr Agra, 24 Sept. 1864, NWP Genl Procs., 28 Jan. 1865, 106, 216/19 OIOC.
16   K.L. Singh, A Historical and Statistical Memoir of Zila Bulandshahar (Allahabad, 1874).
17   A.O. Hume, Magt. Etawah, to Sec. Govt NWP, 10 Jan. 1861, NWP Genl Procs., 26 Jan. 1861, 55 and 56, 216/4.
18   See NWP Genl Procs., 26 May 1866, 125–45, 438/27.

would also be 'the government's friend'.[19] Ironically, Hume also fell victim to a petitioning campaign against him by some Etawah residents who disliked his judgement in a property case. While enraged that the complainants had gone over his head to the Commissioner, he gamely wrote 'The power of petitioning at once to higher authorities is a most invaluable check on the great and perhaps not always wisely exercised powers of the district officer.' He thought the greatest triumph for an Indian besides winning a case was to say in the bazaar: 'Humare mokuddumah men Lat Sahib ne Collector Sahib se jawab talab ki' ('In my case the Lieutenant-Governor ordered an answer from the Collector Sahib').[20] Caught between a swell of popular sentiment, now empowered by the mass media, and a government which stood above the battle of opinion but tried ineffectually to suppress it, Hume ultimately abandoned his official position in order to help articulate that popular sentiment more clearly through national political associations.

Social communication and the expansion of the Indian press

Whatever officials tried to do, by the mid-1860s the Indian press and other internal lines of communication were increasingly running out of the government's control. The power of the publicist and newspaper proprietor was manifest years before formal nationalist organisations began to emerge. The new generation of pleaders, mukhtars and schoolmasters in town and country afforced the lively debates of the ecumene with new tools of publicity. As early as 1865, an official wrote that 'Rich natives now make handsome presents to the editors of Native papers, as well as subscribe for their publications, and the sense of their editorial power is increasing.'[21] George Grierson, the scholar of Indian languages, put it in similar terms: 'there is now scarcely a town of importance which does not possess its printing-press or two. Every scribbler can now see his writings in type or lithographed for a few rupees, and too often he avails himself of the power and the opportunity.'[22] The range and self-sufficiency of Indian printed media was deepening. Whereas the press of Bentinck's time and the schoolbooks of Raja Shiva Prasad's early experiments in the 1850s had often been translations of English or Bengali newspapers and books, most printed

[19] Remarks on Hume to Govt, 10 Jan. 1861, NWP Genl Procs., 26 Jan. 1861, 55 and 56, 216/4.
[20] Hume to Commr Agra, 24 Jan. 1865, NWP Genl Procs., 3 Jun. 1865, 150, 216/19.
[21] Director Public Instruction to Govt, 22 Feb. 1864, NWP Genl Procs., 10 Jun. 1865, 162, 216/19.
[22] G.A. Grierson, *Vernacular Literature*, p. 145.

works were now original publications. In the 1820s it had been only the Maharaja of Banaras and a few other princes who could afford to print copies of the Ramayana and Hindi religious works. Now small towns and large villages boasted their own presses. In 1870, for instance, it was reported that Thakur Girpershad of Beswan village in Aligarh District had 'established a press in a village, and busies himself in the publication of editions of Bhasha [i.e. Hindi] versions of Sanskrit works'.[23] Girpershad professed his aim was the revival of 'the old Hindoo religion in its integrity', but, publishing for a voracious market in religious books, he also turned out thousands of copies of the Puranas despite his aversion to post-vedic Hinduism.

The Indian press, bookseller and publicist were able to use those deeply recessed lines of communication within society and religion to which the colonial authorities had only minimal access. This explains the apparent puzzle that political print culture and pressure-group politics took off so rapidly after 1860 in a society which was still generating only very slow economic growth. In fact, the new media and interests expanded along the older networks of the ecumene. Newspapers such as the *Hindi Pradipa* and *Bharat Jiwan* seem on the surface to resemble their Anglo-Indian contemporaries. They reported on prices, the peregrinations of the Viceroy and on foreign affairs. Slyly, they also reported on 'panics' among the European residents, concerning supposed links between the Russians and dissident Indian princes[24] in much the same way as the older Anglo-Indian papers used to report 'wild rumours' amongst the natives.

The Indian editors, however, were able to tap into networks which were largely inaccessible both to the government and to Anglo-Indian editors. Many of their reports were picked up through marriage connections; others from the reports of the yet larger numbers of pilgrims coming into Banaras and Allahabad by railway. Acts of public charity, such as the feeding of the poor, Brahmins and cows, were heavily represented in their columns, but so too was a more modern form of charity, the subscription movements initiated by wealthy people to respond to famines in distant parts of India.[25] The press was, indeed, discovering India. It was a discovery powerfully reinforced by those inherent links of social communication embodied in the virtues of *shadi* (marriage), *dan* (pious donation) and *yatra* (pilgrimage). If the 'pure

---

[23] Director Public Instruction to Govt, 18 Feb. 1870, NWP General Procs., 19 Mar. 1870, 63–5, 438/35.

[24] *Hindi Pradipa*, 1 Sept. 1877; *Rohilkhand Akhbar*, 11 July 1868, NWPNNR, 1868, 364–5.

[25] 'Famine in Madras', *Hindi Pradipa*, 1 Oct. 1877.

Hindi' language of these newspapers was 'artificial' as critics such as Grierson claimed, it must also be acknowledged that it created a definite sense of the unity of culture and territory which was ultimately Hindu.[26] Hindustan in these consciously Hindi newspapers became 'Bharat Varsh'.

Caste was one pillar of this reinvigorated culture of communication. In the 1860s, before Indians began to probe the statistical and moral health of the wider national community, publicists had begun to report in print on their own communities. Caste associations developed in many cities; lecturers using the printing press, the railway and the community meeting again built on older patterns of commensality and marriage. Some historians have argued that these emerging caste movements were a direct reaction to official census activities; that is latent 'communities' responded to government intervention by organising in the public arena to preserve their status. Government action often acted as a catalyst, but internal divisions over the status of community leaders, marriage and morality were already forging new alliances and organisations independently of the intervention of government. It was the post and the printed media rather than the state which facilitated new links and revivified old ones. Even quite humble caste councils (*panchayats*) already used the 'technology of the list', the signature of the family head and forms of publicity in more localised decision-making. Their counsels were now widened in scope and recorded in print. One feature of the campaign of the Kayastha reformer Munshi Pyare Lal, for instance, was the way in which his lecture tours against expensive marriages produced directories of leading Kayastha elders in different towns and sub-divisions of Bihar and the North-Western Provinces.[27]

It was only a brief step further for the vernacular newspapers to turn the technique of community surveillance back on its British authors. The relations between communities became as contested an issue as the meaning of community itself. Large numbers of articles in the early Hindi newspapers dwelt on the balance between Hindus and Muslims, Bengalis and upper Indian Kayasthas, Brahmins and commercial people, in the expanding government offices. These 'Indian statistics' were used to argue for new positions and for preferential treatment.[28]

[26] ibid. The Hindu tone of this newspaper and the *Bharat Jiwan* (Banaras) was reinforced by the publication of pieces of translated Sanskrit religious works, religious sermons; *Hindi Pradipa*, 1 Dec. 1877, uses the word *jati* (race or genus) to distinguish Hindus from others (Christians, Muslims, etc.), '*kisi aur jati*'.

[27] *Paddhati vivaha ki* (Marriage Rules adopted by the Kayasthas of Allahabad) (Allahabad, 1870), contains lists of family heads who subscribed, pp. 55–65.

[28] e.g. a leader on 'Hindus and Government service in the North-Western Provinces', *Hindi Pradipa*, 1 Dec. 1877.

The rise of the public man

Many features of the rapid development of the public arena after 1857 were reflected in the contrasting careers of the two foremost men of letters in contemporary north India: Raja Shiva Prasad and Bhartendu Harishchandra. Harishchandra, hero of the Hindi movement, has tended to overshadow his loyalist rival, but the political influence of Shiva Prasad was much greater in his lifetime. We have already encountered Shiva Prasad as one of the 'new munshis' of the Thomason era. Beginning as vakil and native informant, his English education qualified him as most senior Indian player in the 'useful knowledge' movement.[29] As Inspector in the Department of Public Instruction (1856) he had a formative influence on the syllabus of district- and sub-district level schools in the North-Western Provinces. A Jain and mercantile background moulded his vision of a charitable public Hindu Dharma in which blemishes such as child marriage and infanticide were to be erased, and Hindu belief and practice would be standardised into a system similar to Christianity or Islam. He wrote or translated more than thirty works many of which were produced under the auspices of the Department of Public Instruction or with the patronage of British officials.[30] Association with the British led him to a loyalist stance and he was eventually to denounce the Indian National Congress.[31] Although privileged, he was far from being a typical landed reactionary; he came from the Jagat Seth mercantile family and his great-grandmother was a noted poetess.[32] Shiva Prasad was a self-created man of publicity whose status as a native informant and opinion-maker resulted from his exceptionally wide contacts. The family's Bengali interests acquainted him with the new literature in that language, but he was also a good scholar of Persian and Sanskrit. It is interesting that though he aimed for a high and somewhat formal style of Hinduism (he translated the 'Laws of Manu' into Hindi, for instance), his plan for a unified north Indian language was much less purist. Here he argued for a 'Hindustani' which would draw on 'the colloquial speech of Agra, Dilli and Lacknau, or of Hindustan proper, midway between the Persian-ridden Urdu and the Sanskrit-ridden Hindi'.[33] Shiva Prasad's interest in promoting a popular Hindustani language was shared by many British officials, but not by the cultural revivalists among his Banaras contemporaries. The newspaper

[29] See above, pp. 234–5.   [30] Grierson, *Vernacular Literature*, pp. 150–2.
[31] J. Lutt, *Hindu Nationalismus in Uttar Prades, 1867–1900* (Stuttgart, 1970), pp. 131–2, cf., 53–64.
[32] K. Sajun Lal, 'Rajah Shiv Pershad. Early Life and Career', *Indica*, p. 351.
[33] Grierson, *Vernacular Literature*, p. 148.

Sudhakar, founded in 1847, was a response from the champions of 'pure' Hindi to an Urdu newspaper produced by Tara Mohan Mittra under Shiva Prasad's patronage.[34]

In many ways Harishchandra's background was similar to Shiva Prasad's. He was drawn from the aristocratic mercantile elite of Banaras and his father had also been a significant poet, like Shiva Prasad's great-grandmother.[35] While Shiva Prasad became a public educator, Harishchandra became a public poet and litterateur through the medium of the press. In the old north Indian ecumene literary excellence had been judged by circles of poets in mushairahs and their Hindi equivalents, by the plaudits of princes and by inclusion in the written anthologies of great verse which were circulated among learned families. By contrast, Harishchandra promoted himself and his poetry through his journal *Harishchandra Chandrika*. In 1880, a group of Indian literati, led by a Calcutta editor, formally conferred on him the 'title' of *Bharatendu*, or 'Moon of India', which had apparently once been given to him as a joke.[36] The 'title' carried the ironic implication that Harishchandra was being promoted as a rival and people's champion against the loyalist Shiva Prasad who had been awarded the title of 'Sitara-i-Hind' (Star of India) by the British.[37] Harishchandra advertised himself as a cultural iconoclast as well as a popular champion. His life-style was calculated to subvert the norms of methodical and sober Vaishnavism which had distinguished his merchant ancestors.[38] He was fatally liberal with money and friendship, eating betel nut to excess until he smelled like a *pan* tree. He consorted with dancing girls and Muslim women. He was attempting to represent himself as a new type of Indian public man, to stand comparison with European public men of the modern era. He displayed a sustained interest in 'great men' in his *Prasidh Mahatmaon ka Jivan Charitra* ('The Lives of Famous Great Souls'), and magazine articles;[39] his subjects ranged from great Hindu poets and philosophers such as Kalidasa and Shankaracharya to Socrates and Napoleon III.

In his journalism and literary work Harishchandra also drew on a wide range of the specialist knowledges of north India which officials found difficult to penetrate. His newspaper, *Kavi Vachan Sudha*, like other

---

[34] Madan Gopal, *Bhartendu Harishchandra* (Delhi, 1971), p. 21; Lutt, *Nationalismus*, pp. 65–98; Sudhir Chandra, *The Oppresive Present: literature and social consciousness in colonial India* (Delhi, 1992).

[35] Gopal, *Harishchandra*, pp. 6–7; *LH*, II, 577–8.

[36] Gopal, *Harishchandra*, p. 15; Vrajratnadas, *Bhartendu Harishchandra* (Allahabad, 1962), p. 114.

[37] Gopal, *Harishchandra*, p.15.   [38] Bayly, *Rulers*, pp. 453–5.

[39] Published, Banaras, 1882.

newspapers of the period,[40] maintained networks of contacts who were called sub-editors. It is said that the founder of the Arya Samaj, Swami Dayananda Saraswati, was a sub-editor at one period.[41] A pilgrimage to Jagannath-Puri in Orissa had introduced Harishchandra to some leading figures of the Bengali literary renaissance who kept him informed of developments there.[42] As a Vaishnavite devotee (bhakta), he wrote regularly to Radhacharan Goswami of Brindaban,[43] a leading Gosain. His literary works reveal the influence of writers located in the small court centres which had continued to nurture the prose and poetry of proto-Hindi through the days of the supremacy of Persianised Urdu. At the same time, Harishchandra's Urdu and Persian were good, and he frequently borrowed both from Persian classics and from Urdu periodicals and newspapers. His dancing-girl mistress, Ali Jan, was a Muslim convert, though he later 'reconverted' her to Hinduism.[44] Harishchandra was equally well versed in British orientalism and Anglo-Indian journalism. His essays on social themes draw on nineteenth-century British historians and orientalists.[45] He appears to have known the linguist, George Grierson.[46] In the later years of his short life, Harishchandra's house at Chaukhambha in Banaras resembled a kind of court to which large numbers of literary and cultural specialists repaired. He interrogated bards and musicians about their songs,[47] genealogical priests about their family histories,[48] pilgrims about their home towns. He was particularly interested in the knowledge that women swapped in their quarters and private social gatherings. The poetic and literary society the Tadiya Samaj,[49] which he held in his house, represented a compromise between the old majliss (councils) and mushairahs (poetry meetings) of the ecumene and a western debating society.

Harishchandra's books reflect this extraordinary and eclectic discovery of India. Works of precise European and Muslim historical scholarship and analyses of ancient charitable grants are put side by side with quotations from the Puranas and his own poetry.[50] The horoscopes of 'great men' are analysed in detail. Again, though Harishchandra held

---

[40] Surendra Gopal, *Patna in the Nineteenth Century* (Calcutta, 1982), p. 73.
[41] Gopal, *Harishchandra*, p. 38.   [42] ibid., pp. 10, 28.
[43] ibid., p. 24.   [44] ibid., p. 14.
[45] e.g., Vrajratnadas (ed.) *Bhartendu Granthavali* (Banaras, 1953), III, 128–9, Grote and Cunningham, and Buchanan, 131; or his '*Udaipurodaya*', 220–33, which uses Tod, *Bombay Journal*, and translates the feudal system as *sainik niyam*.
[46] Grierson, *Vernacular Literature*, p. 124.   [47] Gopal, *Harishchandra*, 22–3.
[48] ibid.
[49] Proceedings of the Samaj, microfilm in author's possession.
[50] This is particularly true in his essays on castes, e.g., *Granthavali*, III, 7–12 ('*Agravalon ki utpatti*'), ibid., 246–54 ('*Khatriyon ki utpatti*'), or local histories, e.g., '*Maharashtra desh ka itihas*', ibid., 163–93.

that all religions were equal, he had nonetheless elevated his own brand of Vaishnavite devotionalism to the status of a universal religion.[51] The expansion of sectarian devotionalism and eclectic scholarship was as influential a route to modern north Indian sensibilities as the more abstract, pietistic and conventional thought of Raja Shiva Prasad.

In addition to older lines of communication the Indian public man could also now draw on longer institutional memories. Alongside municipal clock towers and works of public utility, north Indians began to build public libraries in the Indian interest. Of course, this had happened earlier in Bengal and in the north the libraries sometimes resembled the older collections of sacred texts rather than repositories of 'useful knowledge'. The major Hindi libraries collected Sanskrit religious manuscripts in large numbers, because they were religious manuscripts. Sayyid Ahmad's Ghazipur Literary Society was criticised by the Director of Public Instruction for concentrating on antique Arabic and Persian texts which would serve to promote not modernity, but tradition. Nevertheless, these new collections were to become a formidable store of information for use in the process of Indian public instruction, and somewhat later, in the battle against government control of public information. The Bharati Bhawan (India House) Library[52] in Allahabad which was closely associated with Madan Mohan Malaviya collected government blue books and treatises on social subjects as well as examples of early Hindi prose literature. It was a free library and attracted educated youth in the old city, who were repelled by the cost of access and racial exclusiveness of the Thornhill-Mayne Library in the European Civil Lines and were not members of Allahabad University.

The 'archival depth' of Indian society in general was considerably enhanced in the 1860s and 1870s. Beginning with the Oudh Branch of the British Indian Association,[53] many private societies began to collect documents and statistics along the lines of government departments. A spur to this process was the striking growth of the legal profession and a more widespread desire for written precedent and documentation validated in British courts. By 1880 Allahabad and Lucknow possessed perhaps twenty public archival collections and libraries and fifty or more private ones associated with publicists and barristers. This represented

[51] V. Dalmia-Luderitz, 'Hariscandra of Banaras, the reassessment of Vaisnava bhakti in the late nineteenth century' in R.S. McGregor, *Devotional Literature in South Asia. Current Research, 1985–88* (Cambridge, 1992), pp. 281–97.
[52] R.N. Chaturvedi, *Mahamana Pandit Madan Mohan Malaviya* (Banaras, 1936), pp. 35–7; *Leader* (Allahabad), 14 May 1913.
[53] Papers of the Oudh Branch of the British India Association, 1863–7, Nehru Memorial Museum and Library, New Delhi.

an enormous advance in collective memory over the previous fifty years. In 1830 these towns had supported perhaps four royal and noble libraries each, to which access was severely restricted, and half a dozen small libraries of English, Hindi and Urdu books associated with the government high schools and mission schools.

While the existence of the technology of communication did not predetermine access or a commensurate change in mentalities, it is evident that in a few major centres north India's information order had undergone a change perhaps more dramatic even than had been felt by its social and economic structures. Knowledge, information and standard time were 'internalised' by the leading men of the post-Mutiny era in ways that were qualitatively new. Pre-colonial public authorities kept 'diaries' (*waqyai*) of events. There are, of course, distinguished examples of pre-colonial private journals. Statesmen such as Babur, Jahangir and Nana Fadnavis all recorded their 'life and times', and one or two more humble examples such as the journal of the Jain merchant, Banarsi Das, have also survived. These are more in the mode of 'life stories' and they generally had a didactic purpose. The Hindi word was *atmakahani* or 'tale of the self'. The lawyer-public men of the later nineteenth century began to keep personal diaries as a record of their division of time between the private and public arenas, and a measure of the routines of their lives. For example, Sunder Lal Dave, an Allahabad lawyer, recorded railway journeys, legal meetings and fees and his political meetings in his English journals.[54] But he also detailed in them attendances at the local Freemasons' Lodge and the intimate details of his illnesses, medicines and diets. Men had begun to make archives of their own lives. We have already noted how the capacity to keep a journal was an important indicator of modernity for the British in the 1820s and 1830s. Here at least, in the reconstructed sphere of inner space, Macaulay was beginning to win the day.

The men active in the public arena of the later nineteenth century had put together a powerful and flexible range of communications which informed them about a newly emerging India while maintaining their stake in regional society. To the formal knowledge purveyed through the press and public meeting they were able to add what we have called affective knowledge – the insights that came from membership in Sufi orders, Vaishnavite sects and other communities of emotion. Patrimonial knowledge was also open to them through their links to old court centres such as Bharatpur, Rewah and Orchcha and their relations with landed magnates. The grafting on to the north Indian ecumene of new

---

[54] Diaries of Sir Sunder Lal Dave, *c.* 1875–85, formerly in possession of Admiral R.N. Dave, Allahabad.

methods of organisation and communication served the indigenous intelligentsia and publicist well. The concerns over religion and right government of the former could now be articulated through newspapers such as the *Oudh Akhbar, Oudh Punch* and even the modernist *Aligarh Institute Gazette*. Equally, an appearance of social weight, which concerned the British so much, could be imparted to a campaign of public meetings by the presence of men of importance in the older public sphere: maulvis, pirzadas of shrines, mahants, and others.[55] Early nationalist newspapers planned their campaigns to coincide with flurries of placarding or the presentation to the authorities of traditional petitions. Such merging of older and more modern forms of publicity could, however, deepen conflict. The intelligentsia of the ecumene were paternalists, seeing themselves as shepherds of communities and people. Numerical representation was an alien concept to them. In the longer term, the face-to-face contacts of the ecumene and its traditions of high-minded friendship conveyed by letter began to be eroded by considerations of religious community, caste and class.[56] The formal, abstract massing of opinion in printed books and newspapers tended to stereotype social situations. Newspapers, by opting for one script or form of language, tended to identify themselves with one 'community' or another. Yet we have noted that even the debates and public action of the earlier ecumene were imbalanced. Important areas of life outside the Islamic domain were less well represented than those inside it. Thus the technology of communications and the new public were to fracture social relations along fault lines of ambiguity and difference which already existed.

Even in the 1830s, of course, Indians had understood massively more about their own societies than had the British. But in modern public and political arenas it was the British who led the way; Indian publications, meetings and speeches borrowed from European contemporaries. By the 1870s this was no longer the case. Government and police reports now drew on Indian-controlled newspapers and books. British knowledge had become more reactive and static. This later colonial knowledge was still most influential when it could serve in the political conflict with nationalist aspirations. It was not simply a precipitation of power, however, since it was also inflected by new aesthetic and intellectual interests deriving from outside the Indian context.

[55] See below, pp. 375–6.
[56] Kenneth Jones (ed.), *Religious Controversy in British India. Dialogues in South Asian Languages* (New York, 1992); Francis Robinson, *Separatism among Indian Muslims. The politics of the United Provinces' Muslims, 1860–1923* (Cambridge, 1974).

Later 'colonial knowledge': Little Indias

British and Indian systems of information collection and diffusion were not, of course, entities which stood outside society, or the wider conceptions of what knowledge was and should be. In the years after the Rebellion, the British came to see India more clearly than before as an agglomeration of small societies. This shift in perspective had empirical, functional and idealist dimensions. British interests and intellectual culture played their part in the selection and presentation of topics. The new orientalism also picked up and manipulated certain Indian conceptions of internal difference. By contrast, Indians began to insist on the integrity and vitality of their own society. The British sought diversity in unity; Indian publicists unity in diversity. Ironically, however, many of the old systems of specialist knowledge and some of the diversity of India were vanishing at the very time it was being catalogued and enlisted in the political battle.

Kaye had said that in India British knowledge of books preceded knowledge of men. The classical orientalists' concerns were with understanding unified Indian traditions, whether it be the classical languages, religious texts, or the 'constitution' of Mughal government. The increasing density of government and its institutions naturally revealed to the British many smaller Indias within the two great traditions. The movement towards taxonomising castes which proceeded from the work of Mackenzie,[57] Walter Elliot[58] and Brian Houghton Hodgson[59] in the first forty years of the nineteenth century resulted in a spectacular increase in the British understanding of such little traditions. Hodgson began to reveal the linguistic variety and complexity of the subcontinent, while H.H. Wilson marked out the sectarian diversity of Hinduism: that religion he had remarked was not a single entity but 'a heterogeneous compound, made up of not infrequently incompatible elements'.[60] The difficulties of judicial officers grappling with Hindu–Muslim conflicts also caused them to conceive of local custom and precedent in a way which fragmented the unity of Hinduism and Islam.[61] Still, the general tendency of the intellectual life and discourses of the period of the

---

[57] Nicholas B. Dirks, 'Castes of Mind', *Representations*, 37, winter 1992, 56–77.
[58] e.g., his collections of local history, Walter Elliot, Papers, Mss. Eur. D317–20, OIOC.
[59] B.H. Hodgson, *Essays on the Languages, Literatures and Religion of Nepal and Tibet* ... (London, 1874).
[60] H.H. Wilson, *Two lectures on the Religious Practices and Opinions of the Hindus delivered before the University of Oxford* (Oxford, 1840), p. 35.
[61] K.H. Prior, 'Making History; the state's intervention in urban religious disputes in the North-Western Provinces in the early nineteenth century', *MAS*, 27, i, 1993, 179–203.

Company's rule was to find unity in tradition, to codify and to seek out authentic informants among Brahmins, munshis and maulvis.

The shift in British attitudes after mid-century was palpable. At one level, of course, it was caused by the events of 1857. The epistemological balkanisation of India accorded well with the post-Mutiny official plan of installing a paternalist bureaucracy to overmaster feudal or 'natural' leaders of the people and a pliant peasantry. The covert evangelicals who had won the war of the Rebellion were deeply suspicious of both Brahminism and Islam. They approved of any policy which broke down India into shards of local custom. Not surprisingly, Robert Montgomery and the members of the Punjab Commission, who were brought back into the NWP and eastern India as apostles of paternalism, emphasised the irreducibility of the local unit. For his part Montgomery had no doubt that the people of the NWP and Oudh 'care little' for Hindu and Muhammadan Law. Knowledge of the Shastras and the Koran had been 'mainly imported by government'.[62] But this 'effete' Hindu and Muslim law was now dying, to be replaced by the arbitration of local Indian judges dispensing verdicts according to custom and aided by jurors and local assemblies. In the Punjab, officials spent the latter part of the nineteenth century seeking out and recording hundreds of local circles of customary law. Just as the earlier Hindu and Muslim law had been distilled from the testimonies of pandits and kazis, and often torn out of their context, so now the testimony of village headmen was often elevated to the standard of a binding code, though in a much smaller geographical compass. This rage for village tradition never occurred to the same extent in the NWP, though in the west of the provinces, judges paid much greater attention to custom in the generation after the Rebellion than they had before.[63] The great accumulation of local information which arose from the more systematic and detailed operations of the census and revenue surveys after 1851 and the explosion of land litigation made this possible.

Such a turn in the official mind toward the rustic and the customary, and away from the towns and high culture, was particularly noticeable in the realms of language, culture and ethnology. It was speeded by intellectual changes in Britain and India, but there is no doubt that much of this thinking fitted well with the politically conservative but culturally radical temper of the bureaucracy as it faced up to the first generation of overt nationalist criticism. Shahid Amin has shown how

[62] Memorandum of 21 Sept. 1858 on Oudh judicial arrangements, Montgomery Papers, 4, Mss. Eur. D1019/4, OIOC.
[63] e.g., C.L. Tupper, *Statements of Customary Law in different Districts* (Calcutta, 1881); H.C. Beadon, *Customary Law of Delhi District* (Lahore, 1911).

William Crooke's *Glossary of North Indian Peasant Life*, a highly empirical listing of words in common use for daily objects, soils, crops, houses, carried a concealed ideological message.[64] As a settlement officer and manager of the Awa Estate under the Court of Wards, Crooke was able to accumulate a detailed archive of rural nomenclature. Crooke's India was the traditional village India, immune to the diseases of modernity. Borrowed anglicisms, words for industrial milling apparatus, for railways, telegraphs and other badges of modernity were excluded. Even the powerful effect of urban capital and village moneylending on 'peasant life' was neglected. Amin suggests that such classification and taxonomising was, in effect, a discursive strategy to bury change within tradition. The only broadly ideological category Crooke recognised was a reified and rigidly understood distinction between Hindu and Muslim. It is true that native informants continued to play a role in the preparation of this sort of material, and some of these people were 'lower down the *sarkari* [service] ladder'. One such was Pandit Ram Gharib Chaube, a prolific Indian ethnographer from eastern NWP, who offered himself as an informant to Crooke, and specifically as an expert on local custom *not* mentioned in the Sanskrit texts.[65] In Amin's view, however, these men were simply providers of fact; they did not really influence the form of colonial knowledge.

Crooke's *Glossary* bears comparison with George Grierson's *Bihar Peasant Life*,[66] a similar, but much larger compilation which bore traces of the influence of Crooke who was a coeval and friend of Grierson from Trinity College, Dublin. In Grierson's work 'ceremonies and superstitions of rural life' were sandwiched between a table of words for foodstuffs and 'accounts between landlord and tenant'. The link between so-called 'superstitions' and religious beliefs was largely ignored. Castes were perceived essentially as bodies of artisanal servants; the interconnections between them were not explored. Many of the early official works of anthropology, the disquisitions on tribes and castes put together by Crooke, Nesfield,[67] Ibbetson and others, convey the same impression. So by placing articles on 'Brahmins' or 'Kayasths', replete with photographs of family groups, alongside Pasis (pig-keepers and watchmen) or Malis (gardeners), the former are minimised and relativised. In fact, by the 1880s, the most important attribute of many

---

[64] S. Amin (ed.), W. Crooke, *A Glossary of North Indian Peasant Life* (orig. 1888, rep. Delhi, 1989), p. xxxix.

[65] ibid., pp. xxx–xxxi.

[66] G. Grierson, *Bihar Peasant Life* (Calcutta, 1885), pp. 331–431.

[67] W. Crooke, *The Tribes and Castes of the North-western Provinces and Oudh*, 4 vols., (Calcutta, 1896); J. Nesfield, *A Brief View of the Caste System of the North-Western Provinces and Oudh . . .* (Allahabad, 1885).

Kayasthas and Brahmins was not their caste status, their superstitions or marriage customs, so much as the new conviction amongst some of them that they were Indians. In these cases official ethnology and typology certainly tended to make Indian subjects specimens, and to deny them any kind of active public or political agency. Perhaps the most extreme form of empirical, taxonomising scholarship was that of Capt. Richard Temple, founder of the *Punjab Notes and Queries*. Temple published a *Dissertation on the Proper Names of Panjabis, with special reference to the Proper names of Villages in the eastern Panjab*. This huge glossary of personal names was supposed to 'indicate the national life, racial ancestry and course of civilisation within India'.[68] It was compiled from the newly available census records of a large number of villages and the cantonments of Ambala, and from a huge inventory of Temple's own making. The head munshi of two regiments stationed at Ambala aided in this compilation.[69] Temple was another correspondent of Crooke and Grierson.

This generation of officials and their missionary and educationist colleagues were, nevertheless, more than simply rustic archaicisers who pictured unchanging rural India as a heroic stage for the enactment of British justice. What they saw beyond this was a range of conservative popular cultures resisting the 'artificiality' of the modern. They were conservationists as well as orientalists, and their perception owed much to the turn in contemporary European sensibilities towards popular culture, represented in the British case by the legal thought of Sir Henry Maine.[70] This new thinking about race, popular culture and authenticity was consciously radical and modern. Temple, Grierson, Crooke and their classmate, Growse, were all influenced by the folklorist revival of their native Ireland which also found an echo in the English 'Arts and Crafts' movement. These men had much in common with their compatriots in Bihar, O'Donnell and MacDonnell, who championed the peasant against the landlord and the 'corrupt' Muslim official. It was MacDonnell who was to allow the adoption of Hindi as an official court language when he was Lieutenant-Governor of the United Provinces in 1900, a measure which completed the earlier work of Grierson in bringing to official attention the 'vernacular literatures of Hindustan'. In some respects, then, this new direction in British official orientalism mirrored and stimulated north Indian nationalism, even as it sought to block and deny it. As changes in communication revealed new levels of

---

[68] R.C. Temple, *A dissertation on the Proper Names of Panjabis...* (Bombay, 1883), p. 1.
[69] ibid., Introduction, p. viii.
[70] Alan Diamond, *The Victorian Achievement of Sir Henry Maine. A centennial reappraisal* (Cambridge, 1991).

Indian thought, this changed the pace of both official and nationalist thinking.

This can be seen most clearly in Grierson's early analysis of north Indian language and literature. It is true that he denounced the 'artificial' Sanskritic Hindi of the Nagari Pracharini Sabha and the linguistic nationalists of Banaras.[71] This was in line with his cool view of Sanskrit literature which reversed a hundred years of official thinking. He was to write that the medieval Sanskrit and Prakrit poems were 'artificial productions written in the closet by learned men for learned men' while the later vernacular writers were addressing those 'unsparing critics – the people'.[72] Grierson wanted to promote a folk-language somewhere between the high Hindi espoused by cultural nationalists and the 'artificial', Persianised Urdu of the courts. Ironically, an earlier generation of officials had themselves put in hand the translation and diffusion of Lalluji's *Prem Sagar*.[73] Grierson emphasised the variety of local variants of this popular Hindi found throughout north India, terming them Awadhi, Chattisgarhi, Braj Bhasha, and so on. On the other hand, Grierson adored and eulogised the great Hindi religious poet Tulsi Das, who had written his story of Ram, the 'Ramcharitmanas', in the vernacular. Grierson hailed Tulsi Das as the 'Shakespeare' of modern Indian literature, acclaiming his poetry and religious thought as a force which would build both a civilised Hindu race and an Indian nation.[74] With his friend F.S. Growse, Collector of Mathura,[75] he accorded Tulsi Das a position in Indian tradition similar to that bestowed on the Sanskrit grammarian Panini by the earlier generation of orientalists. Tulsi Das had forged a common language which created naturalistic similes in preference to the high-flown conceits of Sanskrit.[76] More important still, his work carried a message of moral reformation. He taught 'the vileness of sin and the infinite graciousness of the Deity' and, as 'an old missionary' had told Grierson, one could only hope to understand north Indians 'after he had mastered every line Tulsi Das had written'.[77] The particular sin Grierson had in mind was sexual licence which had degraded 'Tantra-ridden Bengal' and was ever present in the 'wanton orgies of Krishna'. This theme was echoed by Growse in Mathura who, praising Tulsi Das for his simple and pure

---

[71] Grierson, *Vernacular Literature*, p. xi.   [72] ibid.
[73] McGregor, *Hindi Literature of the Nineteenth and Early Twentieth Centuries*, pp. 6–7; F. Pincott (tr., ed.), *The Prem-sagara or Ocean of Love*. (London, 1897), pp. v–viii.
[74] Grierson, *Vernacular Literature*, pp. xviii–xxi.
[75] F.S. Growse, *Mathura. A District Memoir* (Allahabad, 1882).
[76] Grierson, *Vernacular Literature*, p. 48.
[77] Grierson, *Linguistic Survey of India*, I, part 1 (Calcutta, 1927), 160.

language,[78] had translated the Ramayana into English. Growse, too, expressed amazement that respectable married men at Mathura should recite indelicate and 'abandoned' verse in praise of Krishna. The theme was taken up in turn by Crooke who foresaw a kind of reformation in north India spearheaded by sober and industrious Ramanandis, a religious grouping for whom Tulsi Das was particularly significant.[79]

This group of officials believed north India to be a constellation of rustic cultures on the brink of a popular ethical reformation. These ideas stood in marked contrast to the orientalism of the generation of Colebrooke and Jones, or even of Wilkinson or Ballantyne, all of whom had hoped for an intellectual revival of the great Sanskritic tradition through the efforts of a Brahmin intelligentsia which had been weaned on western knowledge. Grierson, Growse and their colleagues hoped to encourage a popular moral nationalism which would counteract the anti-colonial nationalism of the English-educated upper castes. Their understanding of India, however, was more than the cultural reflection of a political agenda as Shahid Amin's approach might suggest. In the first place, the folklorist turn of contemporary thinking was an international phenomenon, and it is significant that several of these officials were actively involved in contemporary movements of Celtic cultural revival. Secondly, their representations of India were informed by powerful undercurrents in Indian life itself; to this extent they mirrored and contested Indian discourses rather than simply seeking to overwhelm them with western science. The reverence of these British officials for Tulsi Das is a case in point; they were responding to powerful changes in Indian sensibility. Tulsi Das's work, the Ramcharitmanas, was probably the most widely known text in circulation before the print revolution – hence Grierson's view that it was a 'bible' for north Indians. Ram's story had also been glorified by the newly emergent Hindu courts of the eighteenth century, particularly Banaras, Bharatpur and Orchcha.[80] In the course of the early nineteenth century small-scale carnival displays of the story were replaced by the massive public celebration of Ramlila, complete with the storming of Ravana's Castle by large bodies of armed men. The Company's Indian troops celebrated the festival with particular elan,[81] and perhaps spread their version back to their home territories. Ram was a symbol not only for the warrior castes, but for travelling merchants and even for the sober and

---

[78] Extract from reply of Mr F.S. Growse, Jun. 1875, NWP Genl Procs., Aug. 1876, 54, 837; cf. Raja Shiva Prasad's view, ibid. no. 55, ibid.
[79] W. Crooke, *The North-Western Provinces of India* (1897, repr., Karachi, 1972), pp. 255–6.
[80] Lutgendorf, *Ramcharitmanas*, passim.   [81] Leupolt, *Recollections*, p. 80.

industrious peasantry which followed his precepts of struggle and familial devotion. Ram as a personal name was gaining notably in popularity during the course of the nineteenth century.

The coming of print brought a great increase in circulated versions of Ram's story, which were distributed to local schoolmasters and libraries, and even sold at fairs by itinerant hawkers. According to Grierson, the Ramcharitmanas 'is in every one's hands from the court to the cottage, and is read or heard or appreciated alike by every class of the Hindu community, whether high or low, rich or poor young or old'.[82] Quite apart from the growing British interest in the text, Indian scholars and printers began to be concerned with authentic versions. Shiva Prasad had found an early copy (dated 1647) in the possession of the Maharaja of Banaras and had had it photographed for his own and Grierson's use. Later commentators and anthologists sought to modify and purify the text. Of these 'restorations', Pandit Ram Jasan's was the best known, but there were many printed bazaar editions in which the 'dialect is altered to the standard of the modern Hindi, and the spelling improved according to the rules of Panini'.[83] This outraged Grierson, but it is an indication of the close connection between Ram's story and linguistic modernisation and nationalism.

Since women were often protectors of folk traditions and the values of the little community, European commentators on Indian life in the mid-nineteenth century began to investigate domestic and female space with greater thoroughness. Women's knowledge, a potent source of information and gossip for the generation of empire-builders, had been pushed to the margins as government became routine. When women were introduced into the debates of the era of 'reform' it had been mainly as symbols; controversy was about the status of Indian tradition, not about women as such. By the 1870s women's lives were better known. S.W. Fallon's *New Hindustani–English Dictionary*, published in 1879 at Banaras, was replete with 'illustrations from Hindustani literature and folk-lore',[84] but also paid special attention to women and women's language. Fallon was a PhD from Halle University and a product of the German school of folklore. His 'dictionary' differentiated between elite and 'rustic' speech but also added a 'third', or female 'dialect'. He wrote:

The Dictionary will include as an important and integral part of the spoken tongue, the vocabulary of women (*rehkti* or *zanani boli*) as yet strangely overlooked and never before given in any work known to the compiler. Some

---

[82] Grierson, *Vernacular Literature*, p. 42.   [83] ibid., p. 50.
[84] S.W. Fallon, *A New Hindustani–English Dictionary* (Banaras and London, 1879), title page.

portion of this vocabulary is more or less current in the language of men; but the greater part is still confined exclusively to women.[85]

What Fallon was interested in above all was the language of the illiterate 'rustic' women, for 'the seclusion of native females in India has been the asylum of the true vernacular, as pure and simple as it is unaffected by the pedantries of word-makers'.[86] He saw his task as preserving the real popular language from the 'professors of Arabic and Persian and ... Brahmin Pundits who have too successfully restored in many instances the Sanskrit forms which the language had already thrown off in the course of development'.[87] Like the district officer seeking to protect the peasant against the wiles of the townsmen and the new, disloyal middle class, Fallon was fighting a new linguistic hegemony. Of course, not all in this popular and female realm was good – 'it is of the greatest importance, for instance, to know to what depths human nature can sink in the vitiated atmosphere of female seclusion'.[88] Only by understanding the obscenity and lewdness of many female stories and ditties could the missionary or legislator hope to eradicate them.

Fallon relied heavily as his preface shows on the expertise of educated Indians: pleaders, university professors, munshis in the education and census departments. His generally accurate references to the poems of the great Urdu writers of the earlier part of the century suggest a deep background in indigenous literature. But he did attempt to get beyond educated native informants and to listen to singers, bards and village story-tellers. These were shadowy and unnamed figures whom he interviewed, apparently in the presence of his elite assistants. He denounced the dismissive tone of the latter who referred to the folk informants as 'boors',[89] but he also frowned on the way in which his semi-literate artistes wished to dress up their own performances with grandiose words when in the presence of the educated. Altogether he found the boundaries between popular and elite culture contentious and problematic. Kabir, the dispassionate mystic of the sixteenth century, was the literary figure best known among the common people. Elite writers such as Nazir and the Lucknow and Delhi satirists, Sauda and Mir, of the eighteenth century were also renowned, even among uneducated rural women. As we have seen, ghazals and stories had passed up and down the social ladder of the ecumene, often being embroidered by popular tradition and then recast in elite poetic forms. There had been less distance than one might think between the poetic salons of the Lucknow courtesans and the world of rural women.

---

[85] ibid., p. iii. [86] ibid. [87] ibid., p. vii. [88] ibid. [89] ibid., p. xxi.

Cohabiting with powerful men, and in a few cases the literary accomplishments of the salon, were one form of escape from the village for Hindu countrywomen. The early Urdu anthologists and writers of dictionaries were well aware of the existence of *rekhti*, women's speech, and were interested in it.[90] Fallon assembled much important data about north Indian women and relations of gender but, like many orientalists, he was less sure of the processes that linked the facts he was describing.

Fallon was a lesser-known member of the generation of neo-orientalists that opened up European knowledge of the 'little Indias'. He can be compared with C.A. Elliott, Magistrate of Farrukhabad, who, in about 1869, assembled four or five different minstrels and had them recite the whole of the 'Lay of Alha' (*Alha Gana*), a tale of Rajput chivalry.[91] The project was similar, again, to that of the Anglo-Indian disciples of the Arts and Crafts movement who tried to categorise and rescue rural artisan trades and promoted an official version of the Indian *swadeshi*, or 'home industry' movement. At its broadest level this turn of mind was represented in the work of census officers such as Nesfield, Hunter and Ibbetson who gathered together the headmen of castes or sub-castes definitely to ascribe them to a rank in the ritual hierarchy.

Oriental scholarship, to repeat, was not a homogenous mode of gaining power over India. It was rather an arena of debate in which the more powerful – the British and the Indian elites – attempted to appropriate themes and symbols which suited their political needs and chimed with features of their intellectual culture. These themes and symbols were of indigenous and often of popular origin. They were distorted or modified as they were appropriated by the British, but they could also fragment in the hands of the colonial rulers and help subvert the very cause they were supposed to uphold.

This chapter has argued that while the knowledge acquired by the 'little tradition' neo-orientalists usually approximated to the interests of colonial taxonomy and control, it also represented a changing Indian reality. At every point, Indians presented themselves as 'native informants' and their own presentations, distorted and sifted out as they often were, could be incorporated into official debates and ideologies. Caste headmen and the representatives of small communities revealed themselves to the rulers because they had to stake out their claims in a

---

[90] Majeed, 'Jargon of Indostan', p. 12, citing Insha Allah Khan, *Darya-e Latafat* (1808, Karachi, 1988) tr. Braj Mohan, pp. 82–104.
[91] W. Waterfield, *The Lay of Alha. A saga of Rajput chivalry as sung by minstrels of northern India*, (Oxford, 1923), p. 10.

situation of accelerating social change. The British sought out the small community, but conversely, the small community began to present itself in the British law courts. Women, tribals and occupational specialists became more visible because the pace of social change had forced them to move into open view. The railways, famine relief operations and the growth of slums on the outskirts of the cities made society more transparent, just as the ever-more-detailed apparatus of revenue surveys swelled out official knowledge.

An important aspect of the increasing capacity and will of Indians to represent themselves was the emergence of a new generation of authors and antiquarians. The munshis of the late eighteenth century were secretaries to great men and had been Muslim gentry or Hindus of the scribal classes. Their world was circumscribed by the rise and decline of Islam and the Mughal Empire, or, sometimes, local Hindu dynasties working within the framework of Indo-Muslim governance. The new men who made a considerable, though largely unacknowledged, contribution to official information at the end of the nineteenth century were residents of towns and large villages, proud of their rootedness. Many were Hindus who knew something of the skills of the old pandits, munshis and maulvis, but had also been exposed to the western knowledge by their English education. The pages of their local histories, descriptions and topologies were crowded indiscriminately with the praise of holy places, legends, and precise social descriptions, the latter sometimes drawn from English originals. Many were local headmasters, government servants and lawyers. They bought books and were often associated with local presses. In envisaging their localities as part of an Indian nation such men as Pandit Ram Gharib Chaube or Kunwar Lachman Singh, or even, in his own way, Harishchandra of Banaras, played as important a part in the development of Indian nationalism as the political critics of the British government.[92] Indian knowledge of the country was now expanding much faster than that of the British.

The fate of indigenous knowledges and communicators

In 1800 north India had been straddled by communities of knowledgeable people serving state and society: spies, runners, astrologers, trackers of animals, bone setters and hundreds of other groups. In theory, knowledge was arranged hierarchically from the highest vedic scholar to

---

[92] See the large number of district accounts, some puranic, some western in style, published after 1860, J. Blumhardt, *Catalogue of the India Office Library*, II, 2, *Hindi, Punjabi, Sindhi and Pushtu Books* (London, 1902), 22–6.

the lowest skinner of animals. In practice the hierarchy was breached by forms of public knowledge and communication which connected Hindu and Muslim, elite and populace in an ecumene of mutual under- standing, wit and political debate. Other widely spread networks gave people affective knowledge of each other in communities of god- devotion across lines of caste and even religion. These little knowledges could also be subversive of hierarchy. Those, like the Chamars, with lowly, earthly skills might find buried treasure to make them rich. By contrast, high-caste physicians might introduce forbidden meat into the diet of a sickly vegetarian Brahmin to preserve life. Astrologers could peer behind the statuses of this life to forbid a marriage because the female outranked the male in some former life. The state shared knowledge and its purveyors with the people, but had neither a monopoly of it nor the capacity decisively to shape it.

The life, death and transfiguration of these different knowledges over the next century was an historical change as dramatic as anything that happened in the realm of politics or economics. The colonial state moved, ineffectively, to appropriate public knowledge and control its diffusion through public instruction and command of the burgeoning press. At the same time, newspapers generally replaced court news- writers; postal peons and telegraph clerks edged aside the communities of runners and spies. Local agents of information in the village were partially subordinated to the police and reported on births, deaths and crimes. Most important, the learned Muslim officials who had mediated between state and society guided by the Law had been relegated to the margins. They survived not as groups of functionaries but as quasi- castes;[93] contract had given way to status.

The penetration of world capitalism into the hinterland had contem- poraneously rendered redundant many old skills. Iron-smelting commu- nities were substantially replaced by factories; weavers by mills; makers of dyes by artificial imports and tanning castes by commercial tanneries. Ironically, British officials and Indian nationalists moved to record and preserve these skills and their teachers before they vanished.

In many cases, however, the old learned traditions and networks of communication retained potency and inflected the language and practice of nationalists or cultural revivalists. In medicine, the outcome was mixed. Many of the humbler specialists began to disappear after 1860. The long battle of the official vaccinator against the 'native innoculator' was gradually going the way of western, or at least hybrid medicine by the 1890s. In large government and private dispensaries,

---

[93] See, e.g., Ghaus Ansari, *Muslim Caste in Uttar Pradesh* (Lucknow, 1960), p. 45.

cataract-cutters and bone setters gave way to 'native assistants' trained on modern lines. Yet the classical Indian medical traditions survived as national icons, though they too felt the impress of modern forms of training, legitimation and retailing. Indigenous specialists also continued to flourish amongst poorer and more remote people, and even the wealthy might have recourse to them from time to time in the face of incurable illness.

A similar process was working in the astral sciences. In practice, the high tradition of Indian astronomy was replaced by post-Copernican theory and instrumentation. In so far as they survived, the learning of Bhaskara and Raja Jai Singh became an emblem of a glorious past, with a handful of Indian scholars trying to show that these sages had anticipated the moderns. Classical traditions were transformed into symbols of excellence which men of modern education could cherish as guarantees of Indian self-respect. On the other hand, astral specialists and forms of diviner remained popular at the local level. The treatise on palmistry *Samudrika*[94] was one of the most frequently republished of all books during the later nineteenth century. Here, as in the case of Puranic readers and religious specialists, the survival of indigenous knowledges was determined by their relevance to the emergence of influential new groups in the localities. Thus in the towns, the invading knowledge communities of western science, medicine and the law generated and legitimated the position of the new dominant classes. In the countryside and the small towns, the old specialisms could survive when they attached themselves to patterns of social mobility among the aspiring. For instance, palmists and astral specialists, alongside the puraniks, were at the heart of the process by which tribals and low castes were 'caught in the net of caste', or rather, domesticated themselves into the hierarchies of plains India. It is for this reason, one which relates to the social context as much as to the virtue of their intellectual content, that indigenous knowledges survived colonialism and the impact of capitalism, or even benefited from their inexorable spread. Colonial rule had encompassed a bifurcation of the information order. Those nationalists and public men who could maintain links in both sectors, men such as Malaviya, Gandhi or Tilak, were in a strong strategic position. Equally, across the borderlands between the older, but still vigorous knowledge communities and the powerful, but still unstable adaptations of western science and communications some of the most critical battles of late colonial and independent south Asia have been fought: should books which insult the Prophet or satellite communica-

---

[94] *Samudrika* (Banaras, 1851, and subsequently).

tions which undermine Hindu female decorum be permitted? Should public instruction privilege scientific archaeology over religious text? Is there history and sociology or 'Pakistan Studies'? Is there a specifically Hindu or Muslim anthropology? How far should the state support indigenous medicine because it is indigenous?

Conclusion: 'Knowing the country'

This book has been intended, firstly, as a contribution to imperial history. It argues that successful intelligence-gathering was a critical feature of the British domination of India. It shows how the British took over and manipulated the sophisticated systems of internal espionage and political reporting which had long been deployed by the kingdoms of the Indian subcontinent. One overriding reason why the East India Company was able to conquer India and dominate it for more than a century was that the British had learnt the art of listening in, as it were, on the internal communications of Indian polity and society. The gap in resources and military technique between Indians and the British has been exaggerated, but, after the 1780s, the superior coherence and effectiveness of British political surveillance and military intelligence were striking. Where indigenous lines of communication did not exist, or where the British were shut out of them by enemies who could control the flow of information more effectively, conquest proved difficult and costly. The wars against Burma and Nepal dramatically demonstrated this.

Even in India itself, however, the British 'empire of information' rested on shaky foundations. Prejudice or ignorance excluded the Europeans from many areas of Indian life. Despite new institutions designed to hoard and preserve information – the science of statistics, trigonometrical surveys, revenue records and oriental societies – much of the deeper social knowledge the European conquerors had once possessed withered away as expatriate society became more hierarchical and government more a matter of routine. Despite the accumulation of records of rights and agricultural statistics after 1830, networks of information beneath the level of the district office remained tenuous. In 1857 much of the British system of espionage and control was swept away in a matter of days and had to be reconstructed from scratch.

The Company's dominion was also an 'empire of opinion' in which Indians were coerced by the reputation or scientific and cultural superiority of their conquerors. Here it never regained the initiative after

1857. North Indians were late starters in printing and lithography, yet the existence of sophisticated patterns of internal political debate and the adaptability of older communities of knowledge ensured that the book, the pamphlet, the newspaper and the British post office had been pressed into use by critics of colonial rule and by those who challenged the West's cultural domination nearly sixty years before the formal date of birth of Indian nationalism. In fact, a study of the information order leads us to query the whole current chronology of the development of that nationalism.

Throughout the book an analytical distinction has been sustained between the information systems of the state and autonomous networks of social communication within Indian society. There was, however, much overlap between the two dimensions, especially in the Indian kingdoms where 'post' (dak) was a 'private' system protected by the ruler, and the political elite relied heavily on the information provided by knowledgeable people: physicians, astrologers and men of religion. In order to bring the analysis of the two dimensions together, we have used the concept of the information order. This has been taken to include the uses of literacy, social communication and the informing knowledge and systems of surveillance of the emerging state. Several other writers have used comparable heuristic concepts. Anthony Giddens, for instance, writes of 'the means of coercion and persuasion' as a domain separate from relations of production. Ernest Gellner's[1] progression of phases of civilisation marries material forces with means of communication: for him, the age of the book and the plough gives way to the age of mass production and multi-media in the modern era. In historiography influenced by Michel Foucault the concepts of 'discourse' and the 'archaeology of knowledge' virtually absorb the whole social space. For writers in this tradition, knowledge and information are properties of the total system of power. Challenging as these last theories are, the assimilation of power into knowledge makes it difficult to analyse systems of communication and surveillance, or the gaps and contradictions within them. This study has, therefore, worked from the premiss that the information order of different societies cannot either be reduced to material factors or be viewed simply as a discursive property of the power of elites and the state. It was, rather, a relatively autonomous domain constituted not only by state surveillance and elite ideological representations but also by affective communities of religion, belief, kinship, pilgrimage, literary or linguistic sensibility and styles of political debate. Societies at similar levels of economic development –

[1] Ernest Gellner, *Plough, Sword and Book. The Structure of Human History* (London, 1991).

late Mughal India and Tokugawa Japan, for example – had created information orders which differed significantly from each other.

The book needed a base line from which to measure the effects of British rule on communications, information and knowledge in north India. At first sight these effects appeared to be substantial, perhaps revolutionary. The first chapter, therefore, advanced some hypotheses about change in immediate pre-colonial India and in the India of the princely kingdoms. While historians have written about posts and communications, indigenous archives, schooling and particular religious controversies, little attempt has yet been made to think about the information order as a whole before the British, and very little indeed is known about the level or uses of literacy. It does appear, however, that later Mughal government and the successor states of the eighteenth century were in some respects becoming more bureaucratic, more reliant on the use of paper and the archive, and more dependent on systems of political surveillance. While these tendencies were only slowly realised, geographically limited and easily reversed, the state's knowledge of a complex society was itself becoming deeper and more complex. Here it was powerfully assisted by an indigenous sociology and theory of government which was elaborated by the Indo-Muslim elites, but drew on earlier classical Sanskritic learning. The most important strand of this was the tradition established by Abul Fazl, Akbar's minister, but it may be seen also in the several attempts to delineate pan-Indian 'Hindu' knowledges during the seventeenth and eighteenth centuries and was associated particularly with the learned cities such as Nadia, Banaras and Jaipur.

Government was not necessarily the prime moving force here for these developments also reflected the growing use of paper, archives, lists and routinised information by many groups in society: religious foundations and specialists, all-India cults, commercial corporations and landholders. India was increasingly a 'literacy aware' society even if it was not a highly literate one by Eurasian standards. Letter writing, the circulation of official and semi-official newsletters and a flexible postal system kept the elites in touch with each other over great distances. Ordinary people also participated in a well-developed culture of oral communication which habitually used these written instruments as points of reference. The very emergence of major new language communities – Indian Persian, Hindustani-Urdu, the various forms of prose Hindi, and ultimately Indian English – is itself a reflection of the dynamism of the information order even during a period of political turmoil and economic stress.

Between this more knowledgeable state and more communicative populace, and reflecting on both, there existed what we have called the north Indian ecumene. This was a routine of political debate and surveillance which subjected both rulers and society to critique through meetings, discussions, placarding and demonstration. It went beyond resistance and religious polemic to constitute a realm of public knowledge in which political ideas were strenuously debated. It took the form of a limited public opinion where the elite ideally represented the interests of the populace and so constrained the despotism of the monarch or ruling group in theory and practice.

This way of looking at Indian society has implications for recent debates amongst historians and sociologists. 'Traditional' India has been depicted as ideologically hierarchical and socially segmented, notably in the anthropological tradition founded by Louis Dumont.[2] Aspects of the information order can certainly be viewed in this light. Many knowledges were indeed passed down within families and remained the properties of certain castes and clans. This line of reasoning, however, can become too reductionist: that is, it concentrates overmuch on how people behaved, rather than on what they thought and how they reflected on their own society. Information, knowledge and debate were not necessarily constrained within segments and hierarchies; the intellectual history of a society cannot be reduced to its social structure. Networks of Hindu sects, the actions of the Mughal chancelleries and the imperial army, the pre-colonial public sphere that we have described – all these subverted the hierarchy and linked the segments. Brahmin makers of almanacs and horoscopes ministered to the lower castes; the medical classics were read in vernacular commentaries by men of humbler caste.

Some historians have recently insisted that it was only after British conquest that centralised knowledges came into existence. History, and alongside it a sense of linear time, was a product of the colonial state, they argue. In particular, it is asserted, no coherent sense of Hindu and Muslim tradition existed before the mid-nineteenth century. The state was not a powerful actor in society beyond the realm of revenue accumulation. In an engaging but ultimately romantic extension of this view, society has been portrayed as a loose congeries of linked communities, a harmonious mélange of syncretic cults and local cultures. Both as a revenue-extracting apparatus and as an accumulation of knowledge, however, the state in immediate pre-colonial India was more formidably developed than this suggests. A dispassionate tradition of state service fortified with a political theory and a sociology of

---

[2]   Louis Dumont, *Homo Hierarchicus. The Caste System and its Implications* (Chicago, 1991); cf. Arjun Appadurai, 'Is Homo Hierarchicus?', *American Anthropologist*, 13, 1986, 754–61.

government already existed. The learned administrators valued precise historical records. Within both Hindu and Muslim society a sense of shared all-India community was already in evidence, though this was rarely energised into an aggressive 'communalism'.

On the other hand, this book has argued against the notion that the pre-colonial state in India was simply an avatar of the modern state. First, the state's information system, though effective at its best, was peculiarly dependent on the collaboration of local elites to keep the runners running and the newsletters flowing. The abruptness with which the system declined, or was subverted by the Mughal Empire's Maratha and Sikh enemies in the course of the eighteenth century, was distantly echoed by the shorter but sharper crisis of the Company's state in 1857. Indian rulers had access to rich information at the higher levels of government, but they rarely aspired to the density of surveillance systems which existed, for instance, in Japan or in the central Chinese provinces. Their information systems took the form of threads of single operatives strung across the country rather than the cross-hatched establishments of local police and state rapporteurs common in some other Asian societies and in Europe. The link between the professional runner and writer system and the village or urban quarter was weak, mediated as it was by headmen and other agents who were part of the village or neighbourhood community and owed ultimate loyalty to it. The state could not communicate with its subjects easily. There was nothing in our period like the regular posting of lithographed notices and orders on the Japanese village noticeboards, though from time to time the village constable's platform may have displayed royal edicts.

As it moved to consider the period of British conquest this study has, inevitably, confronted aspects of the debate on 'orientalism' and has indirectly engaged with some of the important arguments of Talal Asad,[3] Edward Said and Ronald Inden, among others. While accepting that oriental knowledge was to some degree a means of 'dominating and mastering' India, it has often found itself in agreement with recent revisions of these authors' arguments.[4] First, if we mean by orientalism the creation of 'essentialised' stereotypes and modes of classification which abstract social characteristics from complex local identities for the sake of ruling, a sort of orientalism certainly existed in India before the British. Secondly, through the perusal of books and the interventions of 'native informants' these indigenous understandings of society, though distorted and forced into new international hierarchies of racial value, continued to inform the British understanding of India. To different

[3] Talal Asad, *Anthropology and the Colonial Encounter* (London, 1973).
[4] MacKenzie, *Orientalism.*

degrees, European and indigenous discourses both played a role in the construction of modern India. European knowledge may have been hegemonic, but it was never absolute. The creation of colonial knowledge was a 'dialogic process', to use Eugene Irschick's phrase in *Dialogue and History*, which is surely the most balanced contribution to the debate thus far from an Indian perspective.

This book has gone somewhat further in deconstructing the notion of orientalism. We have been uneasy about the assumption that the 'learned' ideas of orientalism played a consistent or determining part in the process of governing and exploiting India. 'Knowledge is power' was a phrase that contemporaries used as often as modern social scientists. But its use is often glib. First, orientalism, in Said's sense (as he sometimes seems to accept), was hardly a coherent system of thought. Even after 1820 it remained self-contradictory, fractured and contested. Stereotypes of India as a 'dream society', ruled by fanaticism and caste, a land where civil society was always on the point of dissolving in the face of the assaults of mindless communities, were more characteristic of what we have called 'information panics' than of day-to-day administration and colonial commercial life. In other words, they were a product of the weakness and blindness of the state at the fringes of its knowledge, rather than a set of governing assumptions at its core. In this, it resembled contemporary governments in the western world which also succumbed from time to time to panics about stranglers, Jesuits, Freemasons, and other malign conspirators.

We have also doubted that the positing of a radical 'other' was the basic intellectual tool of colonial rule. As has been pointed out by several scholars,[5] the construction of Indian 'otherness' always went along with another strategy: to find in India and Indians residues of universal truths or universal values. That position was more characteristic of the later eighteenth century and the circles of Sir William Jones than it was of the mid-nineteenth, but the search in Indian scriptures for clues to the age of the universe, or wondrous drugs known to the ancients, never ceased. By the later Victorian age, European Theosophists and theorists of 'race essence' were again looking to India for spiritual nourishment as their own sense of the sacred was perceived to atrophy. The most common epistemological strategy of colonial rule was, in fact, a form of syncretism in which European knowledge and technique were vaunted as superior, but were required to be grafted onto indigenous stock when planted in the great extra-European civilisations. This was the view that Thomason, Wilkinson and Ballantyne had taken of the engagement

---

[5]   Peabody, 'Tod's *Rajast'han*'.

between European and Indian knowledge. Probably, an intellectual tactic which stressed the radical 'otherness' of India could not have worked except in a situation where massive European immigration was supported by total racial apartheid. Since the British were dependent on Indian administrators, soldiers and merchants, and since Indians controlled the bulk of the means of production, commerce and capital throughout the colonial period, such syncretism was the only possible course. It was therefore a moralised version of the theory of the Scottish Enlightenment, stressing the need for Mankind to pass through 'stages' of development, which informed that moiety of administrative thought which was guided by any leading idea at all. Much of Indian government beyond these charmed circles of thinkers or fashionable metropolitan texts remained resolutely pragmatic and satisficing.

This raises another important point in the debate about orientalist knowledge and colonial rule. Both have to be set in a broader, international framework of the development of the world economy and the modern state. Orientalism was only one element in the wider information order of colonial India. That information order included both Indian and European modes of communication and debate. Moreover, it reflected changes in the external conditions of rule, economy and political thought. Just as information panics about orientals were prolific at the margins of the state's strength, so racist stereotypes were generated out of an increasing fear of 'native' competition, in trade and in employment, between expatriate Europeans and newly educated Indians. These stereotypes were especially pervasive in the journals and newspapers of the Anglo-Indian expatriates. The harshest denunciations of Indians and their culture consequently began to appear from the mid-1820s when English-educated Indians started to intervene in the debates of Europeans about their country's governance and education. Orientalism as a practical philosophy was not the property of a domineering European government in Asia, so much as a reflection of its weakness, and of the fear, bafflement and guilt of its expatriate citizens.

Finally, British knowledge of Indians was not a self-sealed system. It arose as much from natural inquisitiveness and the desire to comprehend the world as it was, as from a simple aim of domination. Colonial knowledge became more sophisticated, more contested and contradictory, even while it was punctuated increasingly with racial pejoratives. Much more was actually known about India in 1880 than in 1780 by both Indians and Europeans, and that knowledge was as much an embarrassment as an advantage to its British rulers. For Indians were increasingly producing their own knowledge from reworked fragments of their own tradition melded with western ideas and conveyed through western artefacts. Orientalism in Said's sense became reactive and embattled before it had taken on any kind of shape at all.

Against this background it is easier to measure the impact of British rule on the north Indian information order in the nineteenth century. What emerged was a dual economy of knowledge: an 'advanced' sector, which used western forms of representation and communication subsisting within an attenuated but still massive hinterland employing older styles of information and debate. Initially, the new colonial government succeeded where it was able to take over the flexible system of information collection and diffusion inherited from its Indian predecessors. The newsletter and running spy systems along with the skills of the native munshi remained valuable at least until the Rebellion of 1857. The networks of rural watch and ward also remained operable. To an extent, the British were able to call on these agencies to perform new duties. From the 1830s, village watchmen had been required to report systematically on births in the village. Enumerating the people had become more important to the British partly because taxation was becoming a matter of individual means rather than community obligation, partly because there were moral panics in Britain and among Christian missionaries over infanticide and other abuses. These local systems, however, also transferred their weaknesses into the colonial system, and in some respects had even begun to decay at the fringes as the craze for statistical knowledge edged out human intelligence after 1830.

The survival of the lowly offices of runner, writer and 'intelligent man', and the old communities which performed these tasks, does not, of course, imply straightforward continuity. The categories in which this information was collected and sorted had become different by the 1830s and 1840s. All sorts of things were quantified for the first time, whereas previously, and even for the purposes of investigators such as Francis Buchanan, statistics had been figurative: ten Brahmins, one hundred cows, seven hundred pen-cases, and so on. By the 1830s all criminals were assigned to 'castes' whereas in the day-books of the pre-colonial 'police' a flexible grid of attributions of caste, occupation, or affiliation to nobles had been used. Likewise, the diffuse pieces of information brought by newswriters and runners, and once filtered and organised by the mind of the aged diwan or clever munshi, were now ordered into files, and processed through official publication and the Anglo-Indian press, giving news a formality and fixity previously unknown.

Some pre-colonial institutions – religious establishments, merchant families, the officers of the army, revenue managers – had kept archives.

In the British period, too, new ranges of knowing institutions emerged to fill the gap left by the decline of the affective and patrimonial knowledge that had once flowed between ruler and subject. The army played an important role as a repository of information about the nature of the Indian subject; it also provided a huge range of connections and contacts which brought in data about rural society. The military and civil medical establishments, ranging well beyond their technical medical expertise, measured, counted and theorised about India. The trigonometrical and revenue survey establishments created a fixed map of India through which to incorporate this knowledge. Oriental scholarship, once the domain of the amateur of humanity's past, had acquired a distinctly official status by the 1850s. Most important, public instruction and the range of schoolbook committees associated with it provided a novel means by which the state could intervene in the ways in which young people thought about family, sect or status group.

In these areas, in the great cities, near the railways and cantonments, we can, indeed, posit a revolution in the information order of colonial India. The Director of Public Instruction remained 'Padre' to villagers, his agents meddling Brahmins or snooping Sayyids. There came into being, nevertheless, forms of social power which drew strength from access to different ways of knowing and communicating: journalism, statistics, science, public instruction, textual criticism. The creation of these new knowledgeable institutions tended temporarily to subordinate Indians to what has been called 'colonial discourse'. In the late eighteenth century Indian informants had been pandits and munshis, secure in their own intellectual cultures. They had called on their own ideologies and training to maintain some degree of independence from their British masters. They explained the rational tradition of the Siddhantas or the traditions of Abul Fazl's statesmanship to the British and some of the British listened because they retained respect for Indian knowledge. By the 1840s the new generation of munshis had been subjected to European disciplines. Where previously the British had been taught Persian, penmanship and the poet Sadi, now the Indian informants were salaried officials. They knew English and they kept European clock-time and had mastered, or been mastered by, the disciplines of diary writing and empirical description in sciences such as geography and topography.

Drawing on earlier traditions of learning, debate and the presentation of knowledge, however, Indians soon reacted to this information revolution in ways which instantly subverted its originators' intentions. Their strength was that, increasingly, they could operate in both of the overlapping domains of the colonial information order. They could engage the colonial authorities and the expatriates in their own arenas of publicity through their own media. At the same time they could draw on the huge resources of affective and patrimonial knowledge within their own societies. Very few of the emerging leaders of professional, national and political associations were radical *évolués* in the sense that they spoke only in English and adopted the conquerors' mores and life-style completely, like some of their comperes in other parts of the colonial world. The deeper, more recessed lines of communication and sympathy within Indian society continued to serve well even the most modish of barristers and editors. It was its huge resources of affective knowledge, rather than its exiguous organisation and pathetically mendicant annual meetings, which was to afford the early Indian National Congress significance. Indian nationalist leaders were able to straddle the fissure which had opened up in the information order between the new knowledge communities and the old ecumene and its networks of informants. This was even more true of those humbler publicists connected with the Arya Samaj, Sanatan Dharma societies, caste associations or Muslim purist movements who were able to demonstrate to people in the localities how their particular grievances and aspirations could be ventilated in wider national and regional arenas.

Of course, many of the specific and localised knowledges of the pre-colonial period were swept away along with their practitioners or were reduced to an impoverished subordinate status. The tradition of 'learned' Indian astronomy-cum-astrology, for instance, became no more than a memory of past glory. The Jantar Mantars remained empty monuments to past intellectual heroes. But at a more local level, armed with 'hybridised' astronomical tables made at government observatories and scattered with astrological predictions and Indian merchants' advertisments, joshis passed into the countryside and the tribal fringes, advancing the process by which people outside the realm of stable cultivation were 'caught in the net of Hinduism'. The conceptual revolution which the Serampore missionaries and 'padres' of the educational establishment had hoped to spread through small books, became a print bazaar in which vast numbers of standardised texts of popular devotional works and epics spread a generalised Hindu or Muslim consciousness to the respectable people of the urban and rural worlds. 'Print capitalism', in Benedict Anderson's formulation, gave many existing communities of knowledge the capacity to operate on a wider scale. It was midwife to intellectual change, not in itself the essence of that change.

Thus the gap between the methods of the ecumene and the new western means of knowing and disseminating information certainly became wider in the later nineteenth century. The distance, however, could be creatively spanned by many of the new publicists of the period. Much the same can be said of divisions between religious and caste communities acting within the wider public sphere. As the new media of publicity modified and was modified by the techniques and concerns of the ecumene, representatives of different interests and ideologies within it began to pull apart from each other. The effect of newspapers, mass publishing and the new voluntary associations was to widen those differentials of participation in public debate and those differences of rhetorical style which already existed. In promoting their message, modernist and purist Muslim leaders all used the routines and media of the ecumene – the letter, the juridical pronouncement, the charisma of the kazi and mufti families – along with the printed page and public meeting. The proponents of revived Hindu Dharma did the same. The shastrartha form, for instance, was widely used in debates between the Arya Samaj and more orthodox reformers. But the differences between these two styles of debate on public doctrine were increasingly infused with antagonism. These fissures were widened by the movement for the Devanagari script which threatened to divide the common speech of the ecumene into two 'languages'. Caste reform movements inevitably promoted division as much as they encouraged self respect amongst formerly subordinate groups. At the same time, the geographical scope of the ecumene was circumscribed. The decline of the learned small towns, the qasbahs, proceeded fast after 1860, isolating the more rural communities of knowledge from the new commercial towns. Late-Nawabi Lucknow represented the last phase of an oriental civilisation, as Abdul Halim Sharar sadly noted. Hyderabad was relegated to the margins, and those distant messages from Kabul, Kandahar and Herat became mere whispers.

On the other hand, the picture was not only one of fragmentation, bifurcation and decline. For a short time in the 1880s the Indian National Congress in northern India seemed capable of concerting an alliance of westernised lawyers and newspaper editors with some of the authorities and methods of the ecumene. Even as late as 1919, the Khilafat and Non-Cooperation movements against British rule witnessed a remarkable resurgence of these well-tried modes of publicity, debate and protest. Mosques became centres of political debate once again. Sufi shrines spread political discussion amongst their Muslim and Hindu devotees. Literary men promoted dissenting Urdu verses and popular songs. The charisma of Sufi leaders, kazi families and the big men of the Hindu Ramlila committees were employed to spread a political message which was common property for many north Indians, if not ultimately for all. The colonial revolution in the north Indian information order had perpetuated many earlier forms of publicity, debate and intellectual style which remained active agents in the creation of modern south Asia.

Bibliography

MANUSCRIPT SOURCES IN EUROPEAN LANGUAGES

ORIENTAL AND INDIA OFFICE COLLECTIONS, BRITISH LIBRARY (FORMERLY INDIA OFFICE LIBRARY), LONDON

Amherst Papers, Mss. Eur. F140.
Elphinstone Papers, Mss. Eur. F88.
Hogg Papers, Mss. Eur. E342.
Jyotish Papers, Mss. Eur. C23.
Kirkpatrick Papers, Mss. Eur. F228.
Montgomery Papers, Mss. D1019.
Orme Mss., OV 69.
'Pharmacopoeia', Mss. Eur. E120.
Reade Papers Mss. Eur. E124.
Shore Papers, Mss. Eur. E307.
Spilsbury Papers, Mss. Eur. D909.
Teignmouth, Lord, *Memoirs of the Life, Writings and Correspondence of Sir William Jones to which have been added some autobiographical letters addressed by Sir William to Charles Wilkins, Esq.* (London, 1804), preface p. xii; a copy with the original letters is in Mss. Eur. C227.
Temple Papers, Mss. Eur. F86.
Westmacott Papers, Mss. Eur. C29.
Wilson Papers, Mss. Eur. E301.

BRITISH LIBRARY, LONDON, ADD. MSS.

Auckland Papers.
Bruce Papers.
Cust Papers.
Elliot Papers.
Hastings Papers.
Wellesley Papers.

CAMBRIDGE UNIVERSITY LIBRARY, ETC.

Edmonstone Papers, Add. Mss. 7616 (additional material in Centre of South Asian Studies).

377

Journal of Sir Paul Joddrell, Cambridge University Library, typescript, Oriental Faculty Library Cambridge (IB 065).
Perry Papers, Add. Mss. 5375.

DEVON RECORD OFFICE, EXETER

Kennaway Papers, B961/M.

NEHRU MEMORIAL MUSEUM AND LIBRARY, NEW DELHI

Papers of the Oudh Branch of the British India Association, 1863–7.

ALLAHABAD

Diaries of Sir Sunder Lal Dave, *c.* 1875–85, formerly in possession of Admiral R.N. Dave, Allahabad.

UNPUBLISHED MSS. AND DISSERTATIONS

Bajekal, M., 'Agricultural Production in selected talukas of the Jaipur State, 1700–70', PhD, London University, 1990.
Cooper, R.G.S., 'Cross-cultural conflict analysis. The reality of British victory in the Second Anglo-Maratha War, 1803–5', PhD, Cambridge, 1992.
Kudaisya, Gyanesh, 'State power and the erosion of colonial rule in Uttar Pradesh, India, 1919–47', PhD, Cambridge, 1992.
Losty, J., 'Note on Durga Shankar Pattack's *Sarvasiddhantattvacudamani*'.
Masselos, J., 'Bombay time'.
McGinn, Patrick, 'Governance and resistance in north Indian towns, *c.* 1860–1900', PhD, Cambridge, 1993.
Myint-U, Thant, 'The crisis of the Burmese state and the foundations of colonial rule in upper Burma, 1840–1900', PhD, Cambridge, 1995.
Prior, K.H., 'British administration of Hinduism in north India, 1780–1900', PhD, Cambridge, 1990.
Robinson, F.C.R., 'Ottomans–Safavids–Mughals; shared knowledge and connective systems'.
Stokes, E.T., 'Bentinck to Dalhousie: the rationale of Indian Empire'.

PROCEEDINGS, ETC., OF GOVERNMENTS AND OTHER BODIES

ORIENTAL AND INDIA OFFICE COLLECTIONS, BRITISH LIBRARY

Bengal Criminal Judicial Consultations.
Bengal Political Consultations.
Bengal Secret and Political Consultations.
Board's Collections.

Home Miscellaneous Series.
North-Western Provinces (later North-Western Provinces and Oudh) General
    Proceedings.
NWP Native Newspaper Reports.
NWP Criminal Judicial Proceedings.
NWP and O Education Proceedings.
NWP and O Police Proceedings.

NATIONAL ARCHIVES OF INDIA, NEW DELHI

Foreign and Political Department Consultations.
Home Political Proceedings.

UTTAR PRADESH CENTRAL RECORD OFFICE, ALLAHABAD

Magistrate of Banaras, Post-Mutiny Correspondence.
Proceedings of the Magistrate, Mirzapur.
Proceedings of the Resident (Agent to the Governor-General), Banaras.

MANUSCRIPT TRANSLATIONS OF PERSIAN, SANSKRIT,
ETC. WORKS, OR MANUSCRIPT WORKS FROM WHICH
TRANSLATIONS HAVE BEEN MADE FOR THE AUTHOR

'Account of Bhul pargana and fort (Hissar)', Mss. Eur. D165, OIOC.
'Tarikh-i Ahmad Shah' (tr. D. Forsythe), Elliot Add. Mss. 30,783, BL.
Durga Shankar Patthak, 'Sarvasiddhantattvacudamani', OR. 5259, OIOC (cf.
    note by Dr J. Losty).
'Muntakhul-t-Tawarikh', Elliot, Add. Mss. 30,786, ff. 106–148, BL.
'Tarikh-i Ibrahim Khan', text and full translation, Elliot Add. Mss., 38,704, BL.
'Taskirat-al umara' and 'Taskirat-al akvam', Add. 27, 255, BL.
Bahadur Singh, 'Yadgar-i Bahaduri', tr. Elliot Papers, Add. Mss. 30,786, BL.
Ghulam Hazrat, Mufti, 'Kifayat-i Zillah Gorakhpur' tr. 'History of Goruckpoor',
    1810, Mss. Pers. 1.0.4540, OIOC.
'Hukumnamah Harkaron', Mss. no. 1,681, Asiatic Society of Bengal Library,
    Calcutta.
Khairuddin Hussain Khan, 'Tarikh-i Jaunpur', Add. Mss. 3866, CUL.
'Akhbarat-i Kotwali-yi Laknau', Bodleian Library, Oxford, Add. Pers. Mss.
    2356.
'Majmu'a Walforti', 'being a general report made to Lieut. Col. Wilford by
    Moghal Beg, son of Muhamad Beg Khan on the topography, state of the
    roads and statistics of the Northwest of India', c. 1790', Mss. Eur. F22,
    OIOC.

PUBLISHED TRANSLATIONS OF WORKS IN PERSIAN
AND OTHER ORIENTAL LANGUAGES AND PUBLISHED
WORKS IN THESE LANGUAGES TRANSLATED FOR THE
AUTHOR

Ahmed, T. (tr.), Ishwardas Nagar, *Futuhat-i-Alamgiri* (Delhi, 1978).
Askari, S.H. (tr.), Shiva Das Lakhnavi, *Shahnamah Munawwar Kalam* (Patna, 1980).
Azfari, Ali Bakht, *Waqi'at-e Azfari. Urdu Translation* (Madras, 1957).
Balfour, Francis, 'Insha-i Hari Karan', tr. as *The Forms of Herkern* (Calcutta, 1781).
Begley, W. and Z. Desai (trs., eds.), Inayat Khan, *Shahjahan Nama* (Delhi, 1990).
Belfour, F.C. (tr.), *The Life of Sheikh Mohammmed Ali Hazin written by himself* (London, 1830).
Bilimoria, J.H., *Ruka'at-i-Alamgiri, or letters of Aurangzebe* (repr. Delhi, 1972).
Bilimoria, J.H., *Ruka'at-i-Alamgiri or letters of Aurangzebe with historical and explanatory notes* (London, 1908).
Curwen, F.C. (tr.), Khairuddin Khan Illahabadi, 'Tuhfa-i Taza', entitled *The Bulwuntnamah* (Allahabad, 1875).
Doniger, Wendy, with Brian K. Smith (tr., eds.), *The Laws of Manu* (London, 1991).
Durgaprasada, Pt. and Pt. Sivadatta (eds.), *The Sisupalavadha of Magha* (Bombay, 1914).
Eastwick, E.B., *The Bagh o Bahar* (Hertford, 1852).
Elliot, H.M. and J. Dowson, *The History of India Told by its own Historians*, 8 vols. (London, 1867–77).
Faruqi, K. A. (tr.), Ghalib, *Dastanbuy* (Delhi, 1970).
Ghulam Abdul Qadir Nazir, *Bahar-i-A'zam Jahi*, tr. S. Muhammad Hussain Nainar, *Sources of the History of the Nawwabs of the Carnatic*, IV (Madras, 1950).
Gladwin, Francis (tr., ed.), 'Ain-i Akbari', translated and edited by Francis Gladwin as *Ayeen Akbery or, the Institutes of the Emperor Akber*, 2 vols. (London, 1800).
Gladwin, Francis, *The Persian Moonshee* (section 2; extracts from the 'Shahjahan Namah', etc.) (Calcutta, 1801), p. 58.
Gladwin, Francis, 'Riyaz-as Salatin', tr. as *A Narrative of the Transactions in Bengal during the Soobahdaries of Azem us Shan . . .* (Calcutta, 1788).
Grierson, G.A. (ed., tr.), *The Bhasha-Bhushana of Jaswant Singh* (Bombay, 1894).
Hoey, W. (tr.), Muhammad Faiz Baksh, 'Tarikh-i Farah Baksh' entitled *Memoirs of Delhi and Faizabad*, 2 vols. (Allahabad, 1889).
Lokhandwala, M.F. (tr.), *Mirat-i Ahmadi* of Ali Muhammad Khan (Baroda, 1965).
Maung Htin Aung, *Epistles Written on the Eve of the Anglo-Burmese War* (The Hague, 1968).
Mitra, Rajendra Lal (ed.), *The Nitisara [Elements of Polity] by Kamandaki*, revised with an English translation by Sisir Kumar Mitra (Calcutta, 1982).

National Archives of India (previously Imperial Records Department), *Calendar of Persian Correspondence*, 18 vols. (Calcutta/ Delhi, 1911–89).

Nota-Manus (tr.), Sheikh Ghulam Hussain Tabatabai, 'Siyyar-ul Mutakhkhirin', entitled *Seir Mutaqirin* (Calcutta, 1789; repr., 3 vols. Lahore, 1975).

Pagan U Tin, *Myanma Min Okchokpon Sadan* ('The Government of the Burmese Kings'), 10 vols. (Rangoon, 1963).

Price, D. (tr.), 'Tuzuk-i Jahangiri' tr. D. Price as *Autobiographical Memoirs of the Emperor Jehangueir* (1829, Calcutta, repr. 1972).

Puntambekar, S.V., 'The Ajnapatra or Royal Edict, relating to the principles of Maratha state policy', *Journal of Indian History*, 8, 1929, 81–105, 207–33.

Rahbar, Daud, *Urdu Letters of Mirza Asadu'llah Khan Ghalib*, 2 vols. (Albany, New York, 1987).

Richards, J.F. (tr., ed.), *Document Forms for Official Orders of Appointment in the Mughal Empire* (Cambridge, 1986).

Russell, Ralph and Khurshidul Islam, *Ghalib, 1797–1869*, I, *Life and Letters* (London, 1969).

Sadat Yar Rangin, *Faras Nama e Rangin, or the book of the horse by Rangin*, tr. D.C. Phillot (London, 1911).

Saran, P., *Persian Documents, being letters, newsletters and kindred documents pertaining to the several states existing in India in the last quarter of the eighteenth century from the oriental collection of the National Archives of India* (London, 1966).

Sarkar, Jadunath (tr.), Sujan Rai, 'Chahar Gulshan', in Jadunath Sarkar, *The India of Aurangzib: topography, statistics and roads compared with the India of Akbar* (Calcutta, 1901).

Sarkar, J.N. (tr.), Karam Ali, 'Muzaffarnamah', tr. in *The Bengal Nawabs* (Calcutta, 1952).

Satish Chandra (tr., ed.), Mehta Balmukund, 'Balmukundnamah', tr. as *Letters of a King Maker of the Eighteenth Century* (Aligarh, 1972).

Shea, D. and A. Troyer (tr., eds.), Muhsin Fani, 'Dabistan-al Madhahib', D. Shea and A. Troyer (tr., eds.), *The Dabistan* (repr., Lahore 1973).

Shejwalkar, T. (ed.), *Nagpur Affairs. A Selection of Marathi Letters from the Menavli Daftar* (Pune, 1954).

Snell, Rupert (tr.), *The Eighty-four Hymns of Hita Harivamsa. An edition of the Chaurasi Pada* (Delhi, 1991).

Stewart, Charles (tr.), *Travels of Abu Taleb Khan* (1814, repr. Delhi, 1972).

Suri, V.S. (tr.), Lala Sohan Lal, *Umdat-ut-Tawarikh. Daftar III* (Delhi, 1961).

Tirmizi, S.A.I. (tr., ed.), *Edicts from the Mughal Harem* (Delhi, 1971).

Tirmizi, S.A.I. (tr., ed.), *Index to Titles, 1798–1855* (Delhi, 1979).

Tirmizi, S.A.I. (tr., ed.), *Persian Letters of Ghalib* (Delhi, 1969).

Vad, G.C. (ed.), *Selections from the Satara Rajas' and the Peshwas' Diaries* (Bombay, 1907–11)

Verma, B.D. (ed.), *News-letters of the Mughal court (reign of Ahmad Shah, 1751–2 A.D.)* (Bombay, 1949).

HINDI BOOKS

Anon., *Dak Bijli* (Allahabad, 1856).

Anon., *Ingland Dvipadipika* (Agra, 1841).

Anon., *Jyotish Vidya ka Varnan* (Agra, 1840).

Anon., *Mahajanon ki Pustaka* (Agra, 1849).

Anon., *Paddhati Vivaha ki* (Allahabad, 1870).

Anon., *Padharthi Vidyasara balakon jan ke liye* (Calcutta, 1846).

Anon., *Panchanga Sambat 1925, Agra, muhar Satsabha,* and other *panchang*s, VT, 1528, OIOC.

Anon., *Patwariyon ki Pustaka* (Agra, 1848).

Anon., *Samudrika* (Banaras, 1851).

Anon., *Vidyabhasa ka Phala aur jojo Vidya pradhan hai* (Agra, 1839).

Bansidhar, Pandit, *Ganga ki Nahar ka Samkhep* (Agra, 1854).

Bhatta, Pandit Omkar, *Bhugolasara arthart Jyotish Chandrika, jis me Purana aur Siddhanta ki Koparnikas Sahib ki Jyotish Vidya se Pariksha ki* (Agra 1841).

Chaturvedi, R.N., *Mahamana Pandit Madan Mohan Malaviya* (Banaras, 1936).

Gurusarana Lala, *Avadhayatra* (Lucknow, 1869).

Harivilasa, *Rogakarshana* (Agra, 1872).

Ratna Lala, Pandit, *Bhugol Darpan Pathshalaon ke liye* (Orphan Press, Agra, 1842).

Ratneswaraji, Pandit, *Patramalika. Sehor niwasi Pandit Ratneswaraji ne Sehor se Bambai tak yatra karne me . . .* (Agra, 1841).

Sharma, G.D. (ed.), *Vakil Reports Maharajgan (1693–1712 A.D.)* (Delhi, 1987).

Shiva Prasad, Babu, *Sikhon ka Udaya aur Asta* (Banaras, 1851).

Shiva Prasad, Babu, *Manava Dharmasara* (Banaras, 1856).

Shiva Prasad, Babu, *Vamamanoranjana* (Banaras, 1849).

Shiva Prasad, Babu, *Vidyankur* (Banaras 1856).

Vrajratnadas (ed.), *Bhartendu Granthavali,* 3 vols. (Banaras, 1953).

Vrajratandas, *Bhartendu Harischandra* (Allahabad, 1962).

CONTEMPORARY WORKS IN EUROPEAN LANGUAGES (TO C. 1890)

Ainslie, Whitelaw, *Materia Indica, or some account of those articles which are employed by the Hindoos and other eastern nations in their medicines, arts and agriculture* (Madras, 1813, revised edn, 2 vols., London, 1826).

Ali, Shahamat, *The Sikhs and Afghans in connection with India and Persia immediately before and after the death of Ranjeet Singh* (London, 1849).

Ali, Shahamat, *The History of Bahawalpur with notices of the adjacent countries of Sindh, Afghanistan . . . ,* 2 vols. (London, 1848).

Annesley, J., *Sketches of the most prevalent diseases of India, comprising a treatise of the epidemic cholera of the East* (London, 1825).

Anon., *The Hindoos. Library of entertaining knowledge,* 2 vols. (London, 1939).

Anon., *Chandra Ghumana Vichar (Does the Moon rotate? A Question argued in Sanskrit and English by the Pandits of the Benares College* (Banaras, 1857).

Anquetil Duperron, A.H. *Recherches Historiques et Geographiques par Anquetil Duperron,* ed. J. Bernouilli, 2 vols. (Paris, 1886).

Arnold, E., *Education in India. A Letter from the Ex-principal of an Indian Government College* (London, 1860).

Bailly, Jean Sylvain, *Traité de l'Astronomie Indienne et Orientale* (Paris, 1787).

Balfour, E.G., *The Cyclopaedia of India and of Eastern and Southern Asia,* 4 vols. (Madras, 1858, rev. edn, 4 vols., London, 1885).

Ballantyne, J.R., *Christianity Contrasted with Hindu Philosophy* ... (London, 1859).

Ballantyne, J.R., *Aphorisms of the Mimansa Philosophy by Jaimini* (Allahabad, 1851).

Ballantyne, J.R., *Lectures on the Nyaya Philosophy embracing the Text of the Tarka Sangraha* (Banaras, 1848).

Ballantyne, J.R., *A Grammar of the Hindustani Language* (Edinburgh, 1838).

Bentley, J., *An Historical View of the Hindoo Astronomy* (London, 1799).

Bernier, François, *Travels in the Mogul Empire A.D. 1656–1668, Constable's Oriental Miscellany* (repr., London, 1891).

Proceedings of the Bethune Society from November 10 1859 to April 12 1869 (Calcutta, 1870).

Bhargava, K.D. (ed.), *Browne Correspondence* (Delhi, 1960).

Boileau, A.H.E., *Personal Narrative of a Tour through the western states of Rajwara in 1835*, 2 vols. (Calcutta, 1837).

Broughton, T.D., *Letters from a Mahratta Camp in the year 1809* (repr. London, 1892).

Brown, James, *History of the Origin and Progress of the Sicks* (London, 1787), repr. in G. Singh (ed.), *Early European Accounts of the Sikhs* (Calcutta, 1962).

Buchanan, Francis, ed. M. Martin, *The History, Antiquities, Topography and Statistics of Eastern India*, 3 vols. (London, 1838).

Buchanan, F., *A Journey from Madras through the countries of Mysore ...* , 2 vols. (London, 1807).

Buchanan (Hamilton), F., *An Account of the Kingdom of Nepaul and of the territories annexed to this dominion by the house of Gorkha* (Edinburgh, 1819).

Burnell, A.C., *A Classified Index to the Sanskrit Mss. in the Palace at Tanjore* (London, 1880).

Burnes, Alexander, *Travels into Bokhara, being the account of a journey from India to Cabool, Tartary and Persia*, 3 vols. (London, 1834).

Burney, Henry, 'On the population of the Burman Empire', 1842, reprint, *Journal of the Burma Research Society*, 31, i, 1941, 19–33.

Chapman, Priscilla, *Hindoo Female Education* (London, 1839).

Chardin, J., *Voyages du Chevalier du Chardin en Perse et autres lieux de l'Orient*, 8 vols. (Paris, 1811).

Christian, G., *Census of the North-West Provinces of the Bengal Presidency taken on 1st June 1853* (Calcutta, 1854).

Chunder, Bholanauth, *Travels of a Hindoo to Various Parts of Bengal and Upper India*, 2 vols. (London, 1869).

Cox, Capt. Hiram, *Journal of a Residence in the Burmhan Empire and more particularly at the court of Amarapoorah* (London, 1821).

Creighton, J.N., *Narrative of the Siege and Capture of Bhurtpore in the Province of Agra, Upper Hindoostan* (London, 1830).

Crooke, William, *An Ethnographic Hand-book for the Northwestern Provinces and Oudh* (Allahabad, 1890).

Crooke, William, *The North-Western Provinces of India. Their history, ethnology and administration* (London, 1897).

Crooke, William, *The Tribes and Castes of the North-western Provinces*, 4 vols. (Calcutta, 1896).

Crooke, William, ed. Shahid Amin, *A Glossary of North Indian Peasant Life* (orig. 1879, repr. Delhi, 1989).

Cust, R.N., *Linguistic and Oriental Essays*, 2nd series (London, 1887).

Das, Satyajit (ed.), *Selections from the Indian Journals* (Calcutta, 1963).

Dirom, Major, *A Narrative of the Campaign in India which terminated the war with Tippoo Sultan in 1792* (London, 1794).

Dow, Alexander, *The History of Hindostan*, 2 vols. (London, 1768).

Elliot, H.M., *Memoirs on the History, Folk-Lore, and Distribution of the Races of the North Western Provinces of India*, ed. J. Beames, I (London, 1859).

Elphinstone, Mountstuart, *Account of the Kingdom of Caubul*, 2 vols. (London, 1815).

Fallon, S.W., *A New Hindustani–English Dictionary* (Banaras and London, 1879).

Ferrier, J.P., *Caravan Journeys and Wanderings in Persia, Afghanistan, Turkistan and Beloochistan* (London, 1857).

Fryer, John, ed. W. Crooke, *A New Account of East India and Persia* (repr., 3 vols., London, 1909).

Garcin de Tassy, J.H., *Histoire de la Littérature Hindouie et Hindoustanie*, 4 vols. (1870, repr. New York, 1972).

Gazetteer of Burma, 3 vols. (Rangoon, 1880).

Gazetteer of the Kangra District. Kangra Proper, 1883–4 (Calcutta, 1884).

Gilchrist, John, *Hindoostanee Philology*, I (Edinburgh, 1810).

Gilchrist, John, *A Collection of Dialogues English and Hindoostanee* (Calcutta, 1804).

Gouger, H., *A Personal Narrative of two years imprisonment in Burmah* (London, 1860).

Grierson, G.A., *The Modern Vernacular Literature of Hindustan* (Calcutta, 1889).

Grierson, G.A., *Bihar Peasant Life* (Calcutta, 1885).

Hadley, George, *A Compendious Grammar of the Current Corrupt Dialect of the Jargon of Hindostan (commonly called Moors)* (orig. *c.* 1772, London, 1796).

Harriot, J., *Soldiers Manual for the use of Infantry in Nagri and English character* (Calcutta, 1824).

Heber, Bishop Reginald, *Narrative of a Journey through the Upper Provinces of India*, 2 vols. (London, 1844).

Hodgson, B.H., *Essays on the Languages, Literatures and Religion of Nepal and Tibet . . .* , 2 vols. (London, 1874).

Hodgson, J.S., *Opinions on the Indian Army* (London, 1857).

Hodson, G.H., *Twelve Years of a Soldier's Life in India; being extracts from the letters of Major W.S.R. Hodson, B.A.* (London, 1859).

Howison, J., *European Colonies in Various Parts of the World* (London, 1834).

Hunter, W.W., *Annals of Rural Bengal* (Calcutta, 1868).

Irvine, R.H., *Some Account of the General and Medical Topology of Ajmeer* (Calcutta, 1841).

Judson, Adoniram (and others), *A Dictionary of the Burman Language with explanations in English from the manuscripts of A. Judson and other missionaries* (Calcutta, 1826).

Judson, Anne Hasseltine, *An Account of the American Baptist Mission to the Burman Empire* (London, 1823).

Judson, E., *Life of Adoniram Judson* (New York, 1883).

Kaye, J. W., *A History of the War in Afghanistan* (London, 1857–8).

Kaye, J.W., *The Administration of the East India Company; A History of Indian Progress* (London, 1853).

Kaye, J.W. and C.B. Malleson, *Kaye's and Malleson's History of the Indian Mutiny of 1857–8*, 5 vols. (1897–8, repr. London, 1971).

Kellie, J., *Dissertation Medica Inauguralis, complectus pauca de morba epidemico, qui nomine cholera spasmodica, per Indiam Orientam nuper grassatus est* (Edinburgh, 1820).

Kirkpatrick, William, *An Account of the Kingdom of Nepaul being the substance of observations made during a mission to that country in the year 1793 by Col. Kirkpatrick* (London, 1811).

Lawrence, H.M.L., *Adventures of an Officer in the Service of Runjeet Singh* (London, 1845, repr. Karachi, 1975).

Leitner, G.W., *History of Indigenous Education in the Panjab since Annexation and in 1882* (Calcutta, 1882).

Leupolt, Revd, C.B., *Recollections of an Indian Missionary* (London, 1846).

Lowrie, John C., *Two Years in Upper India* (New York, 1850).

Malcolm, John, *A Memoir of Central India*, 2 vols. (London, 1824).

Malcolm, John, *Political History of India*, 2 vols. (London, 1826).

Manucci, N., W. Irvine (tr.), *Storio do Mogor, or Mughal India, 1653–1703 by Niccolao Manucci*, 3 vols. (London, 1907).

Masson, Charles, *Narrative of Various Journeys in Balochistan, Afghanistan and the Punjab*, 3 vols. (London, 1842).

Maxwell, W.G., *A Practical Treatise on Epidemic Cholera, Ague and Dysentery* (Calcutta, 1838).

Meer Hassan Ali, Mrs., *Observations on the Mussulmauns of India* (1832, repr. Oxford, 1917).

Mittra, R., *A Catalogue of Sanskrit Manuscripts in the Library of his Highness the Maharaja of Bikaner* (Calcutta, 1880).

Mohan Lal, Munshi, *Journal of a Tour through the Panjab, Afghanistan ...* (Calcutta, 1834).

Mohan Lal, Munshi, *Life of Amir Dost Mohammed Khan of Kabul*, 2 vols. (London, 1846).

Monserrate, Fr, Hoyland, J. (ed., tr.), *The Commentary of Father Monserrate on his journey to the Court of Akbar* (Oxford, 1922).

Muir, William, *Records of the Intelligence Department of the Government of the North-West Provinces of India during the Mutiny of 1857*, 2 vols. (Edinburgh, 1902).

Muir, William, *Mahomet and Islam. A sketch of the Prophet's Life from original sources, and a brief outline of his religion* (London, 1887).

Nesfield, J.C., *The Functions of Modern Brahmins in Upper India* (Calcutta, 1887).

Nesfield, J.C., *A Brief View of the Caste System of the North-Western Provinces and Oudh* (Allahabad, 1885).

Nicholls, G.A., *Grammar of Geography adapted to the Education of Indian Youth* (Calcutta, 1838).

North-Western Provinces, Government of, *Selections from the Records of the Government, North Western Provinces*, 5 vols. (Agra, 1852–6)

Ochterlony, Sinha, N.K. (ed.), *Selections from the Ochterlony Papers 1818–25) in the National Archives of India*, 2 vols. (Calcutta, 1964).

Parliamentary Papers, 'Trial of the King of Delhi', 1859, sess. 1, 18.

Phayre, A.P., *History of Burma, including Burma Proper, Pegu, Taungu, Tenasserim and Arakan* (London, 1883, rep. 1967).

Philips, C.H., *The Correspondence of Lord William Cavendish Bentinck, Governor-General of India, 1825–35*, 2 vols. (Oxford, 1977).

Ramchandra, Yesudas, *A Treatise on the Problems of Maxima and Minima . . . reproduced by order of the East India Company* (London, 1850).

Reade, E.A., *Contributions to the Benares Recorder in 1852* (Banaras, 1858).

Rennell, James, *Memoir of a Map of Hindostan or the Moguls Empire* (3rd edn, London, 1793).

Royle, J.F., *An Essay in the Antiquity of Hindoo Medicine*, 2 vols. (London, 1837).

Sangermano, Fr Vincentius, *A Description of the Burmese Empire compiled chiefly from Burmese Documents by Father Sangermano translated from his manuscript by William Tandy D.D.* (1833, repr., 2 vols. London, 1966).

Saraswati, Dayananda, *Satyarth Prakash*, tr. as *Light of Truth* by G. Bharadwaja (Lahore, 1927).

Sastri, Bapu Deva, *The Surya-Siddhanta, an ancient system of Hindu astronomy; with Ranganatha's exposition, the Gudhartha Prakasaka*, edited by F. Hall, with the assistance of Bapu Deva Sastrin [sic], *Bibilioteca Indica*, 25 (Calcutta 1854–9).

Sastri, Bapu Deva, *A Translation of the Surya Siddhanta by Pundit Bapu Deva Sastri, and of the Siddhanta Siromani by the late Lancelot Wilkinson, esq. C.S.* (Calcutta 1861).

Sen, A.G., *The Post Office of India* (Calcutta, 1875).

Sen, S.N. (ed.), *Indian Travels of Thevenot and Careri. Indian Records Series* (Delhi, 1949).

Shakespear, A. *Selections from the Duncan Records* (Banaras, 1873).

Sherring, M.A., *Hindu Tribes and Castes as represented in Benares*, 3 vols. (London, 1872).

Sherring, M.A., *The Sacred City of the Hindus. An account of Benares in ancient and modern times* (London, 1868).

Shipp, John, *Memoirs of the Extraordinary Military Career of John Shipp, late a Lieutenant in H.H. 87th Regiment*, 3 vols. (London, 1832).

Shoolbred, J., *Report on the progress of vaccine innoculation in Bengal from the period of its introduction in November 1802 to the end of 1803* (London, 1804).

Singh, Kuar Lachman, *A Historical and Statistical Memoir of Zila Bulandshahar* (Allahabad, 1874).

Sleeman, W.H., *Rambles and Recollections of an Indian Official*, ed. V.A. Smith (London, 1915, repr. Karachi, 1973).

Sleeman, W.H., *Ramaseeana, or a Vocabulary of the peculiar language used by the Thugs . . .* (Calcutta, 1836).

Snodgrass, Major J., *Narrative of the Burmese War* (London, 1827).

Sprenger, Alois, *A Catalogue of the Arabic, Persian and Hindustani Manuscripts in the Libraries of the King of Oudh* (Calcutta, 1854).

Sprenger, Alois, *Report of the Researches into the Muhammadan Libraries of Lucknow* (Calcutta, 1896).

Spry, *Modern India. With Illustrations of the Capabilities and Resources of Hindustan*, 2 vols. (London, 1837).

Stewart, Charles, *A History of Bengal from the First Muhammadan Invasion until the virtual conquest of that country by the English, A.D. 1757* (London, 1813).

Stewart, Charles, *A Descriptive Catalogue of the Oriental Library of the late Tippoo Sultan of Mysore* (Cambridge, 1809).

Stuart, R. and B. Philipps, *Report of the Epidemic of Cholera which has raged through Hindostan and The Peninsula of India since August 1817* (Bombay, 1817).

Symonds, Revd A.R., *Introduction to the Geography and History of India* (Madras, 1845).

Tavernier, J-B., *The Six Voyages of John Baptist Tavernier* (London, 1678).

Taylor, Meadows, *Confessions of a Thug* (London, 1839).

Temple, R.C., *A Dissertation on the Proper Names of Panjabis* (Bombay, 1883).

Thomason, James, *Speech Delivered at the Opening of the Benares New College, Jan. 11, 1853* (Benares, 1853).

Thompson, J.T., *A Dictionary in Hindee and English compiled from approved authorities* (Calcutta, 1846).

Thornton, E., *Chapters of the Modern History of British India* (London, 1840).

Tilak, Bal Ganghadar, *Orion, or researches into the Antiquity of the Vedas by B.G. Tilak, BA, LLB* (London, 1892).

Tilak, Bal Gangadhar, *The Arctic Home in the Vedas, being also a key text to many Vedic texts and legends* (Pune, 1903).

Tod, James, *Annals and Antiquities of Rajast'han, or the central and western Rajpoot states of India* (London, 1829–32, repr., 3 vols. 1950).

'Trial of the King of Delhi', *Parliamentary Papers*, 1859, sess. 1, 18.

Tupper, C.L., *Statements of Customary Law in different Districts* (Calcutta, 1881).

Walton, H.G. (ed.), *Almora. A Gazetteer. District Gazetteers of the United Provinces of Agra and Oudh*, 35 (Allahabad, 1911).

Wellington, Arthur, Duke of, *Dispatches* (4 vols., London, 1837).

Wendel, X., J. Deloche (ed.), *Les Mémoires de Wendel sur les Jat, les Pathan et les Sikh* (Paris, 1979).

Wilkinson, Lancelot, tr., *The Goladhia: a treatise on astronomy with a commentary entitled the mitacshara, forming the fourth and last chapter of the Siddhant Shiromuni* (Calcutta, 1842).

Williamson, Capt., ed. J.B. Gilchrist, *General East India Guide and Vade Mecum for the Public Functionary, Government Officer, Private Agent or Foreign Sojourner* (London, 1825).

Wilson, H.H., *Two lectures on the Religious Practices and Opinions of the Hindus delivered before the University of Oxford* (Oxford, 1840).

Wilson, H.H. *Glossary of Judicial and Revenue Terms* (Calcutta, 1864).

Wise, T.A., *Commentary on the Hindu System of Medicine* (Calcutta, 1845).

Yates, W., *Introduction to the Hindoostanee Language* (Calcutta, 1827).

CONTEMPORARY JOURNALS, SERIALS AND NEWSPAPERS, TO 1880

Asiatic Annual Register.

Asiatic Journal.
Asiatic Researches.
Benares Magazine.
Benares Recorder.
Bengal Hurkaru.
Bharat Jivan (Hindi).
Calcutta Journal.
Calcutta Review.
Church Missionary Register.
Delhi Gazette.
Dihli Urdu Akhbar (Urdu), selections. ed. K.A. Faruqi (Delhi, 1972).
East Indian United Service Journal.
Englishman.
Friend of India.
Gleanings in Science.
Hindi Pradipa (Hindi).
Histoire de l'Académie Royale des Sciences. Anné 1772. Seconde Partie. Avec les Mémoires de Mathématique et de Physique pour la même Anné (Paris, 1776).
Indian Journal of Medical Science.
Journal of the Royal Asiatic Society.
Journale Asiatique.
Lahore Chronicle.
Ledlie's Miscellany and Journal for the North West.
Meerut Universal Magazine.
The Missionary Register for MDCCCXXIV (London, 1824).
Mofussilite.
The Pandit. A monthly publication of the Benares College devoted to Sanskrit Literature.
Philosophical Transactions of the Royal Society of London for the year 1792 (London, 1792).
Transactions of the Literary Society of Bombay.
Transactions of the Medical and Physical Society of Calcutta.

JOURNALS, ETC. SINCE C. 1885

American Anthropologist.
Annales.
Bengal Past and Present.
Bharata Itihasa Sanshodhaka Mandala Quarterly.
Cartographica.
The Cartographical Journal.
Comparative Studies in Society and History.
English Historical Review.
Historical Journal.
Indian Economic and Social History Review.
Intelligence and National Security.
Iranian Studies.
Journal of the American Oriental Society.

Journal of Asian Studies.
Journal of the Asiatic Society.
Journal of the Bihar and Orissa Research Society.
Journal of the Economic and Social History of the Orient.
Journal of Indian History.
Journal of Japan Netherlands Research Institute.
Journal of World History.
Mahfil.
Modern Asian Studies.
Past and Present.
Representations.
Southwestern Journal of Anthropology.

SECONDARY WORKS, AFTER C. 1885

Ahmed, Aijaz, *Orientalism and After; ambivalence and cosmopolitan location in the work of Edward Said* (New York, 1993).
Ahuja, A.M. and N.D., *Persecution of Muslims by Aurangzeb. Guru Tegh Bahadaur's Martyrdom Centenary Publication* (Chandigarh, 1981).
Alam, Muzaffar, *The Crisis of Empire in Mughal North India* (Delhi, 1986).
Alam, Muzaffar and Sanjay Subrahmanyam, 'L'état Moghol et sa fiscalité (xviie–xviiie siècles)', *Annales*, 49, 1, 1994, 189–218.
Alavi, Seema, *The Sepoys and the Company* (Delhi, 1995).
Alavi, Seema, 'The Company Army and rural society: the invalid thanah, 1780–1830', *MAS*, 27, 1, 1992, 147–78.
Alavi, Seema, 'The Makings of Company Power: James Skinner in the Ceded and Conquered Provinces, 1802–40', *IESHR*, 30, 4, 1993, 437–66.
Alder, G., *Beyond Bokhara. The life of William Moorcroft Asian explorer and pioneer veterinary surgeon, 1767–1825* (London, 1985).
Ali, Rahman, *Tazkira-i Ulama-i Hind*, 4 vols. (Lucknow, 1914).
Ali, S.M., *The Geography of the Puranas* (New Delhi, 1983).
Allison, W., *The Sadhs* (Calcutta, 1934).
Anderson, Benedict, *Imagined Communities. An Inquiry into the origin of Nations* (revised edn, Cambridge, Mass., 1993).
Andrews, C.F., *Zakaullah of Delhi* (Cambridge, 1929).
Ansari, Ghaus, *Muslim Caste in Uttar Pradesh. A Study in Cultural Contact* (Lucknow, 1960).
Appadurai, Arjun, 'Is Homo Hierarchicus?', *American Anthropologist*, 13, 1986, 754–61.
Archer Mildred and William Archer, *Indian Painting for the British, 1770–1880* (Oxford, 1955).
Archer, Mildred and Falk Toby, *India Revealed. The Art and Adventures of James and William Fraser 1801–35* (London, 1989).
Arjomand, S.A., *The Shadow of God and the Hidden Imam* (Chicago, 1984).
Arnold, David, *Police Power and Colonial Rule. Madras 1859–1947* (Oxford, 1986).
Arnold, David, *Colonising the Body. The State and Epidemic Disease in Nineteenth Century India* (Berkeley, 1993).

Arshi, Imtiaz Ali, *A Catalogue of Arabic Manuscripts in Raza Library, Rampur,* 7 vols. (Rampur, 1963–77).

Asad, Talal, *Anthropology and the Colonial Encounter* (London, 1973).

Asopa, J.N. (ed.), *Cultural Heritage of Jaipur* (Jodhpur, 1982).

Bahura, G.N., 'Glimpses of historical information from the manuscripts in the *potikhana* of Jaipur', J.N. Asopa (ed.), *Cultural Heritage of Jaipur* (Jodhpur, 1982).

Ballhatchet, Kenneth, *Social Policy and Social Change in Western India, 1817–1830* (London, 1957).

Barnett, Richard B., *North India Between Empires. Awadh the Mughals and the British, 1720–1801* (Berkeley, 1980).

Barooah, N.K., *David Scott in North-East India. A Study in British Paternalism* (Delhi, 1970).

Barrier, N., *Banned. Controversial literature and political control in British India, 1907–47* (Delhi, 1976).

Basu, Dilip, 'Early banians in Calcutta: the Setts and Bysacks in their own image', *Bengal Past and Present*, 90, 1971, 30–46.

Bayly, C.A., *Rulers, Townsmen and Bazaars. North India in the Age of British Expansion, 1780–1870* (Cambridge, 1983).

Bayly, Susan, *Saints, Goddesses and Kings. Muslims and Christians in South Indian Society, 1700–1900* (Cambridge, 1989).

Beadon, H.C., *Customary Law of Delhi District* (Lahore, 1911).

Bhat, M. Ramakrishna, *Essentials of Horary Astrology or Prasnapadavi* (Delhi, 1992).

Bhabha, Homi K., *The Location of Culture* (London, 1995).

Bhattacharya, D.P., *Report on the Population Estimates of India, 1820–1830* (Delhi, 1962–5).

Bhatnagar, V.S., *Life and Times of Sawai Jai Singh 1688–1743* (Delhi, 1974).

Bhargava, M., 'Perceptions and Classification of the rights of social classes: Gorakhpur and the East India Company in the late eighteenth and early nineteenth century', *IESHR*, xxx, 2, 1993, 215–37.

Biddulph, Col. J., *The Nineteenth and their Times* (London, 1899).

Blake, Stephen P., *Shahjahanabad. The sovereign city in Mughal India 1639–1739* (Cambridge, 1991).

Blumhardt, J.F., *Catalogue of the Library of the India Office*, II, 2 (London, 1900).

Bose, D.M., S.N. Sen and B.V. Subbarayappa, *A Concise History of Science in India* (Calcutta, 1971).

Bowen, Margaret, *Empiricism and Geographical Thought from Francis Bacon to Alexander von Humboldt* (Cambridge, 1981).

Brass, Paul R., *Language, Religion and Politics in North India* (Cambridge, 1974).

Breckenridge, C. and P. Van der Veer, *Orientalism and the Postcolonial Predicament* (New York, 1993).

Brennand, W., *Hindu Astronomy* (London, 1896).

Brodkin, E.I., 'The struggle for succession. Rebels and loyalists in the Indian Rebellion of 1857', *MAS*, 6, 3, 1972, 277–90.

Buckland, C.E., *Dictionary of Indian Biography* (London, 1906).

Buckler, F.W., 'The political theory of the Indian Mutiny of 1857', *Transactions of the Royal Historical Society*, 4 series, v, 1922, 71–100.

Calhoun, C. (ed.), *Habermas and the Public Sphere* (Cambridge, Mass., 1992).

Carter, H., *Sir Joseph Banks (1743–1820). A Guide to biographical and bibliographical sources* (London, 1987).

Castells, Manuel, *The Informational City. Information technology, economic restructuring and the urban–regional process* (Oxford, 1989).

Chakrabarty, Dipesh, 'Modernity and ethnicity in India', *South Asia*, special issue, 17, 1994, pp. 147–9.

Chandavarkar, R.S., 'Plague, panic and epidemic politics in India, 1896–1914' in P. Slack (ed.), *Epidemics and Ideas. Essays on the historical perceptions of pestilence* (Cambridge, 1992), pp. 203–40.

Chandra, Sudhir, *The Oppresive Present: literature and social consciousness in colonial India* (Delhi, 1992).

Chatterjee, Kumkum, 'Collaboration and conflict: bankers and early colonial rule in India, 1715–1813', *Indian Economic and Social History Review*, 30, 3, 1993, 283–310.

Chaudhuri, K.N., *The Trading World of Asia and the English East India Company, 1600–1760* (Cambridge, 1978).

Chaudhuri, Sukanta (ed.), *Calcutta, the Living City*, I (Calcutta, 1990).

Chopra, H.L., *Pandit Mohan Lal Kashmiri* (Delhi, 1979).

Cohn, Bernard, 'The Command of Language and the Language of Command' in R. Guha (ed.), *Subaltern Studies*, IV (Delhi, 1985), 276–329.

Cole, Juan R. I., *The Roots of North Indian Shi'ism in Iran and Iraq. Religion and State in Awadh, 1722–1859* (Berkeley, 1988).

Cole, Juan R.I., 'Invisible Occidentalism. Eighteenth-century Indo-Persian constructions of the West', *Iranian Studies*, 3–4, 1992, 3–16.

Collins, Randall, *Weberian Sociological Theory* (Cambridge, 1986).

Cort, John E., 'The Jain knowledge warehouses: traditional libraries in India', *Journal of the American Oriental Society*, 115, I, 1995, 77–88.

Crawford, D.G., *A History of the Indian Medical Service, 1600–1913*, 3 vols. (London, 1914).

Crooke, William, *The Tribes and Castes of the North-Western Provinces and Oudh* (Calcutta, 1896).

Dale, Stephen, F., *Indian Merchants and Eurasian Trade* (Cambridge, 1994).

Danvers, C., M. Monier Williams, et al., *Memorials of Old Haileybury College* (Westminster, 1894).

Das Gupta, Ashin, *Indian Merchants and the Decline of Surat, c. 1700–1750* (Wiesbaden, 1979).

Dasgupta, D.C., *The Jaina System of Education* (Calcutta, 1944).

Datta, B.K., *Libraries and Librarianship of Ancient and Medieval India* (Delhi, 1970).

Datta, K.K., 'Raja Jhaw Lal of the Oudh Court', *Journal of the Bihar and Orissa Research Society*, 23, 4, 1937, 502–15.

Davis, Emmett, *The Press and Politics in British West Punjab, 1836–47* (Delhi, 1983).

Daw Mya Sein, *The Administration of Burma* (repr. Singapore, 1973)

Deloche, Jean, *Transport and Communications in India prior to Steam Locomotion* (Delhi, 1993).

Desai, W.S. 'A map of Burma (1795) by a Burmese slave', *JBRS*, 26, 1936, 147–51.

Deutsch, Karl, *Nationalism and Social Communication. An enquiry into the foundations of nationality* (Cambridge, Mass., 1960).

Diamond, Alan, *The Victorian Achievement of Sir Henry Maine. A centennial reappraisal* (Cambridge, 1991).

Digby, Simon, 'The Bhugola of Ksema Karna: a dated sixteenth century piece of Indian metalware', *Art and Archaeology Research Papers*, 4, 1973, 10–31.

Dirks, Nicholas B., 'Castes of Mind', *Representations*, 37, winter 1992, pp. 56–77.

Dumont, Louis, *Homo Hierarchicus. The caste system and its implications* (London, 1970).

Dundas, P., *The Jains* (London, 1992).

Eaton, Richard M., *Sufis of Bijapur, 1300–1700. Social roles in Medieval India* (Princeton, 1978).

Edney, Matthew, 'The patronage of science and the creation of imperial space', *Cartographica*, 30, I, 1993, 61–7.

Edney, Matthew, 'British military education, map-making and military "mapmindedness" in the late enlightenment', *The Cartographic Journal*, 31, I, 1994, 14–20.

Encyclopaedia of Islam, new edn, 5 vols. (London, 1960–).

Enriquez, C.M., 'Bandula – A Burmese Soldier', *JBRS*, 11, 1921, 158–62.

Entwistle, A.W., *Braj. Centre of Krishna Pilgrimage* (Groningen, 1987).

Ethé, H., *Catalogue of Persian Manuscripts in the Library of the India Office* (London, 1903).

Ethé, H., *Catalogue of the Persian . . . Manuscripts in the Bodleian Library* (Oxford, 1930).

Ferrier, R.W., 'The Armenians and the East India Company in the 17th and early 18th century', *English Historical Review*, 2nd. ser., xxvi, 1973, 38–62.

Fisher, Michael H., *Indirect Rule in India. Residents and the Residency System, 1764–1857* (Delhi, 1991).

Fisher, Michael H., 'The office of Akhbar Nawis. The transition from Mughal to British forms', *Modern Asian Studies*, 27, I, 1993, 45–82.

Fisher, Michael H., 'The East India Company's "suppression of the native dak" ', *IESHR*, xxxi, 3, 1994, 319–26.

Foucault, Michel, 'Two lectures' in N. Dirks, G. Eley and S. Ortner (eds.), *Culture/Power/History. A reader in contemporary Social theory* (Princeton, 1994).

Francke, A.H., *Antiquities of Indian Tibet*, II, *Archaeological Survey of India, New Imperial Series*, vol. L (Calcutta, 1926).

Frawley, D., *Ayurvedic Healing. A Comprehensive Guide* (Delhi, 1992).

Freitag, Sandria, *Collective Action and Community. Public arenas and the emergence of communalism in north India* (Berkeley, 1989).

Freitag, Sandria (ed.), *Culture and Power in Banaras. Community, performance and environment, 1800–1989* (Berkeley, 1989).

Fritz, P., 'The anti-Jacobite intelligence system of the English ministers, 1715–45', *Historical Journal*, xvi, 1973, 265–89.

Fussfeld, Warren, *The Shaping of Sufi Leadership in Delhi. The Naqshbandiyya Mujaddidiyya 1750–1820* (Ann Arbor, 1981).

Garrett, H.L.O. and G.L.Chopra, *Events at the Court of Ranjit Singh, 1810–1817* (Lahore, 1935).

Gazetteer of Burma (repr., Rangoon, 1880).

Gellner, Ernest, *Plough, Sword and Book. The Structure of Human History* (London, 1991).

Ghosal, U.N. *A History of Indian Political Ideas* (Madras, 1966).

Gold, D., 'What the merchant-guru sold; social and literary types in Hindi devotional verse', *Journal of the American Oriental Society*, 112, 1, 1992, 22–36.

Gole, Susan, *Indian Maps and Plans from the earliest times to the advent of European Surveys* (Delhi, 1989).

Gommans, J., *The Rise of the Indo-Afghan Empire, c. 1710–1780* (Leiden, 1994).

Gommans, J., 'The Horse Trade in Eighteenth Century South Asia', *Journal of the Economic and Social History of the Orient*, 37, 3, 1994, 228–50.

Gopal, Madan, *Bhartendu Harishchandra* (Delhi, 1971).

Gopal, Surendra, *Patna in the Nineteenth Century. A socio-cultural profile* (Calcutta, 1982).

Gordon, Stewart N., 'Bhils and the idea of a criminal tribe in nineteenth century India' in Anand A. Yang (ed.) *Crime and Criminality in British India* (Tucson, 1985).

Gordon, Stewart N., 'Scarf and Sword. Thugs, marauders and state formation in eighteenth century Malwa', *IESHR*, 6, 4, 1969, 403–29.

Grewal, J.S., *Muslim Rule in India. The Assessment of British Historians* (Calcutta, 1970).

Grey, C. and H.L.O.Garrett (ed.), *European Adventurers of Northern India, 1785–1849* (Lahore, 1924).

Grierson, G.A., *Linguistic Survey of India*, 13 vols. (Calcutta, 1897–1927).

Grove, Richard, 'The transfer of botanical knowledge between Asia and Europe 1498–1800', *Journal of the Japan Netherlands Institute*, 3, 1991, pp. 164–172.

Grover, B.R., 'Land Rights in Mughal India', *IESHR*, I, 1, 1963, 1–23.

Growse, F.S., *Mathura. A District Memoir* (Allahabad, 1882).

Guha, Sumit, 'A pre-colonial Indian penal regime', *Past and Present*, 147, 1995, 101–26.

Gupta, S.P., *The Agrarian System of Eastern Rajasthan* (Delhi, 1987).

Habermas, Jurgen, *The Structural Transformation of the Public Sphere*, tr. T. Burger (Cambridge, Mass., 1992).

Habib, Irfan, *The Agrarian System of Mughal India (1556–1707)* (Bombay, 1963).

Habib, Irfan, 'Postal Communications in Mughal India', *Proceedings of the Indian Historical Congress, 46th Session* (Delhi, 1986), 236–52.

Habib, Irfan, 'Cartography in Mughal India', *Medieval India. A Miscellany*, 4, 1977, 123–34.

Hall, D.G.E. (ed.), *Historians of South East Asia* (Oxford, 1962).

Hall, D.G.E. *A History of South-East Asia* (London, 1981).

Hardy, Peter, *Historians of Medieval India. Studies in Indo-Muslim Historical writing* (London, 1960).

Hardy, Peter, 'Approaches to pre-modern Indo-Muslim historical writing', in P. Robb (ed.), *Society and Ideology* (Delhi, 1993).

Harrison, Mark, *Public Health in British India: Anglo-Indian Preventive Medicine, 1859–1914* (Cambridge, 1994).

Haynes, Douglas, *Rhetoric and Ritual in a colonial city. The shaping of public culture in Surat City, 1852–1928* (Berkeley, 1991).

Heesterman, J.C. *The Inner Conflict of Tradition. Essays in Indian ritual, kingship and society* (Chicago, 1985).

Heitler, R., 'The Varanasi house tax hartal of 1810–11', *IESHR*, 9, 3, 1972, 239–57.

Hill, S.C. (ed.), *Indian Records Series. Bengal in 1756–7*, 3 vols. (London, 1905).

Hill, S.C., *Catalogue of the Home Miscellaneous Series of the India Office Records* (London, 1927).

Hodson, V.P.C., *List of the Officers of the Bengal Army, 1758–1834*, 4 vols. (London, 1927–47).

Holman, D., *Sikander Sahib. The Life of Colonel James Skinner, 1778–1841* (London, 1961), p. 137.

Husain, I., *The Ruhela Chieftaincies. The rise and fall of Ruhela power in India in the eighteenth century* (Delhi, 1994).

Imperial Gazetteer of India, 23 vols. (Oxford, 1908).

Inden, R., *Imagining India* (Oxford, 1990).

Indica. Indian History Research Institute Silver Jubilee Commemoration Volume (Bombay, 1953).

Ingram, Edward (ed.), *Two Views of British India. The Private Correspondence of Mr. Dundas and Lord Wellesley: 1798–1801* (Bath, *c.* 1969).

Innis, H.A., *Empire and Communications* (Oxford, 1990).

Irschick, Eugene F., *Tamil Revivalism in the 1930s* (Madras, 1986).

Irschick, Eugene F., *Dialogue and History. Constructing South India, 1795–1895* (Berkeley, 1994).

Irvine, William, *The Army of the Indian Moghuls. Its organisation and administration* (repr. Delhi, 1962).

Israel, Milton, *Communications and Power. Propaganda and the press in the Indian nationalist struggle, 1920–47* (Cambridge, 1994).

Ivanow, W., *Concise Descriptive Catalogue of the Persian Mss. in the Collection of the Asiatic Society of Bengal* (Calcutta, 1924).

Johal, D.J.Singh, 'Historical significance of *Jhaggra Jatti ke Katrani da*' in F. Singh and A.C. Arora (eds.), *Maharaja Ranjit Singh. Politics, Society, Economics* (Patiala, 1984).

Jones, Kenneth (ed.), *Religious Controversy in British India. Dialogues in South Asian Languages* (New York, 1992).

Kane, P.V., *History of Dharmasastra*, 6 vols. (Pune, 1956–78).

Kaplan, Lionel, *Warrior Gentlemen: 'Gurkhas' in the Western Imagination* (London, 1995).

Karve, I., and M. Dandekar, *Anthropometric Measurement of Maharashtra* (Pune, 1951).

Kaye, G.R., *The Astronomical Observations of Jai Singh. Archaeological Survey of India. New Imperial Series*, 40 (Calcutta, 1918).

Kaye, G.R., *Hindu Astronomy. Memoirs of the Archaeological Survey of India*, 18 (Calcutta, 1924).

Kaye (ed.), G.R., *India Office Library. Catalogue of Mss in European Languages*, 2, ii (London, 1937).

Kejariwal, O.P., *The Asiatic Society of Bengal and the Discovery of India's Past, 1784–1838* (Delhi, 1988).

Khan, A.M., *The Transition in Bengal 1756–1775* (Cambridge, 1969).

Kidwai, S. R., *Gilchrist and the 'Language of Hindostan'* (Delhi, 1972).

King, Christopher R., *One Language; Two scripts; the Hindi Movement in nineteenth century north India* (Bombay, 1994).

Kippen, J., *The Tabla of Lucknow. A cultural analysis of a musical tradition* (Cambridge, 1988).

Koffsky, P.L. 'Postal Systems of India', *Bengal Past and Present*, 90, 1971, 47–69.

Kolff, D.H.A., *Rajput, Naukar and Sepoy. The ethnohistory of the military labour market in Hindustan, 1450–1850* (Cambridge, 1990).

Kroeber, A.L., *The Nature of Culture* (Chicago, 1952).

Kumar, Deepak, *Science and the Raj* (Delhi, 1995).

Lateef, S., *Muslim Women in India* (London, 1990).

Lavan, Spencer, *The Ahmadiyah Movement. A History and Perspective* (Delhi, 1974).

Law, Narendranath, *The Promotion of learning in India during Muhammadan rule by Muhammadans* (London, 1916).

Leask, Nigel, *British Romantic Writers and the East. Anxieties of Empire* (Cambridge, 1992).

Lele, Jayant K., *Tradition and Modernisation in Bhakti Movements* (Leiden, 1981).

Lelyveld, David, 'Colonial Knowledge and the fate of Hindustani', *Comparative Studies in Society and History*, 35, 4, 1993, 678–9.

Leonard, Karen I., *Social History of an Indian Caste. The Kayasths of Hyderabad* (Berkeley, 1978).

Lieberman, Victor, *Burmese Administrative Cycles. Anarchy and Conquest c. 1580–1760* (Princeton, 1984).

Logan, William, *Malabar*, 3 vols. (repr., Madras, 1951).

Luard, C.E. (ed.), *Indore State Gazetteer* (Calcutta, 1909).

Luiz, A.D., *The Tribes of Kerala* (Delhi, 1962).

Lutgendorf, Phillip, *The Life of a Text. Performing the Ramcaritmanas of Tulsi Das* (Berkeley, 1991).

Lutt, Jurgen, *Hindu Nationalismus in Uttar Prades, 1867–1900* (Stuttgart, 1970).

MacKenzie, John, *Orientalism. History, theory and the arts* (Manchester, 1995).

MacLeod, Roy, 'Passages in imperial science from Empire to Commonwealth', *Journal of World History*, iv, 1993, 117–50.

McGregor, R.S., *Hindi Literature from its beginnings to the Early Nineteenth Century* (Wiesbaden, 1984).

McGregor, R.S., *Hindi Literature of the Nineteenth and Early Twentieth Centuries* (Wiesbaden, 1974).

McGregor, R.S. (ed.), *Devotional Literature in South Asia. Current Research, 1985–88* (Cambridge, 1992).

McKenzie, John, *Orientalism. History, theory and the arts* (Manchester, 1995).

Mahesvari, H., *A History of Rajasthani Literature* (Delhi, 1980).

Majeed, Javed, 'The Jargon of Indostan – an exploration of jargon in Urdu and East India Company English', in P. Burke and R. Porter (eds.), *Languages and Jargons* (Cambridge, Mass., forthcoming).

Marshall, P.J., *East Indian Fortunes. The British in Bengal in the eighteenth century* (Oxford, 1976).

Marshall, P.J., and G. Williams, *The Great Map of Mankind. British Perceptions of the World in the Age of Enlightenment* (London, 1982).

Marshall, P.J., *Bengal the British Bridgehead. Eastern India, 1740–1828* (Cambridge, 1987).

Marshall, P.J., *Trade and Conquest. Studies of the Rise of British Dominance in India* (Aldershot, 1993).

Marshall, P.J. (ed.), *The British Discovery of Hinduism in the Eighteenth Century* (Cambridge, 1970).

Matilal, B., *Nyaya-Vaisesika. A History of Indian Literature*, ed. J. Gonda, VI, 2 (Wiesbaden, 1977).

Mines, Mattison, 'Individuality and achievement in south Asian social history', *MAS*, 26, I, 1992, 129–56.

Mishra, K.P., *Banaras in Transition (1738–1790)* (Delhi, 1975).

Moini, S.L.H., 'A critical analysis of the Waqai Sarkar-i Ajmer wa Ranthambore', in Devahuti (ed.), *Bias in Indian Historiography* (Delhi, 1980).

Moore, R.I., *The Formation of a Persecuting Society. Power and Deviance in Western Europe, 950–1250* (London, 1987).

Moriya, K., 'Urban networks and information networks' in C. Nakane and S. Oishi (eds.), *Tokugawa Japan* (Tokyo, 1990).

Mukherjee, Rudrangshu, *Awadh in Revolt, 1857–1858. A study of popular resistance* (Delhi, 1984).

Mukhia, Harbans, *Perspectives on Medieval History* (Delhi, 1993).

Nakane, Chia, *Kinship and Economic Organisation in Rural Japan* (Princeton, 1975).

Nandy, S.C., *Life and Times of Cantoo Baboo, the Banian of Warren Hastings* (Calcutta, 1981).

Natarajan, J., *History of Indian Journalism* (Delhi, 1955).

Nayeem, M.A., *Evolution of Postal Communications and Administration in the Deccan (from 1294 A.D. to the Formation of the Hyderabad State in 1724 A.D.)* (Bombay, 1968).

Nayeem, M.A., *Mughal Administration of Deccan under Nizamul Mulk Asaf Jah (1720–1748 A.D.)* (Bombay, 1985).

Nizami, K.A. *On History and Historians of Medieval India* (Delhi, 1983).

Nourrison, J.F., *Trois Révolutionnaires: Turgot, Necker, Bailly* (Paris, 1885).

O'Hanlon, Rosalind, *Caste, Conflict and Ideology. Mahatma Jotirao Phule and low caste protest in nineteenth century western India* (Cambridge, 1988).

Ohdedar, A.K., *The Growth of the Library in Modern India, 1498–1936* (Calcutta, 1966).

O'Malley, L.S.S., *Bihar and Orissa District Gazetteers. Patna* (Patna, 1924).

Om Prakash, *The Dutch East India Company and the Economy of Bengal, 1630–1720* (Princeton, 1985).

Pakrasi, K.D., *Female Infanticide in India* (Calcutta, 1970).

Pandey, Gyanendra, *The Construction of Communalism in Colonial North India* (Berkeley, 1990).

Parry, J., 'The Brahmanical tradition and the technology of the intellect', in J. Overing (ed.), *Reason and Morality* (Oxford, 1985), pp. 200–25.

Peabody, Norbert, 'Tod's *Rajast'han* and the boundaries of Imperial Rule in Nineteenth Century India', *MAS*, 30, 1, 1996, 141–70.

Pearson, M.N., 'The Thin End of the Wedge. Medical relativities as a paradigm of early modern Indian–European relations', *MAS*, 29, 1, 1995, pp. 141–70.

Peers, Douglas, *Between Mars and Mammon. Colonial armies and the garrison state in India, 1819–1835* (London, 1995).

Pemble J., *The Invasion of Nepal. John Company at War* (Oxford, 1971).

Penner, Peter, *The Patronage Bureaucracy in North India. The Robert M. Bird and James Thomason School, 1820–1870* (Delhi, 1986).

Phillimore, R., *Historical Records of the Survey of India*, 4 vols. (Dehra Dun, 1945–).

Pincott, F. (tr., ed.), *The Prem-sagara or Ocean of Love*. (London, 1897).

Pingree, David, *Jyotihsastra. Astral and Mathematical Literature* (Wiesbaden, 1981), *History of Indian Literature*, VI, fasc. 4.

Pollack, O.B., *Empires in Collision. Anglo-Burmese Relations in the mid Nineteenth Century* (Westpoint, Conn., 1979).

Pollock, Sheldon, 'Ramayana and the political imagination in India', *JAS*, 52, 2, 1993, 261–97.

Powell, Avril, *Muslims and Missionaries in pre-Mutiny India* (Richmond, 1993).

Pradhan, Kumar, *The Gorkha Conquests. The Process and Consequences of the unification of Nepal with particular reference to eastern Nepal* (Delhi, 1991).

Prakash, Gyan, 'Science gone native in colonial India', *Representations*, 40, fall 1992, 153–78.

Prior, K.H., 'Making History; the state's intervention in urban religious disputes in the North-Western Provinces in the early nineteenth century', *MAS*, 27, I, 1993, 179–203.

Pyenson, Lewis, *Empires of Reason. Exact Sciences in Indonesia, 1840–1940* (Leiden, 1989).

Qamber, Akhtar, *The Last Mushairah of Delhi* (Delhi, 1979).

Rai, Amrit, *A House Divided. The origins and development of Hindi-Urdu* (Delhi, 1992).

Ramaswami, N.S., *Political History of the Carnatic under the Nawabs* (Delhi, 1984).

Rao, P. Setu Madhava, *Eighteenth Century Deccan* (Bombay, 1963).

Regmi, D.R., *Modern Nepal*, 2 vols. (Calcutta, 1975/6).

Regmi, M.C., *A Study in Nepali Economic History, 1768–1846* (Delhi, 1971).

Richards, John F., *Mughal Administration in Golconda* (Oxford, 1973).

Richards, Thomas, *The Imperial Archive. Knowledge and the fantasy of empire* (London, 1993).

Rieu, E.V., *Catalogue of the Persian Manuscripts in the British Museum* (London, 1879).

Rizvi, S.A.A. and M.L. Bhargava (eds.), *Freedom Struggle in Uttar Pradesh*, 5 vols. (Lucknow, 1957–9).

Rizvi, S.A.A., *Religious and Intellectual Life of Muslims in Akbar's Reign with special reference to Abu'l Fazl (1556–1605)* (Delhi, 1975).

Rizvi, S.A.A., *A Socio-intellectual History of the Isna Ashari Shi'is in India (16th to 19th century)*, 2 vols. (Canberra, 1986).

Rizvi, S.A.A., *Shah Wali-allah and his Times* (Canberra, 1980).

Rizvi, S.A.A., *Shah Abd-al Aziz. Puritanism, sectarian politics and jihad* (Canberra, 1982).

Robb, Peter, 'The impact of British rule on religious community: reflections on the trial of Maulvi Ahmadullah of Patna in 1865', in Robb (ed.), *Society and Ideology. Essays in honour of Kenneth Ballhatchet* (London, 1994), pp. 142–76.

Robinson, F.C.R., *Separatism among Indian Muslims*.

Robinson, F.C.R., 'Consultation and Control. The U.P. Government and its allies, 1860–1906, *MAS*, 5, 4, 1971, 313–36.

Robinson, F.C.R. 'Scholarship and Mysticism in early eighteenth century Awadh', in A.L. Dallapiccola and S. Z. Lallement, *Islam and the Indian Regions* (Stuttgart, 1994).

Rocher, L., *The Puranas* (Wiesbaden, 1986).

Roseberry, Royal, III, *Imperial Rule in the Punjab. The conquest and administration of Multan* (Delhi, 1987).

Ross, Robert, *Adam Kok's Griquas. A study in the development of stratification in South Africa* (Cambridge, 1976).

Roy, A.K., *History of the Jaipur City* (Delhi, 1978).

Roy, Tapti, 'Visions of the Rebels: a study of 1857 in Bundelkhand', *MAS*, 27, 1, 1993, 205–28.

Russell, Ralph and Khurshidul Islam, *Three Mughal Poets. Mir, Sauda, Mir Hasan* (London, 1969).

Sadiq, M., *A History of Urdu Literature* (London, 1964).

Sagar, S., 'Social change and the *kissas* of the first half of the nineteenth century', in F. Singh and A.C. Arora (eds.), *Maharaja Ranjit Singh. Politics, Society, Economics* (Patial, 1984).

Saletore, G. (ed.), *Banaras Affairs (1788–1810)*, 2 vols (Allahabad, *c.* 1955–58).

Sanwal, B.D., *Nepal and the East India Company* (Bombay, 1965).

Sarkar, B.K., *Inland Transport and Communications in Medieval India* (Calcutta, 1925).

Sarma, K.V., *History of the Kerala School of Hindu Astronomy (in perspective)* (Hoshiarpur, 1972).

Satish Chandra, *Mughal Religious Policies; the Rajputs and the Deccan* (Delhi, 1992).

Schimmel, A., *Islamic Literatures of India* (Wiesbaden, 1973).

Schwartz, Stuart B. (ed.), *Implicit Understandings. Observing, reporting and reflections on the encounters between Europeans and other peoples in the early modern era* (Cambridge, 1994).

Schwartzberg, J. 'Cartography in the traditional Islamic and South Asian societies', in J.B. Harley (ed.), *History of Cartography*, II, 1 (Chicago, 1992).

Sen, S.N. *Administrative System of the Marathas* (Calcutta, 1923).

Sender, H., *The Kashmiri Brahmins. A study in cultural choice* (Delhi, 1988).

Seth, M.J., *Armenians in India from the earliest times to the present day* (Calcutta, 1937).

Sewell, R., and S.B. Dikshit, *The Indian Calendar* (London, 1896).

Sharma, Sanjay, 'The 1837–8 famine in U.P.: some dimensions of popular action, *IESHR*, 30, 3, 1993, 337–70.

Sharp, H. (ed.), *Selections from Educational Records*, Part I, 1781–1839 (Calcutta, 1920).

Shastri, R.N., *Jhala Zalim Singh (1730–1823)* (Jaipur, *c.*1971).

Shejwalkar, T.J., *Panipat 1761* (Pune, 1946).

Shulman, David and Sanjay Subrahmanyam, *Symbols of Substance. Court and state in Nayaka Period Tamilnadu* (Delhi, 1992).

Siddiqi, J.M., *Aligarh District. A Historical Survey* (Aligarh, 1975).

Siddiqi, M.Z., 'The Intelligence Services under the Mughals', *Medieval India; A Miscellany*, 2, 1972, 53–60.

Siddiqi, M.Z., 'The Muhtasib under Aurangzeb', *Medieval India Quarterly*, 5, 1963, 113–19.

Siddiqi, M.Z., 'The institution of the Qazi under the Mughals, *MIM*, I, 1969, 240–60; .

Silver, Harold, *The Concept of Popular Education. A study of ideas and social movements in the early nineteenth century* (London, 1965).

Singh, Daulat, *Astronomical Observatory of Jaipur* (Jaipur, 1981).

Singh, Dilbagh, *The State Landlords and Peasants. Rajasthan in the 18th century* (Delhi, 1990).

Singh, N.N., *British Historiography on British Rule in India. The life and writings of Sir J.W.Kaye, 1814–76* (Patna, 1986).

Singh, R.P., *Rise of Jat Power* (Delhi, 1988).

Singha, Radhika, 'Providential Circumstances. The Thugee campaign of the 1830s and legal innovation', *MAS*, 27, 1, 1993, 83–146.

Sinha, N.K. and A.K. Dasgupta (eds.), *Selections from Ochterlony Papers in the National Archives of India* (Calcutta, 1964).

Smith, D.E., *Religion and Politics in Burma* (Princeton, 1965).

Smith, John D., *The Epic of Pabuji. A study in transcription and translation* (Cambridge, 1991).

Spear, Percival, *Twilight of the Mughals. Studies in Late Mughal Delhi* (Cambridge, 1951).

Steele, Ian K., *The English Atlantic, 1675–1740. An exploration of communications and community* (New York, 1986).

Stein, Burton, *Peasant State and Society in Medieval South India* (Delhi, 1980).

Stiller, L.F., *Prithvinarayan Shah in the Light of his Dibya Upadesh* (Katmandu, 1968).

Stokes, E.T., *The English Utilitarians and India* (Oxford, 1959).

Stokes, E.T., *The Peasant and the Raj* (Cambridge, 1978).

Stokes, E.T., *The Peasant Armed. The Indian Rebellion of 1857* (Oxford, 1986).

Stutley, M. and J. (eds.), *Dictionary of Hinduism. Its myth, folklore and development, 1500 B.C.–A.D. 1500* (London, 1977).

Subrahmanyam, Sanjay (ed.), *Merchants, Markets and the State in early modern India* (Delhi, 1990).

Subrahmanyam, Sanjay, *The Portuguese Empire in Asia, 1500–1700* (London, 1993).

Tarling, Nicholas, *The Cambridge History of South East Asia*, 2 vols. (Cambridge, 1992).

Tegenfeldt, H.G., *The Kachin Baptist Church of Burma* (S. Pasadena, Cal., 1974).

Teltscher, Kate, *India Inscribed. European and British writing on India 1600–1800* (Delhi, 1995).

Temple, Sir Richard, *James Thomason. Rulers of India Series* (Oxford, 1893).

Thompson, Edward, *Life of Charles, Lord Metcalfe* (London, 1937).

Thompson, Edward, *The Making of the Indian Princes* (London, 1943).

Thompson, Leonard, and Monica Wilson, *The Oxford History of South Africa*, 2 vols. (Oxford, 1969).

Tirmizi, S.A.I., *Index to Titles, 1798–1855* (Delhi, 1979).

Troll, C.W., *Sayyid Ahmad Khan. A Reinterpretation of Muslim Theology* (Delhi, 1978).

Troll, C.W., 'A note on an early topographical work of Sayyid Ahmad Khan: Asar-as Sanadid', *Journal of the Royal Asiatic Society*, 1972, 135–46.

Uttar Pradesh Records Office, *An Alphabetic Index of Persian, Urdu and Arabic Manuscripts in the State Archives of Uttar Pradesh* (Allahabad, c. 1968).

Uttar Pradesh Records Office, *Calendar of Oriental Records* (Allahabad, 1959).

Vidyabhusana, S., *History of Indian Logic. Ancient, Mediaeval and Modern Schools* (1920, repr. Delhi, 1971).

Waterfield, W., *The Lay of Alha. A saga of Rajput chivalry as sung by minstrels of northern India* (Oxford, 1923).

Watson, I. B., *Foundation for Empire. English Private Trade in India, 1659–1760* (Delhi, 1980).

Wilson, C.R., *Early Annals of the English in Bengal*, 3 vols. (Calcutta, 1911).

Wilson, W.J. *History of the Madras Army*, 4 vols. (Madras, 1882).

Winichakul, T., *Siam Mapped. The History of the Geo-body of a Nation* (Honolulu, 1994).

Wink, André, *Land and Sovereignty in India: agrarian society and politics under the eighteenth century Maratha Svarajya* (Cambridge, 1986).

Wink, André, *Al-Hind. The making of the Indo-Islamic world*, I (Leiden, 1990).

Woerkens, M. van, *Le Voyageur Etranglé. L'Inde des Thugs. Le colonialisme et l'imaginaire* (Paris, 1995).

Yapp, M.E., *Strategies of British India. Britain, Iran and Afghanistan, 1798–1850* (Oxford, 1980).

Yule, H. and A. Burnell, *Hobson-Jobson. A Glossary of colloquial Anglo-Indian and Indian words and phrases* (Rev. edn, London, 1903).

Zimmermann, Francis, *The Jungle and the Aroma of Meats. An ecological theme in Hindu medicine* (Berkeley, 1987).

Index